אַתָּה וְהַלֵּוִי וְהַגֵּר

Attah, v'HaLevy, v'HaGeir

אַתָּה וְהַלֵּוִי וְהַגֵּר

Attah, v'HaLevy, v'HaGeir

Lessons from the Weekly Torah Portion

Compiled by

Menashe R. Frank

Copyright © 2015, Compiled by Menashe R. Frank

Fourth Printing

ISBN: 9780692513231

Library of Congress Control Number: 2015913310

A collection of *divrei Torah* about the *Yomim Tovim* is available in a second book, complied by Menashe R. Frank, entitled *Ach Sameach*.

DEDICATION

This *sefer* is dedicated to my children,
the most recent links in the Chain:

Yael Rani
יעל רני

Esther Miriam
אסתר מרים

Binyamin Pinchas
בנימן פינחס

Ayden Avraham
עדן אברהם

This *sefer* is in honor of my beloved wife,
who makes it all possible:

Jamie
פייגל לאה

This *sefer* is in gratitude to *Hashem*

CONTENTS

APPROBATION

הנני הבא לתמוך יד הספר "אמרי יהודה" והרי
שלמין ולפ60 ד' הרב אשר שמו אתו סימן ל[...]
[...] גדול חסר ביהודה אשר ביהודה ודבר חכמה
תקים לתורה. לבונה ונחמד, ויש אשר הולך משולל ון
ובכידן שמול את[...] באדרה אשר שלם אחולם
להגבות מתירון וגבהי

[...]רת פלל הספר, וגה[נ]אן מאיר מהסיסראן ודבי
תורה הנאמ[...] תגודו. 1001 הבא רא"ו הדרן פל שם
כל ישראל ואמ[ו]ן יקהו לגהר תורה את שרף ושכן
ככות הרבים ותקיה. כן שלו, לבנון כל הדורים
ה[...]ים בתורה וסכה הוא ואמשן חום כוא[...]
מתקין אלו ואמט, וישור רת לתן נמין, וככר
הקדוד בנוחת ום כל ל ישרא ביחולת בחר[...] ושרד
ואמשן הבוח יוד לפן בחברה ב[...] ואן

אהבת התורה
כ[...] ל[...]ין
ש[...]ב מאיר א[...]

BS'D

I present this letter as acknowledgment of my approbation of this *sefer* "Attah, v'HaLevy v'HaGeir," which was collected and printed by Menashe Shmuel Frank – a man who enjoys the fruits of his labor, always making time to learn and teach *Torah*, and is always going from strength to strength.

I merited to learn with Menashe the last fourteen years and was privileged to enjoy his *Torah* insights.

After reviewing the *sefer*, I found it to be insightful and enjoyable; a true book of *Torah* worthy to have its place on every Jew's table, where he may enjoy a *D'var Torah* for every *Shabbat* of the year.

The merit of this book and the *Torah* contained in it should shield him and his family. May he merit all of the blessings written in the *Torah*. He and his family should enjoy all the good with joy and gladness, they should see much *nachat* from their children and they should merit to see together with their brethren the salvation of the Jewish people with the coming of *Moshiach* soon in our days, Amen

With blessings of the *Torah*,
Rabbi Chesriel Yosef Jankovits
Sivan 5775 / June 2015

ACKNOWLEDGMENTS

The *hakarat hatov* I have for being able to produce this book begins and ends with *Hashem*. "הוּא עָשָׂנוּ. וְלוֹ אֲנַחְנוּ עַמּוֹ וְצֹאן מַרְעִיתוֹ." "He made us, and we are His, the People and the sheep of His pasture." (Tehillim 100:3)

The "Sources and Influences" list sets out the eclectic roster of people who contributed, in most cases unknowingly, to the content of this book. I am indebted to each and every one of them for sharing their words of *Torah*, first with me, and now with a broader audience. Producing the book was a much greater undertaking than I originally anticipated, and it was only because of the tremendous efforts of a talented support group that the project was completed. Dr. Jason Schulman's photography acumen and creativity were critical to the cover design. Rebbetzin Yaffa Spodek Wexler, Mrs. Suzanne Jacoby Offer and Rebbetzin Jen Kroll were indispensable in collecting the inputs for the "Glossary" and "Sources," as well as proofreading and editing the *parshiot* chapters. I also could not have compiled a book of this nature and scope in the days before ArtScroll and the Internet made the source material immediately accessible. I especially want to thank Torah.org and Chabad.org, two superlative Web-based *Torah* resources. Sara Stratton of Business Ghost was near-heroic in patiently walking me through and facilitating my first time at publishing. Most importantly, my *Rebbe*, Rabbi Yossi Jankovits, was the true brains of the operation, applying his encyclopedic knowledge of *Torah*, *Gemara* and all secondary sources to ensure the final work was not only informative and inspirational, but kosher as well. "כִּי מִצִּיּוֹן תֵּצֵא תוֹרָה, וּדְבַר ה' מִירוּשָׁלָיִם," "For from Tzion shall go forth the Torah, and the Word of Hashem from Yerushalayim." (Yeshaiyahu 2:3)

The true genesis for the creation of this *sefer* is contained in my journey to Judaism, which began over twenty years ago. As I set out in the <u>Introduction</u>, I was assisted and influenced by many very special individuals in the process. To recognize some of them will necessarily mean I inadvertently overlook many well-deserving others, but I would be remiss if I did not make an attempt to show my sincere gratitude. Jessica and Keith Wasserstrom were catalysts at the very beginning, with Jana and Michael Chesal also demonstrating how to successfully embrace a *Torah* life. Iris Goldenholz Silverberg unlocked the mysteries of Hebrew, and Yossi Hahn was my eleven-year tour guide through the *Mishnah*. From their "50th Avenue Vortex," Jeanette (ע"ה) and Norman Levine and their wonderful family became our lifelong teachers and friends. Rabbi Seymour Atlas (זצ"ל) served on my conversion *Beit Din*, as did Rabbi Howard Seif and our beloved *Mara Datra*, Rabbi Edward Davis. Sammy Grundwerg, Aaron Moses and Fritz LaPorte have been unconditional brothers.

I am so very grateful to my mother, Nancy Frank Grondin, and my sister Kathleen Frank Young, for their love and support. Losing my father, Ronald A. Frank (ע"ה), at such an early age was difficult on all of us, but we have more than persevered, we have thrived - individually and as a family. My in-laws, Maureen and Douglas Cohn, an enduring inspiration for my family, have shown tremendous patience and understanding in their children's spiritual odysseys.

Each of my wonderful children deserves independent acknowledgement and appreciation. Yaelie, Emma, Benny and Ayden (Gidge) consistently exceed my expectations and provide lasting *nachat* to their family. While I compiled this book in honor and celebration of my son, Binyamin Pinchas, becoming a *Bar Mitzvah*, each child has been a true inspiration for this book. And finally, "אחרון אחרון חביב," "the very last is most beloved," (Rashi on Bereshit 33:2), I want to thank my beloved wife Jamie. In nineteen years of marriage we've already had quite a ride. We have both come so far, and we've done it together: with trust, and love, and laughter, and a few tears. For all of it, I simply say "thank you."

NOTES, DISCLAIMERS, APOLOGIES AND CONVENTIONS

The Parashah Chapters

Nineteen years ago I began compiling the *divrei Torah* set forth in this book. The intention was to include one entry per week, related to the *parashah hashavua*, based on something I heard or read during that week. I also compiled entries on the *Yom Tovim* during the same period which, *b'ezrat Hashem*, I may publish at a later date. I provide the Hebrew year in which each entry was recorded, and have included a "Calendar Converter" to assist the reader in connecting an entry to the corresponding year in the Common Era.

During the time I was compiling these entries my understanding and appreciation of both the substance and process of *Torah* learning advanced. In the early years, I would sometimes capture a concept without identifying its source. I ask forgiveness from those inadvertently omitted, yet are deserving of credit for teaching me. In compiling this book I had to make judgment calls and adopt conventions of uniformity. For example, I have avoided applying my limited and deficient judgment concerning proper titles for attributed "Sources and Influences," and therefore have listed all male religious figures as "Rabbi" (rather than Rav, HaRav, Rosh Kollel, etc.) and, in the case of women, "Rebbetzin." I intended no disrespect and ask for *mechillah* for any offense. Occasionally, where a source himself used an appellation other than Rabbi to quote another, I have included that alternative title (for example Rabbi Edward Davis, and many others, often referred to Rabbi Soloveitchik as "the Rav").

There is an entry for each *parashah* for most, although not every, year. Occasionally, when there was a double *parashat hashavua*, I made one entry. In some case, I made entries that had little, if any, connection to the *parashah*. I generally recorded each entry in the week in which I heard the *vort*. Therefore, in a few isolated instances, I recorded an entry for one *parashah* that is connected to a completely separate *parashah*. The only criterion for inclusion was that the *Torah* thought struck a chord with me to the point that I wanted to retain it and draw inspiration from it again and again.

In a few places I note *halachot* connected in some measure to the *parashah* at issue. While in all cases these *halachic* notes were gleaned from the teachings of my Rabbis (usually Rabbi Edward Davis), they should not be relied upon as authoritative.

In a few cases I include my original *Torah* thoughts, sometimes as an addendum to something I heard, occasionally in the form of a question, and in a few isolated instances, as a free standing thesis. This is indicated by the insertion of "MRF Note" in the text. Where I take what I believed to be any kind of a step out onto the proverbial theological limb, I always tried to check with a *Torah* authority (usually Rabbi Yossi Jankovits) to ensure the idea was genuine and in keeping with normative Jewish thought. In the handful of cases that I presented him with an original *Torah* idea, I cannot recall even a single time time that Rabbi Jankovits showed less that complete enthusiasm for my *chiddush*. While some unattributed entries may have been my original thought, I only claimed the ones about which I was certain.

On occasion I included personal political statements associated with both Israel and the United States and connected in some way to the *parashah*. I do not intend to offend those who have an alternate perspective.

Verses from *Tanach* are presented first in Hebrew and then immediately translated to English. A portion of a verse is presented in transliterated Hebrew, followed by the English translation. For readability, Hebrew words and phrases are transliterated, italicized and defined in the "Glossary of Terms, Places and Persons."

I routinely capitalize Hebrew and English words that I feel are deserving of that respectful treatment. This includes reference to *Hashem* and any Aspect of Him, but is extended to words such as, for example, Holy, and references to the Land of Israel and the People of Israel. I tend to use the Hebrew names of personages (e.g. *Moshe*) rather than the English version (i.e. Moses), but I do provide the English names in the "Glossary."

Many of the *divrei Torah* were originally presented (and often recorded) with *Ashkenaz* transliterated spelling of Hebrew words (e.g. *chanukas habayis*), but I have made most defined words transliterated in the Sephardic pronunciation for uniformity (i.e. *chanukat habayit*). There are exceptions, however, where certain words just sound more natural to me when presented as pronounced in the *Ashkenaz nusach* (e.g. *bris*; *Shabbos*). The same convention also applies to "Sources and Influences" (see below).

Glossary of Terms, Places and Persons

Entries are transliterated (as best as can be) from Hebrew, and occasionally Yiddish or Aramaic, and alphabetically ordered without regard to spacing or punctuation within words or phrases. Entries for which there is both a singular and plural form are separated by a "slash." For entries that are often, but not always, accompanied by another word the second word follows in parentheses (e.g. Yosef (HaTzaddik)).

The definition provide is limited to assisting in understanding the use of the word or phrase in the context in which I present it. Alternate but inapplicable definitions are generally not included. Dates are Hebrew years unless designated with CE or BCE. Hebrew months are reckoned from *Nissan* (with the reckoning from *Tishrei* in parentheses).

Sources and Influences

Entries are presented in alphabetical order based on what I understand to be the most accepted appellation for the source. Accordingly, Rabbi Yisrael Meir Kagan haKohein is presented as the *Chofetz Chaim*, the name of one of his *sefarim*. Where a source is identified as a *sefer*, it is italicized and the author, if known, is provided. Most sources are presented in transliterated Sephardic pronunciation (e.g. Daat Zakainim), but there are notable exceptions (e.g. Chasam Sofer; Sefas Emes) based on how they best sound to me. Only very basic information about each source is provided (e.g. years of life, geographical connection). I have not begun to do justice to the greatness and accomplishments of many of the sources and I ask for *mechillah* for my failure to do so. I encourage each interested reader to do additional research on the personages listed.

Male non-rabbinical sources are called "Reb," or, if applicable "Dr.," neither of which should be read as judgment of individual erudition, which in some cases rivals the Rabbis. For the most part I did not include any honorifics for deceased sources (e.g. alav hashalom; ז״ל; ע״ה), so as not to draw comparisons between individuals. Of course it is my desire and prayer that those whose teachings are set forth in this *sefer* and who are no longer with us should draw merit from their posthumous contributions.

Finally, as this *sefer* was nearing completion, the United States Supreme Court rendered its dishonorable decision in Zivotofsky v. Kerry, striking as unconstitutional the law passed by Congress requiring the U.S. State Department, if requested, to list Israel on U.S. passports as the country of birth for Americans born in Jerusalem. Jerusalem, or, more properly, *Yerushalayim*, is and shall remain the undisputed, undivided capital of the Jewish State, regardless of what the detractors in Washington might say or think. Accordingly, any reference to *Yerushalayim* in "Sources and Influences" is clarified as being in Israel.

This book contains the holy Name of G-d in Hebrew. Please treat it with respect and dispose of it properly.

PREFACE

וְשָׂמַחְתָּ בְכָל הַטּוֹב אֲשֶׁר נָתַן לְךָ ה' אלקיך וּלְבֵיתֶךָ אַתָּה וְהַלֵּוִי וְהַגֵּר אֲשֶׁר בְּקִרְבֶּךָ

And you shall rejoice in all the good that Hashem, your G-d, has given you and your household: you, the Levy, and the convert who is close to you.
— Devarim 26:11

וְהַחוּט הַמְשֻׁלָּשׁ לֹא בִמְהֵרָה יִנָּתֵק

... and a three-strand rope will not be easily broken.
— Kohelet 4:12

The New York City Marathon is unique in the world of sports. With an estimated two million spectators lining the five-borough course, it is arguably the largest one-day professional sporting event in the world. And while the world's top professional running talent annually competes, the vast majority of its 50,000 participants are amateurs who gain entry based on having run the race before, through a lottery system that is blind to athletic ability, or in exchange for a commitment to raise money for charity. Most high-profile professional sports confine the non-professionals to spectator status. In the world's top running events there is also a certain element of elitism. The oldest, and arguably most prestigious, is the Boston Marathon, where one must qualify with an exceptional race time to earn entry. Among the major American races, New York is the exception. The result is a distinctive sporting experience.

In 2010, the winner of the NYC Marathon was Gebregziabher Gebre-mariam of Ethiopia, who completed the race in 2:08:14, a pace of less than five minutes per mile for more than twenty-six miles! For perspective, on that November morning, Mr. Gebremariam averaged more than twelve miles per hour, continually for two hours. It is estimated that 0.01% of all Americans could run even a single mile in less than five minutes, much less twenty-six consecutive miles. For recreational runners, such athleticism is beyond comprehension.

I was one of the tens of thousands of racers who finished hours behind the winner. My time was 4:37:28, an average of 10:35 per mile. That is an average speed of about 5.5 miles per hour, which is just a little faster than a brisk walk. No matter, I still was an active participant in an exciting, world-class athletic event. While I did not come remotely close to matching the performance of the top runners, I ran the same streets, past the same cheering crowd. It was exhilarating. And like everything in *Hashem's* world, it is a metaphor.

Torah is unique. Every Jew can participate in the learning, and even the teaching, of *Torah*. I have been Jewish for almost nineteen years; I studied *Torah* for a little bit longer than that in preparation for my conversion (see "Introduction"). Since the beginning, I took it upon myself to record, on a weekly basis, an interesting, provocative or inspirational *d'var Torah* related to the weekly *parashah*. Those handwritten notes eventually filled an entire three-ring binder, which I reviewed and augmented over the years. Those notes form the content of this book. Interestingly, the entries demonstrate a progression in my Torah outlook over an eighteen-year period.

During that time I have been privileged to learn from some very talented teachers, among them Rabbi Edward Davis, Rabbi Yossi Jankovits and Rabbi Yitzchak Salid. They each, of course, learned from their *Torah* teachers who, they would readily admit, were even greater. I am awed and humbled by their acumen, erudition, intelligence and *middot*. They are, quite literally, in a different league. And yet, like the amateur runner, I have been allowed to participate, to a lesser degree, in their learning. Of course I cannot keep up with them. They are professionals with years of intensive training from the very best "coaches." I will not come close to matching their performance, but I am nonetheless on the same "course." The *Daf Yomi*, for example, that I learn with Rabbi Salid, surveys the same *Gemara* that he, and his *Rebbe*, Rabbi Ephraim Greenblatt, and <u>his</u> *Rebbe*, Rabbi Moshe Feinstein pored over. The *Chumash* that I try to decipher with the aid of Rabbi Jankovits is the same one that he, and his *Rebbe*, Rabbi Ezriel Yehuda Lebowitz, and <u>his</u> *Rebbe*, Rabbi Yonasan Steif investigated deeply. And the *hashkafah* that I ponder with Rabbi Davis explores the same subjects that he, and his *Rebbe*, Rav Joseph B. Soloveitchik, and <u>his</u> *Rebbe*, Rabbi Moshe Soloveitchik gleaned from the Ancient Sages. That is both humbling and exhilarating at the same time.

I sincerely hope that I have faithfully transcribed the thoughts of these *Torah* scholars and the many others whose ideas are included in this book. Ideally, this book will provide some value and inspiration to both the "professional" learned veteran as well as the "amateur" *Torah* novice like me. Indeed, my personal growth over these years has, on a few occasions, prompted me to offer my own *Torah chiddushim*, which are scattered among the gems of others in these pages.

The reader will not be able to fully appreciate the context and the meaning of the *divrei Torah* that I have compiled absent an understanding of how I personally came to *Torah* and Judaism. It is for that reason that I provided an "Introduction," which sets forth the serendipitous journey I have undertaken with my wife, Jamie.

Finally, the title of this book holds great meaning for my family. As described in the "Introduction," through my dating relationship with Jamie I became aware that my father (ע״ה), although he never knew it, was Jewish - actually a *Levy*, by birth. His mother (ע״ה) and father (ע״ה), my paternal grandparents, although raised Jewish, sought to disconnect entirely and forever from Judaism upon arriving in America as refugees in 1940. *Hashem* had other plans, however, and fifty-six years later, I, their grandson, converted to Judaism and adopted a *Torah*-observant life with Jamie. Presently, seventy-five years after their fateful decision, their great grandson, my eldest son, Binyamin Pinchas, is becoming a *Bar Mitzvah*.

It was this event that inspired me to compile a book of *Torah* teachings that would celebrate the continuity of *Yiddishkeit* in our family, recaptured against all odds, and only by the grace of *Hashem*. As the *pasuk* states "and you shall rejoice in all the good that Hashem, your G-d, has given you and your household . . . ," (Devarim 26:11) "Attah, v'HaLevy, v' HaGeir," "You, and the Levy, and the Convert." I view this as an imperative to each of my four children, for each of them is the third link in a repaired, reclaimed chain that reaches back to *Har Sinai*: each of them, with my father and me. This book is a celebration of that reclamation, and living testimony to my children as to why it means so much to me.

Something else extraordinary happened at the New York City Marathon of 2010. Early that summer, the world was riveted by the story of thirty-three Chilean miners trapped 2,300 feet underground for sixty-nine days. Less than a month after their dramatic rescue, one of the miners, Edison Peña, ran in the NYC Marathon. His time was 5:40:51. Based on his background, and what he had endured, that was extraordinary and inspiring. I passed him in Central Park that day, and stopped to shake his hand, in admiration of his resolve and courage. I was moved by the fact that he had emerged from darkness to take his place on the course, among those of varying abilities who were striving to attain more; to be more. I internalized the metaphor – and kept on running.

M.R.F
Summer, 2015 (5775)

INTRODUCTION

I was born as Christopher Ronald Frank, to Ronald Albert Frank (ע"ה) and Nancy Gillen Frank, on December 18, 1966, in Englewood, New Jersey. I grew up in New Hampshire, about an hour north of Boston, with my parents and one sister, Kathleen. My mother's parents were from Ireland, and she was naturally raised a Catholic. We knew of many cousins in New York from her side of the family, but we had limited interactions. My father and his parents were Dutch. Growing up, we were aware that they had emigrated from Holland to America in 1940, when he was only five years old. An only child, he was raised without any religious affiliation to speak of, and so, when he married my mother and started a family, he allowed my sister and me to be raised by my mother in the Catholic faith. Every Sunday we would all drive to church together. My mother, sister and I would attend and my father would sit in the car and read the Sunday newspaper. We were unaware of any family on my father's side except for my grandmother, Elisabeth "Elly" Vis Frank (ע"ה), whom we saw regularly, and her brother who lived far away in Florida, and whom I personally never met. Both my grandfathers died before I was born.

My father passed away one week before my eighteenth birthday, after a lifelong battle with Crohn's disease. His father had also died young, and with the death of my father, my paternal grandmother was truly alone.

I tried to assist her with her affairs, and over time we became very close, due, at least in part, to the fact that she had no other identified family.

By the time I left home for American University, in Washington, D.C., I didn't feel very Catholic. What I did feel was liberated and uninhibited. I joined a fraternity and had a socially superlative but academically unproductive four years. It was during that time that I made my first Jewish friends, including a nice Jewish girl named Jamie Cohn, from Tampa, Florida. Jamie and I dated briefly, but based mostly on my emotional immaturity, we went our separate ways.

After graduating from college, I entered the working world. Within a few years, I began to revisit my childhood ambition of becoming a lawyer. I registered for the LSATs and began the process of applying to law schools. It was during that time that I ran into Jamie again. After four years apart, it turned out we lived within a quarter mile of each other, in Rockville, Maryland. I was instantly interested in resuming dating but she would hear nothing of it. She told me I had three strikes against me: I was a jerk in college, I was likely soon moving to Miami for law school, and, most importantly, I wasn't Jewish.

"Ok," I said, "you're right about number one, I was a jerk in college, but I've changed. I'm nice now. As for number two, who knows what will happen? It's only for three years, maybe I'll move back to Maryland, maybe you'll move to Miami. And as for three," I paused, "well, two out of three ain't bad!"

At the time I did not understand why she would be apprehensive about my religion, since I was unconcerned about hers. Jamie had grown up within Reform Judaism, and whatever opinions she had formed about *Yiddishkeit* were mostly negative. Her brother Greg had become deeply involved in *Chabad* during college, and returned to Tampa with ideas about *kashrut* and *tzniut* that were not at all aligned with Jamie's high school life. I viewed her promise to her parents that she would marry a Jew to be inconsequential, if not mildly racist. Somehow I convinced her to give me a chance and in short order it became clear to both of us that we were meant to be together. My life changed enormously for the better. Even my grandmother Elly, for whom I had become something of a surrogate son, recognized the changes in me. I was in love.

In 1993, after dating Jamie for six months, I moved to Miami to begin law school, leaving her in Maryland. We made a plan that she would soon move to Florida as well. My grandmother did not approve. I would travel on a regular basis to visit her small apartment in (of all places!) Teaneck, New Jersey, to manage her affairs and spend quality time together. During one such visit, when we were driving to her favorite diner for lunch, she told me that Jamie wasn't right for me.

"There are plenty of fish in the sea," she quipped. "You should keep looking."

I was shocked. My grandmother had never taken a position before as to other girlfriends. And moreover, nobody that met Jamie, and saw the effect she had on me, had anything negative to say about our relationship.

"I don't like her," my grandmother continued, avoiding any eye contact. For the first time I entertained a horrific idea: could it be that my grandmother was an anti-Semite?

I asked her "is the reason that you don't like Jamie because she is Jewish?" She nodded, yes. Now I was indignant. "Why should that matter to you?" I demanded.

For the first time she turned to me. In a very direct manner she said "Because I am Jewish, and life is hard enough without being Jewish."

I remember almost driving off the road. My blood ran cold the same way that it had when I received the news my father had died. My mind was spinning with questions.

"You are Jewish?!" I repeated.

"Yes," she said, "life is hard enough without being Jewish, and I never wanted that for you."

That was all she would say on the subject. After fifty-three years, the secret was out, but she was not going to fill in the pieces of the puzzle. That she would leave up to me.

"What does that mean?" Jamie sputtered, when I called her that night with the news. "Does that mean you're Jewish?"

I had no idea, but I was determined to find out. My quest for answers began with an address I got from my grandmother's personal papers. As the pre-appointed executor of her estate, she once told me that upon her passing I should contact a gentleman named Leonard Vis in Toronto. I knew that "Vis," which is the Dutch word for "fish," was my grandmother's maiden name. I immediately wrote to Mr. Leonard Vis to introduce myself, obliquely mentioning that my grandmother, Elly Vis Frank, had recently mentioned some "interesting facts" about my "Dutch heritage," and asking if he "would be so kind as to pass along anything he could add about my family roots?" The day he received my letter, Leonard telephoned me.

"Chris," he said "I've known about you and your sister your entire lives, but I was forbidden by your grandmother from contacting you. Now that you have contacted me, however, all bets are off. Welcome to the family."

He went on to explain that, "yes, your grandmother is Jewish, your grandfather was Jewish and your father, may he rest in peace, was 100% Jewish. You have observant Jewish family in Canada, Holland and Israel." He concluded by saying "Chris, I know that there is a G-d, because he led you back to me."

These two conversations – the first with my grandmother and the second with my cousin Leonard – were the beginning of the most incredible personal journey, bringing me and Jamie all the way to an observant *Torah* life in Hollywood, Florida. How did that happen?

When we began dating, and it became clear to both of us that it was a serious, potentially long-term relationship, Jamie once asked if I would consider converting to Judaism. I was unenthusiastic. To me the idea was absurd. Me? Convert to Judaism? You might as well ask me to become a woman. One doesn't choose Judaism, one simply is or is not Jewish. With my grandmother's revelation that my father was Jewish, however, I did feel compelled to learn something, anything about Judaism. At age twenty-six, for the first time in my life, I tentatively stepped foot into a synagogue, in Miami Beach. The Conservative rabbi there dutifully told me to go somewhere else; assuming my questions indicated an interest in converting. Soon after, I realized that the Jewish approach is to dissuade a potential convert. With this in mind we tried another Conservative rabbi in Miami. I tried to be very clear.

"I'm not saying I want to be Jewish," I told him, "I'm just looking for information."

"That's good" he replied, "because I'm not saying we want you!"

To learn about Judaism he recommended a Conservative-sponsored course, and so, every Wednesday evening, after law school let out, I would pick up Jamie and drive an hour north for our "Jewish class." The first hour was learning Hebrew reading ("letter-vowel, letter-vowel"), followed by an hour of "Judaism 101." Jamie and I learned together about the events of the Jewish life cycle, the *Yom Tovim*, and the history of the Chosen People. For her it was a valuable supplement to her incomplete Jewish education. For me, it was an awakening. Both my intellect and my soul were immediately and irrevocably drawn to *Yiddishkeit*. Soon, I was reading every English book about Judaism that I could get my hands on, and advancing in observance along the way. I can't say I remember the point in time when I realized that I was going to convert, because truly, I never had a transitional moment. Instead, I felt like I was reconnecting to something that was a part of my already existing Jewish *neshamah*. In essence, I had no choice.

At the conclusion of the course the instructor wished us well.

"Now go back to your sponsoring rabbi and he will convert you," we were told.

For me, a Conservative conversion was never a real option. Rather than having finished the process, I believed I had merely begun. My intention was to fully embrace Judaism at the Orthodox level. There was only one problem: Jamie. At this point, she had more than she had ever bargained for. Here she had been dating "Catholic Chris," concerned about the fact that he wasn't Jewish, and now she was dealing with the new and improved Chris, talking about becoming *frum*. Based on her childhood experiences, embracing *frumkeit* was, to put it mildly, not on Jamie's agenda. I realized I would have to win her over, stealthily and incrementally, and that is what I set out to do.

We would each drive to *shul* on *Shabbos* (until Jamie's car was stolen from the parking lot, after which we both decided to walk), and I'd watch Jamie light *Shabbos* candles on Friday evening before I would take her out to happy hour. All the while I kept learning, mostly on my own. In the summer of 1995, between my second and third years of law school, I interned at a Miami law firm. A lawyer there, who herself was Orthodox, called me into her office one day, demanding some answers.

"Okay" she inquired, "what's your deal? Your name is Chris, you keep kosher and your girlfriend lights *Shabbos* candles. What's going on?"

I explained my background to her, and the fact that I was stalled in my *Torah* journey, having "graduated" from the Conservative class, but without an Orthodox mentor with whom to continue my studies.

She was fascinated by my story and eager to help. "I live in Hollywood," she told me. "You have to meet Rabbi Edward Davis. He would work with you."

Our first meeting with Rabbi Davis in September 1995 was a mixed bag. While I was very intimidated and withdrawn (although his uncommon affinity for both the Boston Red Sox and the Washington Redskins was a welcome surprise), Jamie found a new best friend. She and Rabbi Davis clicked, which made any next steps at least possible. Rabbi Davis set out the ground rules from the start. He would work with me towards conversion only if Jamie would agree to adopt an Orthodox life herself.

"What does that mean?" Jamie inquired, feigning ignorance of a subject she knew all too much about.

"It means committing at the very least to observing the laws of *Taharat HaMishpachah*, *Shabbat* and *kashrut*," he replied.

"Give me an example about the laws of keeping kosher," she countered.

"Well," the Rabbi proceeded cautiously, "it means waiting six hours after eating meat before eating dairy."

"Not so!" exclaimed Jamie, playing her ace-in-the-hole. "His father was Dutch! We only have to wait one hour!"

Rabbi Davis was amused. I was mortified. Being a *goy* and a vegetarian at the time, I stayed out of it.

"That won't work," he said, gently. "First off, he's not Jewish, and his father did not keep that *minhag*. No one in this Community keeps one hour. I cannot permit it."

Jamie was undaunted. "Well Rabbi," she asserted, crossing her arms for effect. "I simply cannot do six hours. We'll need to figure that one out."

Rabbi Davis thoughtfully stroked his beard. "You know, my in-laws are *Yekkish*, and they and some others here in Hollywood keep three hours ...."

"Done!" Jamie interjected, slapping her hand on his desk.[1] Jamie and the Rabbi worked through a few more *halachic* items while I sat there stunned, and we left his office with a new lease on our Jewish life. Rabbi Davis proved to be the ideal mentor and *Rav*, managing and refereeing for two independent minds with disparate growth rates. Jamie and I did learn and grow together. The process was sometimes sad, sometimes funny, often difficult, but always interesting.

Rabbi Davis insisted that we learn about *kashrut* from a reliable expert, and recommended Norman Levine as our instructor. I began pestering Norman to meet Jamie and me, but it was March, and as the *mashgiach* for both Coca-Cola and Pepsi in their pre-*Pesach* runs, he kept putting me off. Finally out of guilt or embarrassment, his wife Jeanette (ע״ה) agreed to meet us one early morning at the supermarket in Hollywood to begin our training. Jeanette and Jamie instantly bonded, despite the obvious difference in their backgrounds and levels of *Torah* observance. They went arm-in-arm down each aisle chatting like old friends, while I scampered behind with a clipboard scribbling notes and pictures of allowable kosher symbols from products. It was the beginning of a precious relationship with the Levine family that has lasted and strengthened even to today, despite Jeanette's tragic passing in 2009. The Levines also welcomed us into the magical world of *Shabbos*, and along with Rabbi Davis, were the primary reason we ultimately settled in Hollywood.

---

[1] Years later, I decided to abandon my vegetarian ways and resume eating meat. I called Rabbi Davis for guidance on how long I should wait between eating meat and milk, since I had never faced that issue since conversion. "Your wife negotiated a good deal for you," he quipped. "Wait three hours, but give her a big kiss!"

In my final year of law school, apart from learning the law, I did my best to learn Hebrew, at least well enough for *davening* and elementary *Torah* learning. We began planning a wedding and, at the same time, I undertook to read *Tanach*, in English, in its entirety. In the process, I came across two particular verses in *Navi* that really resonated with me, for they spoke to the reestablishment of Jewish joy through marriage. I telephoned my Hebrew tutor with an idea. I asked if she could translate the *pasukim* into Hebrew for inclusion on our wedding invitation.

"Sure," she said. "What are the verses?"

"They're from Jeremiah," I replied. "'So said the Lord, "Again there shall be heard, ... in the streets of Judah, and the courtyards of Jerusalem ...."'" I was interrupted by singing on the other end of the line. "Kol sasson, v' kol simchah, kol chattan, v' kol kallah!"

I was perplexed. "Sorry, what's going on?" I asked.

She kept on joyously singing, now joined by her father in the background. At some point she finished and got serious. "Chris," she told me, "you picked the one part in all of *Tanach* that is on every Jewish wedding invitation. עוֹד יִשָּׁמַע ... ,בְּעָרֵי יְהוּדָה וּבְחֻצוֹת יְרוּשָׁלַם ... ,קוֹל שָׂשׂוֹן וְקוֹל שִׂמְחָה קוֹל חָתָן וְקוֹל כַּלָּה," "Again there shall be heard, ... in the streets of Yehudah and in the courtyards of Yerushalayim, ... the sound of joy and the sound of gladness, the voice of the groom and the voice of the bride." (Yirmiyahu 33:10, 11) I took that as a positive sign.

In the summer of 1996 I underwent my conversion, adopting the Hebrew name Menashe Shmuel. In 1998, I legally changed my name to Menashe Ronald Frank. I chose Menashe because, as a result of my journey through *Tanach*, more than any other *Torah* personage, I felt a kinship to *Yosef's* elder son, based on some similarities in our backgrounds. *Menashe* grew up in *Mitzrayim*, after his father had become estranged from *Bnei Yisrael*. Years later, after his father's death, *Menashe* and his brother *Ephraim* left the Egyptian society of their birth to rejoin their People. I found his story poignant, as well as relevant.

I also chose Shmuel because, as best as I could determine, that was my father's Hebrew name: שמואל בן אברהם הלוי ע"ה. Much of the Jewish records in Holland were destroyed during the War. Of course, as a convert, I am not called "ben Shmuel," "son of Shmuel," but rather "ben Avraham," "the son of Avraham," the Father of the Jewish People. Nonetheless, I wished to honor my father in some way through adding his name to mine.

My research into the extended family tree was a separate odyssey that began in earnest following our wedding in autumn of 1996. Cousin Leonard introduced me to his brother Arthur Vis, his nephew Reuben Vis and his niece Maureen Vis-Glaser of Amsterdam, and I traveled there to do research on the family with their help. My grandfather, Albert Siegfried Frank (אברהם בן שמואל הלוי ע״ה), was the son of Samuel Frank (שמואל בן אברהם הלוי ע״ה) and Rosalie Schoolmeester-Frank, whose *kevarot* in Holland I have visited. Albert and my grandmother Elly (בילא הנא בת משה ע״ה) were married in a traditional Jewish ceremony, and I was thrilled to find a copy of their *ketubah* in the Amsterdam public archives. Albert owned a factory in Haarlem, Holland, that produced a medicinal elixir called "Haarlemerolie," which he successfully marketed through European and American pharmaceutical companies. My father, their only child, became chronically ill at a young age, but that was the least of their worries. In August 1940 they were vacationing in the south of France. It seems they had an inkling that something dreadful was afoot, for they took with them certain family heirlooms, including my grandmother's silver candlesticks. When the Germans, *yemach shemam*, invaded Holland, my grandparents knew they could not return. Astonishingly, based on their business contacts, they were able to obtain visas to come to the United States that year, something almost unheard of for Jewish refugees at that time. They came to America with only those items they had with them, and the bulk of their wealth, including the family factory, was never reclaimed. When they arrived in America they promptly dropped all Jewish connections and distanced themselves from their family now trapped in Europe.[2] They were now

---

[2]In the course of my family research I discovered that Elly and Albert sent care packages to family and friends in Europe after the war, and even formally sponsored some Jewish families who sought to immigrate to the United States.

officially "non-Jews." They registered at a local church but seldom attended, instead raising my father without any religion or awareness of his heritage.

On that fateful day, when she disclosed to me her long-kept secret, my grandmother said two things that spoke volumes and proved prescient: "Life is hard enough, without being Jewish," and "I never wanted that for you." Her life was certainly difficult, despite her attempts to hide her faith. She was a war refugee who lost both her husband and her only child to early deaths. She herself passed away in the summer of 2000, and I recall thinking of how distressed she would have been had she lived to see the horror of September 11, 2001. Grandma was absolutely right about the dangers of being Jewish. In the nineteen years since my conversion, latent anti-Semitism around world has become increasingly and alarmingly manifested. It truly is dangerous to be Jewish. Yet I have never regretted my decision. Perhaps even more prophetic was Grandma's statement that she never wanted me to adopt Judaism, suggesting then what even I did not know: that, by virtue of being with Jamie, I would one day choose to become Jewish. Yet that is exactly what happened

Since embracing *Yiddishkeit* my life has taken more amazing turns. My wife and I continue to strive to grow in *Torah* and *mitzvot*. We've become very connected to my extended family in Canada, Holland and Israel, while at the same time retaining close ties to my mother and sister, who have respectfully accepted and supported my decisions. *Hashem* has blessed Jamie and me with two daughters, Yael Rani (Ronny was my father's nickname) and Esther Miriam, and two sons, Binyamin Pinchas and Ayden Avraham. Binyamin Pinchas was the first Jewish Frank boy born in America and, *Baruch Hashem*, he is now becoming a *Bar Mitzvah*. In some ways, of course, this represents the total frustration of my grandmother's plan, for she wanted my father to be the last Jewish Frank baby anywhere in the world. Yet against all odds, *Hashem* orchestrated a completely different outcome. Recall that when my grandmother made her shocking admission she did not say to me "I was Jewish," or "I used to be Jewish," but rather she said "I am Jewish." I think that, in the end, prior to her death, my grandmother came to terms with my decision, which she may have viewed as inevitable. After all, as a wedding present, she gave Jamie those silver candlesticks that had survived the War. The fact that they are continually used to hold our weekly *Shabbos* lights is ironic, as well as beautiful.

In Parashat Behaalotecha, *Moshe* pleads with his father-in-law *Yitro,* a convert to Judaism, not to return to his native *Midyan,* but rather to remain with *Bnei Yisrael* in their journey to the Promised Land. "וַיֹּאמֶר אַל נָא תַּעֲזֹב אֹתָנוּ כִּי | עַל כֵּן יָדַעְתָּ חֲנֹתֵנוּ בַּמִּדְבָּר וְהָיִיתָ לָּנוּ לְעֵינָיִם," "He said, 'Please don't leave us, for you know of our encampments in the desert and you will be <u>eyes for us</u>." (Bamidbar 10:31) There are many interpretations of what, exactly, *Moshe* was telling *Yitro.* Rabbi Yaacov Sipper brings a provocative idea. *Bnei Yisrael* was living a unique and miraculous existence since leaving *Mitzrayim.* They received nourishment daily in the *Mon* from *Shamayim.* They traveled in the climate-controlled *Anani HaKavod,* immune from all environmental dangers. Most importantly, they merited to learn *Torah* constantly and continually. It was by all objective reasoning a charmed life. Any yet, there was among them complaining, rebellion, and rejection, even under such pristine conditions. *Yitro's* decision to reject his past and embrace *Torah* gave him a perspective that the born-Jew did not have. *Moshe* rightly reasoned that *Yitro* could be "eyes" for those born-Jews by which to see and appreciate the tremendous gifts that they had been given, so as to not take any of them for granted. Rabbi Sipper told me that every *geir* can make this same unique contribution to the Jewish People, and I sincerely hope and pray that this *sefer,* in light of the personal story that made it possible, will be mine.

May it be that my children, and their children, and all of *Am Yisrael,* will treasure forever, with true gratitude to *Hashem,* the priceless gift that has been passed to them, and as a result of that appreciation, will live lives of *Torah,* and *mitzvot,* worthy of the splendorous legacy of *Hashem's Am Segulah.*

Albert S. Frank and a young Ronald A. Frank

Elisabeth Vis Frank, Ronald A. Frank
and Christopher R. Frank

Ronald A. Frank (1934-1984)

Graves of great grandparents, Samuel and Rosalie Frank

Graves of great grandparents, Maurits and Louisa Vis

Ketubah of Albert S. Frank and Elisabeth Vis Frank.

PARSHIOT

SEFER BERESHIT
BERESHIT

5757

Hashem tells *Chavah* that her husband will rule over her. (Bereshit 3:16) Husbands have a duty to reduce this curse. The serpent was cursed that it should crawl upon its belly and strike at the heels of man, yet just as one does not walk barefoot in the forest so as to allow the snake to bite his heels, so too must one strive to ensure that the curse of *Chavah* should not be fulfilled.

5758

The *Torah* makes clear that one should not add to the *mitzvot* of *Hashem*. *Chavah* told the snake that *Hashem* had instructed her "to neither eat nor touch" the tree (Bereshit 3:3), yet *Hashem* instructed *Adam* only not to eat of the tree. (Bereshit 2:17) The *Gemara* tells us (Sanhedrin 29a) that when *Chavah* touched the tree and did not die, her willingness to comply with the prohibition of eating from the tree was diminished and disaster ensued. One lesson is that if one seeks to add a *chumrah* with respect to serving *Hashem*, one must identify it as his own, not the Will of *Hashem*.

5759

Rabbi Israel Schepansky – Why was *Kayin* not executed by *Hashem* for *Hevel's* murder? Perhaps because the rationale of the death penalty is deterrence and not retribution. Since *Adam* and *Chavah* were the only remaining humans, nothing would be served in killing *Kayin*.

5760

The *parashah*, in describing the Creation of the world, begins with a "ב", "bet," while the Ten Commandments begin with an "א", "aleph." (Shemot 20:2) This teaches that the *mitzvot* existed before Creation, and that the purpose of Creation is the fulfillment of *Torah* and *mitzvot*.

Mankind destroyed much of the *Kedushah* of Creation on Friday, Day Six of Creation, however *Shabbat* had not yet been created and was therefore not impacted. For this reason, we have a special responsibility not to ruin the special day of *Shabbat*, our gift from *Hashem*.

Rabbi Elias Schwartz – The curse of the serpent was to eat dust all the days of its life. (Bereshit 3:14) But since dust is plentiful and accessible everywhere, was this really the harshest curse? In truth, the curse is the worst, because at no time does the snake raise his eyes to Heaven in search of sustenance. Bound to earth, he has no occasion to connect to his Creator. Man, conversely, in his limited time between emerging from the dust and returning to the dust, has the potential to connect to *Hashem* as the Source of all nourishment – spiritual or otherwise. Man, unlike the serpent, can look upward to better himself.

Rabbi Edward Davis – Woman was created from man by *Hashem* while *Adam* was sleeping. (Bereshit 2:21) Sleep is seen by *Chazal* as a relinquishing of control, as is *Shabbat*. Man has no claim to control woman, as *Hashem* took man out of the Creation equation. As with *Shabbat*, man must realize he is not in control of his wife.

Before *maariv* on Friday afternoon, as we are accepting *Shabbat*, we read the *Mishnah* that directs that a person is required to examine his clothing on *Erev Shabbat*, just before dark. (Shabbat 12a) *Chazal* (Avodah Zareh 3a) compare this world to *Erev Shabbat* and the World to Come as *Shabbat*. *Rabbi Chananya* is admonishing us to check our "clothes," which are the *mitzvot* that we are "wearing," before we leave this world, to ensure a pleasant "*Shabbat*" in the world to come. Since one never knows the date and time of his departure from this world, continual *mitzvot* performance and reflection is essential.

5761

Dr. Gerald Schroeder – The Creation story is punctuated with a narrative repeating the words "vayehee erev, vayehee vokeir … ," which is commonly translated as "and it was evening and it was morning … ," yet because the sun was created on Day Four, the understanding must be deeper. The word "erev" connotes chaos (an "eruv" is a mixture) and "boker" is connected to order. The Universe was organizing in stages, where disarray became ordered day by day.

5762

Rabbi Edward Davis – According to *Rabbi Akiva* "v'ahavta l'raiacha k'mocha," "love your neighbor as yourself," (Vayikra 19:18) is the *pasuk* conveying the essence of the *Torah*, but *Ben Azai's* opinion, recorded in the *Yerushalmi* (Nedarim 9:4) holds that it is actually "zeh sefer toldot *Adam*," "this is the book of the generations of man." (Bereshit 5:1) These stories in *Parashat Bereshit* signify the essence of the human condition – the choice to do good or evil was in the hands of *Adam* and *Kayin*, and is the choice we all face on a daily basis.

5763

Rabbi Edward Davis – There is a misunderstanding regarding the first mitzvah of the *Torah*. *Hashem* did not make the first command to *Adam* and *Chavah* that they may not eat from the "Eitz HaDa'at Tov v'Rah", "the Tree of Knowledge of Good and Evil." (Bereshit 2:17) Rather the *pasuk* says "וַיְצַו ה׳ אלקים עַל הָאָדָם לֵאמֹר מִכֹּל עֵץ הַגָּן אָכֹל תֹּאכֵל," "And *Hashem* G-d <u>commanded</u> the man, saying 'Of every tree of the garden you may eat freely.'" (Bereshit 2:16) By using the language of commandment, the *Torah* is first instructing man to enjoy: a *mitzvah aseh*, not a *mitzvah lo t'aseh*! Of course there have to be limits, but *Hashem* demands that we enjoy ourselves in this wonderful world that He has created for us. Rabbi Yossi Jankovits points out that the *Yerushalmi* (end of Kedushin) says that in the future, *Hashem* will exact justice against someone who sees something nice to eat and does not partake of it.

5764

Rabbi Chaim Flom – The *pasuk* says "וַיֹּאמֶר ה׳ לֹא יָדוֹן רוּחִי בָאָדָם לְעֹלָם בְּשַׁגַּם הוּא בָשָׂר וְהָיוּ יָמָיו מֵאָה וְעֶשְׂרִים שָׁנָה," "And *Hashem* said, 'My Spirit shall not contend evermore concerning man because he is flesh; besides his days shall be 120 years.'" (Bereshit 6:3) The word "b'shagam," is translated as "because," or "on account of." The *Gemara* (Chulin 139b) tells us that the *gematria* of "Moshe" is equal to "b'shagam." *Moshe's* greatness was overcoming his undeniable humanness. He was a flesh and blood human, yet <u>because</u> or <u>on account of</u> this, what he achieved is all the more impressive.

Rabbi Eli Mansour – In the *Chumash* there is a reference to everyone and everything that was and will be. *Haman, yemach shemo*, is mentioned in *Parashat Bereshit*. The *pasuk* states "וַיֹּאמֶר מִי הִגִּיד לְךָ כִּי עֵירֹם אָתָּה הֲמִן הָעֵץ אֲשֶׁר צִוִּיתִיךָ לְבִלְתִּי אֲכָל מִמֶּנּוּ אָכָלְתָּ," "And He Said, 'Who told you that you are naked? Have you eaten of the tree from which I commanded you not to eat?'" (Bereshit 3:11) The *Gemara* (Chulin 139b) states that "hamin" ("the type [of tree]") and "*Haman*" are spelled the same, and *Chazal* see similarities in the behavior of *Adam HaRishon* and *Haman*. *Adam* had everything he could ever want but was not satisfied. *Haman* also had everything except the respect and obedience of *Mordechai*. In both cases what was lacking brought about the destruction of an otherwise ideal situation.

5765

Rabbi Yossi Jankovits – The *pasuk* reads "אֵלֶּה תוֹלְדוֹת הַשָּׁמַיִם וְהָאָרֶץ בְּהִבָּרְאָם בְּיוֹם עֲשׂוֹת ה' אלקים אֶרֶץ וְשָׁמָיִם," "These are the generations of the heavens and the earth when they were created on the day of *Hashem's*, G-d's, making of earth and heavens." (Bereshit 2:4) According to the Baal HaTurim, the word "b'heebaram," "when they were created," can be rearranged to spell "b'Avraham," meaning with *Avraham* the purpose of *Hashem's* Creation was achieved. This is hinted at by the spelling of "b'heebaram" in the *Sefer Torah*, where the "heh" is written smaller than the other letters. Of course a "heh" was ultimately added to *Avram's* name to complete him as a servant of *Hashem*. (Bereshit 17:5)

5767

Reb Sammy Grundwerg – Rabbi Eliyahu Schlesinger tells us that where the *pasuk* states "na'aseh adam," "let us make man," (Bereshit 1:26) *Hashem* is referring to the eternal "shituf bein Adam l'Makom," the partnership between Man and G-d. As the only creation with *bechirah*, each human is eligible at any time to be a true partner with *Hashem* in turning (i.e. "creating") himself to be a faithful servant to He who created him.

5768

Reb Ephraim Sobol – *Rashi* indicates that "Bereshit" can mean "for reishit," meaning "for the sake of the first." (*Rashi* on Bereshit 1:1) Much commentary is developed on the question of what is "reishit." Every morning, upon arising, we declare "Reishit chachmah yirat Hashem ... ," "The beginning of wisdom is fear of Hashem ...." (Tehillim 111:10) From this we can learn that "reishit" is fear of *Hashem*, and therefore for the sake of man's fear of *Hashem* the world was created. Through fear of *Hashem*, as manifested in following his *mitzvot*, we fulfill the purpose of Creation.

5769

Rabbi Yitzchak Salid – "Bereshit" is often read as "In the beginning ..." but it can be read as "with the beginning ..." meaning "with the advent of a beginning" (i.e. with the creation of time), *Hashem* made the Heavens and the Earth. This would support the timelessness of *Hashem* and His *Torah*, and present time as a construct for aiding Jews in performing the *Torah* in fulfillment of our Divine Mission.

5770

Rabbi Yosef Weinstock – *Hashem* declares "lo tov heyot haadam l'vado ... ," "it is not good for man to be alone ...." (Bereshit 2:18) Certainly, we can say that *Hashem*, as *Adam's* Creator, knew that *Chavah* was the ideal mate for him, yet Hashem first formed from the ground every beast and bird and presented them to *Adam*. *Adam* named all the animals, yet the *Torah* tells us "ul'Adam lo matza eizer k'negdo," "but the man did not find a helper for himself." (Bereshit 2:20) Only then did *Hashem* present *Adam* with his perfect mate. We see here that *Hashem* alone determines the timing on delivering the solutions we expect for our problems, and sometimes He deems it necessary for us to wait and struggle in order to receive His intended benefits.

5771

What is meant by the term "eizer k'negdo?" (Bereshit 2:20) Literally, the words mean "a helper against him." Many commentators indicate that a helper in opposition to a husband can be a wife who will disagree respect-fully with him and guide him when he is acting rashly or improperly. By placing him on the correct path, she is truly a helper to him.

5772

Rabbi Daniel Kunstler – The *pasuk* says "vayivarech Elokim et yom hash'vee'ee vaikadeish oto ... ," "G-d *blessed* the seventh day and *sanctified* it ...." (Bereshit 2:3) From here we see that Hashem made *Shabbat* special by both blessing it and sanctifying it, and was instructing the Jews on how, by emulating His ways, we too make *Shabbat* special. In the *zemer* we sing of Friday night we say ",כָּל מְקַדֵּשׁ שְׁבִיעִי כָּרָאוּי לוֹ, כָּל שֹׁמֵר שַׁבָּת כַּדָּת מֵחַלְּלוֹ, "שְׂכָרוֹ הַרְבֵּה מְאֹד עַל פִּי פָעֳלוֹ, אִישׁ עַל מַחֲנֵהוּ וְאִישׁ עַל דִּגְלוֹ," "Whoever <u>sanctifies</u> the *Shabbat* as befits it, whoever <u>safeguards</u> the *Shabbat* properly from desecration, his reward is exceedingly great in accordance with his deed." The Chofetz Chaim states that this song describes the two necessary ingredients of a successful *Shabbat*: not merely <u>safeguarding</u> *Shabbat* (by avoiding transgressions of the negative commandments) but also <u>sanctifying</u> it (through learning *Torah, oneg,* etc.). Similarly, based on the *pasuk* in Bereshit, *Hashem* does not merely want us to "bless" the *Shabbat* by making *kiddush* Friday night and at lunch, but to also "sanctify" *Shabbat* and make it Holy through our entire approach to the day.

5773

Rabbi Menashe ben Yisrael – With respect to all Creation except for man, Hashem said "yehi," "let there be," which implies separation and distance between Creator and His Creation. With respect to humans, *Hashem* said "naaseh adam," "let us make man," (Bereshit 1:26), which implied intimate connection between Creator and Man. *Hashem* associated Himself with the act of creating Man to demonstrate Man's inherent greatness and superiority over animals.

NOACH

5759

Kotzker Rebbe – *Noach* was a *tzaddik*, yet in the *Haftorah* (Yishaiyah 54:9) the destructive waters of the *mabul* are called "the waters of Noach." This shows that *Noach* bears some responsibility for the Flood. Unlike *Avraham*, *Noach* did not plead to *Hashem* for the people of the world, nor did he actively work to bring about their repentance. This is similar to a situation where many people are sitting in a bitterly cold room, and one departs the room and returns to join them wearing a big warm fur coat. *Noach* is compared to a "*tzaddik* in peltz," a righteous man in a fur coat. *Avraham*, by contrast, departs the room and returns with wood by which to make a fire to warm everyone. The lesson is that we need to be concerned with the spiritual development not only of ourselves but of those around us.

5760

It has been suggested that *Noach* made himself naked following the Flood in an attempt to return man to his state in *Gan Ayden*. After witnessing the extreme devastation of the world, he wanted to change the role of man in the world back to its original conception. To accomplish this he planted a vineyard to make wine to release inhibition. His sons saw clearly that the chance of *Gan Ayden* was lost, and covered him to symbolize that we must live in the world as we find it, not as we wish it to be.

Shem walked backwards to cover his drunken father so as to avoid seeing his nakedness, and by honoring his father in this way was rewarded with children who were commanded in the mitzvah of *Tzitzit* (Rashi on Bereshit 9:23). This is a logical connection, for *Tzitit* are meant to remind us to direct our eyes to avoid sin.

With regard to the Tower of Bavel the Torah says "vayered Hashem lirot et ha'ir v'et hamigdal ...," "and *Hashem* descended to look at the city and the tower ...." (Bereshit 11:5) Of course, *Hashem* did not actually descend or spend time analyzing the situation. Instead, Rashi, based on the Midrash Tanchuma, tells us that we learn that *Hashem's* example is meant to show judges (and all humans for that matter) not to pass judgment without getting all the facts first.

While humor is often used to neutralize a serious situation, it can sometimes be dangerous. When *Noach* became drunk and exposed, his son *Cham* saw his condition as humorous, rather than requiring serious remediation, and for this he is forever faulted.

5761

In the process of attempting to abstain from speaking *lashon hara* one struggles greatly with the *yetzer hara*. The urge to tell others how someone wronged us is great and exhausting. One technique to lessening this burden is to be "dan l'kaf zechut," to judge others favorably. People generally don't eagerly seek to relay information that is either favorable or *pareve*. By reframing an incident in one's mind to give others the benefit of the doubt and refusing to see the event as negative when the situation could be read as an affront, one is able, so to speak, to outwit the *yetzer hara*. A human will struggle to contain negative information he has already internalized, but it is less difficult to transform a negative interaction into a positive one before it ever enters one's psyche.

Sefas Emes – A classic question exists concerning the disparate punishments meted out for the *Dor HaMabul* and those who worked on the *Migdal Bavel*. In the case of those preceding the Flood, they engaged in robbery and illicit relations and were exterminated. For the Tower builders, they waged war with G-d yet were merely dispersed. The common answer is that *Hashem* can tolerate affronts to Him so long as people respect one another, but when they treat each other poorly the purpose of Creation is seen as frustrated and the only choice is to start over. The Sefas Emes gives a different answer. The generation of the Flood was steeped in physicality: illicit relations and stealing property from one another. Such behavior leaves humans indistinguishable from the animals and unable to fulfil their mission. The generation of the Tower was operating in a spiritual context: severely misdirected but spiritual nonetheless. *Hashem* can, so to speak, work with people who are willing to struggle with spiritual ideas. Ultimately, such people can embrace the proper path, and therefore such a generation need not be destroyed.

5762

Rabbi Yissocher Frand – *Noach* is credited with inventing the plow and thereby revolutionizing farming, in effect lessening the curse imposed upon

Adam at the expulsion from *Gan Ayden*. Rav Avraham Pam points out that while it was *Noach's* generation that enjoyed an easier life by virtue of the plow, it was also the generation that became corrupt and deserving of death. Rav Pam draws a correlation between leisure time and moral depravity. There is a great *mussar* lesson concerning the danger of adopting time and effort saving tools in our lives.

5763

Rabbi Yosef Kalatsky – The *parashah* begins "אֵלֶּה תּוֹלְדֹת נֹחַ נֹחַ אִישׁ צַדִּיק תָּמִים הָיָה בְּדֹרֹתָיו אֶת הָאלקים הִתְהַלֶּךְ נֹחַ," "These are the offspring of Noach, Noach was a righteous man, perfect in his generations; Noach walked with G-d." (Bereshit 6:9) As the sole survivor of the Flood, it is fair to say that all mankind descends from *Noach*. As such, it is important for the *Torah* to inform mankind that just as *Noach* was a *tzaddik*, so it is within the reach of all of his descendants.

5764

Rabbi Eli Mansour – The *Torah* teaches that *Nimrod*, a descendant of *Cham*, was a "mighty hunter before Hashem." (Bereshit 10:9) The Ibn Ezra writes that *Nimrod* would bring great animals that he hunted as sacrifices to *Hashem*. The Ramban criticizes this approach of making a known *rasha* into a *tzaddik*. The Alter of Kelm reconciles the two positions. The Jewish measurement of the value of a man is the sum of the "little things" that he does. Small acts of *chesed* and service show loyalty to *Hashem*, more so than dramatic actions. *Nimrod* advocated isolated dramatic actions to indicate moral status, and that's why he is a *rasha*. He was trying to assert that it is only our "big deeds" that count, when in fact it is all the "little things" for which we ultimately are judged. MRF Note – I originally gave this *vort* at a *kiddush* in honor of Rabbi Dr. Paul Ginsberg, a *gabbai* extraordinaire and tremendous contributor to the Hollywood Jewish Community.

Rabbi Yossi Jankovits — How is it possible that *Noach* planted a vineyard and got drunk immediately after exiting the Ark? *Hashem* gave him a *berachah* that the first thing he would do after leaving would be successful.

5765

Rabbi Yossi Jankovits — The *pasuk* says "Noach, Noach, ish tzaddik ...." "Noach, Noach was a righteous man ...." (Bereshit 6:9) *Noach* is spelled identical to "Nach," "rest," a word that is used to describe the Rest of *Hashem* and all of Creation on *Shabbat*. The lesson of the *pasuk* is as set forth in the Talmud (Shabbat 118b) that if the world would observe two consecutive *Shabbatot* (nach, nach), then "ish tzaddik," a righteous man (i.e. *Moshiach*) would arrive.

Rabbi Yitzchak Assouli — It says in the *Talmud* (Zevachim 113b) that there was a huge creature named the *re'eim* that did not fit into the *Teivah*, but was preserved during the *Mabul* by placing its head inside the Ark while its body remained outside. This is a lesson for survival in the spiritual "flood" we are experiencing in our times. We must have our thoughts and attention in the *beit midrash* or *shul* in order to survive.

5767

Rabbi Yossi Jankovits — Rashi comments on the apparent problem in the first *pasuk* of the *parashah*. "Ailah toldot Noach, Noach ish tzaddik ...." "These are the generations of Noach: Noach was a righteous man ...." (Bereshit 6:9) The *pasuk* mentions the offspring of *Noach* and then delays in naming them until the following verse. Perhaps the message is that the offspring of a man will ultimately be a reflection of the actions of that man. As Rabbi Eli Mansour points out, the truest *chinuch* for a child is providing a *Torah* example for that child. In indicating that *Noach* was a *tzaddik* before naming his sons, the *Torah* is telling us that he was righteous and, as Rashi indicates there, the primary offspring of a man are his good deeds. And taking it one step further, a man's children will learn from and adopt the positive character traits of their father and become his literal and figurative offspring. Yet the question then arises, what of the *tzaddik* who, despite his good deeds, has an evil son (for example *Avraham* had *Yishmael*; *Yitzchak* had *Eisav*)? In separating *Noach* from his sons, including *Cham*, the *pasuk* may be indicating that in such cases, where the father has led a virtuous life and is not therefore liable for his son's divergence from *Torah*, *Hashem* will still judge the father as a *tzaddik*.

5768

Rabbi Michael Jablinowitz – A classic question, raised by Rashi, is why the *Torah* states "Ailah toldot Noach, Noach ...." "These are the offspring of Noach, Noach ...." (Bereshit 6:9), and then fails to immediately recite his "toldot," offspring. The Torah states "Noach ish tzaddik ...." "Noach was a righteous man ...." Here Rashi states that the "toldot" of a *tzaddik* are his *maasim tovim*. The *Gemara* teaches "The Rabbis taught in a *Baraita*: There are three partners in the creation of a person: The Holy One, Blessed is He, and the father and the mother." (Niddah 31a) Clearly, based on this *Gemara*, one cannot take sole credit for one's children. What one can take credit for are his good deeds, and as such, these are one's "toldot."

5769

Rabbi Yitzchak Salid – We commonly consider *Noach* to be deficient in his religious standing in comparison to *Avraham*, and the traditional understanding is that *Noach's* failure in *kiruv* is the difference. Yet the only person in all of *Tanach* described as a *tzaddik* is *Noach* (it is the Rabbis, not the *Torah*, that refer to *Yosef* as a *tzaddik*). We do see that *Noach* fell far in his righteousness following the *Mabul*, when, with all of mankind destroyed, the opportunity for *kiruv* had left him. Perhaps we can say that *Noach's* fall from grace was a simple manifestation of the fact that following the Flood there was no one to *mikareiv*, and that it was by the merit of the existence of a continuing population of people to bring closer to *Hashem* that *Avraham* was able to maintain his righteousness.

5770

Rabbi Edward Davis – The story is told of the Berditchever Rebbe who came to a certain city. When the time came to *daven* they needed to make a *minyan*. The Rebbe inquired about a particular *Yid*, and the townsfolk told him "oh, you mean Reuven the Thief." The Rebbe scolded the townsfolk for referring to a fellow Jew in such a pejorative manner. Days later, the Rebbe was leaving town and wanted to deposit some money for safekeeping until his return. Someone suggested Reuven and the Rebbe quickly dismissed the suggestion, questioning how one could recommend "Reuven the Thief." When the townsfolk challenged the Rebbe based on his apparent double standard, he brought support for his approach from Parashat Noach. When describing the animals to be brought into the *Teivah* for saving, the *Torah* mentions both the "tahora," the "pure" and the "lo tahora," the "not pure." (Bereshit 7:2) Here the impure animals are not called "tameia," "impure," but rather are euphemistically referred to as not being the desired thing – pure. Yet later in the *Torah*, in the context of the animals that are fit to be used for food, the *Torah* unequivocally designates some animals as *tahor* and some as *tamei*, and therefore unfit for Jewish consumption (*Noach* did not have these laws so it was not of practical concern for him). Explained the Rebbe, "I was insistent that we show Reuven respect in reference to him as a member of the community, but on the practical question of holding money, then it was necessary to be unequivocal and state clearly that the man was a thief and could not be trusted." The *Torah* compels both approaches. Our job is to identify the context and, from that, the proper way to conduct ourselves.

5771

Rabbi Dovid Feinstein – The *pasuk* states "וַתִּשָּׁחֵת הָאָרֶץ לִפְנֵי הָאלקים וַתִּמָּלֵא הָאָרֶץ חָמָס" "Now the earth had become corrupted before G-d; and the earth had become filled with robbery." (Bereshit 6:11) This clearly indicates that the corruption preceded the robbery. Rashi, based on the *Gemara* (Sanhedrin 57a), tells us this corruption refers to idolatry and immorality, sins against (i.e. "before") Hashem, or what modern society would term "victimless crimes." Yet these private acts inevitably break down human decency to a point where robbery, the sin that sealed the fate of the generation, can prevail. From this we learn that perverse consensual behavior is a gateway to violent crimes and the breakdown of society.

5772

Rabbi Avraham Yitzchak Kook – Often *Noach* is compared unfavorably to *Avraham*. According to the opinion of *Rav Yochanan* in the *Talmud* (Zevachim 113a), *Noach* was aware, based on the dove's return with the olive branch, that while he was imprisoned on the *Teivah, Eretz Yisrael* remained at least partially unscathed. That should have inspired *Noach* to settle the Goodly Land. This is why the *Torah* later drops the original title of "tamim," "perfect" in describing *Noach*. Tamim describes a connection to *Eretz Yisrael*, the "inheritance" described in Tehillim (37:18). This lack of a connection to *Eretz Yisrael* is why *Noach* is not regarded as the progenitor of the Jewish People.

5773

Rabbi Edward Davis – *Mefarshim* indicate that the reason that *Lot* was admonished not to turn back to witness the destruction of *Sodom* was that but-for the *zechut* of *Avraham*, *Lot* would have himself been destroyed. In essence, *Lot* did not merit to witness the destruction he rightfully should have endured. There is a *machloket* among the Commentators as to whether *Noach* was a *tzaddik*, or merely the "best of the worst." There is also a *machloket* as to whether the "tzohar" of the *Teivah* (Bereshit 6:16) was a window or an illuminated precious stone. For those who say that *Noach* was purely righteous, a window would make sense, for witnessing the destruction of the generation would not present any issue. For those who see *Noach* as less than righteous, and perhaps himself deserving of death at some level, the *Tzohar* would be viewed as opaque, not allowing

Noach to view the destruction, applying the principle that was applied to *Lot*. (See Pardes Yosef in the name of Eidut b'Yosef)

LECH LECHA

5757

Contrary to the conventional understanding, *Hashem* does <u>not</u> tell *Avraham* that his children will be as numerous as the stars, but rather that counting them will be <u>as impossible</u> as counting the stars. (Bereshit 15:5)

5758

Avraham is faulted by some commentators for distancing himself from his nephew *Lot*, who *Avraham* believed to be a bad influence. According to this opinion, had he achieved a level whereby he could have kept *Lot* near to himself, *Avraham* could have effected a change of character in *Lot*. The message for observant Jews is to recognize the negative but close forces in our lives and to try to be an example (not a stranger) to the nonreligious people that we love.

5759

We are taught previously in Parashat Noach that the "generations" of *Noach* were the good deeds he performed in his lifetime. (Rashi on Bereshit 6:9) Yet in the story of Avraham Avinu, we learn (Midrash Rabbah 63:2) that had *Avraham* not been the grandfather of *Yaacov Avinu*, then *Avraham* would have been burned alive in the furnace at *Ur Kasdim*, his second of ten tests from *Hashem*. The distinction is acute. *Noach*, as a non-Jew, was essentially "on his own" in terms of righteousness. Yet the merit of *Yaacov* reached back in time to save his grandfather *Avraham* even before he had children. This is the wonder of the "Peoplehood" that comprises the Jewish Nation. The unbroken chain from *Avraham* to the present provides immeasurable protection and favor for every Jew in every era.

5760

By having *Avraham* and *Sarah* travel so much, *Hashem* imbued them with an appreciation for *hachnasat orchim* provided to travelers. This was similar to the life of the Chernobyl Rebbe who dedicated his life to ransoming Jewish prisoners because he himself had once been imprisoned.

Our Sages of the *Talmud* (Yoma 28b) tell us that *Avraham* kept the *mitzvot* before *Matan Torah* with the sole exception of *brit milah*, which *Avraham* waited to perform until commanded to do so. Since *milah* is a *mitzvah* that can only be performed once, *Avraham* wanted to observe it as best as possible, as a "metzuvah v'oseh," "one who is commanded and does," rather than as one who volunteers for the *mitzvah*. The Gemara (Kiddushin 31a) tells us that one who performs an obligatory *mitzvah* is greater than one who observes a voluntary *mitzvah*, because the former must overcome the *yetzer hara* that arises to disrupt his performance.

5761

Rabbi Akiva Tatz – *Avraham's* journey in Parashat Lech Lecha is a proto-typical *Torah* journey, which begins in clarity and proceeds without knowledge of the destination. One does not know what will be. It is like a person who is commanded to climb 10,000 flights of stairs and starts, obviously not knowing how he will accomplish the task. He begins nonetheless, and after struggling to make it up 100 flights, he discovers an elevator that takes him to the top. Something unnatural happens and the one on a *Torah* journey transcends nature and succeeds.

Rabbi Yisroel Ciner – Before entering *Mitzrayim* due to the famine in *Eretz Yisrael*, *Avram* says to *Sarai* "hinei na yadati ki isha yifat mareh at," "now I know you are a woman of beautiful appearance." (Bereshit 12:11) Rashi indicates that "na" means "now," that even after years of marriage and while on a grueling journey *Sarai* retained her beauty, and it was recognized by *Avram*. This is an example to which we must aspire in our relationships. As a marriage matures and develops, one must see the sustained beauty in one's wife, and, importantly, tell her.

Rabbi Yossi Jankovits – At the end of Parashat Balak, *Pinchas* rises up and takes "רמח" a "romach," or spear, in his hand. (Bamidbar 25:7) The word romach is missing a "vav," as it should be spelled "רומח." Without the "vav," the *gematria* of romach is 248, the number of sinews in a person's body, as well as the numerical value of the word "Avraham." *Pinchas* was outraged at the fact that *Zimri* was using his male organ, which had the sign of the *brit* of *Avraham*, for an unholy purpose (cohabitating with a Midianite woman), and he acted with every fiber of his body (248 sinews) in killing them both. As a reward, in Parashat Pinchas, *Hashem* gives *Pinchas* a covenant of peace and a covenant of priesthood. (Bamidbar 25: 12,13) Where the word "shalom," "peace," is written in the *Torah* there is a line through the "vav" (note, another "vav issue"), seeming to indicate that the gift is something other than peace. Without the "vav," the words can be read as "briti shaleim," "My covenant of 'shaleim,'" rather than "My covenant of peace." In Parashat Lech Lecha, after defeating the Four Kings, *Avram* is met by "Malkitzedek, Melech *Shaleim*," who brings out bread and wine for *Avram* and who was, the *Torah* tells us, a "Kohain l'Keil Elyon," "a Priest of G-d, Most High." (Bereshit 14:18) While *Malkitzedek* was a *Kohain* even before *Aharon*, he lost the *Kehuna* at this point in history, for the *pasuk* tells us that he greeted *Avram* with the words "Baruch Avram l'Keil Elyon," "Blessed is Avram of G-d, Most High," giving praise to *Avram* before praising *Hashem*. (Bereshit 14: 19, 20) The *Talmud* (Nedarim 32b) tells us that, due to this error, the *Kehuna* immediately transferred to *Avram*, and was subsequently claimed by *Pinchas*, who became a *Kohain* not through his grandfather *Aharon* but through his spiritual predecessor *Avraham Avinu*.

5762

Rabbi Edward Davis – The Malbim points out that, as with a plant, *Hashem* had to "transplant" *Avraham* into *Eretz Yisrael*, a location uniquely suited for his "blossoming" into the most "fruitful" person he could be. *Hashem* does the same for all of us, leading us to the place best suited for each of us to attain our spiritual mission.

5763

Rabbi Shlomo Riskin – The Sefas Emes tells us that when *Hashem* urged *Avram* to count the stars, and declares "so shall it be with your children," (Bereshit 15:5) *Hashem* was referring to <u>process</u>, not <u>number</u>. *Hashem* tells *Avram* to count the stars, something that is patently impossible, yet *Avram* obediently attempts to do so. <u>That</u>, states *Hashem*, shall be the legacy of the Jewish People: attempting and ultimately accomplishing the impossible.

5765

Rabbi Yossi Jankovits – After *Avram's* victory in the war of the Four Kings, he is greeted by *Malkitzedek, Melech Shaleim*, who brings out bread and wine. (Bereshit 14:18) Why bread and wine? It was a message to *Avram* that the world had been made better through his acts, even though destructive. Normally, food loses spiritual value through destruction. For example, the *berachah* for an orange is *ha'eitz*, yet the *berachah* for orange juice is *shehakol*. Yet wine and bread are exceptions to the general rule, for the process by which each is produced, while destructive, results in a higher spiritual reality, as evidenced by the *berachot* of *ha'gafen* and *hamotzi*. *Avram* engaged in war, an inherently destructive activity, yet the world that resulted was more elevated than that which existed beforehand. Incidentally, *brit milah*, which is strongly connected to *Avraham*, is another example of a destructive act that results in elevation.

5766

Reb Michael Greenwald – The *pasuk* says "V'yikach Avram et Sarai ishto ...." "And Avram took Sarai his wife" to *Eretz Canaan*. (Bereshit 12:5) The Meshech Chochmah tells us that on this *pasuk* the Zohar comments that he persuaded *Sarai* to go, suggesting she was not immediately willing to do so. Yet we know the *halachah*, as set forth in the *Gemara* (Ketubot 110b) is that while a woman is not generally obligated to accompany her husband to relocate to a foreign land, if a man determines to move to *Eretz Yisrael* his wife is obligated to accompany him (and she loses her *ketubah* if she does not). Since the *Gemara* tells us that *Avram* kept the entire *Torah* before it was given (Yoma 28b), should *Sarai* have required convincing? Was she not obligated by *halachah* to accompany *Avram*? One answer is that *Avram* was commanded to go to *Eretz Canaan*, <u>not</u> to the Holy Land of *Eretz Yisrael*. Until *Avram* made a *kinyan* of the Land by traveling its length and breadth, the Land did not have the *halachic* status of *Eretz Yisrael* and *Sarai* could therefore be resistant to going there. This gives us an insight into the tremendous power of *Avraham*, the first Jew, in staking out *Eretz Yisrael* as the Holy Dominion of the Jewish People for all future generations.

5767

Reb Michael Greenwald – The Beis HaLevi questions how, in Parashat Noach, the animals and, for that matter the entire Earth, could be so corrupted before *Hashem* as to warrant total annihilation. (Bereshit 6:12) Being that animals do not have *bechirah*, how could they have chosen to be either good or evil? The answer is made apparent in Parashat Lech Lecha, where, as he crosses into *Mitzrayim*, *Avram* tells *Sarai* "now I know you are a beautiful woman." (Bereshit 12:11) Why now? *Avram* and *Sarai* had been married for decades! Presumably he would have had occasion to notice her beauty during their many years together. The answer lies in where they were at the time. Having crossed into *Mitzrayim*, *Avram*, a tzaddik focused always on spirituality, now noticed the obvious physical attributes of his wife. It was the environment of physicality in *Mitzrayim* that, against his nature, influenced *Avram* to the negative, which is what happened to the animals and the Earth in the times preceding the Flood. With mankind so steeped in sin, the animals could not help but be contaminated. The obvious lesson for us is to be very selective and discerning about the environment we choose for ourselves and our families.

5768

Reb Moshe Stauber – *Hashem* tells *Avram* that He will bless him and make his name great, and "veyay berachah," "and you shall be a blessing." (Bereshit 12:2) This could be read as a commandment, rather than a reward. *Hashem* could be telling *Avram* that while He is giving him wealth and honor, in return *Avram* must <u>be</u> a blessing, in essence to make a *Kiddush Hashem* using the gifts for *Hashem's* honor.

5769

Rabbi Yosef Weinstock – *Hashem* promises *Avram* that he shall be a "blessing," which our Sages indicate means that the first *berachah* of *Shemoneh Esrei* will conclude exclusively with the name of *Avraham* (i.e. "Magen Avraham) (Rashi on Bereshit 12:2), despite the fact that the *berachah* begins naming each of the three *Avot*. This might be an indication to Jews throughout the ages that, like *Avraham Avinu*, they are capable of achieving spiritual growth and self-actualization despite lack of any merit, inspiration or guidance from their fathers. While the merit of all the *Avot* is available to and influential for every Jew, without the example of *Avraham* we might have thought that adopting a spiritual lifestyle absent childhood mentoring by a parent (or grandparent) would be beyond us. Yet since *Avraham* was able to reach for spiritual greatness despite an evil father, so too can we. MRF Note – Perhaps this is why we refer to him as "Avraham Avinu," indicating he will fulfill that role for the Jews throughout the ages.

5770

Rabbi Yossi Jankovits – *Avram's* priorities seem to be out of place when he asks *Sarai* to tell the Egyptians that she is his sister so that (a) things will go well for him (Rashi here indicates so that they will give him gifts) and (b) he will live (i.e. the *Mitzrim* won't kill him) (Bereshit 12:13). Clearly, to remain alive would seem to be a greater priority than to receive gifts.

Avram reasoned that one cannot make two simultaneous requests. He therefore invoked the *pasuk* in *Ashrei* "פּוֹתֵחַ אֶת יָדֶךָ וּמַשְׂבִּיעַ לְכָל חַי רָצוֹן," "You open Your Hand and satisfy the desire of every living thing." (Tehillim 145:16) If *Hashem* were to provide for him by giving from His Hand, it is a given that *Avraham* is "chai," "alive." A similar answer appears in the *Gemara* (Taanit 8b).

5771

Reb Steven Jacoby – The *pasuk* says "וַיְהִי רִיב בֵּין רֹעֵי מִקְנֵה אַבְרָם וּבֵין רֹעֵי מִקְנֵה לוֹט וְהַכְּנַעֲנִי וְהַפְּרִזִּי אָז יֹשֵׁב בָּאָרֶץ," "And there was quarreling between the herdsmen of Avram's livestock and the herdsmen of Lot's livestock – and the Canaanite and the Perizzite were then dwelling in the Land." (Bereshit 13:7) From here we see that when there is strife between those of the family of *Avraham* (i.e. the Jews) the *goyim* have a tighter connection to *Eretz Yisrael*.

5772

Rabbi Michael Jablinowitz – In the first *pasuk* of the *sedra*, *Hashem* instructs *Avram* to go "el haaretz asher arechah," commonly translated as "to the Land that I will show you." (Bereshit 12:1) The Meshech Chochmah reads this language as "to the Land in which I will reveal you," meaning *Hashem* is commanding *Avram* to go to the place that allows Jews to self-actualize, and there *Hashem* will expose *Avram* to an understanding of his inherent greatness. *Eretz Yisrael* is the place where one's *Avodat Hashem* can be fully manifested and realized.

5773

Rabbi Yukutiel Yehuda Halberstam – The *pasuk* says "וַיֹּאמֶר לְאַבְרָם יָדֹעַ תֵּדַע כִּי גֵר | יִהְיֶה זַרְעֲךָ בְּאֶרֶץ לֹא לָהֶם וַעֲבָדוּם וְעִנּוּ אֹתָם אַרְבַּע מֵאוֹת שָׁנָה," "And He said to Avram, 'Know with certainty that your offspring shall be like strangers in a land not their own – and they will serve them, and they will oppress them – four hundred years.'" (Bereshit 15:13) Rashi indicates that "Land" referred to here is not Egypt but *Eretz Yisrael*, and that the Jews were in *Mitzrayim* only for 210 years, for the counting of the 400 years began with the birth of *Yitzchak* in *Eretz Yisrael*. Based on this accounting, a question arises with respect to ownership of *Eretz Yisrael*. If 190 of the 400 years were spent in the *Aretz* in the years preceding the Egyptian exile, how would the children of *Avraham* be considered sojourners there? After all, as the Ramban asks, did not *Avraham* acquire the Land at the time *Hashem* commanded him "קוּם הִתְהַלֵּךְ בָּאָרֶץ לְאָרְכָּהּ וּלְרָחְבָּהּ כִּי לְךָ אֶתְּנֶנָּה," "Arise, walk about the Land through its length and breadth! For to you will I give it." (Bereshit 13:17; see Targum Yonatan ben Uziel; Bava Batra 100a)? The answer is that *Eretz Yisrael* did, indeed, belong to *Avraham* and his descendants from the very beginning, which is why the *pasuk* is very precise and says "ki gair," "like a stranger" shall the Jews be, for clearly, they were not actual strangers in their own Land.

VAYEIRA

5758

The angels that visit *Avraham* ask him "ayei Sarah ishtecha," "where is Sarah your wife?" (Bereshit 18:9) Rashi here brings the *Gemara* (Bava Metzia 87a) that indicates they wished to pass to her the "kos shel berachah," the glass of wine used for *Birkat Hamazon*, which is said to provide fertility to women.

5759

Because of the merit of his familial connection to *Avraham Avinu*, *Lot* and his daughter founded the nation of *Moav*, which give rise to *Rut*, who gave rise to *David HaMelech*, and, ultimately, to *Moshiach*.

5760

Sforno – After *Hagar* is banished with her son from *Avraham's* home, an angel of *Hashem* asks "lamah lach Hagar … ," "What is troubling you Hagar … ," (Bereshit 21:17), seemingly incredulous as to why she would sit and weep in the desert rather than search for water. The *Torah* then states "וַיִּפְקַח אלקים אֶת עֵינֶיהָ וַתֵּרֶא בְּאֵר מָיִם וַתֵּלֶךְ וַתְּמַלֵּא אֶת הַחֵמֶת מַיִם וַתַּשְׁקְ אֶת הַנָּעַר," "Then G-d opened her eyes and she perceived a well of water; she went and filled the skins with water and gave the youth to drink." (Bereshit 21:19) This does <u>not</u> indicate that *Hashem* did a miracle for *Hagar*, but rather that the well was there <u>all the time</u>. *Hagar* simply thought that there would be no chance that a well would exist in a desert and therefore she did not even look for one. The lesson is that when things are going badly we must remember that we may, in fact, be very close to a solution, if only we keep searching.

While Rashi informs us that three angels visited *Avraham*, the *Torah's* plain language calls his guests "anashim," "people," – Arab peasants. (Bereshit 18:2) In contrast, the *Torah* tells us that the two "malachim," "angels" came to *Lot* in *S'dom*. (Bereshit 19:1) We see here that *Avraham's* merit was larger because he took care of what he perceived to be regular people, not just esteemed guests that would owe him, and had the resources to repay, a favor.

Seder Hadorot tells us that *Akeidat Yitzchak* occurred in 2075 on *Har Moriah*, the place from which *Adam HaRishon* was created, where *Noach* built his Ark, where *Kayin* and *Hevel* brought *korbanot* to *Hashem* and where *Shlomo* built the *Beit HaMikdash*.

5761

Rabbi Mordechai Kamenetsky – Rashi tells us that *Avraham* directs that "yukach na m'at mayim … ," "let a little water be brought … ," (Bereshit 18:4), not for drinking but in order to wash the idolatrous sand from feet of the guests. He wanted the sand removed but did not want to do it himself (unlike the meal preparation, which he attended to personally).

Accordingly, he called only for a "little" water so as to minimize the burden on his servant. While he was very stringent with regard to the law of avoiding idolatry, he didn't want to place undue burden of his stringencies on the backs of the members of his household. This may have also been evidenced by *Avraham's* willingness to allow his servants and his comrades who fought the war against the Four Kings to partake in the spoils, even while *Avraham* himself was stringent upon himself and refused to do so. (Bereshit 14:22-24)

The *Mishnah* (Berachot 30b) identifies two things for which one does not interrupt his *Shemoneh Esrai*: a king (who inquires concerning his welfare) or a snake coiled around one's heel. These represent two distraction tactics of the *yetzer hara*, which will tell one during his *davening* either "look how *frum* you are – being an exalted, kingly personage, why bother praying to G-d?," or, alternatively, "look how lowly you are; you are such a sinner – why bother to pray to G-d?" The *Mishnah* cautions us to ignore both distractions when approaching *Hashem* in prayer.

5762

The *Gemara* tells us (Eruvin 17b) that we engage in *mayim achronim* to remove from our fingers the salt of *S'dom*, which can blind the eyes. On a *mussar* level, we do *mayim achronim* to remove the *middah* of *S'dom* from our fingers, which, we are informed in *Pirkei Avot* (5:13), is captured in the phrase "sheli, sheli, shelach, shelach," "what's mine is mine and what's yours is yours." Before we approach *Hashem* through *Birkat HaMazon*, and especially at a time when we are satiated, we must remove the philosophy of *S'dom* from our minds and think about the welfare of others. And just as *mayim achronim* precedes *Birkat HaMazon*, so too can caring about our fellow man precede providing praise to the Creator. Removing *S'dom* from our lives means removing self-centeredness.

Rabbi Yosef Kalatsky – In Parashat Lech Lecha, when *Avraham* asks *Hashem* about his promised son and his concern about *Eliezer*, his servant, inheriting him, he is not faulted by *Hashem* for questioning His promise to him. (Bereshit 15:3-6) This may be because *Avraham* was not questioning the faithfulness of *Hashem* in a <u>spiritual</u> sense. Avraham knew he had taught *Eliezer* all his *Torah* knowledge, and that, in doing so, as per the *Gemara* (Sanhedrin 19b), he had become as a father to him. Rather, *Avraham* was asking an <u>economic</u> question: "who will get my money?," which is not to be included in the spiritual inheritance that *Avraham* assumed was for *Eliezer*. *Hashem* responds that *Avraham* will have a son (born to him in Parashat Vayeira) who will be the recipient of <u>both</u> his spiritual legacy and his wealth. This understanding of *Avraham's* connection to *Eliezer* demonstrated the seriousness of the teacher-student connection and the serious responsibility of the *talmid* to honor his teacher as he would honor his father.

5763

Nowhere in the *Torah* is there a record of *Lot* thanking *Avraham* for the many times he rescued him or for having made him rich. This improper trait of lacking gratitude was passed on to the nations of *Amon* and *Moav*, and forms the basis for the *halachah* that they may not enter into the Nation of Israel.

Rabbi Keith Wasserstrom – There are many examples of *Lot's* ingratitude to his uncle *Avraham*. His daughters sought an incestuous relationship with him based on their belief at the time that, following the destruction of *S'dom*, that the three of them were the only people remaining in the world. Had *Lot* told his daughters at any time previously of his righteous uncle *Avraham*, they would have known that, in at least one case, there were bound to be survivors of *S'dom* and *Amorah* and improper conduct could have been avoided.

5764

Rabbi Donald Bixon – *Chazal* tell us that our *Avot* went to study at *Yeshivat Shem v'Eiver* after three major events: (1) *Avraham* went after his battle with the Four Kings; (2) *Yitzchak* went after the *Akeidah*; and (3) *Yaacov* went after the incident of taking the *berachah* from *Eisav*. In each case the Patriarch needed to go learn *Torah* after a morally challenging event. What was learned in *Yeshivat Shem v'Eiver*? "Mesechet Mabul," "the story and lessons of the Great Flood," which was an investigation into the causes of the *Mabul* (not unlike the report of a "blue ribbon panel" that investigates a major crime/event). The *yeshivah* was essentially a morality "think tank." But if his focus was on ethics, why was *Shem* not the first Jew? Because *Shem* was confined to the *yeshivah* but *Avraham* took morality "to the streets" against *Nimrod* who was constantly trying to assert himself as the highest power in the world. A possible example of *Shem's* detachment is his greeting to *Avraham* following the victory over the Four Kings. The *Torah* tells us that *Shem/Malkitzedek*, the "Khohein l'Keil Elyon," "Priest of G-d Most High," came out to greet *Avraham*. The pasuk then states "וַיְבָרְכֵהוּ וַיֹּאמַר בָּרוּךְ אַבְרָם לְאֵל עֶלְיוֹן קֹנֵה שָׁמַיִם וָאָרֶץ," "He [Shem/Malkitzedek] blessed him [Avraham] and he said 'Blessed is Avram of G-d, the *Most High, Acquirer of Heaven and Earth.*'" (Bereshit 14:19) *Shem* clearly identifies with G-d who is Most High, rather than *Hashem* who is intimately involved in the world.

5765

Rabbi Edward Davis – While it may be appropriate to be a natural skeptic with respect to supposed "design" behind what otherwise seems to be "coincidence," certain occurrences jump out as directed by *Hashem*. One example in the parashah, described by Rashi, is the fact that the cave in which *Lot* and his daughters sought refuge after the destruction of *S'dom* contained wine that was used for immoral purposes. (Bereshit 19:30-32) It is at least notable, therefore, that in the week in which we read (Bereshit 21:22-33) of *Avraham Avinu's* decision to grant rights in *Eretz Yisrael* (specifically Aza/Gaza) to *goyim* (specifically *Avimelech* and the *Plishtim*) the Israeli Knesset, on October 26, 2004, voted to do exactly that through the so-called "Disengagement" from Gaza. It is also worth noting that following the incident of the surrender of the Land, the *Torah* states "vayehi achar hadevarim haeileh v'HaElokim nisah et Avraham ... ," "and it happened after these things that G-d tested Avraham ...." (Bereshit 22:1) The Rashba states that the test of *Akeidat Yitzchak* was a punishment for *Avraham* for lacking faith and giving away a portion of the Land that G-d gave him.

5766

Rabbi Eli Mansour – Parashat Vayeira contains one of the most dramatic and cosmically important events in the history of humankind: *Akeidat Yitzhak*. Based on *mesorah*, we know that *Avraham Avinu* was tested by Hashem ten times, and among all Commentators this was one of the tests. What is less appreciated is the impact of the final paragraph of the *parashah*, where it reads that "It came to pass after these things, that Avraham was told ...." (Bereshit 22:20) The Torah goes on to describe in surprising detail the children born to Avraham's brother and the resulting family. Bearing in mind what Avraham had just endured, we can appreciate that this too may have been a test, perhaps an enormous one. After waiting his entire life, into his old age, *Avraham* is finally granted a worthy son through *Sarah*. They raise him lovingly into adulthood and then, in contradiction to all he knows, *Avraham* is asked by *Hashem* to kill his son. Of course, he dutifully agrees and almost completes the feat, but for the intervention of *Hashem's* angel. "After these things," one might suspect that *Avraham* is worthy of a respite. Certainly, we would think he should not be burdened by hearing of the good fortune of his idolatrous brother. Yet it is at this moment that *Hashem* again tests *Avraham*; to allow him to become despondent at having to try so hard to retain his only son in *Kedushah*, while the wicked are prospering before him. Of course, *Avraham* does not despair at this news and in maintaining his faith in *Hashem*, he creates a spiritual precedence that all Jews can draw from in trying times.

5767

Rabbi Yossi Jankovits – The *pasuk* tells us of the angel and *Avraham*: "וַיֹּאמֶר שׁוֹב אָשׁוּב אֵלֶיךָ כָּעֵת חַיָּה וְהִנֵּה בֵן לְשָׂרָה אִשְׁתֶּךָ וְשָׂרָה שֹׁמַעַת פֶּתַח הָאֹהֶל וְהוּא אַחֲרָיו,", "And he said to him 'I shall surely return to you *at this time* next year, and behold, to Sarah your wife, a son.' And Sarah heard from the entrance of the tent, and it was behind him." (Bereshit 18:10) And soon thereafter *Hashem* Himself tells *Avraham* "ashoov eilecha *kaeit chaya* ul'Sarah vein," "I shall return to you *at this time* and Sarah will have a son." (Bereshit 18:14) A question arises: why must *Hashem* repeat the *berachah* of *Sarah's* pregnancy after it is stated by the angel? *Sefer* Ezer Miyehudah brings that *Sarah* nullified the first blessing of the *malach* by laughing (Bereshit 18:12), rather than responding "amen." This necessitated a repetition of the *berachah* by *Hashem* in order to "reinstate" the blessing for *Sarah*. The lesson for us is to accept and concretize all *berachot* directed towards us from whatever source and however seemingly impossible. Yet a second question emerges: Since *Hashem* (in Parashat Lech Lecha) had previously promised *Avraham* that Sarah would bear him a son (Bereshit 17:16), what new element was contained in the original <u>and</u> replacement *berachot* of Parashat Vayeira? Here both the *malach* and *Hashem* mention "kaeit chaya," which can be translated not as "at this time," but rather "at a living time," an allusion to the fact that despite the fact that *Sarah* was ninety years old she would give birth and <u>survive/live</u>. This, incidentally, could be why *Avraham* had a "weaning party" for *Yitzchak*. (Bereshit 21:8) Insofar as, following his weaning, *Sarah* was no longer needed to nurse *Yitzchak*, and yet she did not die, *Avraham* held a festive "seudat hoda'ah," "a meal of thanks," not for himself or *Yitzchak*, but for *Sarah*, in gratitude that she lived past the birth and the weaning.

5768

Rabbi Yissocher Frand – In describing the opening scene of the *parashah*, in a single *pasuk* the *Torah* twice uses the word "vayar," "and he [Avraham] saw." (Bereshit 18:2) The double *lashon* begs for explanation. Rabbi Meir

Tzvi Bergman indicates that a *baal chesed* not only <u>sees</u> a person but <u>perceives</u> his actual needs. This was why *Avraham* first "saw" the travelers and then "saw" that they were in apparent need of food and drink. There is a story told of the Beis HaLevi: a man asked him if one could use milk for the Four Cups at the *Pesach Seder*, and the *Rav* sent him money by which to purchase wine and meat for his *Yom Tov*. He "saw" within the question about milk not only that the man could not afford wine but that he would not be eating meat during his *Seder* (since milk would be prohibited for the two cups that follow the meal).

5769

The first (of four) *shalshelet* in the *Torah* appears in Parashat Vayeira with *Lot's* delay in fleeing *S'dom*, which Rashi tells us was out of concern for his money that would be lost in the destruction. (Bereshit 19:16) The second *shalshelet* is found at *Eliezer's* attempt to find a wife for *Yitzchak* (Bereshit 24:12), which the *Midrash* tells us was a hesitation based on his conflict of interest, for he secretly wished *Yitzchak* would marry his daughter. The third occurs in *Yosef's* enticement by the wife of *Potiphar* (Bereshit 39:8) and the fourth occurs as *Moshe* slaughters rams in preparation for the inauguration of the sons of his brother *Aharon* as the *Kohanim*, rather than his own sons. (Vayikra 8:23) In each case a spiritual dilemma or conflict exists and is overcome or avoided.

5770

Rabbi Yitzchak Salid – It is clear from the end of the *parashah* of the *Akeidah* that *Avraham* accomplishes more than "merely" almost sacrificing his only son. As the text makes clear, *Avraham* receives abundant blessing for two reasons "ki ya'an asher asita et hadavar hazeh v'lo chasachta et beencha et yacheedecha ... ," "because [1] you have done this thing and [2] you have not withheld your son, your only one ...." (Bereshit 22:16) The Kli Yakar indicates that "hadavar hazeh" was the sacrificing of the *ayil* after being told by the angel to spare *Yitzchak*. (Bereshit 22:13) Clearly *Avraham* was never commanded to bring the *ayil* as a *korban*. His only *mitzvah* was not to kill *Yitzchak*. Yet such was his desire to do *avodah* that, rather than "retire" following the command to stop, he saw the *ayil* and seized on the opportunity to go beyond what was seemingly possible. For that he deserved the enhanced enumerated blessings.

5771

Rabbi Nachman of Breslov – The name "Avimelech" is rooted in the language of a desire to be king. *Avimelech's* arrogance blinded him to the superiority of his contemporary, *Avraham*. In fact, *Hashem* himself had to direct *Avimelech* to ask *Avraham* to pray for him in order to obtain healing. (Bereshit 20:7) Those who disparage the value of asking a *tzaddik* to pray for oneself are, at their core, exhibiting arrogance in the tradition of *Avimelech*.

5772

Rabbi Eli Mansour – After being banished from the home of *Avraham* and *Sarah*, at the point of near death, *Hagar* abandons *Yishmael*, her son. (Bereshit 21:15, 16) Rabbi Samson Raphael Hirsch states that *Hagar's* actions with regard to *Yishmael* are the antithesis of proper parenting. Because she personally felt extreme sadness and discomfort with respect to the suffering of her son, she moved away from him rather than rendering aid. A parent's job is to always put the interests of the child first. It should not matter whether the parent seeks to avoid pain or achieve personal pleasure. The ultimate "giving" parent subordinates all personal concerns for what is best for the child.

5773

Rabbi Edward Davis – *Avraham* teaches us the mitzvah of *hachnasat orchim*, which is a form of *chesed* we do without a *berachah*. The general rule is that for those *mitzvot* that are focused on a human recipient (e.g. *tzedakah*, *bikur cholim*, *m'samaiach chattan v'kallah*) there is no *berachah*, perhaps because the focus of the *mitzvah* is not on the person doing the *mitzvah* but the person receiving the benefit. MRF Note – Perhaps also, where we are engaged in a *mitzvah bein adam l'Makom* we <u>do</u> say a *berachah* on behalf of the beneficiary, which is clearly not *Hashem*, but ourselves.

Rabbi Eli Mansour – Rashi tells us that the three "men" who visit *Avraham* at the beginning of Parashat Vayeira are actually three angels with three distinct tasks: (1) to tell *Sarah* of her impending pregnancy; (2) to destroy *S'dom*; and (3) to heal *Avraham*. (Rashi, Bereshit 19:2) The first and third missions would clearly require a visit to *Avraham's* camp, but why should the angel tasked with destroying *S'dom* first visit *Avraham* and *Sarah*? Insofar as *Lot* would be the progenitor of *Moav* and, therefore, *Rut*, and *Rut* was to be the great grandmother of *David HaMelech*, the line from which *Moshiach* would emerge, a question existed as to the status of the women of *Moav*. The *Torah* clearly states that the men of *Moav* may not convert to Judaism based on their failure to greet the Jews with bread and water in the desert after the Exodus, (Devarim 23:4, 5) however there was a question, raised in the *Gemara* (Yevamot 77a), as to whether the conversion prohibition applied also to the women of *Moav*. The *Torah* in Parashat Vayeira tells us "וַיֹּאמְרוּ אֵלָיו אַיֵּה שָׂרָה אִשְׁתֶּךָ וַיֹּאמֶר הִנֵּה בָאֹהֶל," "[The angels] said to [Avraham] 'Where is Sarah your wife?' And he said "Behold! – in the tent!'" (Bereshit 18:9) The angel charged with destroying *S'dom* needed to know the custom of women in order to determine if the women of *Moav* could be faulted for failing to provide for the Jews. *Sarah's* conduct made clear that it is improper for women to go out of the tent to provide hospitality, which means the women of *Moav* were <u>not</u> liable for the sins of their nation, which in turn meant they <u>were</u> eligible for conversion to *Am Yisrael*. As such, while *S'dom* had to be destroyed, *Lot*, as the progenitor of *Rut*, had to be saved in the process. MRF Note – Perhaps it was not for the *malach* to <u>learn</u> the *halachah* of the women of *Moav* but to <u>teach</u> the *halachah* through his visit. Would it make sense for the *malach* to learn whether or not to save *Lot* when the *Torah*, which existed before the Creation of the world, indicates that *Amon* and *Moav* may not join *Am Yisrael*? Presumably these nations were destined to descend from *Lot*, so had he been destroyed there would have been an inconsistency between *Torah*, the blueprint for reality, and reality itself. But perhaps the story of *Sarah* in the tent gave support to those who argued the law of the acceptance of *Moav* women was a *Halachah l'Moshe m'Sinai*, the position that ultimately prevailed.

CHAYEI SARAH

5759

The *Maarat HaMachpeilah* in *Kiryat Arba/Chevron* was *Avraham's* first attempt to acquire a part of *Eretz Yisrael*. Since the Hittites could not sell the Land to a non-Hittite, *Avraham* had to be semi-adopted by *Ephron*, who, rather than calling *Avraham* a "prince," as the Hittites did (Bereshit 23:6), makes a deal "between you and me," (Bereshit 23:15) indicating a closer relationship. This is how *Avraham* got his "foot in the door," within *Eretz Yisrael*. The result is undisputed ownership.

There are two *parshiot* that describe the death of a great person: Chayei Sarah describes the death of *Sarah Imeinu* and Vayechi describes the death of *Yaacov Avinu*. Both use the word for "life" in describing their deaths. The *Talmud* tells us (Berachot 18b) that wicked people are "dead" whilst they are alive, and (Berachot 18a) the righteous are "alive" even after death. The *Talmud* (Taanit 5b) also states "Yaacov Avinu lo met," "Yaacov, our father, never died." Like *Sarah*, *Yaacov* lives on through *Bnei Yisrael*, his descendants.

5760

The *pasuk* says "v'yakam Avraham mayal maytow," "and *Avraham* got up from before his dead," (Bereshit 23:3) meaning he did not excessively mourn his wife *Sarah* despite the fact that, as Rashi explains, she died as a result of hearing the news of the *Akeidah*. *Avraham* understood that

Sarah's death was a part of *Hashem's* Plan, and to have excessively mourned would have given a public impression either that (a) *Avraham* regretted having done the *Akeidah* or (b) *Avraham* somehow blamed himself or *Hashem* for *Sarah's* death.

5761

Rabbi Yisroel Ciner – *Eliezer* is described in the *parashah* as "zakain beito, hamoshail b'chol asher lo," "the elder of [Avraham's] house, who ruled over all that was [Avraham's]." (Bereshit 24:2) On a simple level, this can be understood that *Eliezer* controlled all of *Avraham's* substantial possessions. Yet when it came time to find a wife for *Yitzchak*, *Avraham* made *Eliezer* swear not to get a Canaanite woman. (Bereshit 24:3) The requirement to swear is jarring: where is the trust of the one in whom so much value has already been entrusted? *Avraham* understood that what was at stake spiritually with respect to *Yitzchak's* marriage was so much more important than what was at stake monetarily. As such, *Avraham* had to demonstrate the seriousness of the mission to *Eliezer*. The lesson for us is clear: we must exercise caution in spiritual matters that transcends the care we take in business deals.

Rabbi Yossi Jankovits – Rashi tells us that *Sarah* died "l'fi she'al y'day b'sorat hakeidah," "because of the news of the Akeidah." (Rashi on Bereshit 23:2) This was not a case of a mother being unable to handle the news of her son's near death experience. *Sarah* died because her mission was completed with the *Akeidah*. The *middah* of *Avraham* was *chesed* and the *middah* of Sarah was *gevurah* (as evidenced, for example, by throwing *Hagar* out of the house). The Jewish People need both *middot* to survive and excel. As the progenitor of the Jewish People, *Avraham* had to learn *gevurah* from his wife, and he ultimately did, as was demonstrated by the *Akeidah*. Moreover, *Sarah* heard that *Yitzchak* had willingly gone to the *Akeidah*, further demonstrating that strength was been passed down the next generation. With her mission complete, *Sarah* could pass on. It is notable that Rashi tells us that upon hearing the news of *Yitzchak's* near slaughter, *Sarah's* soul departed. He does not state that she was distraught, alarmed or experienced anything denoting fear or terror.

Rabbi Yossi Jankovits – *Avraham* was *chesed* and *Sarah* was *gevurah*, and each was a perfect complement for the other in creating the foundation of the Jewish People for eternity. Similarly, *Yitzchak* became the epitome of *gevurah* at the *Akeidah* and *Rivkah* is introduced in the *parashah* as the paragon of *chesed*. In every case Hashem orchestrates the world to find one's perfect mate.

5762

Rabbi Yossi Jankovits – The Midrash Rabbah (56:11) says that *Yitzchak* is not mentioned in the description of the burial of *Sarah*, his mother, because he was then learning at a *yeshivah*. One obvious question is what could someone who was willing to give his life for *Hashem* learn from others about obtaining greater closeness to Him? The answer is: everything! *Torah* learning never ends and personal growth is always possible and necessary. MRF Note – Also, the *Torah* is about living in this world and elevating it through *mitzvot*. While *Yitzchak* certainly guaranteed his place in *Olam Haba*, he needed to master the ways of *Olam HaZeh* in order to gain even greater heights.

Rabbi Mark Spiro – *Avraham* made his servant *Eliezer* swear not to take a Caananite woman for *Yitzchak*, "כִּי אֶל אַרְצִי וְאֶל מוֹלַדְתִּי תֵּלֵךְ וְלָקַחְתָּ אִשָּׁה לִבְנִי לְיִצְחָק," "rather, to my land and to my kindred shall you go and take a wife for my son, for Yitzchak." (Bereshit 24:4) This directive seems strange, since we know that the home of *Betuel* and *Lavan* in *Charan* was idolatrous and corrupt. How could this be appreciably better than obtaining a wife in *Canaan*? In getting a woman from a far away land, *Avraham* could remove her from the negative influences in her life. Even if *Eliezer* could find a righteous woman from among the Canaanites, because, as *Avraham* pointed out, "anochee yoshaiv b'kirbo ... ," "I [Avraham] dwell amongst them ... ," (Bereshit 24:3) the Canaanite influence would ultimately corrupt her, given the continuing proximity. The lesson for all us is that creating distance from the bad influences in our lives can make a critical difference for personal growth.

5763

Rabbi Yochanan Zweig – The Ibn Ezra says the entire story of the negotiations between *Ephron* and *Avraham* regarding the purchase of the *Maarat HaMachpeilah* is to show the importance of being buried in *Eretz Yisrael*. The Ramban doesn't see this point, because since *Sarah* died in *Eretz Yisrael* burying her there would only be logical. Rabbi Zweig suggests that *Sarah* died in *Eretz Canaan* but was buried in *Eretz Yisrael* through the transfer of sovereign rule and ownership to *Avraham*. This is why *Avraham* goes to great lengths to deal with both *Ephron* and *Bnei Cheit*. Rashi points out that on that very day *Ephron* was appointed their leader (Rashi on Bereshit 23:10), which necessitated assent from both the new king and his subjects. Furthermore, by virtue of the sovereign acquisition, Rashi refer to *Avraham* as a "king." (Rashi on Bereshit 23:17). Finally, *Avraham* paid *Ephron* "abra meiot shekel kesef ovair lasochair," "four hundred silver shekels in negotiable currency," (Bereshit 23:16), universally accepted legal tender that would hold value before and after the land changed status and sovereigns.

Maharil Diskin – *Avraham* has a daughter named "Bakol" and she died on the same day as *Sarah*. The *pasuk* in the beginning of the *parashah* states "Vayavo Avraham lispod l'Sarah v'livkotah," "and Avraham came to eulogize Sarah 'ולבכתה.'" (Bereshit 23:2) The word "ולבכתה," is written with a small "chaf," which can be read as "and cry for her," or, if read without the small chaf, the word is "l'bita," meaning "for her daughter," meaning *Avraham* cried for *Sarah* and her daughter. A *pasuk* later in the *parashah* says "וְאַבְרָהָם זָקֵן בָּא בַּיָּמִים וה' בֵּרַךְ אֶת אַבְרָהָם בַּכֹּל," "Now Avraham was old, well on in years, and Hashem had blessed Avraham 'bakol.'" (Bereshit 24:1). "Bakol" is generally translated as "with everything," but the *Gemara* (Bava Batra 16b) indicates the opinion of *Rabbi Yehudah* that this is referring to the fact that *Avraham* had a daughter and, some say, that her name was "Bakol." Rav Moshe Feinstein disputes that *Avraham's* daughter died on the same day as *Sarah* but concedes that she existed. (Igros Moshe, Orach Chaim chelek 4, siman 40, ot 6)

5764

Rabbi Edward Davis – The *Torah* devotes thirty-one verses to the Creation of the universe and sixty-six verses to the *shidduch* of *Yitzchak* and *Rivkah*. This is to stress that a proper union is as essential to the world's continued existence as its Creation. The concept of a *bashert* is explicitly mentioned in this parashah. After *Eliezer* describes the events leading up to his meeting with *Rivkah's* family, both *Betuel* and *Lavan* reply "may Hashem yatza hadavar," "this matter comes from Hashem!" (Bereshit 24:50)

5765

Rabbi Berel Wein – Talk is cheap. The Hittites were especially effusive in their praise and professed love for *Avraham*, but he was rightly skeptical. *Ephron's* true colors came forth in his ultimate willingness to exact a huge sum from his "friend," *Avraham*. We learn from this that the words of the supposed allies of Israel are to be taken with a grain of salt until their actual deeds towards Israel tell the tale.

5766

Rabbi Yossi Jankovits – The Viener Rav pointed out that as *Avraham Avinu* implores his servant *Eliezer* to travel to find a wife for *Yitzchak*, *Avraham* states "וְאַשְׁבִּיעֲךָ בַּיהוָה אלקי הַשָּׁמַיִם ואלקי הָאָרֶץ אֲשֶׁר לֹא תִקַּח אִשָּׁה לִבְנִי מִבְּנוֹת הַכְּנַעֲנִי אֲשֶׁר אָנֹכִי יוֹשֵׁב בְּקִרְבּוֹ," "And I will have you swear by Hashem, G-d of Heavens and G-d of the earth, that you not take a wife for my son from the daughters of the Canaanites, *among whom I dwell*." (Bereshit 24:3) The language "Asher anochi yoshaiv b'kirbo" could be translated either as "Among whom I [Avraham] dwell," or as "Among whom 'I' dwells." The later interpretation would indicate that daughters of *Canaan* were self-centered people, concerned only for the "I," devoid of *chesed* and concern for others. Such a cultural character flaw would disqualified them from being forbearers of the Jewish People. This is also why *Eliezer* was justified in devising a test by which to measure the extent, if any, that the "I" was present in *Rivkah*. (Bereshit 24:14)

5768

Yael Jaffee – The Baal HaTurim teaches that from the small "chaf" in the word "v'livkotah," "and to cry for her," (Bereshit 23:2) we learn that *Avraham* did not excessively bewail the death of *Sarah*. This demonstrated *Avraham's* mastery over the *yetzer hara* which often will attempt to steal one's merit in performing a *mitzvah*. *Sarah*, Rashi indicates, died upon hearing of the *Akeidah*. (Rashi on Bereshit 23:2) Knowing this, *Avraham* could have been saddened and angry, based on the cynical dictum that "no good deed goes unpunished." Instead, he accepted *Hashem's* judgment and did not dwell on *Sarah's* death.

5769

Rabbi Yitzchak Salid – As part of his mission to secure a wife for *Yitzchak*, *Eliezer* the servant of *Avraham* famously relates to *Lavan* and *Betuel* the charge that *Avraham* gave him. *Eliezer* tells them "וָאֹמַר אֶל אֲדֹנִי אֻלַי לֹא תֵלֵךְ הָאִשָּׁה אַחֲרָי," "And I said to my master 'perhaps the woman will not go after me?'" (Bereshit 24:39) Rashi on that *pasuk* points out that the word "oolai," "perhaps," is written without a "vav," which renders it "alai," "to me." (Rashi on Bereshit 24:39) This was a subtle indication that *Eliezer* had an "agenda." Rashi tells us that he had a daughter whom he wanted to marry to *Yitzchak*, an idea that was rejected by *Avraham*. The problem with this interpretation is that in the original *pasuk* by which *Eliezer* received his original directive from *Avraham* we see no such indication of *Eliezer's* conflict of interest, as the same word "oolai" is written complete and with a "vav." (Bereshit 24:5) One would expect that, if truly conflicted about his own daughter's prospects, *Eliezer* would have "tipped his hand" in this earlier conversation, and communicated "oolai" without the "vav." Actually, he demonstrated his issue through his choice of words, for there was a more appropriate word to use when questioning *Avraham* rather than "oolai": "pen," meaning "lest," or "perhaps not," which is the negative form of "oolai," which means "perhaps." In fact, in the next *pasuk*, in response to *Eliezer*, it says "Vayomair ailav Avraham hishamer l'cha <u>pen</u> tasheev et b'ni shama," "Avraham said to him 'Beware <u>lest</u> you return my son to there,'" (Bereshit 24:6), specifically invoking the word "pen" as if to correct *Eliezer* for having used the word "oolai." *Avraham* was alarmed at the language employed by his loyal servant *Eliezer*, who had never before questioned *Avraham* with respect to any mission assigned to him. *Avraham* sensed that this was due to the self-interest of *Eliezer*, and therefore he gently pointed this out in order to let *Eliezer* self-correct. By the time *Eliezer* was completing the mission and relaying to *Rivkah's* family the original conversation he was essentially admitting his original error through the use of the incomplete word "oolai."

5770

Rabbi Yitzchak Salid – In his dealings with *Ephron haChiti*, *Avraham* first asks that the *Maarat HaMachpeilah* be "given" to him. "v'yitain li et M'arat HaMachpailah … ," "and give me the Maarat HaMachpailah …." (Bereshit 23:9). The word "sell" is never used in the dialogue, although the word "purchase" is. (see Bereshit 23:18) It seems *Avraham* was "covering his bases," allowing for all potential future disputes to his claim of ownership. If the transfer was regarded as a gift, the plot would not be subject to the *din* of "bar metzra," the halachic concept that gives the owner of a property adjoining a for-sale property a right of first refusal, and if regarded as a sale, *Avraham's* payment of a significant purchase price would eradicate any claim of an invalid or voidable sale.

5771

Rabbi Yossi Jankovits – Rashi tells us that *Rivkah's* father *Betuel* tried to kill *Eliezer* and was himself killed. (Rashi on Bereshit 24:55) Perhaps this is what the *Haggadah* means by the verse "An Aramean tried to destroy my father." *Betuel* was clearly from *Aram*, but how would killing *Eliezer* destroy *Yaacov Avinu* and *Klal Yisrael*? The *halachah*, set forth in the *Gemara* (Nazir 12a) is that a *shliach* sent to betroth a wife to a man who subsequently dies before returning to the man is presumed to have been successful. Insofar as *Eliezer* could have betrothed anyone to *Yitzchak*, *Yitzchak* could have been prohibited from marrying anyone for fear that his chosen wife was the sister of the originally betrothed (but unknown) woman. *Yitzchak* never marrying would obviously have "destroyed" *Yaacov* and the Jewish People. Yet since *Avraham* sent *Eliezer* to *Aram Naharaim* to find a woman for *Yitzchak*, would not a Canaanite woman have been allowed to *Yitzchak*, as we would be certain that a Canaanite girl would not be the sister of an Aramean girl? Here the net effect would also be to "destroy" *Yaacov* and his descendants spiritually, since *Avraham* was adamant that the Canaanites were unfit to be the progenitors of the Jewish People.

5772

Rabbi Edward Davis – Rashi famously cites the *Midrash* that states that when *Rivkah* entered *Sarah's* tent three miracles that existed during *Sarah's* lifetime returned: (1) a lamp burned in the tent from one *Erev Shabbat* to the next *Erev Shabbat*; (2) the dough of her *challah* was blessed; and (3) the cloud of the *Shechinah* hovered over the tent. (Rashi on Bereshit 24:67) The *Midrash* in Bereshit Rabbah (60:16) actually cites a fourth attribute of *Sarah's* tent; that the walls were open on all four sides. Yet Rashi makes no mention of this at all! This might be the ultimate compliment to *Sarah*. The three items that were restored through *Rivkah* mirror the miracles that took place in the *Mishkan*. Yet the *Mishkan* – the ultimate manifestation of *Kedushah* in the world – was closed on its sides, unlike

Sarah's tent, which, although also a Makom Kedushah, was open on all sides. This tells us that *Sarah* had been successful during her lifetime not merely in creating a "Mishkan" for her family but for allowing its spiritual radiance to shine for the entire world. The fact that only three attributes returned with Rivkah tells us that although Rivkah was a worthy successor to Sarah's legacy, she did not have the same obligation (nor reward) of kiruv.

Rabbi Meir of Premishlan – There is a dichotomy in the dialogue between *Avraham* and *Bnei Cheit*. *Avraham* states "geir v'toshav anochi imachem … ," "a stranger and a resident among you I am … ," (Bereshit 23:4) underscoring his unsettled status in the Land. In contrast, *Bnei Cheit* respond to him "nassi Elokim atta b'tochainu … ," "a prince of G-d are you among us … ," (Bereshit 23:6) seemingly emphasizing his elevated position (and connection) amongst them. Their response was hardly meant to honor *Avraham*. Rather, the inhabitants of the Land were well aware of the prophecy that *Avraham's* children would wander for 400 years before finally settling and exercising dominion over the Land. While *Avraham* surely sought to have his days credited towards the 400 years and therefore called himself a "sojourner," the *goyim*, who were to lose the Land after the 400 years, sought the opposite. Accordingly, they took efforts to characterize him as a "prince" in their society, to push off the countdown of the 400 years.

TOLDOT

5758

In orchestrating her son *Yaacov's* masquerade, *Rivkah* employed a talent learned in a home of deceivers to ensure that the proper and desired outcome took place. In distinction to her brother *Lavan*, a known self-interested deceiver, *Rivkah* acted against her own interests in deceiving her husband *Yitzchak*, for, as a result of *Yaacov's* deception and *Eisav's* ensuing wrath, she was forced to send *Yaacov* away and never saw him again.

5759

There is plenty of "deception" described in the *Torah*, even before the ruse in Parashat Toldot when *Yaacov* stands in for *Eisav* before his father *Yitzchak*. (Bereshit 27:18-29) In Parashat Lech Lecha, *Avraham* coordinates with his wife *Sarah* to tell those in *Mitzrayim* that they are brother and sister, rather than husband and wife. (Bereshit 12:13) In Parashat Vayeira *Hashem*, Himself, in relating to *Avraham* that *Sarah* laughed when given the news of the impending pregnancy, tells *Avraham* that *Sarah* commented only on her advanced age (when, in fact, she had said explicitly that *Avraham* too was old). (Bereshit 18:12-15) And in Parashat Chayei Sarah, *Eliezer* tells *Betuel* that he inquired of *Rivkah's* name before giving her gifts, yet the opposite was true. (Bereshit 24:22, 23 and 24:47) In each of these cases, along with the matter of *Yaacov's* ruse, the *Torah* is demonstrating the judicious use of words to bring about a positive outcome without the taint of personal gain.

5760

Rabbi Yosef Kalatsky – *Eisav* used logical reasoning to rationalize his *avodah zareh*, and chose to blame *Hashem* for the death of his righteous grandfather *Avraham*, when he, himself, was responsible. *Chazal* state that *Avraham* was meant to live a full life of a *tzaddik* of 180 years. *Eisav* was aware of this expectation. Yet *Hashem* took *Avraham* from this world at age 175, five years early, because He wished to spare *Avraham* the pain of seeing all the evil that *Eisav* would do. (Rashi on Bereshit 25:30) In fact, on the day of *Avraham's* death, *Eisav* was out committing multiple cardinal sins. Yet while *Eisav's* behavior was responsible for his grandfather's death, rather than take responsibility, *Eisav* declared that the early death of a *tzaddik* was proof of the lack of a Just G-d in the world, which he used as an excuse to engage in idolatry, the course of action he always intended but could now rationalize and justify. The distinction of the wicked *Eisav* and the righteous *Avraham* in dealing with death is startling. In bringing *Yitzchak* to the *Akeidah*, *Avraham* (1) acted in accord with

Hashem's wishes; (2) accepted that the consequence of following *Hashem's* Will was the death of his beloved wife *Sarah*; (3) praised *Hashem* as the source of all goodness, despite his loss; and (4) made a *Kiddush Hashem* in burying her. With regard to the death of *Avraham*, *Eisav* (1) acted against the *Torah*; (2) produced, as a consequence, the death of *Avraham*; (3) denied responsibility and blamed *Hashem*; and (4) used the situation as an excuse to forsake the *Torah*. MRF Note – The Ramchal discusses the phenomenon of rationalization in his work Mesilat Yesharim, "The Path of the Righteous." In pointing out the two ways in which the *yetzer hara* blinds a person, the Ramchal says that, worse than making an individual unaware of danger posed, the *yetzer hara* can allow one to perceive reality in a way that is warped and contrary. In such cases, as with *Eisav*, "they see fit to find powerful substantiations and empirical evidence supporting their evil theories and false ideas." (Mesilat Yesharim Chapter 3)

5761

In Parashat Bereshit, in describing the products of Heaven, the *Torah* spells "toldot," or "products," as "תּוֹלְדוֹת," with two "vavs." (Bereshit 2:4) This indicates that the "toldot" of Heaven are all good. In Parashat Chayei Sarah, with respect to *Yishmael*, the Torah spells "toldot" as "תֹּלְדֹת," with no "vavs." (Bereshit 25:12) This indicates the offspring of *Yishmael* were no good, meaning none of his descendants were righteous. In Parashat Toldot, with respect to *Yitzchak*, the Torah spells "toldot" as "תּוֹלְדֹת," with one "vav." (Bereshit 25:19) This indicates *Yitzchak* produced half goodness, in the form of *Yaacov* and half evil, in the form of *Eisav*.

Rabbi Yissacher Frand – When *Eisav* comes to *Yaacov* and requires food, *Yaacov* requests that *Eisav* sell him the *bechorah* "chayom," "as this day." (Bereshit 25:31) Why this seemingly superfluous addition? The term is meant to connote *Eisav's* perspective on life. It is "this day," here and now, self-gratification and *Olam HaZeh* that matter. *Yaacov* correctly intuited that such an outlook was inconsistent with being the standard bearer of *Avraham's* movement, and rightly worked to ensure *Yaacov*, the more worthy of the two, would be the successor to the philosophy based upon serving others and attaining closeness to *Hashem* both in this world and the next. One must engage in serious introspection to determine the degree to which he, like *Eisav*, warps his perception and priorities in this world.

5762

The *Gemara* (Nedarim 32a) derives from Parashat Toldot the position that *Avraham* understood and followed *Hashem* from the age of three, based on the *pasuk* that reads "עֵקֶב אֲשֶׁר שָׁמַע אַבְרָהָם בְּקֹלִי וַיִּשְׁמֹר מִשְׁמַרְתִּי מִצְוֺתַי חֻקּוֹתַי וְתוֹרֹתָי," "Because [eikev] Avraham obeyed My Voice and observed My Safeguards, My Commandments, My Edicts and My Torahs." (Bereshit 26:5) The *gematria* for the word "eikev" is 172, meaning that *Avraham* had consciousness of *Hashem* for 172 years. Since *Avraham* lived 175 years, (Bereshit 25:7), we deduce that he became aware of G-d at the age of three.

5763

Rabbi Yosef Kalatsky – *Rivkah* told her son *Yaacov* to flee to her brother *Lavan* for a "yamim achadim," "a short while." (Bereshit 27: 43, 44) *Yaacov* ended up being gone for thirty-six years! At the end of Parashat Toldot, Rashi tells us that for the first fourteen years *Yaacov* secluded himself and studied at the *Yeshivah* of *Eiver*. (Rashi on Bereshit 28:9). Thereafter, in reference to Parashat Vayeishev, Rashi states that for the ensuing twenty-two years *Yaacov* was traveling or sojourning with *Lavan*. (Rashi on Bereshit 37:34) The *Gemara* (Megillah 17a) tells us that for not returning to his parents during those twenty-two years, *Yaacov* was punished, *middah keneged middah*, in being separated from his son *Yosef* for twenty-two years.

5764

The *pasuk* says "עֵקֶב אֲשֶׁר שָׁמַע אַבְרָהָם בְּקֹלִי וַיִּשְׁמֹר מִשְׁמַרְתִּי מִצְוֺתַי חֻקּוֹתַי וְתוֹרֹתָי," "Because Avraham obeyed My Voice, and observed My Safeguards, My Commandments, My Edits and My Torahs." (Bereshit 26:5) Here,

Rashi, quoting the *Gemara* (Yoma 28b) tells us, the plural form of *Torah* indicates a clear reference to the Written *Torah* and the Oral *Torah*, both of which were given to *Moshe* at *Har Sinai*, as well as the "mishmarti," the Safeguards that would be instituted by the Rabbis to protect the observance of the *Torah*.

5765

Rabbi Avi Weiss – After *Yaacov* was told by *Rivkah* to flee *Eisav*, the *Torah* states that *Rivkah* was the mother of *Yaacov* and *Eisav*. (Bereshit 28:5) Is this not obvious? In fact, Rashi on this *pasuk* famously states "איני יודע מה מלמדנו," "I do not know what it teaches us." The Tzedah Laderech says that despite *Rivkah's* concern for *Yaacov's* safety, she was also concerned for her other son. If, as she feared, *Eisav* killed *Yaacov* (her favorite) he would be a murderer. This is why she says "... lamah eshkal gam shenaychem yom echad," "why should I be bereaved of both of you on the same day?" (Bereshit 27:45) For on such a day she would lose her physical connection to *Yaacov* and her motherly connection to *Eisav*, something she assuredly did not want to lose. Within *Rivkah's* calculus is a strong lesson for parents of challenging children.

5767

Rabbi Eli Mansour – Rather than ascribing falsehood to *Yaacov*, we must be impressed with his attempts to speak the truth. To his father he said "Anochi, Eisav b'chorecha ... ," which can be translated as "I am who I am, Eisav is your firstborn." (Bereshit 27:19) While *Yaacov* had to engage in the charade, having been directed to do so by his mother *Rivkah*, an unquestioned prophetess, he still could not suppress the *middah* of *emet*. This may also be why he told his father that he returned quickly from his hunt "... ki hikrah Hashem Elokecha l'fanav," "because Hashem, your G-d, arranged it for me," (Bereshit 27:20), which was not only true, but something *Eisav* the Wicked would never have said.

5768

Rabbi Yossi Jankovits – As with *Yaacov* when he blesses *Menashe* and *Ephraim*, *Yitzchak*, in blessing *Yaacov*, employs all five senses. He <u>hears</u> that "kol" (voice) of *Yaacov* and <u>feels</u> the "yadayim" (hands) of "Eisav," (Bereshit 27:22), <u>smells</u> the odor of *Gan Ayden* in the clothing of *Yaacov*, (Bereshit 27:27) <u>tastes</u> the food prepared by *Rivkah*, (Bereshit 27:25) and, significantly, although blind, *Yitzchak* says "Re'ay rayach b'ni ... ," "<u>see</u> the fragrance of my son ...." (Bereshit 27:27) The *tzaddik* employs all his physical assets in bringing Holiness to the world through a *berachah*.

5769

Rabbi Yosef Weinstock – Having been childless for close to twenty years, *Yitzchak* and *Rivkah* each *daven* for children. The *pasuk* informs us that *Hashem* allowed himself to be entreated by him alone. (Bereshit 25:21) There, Rashi points out "לו ולא לה, שאין דומה תפלת צדיק בן צדיק לתפלת צדיק בן רשע לפיכך לו ולא לה," "His [prayer] but not hers, for the prayer of the righteous person [Rivkah] who is the child of a wicked person [Betuel] is not comparable to the prayer of a righteous person [Yitzchak] who is the child of a righteous person [Avraham], therefore to him, but not to her." This might be understood to mean that *Rivkah* could pray at any level and her prayer would transcend the level of her wicked father, but *Yitzchak* had to truly extend himself to successfully distinguish his prayer from that of his righteous father *Avraham*. Such a prayer is much more potent because such effort goes into bringing it forth from the petitioner.

5770

Rabbi Yitzchak Salid – *Yaacov* flees for his life upon receiving the *berachot* from *Yitzchak*. The *Midrash* tells us that *Eisav* sent his son *Eliphaz* to pursue and kill *Yaacov*. *Eliphaz*, upon finding *Yaacov*, was faced with an apparent dilemma: he wanted to honor his father's directive, yet he felt badly about killing his uncle. *Yaacov* famously proposed a solution to *Eliphaz's* conflict: by taking all his wealth and impoverishing *Yaacov*, *Eliphaz* would, according to the *Gemara* (Nedarim 64b), essentially have killed him, since a poor man is consider as if dead. What is not fully appreciated from this story is the twisted premise – that *Eliphaz* actually understood the *mitzvah* of *kibbud av* to include requiring him to commit murder! This he could only have learned from his twisted father, who warped the idea of *kibbud av* in his own right by dutifully serving *Yitzchak* and then causing mayhem towards others. *Eliphaz*, as the progenitor of *Amalek*, is rightfully faulted for failing to refuse to follow his father's orders.

5771

Rabbi Yosef Weinstock – The *pasuk* tells us "... v'Yaacov eesh tam yoshaiv ohalim," "but Yaacov was a wholesome man, dwelling in <u>tents</u>." (Bereshit 25:27) Why "tents" and not simply in a "tent?" In referring to *Eisav*, the *Torah* calls him "eesh sadeh" "a man of a field [singular]." *Yaacov* was intent on growing spiritually and sought to be spiritually educated from any source. In contrast, the name "Eisav," Rashi tells us, comes from the word "Asay," meaning "made [complete]." (Rashi on Bereshit 25:25) *Eisav's* belief was that he had nothing more to learn. *Yaacov* was always seeking to grow. That may be why the word "יֵשֵׁב," "dwelling," is written incomplete, without a "vav," for while Yaacov certainly "sat and learned," he never felt complete in his *Torah* learning or spiritual journey.

5772

Maharsha – The *pasuk* relates "וַיֶּעְתַּר יִצְחָק לה' לְנֹכַח אִשְׁתּוֹ כִּי עֲקָרָה הִוא וַיֵּעָתֶר לוֹ ה' וַתַּהַר רִבְקָה אִשְׁתּוֹ," "And Yitzchak prayed to Hashem opposite his wife because she was barren, and Hashem accepted <u>his</u> prayer, and Rivkah his wife conceived." (Bereshit 25:21) Rashi quotes the *Gemara* (Yevamot 64a) that *Hashem* heard the prayer of *Yitzchak* over the prayer of *Rivkah* because there is no comparison of the prayer of a "tzaddik ben tzaddik," "a righteous person, child of a righteous person," and that of a "tzaddik ben rasha," "a righteous person, child of a wicked person," meaning the former is superior. This rule applies only with respect to praying for children, where the prior generation's merit comes to bear in the formation of the next generation. The *Gemara* (Yevamot 62b) states that grandchildren are like children, and in this area alone the merits or sins of the grandfather can have a very real effect on whether *Hashem* grants another generation in the family tree.

5773

MRF Note – When the *Torah*, towards the end of Parashat Toldot, calls *Rivkah* "eim Yaacov v'Eisav," "the mother of Yaacov and Eisav," (Bereshit 28:5) Rashi admits "ani yodaya mah m'lamadaynu," "I do not know what it teaches us." Perhaps we can say that her response to hearing that *Eisav* wanted to kill *Yaacov* (i.e. her decision to send *Yaacov* away) indicated she was the loving mother of <u>both</u> sons, since, *Eisav*, in declaring his intention to kill *Yaacov*, had the *din* of a *rodeiph*, making it permissible for either *Rivkah* or *Yaacov* to justifiably kill him first. Instead, *Rivkah* chose to send *Yaacov* away, against her own interest, but to save her other son from death.

VAYEITZEI

5758

Following his famous dream, *Yaacov* prayed to *Hashem* that his wicked uncle *Lavan* should not have a negative spiritual impact on him. (Rashi on Bereshit 28:21) This prayer seems to have been granted when, in next week's *parashah*, *Yaacov* instructs messengers to declare to his brother *Eisav* "eem Lavan garti," literally "with Lavan I have sojourned." (Bereshit 32:5) There Rashi points out that "garti," "גרתי,"comprises the same letters as "taryag," "תריג," which has a *gematria* of 613, which is the total number of *mitzvot*. The message for *Eisav* is that *Yaacov* has, despite the negative influence of his wicked uncle, remained true to the entire *Torah*, as was originally requested of *Hashem* in Parashat Vayeitzei.

5759

Yaacov dreamed of a ladder and was, in fact, a sort of ladder between *Avraham*, the idealist with a heart in the proverbial clouds, and *Yitzchak*, a pragmatist with his head "down to earth." *Yaacov* bridged the two realms of Heaven and Earth. The Baal Haturim points out that the words "Sinai" and "Sulam" (ladder) share the same *gematria*, as each indicates a bridge between the physical world and the spiritual world.

5760

Chasam Sofer – In the beginning of Parashat Vayeitzei, the *Torah* makes special mention that *Yaacov* left *Be'er Sheva*, which Rashi says is for the purpose of teaching us that the departure of a righteous person from a city leaves a resulting spiritual void. (Rashi on Bereshit 28:10) Why, then, in Parashat Lech Lecha, does the *Torah* not tell us that *Avraham* went out of *Charan*? (Bereshit 12:4) Perhaps because in leaving *Be'er Sheva Yaacov* left behind *Yitzchak* and *Rikvah*, righteous individuals who could appreciate the loss of a *tzaddik*. Yet when *Avraham* went out of *Charan* he left behind him only idol worshipers with no concept of what they had lost.

5761

Rabbi Yisroel Ciner – *Yaacov's* dream of a ladder originating on Earth and stretching to Heaven demonstrates man's role in bridging the physical and spiritual. Indeed, man comprises both elements: a *guf* and a *neshamah*, and is the only being so created by *Hashem*. The duty to reconcile these competing forces is put to the test when we are forced to deal with unscrupulous people in this world, such as *Lavan*. As Jews, we are obligated to reflect the *middah* of spirituality, and the beauty of spirituality, to the world at large, showing even the bad people with whom we interact that we, ourselves, are ladders.

5762

Rabbi Yossi Jankovits – Bnei Yissaschar (Chodesh Adar 1:10) teaches that because *Chavah* used four of her five senses (excluding smell) when she committed her sin, *Leah* sought to correct the error of *Chavah* through her children. *Reuven* was a *tikkun* for <u>sight</u> (Rashi on Bereshit 29:32); *Shimon* for <u>hearing</u> (Bereshit 29:33); *Levy* for <u>touch</u> (for when a third child is born, because the mother's two hands are otherwise occupied, the father must hold the newborn) (Bereshit 29:35; see Meshech Chochmah); and *Yehudah* for <u>using the mouth</u> (in giving thanks, Bereshit 29:35). Yet *Leah's* children realized that all five senses, not only these four, are required in service to *Hashem*, and *Reuven* therefore brought *Leah* "dudaim," a type of fragrant flower, for her to smell. (Bereshit 30:14; see Shir HaShirim 7:14) The *gematria* of *Leah* is thirty-six, which corresponds to the thirty-six sparks of Holiness that the Ohr HaChaim HaKadosh (Devarim 21:11) states were originally contained in *Adam HaRishon* and were dispersed in the world as a result of *Chavah's* sin. *Leah* was destined to gather these sparks through six of the Twelve Tribes that came through her.

Rabbi Binyamin Kamenetsky – After fleeing his home, the *Midrash* tells us that *Yaacov* studied for fourteen years at the *Yeshivat Shem v'Eiver* on the subject of how to survive in an environment contrary to Torah, which was preparation for his time with *Lavan*, his evil uncle. *Shem* became an expert on the subject, having been a part of the generation of the Flood, and *Yaacov* was successful in passing the lessons on to his son *Yosef*, which kept him from sinning with the wife of *Potiphar* in *Mitzrayim* (see Bereshit 39:11, where Rashi comments that *Yosef* saw *Yaacov's* face). Our challenge in modern times is to do anything and everything to teach ourselves and other Jews these ancient secrets to surviving as a Jew in a world anathema to Torah.

MRF Note – The Five Books of Moses reflect the areas in which a Jew can and should bring *Kedushah* to the world. Bereshit, "in the beginning," connotes time; Shemot, "names," connotes interactions between people (which is why we use names); Vayikra, "calling out," connotes speech; Bamidbar, "in the desert," indicates place; and Devarim, "things [or words]," refers to objects. By making all aspects of our lives Holy we fulfill the reason the Five Books were given to *Bnei Yisrael*. Connected to this idea, the *siddur* sets forth *Sheish Zichronot*, six remembrances that the *Torah* mandates must be recalled daily. They are (1) the giving of the *Torah*; (2) the Exodus from Egypt; (3) *Shabbat*; (4) the attack of *Amalek*; (5) the sin of the golden calf; and (6) the incident of *Miriam* speaking *lashon hara* about *Moshe Rabbeinu*. These items can also be applied to the same pathways for *Kedushah* in our lives. The *Torah*, through its interpretation by the *Chachamim*, provides the necessary guide for how to *miKadaish* each area. Egypt, a location, indicates place. *Shabbat*, a weekly occurrence, indicates time. *Amalek* attacked *Bnei Yisrael*, providing an infamous example of human interaction. The incident of the golden calf demonstrated the most negative use of an object, and *Miriam*, in speaking *lashon hara*, failed to use speech to achieve Holiness. Our challenge and mission is to apply the teachings of the *Torah* to bring Holiness in all aspects of our lives: whenever possible, in dealing with others, through our speech, wherever we are, and with whatever we have at our disposal.

Yaacov, like his father *Yitzchak* (through *Eliezer*) before him (Bereshit 24:13) and *Moshe* after him (Shemot 2:16), met his *bashert* at a well containing water. Water symbolizes *Torah* wisdom (Derech Eretz Zutah 8), and water drawn from a well below the ground indicates wisdom that is not readily apparent but is accessible to those willing to extend their reach and work for it. Women are especially important in assisting in that endeavor.

Rabbi Yossi Jankovits – The predominance of water in the acquisition of the wives of Jewish leaders (*Yitzchak*, *Yaacov* and *Moshe*) teaches an important lesson. The Kli Yakar (Bereshit 6:15) draws a connection between water and sexual immorality. Relations with one's wife must be tempered and in measure, as water is drawn from a well.

5763

Rachel demands that *Yaacov* assist her in having a child, for, if not, she states "I am dead." (Bereshit 30:1) What bothered *Rachel* was not her inability to fulfill her personal desire to have children – it was not about her at all. Rather, her complaint was that she was created to be a link in the *mesorah* of *Bnei Yisrael,* and if she could not fulfill her destiny, she would be considered as a "dead woman walking." Her sole concern was service to her Creator. We must keep *Rachel's* example in mind when we are blessed to raise children. Our purpose is not to get *nachas* for our own satisfaction, but rather to have a role in completing the Jewish mission of perfecting the world.

HaK'tav v'HaKabbalah – Why did *Yaacov* wait seven years to marry *Rachel?* He wanted to wait until she was twelve and able to conceive, meaning she was five when they met. MRF Note – perhaps this explains why Yaacov was able to kiss Rachel at the time he met her. (Bereshit 29:11)

5764

Rabbi Edward Davis – After stopping and sleeping on what was to one day become the Temple Mount, the *Torah* tells us concerning *Yaacov* "וַיִּירָא וַיֹּאמַר מַה נּוֹרָא הַמָּקוֹם הַזֶּה אֵין זֶה כִּי אִם בֵּית אלקים וְזֶה שַׁעַר הַשָּׁמָיִם", "And he became frightened and said 'How awesome is this place! For this is none other than the abode of G-d and this is the Gate of the Heavens!'" (Bereshit 28:17) This was *Har Moriah*, the site of the *Akeidah*. How could *Yaacov* not have known of such an important place – or did he forget? Currently, a "Geneva Plan" is being proposed under which Israel would surrender sovereignty over the Temple Mount to the Arabs. The fact that such a disastrous proposal could even be suggested is understandable since even Orthodox Jews do not appreciate the importance of *Har HaBayit*. Most Jews who follow the *Torah* would assert that the *Kotel* is Judaism's Holiest site, yet the *Kotel* is a mere outer retaining wall for the Mount. If we, the supposed true keepers of our hallowed tradition, fail to stress the fundamental importance of *Har HaBayit*, we should not be surprised when the Yossi Beilens of the world work to give it away.

It is remarkable that despite the fact that *Hashem* Himself spoke to *Lavan* in a dream (Bereshit 31:24), *Lavan* still strongly desired his "tiraphin," idols for worship that *Rachel* stole (Bereshit 31:19), and demanded their return! Perhaps the answer comes at the end of the *parashah*, where the *pasuk* indicates "... vayaylech v'yashav Lavan limkomo. V'Yaacov halachah l'darko ... ," "... then Lavan went and returned to his place. And Yaacov went on his way ... ," (Bereshit 32: 1,2) indicating that *Lavan* was spiritually stagnant, stuck in "place," while *Yaacov* was always in growth mode, continuing on his "path" to *Torah* greatness.

5765

Rabbi Edward Davis – *Yaacov* famously takes his vow, pledging fidelity to Hashem if "... He will give me bread to eat and clothes to wear; . . ," (Bereshit 28:20) Why are the words "to eat" and "to wear" included? Is it not understood that the bread is for eating and the clothes for wearing? The concern is that, on the verge of going into *galut*, *Yaacov* was fearful of being influenced to eat food or wear clothing that is not kosher for a Jew. Here he was simply asking *Hashem* to assist him in remaining faithful to the teachings of his father and grandfather while traveling away from home.

5767

Reb Ben Greenberg – The *pasukim* tell us that *Yaacov* planned to build a *Beit HaMikdash* and give *maaser* seemingly only under certain conditions: "וַיִּדַּר יַעֲקֹב נֶדֶר לֵאמֹר אִם יִהְיֶה אלקים עִמָּדִי וּשְׁמָרַנִי בַּדֶּרֶךְ הַזֶּה אֲשֶׁר אָנֹכִי הוֹלֵךְ וְנָתַן לִי לֶחֶם לֶאֱכֹל וּבֶגֶד לִלְבֹּשׁ וְשַׁבְתִּי בְשָׁלוֹם אֶל בֵּית אָבִי וְהָיָה ה' לִי לאלקים," "Then Yaacov took a vow, saying 'if G-d will be with me, and He will guard me on this way that I am going; and he will give me bread to eat and clothes to wear; and I will return in peace to my father's house, and Hashem will be a G-d to me ....'" (Bereshit 28:20, 21) It is startling that *Yaacov Avinu* here seems to be conditioning his religiosity! In reality, *Yaacov* was showing his vulnerability and admitting to being human. He understood that all protection and blessings from *Hashem* are dependent on one's *avodah* and worthiness. Yet while he knew the formula for success, he was expressing his anxiety that, without help, he might be unable to uphold his end of the bargain.

5769

Rabbi Yossi Jankovits – At the very end of the *parashah* the *Torah* tells us that angels came to meet *Yaacov*, and Rashi there indicates, based on the Midrash Tanchuma, that they came out of *Eretz Yisrael* for the purpose of escorting *Yaacov* on his return into the Land. (Bereshit 32:2) Yet this seems to contradict what we are told earlier in the *parashah* concerning the angels of *Yaacov's* famous dream. There, when the *Torah* describes angels "ascending and descending on a ladder," (Bereshit 28:12) Rashi states specifically "the angels who escorted [Yaacov] in the Land do not go out of the Land," which, he explains, is why those angels first ascended, after which the angels for *chutz l'Aretz* descended to accompany him. The answer might be that the "*Eretz Yisrael*" angels will not, indeed cannot, leave the Land for the purpose of facilitating a *yerida*, but they can exit the Land to greet an *oleh* who is making *aliyah*.

5770

Reb Levy Cohn – Rabbi Yosef Y. Jacobson states that there is a common perception that the *bedeken* ceremony is designed to ensure that the *chatan* is marrying the proper bride – an antidote to the trickery of *Lavan* in the matter of his switching of *Rachel* and *Leah* on *Yaacov's* wedding night. (Bereshit 29:23) *Yaacov* was attracted to and greatly desired *Rachel*, yet, through *Lavan's* deception, *Leah* became his primary wife, at least with respect to spirituality, as she was the mother of six *Shevatim*, three times as many as any other wife. Rather than operating as an "identity check," the *beddeken* can be seen as an affirmation by the *chatan* that the beauty and physicality of the *kallah* should be veiled and, in essence, secondary, and that the *chatan* is, through the ceremony, embracing the spiritual/hidden side of his wife, his *bashert*, which he knows to be his destiny.

5771

Kli Yakar – *Yaacov's* vow to *Hashem* engenders much commentary. The *Torah* relates that *Yaacov* declared that if *Hashem* gives him "bread to eat and clothes to wear" then *Hashem* will be a G-d for him. (Bereshit 28:20, 21) That the bread is "to eat" and the clothes are "to wear" seems redundant and unnecessary. In fact, this language is meant to convey the limited nature of *Yaacov's* request. He was informing *Hashem* that his food and clothing were necessities, required to properly serve Hashem, not luxuries for his own benefit.

5772

Rabbi Chaim Tuvi – *Hashem's* perfect justice is on display in *Sefer Bereshit*. In Parashat Vayeitzei *Yaacov* angrily responds to *Rachel's* demand for children with the following words: "hatachat Elokim anochi?!," "am I instead of G-d?!," (Bereshit 30:2) a clearly rhetorical question delivered in a harsh manner. Years later, as described in Parashat Vayechi, after *Yaacov's* death, the brothers plead with *Yosef*, son of *Rachel*, not to do them harm. *Yosef's* reply is ironic "וַיֹּאמֶר אֲלֵהֶם יוֹסֵף אַל תִּירָאוּ כִּי הֲתַחַת אלקים אָנִי," "But Yosef said to them, 'Fear not, for am I instead of G-d?!'" (Bereshit 50:19)

5773

Near the conclusion of the *parashah* there is an interesting exchange between *Lavan* and *Yaacov*. On the verge of reconciliation, *Lavan* lists the "assets" that Yaacov has amassed during his years of service to *Lavan*, including daughters, grandchildren and flocks. *Yaacov* does not reply directly, but rather directs "l'echav," "to his brothers," to gather stones for the purpose of building a memorial to their treaty with *Lavan*. (Bereshit 31:46) Who are *Yaacov's* brothers? Rashi tells us "הם בניו, שהיו לו אחים נגשים אליו לצרה ולמלחמה," "These are his sons, who were like brothers to him, who would come forward in times of trouble and war for him!" (Rashi on Bereshit 31:46) The contrast between *Lavan's* characterization of *Yaacov's* family as passive possession and *Yaacov's* description of empowerment and co-reliance is startling. Here *Yaacov* is providing us with the blueprint for the Jewish way of building a family.

MRF Note – The Torah tells us that when *Yaacov* met *Rachel* he wept. (Bereshit 29:11) One reason provided by Rashi is "לפי שצפה ברוח הקודש שאינה נכנסת עמו לקבורה," "Because he foresaw through *Ruach HaKodesh* that she would not go in with him to the grave." Read literally, this Rashi <u>does not</u> mean that he was upset that they would not be buried in the same <u>place</u>, but rather that they would not be buried at the same <u>time</u>. Perhaps *Yaacov* was feeling the pain of knowing that, after having found his soul mate, he would end up living in this world without her for some period after her death, which would mark a painful and incomplete phase of his life. Certainly this Rashi could be interpreted to mean that *Yaacov* was upset that they would not be buried in the same <u>place</u>. Yet it is also true that upon their deaths *Yaacov* and *Rachel* would be reunited in the Afterlife, at which point where they were buried would be of lesser consequence. To read the Rashi to indicate that *Yaacov's* sadness was in knowing that death would separate him and *Rachel* for a period in this world underscores what we know to be true: how painful the loss of a spouse can be. Yet this interpretation can also prompt us to rejoice and be ever thankful for the time we do spend in serenity and love with our soul mates.

VAYISHLACH

5758

Eisav is regarded badly by *Chazal*, who compare him to the *yetzer hara* in all of us. Why, then, does the *Torah* continually refer to him as *Yaacov's* "brother," a seemingly affectionate term? There are, in actuality, two types of "*Eisavs*" representing the two types of societies that Jews have found themselves in over the millennia, each of which represents a separate test. One model is where *Eisav* hates and ostracizes the Jews, and the other is where *Eisav* loves the Jews and assimilation ensues. The latter is the "*Eisav*, my brother*" model, and, in many ways, it is more dangerous than the "*Eisav*, my enemy" model. The more benign *Eisav* forces every Jew to ask himself "How far will I allow *Eisav* my brother into my life?"

5759

The *Gemara* (Berachot 26b) teaches that each of the *Avot* instituted one of the three daily prayer services, which occur morning, afternoon and evening. *Avraham* instituted *Shacharit*, which occurs in the "boker," morning. בוקר begins with a "ב," which is the second letter of *Avraham's* name. *Yitzchak* instituted *Minchah*, which occurs in the "tzararayim," afternoon. צהריים begins with a "צ", which is the second letter of *Yitzchak's* name. Finally, *Yaacov* instituted Maariv, which occurs in the "erev," evening. ערב begins with a "ע," which is the second letter of *Yaacov's* name.

5760

Rabbi Yisroel Ciner – One way *Yaacov* prepared for his confrontation with *Eisav* was through prayer. (Bereshit 32:12) The *Talmud* (Yoma 69b) tells us that *Yirmiyahu HaNavi*, upon seeing the nations rejoicing at the destruction of the *Beit HaMikdash* left out "norah," "awesome," in describing *Hashem*. *Daniel*, upon seeing the nations enslave *Bnei Yisrael*, left out "gibor," "powerful." When the *Men of the Great Assembly* codified the *Shemoneh Esrei* they included reference to *Hashem* as "HaGadol (the Big), HaGibor (the Strong) v'HaNorah (the Awesome)." The *Men of the Great Assembly* lived at the end of the Babylonian Exile, following the *Purim* miracle. Their inclusion of these references to *Hashem* conceded the point well understood by *Yaacov*: that our ups and downs are awesome displays of *Hashem's* Power and Greatness.

Rabbi Yitzchak Etshalom – One can ask a question as to whether *Yaacov* was truly mad at *Shimon* and *Levy* for their dealings with *Schem*. (Bereshit 34:1-31) In any event, whether mad or not, it is not at all clear that *Yaacov* thought their actions were morally wrong. Consider the following: (1) Ultimately, in Parashat Vayechi, *Yaacov* "blesses" all of his sons on his deathbed; (2) the actual language *Yaacov* uses with respect to *Shimon* and *Levy* seems to downplay the action, as it says " ... in their rage they killed a man ...," (Bereshit 49:6) suggesting only one (when in fact they killed over one hundred including, including women); (3) *Yaacov's* only objection after the incident is that it will upset the local population (Bereshit 34:30), which turns out to be unfounded. No mention is made of morality; and (4) Although rape of an unmarried girl is not considered a capital offense (even by non-Jews), any attack on the spiritual essence of *Bnei Yisrael* is met with armed resistance (see, for example, the *Chanukah* story).

5761

Rabbi Yossi Jankovits – The Ohr HaChaim (Devarim 21:11) teaches that there are sparks of *Kedushah* spread throughout the world. When *Adam HaRishon* ate from the *Eitz HaDa'at*, the result was a scattering throughout the world of the "sparks of light" that were once singly sourced with him. Gentiles who possess one of these sparks of *Kedushah* seek out Jews, who form the group that is closest to G-d and contain the largest concentration of *Kedushah* in the world. These gentiles seek to cleave to the Jews so as to return to the source of their being, and to match the *Kedushah* spark within them to the larger source. This is the sole reason for the *galut*. According to the Baal Shem Tov, Jews must inject themselves into the world at large in order to "redeem" these Holy sparks. The two examples given by the Ohr HaChaim are the cases of *aishet yefat toar* in Parashat Ki Taitzei (Devarim 21:10-14) and the case of *Schem* in Parashat Vayishlach. (Bereshit 34:1-31) In the case of the abduction of *Dinah* by *Schem*, the *Torah* states in three places that he did not merely "desire" her but that his *neshamah* "deeply desired" and "cleaved" to her. (Bereshit 34:3, 8 and 19)

The text seems to suggest that something much more than mere physical lust was driving *Schem's* conduct. Of course, *Schem* should have controlled himself by first having a *brit milah* through a valid conversion. Instead, by reacting too quickly and raping her, he committed an unpardonable sin. Yet it seems he and his people were allowed to convert, to have a *brit milah*, to complete the *Kedushah* connection to the Jewish People, and only then to die, as Jews. The other example is also instructive, describing how the *tzaddikim* of *Bnei Yisrael* would, during the throes of war and based on the spark of *Kedushah*, be attracted to a non-Jewish woman, and thereafter undertake a thirty day process of waiting (according to Rashi and Ramban) to ensure that it was the *neshamah*, and not the *guf*, that was driving the attraction.

5762

Rabbi Yissacher Frand – The Baal HaTurim tells us that the three pilgrimage holidays mandated by the *Torah* correspond to the three *Avot*. *Avraham* represents *Pesach*, as that is the time in which he welcomed the three angels (Rashi on Bereshit 18:10); *Yitzchak* represents *Shavuot*, as the ram's horn from the *Akeidah* was blown at *Matan Torah* (Rashi on Shemot 19:13), which *Shavuot* commemorates; and *Yaacov* represents *Sukkot*, for he made "sukkot" for his livestock in Parashat Vayishlach. (Bereshit 33:17) The Ohr HaChaim says that *Yaacov* was the first person ever to make shelter for animals, by which he was demonstrating *hakarat hatov*, a *middah* that he passed on to his son *Yosef*. It was this trait, rather than fear of punishment, that ultimately stopped *Yosef* from sinning with *Potiphar's* wife. And this *middah* is strongly connected to the holiday of *Sukkot* when we thank *Hashem* for sustaining us in the *midbar*.

5763

Rabbi Yosef Kalatsky – *Yaacov's* prayer before he meets *Eisav* seem to suggest that he is unworthy because any accumulated merits he may have possessed have been reduced by the kindness granted him by

Hashem. Yaacov states "ki v'makli avarti et haYarden hazeh, v'atah hayiti l'shnay machanot. Hatzilaynee na ... ," "for with my staff I crossed this Jordan [River] and now I have become two camps. Rescue me please ...." (Bereshit 32:11, 12) Rather than a declaration that the abundant *chesed* of *Hashem* (transforming a mere staff to the wealth of two camps) has depleted his merits, *Yaacov* may have actually been invoking a merit. *Yaacov* crossed the *Yarden* with only a staff because all the riches and possessions given to him by his parents were taken by his nephew, *Eliphaz ben Eisav*. In Parashat Vayeitzei, *Eisav* had sent his son to kill *Yaacov*, and *Yaacov* had convinced *Eliphaz* that by impoverishing him *Eliphaz* would have minimally complied with his father's wishes. (Rashi on Bereshit 29:11) In the same *parashah*, we are told that a large, heavy stone covered the well in *Charan*, and while many local men were unable to move it, *Yaacov* did so easily based on his great strength (Rashi on Bereshit 29:8-10). We are told of *Yaacov's* superhuman strength to teach us that *Yaacov* could have easily killed *Eliphaz*, something that would have been justified based on *halachah*, as *Eliphaz* was a *rodeiph*. Yet knowing that he was the progenitor of the Jewish People, *Yaacov* chose to impoverish himself rather than spill blood. Later, in preparing for his confrontation with *Eisav*, *Yaacov* was "reminding" *Hashem* that the reason he had but a single staff when he crossed the river and met *Rachel* was due to his humility and respect for life, hoping that *Hashem* would judge him favorably as a result.

5764

Rabbi Mordechai Ginsparg – Rashi tells us that, prior to the confrontation with *Eisav*, *Yaacov* was attacked by *Eisav's* angel after being "left alone" in retrieving "pachim katanim," "small jars," he had previously forgotten. (Rashi on Bereshit 32:25) Rashi anticipates the obvious question: why would items of minor value matter to *Yaacov*, who was clearly a rich man by this time? The answer lies in the converse of the Western/secular expression that "time is money." For the *Torah* mind, "money is time."

For secular ideology, the goal is money and time is the means to that goal. But for the *tzaddik*, the goal is *Avodat Hashem* through *Torah* and *mitzvot*. Such *avodah* requires time, which can be "bought," as it were, with money. For the *tzaddik*, the only way to acquire money is through honest, *Torah* sanctioned means, such as work, which also requires time. Anything received in the effort of *Avodat Hashem* is supremely valuable and warrants a return to retrieve it.

5765

Rachel dies in Parashat Vayishlach. Before her passing, she names her second son "Ben-Oni," which Rashi tells us means "son of my pain." (Rashi on Bereshit 35:18) *Yaacov* wanted to give the name a more positive connotation and therefore named him בִּנְיָמִין. Ramban says that "oni" is a homonym for "strength," so *Yaacov* used "Ben Yamin," "son of the South," meaning "son of the right side" (for when one is facing eastward, his right side is to the south). The right hand is associated with strength. From this we see an example of a husband trying to honor his wife's dying declaration but modifying the name to accommodate conditions.

5766

Reb Ephraim Sobol – In regards to the ominous approach of *Eisav* and the 400 men accompanying him, the *pasuk* states "vayira Yaacov miod, v'yaizar lo ... ," "and Yaacov became very afraid and it distressed him ...." (Bereshit 32:8) There, Rashi famously comments that the fear was that he would be killed and the distress was that that he would kill others. The Minchat Yehudah there comments that while *Yaacov* would be justified in killing *Eisav*, it would surely cause pain to his father *Yitzchak*, something that distressed *Yaacov*. Perhaps also, *Yaacov* reasoned that in either case, were he to be killed by *Eisav* or to kill *Eisav*, it would mean the death of *Yaacov* as well, since *Rikvah* had unintentionally prophesized that her two sons would die on the same day. (Bereshit 27:45) *Yaacov*, rather than being pained at the thought of slaying his brother, may have simply been concerned that under either scenario, he, *Yaacov*, would die, and since this would mean not having fulfilled his known destiny to father the Twelve Tribes of Israel, he was greatly distressed.

5769

Rabbi Yitzchak Salid – There is a subtle distinction in the language of Rashi in regard to *Yaacov's* hiding *Dinah* from *Eisav* (Rashi on Bereshit 32:23) and *Yosef* shielding *Rachel* from Eisav. (Rashi on Bereshit 33:7) In the case of *Dinah*, Rashi, commenting on why the *Torah* mentions only Yaacov's "eleven sons," states that *Yaacov* placed her in a chest "shelo yitain bah Eisav aynav ... ," "so that Eisav should not set his eyes on her." In the case of *Rachel*, Rashi, commenting on how *Yosef* blocked *Eisav's* view, tells us he did so to avoid a situation where "shema yitleh bah aynav oto rasha ... ," "that evil one may 'hang' his eyes upon her." The difference in *lashon* indicates a distinction in intent. *Yaacov* simply wanted to keep *Dinah* from marrying *Eisav*. *Yosef* was aware that *Eisav* was intent on giving an "*ayin hara*" in regard to *Rachel*, not to marry her but in some way to ruin her for *Yaacov* (hence Rashi describing him there as the "evil one"). In intervening to avoid this result, as Rashi points out, "zacha Yosef l'virkat alay ayin ... ," "Yosef was blessed to be 'above the eye' (i.e. beyond the reach of the *yetzer hara*).

5770

Maggid of Mezritch – *Yaacov* declares to *Eisav* "vaihee lee shor vachamor ... ," "I have acquired an ox and a donkey ...." (Bereshit 32:6) The *Midrash* tells us these are allusions to *Yosef* and *Yissachar*, each of which is a tool for combatting the *yetzer hara*, to which *Eisav* is classically compared. The *yetzer hara*, of course, destroys the Jew in two ways: through enthusiasm for sinning and lethargy in performing *mitzvot*. The antidote in each case should therefore be the opposite: passivity towards sinful conduct and passion for mitzvot. *Yosef*, whom *Moshe* calls an "ox," (Devarim 33:17) is referred to in the *Haftarah* of Parashat Vayishlach as "lehavah," "a flame," (Ovadiah 1:18) which denotes enthusiasm for *mitzvot*. *Yissachar* is compared by *Yaacov* to a donkey, (Bereshit 49:14), which is naturally sedentary (i.e. not "aflame") in the face of sin. The action of *Yosef* is the antidote for passivity towards mitzvot, and the passivity of *Yissachar* is the antidote to an inclination towards sinful action. In fact, the *Gemara* (Makot 23b) tells us that one who has an opportunity to sin and does nothing is credited with a *mitzvah*.

5771

Panim Yafos – The *pasuk* reads "וַיְצַו אֹתָם לֵאמֹר כֹּה תֹאמְרוּן לַאדֹנִי לְעֵשָׂו כֹּה אָמַר עַבְדְּךָ יַעֲקֹב עִם לָבָן גַּרְתִּי וָאֵחַר עַד עָתָּה" "And he commanded them, *saying*, 'So shall you say to my master to Eisav, 'Thus said your servant Jacob, I have sojourned with Laban, and I have tarried until now.''" (Bereshit 32:5) The word "laymor," "saying" seems superfluous. The *pasuk* could have simply started "vayatzav otam, ko tomroon ... ," "and he commanded them "so shall you say ...." The angels that *Yaacov* is here commanding were not told to give his message directly to *Eisav*, but rather to "say" to another party to tell *Eisav* the message. This would be in line with Rashi's explanation in Parashat Vayeitzei that there are angels that escort travelers inside of *Eretz Yisrael* and do not go outside the Land and there are those that escort travelers outside of the Land only. (Rashi on Bereshit 28:12) Since the first *pasuk* in Parashat Vayishlach tells us that *Eisav* was in the Land of Seir (outside of Eretz Yisrael) (Bereshit 32:4) *Yaacov*, being in *Eretz Yisrael* himself, was required to appoint "interior" angels to speak to the "exterior" angels, who would then speak to *Eisav*. This would also explain why these "interior" angels, upon returning to *Yaacov*, state "banu el achicha ... ," "*we* came to your brother ... ," (Bereshit 32:7), indicating that *Eisav* was actually already in *Eretz Yisrael*, on his way with an army (thereby making the involvement of the "exterior" angels unnecessary).

5772

Rabbi Yochanan Zweig – The *Torah* tells us that *Eisav* took *Machlat bat Yishmael* as a wife (Bereshit 28:9) and also took *Basmat bat Yishmael* as a wife. (Bereshit 36:3) The *Talmud* Yerushalmi (Bikkurim 3:3) identifies these women as one in the same and deduces that "machlat" is from the word "machal" – to forgive. Further, the *Gemara* learns that one is forgiven on one's wedding day, which is the source of the customs of both fasting and *vidui* on that day. What is the connection between marriage and forgiveness? Sin comes from self-gratification and self-absorption. Being married affords us an opportunity to show concern and sensitivity towards others, which acts to atone for our sins.

5773

Rabbi Michael Jablinowitz – The *pasuk* says "וַיִּוָּתֵר יַעֲקֹב לְבַדּוֹ וַיֵּאָבֵק אִישׁ עִמּוֹ עַד עֲלוֹת הַשָּׁחַר" "And *Yaacov* was left alone, and a man wrestled with him until the break of dawn." (Bereshit 32:25) The Midrash Rabbah compares the "aloneness" of *Yaacov* to that of *Hashem* as The One and Only, "Ain Od Milvado." It seems clear that once *Yaacov* had achieved an elevated singular status he was attacked, and once he prevailed, he had earned the title of "*Yisrael*." The Jewish People, as the descendants of *Yaacov*, must recognize their inherent transcendent uniqueness and overcome the predictable negative reactions of the non-Jews. In doing so, we claim our destiny of becoming closer to and, so to speak, comparable to, G-d.

VAYEISHEV

5758

Parashat Vayeishev seemingly is a chain of coincidental causes and effects. Nearly every *pasuk* begins with a "vav" indicating connection to the previous *pasuk*; meaning, in the vernacular, "this happened, AND THEN this happened, AND THEN, this happened," etc. However, there are eight *pasukim* that do not begin with a "vav," interrupting the "this AND THEN that" pattern. This comes to show us that we must look beyond what appears to be natural occurring events to see the design behind them. Eight is a number indicating transcendence over nature (compare, for example, the *brit milah* on the eighth day, and the *Sheva Mitzvot Bnei Noach*). Looking beyond the basic understanding of the story of *Yosef* and his brothers we see *Hashgachah Pratit* at each and every moment. *Hashem* did not push the first domino of the narrative (so to speak) and then watch them all fall. Rather he knocked over each and every one! So too, we know *Hashem* renews Creation in every instant of time, although a less informed and "natural" reading would seem to show that the world operates automatically on principles of nature that He created and set in motion.

When *Yosef* is seeking his brothers in *Schem* the *Torah* text tells us "vayeemtzayhu ish," "and a man found him." (Bereshit 37:15) Rashi tells us that this was the Angel *Gavriel*, which we can deduce from that fact that the stranger "found *Yosef*." Why would a stranger be looking for someone unknown to him unless that stranger was sent to do so as a messenger from *Hashem*?

5759

Yosef's second dream is that the sun, the moon and eleven stars were bowing to him. (Bereshit 37:9) When *Yosef* tells his father of his dream, *Yaacov* is incredulous, understanding that the sun represents *Yaacov*, the moon represents *Rachel*, since deceased, and the eleven stars are *Yosef's* brothers. *Yaacov* scolds *Yosef*, asking him rhetorically "mah hachalom haze hasher chalamta ... ," "what is this dream that you dreamed ... ? (Bereshit 37:10) The letters embedded in the words "אֲשֶׁר חָלָמְתָּ הֲבוֹא" can be read as "רחל מתה," "Rachel mata," "Rachel is dead." *Yaacov* was alluding to the fact that because the "moon" in the dream was gone, the dream, as stated by *Yosef*, was impossible. Yet *Yaacov*, Rashi tells us, focused on the impropriety of *Yosef's* declaration of his dream rather than its impossibility, perhaps to spare *Yosef* (or perhaps himself) the pain that would result from a direct reference to *Rachel's* death.

5760

Rabbi Yosef Kalatsky – At the end of the *Chumash* in Parashat V'zot HaBerachah, *Moshe* praises *Yehudah* (and *Reuven*). (Devarim 33:7) *Chazal* say in the *Gemara* (Makot 11b) that *Yehudah's* praise relates to this incident in Parashat Vayeishev regarding *Tamar* – that when faced with evidence of his sin, he declared her innocent and publicly admitted his guilt. (Bereshit 38:26) Yet we can ask why this is especially laudable? *Yehudah*, after all, was a *tzaddik*. Should we not expect such behavior? The answer is profound. Because of human nature, being what it is, someone of *Yehudah's* station could easily have rationalized and provided a tenable reason to carry forth publicly the execution of *Tamar*, even while internally recognizing his own true guilt. Perhaps, he could have reasoned, that admitting guilt and undermining his standing with the local population would have broader negative consequences to the House of *Yaacov*, who were regarded as royalty. *Yehudah* had clarity to know that such a judgment would be based on his own interests rather than true justice. This can be compared to the sale of *Yosef*, where the *Torah* tells us "וַיֹּאמֶר יְהוּדָה אֶל אֶחָיו מַה בֶּצַע כִּי נַהֲרֹג אֶת אָחִינוּ וְכִסִּינוּ אֶת דָּמוֹ" "And Yehudah said to his brothers, 'What is the gain if we slay our brother and cover up his blood?'" (Bereshit 37:26) This is a seemingly strange question for a judge to ask at the time of applying the law and passing a sentence. *Yehudah* knew that the Brothers were driven at some deep level by personal jealousy, and their gain from eliminating *Yosef* was affecting what would otherwise have been a tenable judgment. We are not on *Yehudah's* level and we often make critical decisions affecting others without this degree of personal introspection. This is why Pirkei Avot (1:6) tells us "aseh l'cha Rav ... ," "take upon yourself a Rabbi ... ," meaning one should appoint someone with one's interests at heart to advise him and help him arrive at *emet*.

5761

Beis HaLevi – *Yosef* had two distinct dreams: one representing material gain and one spiritual gain. Where the brothers' bundles bowed to *Yosef's* bundle (Bereshit 37:7), the allusion was to physical gain, for in this world getting rich and powerful does not inherently change a person, it merely gives him a larger "bundle" of possessions. But when the stars, the sun and the moon bowed to him (Bereshit 37:9), *Yosef* was foreseeing spiritual growth that <u>does</u> change a person, making him <u>inherently</u> greater.

5762

Rabbi Yisroel Ciner – *Leah* made a supreme sacrifice in *davening* that her seventh child be a girl, not a boy, because she desired that her sister *Rachel* should be mother to at least one of the *Shevatim*. That child was *Dinah*, who was violated by *Schem*. (Bereshit 34:2) The *Midrash* Yalkut Shimoni (end of remez 134) states that the product of that union was a daughter that *Yaacov* banished to *Mitzrayim*. That girl became the adopted daughter of *Potiphar*, Yosef's erstwhile master, who named her *Asnat*, who eventually became *Yosef's* wife. (Bereshit 41:45) From that union came not one but <u>two</u> Tribes, *Ephraim* and *Menashe* (for *Yaacov*, near his death, declared that *Ephraim* and *Menashe* shall be to him like *Reuven* and *Shimon*- Bereshit 48:5). At the time of the *Schem* affair, *Leah* very well might have asked herself why her *chesed* resulted in such a catastrophe, but *Hashem* orchestrated the events, and *Leah* ultimately received an unimaginable reward. Often people cynically state that "no good deed goes unpunished," but this story stands for the idea that no good deed goes unrewarded, often in a much larger measure than could ever have been anticipated.

Rabbi Eli Mansour – *Yosef* is the master of *bitachon*. We know this from his interactions with the *Sar Hamashkim* and the *Sar Haofim*. *Yosef* finds himself in a dungeon after having originally been sold into slavery by his family and later framed by his master's wife. Certainly he had every reason and right to be depressed. Yet the *pasuk* tells us that *Yosef* noticed that two other prisoners, the *Sar Hamashkim* and the *Sar Haofim*, were sad, and he asked them "maduah p'naichem ra'im hayom?" "why are your faces downcast today?" (Bereshit 40:7) The Malbim tells us that the word "hayom," "today" is the key. *Yosef* actually noticed the disposition of fellow inmates from one day to the next, as if he himself was not actually an inmate but a casual guest in an otherwise horrible place. In fact, *Yosef* was confident that *Hashem* was "calling the shots," and he simply lived his life in the dungeon as if things were perfectly fine. This is the unbelievable level of belief possessed by the *tzaddik*, who knows that *Hashem* is orchestrating everything in his life.

5763

Reb Steven Jacoby – Rebbetzin Esther Jungreis points out that the Brothers asked *Yaacov Avinu* "hakitonet bincha hee eem lo?" "is this your son's tunic or not?" (Bereshit 37:32) By not naming *Yosef* by name to *Yaacov*, they displayed hatred towards their brother. This is similar to the upset parent who declares to the spouse "look what your son did!" (Interestingly, when *Yosef* reveals himself to his Brothers he declares "Ani Yosef," "I am Yosef," (Bereshit 45:3) emphasizing his identity and, perhaps, underscoring their shame.) We can learn a message from this concerning our attitude towards those that upset us. By using their names and humanizing them, we can empathize and connect, thereby diffusing the conflict.

5764

Rabbi Eli Mansour – When *Yaacov* sends *Yosef*, he tells him to look into the welfare of his Brothers and the welfare of the flock. (Bereshit 37:14) Why the concern over the animals? Because one must have gratitude to that which provides sustenance. The *Gemara* (Sotah 36b) tells us that *Yosef* was able to withstand the advances of *Potiphar's* wife because at the moment of his greatest temptation he saw *Yaacov's* face. This caused *Yosef* to recall *Yaacov's* lesson concerning having gratitude for one's sustenance. This is reflected in *Yosef's* earlier protestations that sinning with his master's wife would be a betrayal of all his master had done for him. (Bereshit 39: 8, 9) The lesson for all of us is that we must exhibit *hakarat hatov* for those who are sent by *Hashem* to aid us in providing for our families.

5765

Rabbi Yossi Jankovits – Why does the story of *Yehudah* and *Tamar* interrupt the story of *Yosef*? Perhaps it implicitly answers the question of why *Yosef* did not contact *Yaacov* during the time in *Mitzrayim* when he was not imprisoned. The Ohr HaChaim (Bereshit 45:26) states that there is a *halachah* that one is required to face death rather than embarrass another. (Sotah 10b) *Tamar* did just that, for Rashi tells us when *Tamar* declared "By the man to whom these [items] belong I am pregnant," (Bereshit 38:25) she was intentionally being oblique so as not to embarrass *Yehudah* publicly. Similarly, *Yosef*, despite the pain resulting from his separation from his father, did not send word to *Yaacov* of what the Brothers had done, for to do so would have been to embarrass them significantly. Perhaps this is what is meant in Parashat Mikeitz when the *Torah* states "וַיִּקְרָא יוֹסֵף אֶת שֵׁם הַבְּכוֹר מְנַשֶּׁה כִּי נַשַּׁנִי אלקים אֶת כָּל עֲמָלִי וְאֵת כָּל בֵּית אָבִי" "And Yosef named the firstborn Menashe, for 'God has caused me to forget all my toil and all my father's house.'" (Bereshit 41:51) Such a name might otherwise be an unbearable reminder of his separation from his father, yet *Hashem* had allowed *Yosef* enough serenity to "forget his father's house," something he was compelled to do based on Jewish law.

5767

Yosef is commonly regarded as a "lover of Eretz Yisrael." We learn in Parashat Shelach that the daughters of *Tzalaphchad* were lovers of the Land descended from *Yosef HaTzaddik* who also loved the Land. (Rashi on Bamidbar 27:1) This may be evidenced in the first *pasuk* of Parashat Vayeishev, when the *Torah* itself refers to the Land as "Eretz Caanan," (Bereshit 37:1) and yet, at the end of the *parasha, Yosef*, in speaking to the

Sar Hamashkim, describes himself as "may Eretz HaIvrim," "from the Land of the Hebrews." (Bereshit 40:15) Even incarcerated in the *galut*, *Yosef* identified with the Land and refers to It as the possession of the descendants of *Avraham*.

5768

Reb Ephraim Sobol – On *Yom Kippur* (and *Tisha B'Av*) we read about the "Asarah Harugei Malkut," "The Ten Martyrs" who, we are told, were murdered as atonement for the Sale of *Yosef*. According to the *Midrash* (Pirkei D'Rabbi Eliezer 37 and Targum Yonatan, based on Amos), many of the five prohibitions of *Yom Kippur* can be connected to the Sale. The Brothers bought shoes with the twenty pieces of silver (wearing shoes is prohibited); they sold *Yosef* to *Mitzrayim*, the epitome of sexual immorality, as with *Potiphar's* wife (marital relations are prohibited); the pit into which they threw *Yosef* had no water in it (washing is prohibited) and after selling *Yosef*, the Brothers sat down to a meal (eating is prohibited). Perhaps there is a connection between the story of the Sale and the prohibition of anointing with oil as well.

5769

Rabbi Yitzchak Salid – The two persons in *Tanach* known for their dreams are *Yosef* and *Daniel*. Each conquered his *yetzer hara*, *Yosef* with respect to the wife of *Potiphar* (Bereshit 39:12) and *Daniel* with respect to partaking of the non-kosher food and wine in the court of King *Nevuchadnezair*. (Daniel 1:8) Unlike most of us, where our dreams reflect a personal *taivah*, because *Yosef* and *Daniel* were each able to overcome their unhealthy personal yearnings, their dreams represented pure messaging from *Hashem*.

5770

Ohr HaChaim – The *pasuk* tells us "וַיִּשְׁמַע רְאוּבֵן וַיַּצִלֵהוּ מִיָּדָם וַיֹּאמֶר לֹא נַכֶּנּוּ נָפֶשׁ" "And Reuven heard, <u>and he saved him</u> from their hand, and he said, 'Let us not deal him a deadly blow.'" (Bereshit 37:21) But if *Reuven* subsequently allowed the Brothers to throw *Yosef* into a pit full of snakes and scorpions (Rashi on Bereshit 37:24), can he really be regarded as *Yosef's* savior? *Reuven* reasoned that since animals do not have free will independent of their Creator, should *Yosef* survive in such an environment it would be a miracle of *Hashem* based on *Yosef's* righteousness, and *Reuven* would be regarded as a savior. However, if *Yosef* were to die, it would demonstrate that the Brothers were right in their indictment of him.

5771

Rabbi Yosef Weinstock – The Netziv explains the two troubling dreams of the *Sar Hamashkim* and the *Sar Haofim*. Neither actually offended *Paroh* to be incarcerated. Rather, they were supervisors whose employees made mistakes: a fly found in the wine and a pebble found in the bread. (Rashi on Bereshit 40:1) Each had a different reaction to the offending event. The *Sar Hamashkim's* dream was benign and *Yosef* properly predicted that he would be restored to his post in three days. The key indicator in the dream was that he himself squeezed the grapes into *Paroh's* cup, (Bereshit 40:11) indicating that he took personal responsibility for the functional failure. The *Sar Haofim*, by contrast, did not bake or hold the bread described in his dream, but rather it is merely in baskets resting on his head, (Bereshit 40:16) a sure sign that he did not take personal responsibility for the original offending stone

5772

Rabbi Chaim Volozhin – *Reuven* advised putting *Yosef* in a pit full of snakes and scorpions and is credited with saving *Yosef*. *Yehudah* advised to remove him from the pit and sell him into slavery and the *Gemara* (Sanhedrin 6b) tells us that praise for *Yehudah* angers *Hashem*. Yet the *Gemara* (Yevamot 121a) states that one who falls into a pit of snakes and scorpions is presumed dead for *agunah* purposes. Was *Reuven* therefore really better than *Yehudah* in his treatment of *Yosef*? Yes, because *Reuven* tried to retain *Yosef* in *Eretz Yisrael*, where physical danger can be managed by spiritual elevation. *Yehudah* facilitated *Yosef's yerida*, an unpardonable error.

MIKEITZ

5757

Yosef's brothers entered the main city of *Mitzrayim* through ten separate gates not only to keep a "low profile," as their father *Yaacov* had instructed them (Rashi on Bereshit 42:5), but also in an attempt to find *Yosef*. (Rashi on Bereshit 42:13) This was the beginning of their *teshuvah* process. Yet because the worldwide famine made all of civilization travel to *Mitzrayim* for food, *Yosef* was expecting them. His scouts trailed them through the city and gave *Yosef* the ammunition to realistically and rationally accuse them of being spies.

Chazal provide three reasons that *Reuven* was not ultimately chosen to be king of the Jewish People, despite the fact that he was the oldest (*Yehudah*, who was fourth oldest, was ultimately chosen). First, *Reuven* moved his father's bed from the tent of *Bilhah* to the tent of *Reuven's* mother *Leah* (Rashi on Bereshit 35:22), a serious offense to the sanctity of the marital arrangement. Second, while *Reuven* recognized the need to save *Yosef* from his Brothers, he did not bring him back safely to his father *Yaacov*. (Bereshit 37: 21, 22) Third, in Parashat Mikeitz, *Reuven* makes the well-intentioned but misplaced guaranty of *Binyamin's* safe return to *Yaacov* by pledging the lives of his two sons. (Bereshit 42:37) In all three cases *Reuven* was partially right and partially wrong, but ultimately did not execute properly.

5758

Kli Yakar – As the narrative of Parashat Mikeitz unfolds, *Yosef* is hard on his Brothers, making them "jump through hoops" to correct the original wrong committed. Why was this allowed? The actions of the Brothers created an enormous gap in Jewish unity. Only when *Yehudah* declared before *Yosef* "HaElokim matza et avone avadecha ... ," "G-d has uncovered the sin of your servants ... ," (Bereshit 44:16) did *Yosef* know that the Brothers fully understood the gravity of their wrongdoing.

5759

Iturei Torah – The Torah Temimah points out a connection between *Chanukah* and the *parashah*. Parashat Mikeitz has 2025 words. The *gematria* of the word "ner," "candle," is 250. There are eight days of *Chanukah*, which starts on the twenty-fifth day of the month of *Kislev*. Eight times 250 equals 2000, plus 25 equals 2025!

5760

Rabbi Yosef Kalatsky – *Yosef's* Egyptian appellation, "Tzaphnat Paneiach," refers to *Yosef's* interpretation of *Paroh's* dream. (Rashbam and Rashi on Bereshit 41:45) This was done by *Paroh* to ensure he would always retain ultimate power in *Mitzrayim*, as this name would be a constant reminder of the story of *Yosef's* ascension from the dungeon and his humble roots. The Zohar, however, explains that this name was Divinely ordained to shield *Yosef's* identity from his Brothers when they eventually came to *Mitzrayim*.

Rabbi Moshe Bogomilsky – The *pasuk* tells us that at the time of the reunion of all Twelve Brothers "vayishtoo vayishkaroo imo," "they drank and they became intoxicated with him [Yosef]." (Bereshit 43:34) Rashi tells us that since the sale of *Yosef* neither he nor his Brothers had consumed wine, yet on that day all drank. It makes sense that *Yosef* would drink insofar as he was the only one present who realized the family was again reunited, but why would the Brothers drink, believing as they did that *Yosef* was still missing? The answer may lie in the preceding portion of the same *pasuk*, where we are told *Yosef* "played favorites" in giving *Binyamin* a portion five times greater than each of the Brothers (Bereshit 43:34), not unlike what *Yaacov* had done with *Yosef* so many years earlier. The Brothers responded positively, and showed no jealousy with regard to *Binyamin's* treatment, and for this they were proud and happy, and celebrated their improved *middot* with wine.

5761

Rabbi Yisrael Ciner – There is a distinction between the *Paroh* of *Yosef's* story and the *Paroh* that *Moshe* experienced. When *Yosef* gives his *Paroh* the blueprint on how to become the richest man in the world, *Paroh* recognizes *Hashem* and welcomes the tidings. (Bereshit 41:37-40) Conversely, when *Moshe* tells his *Paroh* that he is about to lose his entire workforce and wealth, the *Paroh* refuses to acknowledge *Hashem's* existence. (Shemot 5:2) This is indicative of the warped notion that a G-d bringing "good" news is always welcome, but a G-d bringing "bad" news is not G-d at all! Rabbi Yaakov Nayman points out that this is not a Jewish perspective, for we recognize *Hashem's* hand in what we perceive as good and bad. Like a doctor, *Hashem* is dispensing exactly the medicine we need, both good tasting and bitter, but all meant to heal us. Rabbi Yossi Jankovits adds that this may be the reason that the *Gemara* (Berachot 48b) says that the same way a person blesses for the good, he must also bless for the "bad."

5762

Rabbi Eli Mansour – *Yosef* is regarded as a "baal bitachon," a "master of faith in Hashem," which is evidenced in many ways. One clear indication is when he is summoned by *Paroh*, yet takes the time to shave and change his clothes before appearing. (Bereshit 41:14) Others might have run directly to *Paroh*, petrified to make the king wait even for a moment, yet *Yosef* was at peace, knowing *Hashem* was orchestrating the entire situation.

5763

Rabbi Yosef Kalatsky – Why would *Potiphar*, a heathen, tolerate a slave who, according to Rashi, always had the Name of Heaven in his mouth (i.e. *Yosef* was always speaking of *Hashem* and His Influence in his life)? (Rashi on Bereshit 39:3) The answer is that every part of *Yosef's* being was *emet* and *emunah. Yosef* lived openly as a religious Jew, which included praising *Hashem* constantly. Those around *Yosef* respected him and not only tolerated him but were positively influenced by his conduct.

5764

Rabbi Eli Mansour – The connection between *Chanukah* and Parashat Mikeitz is clear. The improbability of the skinny cows swallowing the fat cows without any change in appearance (Bereshit 41:20, 21) is mirrored by the victory of the *Torah*-true Jews over powerful armies and influences.

5765

Dr. Larry Reiss – Rabbi Yissocher Frand points out that Parashat Mikeitz is unusual in that it ends in "cliffhanger" fashion. At the end of the *parashah*, we are unaware how the catastrophe of *Yosef* finding the "stolen" goblet in *Binyamin's* sack will turn out. We must "tune in next week" to Parashat Vayigash to hear the positive conclusion of the situation. This is a lesson for life. Often the serious difficulties we experience are not reconciled or explained to us, even in our lifetimes. Yet as Jews, we are well aware that those difficulties come directly from *Hashem*, and we must have faith that what we experience will ultimately and unquestioningly be for the good, despite that fact that we may not immediately experience that reconciliation, if at all, in our lifetimes.

5767

Rabbi Yossi Jankovits – Rabbi Jankovits's grandfather (Reb Menachem Mendel, a'h) was a *shochet* in Romania after World War II. At that time, it was illegal to slaughter meat without the permission of the Communist authorities due to scarcity. When it was almost *Yom Tov*, he *shechted* a cow and his son (Reb Yisroel, a'h, Rabbi Jankovits's father) went to deliver the meat to the local Jewish community. Reb Yisroel was caught by the authorities and his trial was scheduled for *Yom Kippur*. Reb Menachem Mendel went to the Damesek Eliezer for advice. The *Rebbe* quoted a *pasuk* from Parashat Mikeitz. In response to *Yehudah's* plea to *Yaacov* to allow the Brothers to take *Binyamin* to *Mitzrayim*, *Yaacov* says "וקל שקי יִתֵּן לָכֶם רַחֲמִים לִפְנֵי הָאִישׁ וְשִׁלַּח לָכֶם אֶת אֲחִיכֶם אַחֵר וְאֶת בִּנְיָמִין ..." "And may the Al-mighty G-d grant you compassion before the man, and he will release to you your other brother and Benjamin ..." (Bereshit 43:14) Aside from the clear thematic connection, the *rashei teivot* of the beginning of the *pasuk* (disregarding the connector "vav") are "aleph," "shin," "yud," "lamed," and "raish," which are the letters that comprise "יִשְׂרָאֵל" the name of the accused! The *Rebbe* assured Reb Menachem Mendel that his son would prevail and on *Yom Kippur* the case was dropped. This story is brought down in a *sefer* about the Damesek Eliezer, and Rabbi Jankovits confirmed this story with his father in his last days.

In the beginning of the *parashah*, when *Yosef* is asked by *Paroh* to interpret his dreams, the *Torah* tells us "וַיֹּאמֶר יוֹסֵף אֶל פַּרְעֹה חֲלוֹם פַּרְעֹה אֶחָד הוּא אֵת אֲשֶׁר הָאֱלֹקִים עֹשֶׂה הִגִּיד לְפַרְעֹה" "And Yosef said to Paroh, 'Paroh's dream is one; what Elokim is doing He has told Paroh.'" (Bereshit 41:25) Another way to interpret the text is as follows: "The dream of Paroh – Echad Hu (He [Hashem] is One) – what Elokim is doing He has told Paroh." This could be a declaration from *Yosef* that all dreams and all phenomena, "good" and "bad," emanate from the One G-d, as captured in the expression "ain od Milvado," "there is nothing except Him." This would be an important foundational precept for *Yosef* to convey to *Paroh* before interpreting any of his dreams. This would also explain why, in the very next *pasuk*, *Yosef* states "... cholam echad hu," "... it is one dream," (Bereshit 41:26) which would be repetitive and therefore superfluous based on a straightforward reading.

Rabbi Yossi Jankovits – In Parashat Vayeitzei, when *Lavan* accuses *Yaacov Avinu* of stealing his *teraphim*, *Yaacov* famously states "im asher timtza et elohecha lo yichyeh ... ," "with whomever you find your idols, he shall not live ....." (Bereshit 31:32) Rashi there comments that this unintended curse of a *tzaddik* resulted in *Rachel's* premature death, for she had taken *Lavan's teraphim*, unbeknownst to *Yaacov*. This gives rise to a question towards the end of Parashat Mikeitz, when *Yosef's* messenger, sent from *Mitzrayim* (the *Midrash* identifies him as *Menashe, Yosef's* son), overtakes them and accuses them of stealing the silver goblet. The *Shevatim* (the Torah does not indicate exactly who) tell him "אֲשֶׁר יִמָּצֵא אִתּוֹ מֵעֲבָדֶיךָ וָמֵת וְגַם אֲנַחְנוּ נִהְיֶה לַאדֹנִי לַעֲבָדִים" "Whichever one of your servants with whom it is found shall die, and also we will be slaves to my master." (Bereshit 44:9) Why did *Binyamin* not die based on this declaration, in the same way that *Rachel* had? Perhaps because there was an important distinction between *Lavan* and *Menashe* as the receivers of these declarations. *Lavan* readily accepted *Yaacov's* pledge, happy that the perpetrator of the theft should die, yet *Menashe* refused the death suggestion, as the *Torah* tells us "וַיֹּאמֶר גַּם עַתָּה כְדִבְרֵיכֶם כֶּן הוּא אֲשֶׁר יִמָּצֵא אִתּוֹ יִהְיֶה לִּי עָבֶד וְאַתֶּם תִּהְיוּ נְקִיִּם" "And [Menashe] said, 'Now indeed, so it is as you have spoken. [But] the one with whom it is found shall be my slave [not killed], and you shall be exonerated.'" (Bereshit 44:10) By not accepting the negative suggestion that the "thief" should be put to death, *Menashe* neutralized its potency. This is also demonstrated in Parashat Vayeira in the context of a *berachah*, rather than a curse. When the angel announced to *Avraham* the impending birth of a son to him and *Sarah*, *Sarah* laughed. (Bereshit 18:12) Immediately thereafter, *Hashem* Himself again tells *Avraham* that *Sarah* will bear a son, seemingly in response to her laughter. (Bereshit 18:13, 14) Ezer MiYehuda states that this is because by laughing, rather than responding in an affirmative fashion (e.g. answering "amen") *Sarah* nullified the blessing, thereby requiring *Hashem* to restate it. The lesson is that it is within the power of the listener to "activate" the potency of both a *berachah* or a *klallah*.

5768

Paroh tries to "rename" *Yosef* as "Tzaphnat Paneiach," which is used exactly once in the entire *Torah* narrative. (Bereshit 41:45) History is written by the victors, and it is likely that when naming *Yosef* with an Egyptian name (perhaps to disguise his Jewish roots) *Paroh* was assuming the man who saved the Egyptian empire would forever be remembered by his Egyptian name. Yet that empire was doomed to be destroyed within a few hundred years and *Yosef* and his glorious story live on forever.

5769

Rabbi Yitzchak Salid – At the end of Parashat Vayeishev we see that *Yosef* pleads with the *Sar Hamashkim* to remember him to *Paroh* and gain his release from prison. (Bereshit 40:14) Rashi there comments that since *Yosef* relied on an Egyptian he remained in prison for two additional years. A careful reading of the Rashi does not, as is commonly misunderstood, fault *Yosef* generally for making efforts to gain his release, but rather for specifically relying on an Egyptian. Because of the natural arrogance of Egyptians, such a plea, Rashi tells us, was ill-advised. This can be contrasted with the revelation in Parashat Mikeitz that at the time of *Yosef*'s sale (which occurred in Parashat Vayeishev) he pleaded with the Brothers not to harm him. The *pasuk* tells us "אֲשֶׁר אֲנַחְנוּ עַל אָחִינוּ אֲבָל אֲשֵׁמִים אֶל אָחִיו אִישׁ וַיֹּאמְרוּ רָאִינוּ צָרַת נַפְשׁוֹ בְּהִתְחַנְנוֹ אֵלֵינוּ וְלֹא שָׁמָעְנוּ עַל כֵּן בָּאָה אֵלֵינוּ הַצָּרָה הַזֹּאת" "And they said to one another, 'Indeed, we are guilty for our brother, that we witnessed the distress of his soul when he begged us, and we did not listen. That is why this trouble has come upon us.'" (Bereshit 42:21) Despite the fact that *Yosef* pleaded with his Brothers not to kill or sell him, we find no criticism from the *Torah* or its commentators. This was not considered a lack of faith since a Jew, by nature, is not arrogant, but rather is susceptible to pleas of mercy and assistance. In short, *Yosef*'s pleas to his Brothers had a chance of working, but his plea to the Egyptian had none. It was this act of futility that evinced the lack of faith for which *Yosef* was faulted.

5770

It is interesting to note that while *Paroh* "named" *Yosef* "Tzaphnat Panaiach," the continuation of the same *pasuk* indicates "V'yaitzei Yosef al Eretz

Mitzryaim," "Thus, <u>Yosef</u> emerged over the Land of Egypt," (Bereshit 41:45) employing his Hebrew name. Perhaps this is the reason he was regarded as a *tzaddik*; because his "*galut* power name" was never adopted by him or others.

5771

Rabbi Yitzchok Isaac Sher – The *pasuk* tells us "וַיַּכֵּר יוֹסֵף אֶת אֶחָיו וְהֵם לֹא הִכִּרֻהוּ" "Yosef recognized his brothers, but they did not recognize him." (Bereshit 42:8) Rashi indicates that *Yosef* was formerly beardless and presently had a beard, but is that truly a disguise that could fool a brother? Moreover, we know that *Yosef* looked like *Yaacov*, (Rashi on Bereshit 37:2) who presumably had a beard. There were other objective indicia that *Yosef* could be their brother. He showed superhuman strength and "divined" the birth order of the Brothers when seating them for a meal. (Bereshit 43:33) Despite all this, the Brothers could not recognize him based on their preconceived notion that *Yosef* was an arrogant, beardless youth. They even entered *Mitzrayim* through ten gates to search the brothels of *Mitzrayim*, since that's where they expected a self-absorbed *Yosef* would be. They thought the worst of him and were blinded to otherwise obvious truth, which is a strong lesson for all of us.

5772

Rabbi Akiva Tatz – *Hashem* created dreams to teach us the concept of a virtual, seemingly actual reality that, in the end, proves to be false. Absent dreams, after 120 years we could arguably tell *Hashem* that we got overly involved in physicality and material pursuits only because it was not apparent to us that this world was a mere instant in comparison to the real and eternal world of the soul. Yet because we all experience dreams in our lifetime, we forfeit this argument, being familiar with the feeling of "waking" up and understanding the truth. A dream demonstrates that something that seems so real when you are experiencing it can prove, "mikeitz," "in the end" to be *sheker*. MRF Note – Interestingly, the word for "awaken" is "vayeekeitz," the same word as "keitz," which is the end point of a person's life, when they "awaken" from the "dream" that is this world to understand the truth of the world to come.

5773

Rabbi Yissocher Frand – The *parashah* opens with the words "Vaiyihee mikeitz shanatayim yamim ... ," "It happened at the end of two years ...." (Bereshit 41:1) The Midrash Rabbah brings a connection to a *pasuk* in Iyov "Ketz sahm l'choshech ... ," "He [Hashem] put an end to the darkness ...." (Iyov 28:3). *Hashem's* plan, always for the sake of the Jewish People, had to manifest. *Yosef* was not released from prison because *Paroh* had a dream that required interpretation. Rather, *Paroh* had a dream because the time for the end of *Yosef's* imprisonment had arrived!

VAYIGASH

5759

The *pasuk* tells us that *Yaacov* saw "haagalot," the wagons, that *Yosef* had sent to transport him. (Bereshit 45:27) As per Rashi, based on the *Midrash*, the word הָעֲגָלוֹת can be translated as "the calves," meaning *Yosef* sent a hidden sign to *Yaacov* to let him know that he remembered the last *Torah* subject they were learning together prior to their separation. This was the section of *Talmud* describing the *Eglah Arufah*, the Decapitated Heifer. (Devarim 21:1-9) This hidden message let *Yaacov* know that *Yosef* was still "alive" in a spiritual sense, beyond a mere biological one. This is why, when *Yaacov* saw the "wagons," the *Torah* tells us "then the spirit of their father Yaacov was revived." (Bereshit 45:27) This may also be why the *Torah* indicates the wagons were sent by *Yosef*, even though it was *Paroh* who arranged them. (Bereshit 45:19)

Before revealing himself to his Brothers, *Yosef* sent all the Egyptians who were present out of the room. (Bereshit 45:1) This evinces the idea of keeping family shame and strife out of the view of others, a lesson that can certainly be applied in today's unfortunate atmosphere of infighting among the Jewish People.

5760

Rabbi Yosef Kalatsky – The *Torah* tells us that, after revealing himself to his Brothers, *Yosef* instructs them to implore their father *Yaacov* to come to *Mitzrayim* and dwell in *Goshen*, (Bereshit 45:10) and specifically directs them "v'higaltem l'Avi et cal k'voodi b'Mitzrayim, ... " "and tell my father of all my glory in Mitzrayim ...." (Bereshit 45:13) *Yosef* was anticipating *Yaacov's* resistance to descending to Egypt based on his fears of assimilation. *Yosef* wanted to convey his standing as guarantor of *Bnei Yisrael's* separation from Egyptian society. Only someone as highly placed as *Yosef* could give *Yaacov Goshen* as a *shtetl*, in which to be insulated from the *Mitzrim*. Incidentally, setting up *Yaacov* and his family in *Eretz Canaan* was a non-starter. *Paroh* would never have allowed *Yosef* to send assets out of Egypt for fear that *Yosef* himself would eventually leave.

With regard to the family of *Leah* who descended into *Mitzrayim*, the *pasuk* says "kol nefesh banav u'vanotav shloshim v'shalosh," "All the souls, his sons and daughters, thirty-three." (Bereshit 46:15) Yet the *Torah* famously lists only thirty-two names. Rashi there tells us that *Yocheved*, having been conceived in *Canaan*, was born "bein hachomot," "between the walls," as the family entered *Mitzrayim*. We can calculate from this that *Yocheved* was 130 when she gave birth to *Moshe*, which is arguably a greater miracle then *Sarah* giving birth to *Yitzchak* at age ninety. Ibn Ezra therefore rejects that the "thirty-third" soul was *Yocheved*, but rather was *Yaacov* himself. Yet Ramban affirms Rashi's opinion that it was, in fact, *Yocheved*, asserting that while *Moshe's* birth was certainly a miracle, the *Torah* does not expressly recount every miracle that occurred to *Bnei Yisrael* but rather only those that are deemed necessary of mention.

Rabbi Yosef Kalatsky – The *pasuk* tells us "... v'yavoo Mitzraima Yaacov v'chol zaro ito," "and they came to Mitzrayim, Yaacov and all his offspring with him." (Bereshit 46:6) Then the *Torah* goes on to describe in detail the names of all the offspring. This comes to show us *Yaacov's* personal involvement in every aspect of their lives, even as a great grandfather, to provide the ammunition to fight the forces of *Lavan* and, soon, *Mitzrayim*. *Yaacov* realizes this was the only way to spiritually sustain a family – by being "hands on" with respect to their training and development.

Rabbi Samson Raphael Hirsch – At the moment when *Yaacov* meets *Paroh* in *Mitzrayim*, the *Torah* states "וַיֹּאמֶר פַּרְעֹה אֶל יַעֲקֹב כַּמָּה יְמֵי שְׁנֵי חַיֶּיךָ" "And Paroh said to Yaacov, 'How many are the <u>days</u> of the <u>years</u> of your life?'" (Bereshit 47:8) He was asking *Yaacov* how much productivity and growth he had managed to derive through his obvious many years. *Yaacov's* modest response is telling. "וַיֹּאמֶר יַעֲקֹב אֶל פַּרְעֹה יְמֵי שְׁנֵי מְגוּרַי שְׁלֹשִׁים וּמְאַת שָׁנָה מְעַט וְרָעִים הָיוּ יְמֵי שְׁנֵי חַיַּי וְלֹא הִשִּׂיגוּ אֶת יְמֵי שְׁנֵי חַיֵּי אֲבֹתַי בִּימֵי מְגוּרֵיהֶם" "And Yaacov said to Paroh, 'The days of the years of my sojournings are one hundred thirty years. The days of the years of my life have been few and miserable, and they have not reached the days of the years of the lives of my forefathers in the days of their sojournings.'" (Bereshit 47:9) In comparing himself to the *Avot*, *Yaacov* is making the point that travail leaves one with the difficulty of deriving meaning and spiritual quality from his days and makes it hard to fulfill one's mission in life. Where we all have relative respite when compared to the experiences of *Yaacov*, we really have no excuse for not striving to obtain more from our days.

Rabbi Aron Rovner – When *Yosef* reveals himself to the Brothers he says "Ani Yosef. Haod avi chai?" "I am Yosef. Is my father still alive?" (Bereshit 45:3) The Beis HaLevi says that this is not truly a question (for the Brothers had mentioned many times that *Yaacov* was, in fact, alive) but rather it was a stern rebuke that caused enormous shame in the Brothers. Why? Further, this shame is comparable to what we will each endure on the *Yom HaDin* when we stand before *Hashem* at the end of our lives. How so? There are many examples in the *Chumash* of more direct and seemingly harsher rebukes. Yet here, *Yosef* was exposing the double standard in *Yehudah's* plea regarding *Binyamin*. While *Yehudah* argued for the release of *Binyamin* based on the affect his continued incarceration would have on his father *Yaacov*, (Bereshit 44:31) *Yosef* was, in effect, responding "what about <u>my</u> father?! Did you think of him when you sold me to Egypt?!" Neither *Yehudah* nor his Brothers had an answer to this exposed hypocrisy. So too on *Yom HaDin*, we will stand before *Hashem* and argue that we had no extra time for *Torah*, no extra money for *tzedakah*, etc. Then *Hashem* will show us our wasted hours and wasted money, and our shame will be enhanced, having even dared to justify ourselves.

Rashi tell us that with the "wagons" *Yosef* sent to *Yaacov* he was sending a hidden message, for the Hebrew word for "wagon" has the same spelling as the word for "calf," which was a reference to the subject in the *Gemara* (Sotah 44b) of the "Decapitated Calf," which was the last thing *Yosef* and *Yaacov* had studied before their separation. (Rashi on Bereshit 45:27) A question arises: why should *Yosef* feel the need to use such a code? Anticipating that his father may be incredulous that he was still alive, why did *Yosef* not simply tell his Brothers to mention *Eglah Arufah* to *Yaacov* directly? Perhaps in the same way that *Yehudah*, in stepping forward to save *Binyamin*, made a *tikkun* on the original issue of sibling rivalry that tore the family apart, *Yosef* too was demonstrating his desire not to repeat the mistakes of the past. To ask the Brothers to tell *Yaacov* of the *Talmud* subject he and *Yosef* studied together would remind the Brothers of the favoritism that *Yaacov* had earlier shown him. *Yosef* knew that this was a contributing factor to the original conflict and therefore took pains to avoid repeating it.

5761

Rabbi Nisson Alpert – When it comes time in Parashat Vayigash for *Yehudah* to plead on behalf of *Binyamin* he does not use an interpreter. The *pasuk* tells us that he approached *Yosef* directly and asked to "speak a word in [Yosef's] ears." (Bereshit 44:18) *Yehudah* knew that his heartfelt message could be conveyed effectively even though he believed *Yosef* did not speak *Ivrit*. This is because of the well-known dictum, taught by Rabbi Moshe Alshich (Devarim 6:6) that "words from the heart impact the heart."

5762

Rabbi Ephraim Groundland – There is a *Midrash* that says that *Yosef* looked exactly like *Yaacov*. (Bereshit Rabbah 84:8) When he revealed himself to his Brothers he said "Ani Yosef ... ," "I am Yosef ... ," and the Brothers couldn't answer because "nivhalu mipanav," "they were afraid of his face." (Bereshit 45:3) The Brothers suddenly saw their father standing before them in judgment, the most frightening thing imaginable.

5763

Kli Yakar – *Bnei Yisrael* was redeemed from *Mitzrayim* in the merit of four things: (1) they did not change their names; (2) they did not abandon Hebrew as their language; (3) they abstained from *lashon hara*; and (4) they were modest with regard to sexual matters. During his conversation with his Brothers, after he has revealed his true identity, *Yosef* alludes to all of these merits. He says "Ani Yosef," (Bereshit 45:3) employing his Hebrew name rather than *Tzaphnat Panaiach*, the Egyptian name *Paroh* tried to foist upon him. He spoke to them in Hebrew (which is implied from the fact that he was left alone with them and addressed them directly). He sent everyone from the room and did not slander his Brothers before the *Mitzrim*. (Bereshit 45:1) Finally, *Yosef* showed his Brothers the place of his *brit milah*, (Rashi on Bereshit 45:4) which was intact, providing proof that *Yosef* had not engaged in immorality (based on the *Gemara* (Eruvin 19a) which indicates cohabiting with a daughter of an idolater would cause the foreskin to grow back). By demonstrating his success in these four areas *Yosef* gave *Bnei Yisrael* the keys to their ultimate redemption from *Mitzrayim*.

5764

Rabbi Yossi Jankovits – After being summoned by *Yosef* to descend into Egypt, the *Torah* tells us "וַיִּסַּע יִשְׂרָאֵל וְכָל אֲשֶׁר לוֹ וַיָּבֹא בְּאֵרָה שָּׁבַע וַיִּזְבַּח זְבָחִים לֵאלֹקֵי אָבִיו יִצְחָק" "And Yisrael and all that was his set out and came to Be'er Sheva, and he slaughtered sacrifices to the G-d of his father Yitzchak." (Bereshit 46:1) Why not offer to the G-d of *Avraham*? One answer may be that *Yaacov* sought the same ruling from the same G-d Who decreed that *Yitzchak* should never leave *Eretz Yisrael*. Instead, *Hashem* directed *Yaacov* to go to *Mitzrayim*, effectively denying his request.

Reb Eli Librati – The *pasuk* states "וַיֹּאמֶר פַּרְעֹה אֶל אֶחָיו מַה מַּעֲשֵׂיכֶם וַיֹּאמְרוּ אֶל פַּרְעֹה רֹעֵה צֹאן עֲבָדֶיךָ גַּם אֲנַחְנוּ גַּם אֲבוֹתֵינוּ" "And Paroh said to [Yosef's] Brothers, 'What is your occupation?' And they said to Paroh, 'Your servants are shepherds, both we and our forefathers.'" (Bereshit 47:3) This was a significant statement on the part of *Bnei Yisrael*. Sheep are representative of wealth and physicality, and therefore the Egyptians, being steeped in *gashmiut*, raised sheep to a god-like status. Yet the Jews declared themselves shepherds, channeling and guiding, but never exalting, wealth and *gashmiut*.

5765

Ramban – *Yosef* recognized his dreams as prophetic visions that had to be realized, and therefore he did not contact his father until he was elevated to a status at which his Brothers would bow to him. Ramban (Bereshit 42:9) That is why *Yosef* required that *Binyamin* come down to *Mitzrayim* with the Brothers: in order to fulfil the first prophecy of all eleven bundles bowing down to *Yosef's* bundle. (Bereshit 37:7)

5767

Rabbi Yossi Jankovits – The *pasuk* says "וְהַקֹּל נִשְׁמַע בֵּית פַּרְעֹה לֵאמֹר בָּאוּ אֲחֵי יוֹסֵף וַיִּיטַב בְּעֵינֵי פַרְעֹה וּבְעֵינֵי עֲבָדָיו" "And the news was heard [in] Paroh's house, saying, 'Yosef's brothers have come!' And it pleased Paroh and his servants." (Bereshit 45:16) *Paroh* even suggested that *Yaacov* move his entire family to *Mitzrayim*, for he understood that for *Yaacov* to do so during the time of famine would ensure that once the hardship was over, it was likely the family would remain in Egypt and fail to return to their Land. While there was a *gezeirah* that *Bnei Yisrael* would remain in a "land not their own" for many years, *Paroh* was likely not aware of that fact. Rather, *Paroh* was scheming to retain *Yosef*, his family and their brainpower and talents, and applied what he knew about human nature to conclude that once comfortable in the *galut*, the Jews would be unlikely to return to their Land. In many respects the modern American Jewish experience has shown *Paroh's* theory to be true.

5768

MRF Note – *Yosef* instructs his Brothers three times to "hurry" and not delay in returning to *Eretz Yisrael* to retrieving *Yaacov*. (Bereshit 45: 9, 9 and 13) Importantly, he also warns the Brothers "al tirgazu baderech," "don't become agitated on the way." (Bereshit 45:24) Perhaps *Yosef* was adjuring the Jewish People for all times concerning the mode for proper *aliyah*. When ascending to Israel, Jews should not stop to argue or make calculations, which can lead to delay and, ultimately, failure to ascend (e.g. the *meraglim*). Instead, we must hurry, not delay, and as Nike says "just do it."

5769

Rabbi Yitzchak Salid – An obvious question emerging from the interaction between *Yosef* and his Brothers is on what basis does *Yosef* feel justified to essentially torture his Brothers emotionally? It is not enough to say that he desired that they do *teshuvah* and therefore compelled that result. The Kli Yakar (Bereshit 42:7) asks on what basis is a brother allowed to conduct himself in such a way? The answer may be that not as a brother but as a <u>father</u> did *Yosef* deal with the Brothers! We know that *Yosef* was elevated by *Yaacov* to patriarchal status as described in Parashat Vayechi, where

Yaacov declares "וְעַתָּה שְׁנֵי בָנֶיךָ הַנּוֹלָדִים לְךָ בְּאֶרֶץ מִצְרַיִם עַד בֹּאִי אֵלֶיךָ מִצְרַיְמָה לִי
הֵם אֶפְרַיִם וּמְנַשֶּׁה כִּרְאוּבֵן וְשִׁמְעוֹן יִהְיוּ לִי" "And now, your two sons, who were
born to you in the land of Mitzrayim, until I came to you, to the land
of Mitzrayim they are mine. Ephraim and Menashe shall be mine like
Reuven and Shimon." (Bereshit 48:5) Furthermore, *Yosef* is the only one
of the *Shevatim* that is an *Ushpizin* guest. For the sake of *chinuch* a father
can resort to such methods. This may also be why we see *Yosef,* but not the
Brothers, crying at the moment *Yosef* reveals himself to them. Like any
parent, *Yosef* feels pain in dispensing the *chinuch.* This is evident again
in Parashat Vayechi when the Brothers begged for his forgiveness and he
wept, as a father would, having completed the education of his charges.
(Bereshit 50:17)

5770

Rabbi Eli Mansour – At the urging of *Yosef,* the Brothers returned to *Yaacov*
"וַיַּגִּדוּ לוֹ לֵאמֹר עוֹד יוֹסֵף חַי וְכִי הוּא מֹשֵׁל בְּכָל אֶרֶץ מִצְרַיִם וַיָּפָג לִבּוֹ כִּי לֹא הֶאֱמִין לָהֶם"
"And they told him, saying, 'Yosef is still alive,' and that he is ruler over
the entire land of Mitzrayim, but his heart changed, for he did not believe
them." (Bereshit 45:26) Rav Shlomo Zalman Breuer asks how it could be
that *Yaacov* did not believe this welcome news. In fact, it would have made
more sense to *Yaacov* that his son was still alive, insomuch as *Yaacov* was
unnaturally never able to achieve consolation for *Yosef's* death. (Rashi on
Bereshit 37:35, explaining that a person does not accept consolation over
a live person whom he believes to have died) In fact, *Yosef* surviving the
"animal attack" (Bereshit 37:33) and remaining alive somewhere in the
world among idolaters would likely not have surprised *Yaacov.* Rather, *Yaacov*
would have been pleasantly surprised only if *Yosef* had remained true to
Torah and *mitzvot* while in such an environment. In seeing the "agalot,"
"wagons" that *Yosef* sent, and discerning the hidden reference to *Eglah
Arufah,* the Talmudic subject *Yaacov* had been studying with *Yosef* at the
time of their separation, *Yaacov* realized true happiness, as the *pasuk* says
" ... vathee ruach Yaacov Avichem," "then the spirit of their father Yaacov

was revived." (Bereshit 45:27) Knowing *Yosef* remained true to *Torah* despite his exile allowed *Yaacov* to overcome his disbelief that *Yosef* was "alive" in a spiritual sense. The message to us is that one can be breathing and functioning in the same way as an animal, but not be considered "alive" as a Jew. Rather, a Jew who is "alive" is involved constantly in spiritual advancement for the purpose of growing closer to his Creator.

5771

Rabbi Eli Mansour – The Ramban (Bereshit 45:11) indicates that *Yosef* would not send food to *Yaacov* in *Eretz Canaan*, for doing so would be perceived by the *Mitzrim* as unseemly: as a "kickback," or the equivalent of moving assets to an "offshore account." Moreover, we see that *Paroh* needed to decree that supplies be brought to *Yaacov* in advance of his trip to *Mitzrayim*, (Bereshit 45:17-20) in recognition of the fact that *Yosef* was so sensitive to the appearance of impropriety that he would not do so himself. Here we see the "squeaky clean" conduct of *Yosef HaTzaddik*. Although justified, perhaps, in benefiting personally after having saved all of *Mitzrayim*, *Yosef* refused to take any but the highest road.

5772

Rabbi Michael Jablinowitz – The Sefas Emes quotes the *Mishnah* in Pirkei Avot (4:26) which states "רבי יוסי ברבי יהודה איש כפר הבבלי אומר, הלמד מן הקטנים, למה הוא דומה--לאוכל ענבים קהות, ושותה יין מגיתו" "Rabbi Yose bar Yehuda of Kfar HaBavli says 'One who learns Torah from the young, to what can he be likened? – to one who eats unripe grapes or drinks unfermented wine from his vat.'" Yet the very next *Mishnah* disputes this rule. "רבי מאיר אומר, אל תסתכל בקנקן, אלא במה שיש בו: יש קנקן חדש, מלא ישן; וישן, אפילו חדש אין בו" "Rabbi Meir says 'Do not look at the vessel, but what is in it; there is a new vessel filled with old wine and an old vessel that does not even contain new wine.'" (Avot 4:27) *Yosef's* Brothers held like *Rabbi Yose bar Yehudah*, believing *Yosef* to be a foolish lad engaged in frivolous activities and *lashon hara*. (Bereshit 37:2) *Yaacov*, however, held like *Rabbi Meir*, seeing great wisdom in *Yosef* despite his young age. In Parashat Vayigash, as *Yosef* reveals himself, his Brothers are unable to answer him, specifically "ki nivahlu mipanav," "for they were amazed by his face." (Bereshit 45:3) Here they finally saw a face, twenty-two years older, but containing the same original wisdom at which they had originally scoffed.

5773

Rabbi Michael Jablinowitz – The Sefas Emes quotes the *Mishnah* in Pirkei Avot (2:4). "בטל רצונך מפני רצונו, כדי שיבטל רצון אחרים מפני רצונך" "Nullify your will before His Will, so that He will nullify the will of others before your will." This is a reference to National will, where the individual members of *Klal Yisrael* subdue their individual wills for the national fulfillment of *Hashem's* Will (i.e. that we keep His *Torah* and perform His mitzvot). If we do so, He will nullify the will of the nations in ruling over *Klal Yisrael* and bring about a total and complete Redemption. This is reflected in the *pasuk* in Parashat Vayigash that reads "כָּל הַנֶּפֶשׁ הַבָּאָה לְיַעֲקֹב מִצְרַיְמָה יֹצְאֵי יְרֵכוֹ מִלְּבַד נְשֵׁי בְנֵי יַעֲקֹב כָּל נֶפֶשׁ שִׁשִּׁים וָשֵׁשׁ" "All the souls [lit. *soul*] coming to *Mitzrayim* with *Yaacov*, those descended from him, excluding the wives of *Yaacov's* sons, all the souls [lit. *soul*] were sixty-six." (Bereshit 46:26) The Jews went down to *Mitzrayim* as if a single soul, displaying extraordinary unity, which became the catalyst for their ultimate redemption 210 years later. Similarly, in *Megillat Esther*, *Haman* refers to the Jews as an "Am Echad," "One Nation," (3:8) meriting salvation as a united Nation.

VAYECHI

5758

There are two *parshiot* that have the word "chai," "life," within their names: Parashat Chayei Sarah and Parashat Vayechi. Each deals specifically with death: Chayei Sarah about the death of *Sarah* and Vayechi about the death of *Yaacov*. The fact that these narratives about death are labeled with "life" is testament to the fact that "life" expands beyond life in *Olam Hazeh*.

5759

The *Gemara* (Taanit 5b) tells us that *Yaacov Avinu* never died. Rashi notes that the *Torah* describes his passing as "vayigva," "and he <u>expired</u>," (Bereshit 49:33) but does not state that he "died." About *Avraham's* passing the *Torah* indicates "Vayigava vayamat Avraham," "and Avraham expired <u>and died</u>," (Bereshit 25:8) and about *Yitzchak* it states "Vayigva Yitzchak vayamat," "and Yitzchak expired <u>and died</u>." (Bereshit 35:29)

The *Gemara* (Sotah 13a) tells us that when the Sons of *Yaacov* took his remains to *Eretz Canaan* for burial, *Eisav* tried to stop them, claiming that when *Yaacov* buried *Leah* in the *Maarat HaMachpeilah* he used up the one space that had been designated for him, leaving the last space for *Eisav*. The Brothers argued that they had a bill of sale from *Eisav* to *Yaacov* which was retained in *Mitzrayim*, and they sent the fleet-footed *Naftali* to retrieve it. *Chushim*, the son of *Dan*, was deaf, and therefore asked for an explanation of the delay in burying his grandfather. He became incensed to learn that *Yaacov* would remain unburied for such a matter so he decapitated *Eisav*, whose head rolled into the Cave. Rabbi Aharon Kotler stated that this represented *Hashem's* perfect justice, insofar as *Eisav* had the capacity for a *Torah* mind but was overcome by an evil body, and therefore his head merited to be buried with the *Avot*.

5760

Rabbi Yosef Kalatsky – Before blessing his grandchildren *Ephraim* and *Menashe*, *Yaacov* hugs and kisses each of them. (Bereshit 48:10) This teaches us to physically involve ourselves in actions that, in their essence, are conceptual/spiritual, as our physical preparation adds to our intellectual focus and enhances the action. An example would be swaying during *davening* or kissing a *Mezuzah*. The opposite is also true: physical actions that are unrelated to the spiritual task at hand will distract, rather than enhance. That, for example, is why one is cautioned about handling *Tefillin* during the recital of *Kaddish* (i.e. "yehay shmay rabbah ....")

There are Twelve Tribes referenced with regard to *Bnei Yisrael*. For purposes when the *Leviim* are not counted (e.g. the allotment of the Land; encampment in the desert) *Ephraim* and *Menashe* are each counted as one of the Tribes (as each got a full portion as decreed by *Yaacov* – Bereshit 48:5) but where *Levy* is counted (e.g. the breastplate of the *Kohain Gadol*; the blessing and curses at *Har Gerizim* and *Har Eival*), the Tribe of *Yosef* is counted as one Tribe inclusive of *Ephraim* and *Menashe*.

Rabbi Yosef Kalatsky – *Yaacov Avinu* grants a double portion to *Yosef*, effectively making *Ephraim* and *Menashe* Tribes at the level of, for example, *Reuven* and *Shimon*. In making this bequest, *Yaacov* says "וְעַתָּה שְׁנֵי בָנֶיךָ הַנּוֹלָדִים לְךָ בְּאֶרֶץ מִצְרַיִם עַד בֹּאִי אֵלֶיךָ מִצְרַיְמָה לִי הֵם אֶפְרַיִם וּמְנַשֶּׁה כִּרְאוּבֵן וְשִׁמְעוֹן יִהְיוּ לִי" "And now, [as for] your two sons, who were born to you in the land of Mitzrayim, until I came to you, to the land of Mitzrayim they are mine. Ephraim and Menashe shall be mine like Reuven and Shimon." (Bereshit 48:5) Why must *Yaacov* describe *Ephraim* and *Menashe* in such terms? *Yaacov* is essentially telling *Yosef* "You are now a Patriarch! Your sons merit equality with my sons, because they were born to you in a place of spiritual depravity, as were mine when I sojourned with *Lavan*, yet you guided them spiritually and raised them in *Torah*, even before I came to provide that guidance myself! You did it on your own, and for that, *Yosef*, you deserve the greatest reward."

Sforno – One cannot engage in *Torah* learning without proper provisions, as it says in Pirkei Avot (3:17) "if there is no flour there is no Torah." *Zevulun* received a portion of *Yissachar's Torah* learning by paying for it (Rashi on Bereshit 49:13), a system later mirrored by *Bnei Yisrael* and the *Kohanim* and *Leviim*. *Hashem* established this ingenious system that would allow even the least educated *am haaretz* to gain some *Torah* merit through *terumah* and *maaser*. Had such a system not been in place, some Jews would have no *Torah* learning at all, G-d forbid. This would be catastrophic, as *Chazal* say that *Techiyat HaMaytim*, the Resurrection of the Dead, requires "tal Torah," the "dew of Torah," meaning *Torah* learning at some level. (Sforno – Bereshit 49:13)

5761

Rabbi Yisroel Ciner – *Yaacov* declares to *Yosef* "וַאֲנִי נָתַתִּי לְךָ שְׁכֶם אַחַד עַל אַחֶיךָ אֲשֶׁר לָקַחְתִּי מִיַּד הָאֱמֹרִי בְּחַרְבִּי וּבְקַשְׁתִּי" "And I have given you one portion over your brothers, which I took from the hand of the Emori with <u>my sword and with my bow</u>." (Bereshit 48:22) The Oznayim L'Torah says here *Yaacov* has to be referring to a <u>spiritual</u> battle, because on the <u>physical</u> battlefield the order is reversed. Hostilities begin with bows and arrows from a distance and result thereafter in swordplay up close. In spiritual matters one must first push sin and temptation away from his immediate area of influence to create a Holy environment. Thereafter, he must use the bow to keep his purified realm clear from future "invaders."

Yaacov is buried in the *Maarat HaMachpeilah*. (Bereshit 50:13) The Zohar says that those buried there were interred in the following order: *Adam, Chavah, Sarah, Avraham, Yitzchak, Rivkah, Leah* and *Yaacov*. They were buried side by side, with no man lying beside a woman other than his wife.

Rabbi Yossi Jankovits – The *Haftarah* for Parashat Vayechi describes the ascension of *Shlomo HaMelech* to the throne. *Shlomo* is well known for the story of the two women who quarreled about a live baby. (I Melachim 3:16-28) *Shlomo* wisely deduced that the woman who was willing to "split the baby" could not be its mother. In our times, the struggle for *Yerushalayim* is an alarming parallel. The Jews are in danger of failing the Test of Solomon, for they consider the potential division of the Holy City while Arafat steadfastly refuses.

Rabbi Edward Davis –*Chushim ben Dan*, the deaf grandson of *Yaacov*, famously killed *Eisav* over a dispute concerning *Yaacov's* burial site. The lesson of *Chushim* is that often a perceived detriment in the form of a disability can actually be a blessing. Reduced functionality of one sense can avoid confusion and can sharpen another sense. *Chushim* was not interested in debating ownership of *Maarat HaMachpeilah*. It is not the case that he was unaware of *Eisav's* claims to one of the family burial plots at the expense of *Yaacov*. Rather, when *Chushim* realized what his non-deaf family members were debating with *Eisav* he refused to participate, knowing what was *emet* and what was *sheker*. In this way, the People of Israel could use more *Chushims* in dealing with Arab claims to the Land. The Chasam Sofer asks why, during the Plague of Darkness, *Hashem* did not simply blind the Egyptians rather than creating the extraordinary miracle of sticking them in total darkness and giving miraculous light to the Jews. He answers that blinding the Egyptians would actually strengthen them in another area, providing them with something of a blessing, as in the case of *Chushim*. Our challenge is to recognize our difficulties as gifts from *Hashem*, providing us with opportunities in other areas.

In a *Sefer Torah*, there is no space separating Parashat Vayigash from Parashat Vayechi. Rashi indicates that Parasha Vayechi is "closed" because when *Yaacov Avinu* died the eyes and heart of *Bnei Yisrael* were closed due to the Egyptian enslavement. (Rashi on Bereshit 47:28) The obvious question is why should Rashi mention the enslavement here, when it is still many years before it would begin? In fact, in Parashat Shemot (6:16) Rashi also states that so long as the Sons of *Yaacov* were alive there was no Egyptian subjugation, and at the beginning of Parashat Vayechi, as *Yaacov* is dying, all his Sons were clearly still alive. The answer is that the commencement of Parashat Vayechi marked the beginning of the subjugation through the "exile of the mind," when *Bnei Yisrael* was introduced into Egyptian culture. Rashi tells us that the standard space between the *parshiot* were placed there by *Hashem* to give *Moshe* time to pause for contemplation. (Rashi on Vayikra 1:1) Between Vayigash and Vayechi there was no "pause." The combination of injecting *Bnei Yisrael* into *Mitzrayim* and the lack of thoughtful reflection on what that would ultimately mean was the start of their ultimate enslavement.

Rabbi Eli Mansour – *Yosef* had sworn to his father *Yaacov* that he would bury him in *Eretz Yisrael*, (Bereshit 47:30) and, according to the Gemara

(Sotah 36b), had earlier sworn to *Paroh* about not divulging that *Yosef* knew more languages than he did. When *Yaacov* died *Paroh* pressured *Yosef* to break his vow. *Yosef* pointed out that if he were to do so with regard to the vow made to his father, he would likely become accustomed to not keeping his word. In doing so, *Yosef* was hinting that such behavior could ultimately result in him "spilling the beans" about *Paroh's* deficiency. (Rashi on Bereshit 50:6) *Yosef's* point is that we must be forcefully vigilant in avoiding behaviors and influences that could shake our commitments. Similarly, we should embrace behaviors and influences that could strengthen our commitments. Being *dan l'kaf z'chut*, giving people the benefit of the doubt, is a technique towards this end. If one is convinced that his friends are *tzaddikim* he strengthens his own *middot*. Yet if one is convinced that his friends are all bad, one is forced either to fight for his own Holiness or to eliminate all friends in his defense efforts.

5762

Rabbi Yissocher Frand – When *Yaacov* asks *Yosef* to bury him in *Eretz Yisrael* he calls it "chesed v'emet," "kindness and truth," which Rashi describes there as "chesed shel emet," "a kindness of truth," (Rashi on Bereshit 47:29) meaning a kindness done without expectation of payment or reward from the deceased. Yet this would seem to be contradicted by a *Gemara* (Ketubot 72a) that one who buries others will himself receive a burial, which is clearly a reward. When one engages in the *chesed* that is the preparation and burial of a deceased Jew, he experiences *emet* in the realization of the shortness of life and the imperative to focus on what is really important. Such acts of *chesed* show us *emet*, even if only for a fleeting moment. Under such conditions we are not prone to expect payment, even if it would be forthcoming.

5763

Rabbi Yochanan Zweig – The essence of a Jew is reflected in the name *Yehudah*. When *Yaacov* blesses him, he mentioned that *Yehudah* is "u'leven shinayim maychalav," "white toothed from milk." (Bereshit 49:12) While Rashi on this *pasuk* mentions the abundance of milk and other resources that will come to *Yehudah* in the Land of Israel, the *Gemara* (Ketubot 111b) mentions the opinion of *Rabbi Yochanan*, who said, "Better is the one who shows the white of his teeth (in a smile) to his friend, than the one who gives him milk to drink." Smiling at another Jew, even when you have no agenda other than to make them feel good, is the essence of being a Jew, and is why we, as Jews, are named after *Yehudah*.

Abravanel – When *Yosef* protests to his father *Yaacov* that he has improperly placed *Ephraim* over his older brother *Menashe*, *Yaacov* responds "yadati b'ni yadati ... ," "I know, my son, I know ...." (Bereshit 48:19) Why the double language? With regard to the first "I know," *Yaacov* was stating "I know I am unduly favoring one son over the other," and with regard to the second "I know" he was stating "I know that you are concerned that the same situation that created such hostility between you and your Brothers not be repeated." In doing so, *Yaacov* disclosed to Yosef that he knew what the Brothers had done to him, but also provided assurances that the same situation would not occur between *Ephraim* and *Menashe*.

5764

Rabbi Yisroel Ciner – The *gematria* of "Vayechi" is thirty-four, presenting the sum of the first seventeen years of *Yosef's* life spent with his father *Yaacov* and the last seventeen years of *Yaacov's* life spent in *Mitzrayim* after being reunited with *Yosef*. Vayechi means "and he lived," and these two periods represented the true "life" of *Yaacov*. (Rabbeinu Bachaiya – Bereshit 23:1)

5765

Meshech Chochmah – The *pasuk* states "Vayechi Yaacov b'Eretz Mitzrayim ... ," "and Yaacov lived in the Land of Mitzrayim ...." (Bereshit 47:28) *Yaacov* influenced the entire Land of Egypt by virtue of living there. *Yaacov* was a *tzaddik* who felt a responsibility to all people within his world. This is why the famine temporarily ended while *Yaacov* was alive and living there. (Rashi on Bereshit 47:10) Far from being self-centered during his final seventeen years of life, *Yaacov* <u>lived</u> in Egypt and Egypt <u>lived</u> through *Yaacov*.

5768

Rabbi Yosef Kalatsky – Why did *Yaacov* wait until his deathbed discussion to explain to *Yosef* his reasoning for burying *Yosef's* mother *Rachel* on the road to *Efrat*? (Bereshit 48:7) *Yaacov* was the Patriarch of the *galut*, for all his children except *Binyamin* were born outside of *Eretz Yisrael* and, as the *Gemara* (Berachot 26b) teaches, he instituted the *Maariv* prayer service, which is said during the time of darkness, representative of *galut*. *Rachel* also has a key role to play regarding *galut*, since, as the *Midrash* (Bereshit Rabbah 82:10) tells us she was buried not with *Yaacov*, but in a strategic position on the road by which many years later the Jews would exit the Land on the way to the exile of *Bavel* (which was the source of sadness for *Yaacov*, who wept when he met *Rachel*, knowing through prophesy that they would not be buried together – Rashi on Bereshit 29:11). In Parashat Vayechi, when *Yaacov* was about to pass away, he transferred the duty of Patriarch of the *galut* to *Yosef* (which explains how *Ephraim* and *Menashe* were elevated to *Shevatim* status). It was only at that time that *Yosef* could finally appreciate the importance of the roles that he, his mother and his father would play in the destiny of the Jewish People.

5769

Rabbi Yitzchak Salid – In Parashat Vayechi, *Yaacov* tells *Yosef* "va'ani natati l'cha Schem ... ," "and I have given you Schem ... ," (Bereshit 48:22), where Scripture tells us that *Yosef* was ultimately buried. (Yehoshua 24:32) There is a *Midrash* that the *kever* of *Yosef* needed to be at this particular place, since it was here, in the story of *Dinah*, that lust ran amok. (Bereshit 34:2) *Yosef*, who had personally demonstrated superhuman discipline and restraint in the area of illicit relations (Bereshit 39:11, 12), was the model for the *tikkun* of *Schem*.

5770

MRF Note – The *Mishnah* in Pirkei Avot (5:22) itemizes the three *middot* of the students of *Avraham Avinu* (*Ayin Tova*, etc.) and the three *middot* of the students of *Bilaam HaRasha* (*ayin ra'ah*, etc.). The *Mishnah* then asks about what becomes of each of these groups, both in the near term (i.e. this world) and the long term (i.e. the World to Come). The *Mishnah* answers that the students of *Avraham Avinu* "ochlin baolam hazeh, v'nochalin haolam haba," "enjoy rewards in this world, and inherit the World to Come." Surprisingly, as to the students of *Bilaam*, it states "yorishim Geihinom, v'yordeen l'vair shachat," "inherit Hell and descend into the well of destruction." It is reasonable to conclude that the *Mishnah*, in drawing the distinctions between the two groups of students, does not reverse the order for comparison. That being the case, the <u>future</u> of each group is rather predictable: *Avraham's* students achieve the World to Come and *Bilaam's* students descend into the darkness forever. Much more surprising are their respective experiences in the <u>present</u>: while the students of *Avraham* enjoy the fruits of this world, the students of *Bilaam* experience Hell <u>in this world</u>! We can conclude that the character traits of an evil eye, an arrogant spirit and a greedy soul bring a person to "Hell on Earth." This is reinforced by the description of such people in the *pasuk* quoted in the same *Mishnah*: "אַנְשֵׁי דָמִים וּמִרְמָה לֹא יֶחֱצוּ יְמֵיהֶם" "men of blood and deceit shall not live half their days." (Tehillim 55:24) Such people lose half their days in this world, perhaps not through an early death but from the mental suffering they bring upon themselves, turning their existence into a "living Hell."

5771

Reb Shmuel Grundwerg – The *pasuk* records an exchange between *Yaacov* and *Yosef* as follows: "וְשָׁכַבְתִּי עִם אֲבֹתַי וּנְשָׂאתַנִי מִמִּצְרַיִם וּקְבַרְתַּנִי בִּקְבֻרָתָם וַיֹּאמַר אָנֹכִי אֶעֱשֶׂה כִדְבָרֶךָ" "I will lie with my forefathers, and you shall carry me out of Mitzrayim, and you shall bury me in their grave. And [Yosef] said, 'I will do as you say.'" (Bereshit 47:30) Rashi on this *pasuk* brings one of three reasons for *Yaacov's* request: that at the time of *Techiyat HaMaytim* the dead will roll in underground tunnels to *Eretz Yisrael* – something *Yaacov* was seeking to avoid. There is a strong *minhag* among *Bnei Yisrael* of wanting to be buried in *Eretz Yisrael*. With respect to honoring the memory of deceased loved ones, there is a common expression "the *neshamah* should have an *aliyah*," meaning the soul of the departed to be elevated in Heaven based on the good deeds done by the survivor. Moreover, this could be extended to a blessing that the soul of the departed be elevated "above ground" even in this world, thereby avoiding the tunnels mentioned by Rashi. But perhaps an even more appropriate reconfiguration of this aphorism could be "your *aliyah* should have a *neshamah*," which amounts to a blessing that one should merit to go to Israel while alive, with one's *neshamah*, rather than for the sole purpose of burial.

5772

Rabbi Avram Skurowitz – Why do Jewish parents bless their sons on Friday nights that they should be like *Ephraim* and *Menashe*? Perhaps because of their demonstration of mastery over the two exceptions to the Rambam's "Shivil HaZahav," the "Golden Mean" of *middot*. Whereas generally, we are advised to take a middle road for most character traits, not being too full of or too deficient in any one (Hilchot Deiot 1:4), with respect to arrogance and anger the Rambam (Hilchot Deiot 2:3) tells us to take an extreme, zero tolerance position. As Jews, we therefore pray that our children should stay far away from anger on one side and arrogance of the other. *Ephraim* was blessed first by *Yaacov*, despite his younger age, yet displayed no arrogance. *Menashe*, as the elder, was passed over by *Yaacov*, yet did not become at all angry.

5773

Rabbi Yitzchak Isaac Chaver – While *Yaacov* was surely intent on being buried in *Eretz Yisrael*, due, in part, to the *kinim* that would one day plague the soil of *Mitzrayim* (Rashi on Bereshit 47:29), his concern was not that his remains would be desecrated by the lice. Rather, he was concerned that the *Kedushah* of his remains would keep the lice from the soil around his *kever*, thereby minimizing the breadth and the glory of the *maka*. As with the other *makot* and the *Torah's* insistence on ensuring that there would be no opening for the *Mitzrim* to question the Power of *Hashem*, there could be no questions raised with regard to the *Makat Kinim*.

SEFER SHEMOT
SHEMOT

5758

The *parashah* of Shemot begins with the list of names of all those of *Bnei Yisrael* who originally descended into *Mitzrayim*. There are many reasons given as to why the *Torah* finds it necessary to repeat these names, after first providing them in Parashat Vayigash. (Bereshit 46:8-27) Rashi makes clear that *Hashem* again counts *Bnei Yisrael* to demonstrate how precious we are to Him. (Rashi on Shemot 1:1) Furthermore, the repetition demonstrates that this first generation of Jews kept their Hebrew names during their sojourn in Egypt.

5759

Hashem first reveals Himself to *Moshe* from within a thorn bush that was aflame. (Shemot 3:2) This demonstrated that *Hashem* resides even in lowly places, such as with the Jews enslaved in Egypt. Furthermore, a bush containing thorns showed that *Hashem* "suffered" along with *Bnei Yisrael* as a result of the enslavement. (Rashi on Shemot 3:2) Just as the fire did not consume the bush, so too Egypt would not destroy *Bnei Yisrael*, and like the bush, *Har Sinai* would also be aflame at the Giving of the Torah, when *Moshe* would again draw close just as he was originally commanded at the thorn bush.

5760

The education of *Paroh* is demonstrated in his first interactions with *Moshe* and *Aharon*. When first approaching *Paroh* to secure the release of *Bnei Yisrael*, they initially mention *Hashem* as "Elokai Yisrael," "the G-d of Israel." (Shemot 5:1). Note that the word "יִשְׂרָאֵל" contains the letters "reish," "aleph," and "shin," which spell "rosh," or head. This suggested to *Paroh* that *Hashem* was G-d of an <u>exalted People</u>, in distinction to the word "יַעֲקֹב" which is derived from "heel," indicating a lowly People. (Bereshit 25:26) To this, the *Torah* tells us *Paroh* responds "mi Hashem," "who is Hashem?" (Shemot 5:2) To clarify, *Moshe* and *Aharon* then describe *Hashem* as "Elokai Ivrim," "the G-d of the Hebrews," (Shemot 5:3). The word "Ivri" has the same root at the word "aveirah," "sin," indicating a <u>lowly People</u>. To this description *Paroh*, who is then called by the *Torah* the "King of Egypt," responds with a lengthy diatribe, accusing them of rabble rousing. (Shemot 5:4) *Paroh* responds to the humbled description of the Jews because this is how he perceives them. *Paroh* sees *Moshe* and *Aharon's* request as a political movement (hence the use here of his political title of "king"), and warns them not to make trouble among the People.

Rabbi Yissachar Frand – When the daughter of *Paroh* discovers *Moshe*, the *Torah* tells us "וַתִּפְתַּח וַתִּרְאֵהוּ אֶת הַיֶּלֶד וְהִנֵּה נַעַר בֹּכֶה וַתַּחְמֹל עָלָיו וַתֹּאמֶר מִיַּלְדֵי הָעִבְרִים זֶה" "She opened [the basket], and she saw him the child, and behold, he was a weeping lad, and she had compassion on him, and she said, 'This is [one] of the children of the Hebrews.'" (Shemot 2:6) It might have been a more sensible progression if after she opened the basket and found a weeping child that she realized the <u>truth</u> (i.e., that he was of the Hebrews) and <u>thereafter</u> applied <u>kindness</u> (i.e., took pity upon him). Yet the *Torah's* progression is true to the *Torah's* general convention that everywhere *chesed* and *emet* are mentioned together, *chesed* always precedes *emet*. Both attributes are necessary, but had *Paroh's* daughter placed *emet* before *chesed* she never would have saved *Moshe*. Her father's decree was the law of the land, and therefore *Moshe* would have to die. But she opened her heart to hear his cries and to do a *chesed* for him. As a result, her name

was *Batyah*, which means Daughter of G-d, and *Hashem* Himself referred
to *Moshe* by his name as given to him by *Batyah*.

The *Torah* and *Midrashim* tell us the inside story of the Egyptian man
that *Moshe* killed. (Shemot 2:11) The Egyptian was beating *Datan* (of
Datan and *Aviram* infamy), who was the husband of *Shelomit bat Divri*,
after *Datan* discovered the Egyptian has tricked *Shelomit* and slept with
her. The son that *Shelomit* ultimately bore was the blasphemer who was
executed in the *midbar*, (Vayikra 24:10-23) after he cursed *Hashem* for
being shunned by the Tribe of *Dan* (his mother's Tribe) based on his
partial Egyptian lineage. Interestingly, the *pasuk* tells us "וַיִּפֶן כֹּה וָכֹה
וַיַּרְא כִּי אֵין אִישׁ וַיַּךְ אֶת הַמִּצְרִי וַיִּטְמְנֵהוּ בַּחוֹל" "[Moshe] turned this way and
that way, and he saw that there was no man; so he struck the Egyptian
and hid him in the sand." (Shemot 2:12) Rashi explains that *Moshe*
discerned through prophesy that no future offspring of this Egyptian
would ultimately convert to Judaism (thereby justifying *Moshe* killing
him). (Rashi on Shemot 2:12)

5761
Rabbi Mordechai Perlman – Rav Eliyahu Dessler discusses the roots of
Kiddush Hashem, and states that private, not necessarily public, moments of
Holiness set the foundation for sanctifying G-d's Name. Such a moment is
exemplified in the private action described in the *Midrash* (Shemot Rabbah,
2:2), when *Moshe* went to great lengths to track and return a single lost
sheep to the larger flock, and in the process achieved the Divine Revelation
at the Burning Bush. (Shemot 3:4) Alone, with no one to be impressed
with his kindness, *Moshe* ultimately sanctified *Hashem's* Name.

5762
MRF Note – The *pasuk* in the *Haftarah* for *Shemot* reads: "Nashim baot
m'irot otah … ," "women will come and set It [Israel] aflame …." (Yishaiyahu
27:10) This was the week when Hamas and Al Aqsa Martyrs Brigades
(*yemach shemam*) together utilized their first female suicide bomber, the

mother of two, who killed four Jews, including three IDF soldiers, at the Erez/Gaza checkpoint.

5763

Abravanel – There are twelve *parshiot* in Sefer Bereshit describing the actions of the *Avot* and the *Shevatim* and twelve *parshiot* beginning with Parashat Shemot that describe the actions of Moshe Rabbeinu, demonstrating to us that his Holiness and prophesies are equal to all of the *Avot* and *Shevatim* combined.

5764

MRF Note – In Parashat Vayishlach, the *Torah*, in describing the reunion of *Eisav* and *Yaacov*, tells us that *Eisav* kissed *Yaacov*. (Bereshit 33:4) Rashi, on that *pasuk*, tells us the kiss was not from affection, bringing the axiom of *Rabbi Shimon Bar Yochai* "halachah hee b'yadua she'Eisav sonai l'Yaacov," "it is a given fact that is known that Eisav hates Yaacov." Note that the axiom is not "Eisav sonay l'Yisrael." In fact, that would make at least as much sense, for *Yaacov* previously overcame the "Angel of *Eisav*." (Rashi on Bereshit 32:25) Yet *Eisav* hates the *Yaacov* of deception (however justified), named after the "heel." (Bereshit 25:26) This is alluded to in the *Haftarah* of Shemot, "הַבָּאִים יַשְׁרֵשׁ יַעֲקֹב יָצִיץ וּפָרַח יִשְׂרָאֵל וּמָלְאוּ פְנֵי תֵבֵל תְּנוּבָה" "Days are coming when Yaacov will take root, Yisrael will bud and blossom and they will fill the face of the world with fruitage." (Yishaiyahu 27:6) When *Yaacov* fullfils his spiritual destiny he is elevated to *Yisrael*, assuming his role as a "light unto the nations." Perhaps anti-Semitism is a function of Jews failing in their mission to become exalted over the goyim and, perhaps a good deal of hate would disappear if Jews acted as the spiritual leaders of mankind.

Rabbi Yossi Jankovits – Iturei Torah, in name of the Bnei Yissaschar, tells us that there is a connection in Parashat Shemot to *Tefillin*. When *Moshe* asks *Hashem* the Name he should tell *Bnei Yisrael* "וַיֹּאמֶר אלקים אֶל מֹשֶׁה אֶהְיֶה "G-d said to Moshe, אֲשֶׁר אֶהְיֶה וַיֹּאמֶר כֹּה תֹאמַר לִבְנֵי יִשְׂרָאֵל אֶהְיֶה שְׁלָחַנִי אֲלֵיכֶם

'I will be what I will be,' and He said, 'So shall you say to the Children of Israel, "I will be" has sent me to you.'" (Shemot 3:14) The word "אֶהְיֶה" has a *gematria* of twenty-one, and the double mention in "אֶהְיֶה אֲשֶׁר אֶהְיֶה" would then equal forty-two. On the sides of the *Tefillin Shel Rosh* there are two letter "shins": one with standard three "branches" and one with the unusual appearance of four "branches." Why four branches and why a total of seven branches? *Chazal* tell us that the standard letter "shin" is comprised of three letter "vavs" connected at the bottom. In the case of the *Tefillin Shel Rosh* there are seven "vavs." The numerical value of "vav" is six, so seven "vavs" have the numerical value of forty-two, as demonstrated by the *pasuk*! Rashi tells us that "אֶהְיֶה אֲשֶׁר אֶהְיֶה" means that *Hashem* will be with *Bnei Yisrael* in the Egyptian *galut* and He will likewise be with them at the times of future *galut*. (Rashi on Shemot 3:14) When a Jew puts on *Tefillin* he brings Hashem's Presence into the *galut*, just as was promised to *Moshe*!

5765

Rabbi Yossi Jankovits – There is one opinion brought by *Chazal* that *Paroh* gave *Yocheved* and *Miriam* the names *Shifrah* and *Puah* in order to distract each of them from her Hebrew essence, since he realized that identifying with one's Hebrew name results in strong identification as a Jew and adoption of Jewish values that would make killing the male babies impossible.

5766

Baal HaTurim – The *pasuk* states "וַתִּפְתַּח וַתִּרְאֵהוּ אֶת הַיֶּלֶד וְהִנֵּה נַעַר בֹּכֶה וַתַּחְמֹל עָלָיו וַתֹּאמֶר מִיַּלְדֵי הָעִבְרִים זֶה" "[Bat Paroh] opened [the basket] and saw [Moshe], the boy, and behold! a youth was crying! She took pity on [Moshe] and said 'This is one of the Hebrew boys.'" (Shemot 2:6) The "naar," "youth" that the *Torah* is referring to is not "hayeled," "the boy," who is in the basket. The latter was Baby *Moshe*, the former was his older brother *Aharon*, who was watching from the bank of the river. *Aharon* was crying because he thought he was watching his brother die. *Batyah* heard *Aharon's* cry, which led her to understand and declare that *Moshe* was a Hebrew boy, since she was aware that only Jews feel such connection with one another, sharing in each other's sorrows. This is further demonstrated by the fact that the *gematria* of "naar boche" equals that of "zeh Aharon HaKohain," "this is Aharon HaKohain!" There is a strong lesson here as to the necessity of crying for our brothers. Rabbi Eli Mansour finds an additional message: while *Aharon* saw *Batyah's* discovery of *Moshe* as his ruin it was, in fact, a salvation for him as well as for the entire Jewish People. What seems like a disaster can be a victory.

5768

Reb Ephraim Sobol – Parashat Shemot describes *Aharon's* coming to meet his younger brother *Moshe* after his exile. (Shemot 4:27) The *Midrash* (Rut Rabba 5:6) points to three incidents in *Tanach* where, had the subject of the story known that his actions would be recorded and remembered for all time, he would have added much more zeal to the action: *Aharon* meeting *Moshe*; *Reuven* saving *Yosef* (Bereshit 37:21) and *Boaz* feeding *Rut*. (Rut 2:14) Perhaps the point is not that *Aharon*, *Reuven* and *Boaz* would have added grandeur to their respective moment but rather that, had they known the ultimate effect of their actions with respect to the scope of Jewish history, they would have celebrated the significance of the moment. MRF Note – This brings to mind the amazing story of Lily and Charlie Zablotsky, of Hollywood, Florida. Lily, originally an Israeli orphan, was serving in the IDF when she met Charlie, an American tourist. Within two and a half weeks they were engaged to be married, and Lily traveled to America to plan their wedding. Charlie's family had prepared a room in their home for Lily, and had emptied the dresser drawers of all items save one: a calendar, from sixteen years prior, produced by an Israeli orphanage, which was provided as a gift to their donors. Everyone was astonished when Lily declared that the little girl pictured in a photo in the calendar was her, taken in the year she first arrived! Shocked, Charlie's parents explained that many years before, when they first began sending *tzedakah* to Israel, they chose this particular orphanage, and continued to support it financially over the ensuing years, not knowing all the while that they were sustaining their future daughter-in-law. Had they known that the little girl in the calendar would one day give them grandchildren, they would have celebrated every check they wrote over those years.

5769

Rabbi Moshe Meir Weiss – The Zohar states that *Batyah bat Paroh* is a *gilgul* of *Chavah*, meant to correct *Chavah's* sin. (Bereshit 3:13) *Chavah* brought darkness, yet *Batyah* sustained the light of *Torah* (i.e. Moshe). *Chavah* stretched out her hand to grab the forbidden fruit (Bereshit 3:6), yet *Batyah* stretched her hands to retrieve *Moshe* from the river. (Rashi on Shemot 2:5) *Chavah*, as the first woman, did not have a father or mother, and *Batyah*, as a convert to Judaism, had the same status. The word "teivah," "basket" can be spelled "bet," "yud," "tav," and "hey," which, when rearranged, spell "בְּתָיה". *Chavah* was expelled from *Gan Ayden* (Bereshit 3:23), and *Batya* was one of nine people who entered *Gan Ayden* alive. (Derech Eretz Zuta 1)

5770

Rabbi Eli Mansour – The day after he killed an Egyptian who was striking a Jew (Rashi tells us that the Jew was *Datan*) *Moshe* encounters *Datan* and his brother *Aviram* quarreling (Rashi on Shemot 2:13). Moshe tries to intervene but is challenged by *Datan*, who asks whether *Moshe* intends to kill him, just as he killed the Egyptian. *Moshe* becomes fearful, and declares "achain noda hadavar," "indeed, the matter is known." (Shemot 2:14) The common understanding of *Moshe's* reaction is that "the matter" he is referring to is his killing of the *Mitzri*. Yet a deeper understanding is presented by Rashi. By virtue of the reaction of *Datan* and *Aviram*, *Moshe* now knows the reason for the then-current enslavement and all current exiles – namely that Jews criticize, defame, slander and inform on one another. MRF Note – Perhaps a related reason is the lack of *hakarat hatov*, since we know that the *Mitzri* whom *Moshe* killed was beating *Datan* at the time, with the intention to kill him. How *Datan* and *Aviram* could thereafter find any fault with *Moshe's* action must have been an unfortunate yet eye-opening revelation regarding the poor state of Jewish interpersonal relations.

5771

Rabbi Eli Mansour – The *pasuk* states "וּבְנֵי יִשְׂרָאֵל פָּרוּ וַיִּשְׁרְצוּ וַיִּרְבּוּ וַיַּעַצְמוּ בִּמְאֹד מְאֹד וַתִּמָּלֵא הָאָרֶץ אֹתָם" "The Children of *Yisrael* were fruitful and swarmed and increased and became very very strong, and the land became filled with them." (Shemot 1:7) The *Midrash* Yalkut Shimoni (remez 162), commenting on this verse, states that the Egyptians would arrive at their theaters and find that Jews had taken their seats, thus causing animosity. The same pattern has repeated itself over and over in Jewish history. In Persia, during the feast of *Achashveirosh*, in Germany and, perhaps, in America. When Jews abandon "*Goshen*" and integrate with the *goyim*, the *goyim* become alarmed and aggressive.

5772

Rabbi Eli Mansour – It is interesting to note that *Yocheved* and *Miriam*, as genuine heroines by virtue of having stood up to *Paroh* and foiled his plan to kill the male Jewish babies, are nonetheless referred to by the *Torah* as *Shifrah* and *Puah*. (Shemot 1:15) Rashi makes clear these names are related to what each did for the children they helped to deliver: שִׁפְרָה because she "beautified" the children at birth and פּוּעָה because she "cooed" to soothe the babies. The *Torah's* decision to refer to these names in the context of dealing with children is a strong statement about the primacy of parenting, which is the essence of the Jew beyond any other notable and heroic deeds. Rebbetzin Toby Katz adds that this concept is captured in the Song of *Devorah*, when she, having defeated the army of *Sisera*, declared "חָדְלוּ פְרָזוֹן

"בִּישְׂרָאֵל חָדֵלוּ עַד שַׁקַּמְתִּי דְּבוֹרָה שַׁקַּמְתִּי אֵם בְּיִשְׂרָאֵל" "The unwalled cities ceased, in Israel they ceased, until I Devorah arose; I arose as a mother in Israel" (Shoftim 5:7) Even though a prophetess, a judge and a conquering heroine, at her moment of glory, *Devorah* identified as a mother.

5773

Reb Shalom Anidjar – Parashat Shemot opens with the following *pasuk*: "V'ailah shemot Bnei Yaacov habaim Mitzraiymah," "And these are the names of the Children of Israel who are coming to Mitzrayim." (Shemot 1:1) The *Torah* then goes on to name all the *Shevatim*. The identical language appears in Parashat Vayigash as the *Torah* introduces the seventy souls that descended with *Yaacov* to Egypt. (Bereshit 46:8) Two questions arise: why the language "are coming" and why is that phrase repeated in Parashat Shemot? Presumably, the instant narrative is taking place at least seventeen years after the *Shevatim* came to *Mitzrayim*. The *Torah* is therefore indicating that even at this point, they were not established but were still "coming" to Egypt. Also, as noted in the *Midrash*, they had retained their Hebrew names despite sojourning in *Mitzrayim* for many years. *Bnei Yisrael* were and are a distinct People who are never completely at home outside of their Homeland.

Mrs. Jamie Frank – The *pasuk* tells us "וַיִּפֶן כֹּה וָכֹה וַיַּרְא כִּי אֵין אִישׁ וַיַּךְ אֶת הַמִּצְרִי וַיִּטְמְנֵהוּ בַּחוֹל" "[Moshe] turned this way and that and saw that there was no man, so he struck the Egyptian and hid him in the sand." (Shemot 2:12) Rashi on this verse states that *Moshe* saw that there was no man destined to descend from the Egyptian who would convert to Judaism, underscoring the clear, unquestioned status that a convert holds as part of *Bnei Yisrael*, even in *Moshe's* time.

VAEIRA

5758

If it was destined that the Jews would be slaves, why did *Hashem* punish the *Mitzrim*? One answer is that they made the suffering of *Bnei Yisrael* too great. This is demonstrated in the warning contained in *Aharon's* staff that transformed into a serpent. (Shemot 7:10) The message to *Paroh* was that while he was chosen by *Hashem* to enslave the Jews, he was tasked with being like a staff – a tool that causes no harm by itself. Yet through his evil decrees, *Paroh* transformed himself into a snake, which will strike without being directed. For this *Paroh* and the entirety of Egypt needed to be punished.

5759

Baal HaTurim – Of the seven *makot* described in Parashat Vaeira, the first three came through the hand of *Aharon*, not *Moshe*. Rashi (on Shemot 7:19) explains that the *makot* of blood (Shemot 7:20) and frogs (8:2) struck the river, which had previously protected baby *Moshe* (Shemot 2:3), and the *maka* of lice struck the ground (Shemot 8:13), which had previously hidden the Egyptian that *Moshe* slew. (Shemot 2:12) We learn from this that if *hakarat hatov* extends to inanimate objects, how much more so are we obligated to show gratitude to those people who provide us benefit of any kind or amount.

5760

There are four expressions of *geulah* by *Hashem* as set forth in Parashat Vaeira that are the source for the four cups of wine at the *Pesach Seder*. "Hotzaiti," "I will take you out," "Hitzalti," "I will rescue you," "Gaalti," "I will redeem you," and "Lakachti," "I will take you." (Shemot 6:6, 7)

Rabbeinu Bachaiya – *Hashem's* four promises, as contained in the *Arba Leshonot Geulah*, the Four Expressions of Redemption (Shemot 6:6, 7), are all fulfilled over time. 1. "I shall take you out of service" – this began with the first plague of *dam*. (Shemot 7:20) 2. "I shall rescue you from service" – this was walking out of Egypt, from *Ramses* to *Sukkot*. (Shemot 12:37) 3. "I shall redeem you" – this happened at *Yam Suf*, when *Bnei Yisrael* became truly free with the drowning death of their captors. (Shemot 14:30) 4. "I shall take you as a People" – this occurred at *Matan Torah* at *Har Sinai*. (Shemot 19:16) What is not often cited is the continuation of the Four Expressions that immediately follows. "וִידַעְתֶּם כִּי אֲנִי ה׳ אלקיכֶם הַמּוֹצִיא אֶתְכֶם מִתַּחַת סִבְלוֹת מִצְרָיִם וְהֵבֵאתִי אֶתְכֶם אֶל הָאָרֶץ אֲשֶׁר נָשָׂאתִי אֶת יָדִי לָתֵת אֹתָהּ לְאַבְרָהָם לְיִצְחָק וּלְיַעֲקֹב וְנָתַתִּי אֹתָהּ לָכֶם מוֹרָשָׁה אֲנִי ה׳" ... and you will know that I am the Hashem your G-d, Who has brought you out from under the burdens of Mitzrayim. I will bring you to the Land, concerning which I raised My Hand to give to Avraham, to Yitzchak, and to Yaacov, and I will give it to you as a heritage; I am Hashem." (Shemot 6:7, 8) The additional text could be read to require recognition of *Hashem* as a condition precedent to the *Geulah*, and perhaps alludes to *Moshiach* and the time at which the Jews (and all nations) will know for certain that *Hashem* is One.

Rabbi Aron Rovner – In Parashat Vaeira, the *Torah* narration discusses the families of *Reuven* and *Shimon*, then *Levy*. (Shemot 6:14-16) Rabbi Yaakov Kaminetsky commented that this was because *Hashem* first looked at the eldest, then the next eldest son to find the Redeemer, but found no one qualified. The *Torah* then describes in detail the lineage of *Moshe* and *Aharon* and the longevity of their forbearers, indicating that, in association with their individual merit, *Moshe* and *Aharon* were also rewarded for the merit of *Kehat* and *Amram*. (Shemot 6:18)

Rabbi Yosef Kalatsky – The *pasuk* states "וְהֵבֵאתִי אֶתְכֶם אֶל הָאָרֶץ אֲשֶׁר נָשָׂאתִי אֶת יָדִי לָתֵת אֹתָהּ לְאַבְרָהָם לְיִצְחָק וּלְיַעֲקֹב וְנָתַתִּי אֹתָהּ לָכֶם מוֹרָשָׁה אֲנִי ה׳" "I will bring you to the Land, concerning which I raised My Hand to give to Avraham, to Yitzchak, and to Yaacov, and I will give it to you as a <u>heritage</u>; I am Hashem." (Shemot 6:8) The *Torah* here uses the word "morashah" meaning "heritage" rather than "nachalah," meaning "inheritance." This is because a heritage, unlike an inheritance, cannot be squandered or discarded. A heritage is, by definition, meant to be passed on. It is one's whether he wants it to be or not, and it is one's offspring's right and obligation to receive and pass it on as well. If the Land of *Eretz Yisrael* is a heritage of *Bnei Yisrael*, it cannot ever be titled to anyone else, even where possession may temporarily transfer.

Rabbi Yosef Kalatsky – With regard to the first plague of blood, the *Torah* tells us that *Hashem* commanded *Moshe* "כֹּה אָמַר ה' בְּזֹאת תֵּדַע כִּי אֲנִי ה' הִנֵּה אָנֹכִי מַכֶּה | בַּמַּטֶּה אֲשֶׁר בְּיָדִי עַל הַמַּיִם אֲשֶׁר בַּיְאֹר וְנֶהֶפְכוּ לְדָם וְהַדָּגָה אֲשֶׁר בַּיְאֹר תָּמוּת וּבָאַשׁ הַיְאֹר" "So said Hashem, 'With this you will know that I am Hashem. Behold, I will smite with the staff that is in My hand upon the water that is in the River, and it will turn to blood. And the fish that are in the River will die, and the River will become putrid ....'" (Shemot 7:17, 18) *Moshe* then followed *Hashem's* instructions and the Nile turned to blood, the fish died, and the stench ensued. (Shemot 7:20, 21) The *Torah* then goes on to tell us that magicians of Egypt "vayaasu khain," "did the same." (Shemot 7:22) The Sforno points out that they really did not do the same thing. Their witchcraft turned water (purchased from Jews) into red water with the appearance of blood, but it was not turned to actual blood, a fundamental change in nature of which only *Hashem* is capable. No fish died in the magician's trick, which in the case of the Nile was the true proof that the water had been transformed into blood. Yet the following *pasuk* tells us "וַיִּפֶן פַּרְעֹה וַיָּבֹא אֶל בֵּיתוֹ וְלֹא שָׁת לִבּוֹ גַּם לָזֹאת" "Paroh turned and went home, and he paid no heed even to this." (Shemot 7:23) It was enough for him that his magicians had come close to duplicating the plague. Any excuse was required to avoid the truth of *Hashem's* Omnipotence. We, in this way, are much like *Paroh*. We look for refutation of fundamental truths. These refutations are clearly not *emet* but are some evidence by which to avoid our obligations. We then return to our "ivory towers," avoiding personal growth and commitment, until, of course, *Hashem* gives us *emet* we cannot avoid, but which is more painful. MRF Note – This may be reflected in the phenomenon of Jews who scour the secular press for the occasional story of a religious Jew who exhibited unethical public behavior, and then use such an example as a justification not to adopt a *Torah* lifestyle themselves.

5761

Rabbi Yisroel Ciner – In *Sefer* Daniel the wicked king *Nevuchadnezair* decreed "וּמַן דִּי לָא יִפֵּל וְיִסְגֵּד יִתְרְמֵא לְגוֹא אַתּוּן נוּרָא יָקִדְתָּא" "And whoever does not fall and prostrate himself [in idol worship] shall be cast into the fiery furnace." (Daniel 3:11) His three Jewish advisors *Chananyah, Misha'el* and *Azaryah* refused, and opted to be thrown into an oven to sanctify G-d's name. From where did they learn that this was proper conduct? The *Talmud* (Pesachim 53b) states that they learned it from the Plague of Frogs. When *Moshe* warned *Paroh* about the impending plague he said "וְשָׁרַץ הַיְאֹר צְפַרְדְּעִים וְעָלוּ וּבָאוּ בְּבֵיתֶךָ וּבַחֲדַר מִשְׁכָּבְךָ וְעַל מִטָּתֶךָ וּבְבֵית עֲבָדֶיךָ וּבְעַמֶּךָ וּבְתַנּוּרֶיךָ וּבְמִשְׁאֲרוֹתֶיךָ" "And the River will swarm with frogs, and they will go up and come into your house and into your bedroom and upon your bed and into the house of your servants and into your people, and into your ovens and into your kneading troughs." (Shemot 7:28) Some frogs realized that while entering the oven would mean certain death, to not do so would mean risking a question arising about *Hashem's* Powers, G-d forbid. The Yalkut Shemoni (end of remez 182) states that, like *Chananyah, Misha'el* and *Azaryah*, the frogs that did enter the ovens survived when the plague ended.

5762

Rabbi Baruch Leff – *Hashem* gave *Paroh* an offer to release *Bnei Yisrael* only for three days, based on His Understanding that doing so would provide *Paroh* with a <u>real</u> choice. Demanding that *Paroh* release all his slaves immediately would be a non-starter and impossible for him to accept. Such a request would have also been too much for the Jews to handle right away. The message for us is that all our goals and changes for the sake of growth as Jews must come in incremental stages to avoid becoming overwhelmed.

Rabbi Yosef Kalatsky – The Rambam says in Hilchot Talmid Torah that we must study *Torah* until the moment of death because the moment we stop learning we immediately start forgetting. This is demonstrated by a *Midrash*. When *Aharon* and *Moshe* came to *Paroh*, he could not run to the Nile River to relieve himself, as was his custom. Instead, he went to an inner palace chamber to do so and *Hashem* sent ten mice that bit him, causing extreme pain. Yet moments later he met *Aharon* and *Moshe* and refused to recognize *Hashem*. We learn from this *Midrash* that forgetfulness is both a blessing and a curse. It helps us heal and "move on," but can be an impediment to recall of critical information.

5763

Paroh decides that the Plague of Frogs must end and summons *Moshe* to his palace. (Shemot 8:4) Suspecting that the plague will end when he cries "uncle," *Paroh* tries to outwit *Moshe* by telling him that *Hashem* should remove the plague "l'machar," "for tomorrow." (Shemot 8:6) *Paroh* was wagering that *Hashem* would end the plague immediately, which would demonstrate some sort of lacking in His Power in not waiting until the next day. This is an incredible insight into the mania of the human mind: a willingness to take a chance of enduring additional unnecessary pain in order to prove a point.

Rabbi Yochanan Zweig – In describing the *maka* of *tzfardaya*, Rashi brings the opinion of Rabbi Akiva that a single frog emerged from the Nile and the Egyptians kept hitting it and it populated all of *Mitzrayim* with frogs. (Rashi on Shemot 8:2) In the *Talmud* (Sanhedrin 67b), *Rabbi Elazar ben Azaryah* takes *Rabbi Akiva* to task, scolding him not to get involved in *Aggadita*. This is because *Rabbi Elazar ben Azaryah* is invoking the principle that miracles are wrought by *Hashem* only to prove a point, and there is no point to the *Midrash Rabbi Akiva* cites. *Rabbi Akiva* counters that the point in this story is *Hashem* punishing the *Mitzrim middah keneged middah*. By creating a situation whereby the *Mitzrim* would continually strike the single frog and thereby progressively worsen their situation, *Hashem* was giving them the psychological burden that comes with the knowledge that one is responsible for one's own dilemma. This was akin to the treatment of the Jews at the hands of the Egyptians. The enslavement began when *Paroh* created a public works project and enlisted the Jews to help on a voluntary basis. When they agreed and began working, he ultimately enslaved them, always reminding them that they had brought it upon themselves. Someone who believes he is personally responsible for his ordeal has a degree of self-loathing that paralyzes him and forecloses positive change. Therefore, *Rabbi Akiva* held that the Egyptians needed to experience the frustration and despair of filling their land with frogs because of their own actions. Furthermore, according to Rashi, because of this evil enslavement plan, the frogs first entered *Paroh's* house. (Rashi on Shemot 7:28)

Ralbag – The *pasuk* states "וַיְדַבֵּר מֹשֶׁה כֵּן אֶל בְּנֵי יִשְׂרָאֵל וְלֹא שָׁמְעוּ אֶל מֹשֶׁה מִקֹּצֶר רוּחַ וּמֵעֲבֹדָה קָשָׁה," "And Moshe spoke accordingly to Bnei Yisrael, but they did not listen to Moshe because of crushed spirit and hard service." (Shemot 6:9) This describes the "kotzer ruach," "crushed spirit," not of *Bnei Yisrael* but of *Moshe Rabbeinu*! He simply did not have the enthusiasm to "inspire the troops." The proof is in a later *pasuk*. "וַיְדַבֵּר מֹשֶׁה לִפְנֵי ה' לֵאמֹר הֵן בְּנֵי יִשְׂרָאֵל לֹא שָׁמְעוּ אֵלַי וְאֵיךְ יִשְׁמָעֵנִי פַרְעֹה וַאֲנִי עֲרַל שְׂפָתָיִם," "Moshe spoke before Hashem, saying 'Behold, Bnei Yisrael has not listened to me, so how will Paroh listen to me? And I have blocked lips.'" (Shemot 6:12) If *Bnei Yisrael* were "of crushed spirit" it would have no bearing on whether or not *Paroh* would listen to *Moshe*, because *Paroh* was neither "of crushed spirit," nor enslaved. It was, in fact, *Moshe* who was disillusioned and distressed.

5764

Rabbi Yissocher Frand – The attacks on the legislative, military and financial symbols of America on September 11 amount to a strong message from *Hashem* as to on what, or rather Whom, we can truly rely. MRF Note – The Warren Zevon song "Lawyers, Guns and Money" suggests the three things western man relies upon in a crisis. It's significant to note that it was precisely these three symbols that were the intended targets of the terrorist attacks: lawyers=the capitol; guns=the Pentagon; and money=Wall Street.

5766

Rabbi Yosef Weinstock – The *Gemara* teaches (Pesachim 53b) that, as described in the Book of Daniel, *Chananyah*, *Misha'el* and *Azaryah* learned that they should enter the *kivshon haaish* from the frogs that entered the ovens of *Mitzrayim* in the second *maka* (Shemot 7:28). They drew a *kal v'chomer* that since the frogs had not been commanded by *Hashem* to jump into the ovens, yet chose to do so, so much more so should they observe *Hashem's* command to give one's life rather than bow down to the idols (as the evil *Nevuchadnezair* had commanded). The problem with this approach is that the frogs were, in fact, commanded to enter all parts of *Mitzrayim*, including "tanurecha," "your ovens." The true lesson of the story lies in the fact that not all frogs were commanded to enters the ovens, and, correspondingly, to die. Some could enter beds, houses and kneading bowls. The message drawn from the frogs and applied to *Chananyah, Misha'el* and *Azaryah* was one of personal responsibility; that at times one has to volunteer for the tough assignment, even when the task could be left to others.

5769

Rabbi Yosef Kalatsky – Most Jews in *Mitzrayim* were idolators who were not engaged in *Torah* study. As such, they are described as having "kotzair ruach," "shortness of breath." (Shemot 6:9) The Ohr HaChaim indicates that they had no capacity to handle the travails of the *shibud* based upon their lack of *Torah* learning. He states that "Torah broadens the heart," which gives a person the capacity to understand the source of difficulties to properly deal with and address them. A non-*Torah* learner is a slave to the setbacks in life and cannot overcome the bondage associated with difficulties.

5770

Rabbi Avraham Dov Berish Flamm – A classic question concerns the fairness of *Hashem* "hardening" *Paroh's* heart in the face of the Ten Plagues. The Plagues were less a punishment for *Paroh* than an education for *Bnei Yisrael*, who had "forgotten" *Hashem* and engaged in idolatry in Egypt.

This is supported by the language of the first of the *Aseret HaDibrot*: "Ani Hashem," "I am Hashem," (Shemot 20:2) which continued their education in understanding Hashem. But if that were the case and the *makot* were only to educate the Jews, why was it fair to inflict so much suffering on *Paroh*? Perhaps because he himself required the same lesson, for he had asked out loud "mee Hashem asher eshma b'Kolo," "Who is Hashem that I should heed His Voice?" (Shemot 5:2) Also, to the extent the Jews forgot about *Hashem* during their enslavement, *Paroh* bore primary responsibility and for that he deserved to be punished.

5771

Rabbi Yechezkel Abramsky – The *pasuk* tells us that *Hashem* told *Moshe* "Aharon achicha yiyeh naviecha," "Aharon your brother will be your navi." (Shemot 7:1) Rashi understands "navi" here to mean "spokesman," citing the verse in *Yishaiyahu* (57:19), where the word "niv" means "utterance of the lips," not only prophesy. This is supported by the Rambam in Mishneh Torah (Hilchot Yesodei HaTorah 7:7), where he says there are two kinds of *naviim*: a *navi* who gives prophesy for a city or a nation, and a *navi* who has prophesy only for himself. One who engages in the study of *Torah*, which we know is *Hashem's* Message to man, is a *navi* to himself; a spokesman for *Hashem*.

5772

Meshech Chochmah – The *Torah*, while describing the mission of *Aharon* and *Moshe* in *Mitzrayim*, seems to take a detour to describe "rashei veit avotam," "the heads of the houses of the fathers," for the Tribes of *Reuven*, *Shimon* and *Levy*. (Shemot 6:14-25) *Hashem* orchestrated events in the *midbar* to ensure *Moshe* was continually challenged as a leader, serving to confirm his ultimate authority for later generations. These distractions came from the three *Shevatim* named at the beginning of the *parashah*: *Datan* and *Aviram* from *Shevet Reuven* (Bamidbar 16:1); *Zimri ben Salu* from *Shevet Shimon* (Bamidbar 25:14); and *Korach* from *Shevet Levy*. (Bamidbar 16:1)

5773

Rabbi Eli Mansour – Rabbi Mordechai Gifter states that in Parashat Vaeira, as the *Torah* traces the lineage of *Aharon* and *Moshe*, it first states "hu Aharon u'Moshe" "this is Aharon and Moshe," (Shemot 6:26) and then reverses and says "hu Moshe v'Aharon," "this is Moshe and Aharon." (Shemot 6:27) It is clear that they were the ones who spoke to *Paroh* throughout the Exodus experience. Why then repeat their names but in reverse order? Perhaps the *Torah* is showing us that they remained unchanged throughout the process. They never lost their focus nor their idealism, and their motive was never corrupted. We can apply this lesson to the projects we undertake *l'Sheim Shamayim*. We must fight the urge to grow disconnected, stale or even arrogant in the process.

BO

5758

Contrary to the conventional understanding, when *Hashem* hardened *Paroh's* heart he did not remove his free will. Rather, he gave him <u>total</u> free will. By not allowing the miracles around him to decide his fate (i.e. not causing *Paroh* to concede to His Will), *Hashem* actually gave *Paroh* the ability to decide how to handle the Jews based only on his own will.

5759

Bnei Yisrael placed blood on their doorposts on the "inside" of their houses, not as a sign on the outside. Rashi says this is because *Hashem* did not need to see it, Bnei Yisrael did. (Rashi on Shemot 12:13) The blood was a sign that they were rejecting the *avodah zareh* of *Mitzrayim* and to demonstrate to them that they had an active role in their own redemption. The imagery of blood on the inside (as opposed to the outside) of the doorway is a message to attend to ourselves first. "Ourselves" is defined as our family, essentially our *bayit*. Also mentioned in Parashat Bo is the mitzvah of *Tefillin* (Shemot 13:16), where the *Shel Yad* represents our inner selves and the *Shel Rosh* represents our connection to the *Tzibbur*. We cannot don the *Shel Rosh* until we have secured the *Shel Yad*.

The *pasuk* says "וְעָבַרְתִּי בְאֶרֶץ מִצְרַיִם בַּלַּיְלָה הַזֶּה וְהִכֵּיתִי כָל בְּכוֹר בְּאֶרֶץ מִצְרַיִם מֵאָדָם וְעַד בְּהֵמָה וּבְכָל אלהי מִצְרַיִם אֶעֱשֶׂה שְׁפָטִים אֲנִי ה'," "I will pass through the land of Mitzrayim on this night, and I will strike every firstborn in the land of Mitzrayim, both man and beast, and upon all the gods of Mitzrayim will I impose judgments I am Hashem." (Shemot 12:12) If *Hashem* Himself was to strike the first born of *Mitzrayim*, why does *Moshe* thereafter tell *Bnei Yisrael* that *Hashem* will hold back the "Destroyer" (i.e. the "Angel of Death") and not allow him to enter their homes? (Shemot 12:23) Why would the Jews think they were at risk of the Angel of Death on a night when *Hashem* was imposing justice on the Egyptians? *Moshe* was indicating that even those of *Bnei Yisrael* who were scheduled to die naturally on that night were spared; not one Israelite was killed. This was to ensure that the Egyptians would not claim that the plague equally affected everyone, thereby diminishing the resulting Glory to *Hashem*.

Baal HaTurim – "Bo," bet-aleph, has the numerical value of three, representing the last three plagues.

5760

The untenable assertion that G-d is merely the Originator of Creation but is not thereafter involved in the details of the world is belied by the first of the Ten Commandments and related to this week's *parashah*, which is the identification of *Hashem* as the One who took *Bnei Yisrael* out of Egypt, and not as the Creator of the World. The entire plague process is a study in *Hashem's* absolute control of His World and actualization of His Will to elevate the Jews and crush *Mitzrayim*. This critical realization on the part of *Bnei Yisrael* required immediate institution of a formal mechanism to retain this clarity. The *Torah* therefore gives the *mitzvot* of *Pesach* before *Matan Torah* as an "eternal decree." (Shemot 12:14) Freedom therefore came before the cessation of servitude, for it was rooted in properly understanding the Omnipotence of *Hashem*.

Paroh was one stubborn despot. The *pasuk* says "v'yihee bachatzi halailah v'Hashem hikah chol bechor b'Eretz Mitzrayim ... ," "and it was exactly at midnight that Hashem smote every firstborn in the Land of Mitzrayim." (Shemot 12:29) In the next verse the *Torah* tells us that *Paroh* awoke during that night (Shemot 12:30), presumably as a result of the screams and outcry of his nation. He was sleeping! Nine devastating plagues later and he had to be awakened to witness the final nail in the Egyptian coffin. This is a study in human nature and a characteristic that we all fight. MRF Note – It is interesting to measure the stubbornness and arrogance of *Paroh*. In the previous Parashat Vaeira, *Hashem* sends *Moshe* to speak to *Paroh* at the Nile, in the morning. Rashi tells us that *Paroh* went daily to secretly relieve himself in an effort to convince his subjects that he was "god-like," and did not relieve himself in an ordinary human fashion. (Rashi on Shemot 7:15) Rashi also informs us that *Hashem* specifically struck the Nile with *dam* because it was worshipped as a god by the Mitzrim. (Rashi on Shemot 7:17) *Paroh* was so concerned with being perceived as god-like that he was willing to quite literally relieve himself on a "god" of *Mitzrayim*. Stubbornness and arrogance: two traits we all must try to personally eradicate.

5761

Rabbi Yossi Jankovits – *Hashem* tells Moshe "דַּבֶּר נָא בְּאָזְנֵי הָעָם וְיִשְׁאֲלוּ אִישׁ מֵאֵת רֵעֵהוּ וְאִשָּׁה מֵאֵת רְעוּתָהּ כְּלֵי כֶסֶף וּכְלֵי זָהָב |," "Please speak in the ears of the People and let them ask every man of his fellow and every woman of her fellow vessels of silver and vessels of gold." (Shemot 11:2) This is commonly understood to mean that the Jews took valuables from the Egyptians, but there is an opinion that this is meant to be as it sounds, that the Jews exchanged valuable gifts between each other. The *Midrash* (Shemot Rabbah 9:10) tells us they had gotten rich from the sale of water to the Egyptians during the Plague of Blood, but *Hashem* wanted them to exchange gifts in the spirit of *achdut* to help them develop as a People. This is the same idea that is behind *Mishloach Manot* on *Purim*.

5762

Rabbi Simcha J. Cohen – When the *Torah* uses the *lashon* "v'zot" or "v'zeh" it alludes to the pointing of a finger. For example, in Parashat Bo, the pasuk says "הַחֹדֶשׁ הַזֶּה לָכֶם רֹאשׁ חֳדָשִׁים רִאשׁוֹן הוּא לָכֶם לְחָדְשֵׁי הַשָּׁנָה," "<u>This</u> month shall be to you the head of the months; to you it shall be the first of the months of the year.'" (Shemot 12:2). Rashi states that with the word "hazeh," *Hashem*, so to speak, pointed "b'etzba," "with His 'Index Finger,'" to show *Moshe* the moon when it was new. During *Hagbah*, we recite the *pasuk* that begins "v'zot HaTorah ... ," "and this is the Torah," (Devarim 4:44) and we point at the *Sefer Torah*, using our "pinky" finger (not the *etzba*). This is done out of humility, because only *Hashem* and *Moshe* have a connection to *Torah* allowing for pointing at it with the use of the *etzba*.

Reb Ricky Turetsky – In Parashat Bo, *Hashem* informs *Bnei Yisrael* that the reason for the wondrous plagues in *Mitzrayim* is "וּלְמַעַן תְּסַפֵּר בְּאָזְנֵי בִנְךָ וּבֶן בִּנְךָ אֵת אֲשֶׁר הִתְעַלַּלְתִּי בְּמִצְרַיִם וְאֶת אֹתֹתַי אֲשֶׁר שַׂמְתִּי בָם וִידַעְתֶּם כִּי אֲנִי ה'," "in order that you tell into the ears of your son and your son's son how I made sport of the Egyptians, and that you tell of My signs that I placed in them, and [then] you will know that I am Hashem." (Shemot 10:2) HaRav Yochanan Zweig states that the *lashon* of the *pasuk* tells us that one must tell the story of the Exodus into the ears of your children and his grandchildren, and "<u>then</u> you will know I am G-d." When there are three generations of *frum* Jews gathered to recount the story of the Exodus, <u>then</u> one has proof positive of Hashem's existence.

5763

It is interesting to note that in Parashat Bo, immediately upon the moment of liberation for the Jews after 210 years of slavery, *Hashem* dictates a host of mitzvot binding upon the People – essentially creating freedom through alternate servitude. The song "Gotta Serve Somebody" by Bob Dylan (שבתאי אברהם בן זיסל) comes to mind: "But you're gonna have to serve somebody, yes indeed, you're gonna have to serve somebody. Well, it may be the devil or it may be the Lord, but you're gonna have to serve somebody."

5764

Rabbi Zvi Grumet – The splashing of the blood on the doorposts and lintel of the Jewish homes (Shemot 12:22) was not a sign for Hashem but for the Jews. Just as the essence of the *avodah* was the sprinkling of the blood on the *Mizbeach*, so too was putting the blood in the doorway a means of sanctifying the Jewish home. Rabbi Yossi Jankovits connects this to the *Gemara* (Pesachim 96a) that states that in *Mitzrayim*, *Bnei Yisrael* had three altars: the two doorposts and the lintel of every Jewish home.

Rabbi Edward Davis – Rav Soloveitchik would say that in *Havdalah* we refer to "הַמַּבְדִּיל בֵּין קֹדֶשׁ לְחוֹל, בֵּין אוֹר לְחֹשֶׁךְ, בֵּין יִשְׂרָאֵל לָעַמִּים, בֵּין יוֹם הַשְּׁבִיעִי לְשֵׁשֶׁת יְמֵי הַמַּעֲשֶׂה," "The distinction between Holy and profane, between light and darkness, between the Jews and the non-Jews, between the Seventh Day and the working days." The message is that just as it is irrefutable to distinguish day and night, it should be crystal clear that someone is Jewish, or that one has entered a Jewish home.

5765

Rabbi Yaacov Kamenetsky – The Sforno asks why we celebrate a *Pidyon HaBen* with a *seudat mitzvah*? After all, isn't this in some respects a defeat, since, but for the *cheit haeigel*, the first born of *Bnei Yisrael* should have served as the *Kohanim*? The answer is that the child has an opportunity to sanctify himself, and, by extension, *Hashem's* name, by engaging in a mundane livelihood but in a Holy manner. This is something that, as a *Kohain*, would have otherwise been prohibited to him. This is why the *Kohain* at the *Pidyon HaBen* blesses the child to be G-d fearing, a necessary condition in dealing with the temptations of the mundane world (see also 5771, below).

5767

Rabbi Yosef Weinstock – Prior to the *Makat Arbeh* in Parashat Bo, *Paroh* concedes that the Jewish men may leave for a holiday in the desert, but not the young children and *zakenim*. (Shemot 10:10) He wisely understood that *Bnei Yisrael* requires both the *mesorah* of its elders and the future in its children. *Moshe* unequivocally demanded all Jews of all generations be together for *Yom Tov*, an element of our celebrations even until today.

5769

Rabbi Chaim Zvi Senter – The *pasuk* states that during the Plague of the Firstborn, "וּלְכֹל | בְּנֵי יִשְׂרָאֵל לֹא יֶחֱרַץ כֶּלֶב לְשֹׁנוֹ לְמֵאִישׁ וְעַד בְּהֵמָה לְמַעַן תֵּדְעוּן אֲשֶׁר יַפְלֶה ה' בֵּין מִצְרַיִם וּבֵין יִשְׂרָאֵל," "But to all Bnei Yisrael, not one dog will whet its tongue against either man or beast, in order that you shall know that Hashem will separate between the Mitzrim and between Yisrael." (Shemot 11:7) The original cause of the Egyptian *galut* was the *lashon hara* of *Yosef* that generated strife with his brothers. (Bereshit 37:2) This was what prompted *Moshe* to declare "indeed, the matter is known," (Shemot 2:14), meaning the exile persists because of the *lashon hara* that *Datan* and *Aviram* spoke about *Moshe* to *Paroh*. The *Gemara* (Pesachim 118a) says that a person who speaks or even believes *lashon hara* deserves to be thrown to the dogs. That no dog barked was an indication that the original sin has been corrected, if only temporarily.

5770

The Noda B'Yehudah asks why a man is able to recite *Kiddush* on behalf of his wife after reciting *Maariv* in *shul* on Friday night. The man recites "vayechulu" and "mikadaish haShabbat," which arguably fulfills the *Torah* obligation to recite *Kiddush*. The wife, who is, in fact, obligated in the *mitzvah* of *Kiddush*, would therefore have a stronger obligation at the *Shabbat* table. Minchat Chinuch answers that the man, in fact, has not fulfilled the *Torah* obligation to sanctify the *Shabbat* because there is no mention in the *Maariv davening* of *Yitziat Mitzrayim*. Based on this answer, why is remembering the Exodus a necessary component of *Kiddush* on *Shabbat*? There are two essential elements of Friday night *Kiddush*: acknowledging *Hashem* as Creator of the Universe and remembering the Exodus from Egypt. How are the two elements related? One answer may be that the miracles of the Exodus, in the form of the *makot* and at *Yam Suf*, strengthen our *eidut* regarding *Hashem* as the Creator of the Universe, and Friday night *Kiddush* is *eidut* (which is why many have the custom of standing for all or part of Kiddush). Another answer might be that only the Creator could have performed these miracles and since our ancestors were not witness to the Creation itself (as no man was there), they <u>were</u> witnesses to the miracles in Egypt, which provides us with the direct link to the Creator and, thus, His Creation itself.

5771

MRF Note – Rav Yaacov Kamenetsky maintains that the *Pidyon HaBen* is joyful for the non-Kohain, first born Jew, despite the fact that he will not merit to do the *avodah* of the *Beit HaMikdash*, because he is appreciative of the challenge he will take on in striving to bring *Kedushah* in a mundane world, something with which the *Kohain*, insulated in the Holy Temple, will not struggle (see 5765, above). This is not a slight to the *Kohain*, but rather is a recognition of the spiritual superiority of the *Kohain* as the one designated for the *avodah*. The same is true of the *beracha* of "shelo asani isha," where a man thanks *Hashem* for not having made him a woman. As Rav Kamenetsky taught, just as a regular Jew celebrates the fact that he missed the "easy way" to *Kedushah* of the *Kohanim* and is forced to "grind it out" in a mundane world, so too did a man miss out on the natural spiritual connection that women have to G-d, and is therefore forced to don *Tefillin* and *daven* three times a day to obtain closeness to *Hashem*. Also, significantly, as with the *Pidyon HaBen* where we require the *Kohain* to set us on the path of struggling for closeness to *Hashem* in our daily lives, so too does the man require a wife to set an example and inspire him.

5772

Dr. Larry Reiss – *Moshe* provided the warning before *Makat Arbeh*, knowing it would be the final blow to the Egyptian agrarian economy, then turned and left before *Paroh* or his advisors could respond. (Shemot 10:6) The Ramban says that he left to allow the *Mitzrim* to discuss the situation without feeling the weight of his presence which, based on human ego, would have "forced" them into ignoring the warning despite the facts. In actuality, this worked, for after *Moshe* departed, his advisors implored *Paroh* to relent. (Shemot 10:7) *Moshe* left because he knew that human nature is such that people don't want to be told what to do, even if it is in their best interest. This leaves us with a terrible dilemma: we cannot see our own faults and we are resistant to *mussar* from others. Yet *Hashem* provided a solution: marriage! Your spouse is not you (clouded by your own personal biases) but is you (a voice you will not resent). This is what Rabbi Elazar means in the *Gemara* (Yevamot 63a) which states "a man who has no wife is not an 'adam,'" and so, therefore, by *Sheva Berachot*, we make the *beracha* of "yotzer haadam," "Blessed … is the One who makes man." Why not make this *beracha* at birth? Because the "man" is completed only when he is married and provided with the solution to the described dilemma.

5773

Rabbi Kalman Winter – The Torah tells us "וַיֹּאמֶר ה' אֶל מֹשֶׁה וְאֶל אַהֲרֹן בְּאֶרֶץ מִצְרַיִם לֵאמֹר הַחֹדֶשׁ הַזֶּה לָכֶם רֹאשׁ חֳדָשִׁים רִאשׁוֹן הוּא לָכֶם לְחָדְשֵׁי הַשָּׁנָה," "Hashem spoke to Moshe and to Aharon in the land of Mitzrayim, saying, 'This month shall be to you the beginning of the months; to you it shall be the first of the months of the year." (Shemot 12:1, 2) Why was the *mitzvah* of sanctifying the new moon given to both *Aharon* and *Moshe* together, rather than only *Moshe*? The moon was the first element of Creation to act with jealousy, through rivalry with the sun. (Chulin 60b; Rashi on Bereshit 1:16). *Aharon* was the *tikkun* in the way he dealt with *Moshe*. Though older and a *Navi* before *Moshe*, *Aharon* exhibited no jealousy for his younger brother having been chosen to lead the Jewish People.

BESHALACH

5759

In the *Haftarah* for Parashat Beshalach, *Devorah* and *Barak* defeat the army of General *Sisra* in the Battle of Mount Tabor. (Shoftim 4:4-5:31) *Sisra* flees the battlefield on foot and enters the tent of *Yael*. He asks for water but she gives him milk instead. When he falls asleep she drives a tent peg through his skull. This is the longest of all the *Haftarot*.

The week that Parashat Beshalach is read is known as "Shabbat Shira," the "Shabbat of the Song" entitled *Az Yashir* which the Jews sang after crossing the Yam Suf. (Shemot 15:1-19) The *Torah* documents that after *Bnei Yisrael* sang to *Hashem*, "וַתִּקַּח מִרְיָם הַנְּבִיאָה אֲחוֹת אַהֲרֹן אֶת הַתֹּף בְּיָדָהּ וַתֵּצֶאןָ אַחֲרֶיהָ בְּתֻפִּים וּבִמְחֹלֹת כָּל הַנָּשִׁים," "Miriam, the prophetess, Aharon's sister, took a <u>drum</u> in her hand, and all the women came out after her with <u>drums</u> and with dances." (Shemot 15:20) But from where did the women obtain musical instruments? Rashi explains that they were so confident that *Hashem* would perform miracles for them that they fashioned the instruments <u>before</u> leaving *Mitzrayim*!

There is a custom to leave bread outside for birds *Erev Shabbat* before Parashat Beshalach. Two reasons are given: (1) some rebellious elements of *Bnei Yisrael* left *Mon* outside the camp on *Erev Shabbat* in an attempt to show *Moshe* was wrong when he claimed that no Mon would fall on *Shabbat*, but the birds came and ate it, thus foiling their plan; and (2) the beautiful singing of birds reminds us of the *Az Yashir* song that Bnei Yisrael sang at *Yam Suf*.

Chofetz Chaim – *Hashem's* directive to *Moshe* to lead *Bnei Yisrael* into the wilderness rather than by the way of the *Plishtim* (Shemot 13:17), was in order not to jeopardize them spiritually (by exposing them to the idolaters who inhabit that route), although perhaps to challenge them physically. This is a lesson of modern life. One should opt for the less spiritually dangerous environment even though his *parnassah* may come through greater difficulty. Our livelihood is G-d's problem but our spiritual connection to *Hashem* rests only with us.

The most faithful of *Bnei Yisrael* went into the water at *Yam Suf* up to their necks before the miracle of the Splitting of the Sea. Because the *Gemara* (Pesachim 118a) compares the difficulty in acquiring one's *parnassah* to crossing the *Yam Suf*, the lesson is to go "in" to one's livelihood up to one's neck, have faith in *Hashem*, and He will provide!

5760

Rabbi Asher Brander – The *pasuk* states "וַיְהִי בְּשַׁלַּח פַּרְעֹה אֶת הָעָם וְלֹא נָחָם אלקים דֶּרֶךְ אֶרֶץ פְּלִשְׁתִּים כִּי קָרוֹב הוּא כִּי | אָמַר אלקים פֶּן יִנָּחֵם הָעָם בִּרְאֹתָם מִלְחָמָה וְשָׁבוּ מִצְרָיְמָה," "It came to pass when Paroh sent the People, that Elokim did not lead them <u>on the way of the land of the Plishtim</u> for it was near, because Elokim said, 'Lest the People reconsider when they see war and return to Mitzrayim.'" (Shemot 13;17) Rather than read the *lashon* "derech eretz Plishtim," as "the way of the land of the Plishtim," it can be read as "the ways of the Plishtim." What are the ways of the *Plishtim*? Hypocrisy and cynicism. The first of the *Plishtim* mentioned in *Chumash* is *Avimelech*. (Bereshit 20:2) *Avraham* lied to *Avimelech* about his marital relationship with *Sarah* because he sensed no "fear of Hashem" amongst the *Plishtim*, yet *Avimelech* castigated *Avraham* for bringing "sin" upon his people. (Bereshit 20:9-11) In fact, the entire difficult experience with the *Plishtim* was repeated by *Yitzchak* years later. (Bereshit 26:8-33) *Avimelech* and his people were pretenders, paying only lip service to fearing and serving *Hashem*. This influence would have been very damaging to the Jewish Nation that had recently left the same type of society in *Mitzrayim* and was trying to become elevated as a People, and for that reason *Hashem* directed them to take a circuitous route. MRF Note – In *Mitzrayim*, *Paroh's* hypocrisy was even more blatant. Rashi comments that *Hashem's* decision to turn the Nile into blood was based on the fact that the Nile was an Egyptian diety. (Rashi on Shemot 7:17) Rashi further comments that Hashem tells Moshe to warn *Paroh* of the impending plague at the Nile River because that was where *Paroh* would daily go to relieve himself outside of the public eye, so as to maintain the illusion that he, being a deity himself, was not burdened with the physical concern of relieving himself. (Rashi on Shemot 7:15) *Paroh* was willing to relieve himself on Egypt's god for the sake of personal *kavod*. Obviously he (and by extension his people) was a hypocrite, and not a true believer. *Bnei Yisrael* could ill afford exposure to such an outlook as a nascent People hoping to connect to their Creator.

In *Hallel* we recite the verse "the sea saw and fled." (Tehillim 114) *Midrash Shocher Tov* states that this is a reference to the *Yam Suf*, which split in deference to the bones of *Yosef HaTzaddik* (which *Moshe* ensured would be brought out of Egypt). The *Gemara* (Sotah 13a) relates that *Moshe* had retrieved *Yosef's* bones to take from *Egypt* during the *Exodus*, while *Bnei Yisrael* collected booty of gold and silver (a lesson to busy oneself with acquiring a *mitzvah* as opposed to getting rich – that gold was later used, in part, in the sin of the golden calf). The sea went against its nature much as *Yosef* had when he ran from *Potiphar's* wife. It was not merely that he ran away, but also that he did not return to retrieve the garment she had snatched from him, despite knowing that leaving it with the woman would be disastrous and most certainly land him in jail, or worse. Running, in the first instance, was righteous. But knowing his own limitations and refusing to use the garment as an excuse to face the same temptation again was heroic; so much so that the sea split in deference to him.

5761

Rabbi Pinchas Winston – At *Marah* in the desert, *Hashem* "gave [the Nation] statutes and judgments." (Shemot 15:25) Bnei Yisrael then went on to *Refidim*, which *Chazal* say was a contraction of "rifyon yadayim," laxity of the hands. When they failed to study the *Torah* given to them prior to *Sinai* at *Marah*, *Amalek* struck. (Shemot 17:8) The *gematria* of *Amalek* is

240, which is the same as for "safek," "doubt." The idea is that laziness in *Torah* leads to ignorance, which accordingly leads to spiritual doubt.

5762

The *pasuk* says that *Bnei Yisrael* went through *Yam Suf* "on dry land" (Shemot 14:16), not on the otherwise wet ocean floor, but <u>as if</u> on dry land. *Chazal* say that "dry land" is *Torah*, which will keep *Bnei Yisrael* "grounded" during the various exiles of time, even where terrifying "walls of water" are on either side, threatening to "sweep" away the Jews into the ocean of assimilation and, G-d forbid, death. The *Gemara* (Bava Batra 73b) cites a *Midrash* about Jews who stopped on an island, built fires and had a picnic. When the fires heated up they realized it was not an island but sand on the back of a giant whale. When the whale got too hot it rolled over, and had the boats not been nearby, all would have drowned. The point is that only *Torah* is authentic "dry land," upon which a Jew can feel secure.

5763

Rebbetzin Toby Katz – Judaism does have exceptional women in history who succeeded at non-traditional undertakings, but even so, the centrality of the woman in the home as primary family builder is evident. Witness the song of *Devorah* in *Haftarah* for Parashat Beshalach. At the apex of her military career, having led *Bnei Yisrael* to an astounding victory over *Sisra, Devorah* sings "... Devorah shakamti eim b'Yisrael," "I, Devorah, arose, a <u>mother</u> in Israel." (Shoftim 5:7) Her self-identification at such a glorious time was not one of military conqueror but one of nurturer, which is a timeless example for all Jewish women.

Rabbi Shlomo Riskin – Because *Bnei Yisrael* journeyed three days in the desert without water (Shemot 15:22), the *Gemara* (Bava Kama 82a) tell us that we do not go three days without public *Torah* reading. Although we do pray to *Hashem* every day in our statutorily-mandated services, we don't go three days without listening to Him speaking <u>to us</u> through the *Torah*.

5764

Rabbi Yossi Jankovits – In orchestrating the song of the Jewish women, the *Torah* tells us "וַתַּעַן לָהֶם מִרְיָם שִׁירוּ לה׳ כִּי גָאֹה גָּאָה סוּס וְרֹכְבוֹ רָמָה בַיָּם," "And Miriam answered <u>to them</u>, 'Sing to Hashem, for very exalted is He; a horse and its rider He cast into the sea.'" (Shemot 15:21) Who was *Miriam* answering? And further, why did she paraphrase in <u>her song</u> the language of the first verse of <u>Moshe's song</u> which included "ashirah l'Hashem ki gaoh ga'ah soos v'rochvo ramah bayam," "I will sing out to Hashem for He is exalted above all exaltedness, a horse and its rider He cast into the sea." (Shemot 15:1)? One thought is that the "question" came from the Jewish women. Knowing that the Jewish men were destined to receive and then learn the *Torah*, and that the reward for the women would be in some way linked to the learning of the Jewish men, the women were concerned with their ability to amass reward in the eyes of *Hashem*. In answering <u>them</u> (i.e. these concerned women), *Miriam* quoted *Moshe's* song, indicating that if the horse was punished before the rider for being an unwitting accomplice to the evil of the *Mitzrim*, how great would be the reward of the women's willing facilitation of Holiness in the form of their husband's *Torah* learning. This argument won over the women who dedicated themselves to building solid homes to support their husbands. MRF Note – This may also explain why, when it comes time for *Miriam* and the women to sing at *Yam Suf*, the *Torah* calls *Miriam*, "achot Aharon," "sister of Aharon." (Shemot 15:20) Perhaps, as a result of *Miriam's* placating the Jewish women, the *Torah* is telling us she was demonstrating *Aharon's* known trait of making peace among Jewish couples. (Rashi on Bamidbar 20:29) Miriam's answer to the women of *Bnei Yisrael* promoted peace amongst the couples of *Bnei Yisrael* in the tradition of her brother *Aharon*.

5765

Rabbeinu Bachaiya – The *pasuk* says that *Bnei Yisrael* went out "v'chamushim," which Rashi indicates can mean "armed." (Shemot 13:18) Why would a Nation for which Hashem decimated the world's most powerful empire need to carry weapons upon leaving Egypt? It is the way of *Torah* that people should conduct themselves in a natural manner and that *Hashem* will then assist them in miracles. MRF Note – Is it not, therefore, sensible that Jews should arm themselves in this very dangerous, Jew hating world?

5767

Rabbi Yossi Jankovits – The *pasuk* describing the *Mon* reads "זֶה הַדָּבָר אֲשֶׁר צִוָּה ה' לִקְטוּ מִמֶּנּוּ אִישׁ לְפִי אָכְלוֹ עֹמֶר לַגֻּלְגֹּלֶת מִסְפַּר נַפְשֹׁתֵיכֶם אִישׁ לַאֲשֶׁר בְּאָהֳלוֹ תִּקָּחוּ" "This is the thing that Hashem has commanded, 'Gather of it each one according to his eating capacity, an omer for each person, according to the number of persons, each one for those in his tent you shall take.'" (Shemot 16:16) Significantly, all the letters of the *aleph-beit* are contained in this single *pasuk*, the only place in the *Torah* this occurs. Since the *Mon* was Heaven-sent to sustain the Jewish People, the *mussar* lesson is that fulfilling the *Torah* from "aleph" to "taff," will result in Divine Assistance in achieving one's *parnassah*.

5769

Reb Ephraim Sobol – *Bnei Yisrael* is referred to as "B'not Yerushalayim" "Daughters of Yerushalayim" in *Shir HaShirim* (8:4), and the reference applies even to the Jews in the desert following the Exodus, before they ascended to *Eretz Yisrael*. Also the *Az Yashir* song is referred to as "hashira hazot" "this song", in the feminine form (Shemot 15:1), not the otherwise expected masculine form. In other contexts in *Tanach*, however, for example in *Tehillim*, a song is referred to as a "shir" (masculine form). The *halachah* of *yerushah* is that a daughter receives ten percent of her deceased father's estate (as a dowry) and a son inherits the remainder. (Ketubot 68a) Upon leaving *Mitzrayim*, the Jews were destined to replace the Seven Nations inhabiting *Eretz Yisrael*. There is a tradition that there are seventy nations in the world. Like a daughter, the Jews were destined in the time of the Exodus to inherit ten percent of the world (seven of seventy), but in the times of *Moshiach*, they will inherit the entire world.

5770

Rabbi Uri Feivel – In the battle between *Bnei Yisrael* and *Amalek*, the *pasuk* tells us "וְהָיָה כַּאֲשֶׁר יָרִים מֹשֶׁה יָדוֹ וְגָבַר יִשְׂרָאֵל וְכַאֲשֶׁר יָנִיחַ יָדוֹ וְגָבַר עֲמָלֵק," "And it was that when Moshe raised his hand[s] Yisrael would prevail and when he lowered them Amalek would prevail." (Shemot 17:11) The *Mishnah* (Rosh Hashanah 3:8) indicates that by raising his hands, *Moshe* directed the focus of the Jews beyond the physical on this world, upward, toward their Father in Heaven. This recalls the statement of *Yitzchak*, that the "the voice is the voice of Yaacov but hands are the hands of Eisav [ancestor of Amalek]." (Bereshit 27:22) Hands connote the physicality of the sword, which was, in fact, part of *Yitzchak's* ultimate *berachah* to *Eisav*. (Bereshit 27:40) Voice represents the spirituality of *Torah*. *Moshe* was indicating to the Jews that their victory over *Amalek* would not come by brute force, but from beyond the hands, from spiritually connecting to *Hashem*.

5771

Rabbi Yitzchak Salid – At the climactic scene on the shores of Yam Suf, the Torah tells us that, "Mitzrayim Nosaiya acharaichem" "Mitzrayim (singular) was journeying after [Bnei Yisrael) ...." (Shemot 14:10). There, Rashi says "b'lev echad, k'ish echad," "with one heart, like one man." This can be contrasted with the *pasuk* in Parashat Yitro which describes the scene at *Matan Torah* as "v'yachan sham Yisrael," "and Israel encamped there." (Shemot 19:2) There Rashi, in describing the Jews, famously states the reverse of his description of the Egyptians: "k'ish echad, b'lev echad," "as if a single man, with one heart." What ultimately makes the Jews successful in our endeavors is the perceived singularity of our Peoplehood. Despite differences of opinion (i.e. "the heart"), Jews see themselves as a single family (i.e. "one entity or man"). From that *achdut* comes, in certain rare but powerful circumstances, unity of purpose. The *goyim* are more apt to rally around an idea ("lev echad") and, from that, attempt to draw unity in a corporeal sense. But this is short lived, since the philosophical basis of the unified mission will break down over time, leading to a breakdown of affinity among the *goyim*.

The Lubavitcher Rebbe – The *Mishnah* in Pirkei Avot (3:15) lists the five things by which a person forfeits his share in the World to Come: (1) profaning sacred things; (2) degrading the Festivals; (3) shaming another person; (4) refusing to get a *brit milah*; and (5) misinterpreting the *Torah*. Each area indicates an area of life that a human being can *miKadaish*. Despite having learned *Torah* and engaged in *maasim tovim*, the person described in the *Mishnah* refuses to bring Holiness to the world, which is the primary life objective of the Jew. MRF Note – This *Mishnah* shows the negative inverse of the areas of *Kedusha*h linked to the *Chamishah Chumshay Torah* (See MRF Note – Parashat Vayeitzei – 5762): (1) Time: Bereshit; "beginning;" avoiding the *Brit Milah* on the eighth day; (2) People; Shemot; "names;" embarrassing a friend in public; (3) Words: Vayikra; "calling out;" misinterpreting the *Torah*; (4) Places: Bamidbar; "desert;" degrading the Festivals, which are celebrated in *Yerushalayim*; and (5) Things: Devarim; "things;" profaning sacred things.

5773

Rabbi Yitzchak Salid – The *Gemara* (Megillah 10b) cites a well-known *Midrash* of the angels being rebuked by *Hashem* for wanting to sing a song to *Hashem* during *Kriyat Yam Suf*. *Hashem's* stern warning to the *malachim* may be his simple indication to them that while *Bnei Yisrael* was justified, and perhaps obligated, to sing *Hashem's* praises, having just benefitted from His salvation, they, the angels, as mere spectators, were not allowed to rejoice, insofar as humans were dying in the process.

YITRO

5757

One should not regard the *Aseret HaDibrot* as the only *mitzvot*, or even the primary *mitzvot*. Rather, they are at the same time *mitzvot* and categories of *mitzvot* under which all 613 *mitzvot* can be grouped. The confusion of some is evidenced by a *mashal*. A man desires to enter the fabric industry. As training, he observes wholesalers and retailers in the industry. When he feels he is ready, he buys fabric samples and approaches potential buyers. When his customers are ready to make a deal they ask him when they can expect the merchandise. He is confused, for he thought all he needed was fabric samples, and did not appreciate that the samples were only representative of a bigger deal.

5758

The first five of the Ten Commandments are essentially spiritual in nature: (1) belief in *Hashem*; (2) no idolatry; (3) no taking *Hashem's* name in vain; (4) honor and guard the *Shabbat*; and (5) honor one's parents. The second five are essentially physical in nature: (6) don't murder; (7) don't commit adultery; (8) don't kidnap; (9) don't give false testimony; and (10) don't covet. (Shemot 20:1-14) There are many ways to compare and connect *mitzvot* in these two groups. For example, the fourth of the first set (*Shabbat*) and the fourth of the second set (prohibition of false testimony) are linked in Friday night *Kiddush*, during which we provide testimony that *Hashem* created the world. Another example is the first *mitzvah* (acknowledging *Hashem*) and the last mitzvah ("lo tachmod," "do not covet"). *Hashem* cares about us and is involved in our lives. The Ten Commandments begin with a reference to leaving Egypt rather than G-d's Creation of the world in order to underscore His *Hashgacha Pratit*. The Tenth Commandment prohibiting coveting suggests an acceptance of that *hashgacha* and the belief that one has whatever *Hashem* deems appropriate for him. With such an understanding, jealousy becomes impossible.

5759

Rabbi Yissocher Frand – The *Torah* tells in Parashat Yitro that *Moshe's* first son was named *Gershom*, "because he said 'I was a stranger in a strange land.'" (Shemot 18:3) His other son was *Eliezer* "for the G-d of my father has come to my aid ...." (Shemot 18:4) The Baal HaTurim asks why is the additional language of "he said" added with respect to *Gershom*? He tells us that *Moshe* was defending a deal he had made with *Yitro* to marry his daughter *Tzipporah*. The agreement was to allow his first born son to become an idol worshipper which, according to Targum Yonatan ben Uziel, is why *Moshe* failed initially to circumcise *Gershom*. (Rashi on Shemot 4:24) Why would *Yitro* ask for this, being that he was a *geir tzedek* and had rejected idol worship? *Yitro*, who was earlier a renowned idolater, wanted the boy to come to embrace *Torah* through the same process of experimentation and questioning that he had. *Yitro* erroneously thought the only way to arrive at *emet* is to go through everything else, try everything out, reject everything else, and then accept the *Torah*. This approach did work for *Yitro* but was inappropriate for *Gershom* because at its deepest levels, this is not a Jewish perspective. The goal of Judaism is deed over philosophical creed.

5760

Baal HaTurim – There are 613 *Torah mitzvot* and seven rabbinical *mitzvot*: (1) *netilat yadayim*; (2) *eruv*; (3) *berachot*; (4) lighting *Shabbat* candles; (5) reading *Megillat Esther*; (6) *Chanukah*; and (7) *Hallel*. This is a total of 620 *mitzvot*, and there are 620 words that make up the portion of the Ten Commandments in Parashat Yitro. (Shemot 20:1-14)

The *pasuk* says "וּמֹשֶׁה עָלָה אֶל הָאֱלֹקִים וַיִּקְרָא אֵלָיו הִי מִן הָהָר לֵאמֹר כֹּה תֹאמַר לְבֵית יַעֲקֹב וְתַגֵּיד לִבְנֵי יִשְׂרָאֵל," "Moshe ascended to Elokim, and Hashem called to him from the mountain, saying, 'So shall you say to the house of Yaacov and tell Bnei Yisrael.'" (Shemot 19:3) Rashi, based on the Mechilta, tells us that "Beit Yaacov" refers to the women, and "tomar," "say," implies a mild tone of speech, befitting their kind and mild nature and setting a tone for the Jewish homes they will create and nurture. The command to "tagid," "relate," given to the men, implies harshness, derived from גיד, "gid," which is a bitter herb. Rashi states that *Hashem* told *Moshe* to state explicitly the fine details and punishments, more consonant with the nature of men.

The first "statement" of the Ten "Commandments" states "אָנֹכִי ה' אלקיך", "אֲשֶׁר הוֹצֵאתִיךָ מֵאֶרֶץ מִצְרַיִם מִבֵּית עֲבָדִים," "I am Hashem, your G-d, who has taken you out of the Land of Mitzrayim, from the house of slavery." (Shemot 20:2) This specifically identifies *Hashem's* special relationship with *Bnei Yisrael*, and sets the foundation for His Authority to command them. But it also makes clear that He is speaking particularly to those He saved from Egypt, not the nations of the world, which were either absent from the event or there as oppressors! And *Hashem* was not speaking to the *Erev Rav*. This raises the question as to why the *goyim* claim the "Ten Commandments" as part of their religion. While they are excellent principles upon which to base one's life, they were not addressed to anyone other than the Jews.

Ohr HaChaim – Before *Matan Torah*, *Moshe* ascended *Har Sinai* where *Hashem* spoke to him. *Moshe* knew that this was the place from a prophetic vision he received at the Burning Bush, and took the initiative to go up before being called by *Hashem* to do so. (Shemot 19:3) The lesson is that *Hashem* often waits for human effort before providing Divine Intervention.

5761

Rabbi Yossi Jankovits – The *Torah* indicates "vayshma Yitro," "Yitro heard," which indicates more than just hearing but internalizing, as in the mitzvah of "Shema Yisrael." (Shemot 18:1)

Rabbi Yossi Jankovits – *Yitro* approached *Bnei Yisrael* to convert only after hearing about the crossing of *Yam Suf* and the war with *Amalek*. (Rashi on Shemot 18:1) One could understand why the great victory at *Yam Suf* would motivate *Yitro* to join *Bnei Yisrael*, but why the war with *Amalek*? The *Gemara* (Yevamot 24b) states that the *halachah* of conversion is that there are no converts allowed during times when Jews are at their most powerful (e.g. during times of *David HaMelech* and the time of the future *Moshiach*). *Yitro* concluded he was prohibited from joining the Jewish People following their triumphant Exodus from Egypt, until he heard that *Amalek* had attacked them, which indicated to him that there was now an opportunity to convert.

Rabbi Yossi Jankovits – There is a *machloket* as to whether *Yitro* joined *Bnei Yisrael* before or after *Matan Torah*, but all agree he was not present for *Matan Torah*. Yalkut Shimoni (remez 271) explains that Hashem declared that because he did not endure the hardships of the enslavement in *Mitzrayim*, *Yitro* was not entitled to the reward of receiving the *Torah* (the same might hold true for a *geir* who wanted to marry into a family that lost members in the Holocaust). Why then name the *parashah* after someone who was not even present? One possible answer, suggested by the *Gemara* (Bava Kama 99a), is that *Yitro*, in suggesting to *Moshe* the appointment of a system of judges over the People, stressed development of fine character as a necessary element to proper *Torah* teaching and interpretation. Perhaps that connection warranted the mention of his name with the giving of the *Torah*.

5762

Rabbi Edward Davis – Rav Moshe Feinstein stated that the miracle that *Yitro* heard of and which impressed him the most was the Exodus from *Mitzrayim*. That the Jews, as de facto conquerors of the country, went out of Egypt was amazing. The Egyptian army was dead and the Egyptian people were mentally subjugated. Based on conventional analysis, one would expect the Jews to stay in *Mitzrayim* as its new rulers. They had been there for more than two hundred years and there was an economic infrastructure (i.e. the Nile River). Why not stay? Because an integral part of the <u>exit</u> from *Mitzrayim* was the <u>entry</u> into *Eretz Yisrael*. This is what amazed *Yitro*: the integration of the Land into the destiny of the People. Understood in this way, every reference to *Yitziat Mitzrayim* (e.g. in the *Aseret HaDibrot*, in *Shabbat Kiddush*, etc.) is an affirmation that *Hashem* took us out specifically for the purpose that we should go into the Land. We must go to *Eretz Yisrael* to keep our side of the bargain.

Rabbi Yosef Kalatsky – In Parashat Devarim, *Moshe* rebukes the Jews (Rashi on Devarim 1:14) for the fact that they accepted the stratified judicial system suggested by *Yitro* in Parashat Yitro (Shemot 18:19-23) without complaint. The structure, which may have been functionally necessary, nonetheless resulted in the People getting *Torah* judgments from a source necessarily less reliable than *Moshe Rabbeinu*. This would be a system that could be influenced and potentially perverted. The People should have, at the very least, lamented the fact that they would be distanced from *emet* under the *Yitro* system.

5763

Rabbi Yossi Jankovits – The *Midrash* Pirkei d'Rabbi Eliezer (perek 40) informs us that before offering the *Torah* to *Bnei Yisrael*, *Hashem* offered it to the other nations of the world. A question emerges: if in each case *Hashem* presented the most difficult *mitzvah* for the nation in question (for example, He told *Edom*, a murderous people, that the *Torah* prohibited murder), then is it not unfair that he never tested *Bnei Yisrael* with their most difficult *mitzvah*? The question is not a question, since the *goyim* were already *chayav* in the *Sheva Mitzvot Bnei Noach*. In those cases, *Hashem* was actually making the decision easy; offering the *goyim Torah* without additional obligations or limitations. Of course, their commitment was lacking, even as to the *Sheva Mitzvot Bnei Noach,* and they were therefore uninterested in the greater rewards of *Torah*.

5764

The first of the Ten Commandments is "Anochi Hashem Elokecha ...." "I am Hashem, your G-d." (Shemot 20:2) Most commentators see this as a positive commandment to believe in *Hashem*. *Hashem* reveals Himself to the Jews as "your G-d," and the Sforno reads this as "your only G-d."

5765

Rabbi Yossi Jankovits – *Yitro* tells *Moshe* to appoint "anshei chayil" to judge *Bnei Yisrael.* (Shemot 18:21) Rashi says these are men of means whose wealth will ensure they are not compromised with bribes. The Ben Ish Chai says "anshei chayil" are soldiers who are known for doing much work without expectation of honor or acknowledgement.

5766

Rabbi Eli Mansour – *Yitro* joins *Bnei Yisrael* and, in doing so, reunites *Moshe's* sons with him after the amazing Exodus from *Mitzrayim.* (Shemot 18:1-4) The pasuk states "וַיֹּאמֶר אֶל מֹשֶׁה אֲנִי חֹתֶנְךָ יִתְרוֹ בָּא אֵלֶיךָ וְאִשְׁתְּךָ וּשְׁנֵי בָנֶיהָ עִמָּהּ," "And [Yitro] said to Moshe, 'I, Yitro, your father in law, am coming to you, and [so is] your wife and her two sons with her.'" (Shemot 18:6) Prior to the reunion, the Torah makes a point to mention that the derivation of the names of the sons, Gershom "because he [Moshe] said, 'I was a stranger in a foreign land,'" (Shemot 18:3) and Eliezer "for the G-d of my father came to my aid, and He saved me from the sword of Paroh." (Shemot 18:4) The Pardes Yosef asks why the *Torah* must reemphasize the sons' names and the meaning behind each name. He answers that *Moshe* found it necessary to provide names relating to his fugitive status because he foresaw that his sons would grow up in *Midyan,* away from the trials of *Mitzrayim.* It was important for *Moshe* to convey to his children that notwithstanding the relative comfort they experienced in *Midyan,* they were, in fact, in exile and could not be at peace until they ultimately joined their brethren as one Nation. Perhaps the *Torah,* through *Yitro,* was reinforcing this message at a time when *Moshe* and *Bnei Yisrael* had felt the heady success of *Yitziat Mitzrayim* and *Kriyat Yam Suf.* True, they were now one Nation, but their *galut* was not to come to an official end until they entered *Eretz Yisrael.* When they would finally enter the Land, they would have the means to achieve their mission of being a Light unto the World.

5767

Rabbi Yossi Jankovits – The fourth of the *Aseret HaDibrot* is "זָכוֹר אֶת יוֹם הַשַּׁבָּת לְקַדְּשׁוֹ," "remember the Shabbat day to sanctify it." (Shemot 20:8) The commandment begins with the letter "zayin." The Baal HaTurim notes that zayin has *gematria* seven, and *Shabbat* is the seventh day of the week. The Yerushalmi (Berachot: perek 1, halachah 7) cites the *pasuk* in *Mishlei* that reads "בִּרְכַּת הי הִיא תַעֲשִׁיר וְלֹא יוֹסִף עֶצֶב עִמָּהּ," "The blessing of Hashem will make you wealthy, and toil will add nothing to it," (Mishlei 10:22), and indicates the referenced "blessing" is to *Shabbat*, whereby the degree to which one honors *Shabbat* will come back to him in the form of personal wealth. "Zayin" also means "feeder," (from the word "mazon," "food") and "sheva" (seven) can also be read as "sovea," "satiated." The lesson is clear: personal riches and satisfaction flow from the proper "remembrance" of *Shabbat*.

5769

Rabbi Michael Jablinowitz – The fourth command of the *Aseret HaDibrot* reads "זָכוֹר אֶת יוֹם הַשַּׁבָּת לְקַדְּשׁוֹ," "Remember the Shabbat day to sanctify it." (Shemot 20:8) This is a two part *mitzvah*: to remember (zachor) the *Shabbat* and to keep it Holy (l'kadesho). "Kadesho" is accomplished by *Kiddush* and "zachor" is accomplished on a daily basis either by the *Shir Shel Yom* (which references *Shabbat* no matter what the day) or by acquiring things during the week in honor of the upcoming *Shabbat*. The Ramban understands that since *Shabbat* is a reminder that *Hashem* created the world, a daily reference helps us follow the advice of the Ramchal: to treat this world that *Hashem* created only for its true purpose which is to prepare our places in the World to Come. Accordingly, *Shabbat* is referred to as "m'ein Olam Haba," "a taste of the World to Come."

5770

Mrs. Jamie Frank – Why does the *Torah* indicate that before *Moshe* told *Yitro* everything that *Hashem* has done to *Paroh* and *Mitzrayim* for the sake of *Bnei Yisrael*, he and *Yitro* inquired about each other's wellbeing? (Shemot 18:7, 8) In the scope of world events to that date, and since, there has never been bigger news. The answer may be as set forth in Pirkei Avot (2:2) "Yafeh Talmud Torah im derech eretz." "The study of Torah is beautiful with proper behavior;" which is supported by the well-known *Midrash* (Vayikra Rabbah 9:3) "Derech eretz kadmah l'Torah," "Proper behavior precedes Torah learning." Rabbi Eli Mansour indicates this was also the guiding principle in *Moshe* asking *Yitro's* permission to leave *Midyan* and return to Egypt (Shemot 4:18), after and despite *Hashem's* clear directive at the Burning Bush to do so. (Shemot 3:10)

5771

Rabbi Aharon Ziegler – Commonly, the *Torah* introduces text with the phrase "vayedaber Hashem el Moshe leimor, ... " "and Hashem spoke to Moshe saying .... " This is usually regarded as license for *Moshe* to relay the statement to *Bnei Yisrael*. Yet when the pasuk that precedes the giving of the *Aseret HaDibrot* in Parsashat Yitro reads "וַיְדַבֵּר אלקים אֵת כָּל הַדְּבָרִים הָאֵלֶּה לֵאמֹר," "And Elokim spoke all these words, to say." (Shemot 20:1) Rashi provides the Mechilta's quoting of *Rabbi Yishmael's* opinion that "leimor" here teaches that *Bnei Yisrael* said "yes" to each positive command and "no" in response to each negative. (Rashi on Shemot 20:1) This opinion conflicts with *Rabbi Akiva*, who holds that as to every command, both positive and negative, they responded "yes." Rav Soloveitchik explained that according to *Rabbi Yishmael*, by responding "no" to the negative commands, *Bnei Yisrael* stated they would not steal, murder, etc., as these prohibitions are intellectually sound for incorporation into an orderly society. *Rabbi Akiva*, by contrast, stressed that applying logic to keeping the *mitzvot* was a dangerous proposition, since logic can lead to results contrary to *Hashem's* Will. Instead, *Rabbi Akiva* holds that by replying "yes" to each commandment, *Bnei Yisrael* indicated that they would suspend logic and simply follow the Divine Will. The *halachah* follows *Rabbi Akiva*.

5772

Rabbi Yosef Weinstock – The portion following the Ten Commandments (or, the "Epilogue of the Decalogue") is the description of the altar to be used in the *Mishkan* (and, ultimately, the *Beit HaMikdash*) and the requirement that the mechanism for "ascending" to the altar be, as Rashi explains, a smooth and upward inclined ramp, rather than stairs with ascending levels. (Rashi on Shemot 20:23) Following on the heels of the giving of the *Torah*, this could be an adjuration to grow spiritually constantly and consistently, not to ascend to levels where you can then rest. The point is to always keep striving upward in spirituality.

5773

Rabbi Eli Mansour – One can raise two questions with respect to *Yitro's* coming to join *Bnei Yisrael* in the desert. First, why did the war with *Amalek* (in part) inspire him (Rashi on Shemot 18:1), and second, why did he "pre-announce," through a messenger, his arrival to *Moshe* (Rashi on Shemot 18:6) , thereby ensuring a high profile, honored welcome from Moshe and the Elders of *Bnei Yisrael*? (Rashi on Shemot 18:7) The Be'er Yosef links the two, holding that *Yitro* joined *Bnei Yisrael* not based on spiritual inspiration, but as a practical rectification of *Amalek's* unprovoked attack, which publicly took the luster off of *Bnei Yisrael* which had attached to them since *Kriyat Yam Suf.* He wanted to cast his lot with the Jews in a very public way as a *Kiddush Hashem*, as an antidote to *Amalek's chillul Hashem*.

MISHPATIM

5757

Parashat Mishpatim often coincides with *Shabbat Shekalim*, one of four special *Shabbat parshiot* (which are *Zachor, Parah, Shekalim* and *HaChodesh*). For *Purim*, each Jew gave a half *shekel* to outweigh *Haman's* bribe of 10,000 *kikar* of silver to *Achashveirosh* to kill all the Jews. "וַיֹּאמֶר הָמָן לַמֶּלֶךְ

אֲחַשְׁוֵרוֹשׁ יֶשְׁנוֹ עַם אֶחָד מְפֻזָּר וּמְפֹרָד בֵּין הָעַמִּים בְּכֹל מְדִינוֹת מַלְכוּתֶךָ וְדָתֵיהֶם שֹׁנוֹת מִכָּל עָם וְאֶת דָּתֵי הַמֶּלֶךְ אֵינָם עֹשִׂים וְלַמֶּלֶךְ אֵין שֹׁוֶה לְהַנִּיחָם," "And Haman said to King Achashveirosh, 'There is a certain people <u>scattered and separate</u> among the peoples throughout all the provinces of your kingdom, and their laws differ from other peoples, and they do not keep the king's laws; it is of no use for the king to let them be.'" (Esther 3:8) We give a half shekel to display our understanding of the importance of Jewish unity: that we are each only a part of the bigger picture, and without a community, we can never reach a state of completeness.

5758

The *parashah* begins "וְאֵלֶּה הַמִּשְׁפָּטִים אֲשֶׁר תָּשִׂים לִפְנֵיהֶם," "Now these are the ordinances that you shall place before them [Bnei Yisrael]." (Shemot 21:1) Rashi states that this is likened to a "shulchan aruch," "a set table," prepared for a great feast. Mishpatim is a *parashah* focused extensively on business ethics. One can connect these two concepts, and match the care one applies to the *kashrut* on his dining table with the attention that is required to conduct business truthfully. In all cases one must strive to fulfill the *Torah's* requirements.

5759

The laws of the *Torah* are divided into three categories: (1) "mishpatim": laws that are understandable and logical from an earthly perspective (e.g. do not murder); (2) "eidot": laws that are understandable in bridging *Hashem* and man (e.g. blowing the *Shofar* on *Rosh Hashanah*, which stirs repentance); and (3) "chukim": laws that defy logic and are entirely G-dly (e.g. *shaatnez*).

5761

The *Gemara* (Taanit 29a) cites the well-known expression: "mishenichnas Adar marbim b'simchah," "when Adar arrives we increase our happiness."

If we are compelled to increase our happiness upon the arrival of Adar this implies we must already be in a state of happiness, for you cannot increase what does not already exist.

5762

Rabbi Edward Davis – The pasuk states "אִם אֲדֹנָיו יִתֶּן לוֹ אִשָּׁה וְיָלְדָה לוֹ בָנִים אוֹ בָנוֹת הָאִשָּׁה וִילָדֶיהָ תִּהְיֶה לַאדֹנֶיהָ וְהוּא יֵצֵא בְגַפּוֹ," "If his master gives him a wife, and she bears him sons or daughters, the woman and her children shall belong to her master, and he shall go out alone." (Shemot 21:4) This could be read to apply not only to the departure of a freed slave from his master's home but the departure of one's soul from this world at death. What one leaves is his wife and children, whom he entrusts into his Master's care. What those he leaves behind accomplish are a reflection upon the deceased. Rabbi Eli Mansour explains that this is the meaning of the discussion in the *Gemara* (Rosh Hashanah 32b) that Hashem inscribes a "Book of Life" and a "Book of Death." The Book of Life is actually the Book of the Living, where the actions of the living are recorded by *Hashem*. The Book of Death is where *Hashem* adds merits (and sins) accomplished by those that the deceased have left behind.

Rabbi Yossi Jankovits – An enigmatic *pasuk* toward the end of Parashat Mishpatim tells us that, in connection with the giving of the *Torah*, "וְאֶל אֲצִילֵי בְּנֵי יִשְׂרָאֵל לֹא שָׁלַח יָדוֹ וַיֶּחֱזוּ אֶת הָאֱלֹקִים וַיֹּאכְלוּ וַיִּשְׁתּוּ," "and upon the nobles of Bnei Yisrael, He did not lay His Hand, and they perceived HaElokim, and they ate and drank." (Shemot 24:11) Rashi tells us that the "nobles" included *Nadav* and *Avihu*, who gazed at *Hashem*, and ate and drank. Rashi also indicates that this was a sin of arrogance that resulted in their deaths later in Parashat Shemini. (Rashi on Shemot 24:10) The question is why was their punishment delayed? The Ohr HaChaim answers that perhaps *Hashem* did not want to diminish the joy of the People in receiving the *Torah*, which would have been the case if their prominent leaders were killed immediately.

5763

Rabbi Yossi Jankovits – The pasuk states "וְאַנְשֵׁי קֹדֶשׁ תִּהְיוּן לִי וּבָשָׂר בַּשָּׂדֶה טְרֵפָה לֹא תֹאכֵלוּ לַכֶּלֶב תַּשְׁלִכוּן אֹתוֹ," "People of Holiness shall you be unto Me; and any flesh torn of the beasts of the field you shall not eat; you shall cast it to the dogs." (Shemot 22:30) The Daat Zakainim states that the "dog" mentioned in the *pasuk* is the sheep dog that was supposed to guard the "beast" that was torn apart. Why then is this dog rewarded? Because had the dog failed entirely in its mission the *treifa* would be missing entirely, dragged away by the predator. The dog is rewarded with the carcass because he was partially successful in defending the herd. The lesson is that *Hashem* rewards us for any victories claimed over the *yetzer hara*, even partial ones.

Dr. Mark Jaffee – There are fifty-three *mitzvot* in Parashat Mishpatim. Fifty-three is "נג," which reversed spells "gan," as in *Gan Ayden*. The message is that the *mitzvot* are the way to *Gan Ayden*.

5764

Rabbi Yissocher Frand – It is interesting to note the immediate proximity of the prohibition against taking bribes (Shemot 23:8), and the prohibition against oppressing the convert. (Shemot 23:9) Bribes are not merely monetary gifts but influences that cloud judgment in any way. There is a human tendency if one has overcome adversity to be less sympathetic to someone facing the same issue. In such a case, the difficulty was a gift or a "bribe" to the one who conquered it. The *Torah* admonishes the Jew to remember not the thrill of freedom but the feeling of slavery that we felt in *Mitzrayim*. Rather than taking the "bribe" of believing in our own superiority and efforts, we recall how lowly we felt, thereby empathizing with the convert.

5765

Rabbi Yossi Jankovits – In Parashat Vayikra, after *Moshe* received the *Torah*, the first word is written "ויקרא," "and He [Hashem] called [to Moshe]," with a "small aleph." *Moshe* was forced by *Hashem* to add the aleph to the word "ויקר," as an indication of affection, in distinction to the same word without the "aleph," which *Hashem* used with regard to *Bilaam HaRasha* (Bamidbar 23:4), and which denotes impurity. (Rashi on Vayikra 1:1) *Moshe*, accordingly, was humbled by *Hashem's* affection, so he attempted to write the aleph in small script. But if this is true, why does a previous *pasuk* toward the end of Parashat Mishpatim, describing preparation to receive the Torah, read "וַיִּקְרָא אֶל מֹשֶׁה," "... and He [Hashem] called to Moshe" (Shemot 24:16), using the longer, less humble form of the word? Perhaps *Moshe's* writing exhibits more humility in Parashat Vayikra because it was only after receiving the entire *Torah* from *Hashem* that *Moshe* appreciate *Hashem's* greatness and his comparative insignificance.

5766

Rabbi Yossi Jankovits – The *pasuk* states "כִּי תִרְאֶה חֲמוֹר שֹׂנַאֲךָ רֹבֵץ תַּחַת מַשָּׂאוֹ וְחָדַלְתָּ מֵעֲזֹב לוֹ עָזֹב תַּעֲזֹב עִמּוֹ," "If you see someone you hate whose donkey is lying under its burden, would you refrain from helping him? You shall surely help along with him." (Shemot 23:5) In such a case the Jew is obligated to assist the donkey and its hated owner. The *Gemara* (Bava Metzia 32a) adds a clarification to this verse by informing us that the obligation attaches only when your enemy is engaged in an effort to assist himself, but not when the owner refuses to assist his own cause. A practical modern example would be where someone whom you do not like, but who is enduring difficult economic times, will not attempt to remedy his own situation, despite your insistence. In such a case you are relieved from the obligation to assist him. Surprisingly, this law recognizes that there will always be Jews who act wickedly towards other Jews, thereby becoming their enemies, but that all remain brothers, responsible in some respect for our own and each other's wellbeing.

5769

Hashem informs *Moshe* "הִנֵּה אָנֹכִי שֹׁלֵחַ מַלְאָךְ לְפָנֶיךָ לִשְׁמָרְךָ בַּדָּרֶךְ וְלַהֲבִיאֲךָ אֶל הַמָּקוֹם אֲשֶׁר הֲכִנֹתִי," "Behold, I am sending an angel before you to guard you on the way and to bring you to the place that I have prepared [Eretz Yisrael]." (Shemot 23:20) There is no recorded reaction by *Moshe*, and Ramban points out this never happened in *Moshe's* lifetime (however an angel did guide *Yehoshua* into the Land [Yehoshua 5:13-15]). Rather, Rashi tells us, that here *Hashem* is alluding to the sin of the golden calf, where, as punishment, *Hashem* proposed to withdraw from the Jewish People to be replaced by an angel, a plan that *Moshe* successfully "convinced" *Hashem* not to implement. (Rashi on Shemot 23:20)

5770

Rabbi Chaim Yaacov Goldvicht – When a Jewish slave decides not to go free from his master his ear is pierced. (Shemot 21:5, 6) Rashi tells us that his ear heard on *Har Sinai* not to steal and yet he did, resulting in mandatory servitude. He also heard on *Har Sinai* that we are slaves to *Hashem* and not to man. (Vayikra 25:55) Because his "hearing" is flawed, his ear is pierced. This indicates the centrality of "hearing" for a Jew. "L'shmoa" means "to hear," "to obey," and "to understand." Rabbeinu Yonah, in Shaarei Teshuvah, tells us that the ear is the most notable limb of a human. How so? If a person were to physically suffer a major fall he would need a cast for his entire body. If he sins with all his limbs all he needs is an ear by which to hear rebuke, after which he may engage in *teshuvah* and purify himself spiritually. This is why one who blinds a person pays only the value of the lost sight, whereas one who deafens another pays for the entire life value of his victim.

5772

Rabbi Eli Mansour – Parashat Mishpatim famously begins with a "vav," which Rashi explains indicates a connection to the end of Parashat Yitro. (Rashi on Shemot 21:1) Rashi connects the *Mizbeach* described in Yitro to the laws set forth in Mishpatim to conclude that the *Sanhedrin* (which adjudicates the laws) must sit adjacent to the *Beit HaMikdash* (where the

Mizbeach is used for *korbanot*). (Rashi on Shemot 21:1) This indicates two things: first, civil law is not separated from religion in the ideal *Torah* based society (i.e. no separation of "church" and state), and second, just as the *korban* makes peace between man and G-d, the *Beit Din* is the only way to solve disputes between man and man.

5772

Rabbi Michael Jablinowitz – Parashat Mishpatim begins with the following pasuk "וְאֵלֶּה הַמִּשְׁפָּטִים אֲשֶׁר תָּשִׂים לִפְנֵיהֶם," "And these are the judgments that you shall set <u>before them</u>." (Shemot 21:1) Rashi notes that "lifneihem," "before them," requires that even if one knows a certain matter of Jewish law and that a non-Jewish court would judge it identically to the laws of Israel, one must nonetheless bring the question to the *Chachamim*, for to bring it to the *goyim* would be a *chillul Hashem*. We see here that the ultimate outcome of an issue is not the objective of the *Torah's* judicial system. Rather, it is subservience to *Hashem* and His *Torah* and those steeped in its ways. MRF note – This idea is manifested in a story Rabbi Akiva Tatz tells about a very inspired potential *geir*. There is a *halachah* that a *goy*, even an aspiring convert, must do at least one *melachah* on *Shabbat*, so as not to keep *Shabbat* perfectly, which is the sole dominion of the Jew. The potential *geir* told the rabbi with whom he was learning that he was so connected and inspired by his first *Shabbat* that had not been able to bring himself to observe this *halachah* and "desecrate" the *Shabbat*. The rabbi promptly eliminated him as a conversion candidate, in large part because he had failed to see that obedience to the *Torah* is the central point of Judaism, not how it makes one feel. This is *naaseh v'nishmah* at its essence.

5773

Rabbi Yosef Weinstock – In asking and answering the question as to why the ear of the Hebrew slave is pierced when he refuses to go free after his imposed period of servitude (Shemot 21:6), Rashi answers, in part, that he failed to hear the words at *Har Sinai* "ki li v'nai Yisrael evadim ... ," "for Bnei Yisrael are slaves unto Me [Hashem]." (Vayikra 25:55) Perhaps the *Beit Din* implies negativity to the slave's decision because he has chosen an easy way to live: structured servitude without personally having to navigate life's challenges. In fact, perhaps we can say that the *avodah* of serving *Hashem* is that exact work: making *Torah* based decisions in the face of ever-changing, ever-challenging human conditions, and being responsible for those choices. MRF Note – Perhaps that is also why *David HaMelech* is referred to so often as "David Avdecha," "David Your [Hashem's] servant," as his life exemplified having to navigate an overwhelming number of challenges to remain true to *Torah*.

TERUMAH

5757

The second *aliyah* of Parashat Terumah gives instruction for making a cover for the Ark that will contain the Tablets. It calls for creating two gold Cherubim with the faces of children with spreading wings. (Shemot 25:17-22) Does this not violate the *Torah* prohibition of engraved images? (Devarim 7:25-26) It is not violative of the *Torah* if the *Torah* specifically commands it.

Parashat Terumah begins with the commandment "v'yichu li terumah," "you [Bnei Yisrael] shall take for Me [Hashem] a donation." Why does the *Torah* use the language of "take" rather than "give" with respect to the donations required for the *Mishkan*? In this case, giving is taking. Since all is *Hashem's*, we cannot give anything to Him. Rather, through the donation process, we are taking the benefits that come from establishing a *Mishkan*. As the *pasuk* says, "וְעָשׂוּ לִי מִקְדָּשׁ וְשָׁכַנְתִּי בְּתוֹכָם," "And they shall make Me a Sanctuary so that I will dwell in their midst." (Shemot 25:8)

5758

Rabbi Yissocher Frand – With regard to the *Mishkan*, the mention of the *Shulchan* (Shemot 25:23-30) is adjacent to the discussion of the *Menorah*. (Shemot 25:31-40) The *Menorah* gives off light, which represents the *Torah*, while the *Shulchan* contains the bread, which represents *parnassah*. Balanced striving in both areas is needed for successful Jewish living.

5759

Unlike the *Batei Mikdash*, the *Mishkan* never deteriorated nor fell into enemy hands. (Sforno on Shemot 38:21) One theory is that the pure intention of its donors was a protection over the centuries. The *Talmud* (Sotah 9a) tells us that this was due to the fact that the *Mishkan* was constructed by *Moshe Rabbeinu*, and that nothing he created was ever destroyed.

5760

Kotzker Rebbe – The literal translation of "terumah," is not "donation," but an "uplifting," transforming the physical contribution into a spiritual elevation.

5761

Shabbat Zachor requires that we remember that *Amalek* attacked *Bnei Yisrael* in the desert, not long after we left *Yam Suf.* (Shemot 17:8) This is one of the four *Shabbatot* with a special *Maftir* and *Haftarah*, along with *Shekalim, Parah* and *HaChodesh*. The Yalkut Shimoni (remez 261) asks from where did *Amalek* draw the strength to attack *Bnei Yisrael*? When the Jews stopped learning *Torah* and began to question *Moshe's* leadership, they became susceptible to such an attack. Reb Avi Frier points out a modern example of this phenomenon of distraction leading to destruction. In the film Fiddler on the Roof, after every scene of assimilation, the Jews are attacked.

Rabbi Akiva was descended from *Amalek*, as the *Gemara* (Gittin 57b) states that the grandchildren of *Haman* learned *Torah* in *Bnei Brak*. This would suggest that *Amalek* is not necessarily only a genetic reality, but a state of mind.

Rabbi Yossi Jankovits – Parashat Terumah deals with donations by *Bnei Yisrael* for the building of the *Mishkan*. The spelling of the word "תרומה," "donation," can be rearranged to read "המותר," "the permitted." The point is that donations to the Community must be from a kosher source. There is no concept in Judaism of Robin Hood, where one can steal from the rich to give to the poor.

5762

Rabbi Yosef Kalatsky – There were thirteen types of materials donated for the *Mishkan*. The Maharal says that thirteen is the *gematria* of "אחד," "one." There were, functionally, thirteen Tribes of *Bnei Yisrael*, for *Menashe* and *Ephraim* were, by virtue of their grandfather *Yaacov's* blessing, treated as full tribes for many purposes. (Bereshit 48:5) The thirteen Tribes are an allusion to the oneness of *Am Yisrael*. Among the thirteen, *Levy* is "א," meaning the first, and most Holy. *Rachel* and *Leah*, the preferred wives, bore *Yaacov* eight, or "ח," sons, and *Bilha* and *Zilpah* together bore *Yaacov* four, or "ד," sons. The varying spirituality all combines for one unity, אחד.

5763

Emes L'Yaacov – Concerning the poles by which the Holy Ark was carried, the *pasuk* states "בְּטַבְּעֹת הָאָרֹן יִהְיוּ הַבַּדִּים לֹא יָסֻרוּ מִמֶּנּוּ," "The poles of the Ark shall be in the rings; they shall not be removed from it," (Shemot 25:15) which Rashi indicates means "shall never be removed eternally." The Ark symbolizes *Torah* and the poles supporting the Ark represent those who support the learning of *Torah*. The verse therefore tells us that just as the poles, though not needed to carry the Ark when it is stationary, are nonetheless always connected to it, so too do the contributions for the support of *Torah* learning when needed connect eternally to the merit of that *Torah* learning.

5764

Ohr HaChaim – The list of materials for the *Mishkan* appearing at the beginning of Parashat Terumah seem to be in descending order of value, beginning with gold and silver and ending with the penultimate item, spices. (Shemot 25:3-7) Yet the final items listed are "אַבְנֵי שֹׁהַם וְאַבְנֵי מִלֻּאִים לָאֵפֹד וְלַחֹשֶׁן," "Shoham stones and filling stones for the Ephod and for the Choshen," (Shemot 25:7) which would presumably be the most valuable of all materials. The *Talmud* (Yoma 75a) states these stones came miraculously to the *nasiim* of *Bnei Yisrael*. While they were very valuable, because they were obtained with no real effort on the part of the People, they are listed last.

5765

Rabbi Yossi Jankovits – The Midrash Rabbah (Parashah 33, Siman 1) describes *Hashem's* so-called "sadness" at having to "part" with the *Torah* in Heaven and His exhortation to *Bnei Yisrael* to build a *Mishkan* on Earth for its safekeeping. The *Midrash* states this is like the father who, upon giving away his daughter in marriage, requests that the son-in-law build him a room so he can come visit and remain close to his daughter. But is there a place *Hashem* cannot go? Where there is *tumah*, *Hashem*, as it were, wants to be absent. Here, He is asking the Jews to maintain a location in their midst designated for *Kedushah*, where no *tumah* shall be present. Perhaps there is a parallel in our personal lives as well. Given the daily *tumah* to which we are exposed, we need at least the Holy *Shabbat*, for example, to reintroduce *Hashem* into our lives on a regular basis.

5766

Reb Aaron Moses – Why did *Hashem* require the intricate assembly of so many pieces of the *Mishkan*? Certainly He had, at other times, wrought miracles for *Bnei Yisrael* and He could have created the *Mishkan* as one finished piece. Perhaps He directed the Jews to assemble the *Mishkan* from many parts to make the point that His Presence could only dwell where there is *achdut* among all the component parts of *Bnei Yisrael.*

5767

Rabbi Yossi Jankovits – The *Mishkan* served *Bnei Yisrael* for about 500 years, until the establishment of the first *Beit HaMikdash.* The first *Beit HaMikdash* stood for 410 years, the second for 420 years. The *pasuk* states "וְעָשׂוּ לִי מִקְדָּשׁ וְשָׁכַנְתִּי בְּתוֹכָם," "They shall make for Me a Sanctuary – so that I may dwell among them." (Shemot 25:8) The Baal HaTurim points out that the word "shachanti," "that I may dwell," can be read as "שכן תי," "rest, 410," the years of the first *Beit HaMikdash.* It can also be rearranged to read "שני תכ," "[the] second, 420," the years of the second *Beit HaMikdash.*

5769

Rabbi Yosef Kalatsky –At the beginning of Parashat Terumah, *Hashem* commands *Moshe* "דַּבֵּר אֶל בְּנֵי יִשְׂרָאֵל וְיִקְחוּ לִי תְּרוּמָה מֵאֵת כָּל אִישׁ אֲשֶׁר יִדְּבֶנּוּ לִבּוֹ תִּקְחוּ אֶת תְּרוּמָתִי," "Speak to Bnei Yisrael and let them take for Me a portion ["terumah"] from every man whose heart motivates him." (Shemot 25:2) Why did the *Mishkan* need to be built with the heartfelt voluntary donations of *Bnei Yisrael*? And related, why did these donations have to be "in kind," meaning why donate the actual materials as opposed to the money or value to buy those materials? The *Mishkan* was not built on *Shabbat*, because, just like with Creation, on the Seventh Day the work stopped. (Rashi on Shemot 35:2) The Daat Zakainim (Shemot 38:25) tells us that every aspect of Creation was alluded to in the *Mishkan.* For example, the Curtains correspond to the Heavens, the Laver to the water, the *Menorah* to the light of the sun, etc. It states in Tehillim (89:3) that "... olam chesed yiboneh," "... [Hashem] built the world through chesed." Accordingly, as an emulation of *Hashem's* Creation, the Jews had to give through *chesed* (i.e. voluntarily) and give the actual ingredients and materials to bring about the replication of His Creation.

5770

Imrei Yosef – The language of Parashat Terumah mentions the *Menorah* (Shemot 25:31-40) adjacent to the *Shulchan*. (Shemot 25:23-30) These items were also physically proximate to each other in the *Mishkan* to stress the relationship of *Zevulun* (the business maker) and *Yissachar* (the *Torah* scholar). The requirements of *Yissachar* go far beyond mere *Torah* study. *Yissachar* takes responsibility for the spiritual well-being of *Zevulun*, guiding him to ensure his business practices are compliant with the precepts of the *Torah* he learns on his behalf. Understood in this way, the image of the detached *kollel* man is inaccurate. Instead, we see a dynamic relationship through which each partner, the learning and the earning, grows both spiritually and economically.

5771

Chofetz Chaim – There is a *Midrash* Yalkut Shimoni (on Yechezkel, remez 382) that when *Hashem* showed the prophet *Yechezkel* the structure of the third and final *Beit HaMikdash* so that he would describe it to *Bnei Yisrael*, the *navi* protested that, insofar as the Jews are in *galut*, it is not the right time to instruct them on the laws of *Bayit Shlishi*. Rather, *Yechezkel* implored *Hashem* to let the Jews leave exile and then he would relay the information. *Hashem* replied that even while in exile, if the Jews study the laws of the Temple, in that merit *Hashem* will view it as if we had rebuilt it.

5772

Rabbi Eli Mansour – The *Torah* commands the Jews "וְיָצַקְתָּ לּוֹ אַרְבַּע טַבְּעֹת זָהָב וְנָתַתָּה עַל אַרְבַּע פַּעֲמֹתָיו וּשְׁתֵּי טַבָּעֹת עַל צַלְעוֹ הָאֶחָת וּשְׁתֵּי טַבָּעֹת עַל צַלְעוֹ הַשֵּׁנִית," "And you shall cast four golden rings for [the Ark], and you shall place them upon its four 'paamotav,' two rings on its one side, and two rings on its other side." (Shemot 25:12) Rashi indicates that "peamot" are the corners of the *Aron*. The Ibn Ezra states that "peamot" are the "legs" of the *Aron*, based on the use of the word in Tehillim (85:14) (Ibn Ezra says that it would not be honorable and proper to place the *Aron* on the ground, hence the need for legs). Assuming they are legs, why not use the more common word "reglayim?" "Reglayim" refers to stationary legs, while "peamot" alludes to legs in motion. Since the *Aron* represents the *Luchot* and *Torah* learning, the message is the importance of continual and active spiritual advancement in *Torah*.

5773

Rabbi Samson Raphael Hirsch – The poles by which the *Aron* was carried are declared by the *pasuk* to remain permanently attached to the *Aron*. (Shemot 25:15) The *Gemara* (Yoma 54a) brings the verse in I Melachim (8:8), which makes clear that the space allotted to the *Aron* in the Holy of Holies in the *Mishkan* was insufficient to contain the poles and they therefore pushed the *Parochet* outward in a manner that was noticeable from outside the Holy of Holies. These poles pushed the curtain in a way that provided the sole evidence to *Bnei Yisrael* that there was an *Aron* behind the Curtain. This was a constant reminder of the centrality of *Torah* (represented by the *Aron*) in the lives of *Bnei Yisrael*. MRF Note – The push of the poles into the *Parochet* also provided support for the notion that even when *Torah* eludes us on a clearly accessible, rational basis, and therefore we cannot "see" it, it remains pure, unchanged and valid nonetheless.

TETZAVEH

5757

Parashat Teztaveh continues the *Torah's* discussion of the *Mishkan* and the service of the *Kohanim*. Both *Moshe* and *Betzalel* were instrumental in building the *Mishkan*. The Talmud (Berachot 55a) recounts that *Hashem* told *Moshe* to build a *Mishkan* and then to create the *Aron* and vessels for service. When *Moshe* instructed *Betzalel* to first build the *Aron* and the vessels, and only then build the *Mishkan* to house them, *Betzalel* objected, questioning where one would put the contents when no structure existed to house them. *Moshe* was persuaded by the question and reverted to Hashem's instruction, and praised the wisdom of *Betzalel*, and invoking the meaning of his name, as "in the shadow of [i.e. thinking in alignment with], G-d."

5758

Tzror Hamor – Why may only "shemen zayit zach, katit lamaor" "pure, crushed olive oil," be used in lighting the *Menorah*? (Shemot 27:20) The oil may be compared to *Bnei Yisrael*. Both must be crushed to be at their finest and both separate and inevitably "rise to the top." Even when faced with great difficulties, *Bnei Yisrael* separates out and rises, remaining distinct from the other nations.

5759

Rabbi Yechiel Dancyger – The *Torah* mandates that we use "pure oil of olives crushed for lighting." (Shemot 27:20) There is a lesson within this verse. When one speaks crushing words of rebuke, it must be for the sole purpose of enlightening and illuminating. MRF Note – Beyond intention, method also matters. Before administering the "needle" of rebuke, it is critical to prepare and clean the area of "injection" so as to not contaminate (with untrue or excessive criticism) and G-d forbid "lose the patient."

5760

The Vilna Gaon – Of all the *parshiot* from *Shemot* to the end of *Sefer Devarim*, Tetzaveh is the only one where *Moshe's* name does not appear. *Moshe* died on 7 *Adar*, which usually falls out during the week Parashat Tetzaveh is read. Rather than viewing the omission in a negative light, in removing his name, *Hashem* was, in fact, paying *Moshe*, the teacher par excellence of *Bnei Yisrael*, the highest compliment. A teacher is regarded as most effective when his pupils perform on their own, absent the teacher's involvement. *Bnei Yisrael* had become attached to *Hashem's Torah*, rather than *Moshe's* cult of personality. This had come about, in part, due to *Moshe's* speech impediment (Shemot 4:10, 6:12 and 6:30), which ensured that the content of his words, not their delivery, would matter most. This is a tribute to *Moshe* which is also reflected the fact that we read about his death (in Parashat V'Zot HaBerachah) on the day we celebrate the *Torah* (*Simchat Torah*).

Baal HaTurim – After the golden calf incident, Moshe pleaded with Hashem "וְעַתָּה אִם תִּשָּׂא חַטָּאתָם וְאִם אַיִן מְחֵנִי נָא מִסִּפְרְךָ אֲשֶׁר כָּתָבְתָּ," "And now, if You forgive their sin, but if not, erase me now from Your book that You have written." (Shemot 32:32) His offer to *Hashem* was that his name be omitted from the *Torah* rather than have *Hashem* destroy the Jewish People. The words of the righteous have an effect to some extent (e.g. *Yaacov* to *Lavan* regarding the stolen idols, [Bereshit 31:32]), but in order to make that effect as minimal as possible, *Hashem* removed *Moshe's* name in the *parashah* (Tetzaveh) furthest (in the annual reading cycle) from the *parashah* in which he made the declaration (Ki Tisa).

5762

Reb Louis Barr – Parashat Tetzaveh describes that the *Kohain Gadol* wore a robe with bells attached to announce his presence in the Sanctuary. (Shemot 28:34, 35) The Rashbam cites this as the basis of the practice, recorded in the *Gemara* (Niddah 16b), of *Rabbi Yochanan* knocking on the door to his own house before entering. The *Torah*, in Parashat Terumah, states "וְעָשׂוּ לִי מִקְדָּשׁ וְשָׁכַנְתִּי בְּתוֹכָם," "they should build for Me a Mikdash and I will reside in them," (Shemot 25:8) not reside in it but reside in them: *Bnei Yisrael*. This is a reference to the idea that *Hashem* will dwell in the homes of the Jewish People, and is a reason that we therefore announce our entrance.

For man to actualize his potential for character development, he must perfect three areas of *Torah* observance: (1) "bein adam l'atzmo" (between a man and himself); (2) "bein adam l'chaveiro" (between a man and his friend); and (3) "bein adam l'Makom" (between a man and Hashem). These three areas are each represented in the dispute among the Sages as to which verse of the *Torah* captures the very essence of the *Torah*. The *Talmud* Yerushalmi (Nedarim: chapter 9, halachah 4) quotes *Ben Azai* who invokes a *pasuk* in *Sefer Bereshit* (5:1) in support of bein adam l'atzmo: "זֶה סֵפֶר תּוֹלְדֹת אָדָם בְּיוֹם בְּרֹא אלקים אָדָם בִּדְמוּת אלקים עָשָׂה אֹתוֹ," "This is the account of the descendants of Adam – on the day that G-d created man, he made him in the likeness of G-d." The same source quotes *Rabbi Akiva* who cites a *pasuk* in *Sefer Vayikra* (19:18) in support of bein adam l'chaveiro "לֹא תִקֹּם וְלֹא תִטֹּר אֶת בְּנֵי עַמֶּךָ וְאָהַבְתָּ לְרֵעֲךָ כָּמוֹךָ אֲנִי הי," "You shall neither take revenge from nor bear a grudge against the members of your People; <u>you shall love your neighbor as yourself.</u> I am Hashem." The Ein Yaakov cites *Rabbi Shimon ben Pazi* who invokes a *pasuk* in Parashat Tetzaveh (Shemot 29:39) in support of bein adam l'Makom "אֶת הַכֶּבֶשׂ הָאֶחָד תַּעֲשֶׂה בַבֹּקֶר וְאֵת הַכֶּבֶשׂ הַשֵּׁנִי תַּעֲשֶׂה בֵּין הָעַרְבָּיִם," "you shall offer [to Hashem] one lamb in the morning and a second lamb shall you offer in the afternoon."

5763

Kli Yakar – Throughout Parashat Tetzaveh, *Hashem* commands *Moshe* with respect to the vessels of the *Mishkan* saying "v'asita," "and <u>you</u> shall make" but with regard to the *Ephod*, Hashem says "v'asoo," "and <u>they</u> shall make." (Shemot 28:6) The *Ephod* comes to atone for idolatry, a violation made by all the Jews, excluding *Moshe*, in the incident of the golden calf.

5764

Rabbi Yisroel Ciner – It is interesting to note that *Moshe*'s name is missing from Parashat Tetzaveh, and Hashem's name is missing from *Megillah Esther*, and these often are read mere days apart in the Jewish calendar. In both cases, the Principal is operating, just not by name.

5765

Rabbi Yossi Jankovits – The *Luchot* represent the Written Torah and the seven branched *Menorah* (Shemot 25:37), the Oral Torah. The *Tefillin* have a bifurcated seven-branched *Menorah* with two "shins" on the *Shel Rosh* – one having the traditional three arms (ש) and one having four arms. The specifications and details of *Tefillin* are not set forth in the Written Torah but are described in detail in the *Oral Law*. By donning the *Tefillin Shel Rosh*, we are accepting the *Oral Law* as presented by the *Menorah*. In fact, immediately after we don the *Shel Rosh* we recite the verse from the *Siddur* "וְשֶׁמֶן הַטּוֹב תָּרִיק עַל שִׁבְעָה קְנֵי הַמְּנוֹרָה," "[May] You pour goodly oil upon the seven arms of the Menorah."

Rabbi Yossi Jankovits – It is well known that *Moshe's* name is absent from Parashat Tetzaveh, the only such *parashah* from the birth of *Moshe* in Parashat Shemot through the conclusion of the *Torah*. What is less well known that *Aharon's* name is absent from the preceding Parashat Terumah (which is the only such *parashah* in *Sefer Shemot*). One opinion is that *Moshe*, as an exceedingly humble man, asked *Hashem* to leave his name out of Tetzaveh so as to deflect attention from the prior omission of *Aharon* in Terumah.

5768

The *Choshen*, which contained the *Urim v'Tumim*, was used, according to Rashi, to arrive at perfect judgment and to atone for the perversion of justice. (Rashi on Shemot 28:15) This year, *Erev Shabbat* for Parashat Tetzaveh, we witnessed the perversion of justice in the criminal case against Keith Wasserstrom.

5769

Rabbi Zalman Sorotzkin – We know from the traditions of *Chazal* that *Moshe's* birthday (and death) were 7 *Adar*, which traditionally falls around the time of year we read Parashat Tetzaveh; the only *parashah* from Parashat

Shemot onward in the *Torah* where *Moshe* is not mentioned by name. This indicates the wisdom of *Torah* and the glory of Judaism. Whereas other religions deify their leaders and have festivals on their birthdays, Judaism, while paying due homage to its greatest leader, does not confuse him with the Source and does not pay undue attention to the date of his birth. It is interesting to note that while the Rabbis ascertained the date of *Moshe's* birth, it is not explicit in the *Torah* and was not generally known among the common people.

5770

Rabbi Michael Jablinowitz – What is the significance of the *Bigdei Kehuna*? The Sefas Emes says that the body is a covering for our soul, and our clothing is a covering for our body. Just as one's actions with one's body reflect the essence of one's soul, so too do one's clothes represent the actions of one's body. In Kohelet (9:8), *Shlomo HaMelech* says "b'chol et yihyu begadecha levanim ... ," "at all times your clothes should be white." This indicates that our actions should be pure. Understood this way, the clothes of the *Kohanim* described in Parashat Tetzaveh had to be coverings of such esteem as to reflect the Holy and pure actions of the *avodah* in the Temple.

5771

Rabbi Naftali Kalter – The *parashah* describes the *Bigdei Kehuna*, including the *Choshen*, worn by *Aharon HaKohain*. (Shemot 28:15-30) Rashi indicates in Parashat Shemot that the heart that rejoiced for his brother (*Moshe*) being chosen to lead *Klal Yisrael*, despite being older, had the merit to wear the *Choshen*. (Rashi on Shemot 4:14) This excellence in character is described by the Ramban as "v'ahavta l'rayacha komocha," "love your friend as yourself," which requires a Jew, like *Aharon*, to feel the joys of another Jew as if they were his own.

5772

Rabbi Michael Jablinowitz – The omission of *Moshe's* name from Parashat Tetzaveh, rather than being a punishment, is an indication of closeness between *Hashem* and *Moshe*. Throughout the *parashah*, beginning with the first word, *Hashem* refers to Moshe not by name, but by using the pronoun "attah," "you." A name is descriptive and speaks to the essence, but not the totality, of a person. Unlike the pronoun "you," a name is, by definition, limiting. For *Hashem* to call *Moshe* "You" was to pay him the highest deference. MRF Note – Rabbi Akiva Tatz states that a name is a "handle" by which others can "grasp" you. But "you" are "you," without limit. Therefore, when *Hashem* refers to *Moshe* as "you," He indicates the great power, in its totality, that *Moshe* possesses. This is *middah keneged middah*. *Moshe* was so selfless that he offered to eliminate himself in defense of his People. (Shemot 32:32) *Hashem* rewarded him with the most expansive and individualized reference possible.

5773

Rabbi Avi Weiss – The *pasuk* says "וְעָשִׂיתָ בִגְדֵי קֹדֶשׁ לְאַהֲרֹן אָחִיךָ לְכָבוֹד וּלְתִפְאָרֶת," "You shall make garments of sanctity for Aharon your brother for honor and for splendor." (Shemot 28:2). Rabbi Aharon Soloveichik asks why the *Kohain* would need or want clothes of honor, since we understand honor to be contrary to the *Torah* ideal of humility. *Kavod*, he answers, is based on the root word "kaved," meaning "heavy." Heaviness is linked conceptually to the weight of responsibility. The greater the level of responsibility, the greater the resulting *kavod*, once the responsibility is fulfilled. The *Kohain* has clothes that remind him of his awesome responsibility to *Am Yisrael*.

KI TISA

5757

Rabbi Chaim Shmuelevitz – The usual rule is that the *yetzer hara* works incrementally to ultimately move us to great evil through small steps. The exception is where we are despondent, in which case we are susceptible to a greater leap based on our negative mood. This was the case with the sin of the golden calf. *Bnei Yisrael* thought *Moshe* was dead and became depressed, allowing for their dramatic descent. The clear lesson is that we must actively work to keep ourselves in a good mood, allowing us to resist the greatest damage by our *yetzer hara*.

5758

Noam Elimelech – In Parashat Ki Tisa, *Hashem* commands that each Jew give a half-*shekel* donation as part of an "atonement" census of *Bnei Yisrael*. (Shemot 30:15) According to the Midrash Tanchuma (siman 9), *Hashem* showed *Moshe* a half-*shekel* coin on fire because *Moshe* did not understand how money could ransom the soul. *Hashem* used fire to show the duality of money. Like fire, money can be for good or evil, depending on application. Fire can warm or burn, illuminate or blind. Money, when used properly, can allow the Jews to accomplish tremendous spiritual results, something about which *Moshe* may have been skeptical.

5759

Daat Zakainim – Parashat Ki Tisa documents the unfortunate incident of the *cheit haeigel*. (Shemot 32:1-6) Because of their reluctance to participate in the sinful event, Jewish women were specifically given *Rosh Chodesh* as a quasi-*Yom Tov*. (Daat Zakainim Shemot 35:22)

Meshech Chochmah – The *pasuk* says "וַיְהִי כַּאֲשֶׁר קָרַב אֶל הַמַּחֲנֶה וַיַּרְא אֶת הָעֵגֶל וּמְחֹלֹת וַיִּחַר אַף מֹשֶׁה וַיַּשְׁלֵךְ מִיָּדָו אֶת הַלֻּחֹת וַיְשַׁבֵּר אֹתָם תַּחַת הָהָר," "Now it came to pass when he drew closer to the camp and saw the calf and the dances, that Moshe's anger was kindled, and he flung the tablets from his hands, shattering them at the foot of the mountain." (Shemot 32:19) Moshe broke the *Luchot* out of fear that they would simply become a physical substitute for the golden calf. He sought to teach the lesson that *Kedushah* existed in *Hashem* alone, not in physical objects.

5760

Rabbi Yisroel Ciner – In Parashat Ki Tisa, *Hashem* again commands *Bnei Yisrael* concerning *Shabbat*. The *Torah* tells us of the essence of *Shabbat*: "בֵּינִי וּבֵין בְּנֵי יִשְׂרָאֵל אוֹת הִוא לְעֹלָם כִּי שֵׁשֶׁת יָמִים עָשָׂה ה' אֶת הַשָּׁמַיִם וְאֶת הָאָרֶץ וּבַיּוֹם הַשְּׁבִיעִי שָׁבַת וַיִּנָּפַשׁ," "Between Me and Bnei Yisrael, it is a sign forever that for six days Hashem created the Heaven and the earth, and on the seventh day He <u>rested and was refreshed</u>." (Shemot 31:17) On *Shabbat* we are given a *neshamah yetairah*, an extra soul. The *Gemara* (Beitzah 16a) tells us that the words of this *pasuk*, "shavat v'yinafash," literally translated as "[He] rested and was refreshed," can also be read as "[Shabbat] stops (shavat), woe (vai) to the soul (y'nafash)" which has departed (i.e. the *neshamah yetairah*). Rashi describes the *neshamah yetairah* as a "widened" heart. Normally the *neshamah* is repulsed by physicality. On *Shabbat*, *Hashem* widens our *neshamot* to accept food, sleep and other pleasures as enjoyable to our <u>souls</u>, not merely our bodies, and it difficult to lose that reconciliation between body and soul when *Shabbat* comes to an end each week.

Rabbi Yissocher Frand – The *pasuk* says "שָׁלֹשׁ פְּעָמִים בַּשָּׁנָה יֵרָאֶה כָּל זְכוּרְךָ אֶת פְּנֵי הָאָדֹן | ה' אלקי יִשְׂרָאֵל," "Three times in the year all your males should appear before the Master, Hashem, G-d of Israel." (Shemot 34:23). This refers to the *mitzvah* of *aliyah l'regel* – going to *Yerushalayim* for the holidays of *Pesach*, *Shavuot* and *Sukkot*. The *Torah* says that while the People are in *Yerushalayim* no foreigners will covet their lands. (Shemot 34:24) This command and the corresponding promise remind one of the commandment "you shall not covet." (Shemot 20:14) There is a question: how can the *Torah* legislate what one thinks? The Ibn Ezra answers that if one were to view what he has as from *Hashem*, and what others have as what *Hashem* has designated for them, one would break any perceived connection he has to his neighbor's wife, house, etc. The Mikdash Mordechai applies the same principle to *aliyah l'regel*. If *Bnei Yisrael* truly keeps the *Torah* and *mitzvot* in the Land, we will be perceived by the *goyim* as an "Am Kadosh," a different type of "People imbued with special Holiness." As such, they will not covet what we have, as they will view it as a gift from *Hashem* to his Holy People, not even in their league as an obtainable object for acquisition.

5761

Rabbi Avraham Pam – Why was *Moshe* so hard on *Bnei Yisrael* regarding the *cheit haeigel*? Indeed, just weeks before in *Mitzrayim* they had been practicing idolatry along with the Egyptians. The answer is that when they were in Egypt, they knew that *avodah zareh* was wrong but had no substitute for serving *Hashem*. Here, in Parashat Ki Tisa, convened at *Har Sinai*, they were proclaiming "this is your god o'Yisrael, who brought you up from the land of Mitzrayim." (Shemot 32:4) They were not merely lapsing, but were perverting the *Torah* they had recently received. They tried to fuse *avodah zareh* with Judaism, which is a major problem worthy of the harshest rebuke.

5762

Rabbi Yosef Kalatsky – In the *Gemara* (Nedarim 32a), *Avraham* is faulted for missing the opportunity to convert the captured subjects of the King of Sodom to monotheism. (Bereshit 14:21-24) This failing is given as one of the reasons for the Egyptian enslavement. *Moshe* was aware of this and therefore took the *Erev Rav* out of Egypt with the Jews as a *tikkun*. Rashi informs us that the *Erev Rav* were the instigators of the sin of the *eigel hazahav*, and the *pasuk* says "וַיְדַבֵּר ה' אֶל מֹשֶׁה לֶךְ רֵד כִּי שִׁחֵת עַמְּךָ אֲשֶׁר הֶעֱלֵיתָ מֵאֶרֶץ מִצְרָיִם," "Hashem told Moshe 'Go, descend, for your people that you have brought up from the land of Mitzrayim [the Erev Rav] have acted corruptly.'" (Shemot 32:7) *Hashem* faulted *Moshe* insofar as *Moshe* was creating the Jewish People, not merely monotheists, and the *Erev Rav* that he decided to bring out with *Bnei Yisrael* jeopardized the mission. This shows how careful we must be in exposing our families to influences that are not in line with the Jewish mission.

5762

Rabbi Shimon Krasner – The special *Maftir* for *Shabbat Parah*, taken from Parashat Chukat says "This is the chok of the Torah...." "this is the statute of the Torah ...." (Bamidbar 19:2) One would expect the *pasuk* would say "this is the *chok* of the *Parah Adumah* ... ," not of the entire *Torah*. The message is that even while *Parah Adumah* is the prototypical *chok*, as for the entire *Torah*, mishpatim and *eidot* included, we cannot really ever know the deep mysteries and meanings of the *mitzvot*.

5763

Rabbi Yosef Kalatsky – *Moshe* went forty days in learning *Torah* from *Hashem* (Shemot 24:18) and the Midrash Rabbah (parashah 41: siman 6) says that every day *Hashem* would teach him the entire *Torah* and at the end of each day *Moshe* would forget it all. On the fortieth attempt *Moshe* retained it all. The number forty represents completion of process (as in forty weeks of a pregnancy; forty days of the Flood), so why should a process of this nature have been used by *Hashem* to convey the *Torah* to *Moshe*? The *Gemara* (Nedarim 55a) tells us the *Torah* itself is a gift of G-d, and the *Gemara* (Megillah 6b) also says that one who claims to have toiled in *Torah* and "found" it, he should be believed. Rabbi Chaim Volozhin says "found" should be read as "understood." The lesson is that *Torah* learning is not solely an intellectual process, but is also a gift to those who toil sufficiently.

5764

Rabbi Yossi Jankovits – The Chasam Sofer points out that immediately following the *Torah's* discussion of the vessels for use in the *Mishkan* (Shemot 31:7-11), *Hashem* commands *Moshe* "וְאַתָּה דַּבֵּר אֶל בְּנֵי יִשְׂרָאֵל לֵאמֹר אַךְ "And אֶת שַׁבְּתֹתַי תִּשְׁמֹרוּ כִּי אוֹת הִוא בֵּינִי וּבֵינֵיכֶם לְדֹרֹתֵיכֶם לָדַעַת כִּי אֲנִי ה' מְקַדִּשְׁכֶם," you, speak to Bnei Yisrael and say 'However, keep My Shabbatot! For it is a sign between Me and you for your generations, to know that I, Hashem, make you Holy.'" (Shemot 31:13) Rashi focuses on the word "ach," meaning "however," which he says indicates there that while work of the *Mishkan* is important, the sanctity of *Shabbat* overrides making a dwelling place for *Hashem*. *Chazal* (Mechilta on Yoma 85a-b) indicate "ach" also is the basis for the exception of observing the *Shabbat* prohibitions when a life is at stake. In such cases it is prohibited <u>not</u> to do the activity necessary to save a life! Such an "exception to the exception" might leave the Jews confused. Why should human life take precedence over *Hashem's* abode or His *Shabbat*? *Hashem* answers in last part of the same *pasuk* "אֲנִי ה׳ מְקַדִּשְׁכֶם," "I am Hashem who makes You Holy." *Hashem* tells us "I decide that you, your human life, should be your highest priority!"

5765

In describing the *Luchot* given by *Hashem* to *Moshe* on *Har Sinai*, the *pasuk* states "וְהַלֻּחֹת מַעֲשֵׂה אלקים הֵמָּה וְהַמִּכְתָּב מִכְתַּב אלקים הוּא חָרוּת עַל הַלֻּחֹת," "And the Tablets were Elokim's work, and the inscription was Elokim's inscription, <u>engraved</u> on the tablets." (Shemot 32:16) The *Gemara* (Eruvin 54a) teaches that the word "חרות," "engraved," can be read as "חירות," "freedom." This indicates that true freedom comes from the submission to the Will of the Al-mighty by living as He instructed us through his *Torah*.

5767

Rabbi Yossi Jankovits – The text of Parashat Ki Tisa is silent on the question as to whether *Shevet Levy* participated in the sin of the golden calf, or even stood by in silence as it took place. And yet, the *pasuk* tells us that after the sin, "וַיַּעֲמֹד מֹשֶׁה בְּשַׁעַר הַמַּחֲנֶה וַיֹּאמֶר מִי לה׳ אֵלָי וַיֵּאָסְפוּ אֵלָיו כָּל בְּנֵי לֵוִי," "Moshe stood in the gate of the camp and said: 'Whoever is for Hashem, [come] to me!' And all the sons of Levy gathered around him." (Shemot 32:26) More than merely joining *Moshe*, we are told the Tribe of *Levy* took up arms to kill their offending brethren. (Shemot 32:28) Perhaps the lesson is that when their *Rebbe* pointed out the seriousness of the situation and demanded immediate *teshuvah*, they responded and made the right choice. The same could be said about the Jews in the *Chanukah* story (where, incidentally, the identical language "מִי לַה' אֵלָי," was stated). The point was that even where the members of *Bnei Yisrael* might have engaged in prohibited acts of assimilation up to that point, at the moment their *Rebbe* demanded *teshuvah*, some responded and were saved, and many others were slaughtered in a civil war. The message for all of us is clear: when we are made aware of our sinful acts by the wise persons around us, we must take heed and save ourselves from the penalties associated with sinning <u>and</u> failing to listen to the Sages.

5768

The *Torah* goes to great lengths to avoid embarrassment for Jews. It is a known *inyan* that *gabbaim* will not call someone for an *aliyah* where that person is suspected of being guilty of an *issur* set forth in that *aliyah*. In the case of the *cheit haeigel*, the *Torah* has extreme sensitivity. The *Kohain* and the *Levy aliyot* together comprise two-thirds of Parashat Ki Tisa, and the entire *cheit haeigel* episode is covered in the *Levy aliyah*. Since the Tribe of *Levy* did not participate in the sin, they do not experience embarrassment in getting called upon for that *aliyah*.

5769

Rabbi Yitzchak Salid – The rule that we violate *Shabbat* in order to save a life has grounding in five *Torah pasukim*, including, as expected, from Parashat Kedoshim "... vachai b'chem," "... you shall live through them" (Vayikra 18:5) but also, surprisingly, from Parashat Ki Tisa "v'shamru Bnei Yisrael ... ," "and Bnei Yisrael shall keep [the Shabbat] ...." (Shemot 31:16) Our Rabbis learn that because saving a life will ensure the subject of your assistance will keep additional *Shabbatot*, you violate the current *Shabbat* to bring about that result. The question is then asked, what if the person you are assisting has assuredly only days to live (and therefore will not experience another *Shabbat*)? The concept of enabling the person to perform the *mitzvot* of *Shabbat* is extended to other *mitzvot* that more regularly present themselves (e.g. saying *Shema*). This would explain why one may also violate the *Shabbat* to save an unborn baby's life. It cannot be "vachai b'chem," for that implies continued living, and the unborn fetus is not yet "alive" in the sense that it will continue doing *mitzvot*. Yet the prospective promise of *mitzvah* performance by the unborn person provides adequate *Torah* justification for the *Shabbat* violation. This is also the basis for allowing *Shabbat* violations in the area of *kiruv*, although that is an admittedly stickier situation.

5770

Rabbi Yitzchak Salid – *Shabbat Parah* always immediately precedes *Shabbat* HaChodesh, which is an aberration in the conventional logic of Jewish calendar. The laws of the *Parah Adumah* deal with removing *tumah*, which is generally contracted through laziness and being less than careful about what one touches. *HaChodesh* heralds the pre-*Pesach* period where we are uber-observant and careful in ridding our dwellings of *chametz* and in preparing the *matzah* in the prescribed manner. The homiletic message is an exhortation to overcome our spiritual laziness and immediately transition to scrupulous adherence to the *Torah* to prepare for our imminent redemption.

5771

Reb Arie Hizkiya – The *Torah* tells that *Betzalel* had the wisdom and knowledge to construct the *Mishkan*, as well as the ability "לַחְשֹׁב מַחֲשָׁבֹת לַעֲשׂוֹת בַּזָּהָב וּבַכֶּסֶף וּבַנְּחֹשֶׁת," "to weave designs, to create with gold and the silver, and the copper." (Shemot 31:4) Rashi indicates this means he could weave things "choshev." The difference in weaving something "choshev" rather than "rokem" is instructive. "Rokem" means a design affixed to an already finished object, while "choshev" means the design is integrated into the object in such a fashion that its removal would be destructive to the object itself. The idea is paralleled by the *Gemara* (Shabbat 59b), where there is a debate about wearing a piece of jewelry called an "ir shel zahav," a "golden city," in a place where there is no *eruv*. There are three opinions. One opinion indicates that it is *assur*, since it is a burden and the wearer could likely come to remove it and impermissibly carry it in the public domain. The second opinion concedes it is a burden but allows it to be worn since it looks good in public, thereby making it unlikely the wearer would remove it. The final opinion holds that the beauty of the piece makes it so beloved to the wearer that it would never be considered a burden and would never be removed. This latter category is the type of Jew that *Betzalel* was, and the kind of Jews we must be. Our *Yiddishkeit* must not be merely "rokem," but "choshev" to us. It must be a part of who we are and may never be a burden.

5772

Rabbi Eli Mansour – The *machzit hashekel* donation was used after its first collection to make the "adanim," the silver sockets at the base of the *Mishkan* that formed the foundation. (Rashi on Shemot 30:15) Be'er Yosef equates the foundation of the *Mishkan* with the foundation of Judaism, which he identifies as *emunah*, faith: the belief in G-d's Existence and Providence. There is a strong connection to faith and the "machzit," "half" *shekel*. We have clarity with respect to the things in the world that challenge one's faith. The incomplete view requires faith. This is demonstrated later in Parashat Ki Tisa where *Moshe* begs *Hashem* for the clarity to "see" His Ways; to which *Hashem* famously responds "וַהֲסִרֹתִי אֶת כַּפִּי וְרָאִיתָ אֶת אֲחֹרָי וּפָנַי לֹא יֵרָאוּ," "Then I will remove My Hand, and you will see My Back, but My Face shall not be seen." (Shemot 33:23) *Moshe* was only allowed to see Hashem "from behind," a "half" view of the whole.

5773

Reb Ronen Elefant – It is startling that when *Hashem* displays anger at the incident of the golden calf, the Torah tells us "וַיֹּאמֶר ה' אֶל מֹשֶׁה רָאִיתִי אֶת הָעָם הַזֶּה וְהִנֵּה עַם קְשֵׁה עֹרֶף הוּא," "And Hashem said to Moshe 'I have seen this People and, behold, it is a stiff necked People.'" (Shemot 32:9) Rashi states that their issue was their refusal to listen to their leader. Yet later in Parashat Ki Tisa, when *Hashem* provides *Moshe* with His Thirteen Attributes of Mercy as a formula to elicit forgiveness for the Nation (Shemot 34:5-7), Moshe implores Hashem to "go in the midst" of *Bnei Yisrael*, stating "... ki Am k'shei oref hu ... ," "for it is a stiff necked People!" (Shemot 34:9) *Moshe*, in essence, was invoking that same attribute for which *Hashem* chastised *Bnei Yisrael* as a merit for them; as a reason for *Hashem* to dwell amongst them. *Chazal* indicate that *Moshe* was indicating to *Hashem* that the same *middah* that gave rise to the sin of the golden calf would sustain the Jewish People in a positive way over the ensuing centuries in the face of concerted efforts by the nations of the world to convert them away from their *Yiddishkeit*. The stiff necked People would remain true to *Hashem* and His *Torah*.

VAYAKHEL

5757

The *pasuk* states "וַיַּעַשׂ אֵת הַכִּיּוֹר נְחֹשֶׁת וְאֵת כַּנּוֹ נְחֹשֶׁת בְּמַרְאֹת הַצֹּבְאֹת אֲשֶׁר צָבְאוּ פֶּתַח אֹהֶל מוֹעֵד," "And he made the washbasin of copper and its base of copper from the mirrors of the women who had set up the legions, who congregated at the entrance of the Tent of Meeting." (Shemot 38:8) The bottom of the *Kiyor* was made of copper mirrors donated by the Jewish women, who used them while in *Mitzrayim* to make themselves appealing to their husbands so as to perpetuate and increase the Jewish Nation. Their husbands did not necessarily want to fulfill the *mitzvah* of procreation, reasoning that their children would be born into slavery, but the women had faith that *Hashem* would ultimately redeem His People. This made these mirrors extremely dear to *Hashem*, who wanted them intimately connected to the *Mishkan*. (Rashi on Shemot 38:8)

5758

Parashat Vayakhel discusses the details of the *Mishkan*, of which *Betzalel* was the primary builder. In Parashat Ki Tisa, the *pasuk* says "רְאֵה קָרָאתִי

בְּשֵׁם בְּצַלְאֵל בֶּן אוּרִי בֶן חוּר לְמַטֵּה יְהוּדָה," "See, I [Hashem] have called by name Betzalel, the son of Uri, son of Chur, of the Tribe of Yehudah." (Shemot 31:2) The Midrash Rabbah (Parashah 40) says that the words "by name," which seem superfluous, refer to the "good name" that *Betzalel* has earned for himself through good deeds. The *Midrash* goes on to state that of all the names a person has, the name he acquires through deeds and behavior is as important as the one he gets from his parents or what he is called by others.

5759

The Torah tells us, in regards to the donations of *Bnei Yisrael* to the *Mishkan*, "וְהַמְּלָאכָה הָיְתָה דַיָּם לְכָל הַמְּלָאכָה לַעֲשׂוֹת אֹתָהּ וְהוֹתֵר," "And the work was <u>enough</u> for them for all the work, to do it, and there was <u>extra</u>." (Shemot 36:7) This seems to be contradictory. If the volume of donations was "enough" (i.e. just enough) then there would be no extra, while if there was "extra" there was <u>more</u> than enough. *Moshe* sought to avoid false pride on the part of the People in completing the *Mishkan*. If exactly enough was raised, many individuals would claim it was his or her single contribution that completed the *Mishkan*. By raising more than required, *Moshe* created the possibility that at least one individual's donation was superfluous, thereby avoiding any false sense of pride for all donors. In that way, too much <u>was</u> enough. We should extend this rationale to the good things we do that result in good outcomes. Perhaps *Hashem* has already deemed the positive outcome to occur, in which case we are simply His tool, in a way, superfluous. By bearing this in mind we avoid a false sense of conceit, thereby making our good deeds not merely enough, but more!

5760

Rabbi Yissocher Frand – The *mitzvah* of *Shabbat* appears in the middle of the instructions for building the *Mishkan*. The *Gemara* (Shabbat 49b) thereby links the prohibited *melachot* of *Shabbat* to those activities required to construct the *Mishkan*: thirty-nine distinct labors. We refrain from these activities on *Shabbat* because they involve creating, which is mastery over nature, and on *Shabbat* we recognize *Hashem* as the original Creator and ultimate Master. This actually applies to thirty-eight of the thirty-nine *melachot*. The thirty-ninth prohibition of "carrying" has a different significance. *Kiddush* on *Shabbat* is recited in commemoration of both the Creation and the Exodus, representing, respectively, *Hashem's* original and continuing involvement in our lives. Carrying represents involvement between two or more people (for example carrying between a private and public domain, which is prohibited). Involvement between people is the history that has unfolded since *Hashem's* Creation, and on *Shabbat* we need to reduce that involvement to a certain extent in order to recognize that *Hashem* is the cause of continuing history, not merely the Force that put it all in motion.

5761

Rabbi Mordechai Kamenetsky- In regard to the donations for the *Mishkan*, the *Torah* states "וְהַמְּלָאכָה הָיְתָה דַיָּם לְכָל הַמְּלָאכָה לַעֲשׂוֹת אֹתָהּ וְהוֹתֵר," "the work [contributions] had been <u>enough</u> for all the work, to do it – and there was <u>extra</u>." (Shemot 36:7). The use of "enough" and "extra" is difficult, for it would make sense to have one word or the other, but not both. One idea is that the enthusiasm generated for giving to the *Mishkan* was enough to finish that project, yet there was excess enthusiasm that carried forth among the generations of Jews, which we see manifested today among otherwise secular Jews who still give *tzedakah* in abundance.

5762

Rabbi Yossi Jankovits – In describing the prohibited *melachot* of *Shabbat*, the *Torah* provides only a single representative example: "לֹא תְבַעֲרוּ אֵשׁ בְּכֹל מֹשְׁבֹתֵיכֶם בְּיוֹם הַשַּׁבָּת," "You shall not kindle a fire in any of your dwelling places on the Shabbat day." (Shemot 35:3) The mention of only "aish," "fire," from the thirty-nine *melachot* alluded to in the parasha has many interpretations: (1) fire is destructive and unless specifically mentioned one could think kindling a fire is not prohibited as are the constructive actions;

(2) according to the *Gemara* (Shabbat 70a), this single example comes to teach that one need not do <u>all</u> the *melachot* to be liable; (3) even acts that provide comfort (like kindling a fire) are nonetheless still prohibited; and (4) since the *Gemara* (Pesachim 54a) says that "man-made" fire was created *Motzei Shabbat* and was, therefore, not included in the *melachot* that *Hashem* used in Creation before the first *Shabbat*, Tiferet Yonatan states the *Torah* mentions it expressly to include it as prohibited.

5763

Meshech Chochmah – In Parashat Vayakhel, *Betzalel's* name is mentioned in connection with the creation of the *Aron* (Shemot 37:1), but not with the other *kaylim*. This was because only *Betzalel* could make the *Aron* due to the requirement of *Keruvim* on top. (Shemot 37:7-9) Anyone else would think idolatrous thoughts in connection with the human-like forms, but *Betzalel*, whose grandfather was *Chur*, had pedigree for rejecting idols. *Chur* had been killed earlier when he protested the creation of the golden calf. (Rashi on Shemot 32:5)

5764

Rabbi Chaim Flom – In Parashat Vaykhel, the *pasuk* tells us "and all those came whose heart motivated them," to craft the *kaylim* for the *Mishkan*. (Shemot 35:22) The Ramban says their hearts motivated them because, as former slaves, *Bnei Yisrael* had no training in the skills necessary to craft the *kaylim*. Nevertheless, their earnest desire to participate merited for them ability to do so.

5765

Rabbi David Hollander – The *sedra* opens with the *pasuk* "וַיַּקְהֵל מֹשֶׁה אֶת כָּל עֲדַת בְּנֵי יִשְׂרָאֵל וַיֹּאמֶר אֲלֵהֶם אֵלֶּה הַדְּבָרִים אֲשֶׁר צִוָּה ה' לַעֲשֹׂת אֹתָם," "And Moshe gathered all the Congregation of Bnei Yisrael saying, 'these are the things that Hashem commanded, <u>to do them</u>.'" (Shemot 35:1) Adherence to Judaism begins with the performance (i.e. the actual <u>doing</u>) of *mitzvot*. The next *pasuk* describes the prohibition of *Shabbat* (Shemot 35:2), to indicate that *mitzvot* are to be performed only because G-d commanded them. Where there is no law, there is no life.

5766

Rabbi Eli Mansour – Parashat Vayakhel opens with *Moshe* assembling *Bnei Yisrael* to admonish them concerning *Shabbat*. Specifically, *Moshe* instructs the Jews not to burn a fire in their residences on *Shabbat*. (Shemot 35:3) *Chazal* comment on the choice of fire as illustrative of the *Shabbat* prohibitions. There are thirty-nine forms of prohibited activity on the *Shabbat*, so why refer only to fire? Homiletically, the verse may be referring to the situation in one's home on *Erev Shabbat*, in which the *satan* tries to frustrate and anger a family so as to ruin their impending *Shabbat*. A fire of anger sparked on Friday afternoon can certainly burn into *Shabbat* and cause enormous spiritual damage to an individual and his family. This may also be explained by the *Mishnah* (Shabbat 2:7) in the "Bameh Madlikin" section of the *siddur*, which we read between *Minchah* and *Maariv* as part of *Kabbalat Shabbat*. It reads: "A person must say three things <u>in his home</u> before dark on Erev Shabbat: Have you tithed; Have you prepared the Eruv; Light the candle." Why must the *Mishnah* stress that these things are said in one's home? This seems superfluous since all the referenced activities take place within the home. The answer may be that these family interactions in preparation for the *Shabbat* must remain "in the home," and that no yelling, resulting from the "fire" of anger, should be heard by others outside the home. The *shalom* of *Shabbat* therefore begins *Erev Shabbat* and continues throughout the night and day.

5768

Rabbi Yossi Jankovits –In Parashat Ki Tisa, we see that *Hashem* first told *Moshe* the laws of the *Mishkan* (Shemot 30:11-31:11) and then the laws of

Shabbat (Shemot 31:12-17), and yet after *Moshe* descends the mountain and following the *cheit haeigel*, at the beginning of Parashat Vayakhel, *Moshe* presents the laws of *Shabbat* (Shemot 35:1-3) prior to addressing the laws of building the *Mishkan* (which constitute the majority of the *parasha*). Why would *Moshe* present *Hashem's* commands in reverse order? In Parashat Beshalach, *Bnei Yisrael* is surprised and confused when on Friday, *Hashem* provides a double portion of *Mon* (Shemot 16:22). *Hashem* faults and rebukes *Moshe* (Shemot 16:28) for their reaction, for he had not taught *Bnei Yisrael* about *Shabbat* (Rashi on Shemot 16:22), despite having been previously instructed by *Hashem* on the pre-*Shabbat* double portion. (Shemot 16:5) This was a lost opportunity to stress the important status and primacy of *Shabbat*. *Moshe*, having learned that lesson, thereafter stresses *Shabbat* at the beginning of Parashat Vayakhel to avoid repeating his mistake.

5769

Rabbi Eli Mansour – Why did *Betzalel*, rather than *Moshe*, merit to lead the building of the *Mishkan*? His grandfather *Chur* opposed the plan to build the *eigel hazahav*, and the Jews killed him. (Rashi on Shemot 32:5) *Betzalel* forgave them and eagerly participated in enabling the atonement for all the People through the *Mishkan*. The Baal Shem Tov quoted the *pasuk* in Tehillim (121:5) "Hashem tzilecha," "Hashem is your shadow," explaining that a shadow perfectly mimics a person's actions. Hashem, as it were, bestows kindness on us when we do so for others. To be forgiven, we must forgive. *Betzalel* was the embodiment of this ideal and therefore merited to build the *Mishkan*.

5770

Rabbi Yossi Jankovits – Parashat Vayakhel begins with another reference to *Shabbat*, mentioned in a *parashah* otherwise devoted to describing the building of the *Mishkan*. Rashi indicates that we learn from this that the work of the *Mishkan* does not push off the prohibitions of Shabbat. (Rashi on Shemot 35:2) This might be evident from our reference to leaving Egypt in Friday night *Shabbat Kiddush*. In *Mitzrayim* the Jews were forced to do all manners of *melachah* on *Shabbat*. Upon leaving Egypt, we became servants of *Hashem* and, accordingly, ceased engaging in these activities – even with regard to building the *Mishkan*.

5771

Rabbi Eli Mansour – On the *pasuk* "וַיֵּצְאוּ כָּל עֲדַת בְּנֵי יִשְׂרָאֵל מִלִּפְנֵי מֹשֶׁה," "The entire congregation of Jews left from Moshe's presence," (Shemot 35:20) Rav Elya Lopian asks why the Torah adds the seemingly superfluous reference of having departed "from Moshe's presence," rather than just "from Moshe?" He answers that the Torah is teaching that it was physically apparent when the People had left *Moshe*, because they were visibly inspired and uplifted. Our challenge is to also become inspired through learning and to make positive outward changes by which others will recognize that we have been inspired.

5772

Rabbi Eli Mansour – The *pasuk* seems redundant: "כָּל אִישׁ וְאִשָּׁה אֲשֶׁר נָדַב לִבָּם אֹתָם לְהָבִיא לְכָל הַמְּלָאכָה אֲשֶׁר צִוָּה ה׳ לַעֲשׂוֹת בְּיַד מֹשֶׁה הֵבִיאוּ בְנֵי יִשְׂרָאֵל נְדָבָה לה׳," "Every man and woman whose heart motivated them to bring for any of the work that Hashem had commanded to make, through Moshe – the Children of Israel brought a free-willed offering to Hashem." (Shemot 35:29) If every man and woman whose heart was stirred brought an offering, why must the *Torah* tell us that *Bnei Yisrael* brought an offering? The term "bnei" could be read literally, with the implication that the parents who were inspired brought their children as an "offering," to be a part of the mitzvah, which is the most powerful method of *chinuch*.

5773

Rabbi Moshe Weinberger – The *mitzvah* of *Shabbat* is set forth (again) in Parashat Vayakhel. (Shemot 35:2, 3) The *Mishnah* (Shabbat 7:2) indicates that number of *melachot* that are the prohibited acts of *Shabbat* are "forty minus one." Why not simply say there are thirty-nine? Why does "minus" have to be part of the definition of *melachot*? The essence of a *melachah* is "chesair," "deficiency," meaning that one engages in *melachah* only if he perceives that something is missing that requires man-made activity to correct it. The idea that one must take action to remedy an imperfection is antithetical to *Shabbat*, where all our needs are satisfied and there is no "chesair," at least not for twenty-five hours. *Melacha*, which is <u>not</u> performed on Shabbat, is therefore described and defined with the language of lacking (i.e. forty <u>lacking</u> one), since no Jew is lacking in any respect on *Shabbat*.

PEDUKEI

5757

Rabbi Yosef Chaim Sonnenfeld – The *Torah's* laws of lending and collateral indicate that it is impermissible for a lender to take as collateral something that is essential to the livelihood of the borrower. So because we know that *Hashem* metaphysically abides by His own *Torah*, on what basis can He have taken both the Temples from the Jewish People? The *halachah* is that one is only prohibited from withholding necessities when the owner cries out for them from true need and want. Therefore, when we finally, collectively and genuinely cry out for restoration of our Temple, *Hashem* will be obliged to return it to us and will do so immediately.

5759

Rabbi Moshe Sternbuch – In Parashat Pekudei, *Moshe* gives an accounting of the silver of the *Mishkan*. The Midrash Tanchuma (siman 7) indicates this was in response to the cynical elements of *Bnei Yisrael* who accused *Moshe* of getting rich through embezzlement from public funds. But if gold and silver were both used in the construction of the *Mishkan*, why provide and accounting only for the silver? *Moshe* knew that those people who would be more accusatory towards him would also likely be the stingier among *Bnei Yisrael*, who would give silver while withholding their gold from the project. As such, he needed to account only for their silver, since they would not have donated gold with a full heart.

5760

Baal HaTurim – The words "as Hashem commanded" appear eighteen times regarding the construction of the *Mishkan*, from which the Rabbis established the eighteen blessings of the *Shemoneh Esrei*. (Shemot 40:32)

Rabbi Yissocher Frand – The *pasuk* says "וַיָּבִיאוּ אֶת הַמִּשְׁכָּן אֶל משֶׁה אֶת הָאֹהֶל" ",וְאֵת כָּל כֵּלָיו קְרָסָיו קְרָשָׁיו בְּרִיחָיו (כתיב בריחו) וְעַמֻּדָיו וַאֲדָנָיו" "And [Bnei Yisrael] brought the Mishkan to Moshe, the tent and all its furnishings its clasps, its planks, its bars, its pillars and its sockets." (Shemot 39:33) Rashi says they were unable to erect it. This seems contradictory. If they brought the *Mishkan* it was complete and ready to be erected, and if they couldn't assemble it then they brought to *Moshe* only the parts but not the *Mishkan* itself. Yet the *pasuk* is faultlessly accurate: *Bnei Yisrael* got the amount of credit earned in assembling the *Mishkan* for merely having tried to complete the task – a valuable lesson for *Avodat Hashem*.

5761

Rabbi Yossi Jankovits – In Parashat Pekudei, *Bnei Yisrael* works diligently to create a magnificent *Mishkan* that is inaugurated in a momentous ceremony. The *pasuk* states "וַיַּרְא משֶׁה אֶת כָּל הַמְּלָאכָה וְהִנֵּה עָשׂוּ אֹתָהּ כַּאֲשֶׁר צִוָּה ה' כֵּן עָשׂוּ וַיְבָרֶךְ אֹתָם משֶׁה," "Moshe saw the entire work, and behold! They had done it-as Hashem had commanded, so had they done. And Moshe blessed them." (Shemot 39:43) Rashi says that when the *Torah* indicates that *Moshe* blessed them, it means he petitioned that the

Shechinah should always dwell upon the handiwork of *Bnei Yisrael*. How would this be accomplished? Through the daily *Avodah*. In essence, the work was just beginning! All the preparation and celebration was a prelude to a lifetime of working to keep things operating correctly. This is the reality for any life changing event, for example a wedding or bar mitzvah. It is both very hard and extremely rewarding to make a successful *simchah*, but the real test rests in the day to day performance thereafter.

5763

Rabbi Yochanan Zweig – Why must the *Torah* rehash the details of the construction of the *Mishkan* over four *parshiot*, when the essence of the *Mishkan* was so that *Hashem* should dwell among *Bnei Yisrael* after the construction was complete? The *Gemara* (Avodah Zarah 3a) tells us that the *goyim* complained to *Hashem* that He did not give them the merit of any *mitzvot*. In response, *Hashem* instructs the *goy* to build a *sukkah* and then He makes the day unbearably hot. The *goy* departs from the *sukkah*, kicking it on the way out. The question arises, what did the *goy* do wrong? Even a Jew would be justified in leaving the *sukkah* under such conditions. The difference is that the Jew would not have kicked the *sukkah*. The *goy* is interested only in the result, and when his objective is not obtained (i.e. he is not able to sit in the *sukkah*), he expresses frustration at the total failure. The Jew appreciates the process, when he knows that building the *sukkah* was an expression of love for *Hashem*, despite the fact that he is unable to sit in it thereafter. Rabbi Zweig uses the example of his wife's cooking for three full days in anticipation of a visit from their married daughter and her family. When the daughter was "snowed-in" and had to cancel her trip, the *Rebbetzin* didn't kick the refrigerator that held all the prepared food. Both she and her daughter knew all the work was worth it, and worth talking about, as an expression of love.

5767

Rabbi Yossi Jankovits – Parashat Pekudei begins "ayleh pikudei haMishkan Mishkan ha eidut ...." "These are the reckonings of the Mishkan, the Mishkan of Testimonies." (Shemot 38:21) The double *lashon* bothers the Baal HaTurim, who points out the three consecutive words making reference (in reverse order) to the second *Beit HaMikdash*, the first *Beit HaMikdash* and the *Mishkan*. The *gematria* of "haeidut" is 479, which is the years the *Mishkan* was operational. "Mishkan" is *gematria* 410, the years that *Bayit Rishon* stood, and "haMishkan," is 415 which, when you add the five letters of the word, equals 420, the years of *Bayit Sheni*. The Chasam Sofer questions why we add five, which seems like a stretch, except when you consider that the *Gemara* (Yoma 21b) tells us that there were five miracles of the first *Beit HaMikdash* that were missing in the second.

5768

Rabbi Avi Weiss – At the end of each *sefer* of the *Chumash* we say "chazak, chazak, v'nitchazaik," "be strong, be strong, and may we be strengthened." Perhaps this is in recognition that in each case there is an unsettled scenario in the *Torah* narrative that requires us to strengthen our faith that the ultimate resolution will come and will be good. In *Sefer Bereshit* the death of *Yosef* portends badly for *Bnei Yisrael*. (Bereshit 50:26) At the end of *Sefer Shemot*, while the *Mishkan* has been completed, it has not yet been inaugurated and put to its intended use. *Sefer Vayikra* ends with the laws of *maaser* (Vayikra 27:1-34) and *Sefer Bamidbar* ends with the laws of *yerushah* for the daughters of *Tzalaphchad* (Bamidbar 36:1-13), all of which pertains to the settlement of the Land of Israel, which had not yet occurred. *Sefer Devarim* famously ends with the death of *Moshe* (Devarim 34:5-12), who never came into the Land. The lesson may be that we must strengthen ourselves when the end result is not apparent; when things seem unsettled. And, more deeply, individuals need to be strong in knowing that as a People we will see the positive end result with the coming of *Moshiach* and the *geulah*. We are a People on a mission over many years.

SEFER VAYIKRA
VAYIKRA

5757

Sefer Vayikra is also known as "Torat Kohanim," the "Law of Priests," since it deals with *korbanot*. There are five *korbanot* mentioned: (1) the "burnt" offering (korban olah); (2) the "peace" offering (korban shelamim); (3) the "sin" offering (korban chatat); (4) the "guilt" offering (korban asham); and (5) the meal offering (korban minchah)

5758

The *pasuk* says "וַיִּקְרָא אֶל מֹשֶׁה וַיְדַבֵּר ה' אֵלָיו מֵאֹהֶל מוֹעֵד לֵאמֹר," "And He called to Moshe and Hashem spoke to him from the Tent of Meeting saying:" (Vayikra 1:1) Why does the *pasuk* mention both "calling" and "speaking"? Rashi indicates that before commanding *Moshe*, *Hashem* would call "Moshe, Moshe" out of endearment. But then why does the *pasuk* read "called to" rather than simply "called" *Moshe*? Here Rashi states that *Hashem's* powerful Voice went only to *Moshe* and not to *Bnei Yisrael*. (Rashi on Vayikra 1:1)

5759

The root of *korban* is "karov," "close." We use the *korbanot* to draw closer to *Hashem* through two main aspects: (1) sprinkling the blood of the *korban* represents the "mitzvot asei," the positive commandments, which require that we "heat up" our blood to do them. (2) burning the fat of the *korban* represents the "mitzvot lo ta'asei," the negative commands, which require us to sit back lazily until the desire to transgress passes. *Hashem* gave us *korbanot* because we got it backwards. We rushed to do that which the negative commandments prohibit and we sat back lazily in regard to those things that are positively commanded. This is like the woman whose husband, a diamond merchant, went to the *beit midrash* and told her not to disturb him. When a customer came to the home to make a substantial purchase, she did not summon her husband, yet when a lender came to collect a debt she urgently called for her husband to return home. She had her priorities exactly backwards.

5760

Rabbi Yosef Kalatsky – Our Sages state that the descendants of *Rachel* are uniquely positioned and qualified to wage war with *Amalek*. This is based on *Rachel's* understanding of how to transcend the physical/material aspects of the world. *Rachel*, her son *Yosef* and Queen *Esther* (of the Tribe of *Binyamin*) were of unparalleled beauty. Despite this physical characteristic, *Rachel* (and *Yosef*) successfully subdued their physical aspects for spiritual elevation (for example, *Yosef* ran away from the advances of his master's wife). That skill/*middah* is the only remedy for combatting *Amalek*, a people solely focused on the physical and entirely uninterested in the spiritual, G-dly pursuits. On *Shabbat Zachor* we are commanded to remember that *Amalek* attacked the weak of Bnei Yisrael and "he did not fear G-d." (Devarim 25:18) *Amalek* made an assessment based on purely physical criteria: the weak and old of *Bnei Yisrael* were worth attacking, but the strong and young were to be avoided. Such a people are like the thief who steals in the nighttime when no one will see or know. They fear people but not an all-seeing Creator. Their perspective is materiality and physicality. *Rachel, Yosef* and *Esther* come to show us that physicality is an illusion: that true *emet* lies in *Avodat Hashe*m, and with that approach, *Amalek* can be defeated.

The *pasuk* says "אֲשֶׁר נָשִׂיא יֶחֱטָא וְעָשָׂה אַחַת מִכָּל מִצְוֹת ה׳ אלקיו אֲשֶׁר לֹא תֵעָשֶׂינָה בִּשְׁגָגָה וְאָשֵׁם," "When ("asher") a ruler [inadvertently] sins and does the prohibited through error." (Vayikra 4:22) Rashi on this *pasuk* says "asher" should be read as "ashrei," meaning "fortunate." The generation whose ruler directs his heart to bring an atonement for inadvertent sins is truly fortunate, for this is an indication that he will admit intentional sins. The recent examples of Bill Clinton (and improper interactions with a subordinate) and Pope Benedict (and his former involvement in Hitler Youth) are indicative of an unfortunate generation.

5761

Rabbi Yaacov Menken – *Hashem* called to *Moshe*, yet *Moshe* intentionally wrote the word "Vayikra" with a small aleph at its end, implying it should be read "vayikar Moshe," which is calling by coincidence (according to Rashi), in the same manner that Hashem called to *Bilaam*. (Rashi on Vayikra 1:1) *Moshe's* modesty was such that he wanted it to appear that he was contacted by *Hashem* by default, not with the language by which He calls to angels.

5762

Rabbi Yossi Jankovits – No honey or *chametz* is allowed on the *Mizbeach* for *korbanot*, because *Hashem* rejects the sweet (i.e. comfortable) and we should never delay (leavening takes time) in serving *Hashem*.

5763

Rabbi Yochanan Zweig – The *pasuk* says "אֲשֶׁר נָשִׂיא יֶחֱטָא וְעָשָׂה אַחַת מִכָּל מִצְוֹת ה' אלקיו אֲשֶׁר לֹא תֵעָשֶׂינָה בִּשְׁגָגָה וְאָשֵׁם," "If a leader sins and unintentionally commits one of all the commandments of Hashem, which may not be committed, incurring guilt." (Vayikra 4:22) Here the *Torah* uses exact language in employing the term "nasi" for "leader," rather than "melech," as each term represents a different aspect of a Jewish ruler. A "nasi" implies the "lifting up" of something, meaning the leader sets the standard of ethical behavior and elevates the People to that example. This makes sense given the context of a ruler admitting a mistake and publicly atoning for it. The "melech" is the political attribute that derives power from the People, which does not apply in questions of ethics. There is no such thing in Judaism (in distinction to America) as screening a potential Supreme Court justice to ensure he holds the moral positions of the people. A true "nasi" possesses *Torah* true ethics and inspires the People to his *madraygah*.

Rabbi Yossi Jankovits – The Midrash Tanchuma (Ki Tisa 37) says that when *Moshe* descended from *Har Sinai* the rays of light that came from his face were a product of the extra ink that remained after completing the writing of the *Torah*, which *Moshe* placed on his forehead. The Iturei Torah states that there was extra ink remaining because *Moshe* made a small "aleph" in the word "ויקרא." Based on this explanation, *Moshe* demonstrated the *halachah* that one may make the letters of a *Sefer Torah* of various sizes and it is still kosher.

5764

Rabbi Shlomo Katz – The second *pasuk* of Parashat Vayikra states "... when a person (adam) among you brings an offering to Hashem ...." (Vayikra 1:2) Rabbi Mordechai Rogow quotes the Zohar, which comments "not the first man and not the last man." This is a reference to *Adam HaRishon* (who had total clarity as to *Hashem* and His Glory) and the "last man" who witnesses *geulah* and, in hindsight, can see clearly the wisdom of *Hashem's* ways. Neither offering is most desired by *Hashem*. Rather, He views with favor that we, those situated in the confusing middle period between the first and last men, are yet able to do our Creator's Will.

5765

Rabbi Yossi Jankovits – What is the connection between *Shabbat Zachor* and *Parashat Vayikra*? We know that "שקול משה כנגד כל ישראל," "Moshe Rabbeinu is comparable to all of Am Yisrael." (Rashi on Shemot 18:1, quoting Mechilta) This can be interpreted to mean he is the representative equivalent of the Jewish People. Therefore, by saying that *Moshe* was specifically called by *Hashem* ("vayikra"), it is as if *Am Yisrael* were specifically called by *Hashem*. This is a refutation of the central philosophy of *Amalek*, namely that there is no *Hashgachah Pratit* in the world. *Amalek* believes in *Hashem*, but only as the Creator not, G-d forbid, as Sustainer and Director of all that happens. Judaism rejects such a view, believing we are called at every moment to do the Will of G-d Who remains an essential and active Force in our lives. This distinction is what we need to "remember" on *Shabbat Zachor*.

5766

Rabbi Yossi Jankovits – The small aleph in the word "ויקרא" is the subject of much commentary. The Baal HaTurim tells us that *Moshe Rabbeinu* was incredibly humble, and was therefore reluctant to draw attention to the fact that *Hashem* called to him by name (which is indicated by the word "vayikra" [Rashi on Vayikra 1:1]). This, however, begs a question: did not *Moshe* realize that in writing the "aleph" smaller than the other letters of the word he would draw attention to the incongruity and, by extension, his humility? Perhaps *Moshe's* modification of the "aleph" is less about himself and more about *Hashem*. *Chazal* tell us that an "aleph" is composed of two "yuds" (top and bottom) and a "vav" connecting them (א). The *gematria* of the intrinsic value of the "aleph" is therefore twenty-six ("vav" equals six, "yud" equals ten), the same value as the ineffable name of *Hashem*. Therefore, we could say that the small "aleph" describes the fact that *Hashem*, as it were, had to make Himself small to speak with *Moshe*! Such an interpretation would be consistent with what we know of *Moshe's* humility, yet would reference the reader not to *Moshe's* greatness in humility but in the awesomeness of *Hashem's* Presence, which the greatest of men can only comprehend in a very limited way.

5769

Rabbi Moshe Soloveitchik – Why does the opening *pasuk* of Parashat Vayikra read "vayikra el Moshe," "and He called to Moshe," rather than stating specifically that *Hashem* called to Moshe?" (Vayikra 1:1) Perhaps the point is that *Hashem* sometimes calls a person without identifying Himself, which suggests that one may choose to heed His "calling," meaning the messages coming from *Hashem*, or, conversely, one can ignore the messages he receives from the Al-mighty. *Moshe* demonstrated at the burning bush and consistently thereafter that he was listening and willing to be called, hence the opening language of this *parashah*.

5770

Rabbi Avraham Aharon Yudelevitch – The *pasuk* describes when an "adam," "man," among you brings an offering. (Vayikra 1:2) Why does the *Torah* here employ the word "adam," as opposed to a similar word like "ish" or "gever?" Interestingly, the word "adam" has no plural form, for it signifies when man is united with his peers. In fact, the *Gemara* (Yevamot 61a) refers to the entire Jewish People as "adam." Sinning distances oneself from the Nation, but through *teshuvah* and bringing an offering, one reconnects to the unity and solidarity of the Nation.

5771

Rabbi Yosef Weinstock – Why are we not allowed to bring a wild, undomesticated yet *tahor* animal as a *korban*? For example, why not a deer or an elk from the wild, each of which is certainly kosher for eating? One answer might be that great energy must be expended to catch such an animal without invalidating it, and while one might believe that such effort in *Avodat Hashem* would be praiseworthy, *Hashem* has specifically indicated through his *Torah* that He does not want such animals brought. This suggests to us that while we may believe a particular course of action is the best way to demonstrate our love for *Hashem*, we must look to His *Torah* and our learned Rabbis for what is, in fact, the proper way.

5772

Reb Moshe Feiglin – On *Shabbat HaChodesh* we read in the *Maftir* the *pasuk* from Parashat Bo "HaChodesh hazeh lachem rosh chadashim ...." "This month shall be for you the beginning of the months ...." (Shemot 12:2). This *pasuk* connects to the first Rashi of the entire *Chumash*, where he famously asks why the Torah starts with the narrative of Creation, rather than with *Rosh Chodesh*, the first *mitzvah* given to the Jewish People. (Rashi on Bereshit 1:1) The implication from the question is that the *Torah* is a book of commandments designed for connecting the

Jewish People to *Hashem*. Rashi brings the famous answer that *Hashem* began the *Torah* with His Creation of the world to allow the Jews to ultimately answer the nations of the world who will question the right of the Jewish People to settle and reside in the Land of Israel. Contained in that answer is a profound thought: while the *Torah* is, in fact, a guide of *mitzvot* for the Jews, the Jews are expected to do all *mitzvot*, starting with *Rosh Chodesh*, in the Land of Israel, and to the extent the nations of the world are intent on denying us access to that Land, we invoke that selfsame *Torah* as the legitimate basis for our presence in the Land. The first Rashi is not merely a "feel good" Zionist *vort*, disconnected from the idea of performing *mitzvot*, it is an undeniable ratification that *mitzvot* are to be performed in *Eretz Yisrael*.

5773

Rabbi Aharon Ziegler – Rav Soloveitchik, quoting the Rosh, indicated that the blessing "Elokai Neshama," which is part of the *siddur's* morning prayers, does not begin with the "Baruch Attah" formation (as is the case with other blessings) because it is connected to the blessing "Asher Yatzar" that precedes it (which <u>does</u> include the "Baruch Attah" wording). Rav Soloveitchik stated that these two *berachot* are connected based on the duality of man that makes him one: a biological essence and a spiritual essence. Accordingly, when we say them one following the other they become one blessing, and no two "Baruch Attah" formulations are necessary or even proper.

TZAV

5757

The original *Shabbat HaGadol* occurred on the Tenth of *Nissan*, on *Shabbat*, of the year the Jews went out of Egypt. This was the day that we were commanded to take a lamb that would ultimately be used as the *Korban Pesach*.

5758

The "Korban Minchah," or Meal Offering, is described in Parashat Tzav. The *minchah* was flour, sometimes mixed with oil and/or incense, and was associated with a poor person. The *pasuk* says "עַל מַחֲבַת בַּשֶּׁמֶן תֵּעָשֶׂה מֻרְבֶּכֶת תְּבִיאֶנָּה תֻּפִינֵי מִנְחַת פִּתִּים תַּקְרִיב רֵיחַ נִיחֹחַ לה'," "It shall be made with oil on a shallow pan, after bringing it scalded and repeatedly baked; A meal offering in broken pieces you shall offer it, as a pleasant fragrance to Hashem." (Vayikra 6:14) Rashi says this means folding the *minchah* twice, once into two parts and again to create four parts. This relates to the honor due a poor person, who brings a meal offering as opposed to an animal. Such a person may feel second class. By folding his offering twice, the *Kohain* fills the pan, thereby making it appear to overflow. Only in regard to a voluntary meal offering does the *Torah* term the offeror as a "nefesh," a "soul," because the *Torah* views such a sacrifice as if the poor man has offered his soul to *Hashem*. (Rashi on Vayikra 2:1)

5759

The words *matzah* (מצה) and *chametz* (חמץ) have virtually the same letters. The only difference is between the "hay" (ה) and the "cheit" (ח), which is merely the small connector on the left side of the letter. This represents the small speck of leaven that we search for in our homes, which is compared to the most minute traces of arrogance that we try to eliminate during the *Pesach* period. The introspection and elimination of our personal spiritual *chametz* ensures our souls will be as kosher as our houses.

5760

The *halachah* tells us that a *keli* that becomes *treif* through cold contact merely requires a cold water rinse to re-kasher, but that for *kaylim* that become *treif* through hot contact, only the application of direct fire can purify. The same concept is true with respect to our *neshamot*. The further one has descended into *treif* conduct and the intensity of the prohibited behavior will dictate the level of intensity by which one must attach to *Torah* and *mitzvot* to redeem and "re-kasher" one's soul.

5761

Rabbi Samson Raphael Hirsch – The *pasuk* says "וּפָשַׁט אֶת בְּגָדָיו וְלָבַשׁ בְּגָדִים אֲחֵרִים וְהוֹצִיא אֶת הַדֶּשֶׁן אֶל מִחוּץ לַמַּחֲנֶה אֶל מָקוֹם טָהוֹר," "And [the Kohain] shall take off his garments and put on other garments and carry forth the ashes out of the camp to a pure place." (Vayikra 6:4) This ceremony occurred every morning, when the ashes from the previous day's *korbanot* would be removed. This ritual expresses the thought that our individual *Torah* mission must be assumed anew each day. Focusing on what has already been accomplished leads to complacency and lack of growth. Every trace of the prior day's sacrifice must be removed.

We are required to learn the portion of *Parah Adumah* prior to *Pesach*, as the ritual was (and again will be) the vehicle for purifying ourselves following contact with the dead, and thereby allowing us to bring the *Korban Pesach*, which may only be offered in a *tahor* state.

5762

Rabbi Yossi Jankovits – The *korbanot* required salt as part of their service. Salt is a preservative, and, homiletically, we seek to preserve the feeling of repentance with which we bring a *korban*. Seeing the *Kohain* salt the *korban* inspired the Jews to retain the feeling of *teshuvah*. In our time, as we recreate the *Mizbeach* at our *Shabbat* and *Yom Tov* tables, it is sensible to include salt to engender this same feeling.

5763

Likutei Kerem Shlomo – The *Torah* tells us that the *olah* is slaughtered in the north. (Vayikra 1:11) The pasuk then tells us "דַּבֵּר אֶל אַהֲרֹן וְאֶל בָּנָיו לֵאמֹר זֹאת תּוֹרַת הַחַטָּאת בִּמְקוֹם אֲשֶׁר תִּשָּׁחֵט הָעֹלָה תִּשָּׁחֵט הַחַטָּאת לִפְנֵי ה' קֹדֶשׁ קָדָשִׁים הוּא," "Speak to Aharon and to his sons, saying, 'This is the law of the chatat: The sin offering shall be slaughtered before Hashem <u>in the place</u>

where the olah is slaughtered. It is a Holy of Holies.'" (Vayikra 6:18) Why does the *Torah* not also say the *chatat* is slaughtered in the north? *Chazal* say that the beginning of sin is thought. One should endeavor to purify his thoughts to avoid sin, for our actions are connected to our original thoughts. This is why the *chatat* is connected not to the north but to the *olah*, because the *olah* atones for one's negative thoughts and the *chatat* atones for one's negative deeds.

5764

Rabbi Avraham Yitzchak Kook – In the *Haftarah* for *Shabbat HaGadol* (and at the end of every *Shemoneh Esrei*), the *pasuk* says "וְעָרְבָה לַה' מִנְחַת יְהוּדָה וִירוּשָׁלָ֥ם כִּימֵי עוֹלָם וּכְשָׁנִים קַדְמֹנִיּוֹת," "Then the minchah offering of Yehudah and Yerushalayim will be pleasing to Hashem, as in days of old and in former years." (Malachi 3:4) Rav Kook indicates that in the future, the animals will have an understanding of *Hashem*, making them *assur* for *korbanot*, just as a proposed human sacrifice would be. Then the *minchah* (flour only) offering will serve in the same manner as the animal offering did in the days of old.

5765

Rabbi Yossi Jankovits – The first part of Parashat Tzav warns the *Kohanim* in detail to be very deliberate concerning the *olah* offering. (Vayikra 6:1, 2) This *korban* is unique insomuch as it is totally burned – there is no portion for the *Kohain* to eat. In that sense, the *olah* is entirely *ruchniut*, as opposed to a mixture of physicality and spirituality. Pure spirituality is dangerous, as it is a conspicuous target for the *yetzer hara*. In fact, throughout Jewish history, *Hashem* has disguised spirituality in contexts involving high levels of physicality in order to "protect" such seeds from detection by the *yetzer hara*. This was true in the story of *Lot* and his daughters (Bereshit 19:30-38), and *Rut* and *Boaz* (Rut 3:8-10), for example. MRF Note – In fact, in such cases, the *yetzer hara* was arguably co-opted to be an unwilling accessory to furthering the spirituality it would have otherwise thought to destroy.

5769

Rabbi Yosef Weinstock – The Baal HaTanya points out that we learn in Parashat Tzav that if meat consecrated to the *Mishkan* or Temple comes in contact with *tumah* it may not be brought on the Altar, but must be burned outside. Similarly, if Holy, consecrated meat comes in contact with an ordinary *tahor* vessel, that vessel becomes sanctified along with the meat and may no longer be used for mundane purposes. Rashi indicates, however, that, for the latter case, heat is required to transfer the Holiness from the meat to the vessel. This underscores the difference between Holiness and impurity. Mere contact transfers impurity but Holiness does not just "rub off." Rather, the transfer of Holiness from one to another requires heat and drive.

5770

Rabbi Yerucham Levovitz – In Parashat Tzav Hashem commands Moshe "וְאֵת כָּל הָעֵדָה הַקְהֵל אֶל פֶּתַח אֹהֶל מוֹעֵד," "Assemble the entire Community at the entrance of the Tent of Meeting." (Vayikra 8:3) Rashi indicates a miracle occurred allowing for millions of people to stand in a small space. The miracle was actually that *Hashem* stretched space to accommodate all the Jews. Space, like time, has no meaning to *Hashem*.

5771

Rabbi Eli Mansour – On *Shabbat Zachor* we are commanded to recall what *Amalek* did to *Bnei Yisrael*. The *gematria* of *Amalek* is 240, which is the same as the word "safek," meaning "doubt." This is demonstrated in the story of *Amalek's* attack. At *Masah u'Merivah*, *Bnei Yisrael* complained about the shortage of water, stating "hayesh Hashem b'kirbenu im ayin," "is Hashem in our midst or not?" (Shemot 17:7) The immediate next pasuk says "וַיָּבֹא עֲמָלֵק וַיִּלָּחֶם עִם יִשְׂרָאֵל בִּרְפִידִם," "and Amalek came and fought with Yisrael at Rephidim." (Shemot 17:8) *Amalek* came right then, following the open doubt expressed by the Jewish People. *Amalek* comes when the Jews express doubt. What is the antidote? In *Pirkei Avot* the *Mishnah* says "aseh lecha Rav, v'histalek min hasafek, ..." "find yourself a Rabbi and remove yourself from doubt ...." (Avot 1:16) Establishing a competent *Rav* will remove all doubt from one's observation, which will, in turn, eliminate *Amalek* from our lives.

5772

Rabbi Yossi Jankovits – Why, except in a leap year, when there is a second *Adar*, is Parashat Tzav always read on *Shabbat HaGadol*, immediately prior to *Pesach*? Perhaps this is because Tzav outlines the *Korban Todah*, which is brought based on one of four occurrences: (1) getting out of prison; (2) crossing a sea; (3) crossing a desert and (4) having a recovery from an illness. These bases for the *Todah* can be recalled by the acronym "חיי״ם‎," where the "cheit" stands for "cholim," "sick persons," the "yud" stands for "yisurim," or "captives," the second "yud" stands for "yam," "sea," and the "mem" stands for "midbar," or "desert." These elements were all at work in the Exodus story, for which *Bnei Yisrael* must show gratitude on *Pesach*. We, in chronological order, (1) got out of jail (*Mitzrayim*); (2) crossed the *Yam Suf*; (3) crossed the *midbar*; and (4) at *Har Sinai*, experienced a *refuah* for all maladies and illnesses the Jews had at that time.

5773

Rabbi Moshe Meir Weiss – There were three major miracles in the *midbar* (the *Be'er Miriam*/Miriam's Well, the *Mon*/Manna and the *Anaini HaKavod*/Clouds of Glory), yet we only formally commemorate the Clouds (during *Sukkot*). The Chida indicates that the *Be'er Miriam* and the *Mon* came about through complaining, and therefore were not worthy of commemoration, but not so with the Clouds of Glory, for which the holiday of *Sukkot* was established.

SHEMINI

5757

We can never know the full reason for a particular *mitzvah*. The highest level of *mitzvah* observance is to do it because *Hashem* so commanded us.

5758

Nadav and *Avihu* were undone by fire, *Moshe* and *Aharon*, to a lesser extent, were undone by water. In Parashat Shemini, *Nadav* and *Avihu* brought a foreign fire to the Incense Altar at a time at which they were not commanded to do so. (Vayikra 10:1) In Parashat Chukat, *Moshe* and *Aharon* were commanded to speak to the rock that it should provide water for *Bnei Yisrael*, but Moshe struck it instead. (Bamidbar 20:9-13)

5759

The exact midpoint of the *Torah* based on a counting of words is in Parashat Shemini, in the pasuk "וְאֵת | שְׂעִיר הַחַטָּאת דָּרֹשׁ דָּרַשׁ מֹשֶׁה וְהִנֵּה שֹׂרָף וַיִּקְצֹף עַל אֶלְעָזָר וְעַל אִיתָמָר בְּנֵי אַהֲרֹן הַנּוֹתָרִם לֵאמֹר," between the words "darosh" and "darash," meaning "[Moshe] thoroughly inquired." (Vayikra 10:16) By placing the midpoint between these two words, the *Torah* may be calling to our attention that rigorous inquiry is required in *Torah*, and that in every generation there should be *Torah*-based inquiry and discovery.

The *Gemara* (Kiddushin 30a) tells us that the midpoint of the *Torah* with respect to letters is the large "Vav" in the word "גָּחוֹן" "gachon," meaning "belly [of a creeping, non-Kosher animal]." (Vayikra 11:42)

Rabbi Shmuel Choueka – The *pasuk* warns *Bnei Yisrael* against contaminating themselves and eating vermin, explaining "כִּי | אֲנִי ה' הַמַּעֲלֶה אֶתְכֶם מֵאֶרֶץ מִצְרַיִם לִהְיֹת לָכֶם לֵאלֹקִים וִהְיִיתֶם קְדֹשִׁים כִּי קָדוֹשׁ אָנִי," "For I am Hashem Who brought you up from the land of Mitzrayim to be a G-d unto you. Thus, you shall be Holy, because I am Holy." (Vayikra 11:45). Normally the *Torah* says "hamotzie," "Who brought you out," but here, in describing the kosher food laws, the word is "hama'aleh" "Who brought you up." The lesson might be that strict adherence to *kashrut* has a uniquely uplifting effect on the Jew.

5760

The Rashbam tells us that when *Nadav* and *Avihu* died, *Moshe* approached *Aharon* and said that he must go forward with the *Avodah* of the *Kohain*

Gadol. He explained that *Aharon* could create a *Kiddush Hashem* by not mourning for his sons. Specifically, the *pasuk* states "וַיֹּאמֶר מֹשֶׁה אֶל אַהֲרֹן הוּא אֲשֶׁר דִּבֶּר ה' | לֵאמֹר בִּקְרֹבַי אֶקָּדֵשׁ וְעַל פְּנֵי כָל הָעָם אֶכָּבֵד וַיִּדֹּם אַהֲרֹן", "Then Moshe said to Aharon, 'This is what Hashem spoke of, "I will be sanctified through those near to Me, and before all the People I will be glorified."' And Aharon was silent." (Vayikra 10:3) *Moshe* was telling *Aharon* that through his silent acceptance of *Hashem's* decision to take away his sons, *Aharon* would sanctify and glorify *Hashem*. "Those close to Me" is not a reference to *Nadav* and *Avihu* but to *Aharon*. This recalls a story about the Alter of Slabodka whose two sons died during *Sukkot*. The Alter rejoiced until he said "hamavdil bein kodesh l'chol" "Who distinguishes between the Holy and the mundane" during *Havdalah* following *Simchat Torah*, and then he collapsed from despair. While we are not on such a level, we can all aspire to create a *Kiddush Hashem* when faced with adversity.

Moshe assembled and disassembled the *Mishkan* for seven full days, and then finally assembled it on the eighth day. This was an acknowledgement that it took seven generations to bring the *Shechinah* back into the world: *Avraham, Yitzchak, Yaacov, Levy, Kehat, Amram* and *Moshe*.

Rabbi Yisroel Ciner – The *pasuk* says "וַיֹּאמֶר מֹשֶׁה אֶל אַהֲרֹן קְרַב אֶל הַמִּזְבֵּחַ וַעֲשֵׂה אֶת חַטָּאתְךָ וְאֶת עֹלָתֶךָ וְכַפֵּר בַּעַדְךָ וּבְעַד הָעָם וַעֲשֵׂה אֶת קָרְבַּן הָעָם וְכַפֵּר בַּעֲדָם כַּאֲשֶׁר צִוָּה ה'," "And Moshe said to Aharon 'draw close to the Altar and offer your Sin Offering and your Elevation Offering, and atone for yourself and the Nation. Then perform the service of the Nation's offering and provide atonement for them, as Hashem has commanded.'" (Vayikra 9:7) *Chazal* say that *Aharon* was afraid and embarrassed to draw close due to his involvement in the sin of the golden calf. Rashi indicates that *Moshe* told him "Why are you embarrassed, for this you have been chosen." (Rashi on Vayikra 9:7) The Imrei Emes, quoting Rav Chaim Vital, says that every person has a life mission: the reason his *neshamah* was sent to this world. The areas of difficulty that challenge us in our lives are indications of the exact areas requiring *tikkun*. The Vilna Gaon says that those areas that either pull us strongly the wrong way or upon which we have often stumbled are such indicators. MRF Note – As a rabbi once told me; those things that you think are <u>in</u> your way, are not <u>in</u> your way, they <u>are</u> your way.

5761

Rabbi Eli Mansour – The *Parah Adumah* is a *chok*, which trains us to accept illogical adversity in our lives. The *mitzvah* of *Parah Adumah* was specifically not given to Aharon, but instead to his son *Elazar* (Bamidbar 19:3), specifically because *Aharon* did not need its lesson. Upon the otherwise incomprehensible death of his other two sons *Nadav* and *Avihu*, *Aharon* was silent, accepting *Hashem's* decree. (Vayikra 10:3)

In Parashat Shemini, we learn that there are two signs that an animal is kosher: split hooves (an outer indication) and chewing the cud (an inner indication). (Vayikra 11:3) The lesson from this is that for a Jew to be kosher he must be *frum* on the outside as well as on the inside.

5762

Rabbi Yossi Jankovits – There is a *Midrash Peliah* which states that *Aharon's zechut* in remaining silent in the face of the deaths of *Nadav* and *Avihu* (Vayikra 10:3), was based on the fact that he had a valid claim against *Hashem* but remained silent nonetheless. *Aharon* reasoned that the fire brought by *Nadav* and *Avihu* (Vayikra 10:1) made them both partners in Creation with *Hashem*. Like in the case of a *brit milah* or in harvesting wheat for bread, *Hashem* requires the action of man to perfect his Creation. Bringing the fire may, arguably, have served this function. *Aharon* is credited by the *Midrash* because he could have raised this claim yet did not.

Rabbi Yossi Jankovits – At the end of Parashat Mishpatim, the pasuk tells us "וְאֶל אֲצִילֵי בְּנֵי יִשְׂרָאֵל לֹא שָׁלַח יָדוֹ וַיֶּחֱזוּ אֶת הָאלקים וַיֹּאכְלוּ וַיִּשְׁתּוּ," "And upon the nobles of Bnei Yisrael He did not lay His Hand, and they perceived

HaElokim, and they ate and drank." (Shemot 24:11) Rashi tells us that *Nadav, Avihu* and the Seventy Elders went up *Har Sinai* and gazed at Hashem with arrogant hearts. The penalty for *Nadav* and *Avihu* was delayed until Hashem imposed it in Parashat Shemini, so as to not diminish the joy of receiving the *Torah*. The *zakainim* were killed later in the episode of *Korach*.

Rabbi Yossi Jankovits – There are many opinions as to what sin *Nadav* and *Avihu* committed that warranted their deaths, yet the Chasam Sofer suggests that all might be reconciled with one: they failed to marry and have children. Raising children provides an invaluable insight into improper *derech eretz*. Actions like, for example, being publicly intoxicated or stating a *halachah* in front of one's *Rebbe*, display childish behavior that *Nadav* and *Avihu* may have avoided if they had seen the same conduct in their own children.

5763

Rabbi Yisroel Ciner – The pasuk says "מַפְרֶסֶת פַּרְסָה וְשֹׁסַעַת שֶׁסַע פְּרָסֹת מַעֲלַת גֵּרָה בַּבְּהֵמָה אֹתָהּ תֹּאכֵלוּ," "Any animal that has a split hoof that is completely split into double hooves, and which brings up its cud, that one you may eat." (Vayikra 11:3) The kosher status of three particular animals is connected to the three main cultures at odds in the modern world. Split hooves represent healthy forward progress and chewing the cud represents an appreciation of the historical past. The Western World descended from *Edom/Eisav* is represented by the pig, which has split hooves but does not chew its cud, thereby displaying an emphasis on the future but no appreciation of the past. The Arab world descended from *Yishmael* is represented by the camel, which chews its cud but has no split hooves, being a regressive culture mired only in the past, without hope of advancement. Only the Jews, represented by the split hooved, cud-chewing cow, blend the value of our amazing past with hopeful yearning for the future, making us worthy to eat the animals that reflect this superior world view.

5764

Rabbi Edward Davis (on *Yom HaShoah*) – According to Rashi, when *Nadav* and *Avihu* died, *Moshe* indicated to *Aharon* that they were martyrs greater than both of them. (Rashi on Vayikra 10:3) The Six Million Martyrs of the Holocaust are also to be regarded as greater to the person than any of us now living.

5765

Rabbi Eli Mansour – Rabbi Dovid Feinstein indicates that Parashat Shemini begins by stating that the inauguration of the *Mishkan* was the eighth day (Vayikra 9:1), which is to say that *Moshe* and the Jews prepared seven days for the inauguration. If the true essence of the day was the fact that the *Mishkan* was erected and put into service, the *parashah* would have been called "rishon," "first" based on the first day it was operational. The fact that the *Torah* pays notice to the seven days that proceeded the first day of operation teaches us an important lesson. There is tremendous worth in preparing to perform a *mitzvah*, and that preparation should be noticed and valued. This is critical as we move towards *Pesach*, the most demanding of holidays in terms of preparations.

5768

Rabbi Yosef Weinstock – *Moshe* is credited by *Chazal* for admitting to *Aharon* that he did not recall the law of the *onen* (Rashi on Vayikra 10:20), but why should this be a merit? Do we expect less of *Moshe*, our great leader? Perhaps this is actually a credit to *Bnei Yisrael*, for Moshe felt he could admit to them that he had forgotten a *halachah* without fear that it would undermine their faith in him as a leader and the system he was propounding. Perhaps the merit of *Moshe* is that as a savvy and truth-based leader, he knew that the People could handle his admission.

5769

Rabbi Yosef Kalatsky – In describing the prohibition of consuming non-kosher animals the *pasuk* reads "אַל תְּשַׁקְּצוּ אֶת נַפְשֹׁתֵיכֶם בְּכָל הַשֶּׁרֶץ הַשֹּׁרֵץ וְלֹא תִטַּמְּאוּ בָּהֶם וְנִטְמֵתֶם בָּם," "Do not make your souls abominable by means of any creeping thing; do not <u>contaminate</u> yourselves through them lest you become <u>contaminated</u> through them." (Vayikra 11:43) In response to the obvious redundancy, the *Gemara* (Yoma 39a) tells us "v'nitmatim" should be read as "v'nitamtem," meaning closed or sealed (note that v'nitmatim is missing an aleph). The message is that consumption of non-kosher food seals the spiritual pipeline between *Hashem* and the Jew. Just as a Jew must aspire to "circumcise his heart" to remove impediments to spirituality, he must also be cautious that physical acts such as eating do not create additional spiritual impediments to connecting to *Hashem*.

5770

Rabbi Zalman Sorotzkin – There were three miraculous occasions in the history of the world when all animals appeared in a single place. The first was when *Adam HaRishon* named all the animals based on their essence. (Rashi on Bereshit 2:19) The second time was when Noach was preparing the *Teivah*. (Rashi on Bereshit 6:20) Here in Parashat Shemini, all animals (including the fish!) appeared before *Moshe* and he identified each as kosher or *treif* for *Bnei Yisrael*. (Rashi on Vayikra 11:2) Each of these moments represented a historical shift of major importance. In the case of *Moshe*, this was the crowning moment of Creation, when *Hashem's* Chosen People were instructed to sanctify Creation by eating the permissible animals in the permissible manner.

5771

Rebbetzin Dr. Pnina Neuwirth – In *Shir HaShirim*, as interpreted by Rabbi Joseph B. Soloveitchik, the maiden misses the great moment of greeting her beloved because she delays. She has an idealized mental image of the beloved and their moment of first meeting, and she therefore delays in seizing the moment when it presents itself. This is precisely the problem with observant Jews in relating to the modern State of Israel. We cannot let idealized notions of what the Land at the time of Redemption would be like keep us from embracing the moment and opportunity that *Hashem* has given to *Am Yisrael*. Instead we must seize the moment where our Beloved [Land] is awaiting us.

5772

Rabbi Avi Weiss – The unquestionable reason for the laws of *kashrut*, as stated by the *Torah* itself, is *Kedushah*, Holiness. (Vayikra 11:44) There are two aspects to *Kedushah*, one being separation or segregation, and the other being transcendence of the Jew through channeling passions and limiting himself in what are otherwise permissible things. There are three major *mitzvot* that are regarded as fundamental to Jewish life: (1) keeping *Shabbat*; (2) keeping *Taharat HaMishpachah*; and (3) keeping *kashrut*. These three *mitzvot* correspond to the three major physical drives of man: (1) to be powerful; (2) to engage in sexual relations; and (3) the desire to eat. The *Torah* does not insist that a Jew abstain in any of these areas, but allows them within permissible boundaries. Power comes from controlling our environment, and for one day out of seven, on *Shabbat*, a Jew cannot do so. On the issue of intimate relations, we must not engage during the time a woman is *niddah*. And while food is delicious and plentiful, thank G-d, some animals and combinations are off limits. The principle of *Kedushah* is at work within this system.

5773

Rabbi Moshe Weinberger – The controversy of propriety of *Nadav* and *Avihu's* strange fire (Vayikra 10:1) is reflected in the disagreement between the Imrei Emes and Rav Avraham Yitzchak Kook. The Imrei Emes believed that, like *Nadav* and *Avhiu*, the modern Zionists disregarded the Elders of their generation and acted impermissibly in establishing the State of Israel. Rav Kook held that, in the absence of a prophet, a generation may transgress and break boundaries to achieve transcendent Holiness, as with settling the Land.

TAZRIA

5759

Parashat Tazria describes the affliction of *tzaraat*, which, contrary to the popular understanding, is not a physical disease but rather is a spiritual malady with physical manifestations. Rashi makes clear that a cause of *tzaraat* is *lashon hara*. (Rashi on Vayikra 13:46) "Evil talk" can be classified into three categories: *lashon hara*, which is true defamatory or harmful speech; *motzei shem ra*, which is untrue defamatory or harmful speech; and *rechilut*, which is speech that can cause strife between Jews. There are seventeen *Torah* violations connected to speaking or listening to *lashon hara*.

Rabbi Edward Davis – About the *metzora*, the *pasuk* says "... v'tamei tamei yikra," "and 'contaminated, contaminated' he shall call out." (Vayikra 13:45) The *Gemara* (Moed Katan 5a) indicates that the double language reflects the two reasons the *metzora* so shouts. The first is so that the community will exclude the individual based on his antisocial behavior, and the second is a plea for forgiveness and for the community to *daven* on his behalf. Rashi cites only the former reason and ignores the latter. Rashi is consistent with the *pasuk* that follows, which reads, in part, "badad yayshaiv," "he shall stay in isolation." (Vayikra 13:46) Ignoring the suggestion that the declaration of the *metzora* is intended to promote empathy, the double language of the original *pasuk* can be read simply as "and the tamei [i.e. metzora] shall call out 'tamei' [i.e. 'I am contaminated']."

5760

Rabbi Yisroel Ciner – Parashat Tazria opens with the laws of *tumah* related to a woman who gives birth. For fourteen days after giving birth to a girl, a woman is *tamei*, while, according to the *Torah*, she is only *tamei* for seven days following the birth of a boy. (Vayikra 12:2, 5) Moreover, she must bring a *korban* for the birth of a girl after eighty days, but for a boy the time is forty days. (Vayikra 12:1-8) Such distinctions have been unfairly used by "progressive" thinking critics of Judaism as proof a woman's subordinated status in the religion. The truth is actually the opposite. Judaism deals with potential – the potential to do good, defined as emulating and drawing closer to *Hashem*. This is specifically accomplished by performance of the *mitzvot*, while we are able. When we lose the potential for closeness to *Hashem* (defined as *Kedushah*) the void created by such a loss is replaced with *tumah* (in essence, un-Holiness). This is why, says the Ohr HaChaim (Bamidbar 19:2), a Jewish corpse is more *tamei* than a gentile corpse: the lost potential is greater. This is also why when a Jew sleeps and is incapable of performing *mitzvot*, a *ruach ra'ah* fills his body (the *Gemara* [Berachot 57b] tells us that sleep is 1/60th of death due to the soul's partial departure from the body). Sleep leaves a residual *tumah* that must be ritually removed through *netilat yadayim*. Having a baby is perhaps the closest a human can come to emulating *Hashem*, the Ultimate Creator. After birth, the void left from the departure of this creation is replaced with real and substantial *tumah*. When the baby is a girl, in essence another potential creator, the potential, and hence the *tumah*, is doubled.

Rabbi Yissocher Frand – Rabbi Nissan Alpert took note of the *Torah's* use of the word "adam" (rather than the expected "ish") when introducing the concept of the "man" who becomes a *metzora*. (Vayikra 13:2) "Adam" is typically viewed as a term of greater prestige than "ish," but why would one that speaks *lashon hara*, and thereby becomes a *metzora*, be honored in such a manner? This is to show us that the problem of *lashon hara* can afflict anyone, even the elevated, yet the true "adam" is the one who learns the lesson of the *tzaraat* and desires to change.

Parashat Tazria contains the *pasuk* that forms one basis of the tradition of taking a haircut on *Lag B'Omer*. The thirty-third (לג) verse of *perek* thirteen begins "v'hitgalach ... ," "then he shall be shaven...." (Vayikra 13:33)

5761

What is the reason that the *Torah* requires a woman to bring a *chatat* following childbirth? One answer is that when she is experiencing the pain of childbirth she recalls all her past sins for which she must then atone. A second answer, given by Shem MiShmuel, is that the *korban* is an atonement for the original sin of *Chavah*. Finally, the *Gemara* (Niddah 31b) tells us that in the pains of labor she swears not to have relations again, a sin for which she must subsequently atone (separate from the necessity of formally annulling such a vow).

5762

Reb Tevi Hirschhorn – The Chofetz Chaim points out that what makes an erstwhile *metzora tamei* or *tahor* is the literal declaration of the *Kohain* who inspects him. (Vayikra 13:3) This provides the *metzora* with an understanding of the powerful effect of words, which is a necessary lesson considering that the condition is brought on by improper use of words through *lashon hara.*

5763

Rabbi Yissocher Frand – The *Torah* dictates that a woman is *tamei*, and therefore Biblically forbidden to her husband, seven days after the birth of a boy. (Vayikra 12:2) The *Gemara* (Niddah 31b) indicates that a boy's *brit milah* takes place on the eighth day following his birth because to do so sooner would dampen the *simchah* surrounding the occasion. For during the first seven days following a birth, a husband and wife would be saddened for being prohibited to one another and that mood would transfer to the guests as well. From here we see the sensitivity of the *Torah* in maximizing a couple's happiness.

5764

Rabbi Yossi Jankovits – The connection between the end of Parashat Shemini and the beginning of Parashat Tazria is obvious. Shemini ends with a discussion of the eating of kosher creatures and Tazria opens with the issue of conception and giving birth. What a woman eats during pregnancy has an effect, for the good (if permissible) or for the bad (if prohibited), not only on her, but also on her unborn child.

5765

Yalkut Shimoni – The *Haftarah* for Parashat Tazria (II Melachim 4:42-5:19) tells the story of *Naaman*, the gentile general, who battled both haughtiness and *tzaraat*. He was great in his ability to recognize the truth, as was evidenced when he famously declared "Now I know that there is no G-d in the whole world, except in Yisrael ...." (5:15) This recognition was greater than that of *Yitro*, who recognized *Hashem* as above all powers by stating "Now I know that Hashem is greater than all the gods, ..." (Shemot 18:11) and of *Rachav*, who recognized *Hashem* as the Source of all powers by declaring "... Hashem, your G-d, He is G-d in the heavens above and the earth below." (Yehoshua 2:11) *Naaman* recognized *Hashem* as the Only Power, as it is said "אין עוד מלבדו" "there is nothing other than Him." (Melachim remez 229)

5768

Rabbi Yossi Jankovits – The *Gemara* comments (Niddah 31b) that the reason a *brit milah* is performed on the eighth day following the birth of a boy is that, according to *Torah* law, for seven days a woman is *tamei* and *Hashem* wants to optimize the *simchah* of the occasion by allowing husband and wife to have physical contact at the party. Yet another way to view this reality is perhaps to say that, based on the immutable laws of the universe, since a *bris* must be held on the eighth day, the *tamei* period of a woman is only seven days following the birth of a boy! MRF Note – This is akin to the contention of Rabbi Akiva Tatz that shellfish are *treif* not because they are found on the bottom of the ocean; rather they were placed by *Hashem* at the bottom of the ocean because they are *treif*!

5771

Reb Aaron Moses – The Sefer Yetzirah (2:7) states that there is nothing greater than "עֹנֶג", "joy," and nothing lower than "נֶגַע", "affliction," as described throughout Parashat Tazria. *Oneg* is associated with *Shabbat*. The Midrash Shocher Tov (Tehillim 92) notes that *Shabbat* has many aspects that are "doubled": for example, the *Tehillah* for the day begins "Mizmor shiur," literally, "a song, a song"; *korbanot* are doubled; we use two loaves of bread for *hamotzi*; the *Talmud* indicates we get a second soul (Beitzah 16a); and the language of *Shabbat* is doubled – "shamor v'zachor, "guard and remember" the *Shabbat*. According to Shem MiShmuel, we see that the very essence of *Shabbat* is doubled. The Jewish People are all equal with regard to the negative prohibitions of *Shabbat* (those commandments subject to "shamor," "guarding" *Shabbat*). On the other hand, *Shabbat* is called "m'ein Olam Haba," "a taste of the World to Come," where everyone obtains a reward based on individual positive *mitzvah* performance, including on *Shabbat* (those commandments subject to "zachor," "remembering" and honoring *Shabbat*). There are two aspects demonstrated here: national unity and personal achievement, both of which are manifested on *Shabbat*. The *metzora* is disqualified in both regards. He is banished from the camp to enforced solitude, disconnecting him from the national purpose. Furthermore, he is locked away for a week, sometimes two, reflecting an individualized penalty as well. Now we understand the Sefer Yetzirah: there is nothing so exalted for the Jew as the *oneg* of *Shabbat* or as low as the *nega* of *tzaraat*.

5772

Rabbi J. Simcha Cohen – Parashat Tazria begins with the discussion of the birth of a child. There is a tradition that a *Shalom Zachor* is held on the first *Shabbat* night following the birth of a boy. The Tanna D'vei Eliyahu (Rabba 26) notes the juxtaposition of the fourth and fifth commands of the *Aseret HaDibrot*. The fourth command, to keep the *Shabbat*, is testimony that *Hashem* ceased creating on that day. Had He not done so, humans would never have been granted the power to create. As such, the fifth command of honoring one's parents, who clearly engaged in creation, is connected to and dependent on the fourth. It is therefore appropriate to celebrate the birth/creation of a child (even a girl) on the day that made it possible – *Shabbat*!

METZORA

5758

Parashat Metzora begins "This is the law of the metzora ... ," (Vayikra 14:2) The *Talmud* tells us in the name of *Reish Lakish* (Arachin 15b) that "metzora" is a conjunction of "motzi shem ra," which is one who slanders another. This follows from the fact that a primary cause of *tzaraat* is speaking *lashon hara*.

Parashat Metzora is sometimes read on *Shabbat HaGadol*, the *Shabbat* that immediately precedes *Pesach*. *Shabbat HaGadol* took place in *Mitzrayim* on the Tenth of *Nissan*, when the Jews led lambs through the streets in preparation for slaughter. The Egyptians were infuriated, for they viewed the lamb as one of their gods, yet miraculously, they never uttered as much as a murmur in protest. Such an event is surely worth commemorating, but why do so on *Shabbat*, rather than on the Tenth of *Nissan* when it occurred? Baal HaTurim (Shemot 10:14) notes that each of the plagues would cease on *Shabbat* in honor of *Shabbat*. Insofar as the taking of the lambs by the Jews occurred during the Plague of Darkness, according to Ramban (Shemot 10:4), *Bnei Yisrael* was required to take them on *Shabbat* so that the Egyptians could see the procession (and feel the angst of having their god humiliated in anticipation of being sacrificed). Incidentally, although the *Mitzrim* were rendered powerless by *Hashem* to react, the Jews were unaware of that fact, adding a great measure of courage to their trust in following *Hashem's* command.

Rabbi Kenneth Auman – Parashat Metzora is often read close to *Yom HaAzmaut*, which celebrates the creation of *Medinat Yisrael*. Israeli Independence Day is significantly different from America's Fourth of July,

which is apparent from verses in Parashat Metzora which reads "כִּי תָבֹאוּ
אֶל אֶרֶץ כְּנַעַן אֲשֶׁר אֲנִי נֹתֵן לָכֶם לַאֲחֻזָּה וְנָתַתִּי נֶגַע צָרַעַת בְּבֵית אֶרֶץ אֲחֻזַּתְכֶם" "When
you come to the land of Canaan, which I am giving you as a <u>possession</u>,
and I place a lesion of tzaraat upon a house in the Land of your <u>posses-</u>
<u>sion</u>." (Vayikra 14:34) Twice in this *pasuk* the word "achuzah" is used,
denoting a "holding." Israel is not for the Jewish People to own or even
possess for our sake, but rather we are commanded to hold it for *Hashem*,
as His representatives. Therefore we must hold it for His Glory, and we
can never let it go.

5759

Why did the *Torah* decree that antisocial behavior results in *tzaraat*? Society
is established not for smooth functioning social order but so people can be
kind and caring to one another. Someone who has forgotten or disregarded
this ideal must be separated from society. By shouting "contaminated,
contaminated!" as required by the *Torah*, he publicly informs society "shut
me out!" (Rashi on Vayikra 13:45)

The Torah commands that the *metzora* shave all his hair, and then outlines
that he must shave his (1) head, (2) beard, and (3) eyebrows. (Vayikra 14:9)
Why the particular directive when the initial general command would
suffice? Perhaps to teach us the hair associated with these three areas is
of particular concern. The beard surrounds the mouth, which is guilty
of *lashon hara*. The head is often held high in a state of haughtiness. The
eyebrows are adjacent to the eyes, which are narrowed with jealousy. As
all these areas are likely to have contributed to the *tzaraat* that a *metzora*
experiences, the *Torah* is providing him with guidance for the future.

5760

Kli Yakar – The word "metzora" is a conjunction of the words "motzi," to
take out, and "ra," evil. The *metzora* displays the physical manifestations
of an underlying spiritual evil. (Shemot 14:2)

5761

Rabbi Yissocher Frand – The *pasuk* states "וְצִוָּה הַכֹּהֵן וְלָקַח לַמִּטַּהֵר שְׁתֵּי צִפֳּרִים חַיּוֹת טְהֹרוֹת וְעֵץ אֶרֶז וּשְׁנִי תוֹלַעַת וְאֵזֹב" "Then the Kohain shall order, and the person to be cleansed shall take two live, clean birds, a cedar stick, a strip of crimson wool, and hyssop." (Vayikra 14:4) With respect to the *metzora's* obligation to bring two birds, the Zohar states that one atones for bad speech and one atones for good speech. One can understand why bad speech requires atonement, but why good speech? The Shemen Hatov says that the *aveirah* stems not from engaging in good speech, but in abstaining from providing necessary and appropriate compliments and greetings to fellow Jews.

5762

Rabbi Yochanan Zweig – The *pasuk* states "כִּי תָבֹאוּ אֶל אֶרֶץ כְּנַעַן אֲשֶׁר אֲנִי נֹתֵן לָכֶם לַאֲחֻזָּה וְנָתַתִּי נֶגַע צָרַעַת בְּבֵית אֶרֶץ אֲחֻזַּתְכֶם" "When you arrive in the land of Canaan that I give you as a possession, and I will place a tzaraat affliction upon a house in the Land of your possession, ... " (Vayikra 14:34) Here Rashi indicates that the *tzaraat* that afflicts the house will be a "good tiding" to [the Jews] ... because the *Emori* hid treasures of gold in the walls of their houses all forty years that *Bnei Yisrael* was in the desert, and as a result of the *tzaraat*, the Jews will break the walls and find the treasure. Why are the *Emori* mentioned (rather than the Canaanites, whom the *Torah* declares to be the owners of the Land), and why the specific mention of the forty years? During the *Brit Bein Habetarim* of Parashat Lech Lecha, the *Torah* states, "וַיֹּאמֶר לְאַבְרָם יָדֹעַ תֵּדַע כִּי גֵר | יִהְיֶה זַרְעֲךָ בְּאֶרֶץ לֹא לָהֶם וַעֲבָדוּם וְעִנּוּ אֹתָם אַרְבַּע מֵאוֹת שָׁנָה" "And He [Hashem] said to Avram, 'You shall surely know that your seed will be strangers in a land that is not theirs, and they will enslave them and oppress them, for four hundred years.'" (Bereshit 15:13) Soon thereafter the *Torah* tells us "וְדוֹר רְבִיעִי יָשׁוּבוּ הֵנָּה כִּי לֹא שָׁלֵם עֲוֹן הָאֱמֹרִי עַד הֵנָּה" "And the fourth generation will return here, for the iniquity of the Emori will not be complete until then." (Bereshit 15:16) On that *pasuk*, Rashi comments that *Hashem* does not punish a nation until its measure of sin is full, implying that the *Emori* had legitimate rights to dwell in the Land up until the expiration of the required exile of the Jews in *Mitzrayim*, at which time the Jews were empowered to rightfully push them out. Yet because of the sin of the *meraglim* the Jews were forced to remain outside of the Land in the desert for forty years, and during that period the *Emori* had no right to live in *Eretz Yisrael*. Therefore, the gold they hid in the walls of their homes was reasonable payment by the *Emori* (the illegitimate inhabitants) to the Jews (the legitimate inhabitants) following the forty years.

The *Haftarah* for *Shabbat HaGadol* contains a famous challenge from *Hashem*. "הָבִיאוּ אֶת כָּל הַמַּעֲשֵׂר אֶל בֵּית הָאוֹצָר וִיהִי טֶרֶף בְּבֵיתִי וּבְחָנוּנִי נָא בָּזֹאת אָמַר ה' צבקות אִם לֹא אֶפְתַּח לָכֶם אֵת אֲרֻבּוֹת הַשָּׁמַיִם וַהֲרִיקֹתִי לָכֶם בְּרָכָה עַד בְּלִי דָי" "Bring the whole of the tithes into the treasury so that there may be nourishment in My House, and test Me now therewith, says Hashem of Hosts, [to see] if I will not open for you the windows of Heaven and pour down for you blessing until there be no room to suffice for it." (Malachi 3:10) While it is considered prohibited to test *Hashem*, the *Gemara* (Taanit 9a) tells us that there is an exception. *Hashem* encourages us to scrupulously give *maaser* which, He assures us, will result in boundless wealth.

5768

Rabbi Yosef Weinstock – The *Torah* describes a purification process for the *metzora* whereby the *Kohain* places the blood of the proscribed offerings on the *metzora's* right earlobe, right hand and big toe of his right foot. (Vayikra 14:14). It is striking that this process is identical to the way in which *Moshe* inaugurated the *Kohanim* for service in the *Mishkan*. (Vayikra 8:23, 24) Perhaps the *Torah* is teaching us that any Jew who seeks to ascend spiritually is praiseworthy and, in a sense, equivalent, whether emerging from the degraded state of the *metzora* to the status of an average Jew or emerging from the favored status as a son of *Aharon* and nephew of *Moshe Rabbeinu* to achieving the greatest heights of the *Kehunah*. Rabbi Edward

Davis asks a related question: Two men are on a ladder of spirituality, who is on a higher level? He answers that the one moving upward is superior to the one moving downward, even if he is positioned lower.

Rabbi Michael Jablinowitz – The Zohar points out that "nega," the blemish of *tzaraat*, is composed on the same letters that spell "oneg," meaning joy. Furthermore, Sefer Yetzirah comments that עננ is an acronym for "ayden, nahar and gan." "Ayden" is Paradise and pertains to spirituality, "nahar" is a river, and suggests process (like the flow of a river), and "gan" is a garden, which involves physicality (in the form of physical growth). The *oneg* that we experience on *Shabbat* comes from the synthesis of these three elements: processing the physical to enable the spiritual. The *nega* of the *metzora* represents the related but opposite reality: using his physicality through a process that disables his spirituality.

5769

Rabbi Yerucham Levovitz – The *pasuk* says "וּבָא אֲשֶׁר לוֹ הַבַּיִת וְהִגִּיד לַכֹּהֵן לֵאמֹר כְּנֶגַע נִרְאָה לִי בַּבָּיִת" "and the one to whom the house belongs comes and tells the Kohain, saying, 'Something like a nega has appeared to me in the house.'" (Vayikra 14:35) Here Rashi comments that even if the homeowner is a *Torah* scholar who knows for sure that the lesion is, in fact, *tzaraat*, he shall not decide the matter but rather use only the words set forth in the *pasuk*. This is reflective of the philosophy set forth in adage of the *Gemara* (Berachot 4a): "Teach your tongue to say 'I don't know.'" Avoiding the perception that one is a "know it all" is a worthwhile goal.

5770

Rabbi Edward Davis – Based on religious considerations, both *Yom HaShoah* and *Yom HaAtzmaut* are out of place on the Hebrew calendar. The originators of the modern State of Israel wanted *Yom HaShoah* to be on the anniversary of initiation of the Warsaw Ghetto Uprising on

April 19, 1943, to align an otherwise somber memorial day with the *hashkafah* of the new Jewish State, which emphasized strength and a rejection of future victimhood. Yet the religious faction of the early State objected, as the corresponding Hebrew date is 14 *Nissan, Erev Pesach*, which is a joyous time when mourning is inappropriate. The non-observant Zionists also wanted *Yom HaAtzmaut* to fall on 5 *Iyar* (except when that is *Shabbat*) as this was the Hebrew date of the Statehood Declaration (May 14, 1948), but the religious were again opposed as this inevitably falls during the *Sefirat HaOmer* period of semi-mourning when celebrations are prohibited. The religious proposed *Tisha B'Av* as *Yom HaShoah* and sometime in *Sivan* for *Yom HaAtzmaut*. Ultimately the religious prevailed in pushing *Yom HaShoah* until after *Pesach* (27 *Nissan*), but still during the festive month when, for example, *tachanun* in not said. The non-religious prevailed in making 5 *Iyar Yom HaAtzmaut*.

5772

Rabbi Yosef Weinstock – There are many lessons one can glean from the fact that the *Torah's* description of the purification process for the *metzora* (Vayikra 14:14) is identical to the inauguration process for the *Kohanim* for service in the *Mishkan*. (Vayikra 8:23, 24) In both cases, blood, then oil, is placed on the person's right earlobe, right hand and big toe of his right foot. Much commentary focuses on the connection between the *Kohain* and the *metzora*, but just as intriguing is the choice of these body parts. Perhaps the answer lies in their functionality. The ear represents listening: a person must not merely talk. The thumb is used for gripping, which is applied not only for physical items but esoteric concepts as well, which is a caution to take firm "hold" of issues and not to be overwhelmed by them. The toe is used by the foot for balance, which alludes to the need to avoid extremes in ideas and positions. Focusing on these attributes brings the *metzora* in line with the Community and allows the *Kohanim* to likewise provide effective leadership.

ACHAREI MOTE

5759

In the *Yom Kippur* service, the *Kohain Gadol* would change clothes and enter the *mikvah* <u>both</u> <u>before</u> going into the *Kodesh HaKadoshim* (Vayikra 16:4) and <u>afterwards</u> (Vayikra 16:28). Surely, going from a less Holy/pure environment to a more Holy/pure environment would dictate changing and dunking before entering the Holy of Holies, but why would the opposite require changing and dunking? Perhaps because retaining *Kedushah* is harder than preparing for it, and people require extra effort and assistance to "hold on" to closeness to *Hashem*. This is certainly a lesson we can apply in making *havdalah*, which is our attempt to hold on to the sanctity of *Shabbat*.

The *pasuk* states "k'maasei eretz Mitzrayim asher yishavtem ba lo ta'asoo u'ch'maasei eretz Canaan ...," "Like the practice of the <u>land</u> of Mitzrayim in which you dwelled do not do; and do not perform the practice of the <u>land</u> of Canaan ...." (Vayikra 18:3) The language seems odd, referencing the land and not the people of Egypt and Canaan. One explanation is that the richness and fertility of these lands leads to wealth and, ultimately, decadence. The *Torah* is warning that bad behavior can result from a comfortable and extravagant environment. This certainly has been the experience for a large segment of American Jews.

5760

Reb Irving Bunin – There is a pyramid of life whereby each level draws strength from the level below and serves the level above. For example, animals may take from the flora but must serve man. Man, at the apogee of the food chain, may benefit from animals, but must serve *Hashem*. The *Gemara* (Pesachim 49b) states that an *am haaretz* has no right to eat meat, specifically because he may not take from the level below if not properly serving the Level Above. The question arises as to whether the use of animals is a *reshut* or a *chovah*. <u>Must</u> a G-d fearing Jew eat meat or <u>may</u> he? And if the use of animals is a requirement, would employing them for clothing or transportation satisfy the requirement? Of course, the ultimate use of an animal is as a *korban*. May *Hashem* send us *Moshiach* soon, so we may restore the *Beit HaMikdash* for fulfillment of that ideal.

Rabbi Samson Raphael Hirsch – The *pasuk* states "... u'v'chukotayhem lo taylaychoo," "and do not do their statutes," (Vayikra 18:3) referring to the people of Egypt and Canaan. "Chukim" are the unexplained, illogical statutes and ways of the *goyim*, such as superstitions, and go beyond the separate prohibition of any custom derived from their religions.

5762

Rabbi Yosef Kalatsky – The *parashah* begins with a mention of the death of *Nadav* and *Avihu* and then goes into an explanation of the *Yom Kippur* service. (Vayikra 16:1) The *Midrash* Pesikta Zutra (Acharei Mote 16:2) teaches that this is to show us that the death of a *tzaddik* brings atonement and that *Hashem's middah* of *rachamim* is ascendant and available to us at such a time.

5764

When Parshiot Acharei Mote and Kedoshim are read together as a "double *parashah*" we read the *Haftarah* from Acharei Mote. (Amos 9:7-15) This is unusual, insofar as usually in such circumstances we read the *Haftarah* for the second *parashah*. In his prophesy, *Amos* describes a glorious future whereby *Hashem* brings the Jews back to their Land and They rebuild desolate cities. Then the promise: וּנְטַעְתִּים עַל אַדְמָתָם וְלֹא יִנָּתְשׁוּ עוֹד מֵעַל אַדְמָתָם אֲשֶׁר נָתַתִּי לָהֶם אָמַר ה' אלקיך," "And I will plant [Bnei Yisrael] on their land, and They shall no longer be uprooted from upon Their Land, that I have given them, said Hashem, your G-d." (Amos 9:15) The day after this *Haftarah* was read (May 2, 2004) was the Likud referendum which soundly rejected the Sharon withdrawal/surrender from Gaza.

5765

Rabbi Yisroel Ciner – The *pasuk* states "אֶת מִשְׁפָּטַי תַּעֲשׂוּ וְאֶת חֻקֹּתַי תִּשְׁמְרוּ לָלֶכֶת בָּהֶם אֲנִי הי אלקיכֶם," "You shall do My Statutes and listen to My Ordinances, to go in them, I am Hashem." (Vayikra 18:4) What is meant by the term "going in" the *mitzvot*? The Ohr HaChaim quotes the Zohar which holds that the 248 positive commandments and the 365 negative commandments correspond to the parts of the human body, and performance of *mitzvot* *miKadaish* a person to the extent that he becomes a *meirkavah* for *Hashem*, whereby *Hashem* goes with him in this world.

5773

Rabbi Yosef Weinstock – The *pasuk* states "וּשְׁמַרְתֶּם אֶת חֻקֹּתַי וְאֶת מִשְׁפָּטַי אֲשֶׁר יַעֲשֶׂה אֹתָם הָאָדָם וָחַי בָּהֶם אֲנִי הי," "You shall observe My Statutes and My Ordinances, which a man shall do and live by them. I am Hashem." (Vayikra 18:5) The *halachah*, based on this verse, holds that we violate the negative *mitzvot* (with the exception of three) to preserve human life. Based on *hashkafah*, however, there is a simpler message: in order to truly live and to experience a life of meaning that is worthy of living, we must fulfill *Hashem's mitzvot*, which were designed by Him for that exact purpose.

KEDOSHIM

5758

On the *pasuk* "v'ahavta l'raiacha komocha ... ," "and you shall love your neighbor like yourself," (Vayikra 19:18), Rashi famously tells us that "Rabbi Akiva says this is a great rule of the Torah." In fact, we are admonished to put the spiritual well-being of our neighbor ahead of our own, which, for instance, could mean to study *Torah* with one less knowledgeable that oneself. However, with regard to physical well-being, a person comes before his neighbor. This is reflected in Rashi's precise language "zeh klal gadol b'Torah," "this is a great rule in Torah," but not in physicality.

5760

Rabbi Yisroel Ciner – The *pasuk* states "you shall judge your neighbor with righteousness... ," (Vayikra 19:15) which Rashi tells us means to give the benefit of the doubt. A *mashal* illustrates the lengths to which one must go in this area. Imagine misplacing one's passport and desperately searching for it on the day of a planned international trip. One's search would start with the likely places but, if unsuccessful, would include obscure, illogical places and then illogical returns to search places already thoroughly searched. If we labored in this same way to find the best possible explanation for perceived faults in others we would be properly performing this critical *mitzvah*.

All ten of the *Aseret HaDibrot* are also set forth individually in Parashat Kedoshim. This teaches us that just as *Klal Yisrael* gathered to hear the Ten Commandments at *Har Sinai* they likewise gathered together to hear the *mitzvot* of Parashat Kedoshim from *Moshe*. (Rashi on Vayikra 19:2)

Rabbi Mordechai Kamenetsky – The Chofetz Chaim teaches that the meaning of the proximity of the *pasuk* "love you neighbor as yourself," (Vayikra 19:18) to "do not bear a grudge," (Vayikra 19:17) is simple. Because one generally "loves" himself, he gives himself plenty of the "benefit of the doubt" and is generally not upset at himself when he is unsuccessful at accomplishing something. Likewise, we should "love" others by giving them the same benefit of the doubt and refrain from blaming them and holding a grudge when things they are involved with do not work out the way we hoped or planned. If a neighbor does not loan you something you expected him to, it is an indication that *Hashem* did not designate him to be your lender. Why be mad? Love him as you do yourself.

5761

Rabbi Yossi Jankovits – "Kedoshim" means "Holiness." The Ramban translates "Kadosh" as "restrained," meaning moderate in all aspects of life. *Kadosh* can also be translated as "separate" or "distinct."

Rabbi Yossi Jankovits – The *pasuk* demands that "you should surely reprove your fellow." (Vayikra 19:17) The Zohar states that *Noach* failed in this area by not reproving those of his generation. The result was his year of solitary confinement upon the Ark. If not for the need to punish *Noach*, *Hashem* could have accomplished the *Mabul* in a single day.

5762

Rabbi Yisroel Ciner – Parashat Kedoshim contains the famous pasuk "v'ahavta l'raiacha komocha, Ani Hashem," "and you shall love your neighbor like yourself, I am Hashem." (Vayikra 19:18) As recorded in the *Gemara*, this *Torah* verse was paraphrased in the negative by *Hillel* in his response to the potential convert who demanded to be taught the entire *Torah* while standing on "one foot." *Hillel* told the man "What is hateful to you, do not to your neighbor: that is the whole Torah, and the rest is commentary; go and learn it." (Shabbat 31a) The classic understanding of the question is that the potential convert wished to know which *mitzvot* of the *Torah* are primary. The classic understanding of the answer is that because *Hillel* failed to include in his response the component of the associated *Torah* verse that connects to *Hashem* (i.e. "Ani Hashem"), *Hillel* would hold that *mitzvot bein adam l'chaveiro* are primary, even in comparison to *mitzvot bein adam l'Makom*. But we can also say that one's failure to keep a *mitzvah bein adam l'Makom* is also a distasteful act towards another, as we see in the *mashal* of the boat passenger drilling a hole in the hull of a boat, directly beneath his seat. In response to the alarm of his fellow passengers, he coolly informs them it is his business only, for only his space is being affected, to which they respond indignantly "you fool, don't you realize a hole under your seat will sink all of us?!" Failing with regard to keeping the *mitzvot* brings *tumah* to the world, contaminating all its inhabitants. If one is reduced in some way by the direct actions of a neighbor he is upset with this neighbor. *Hillel* is forcing us to understand our dealings with *Hashem* as we do our dealings with mankind. Our actions or inactions directly affect our fellow man, even in *mitzvot* seemingly between only man and G-d. This is what is meant by "all of the *Torah* on one foot." Failure to do a positive *mitzvah* or transgressing a negative *mitzvah*, whether relating to man or to G-d, will have an effect on your fellow. What *Hillel* is saying is "if you are offended when your neighbor is careless with fire in a way that could cost you financial loss, then don't wear *shaatnez* or eat *chametz* on *Pesach* because it could result in a financial loss to him!" This is a complete refocusing of the traditional "live and let live" mentality in regard to the *mitzvah* observance of others, based on the fact that the People of Israel are one in all areas of *Kedushah* and *tumah*.

5763

Rabbi Yossi Jankovits – The *pasuk* says "... kedoshim tiyu, ki Kadosh Ani Hashem Elokayhem," "you shall be Holy for I, Hashem your G-d, am Holy." (Vayikra 19:2) The word "kedoshim," referencing *Bnei Yisrael*, is spelled קדשים (without the "vav"), yet "Kadosh," with respect to *Hashem*, is spelled קדוש (with the "vav"). According to the Ma'ayanah shel Torah, this is meant to show us that although we aspire to Holiness, what we achieve will necessarily never rise to the complete and total Holiness of *Hashem*.

5765

Rabbi Yossi Jankovits – The reference to "Eretz zavat chalav u'davash," "a Land flowing with milk and honey," (Vayikra 20:24) appearing at the end of Parashat Kedoshim is not presented in association with other fruit from Israel. From this we learn that the *davash* described here is referring not to <u>date</u> honey (as referenced elsewhere) but to <u>bees'</u> honey, which would need a specific reference in the *Torah* to demonstrate why we can eat the product of a non-kosher animal.

MRF Note – Parashat Kedoshim opens with three consecutive *pasukim* that each references to "Ani, Hashem, Elokayhem," perhaps alluding to the three categories of *mitzvot* for which a Jew is obligated: (1) "Kedoshim tiyu … ," "you shall be Holy," (Vayikra 19:2) could be a reference to the *mitzvot bein adam l'atzmo*; (2) "ish imo v'aviv tiraoo … ," "Every man shall fear his mother and his father," (Vayikra 19:3) seems to deal with *mitzvot bein adam v'chaveiro*; and (3) "al tifoo el haelilim vaylohay masaycha lo taasoo lachem … ," "You shall not turn to worthless idols, nor shall you make molten gods for yourselves," (Vayikra 19:4) deals with *mitzvot bein adam l'Makom*. One could question the second category, since the full *pasuk* reads "אִישׁ אִמּוֹ וְאָבִיו תִּירָאוּ וְאֶת שַׁבְּתֹתַי תִּשְׁמֹרוּ אֲנִי הי אלקיכֶם," "Every man shall fear his mother and his father, and you shall observe My Sabbaths. I am Hashem, your G-d." (Vayikra 19:3) The inclusion of observing *Shabbat* might be regarded as a *mitzvah bein adam l'Makom*, but Rashi on that *pasuk* comments that the inclusion of the *Shabbat* reference teaches that it one's father directs him to desecrate the *Shabbat*, G-d forbid, he should not heed him, which seems to be also in the category of interpersonal relations.

5766

Rabbi Yosef Weinstock – We read Parashat Kedoshim during the semi-mourning period of *Sefirah*, during which time, the *Gemara* (Yevamot 62b) tells us, 12,000 pairs of *talmidim* of *Rabbi Akiva* died in a plague. Our Sages inform us that the cause of the plague was the lack of *kavod* among the students. In Kedoshim, the *Torah* sets forth the *mitzvah* of "v'ahavtah l'reiacha kamocha," "love your neighbor like yourself," on which *Rabbi Akiva* said "zeh klal gadol b'Torah," "this is a central concept of the Torah." (Rashi on Vayikra 19:18) It is fair to assume *Rabbi Akiva's* students mastered *ahavah* (as so directed by their *Rebbe*) while failing in *kavod*. How can this be? *Ahavah* is the emotion resulting from finding commonality with another Jew. We love those who are like us and like things we like. *Ahavah* is a celebration of what we have in common with one another. Conversely, *kavod* is an emotion resulting from recognition and acceptance of the differences between ourselves and others. We must have *kavod* for our parents and teachers because they are different (much better) than we are. Striving to have *kavod* for other Jews is perhaps harder since we must come to terms with what makes us different from them, but the result is a strengthened *achdut* among the Jewish people.

5769

Rabbi Yosef Weinstock – The *parashah* opens with an extraordinary command to *Moshe*: "דַּבֵּר אֶל כָּל עֲדַת בְּנֵי יִשְׂרָאֵל וְאָמַרְתָּ אֲלֵהֶם קְדֹשִׁים תִּהְיוּ כִּי קָדוֹשׁ אֲנִי הי אלקיכֶם," "Speak to the <u>entire</u> Congregation of Bnei Yisrael, and say to them, You shall be Holy, for I, Hashem, your G-d, am Holy." (Vayikra 19:2) The Chasam Sofer teaches that the mention of the <u>entire</u> Congregation is an indication that one may not attain spirituality by oneself, outside of normative Jewish life. Rather all one's congregation, as a congregation, needs to become Holy together.

5770

Rabbi Eli Mansour – In Parashat Kedoshim the *pasuk* reads "hochayach tochiach et amitecha, v'lo tisa alav cheit," "You shall surely rebuke your fellow, but you should not bear a sin on his account," (Vayikra 19:17), which is generally interpreted to mean that in the process of trying to improve a friend, do not act harshly whereby you would incur a sin on yourself. The second part of the *pasuk* could, however, be read "and do not raise over him the sin," meaning "don't suggest that the sin is so serious as to be greater than or 'raised over' the sinner." Rather, emphasize how good the perpetrator is and his ability to overcome the sin. This is a critical concept in raising children. We must inspire them towards success in spirituality, not oppress them with a sense that their sins are insurmountable.

5771

Rabbi Yosef Weinstock – The *pasuk* states "לֹא תִקֹּם וְלֹא תִטֹּר אֶת בְּנֵי עַמֶּךָ וְאָהַבְתָּ לְרֵעֲךָ כָּמוֹךָ אֲנִי הי," "You shall neither take <u>revenge</u> from nor bear a <u>grudge</u>

against the members of your Nation; you shall love your neighbor as yourself. I am Hashem." (Vayikra 19:18) The classic example, provided by Rashi, teaches us how to distinguish taking revenge from bearing a grudge. When Reuven asks Shimon to borrow his sickle and Shimon refuses, Reuven cannot thereafter refuse Shimon's request to borrow Reuven's hatchet (revenge), nor may Reuven lend Shimon the hatchet but, in the process, remind Shimon of his previous failure to lend the sickle (grudge). These two *Torah* prohibitions apply to Reuven, but the Chizkuni asks why the *Torah* does not sanction Shimon for his initial refusal to lend Reuven. One answer the Chizkuni gives is that the *Torah* does not mandate lending, but if this is true, then why is Reuven faulted for not lending Shimon his hatchet? The Chizkuni answers that Reuven was inclined to otherwise lend out his property to Shimon, but Shimon's refusal to lend Reuven a sickle somehow altered Reuven's approach. Understood in this way, the *issur* of taking revenge is "not lending only because of a prior negative occurrence with the requestor" and the *issur* of bearing a grudge is "to lend with negativity only because of a prior negative occurrence with the requestor." MRF Note – Perhaps, in response to the Chizkuni's question as to why the *Torah* doesn't address Shimon for his original failure to lend Reuven, we can say that the *Torah* does, indeed, address Shimon with *mussar* in the same *pasuk*: "v'ahavtah l'reiacha kamocha," "love your neighbor like yourself." (Vayikra 19:18) Interestingly, Rashi's famous example involves similar cutting tools (sickle and hatchet), presumably to be used by similar neighbors. The Torah, then, is saying to Shimon "You are requesting a tool from your friend Reuven, but did you love him as yourself when he asked you for your sickle?!"

5772

Rabbi Edward Davis – Rabbi Akiva Eiger ruled that a *Sefer Torah* found after years of non-use can be ruled kosher if (a) all letters are proper and (b) it was written with the correct *kavanah*. But how may one ascertain the intent of the *sofer*? Traditionally, *soferim* outline the letters in the final *pasukim* of Parashat V'zot HaBeracha, the last *aliyah* of the *Torah* Scroll, in order to allow others to fill them in, thereby having a portion in the *mitzvah* of writing a *Sefer Torah*. While the aesthetics of such letters is perhaps compromised, adopting this process evidences a *hashkafah* of inclusion and *achdut*; which create proof of kosher intent. The *Torah*, after all, is about inclusion.

5773

Rabbi Edward Davis – The *Torah* can provide philosophical truths in places that are also meant to teach us *halachah*. For example, the *Torah* teaches "אִישׁ אִמּוֹ וְאָבִיו תִּירָאוּ וְאֶת שַׁבְּתֹתַי תִּשְׁמֹרוּ אֲנִי הי אלקיכֶם," "Every man shall fear his mother and his father, and you shall observe My Sabbaths. I am Hashem, your G-d." (Vayikra 19:3) On the juxtaposition of the command to honor one's parents and observe *Shabbat*, Rashi famously comments that the proximity of these two ideas obligates one to ignore his father should he tell him to desecrate the *Shabbat*. Yet we can also say that, based on *hashkafah*, the *Torah* is setting forth the family ideal, which contemplates a religious life where a child keeps and celebrates *Shabbat* based on the fear and respect of a parent who insists upon it.

EMOR

5758

Parashat Emor describes the *Arba'ah Minim* that *Bnei Yisrael* are commanded to take on *Sukkot*. (Vayikra 23:40) One of the species is "arvay nachal," "brook willows." The root is "ערב," which is identical to the Hebrew word for guarantor. Every Jew is the guarantor of the safety and wellbeing of every other Jew, which flow from adherence to *Torah*. On *Har Sinai Bnei Yisrael* famously said "naaseh v'nishma," "<u>we</u> will do and <u>we</u> will hear." (Shemot 24:7) That "we" is used with respect to accepting the *Torah* is evidence that we were accepting for the Community as a whole and guaranteeing the future performance of *mitzvot* of all our fellow Jews.

Parashat Emor contains the unfortunate story of the "megadef," "blasphemer." (Vayikra 24: 10-16) While the *Torah's* narrative is enigmatic, the Midrash Tanchuma and Vayikra Rabbah, as quoted by Rashi, provide the "full story" behind the episode. *Shelomit bat Divri* was a Jewish slave married to a Jewish man in *Mitzrayim*, and was prone to chattering. (Rashi on Vayikra 24:11) Her Egyptian taskmaster took her chatter as advances and so, one day, after her husband departed for work, came to her home and forced himself upon her. Her husband returned and discovered the Egyptian, and a struggle ensued. *Moshe* witnessed the Egyptian hitting the Jewish slave and mortally struck him. (Shemot 2:11, 12) *Shelomit* was impregnated by the *Mitzri* and the child from that union was, years later, the *megadef*, as the *pasuk* tells us "וַיֵּצֵא בֶּן אִשָּׁה יִשְׂרְאֵלִית" "The "וְהוּא בֶּן אִישׁ מִצְרִי בְּתוֹךְ בְּנֵי יִשְׂרָאֵל וַיִּנָּצוּ בַּמַּחֲנֶה בֶּן הַיִּשְׂרְאֵלִית וְאִישׁ הַיִּשְׂרְאֵלִי" son of a Yisraeli woman and a Mitzri man went out among Bnei Yisrael, and they struggled in the camp, this son of the Yisraeli woman, and the [other] Yisraeli man." (Vayikra 24:10) Rashi informs us that the struggle concerned where he could pitch his tent, for as the son of a *Mitzri*, he was not considered part of any particular Tribe, which was determined by one's father. Having been excluded from the Jewish camp, the *megadef* cursed *Hashem* and was thereafter put to death at the express directive of *Hashem*. (Vayikra 24:14).

There are two incidents involving the death penalty in the *Chumash*: the incident of the *megadef* in Parashat Emor (Vayikra 24:10-16) and the story of the *mikoshaysh* in Parashat Shelach. (Bamidbar 15:32-36) In each case, which Rashi indicates took place in the same period (Vayikra 24:12), there was a cooling off period before judgment, when *Moshe* went to *Hashem* for guidance.

Parashat Emor introduces the Jewish holidays with the following *pasuk*: "דַּבֵּר אֶל בְּנֵי יִשְׂרָאֵל וְאָמַרְתָּ אֲלֵהֶם מוֹעֲדֵי ה' אֲשֶׁר תִּקְרְאוּ אֹתָם מִקְרָאֵי קֹדֶשׁ אֵלֶּה הֵם מוֹעֲדָי" "Speak to Bnei Yisrael and say to them: Hashem's appointed [Festivals] that you shall designate as <u>Holy Convocations</u>. These are My appointed [Festivals]." (Vayikra 23:2) The words "Mikra'ei Kodesh," "Holy Convocations," connotes a "calling out" for the sake of "Holiness." Following the mention of *Shabbat*, the *parashah* then enumerates the (Biblical) *Yom Tovim* days: *Pesach* (seven days); *Shavuot* (one day); *Rosh Hashanah* (one day); *Yom Kippur* (one day); *Sukkot* (seven days); and *Shemini Atzeret* (one day). (Vayikra 23:4-36) These total eighteen days of Festivals, equal to the *gematria* of "חי," "chai," "life!" The Jewish People acquire Holiness through the Festivals, which are our life!

5759

Parashat Emor outlines the physical deformities for which a *Kohain* is excluded from his Priestly Service. (Vayikra 21:16-24) This exclusion is not based on any "need" of *Hashem* for perfection, but rather for humans, who need to <u>see</u> perfection in order to <u>feel</u> it.

5760

Rabbi Mordechai Kamenetsky – The *pasuk* says "וּשְׁמַרְתֶּם מִצְוֹתַי וַעֲשִׂיתֶם אֹתָם אֲנִי ה׳," "You shall safeguard My Commandments and perform them. I am Hashem." (Vayikra 22:31) What does it mean to both "safeguard" the *mitzvot* and do them? Rabbi Paysach Krohn tells the story of a man named Moshe Cohen, a member of the *kehillah* of Rabbi Yehudah Leib Lewis in Amsterdam. Reb Cohen wanted to participate in the *Chevra Kadisha* but, as a *Kohain*, could not be close to a corpse or enter a cemetery. When the *kehillah* bought and dedicated a new burial area, and it came time to bury the first person there, they found that the first grave had already been dug by Reb Cohen. He was alert to the *mitzvah* opportunities in areas from which he was normally excluded, demonstrating both watchfulness and alacrity to do the *mitzvot*.

5761

Rabbi Yossi Jankovits – The *pasuk* states "שֵׁשֶׁת יָמִים תֵּעָשֶׂה מְלָאכָה וּבַיּוֹם הַשְּׁבִיעִי שַׁבַּת שַׁבָּתוֹן מִקְרָא קֹדֶשׁ כָּל מְלָאכָה לֹא תַעֲשׂוּ שַׁבָּת הִוא לַה׳ בְּכֹל מוֹשְׁבֹתֵיכֶם," "For six days, work may be performed, but on the seventh day, it is a complete rest day, a Holy convocation; you shall not perform any work. It is a Shabbat to Hashem in all your dwelling places." (Vayikra 23:3) While this would seem to be a straightforward reference to the six workdays and *Shabbat*, the Vilna Gaon interprets the "six days" as the two (first and last) days of *Pesach*, one day of *Shavuot*, one day of *Rosh Hashanah* and two (first and last) days of *Sukkot*, when "work can be performed," meaning we may cook and carry for the benefit of the day. The "seventh day" mentioned in the *pasuk* is *Yom Kippur*, "Shabbat Shabbaton," a "complete rest day," when even cooking and carrying is prohibited, as is the case with *Shabbat*.

Rabbi Yissocher Frand – The *pasuk* states "וְלֹא תְחַלְּלוּ אֶת שֵׁם קָדְשִׁי וְנִקְדַּשְׁתִּי בְּתוֹךְ בְּנֵי יִשְׂרָאֵל אֲנִי ה' מְקַדִּשְׁכֶם," "Do not desecrate My Holy Name, rather I should be sanctified among Bnei Yisrael; I am Hashem Who sanctifies you." (Vayikra 22:32) The mention of *chillul Hashem* and *Kiddush Hashem* together indicate that the atonement for the first is the latter. According to Rambam (Hilchot Yesodei Hatorah 5:4-11), there are three ways by which one could come to do a *chillul Hashem* (G-d forbid): (1) to do one of the sins for which a Jew must give his life rather than transgress; (2) to do a sin solely to spite Heaven, where one will get no personal pleasure or benefit; and (3) for a recognized *talmud chacham* to do an act publicly that is questionable, even if it is, in fact, permissible. Rambam goes on to state that all visibly observant Jews are considered *talmidei chachamim*, such that giving the public perception that they have sinned amounts to a *chillul Hashem*.

5762

The *pasuk* states "וְשׁוֹר אוֹ שֶׂה אֹתוֹ וְאֶת בְּנוֹ לֹא תִשְׁחֲטוּ בְּיוֹם אֶחָד," "And whether an ox or sheep, you shall not slaughter it and its offspring in the same day." (Vayikra 22:28) The Zohar says that this applies the whole day (i.e. one cannot separate the mother and its offspring and kill each at different times of the same day). This is because a day is sacred and every day "below" has a corresponding appointed day "Above," and one should be careful not to impair the day Above with such unjust conduct on the same day "below." "Thus if a man does kindness on earth he awakens lovingkindness Above, and it rests upon that day which is crowned therewith through him." (Zohar III, 92b) If one performs mercy on earth (by, for example, not killing the offspring), that deed becomes his protector in his hour of need. The inverse is true with respect to cruelty, based on the principle of *middah keneged middah*. The Chofetz Chaim, in Sefer Shmirat HaLashon, states that forgiving injustices done to us brings forgiveness for both ourselves as individuals and for all of *Bnei Yisrael*.

5762

Rabbi Yochanan Zweig – The *Gemara* (Yevamot 62b) tells us that 12,000 pairs of students of *Rabbi Akiva* died during the period of *Sefirat HaOmer* because they were disrespectful to each other as *talmidei chachamim*. The period of *Sefirat HaOmer* is about acceptance of the entire *Torah*, including the Oral *Torah*. This is evidenced in the *machloket* as to when to start counting the *Omer*. The *pasuk* in Parashat Emor states "וּסְפַרְתֶּם לָכֶם מִמָּחֳרַת הַשַּׁבָּת מִיּוֹם הֲבִיאֲכֶם אֶת עֹמֶר הַתְּנוּפָה שֶׁבַע שַׁבָּתוֹת תְּמִימֹת תִּהְיֶינָה", "And you shall count for yourselves, from the morrow of the "shabbat" from the day you bring the omer as a wave offering seven weeks; they shall be complete." (Vayikra 23:15). Only by virtue of the Oral *Torah* (Menachot 66a) do we know that "shabbat" in this context means the day after the first day of *Pesach* and not the first *Shabbat* that follows *Pesach*. A *talmud chacham* is arguably greater than a *Sefer Torah*, as he knows both the Oral and Written *Torah*. Disrespecting such a person is the opposite of the goal of the *Sefirat HaOmer* period, which is to move toward acceptance of the entire *Torah* on *Shavuot*.

5763

The *pasuk* says "שֶׁבֶר תַּחַת שֶׁבֶר עַיִן תַּחַת עַיִן שֵׁן תַּחַת שֵׁן כַּאֲשֶׁר יִתֵּן מוּם בָּאָדָם כֵּן יִנָּתֶן בּוֹ", "fracture for fracture, eye for eye, tooth for tooth. Just as he inflicted an injury upon a person, so shall it be inflicted upon him." (Vayikra 24:20) It is well known, based on the *Gemara* (Bava Kama 84a), that this *pasuk* is referring to the obligation of compensating an injured party with, for instance, the <u>value</u> of a lost eye, as opposed to the actual eye of the injurer. Yet one could question why, if that is that case, the next *pasuk* says "One who strikes an animal shall make restitution ...." (Devarim 24:21) If the *Torah* can expressly provide for monetary restitution with respect to an animal, why not also say so with respect to a human? The answer, perhaps, is that the *Torah* wishes to teach us that in the case of injury to an animal, money alone can fix the situation, but in the case of a human the actual damage goes beyond economic and the tortfeasor truly deserves to, but does not, lose his eye.

5764

Rabbi Binny Freedman – As described in Parashat Vayishlach, *Shimon* and *Levy* got together and slaughtered the City of *Schem*, to the disapproval of *Yaacov Avinu*. (Bereshit 34:25-31) They expressed passion that their father thought was misplaced. *Levy* made a *tikkun* by siding with *Moshe* during the *cheit haeigel*, but *Shimon* never did. In Parashat Balak, *Zimri*, the *nasi* of the Tribe of *Shimon*, was involved in the sin of *Baal Peor* and the ensuing immorality, for which *Pinchas*, from the Tribe of *Levy*, killed him. (Bamidbar 25:1-9) *Shimon*, as a Tribe, was never really heard from again in Jewish history. The total who died in the incident of *Baal Peor* was 24,000, which coincidentally is the number of students of *Rabbi Akiva* who died during *Sefirat HaOmer*. Those students were the *tikkun* for what took place that day, as the Zohar states that *Rabbi Akiva* was a *gilgul* of *Zimri* and one's students are regarded equivalent to one's children. (Rashi on Bamidbar 3:1)

5765

Rabbi Edward Davis – The Kli Yakar describes what he calls the faulty logic of *Yaacov Avinu* in Parashat Vayishlach. When *Levy* and *Shimon* decimate *Schem*, *Yaacov* objects to their actions. He states "You have decomposed me, making me odious among the inhabitants of the land ...." (Bereshit 34:30) *Yaacov* fears that he and his household will be annihilated, yet we clearly see that this never happened. The Kli Yakar states that no one cared about the people of *Schem* because they had, by virtue of their mass circumcision, become Jews, and the world is generally apathetic toward violence against Jews. This has certainly borne itself out in the recent history of *Medinat Yisrael* and before that, during the Holocaust. Today, this attitude is manifested in the worldwide apathy to the deportation of Jews from their homes in *Gush Katif.*

5767

Rabbi Yossi Jankovits – The *pasuk* "... v'Nikdashti b'toch Bnei Yisrael, Ani Hashem m'Kadishchem," "I should be Sanctified among Bnei Yisrael, I am Hashem Who Sanctifies you," (Vayikra 22:32) is conventionally regarded as the source for the command to sacrifice one's life in G-d's name. Yet another reading of this directive is to make a *Kiddush Hashem* "b'toch," "within" *Bnei Yisrael*, not, for example, from a monastery or through ascetic living, but rather by living within a community, bringing people closer to *Torah* through *kiruv*. Perhaps this can be compared to another *pasuk* in Parashat Emor that reads "וַיֵּצֵא בֶּן אִשָּׁה יִשְׂרְאֵלִית וְהוּא בֶּן אִישׁ מִצְרִי בְּתוֹךְ בְּנֵי יִשְׂרָאֵל וַיִּנָּצוּ בַּמַּחֲנֶה בֶּן הַיִּשְׂרְאֵלִית וְאִישׁ הַיִּשְׂרְאֵלִי," "Now, the son of a Yisrael woman and he was the son of a Mitzri man <u>went out among Bnei Yisrael</u>, and they quarreled in the camp this son of the Yisrael woman, with a Yisrael man." (Vayikra 24:10) The *megadef* also went "b'toch Bnei Yisrael," and made a *chillul Hashem* within the People. The negative forces <u>within</u> the Nation will always be present <u>among</u> the Nation. Those sanctifying Hashem and bringing Holiness should be there as well.

5769

Rabbi Joseph B. Soloveitchik – Parashat Emor mentions the *Chagim*, including *Sukkot*, and we know that, with respect to the *Arba'ah Minim* mentioned in the *parashah* (Vayikra 23:40), we make a *berachah* only on

the *lulav*. The *Gemara* (Sukkah 37b) states that as the *lulav* is the tallest of
the *Arba'ah Minim*, we learn that receiving *Hashem's* gifts is dependent on
"standing tall," apart from the other nations, and cognizant of our worth
as the Chosen People. The Rav explains (Yemei Zikaron, pp. 134-35) that
this message of Jewish identity and pride is applicable to the Jews in Israel
(in how they interact with and try to appease their neighbors), as well as
the Jews in the Diaspora, especially America, who all too often sacrifice
their children's connection to Jewish identity and pride in the name of
conforming to the ways of the *goyim*.

5770

Dr. Mark Jaffee – Wedged between the many *mitzvot* of the *Kohanim* and
the description of the *Yom Tovim* in Parashat Emor are two related *mitzvot*
in a single *pasuk*. ",וְלֹא תְחַלְּלוּ אֶת שֵׁם קָדְשִׁי וְנִקְדַּשְׁתִּי בְּתוֹךְ בְּנֵי יִשְׂרָאֵל אֲנִי ה' מְקַדִּשְׁכֶם"
"[1] You shall not desecrate My Holy Name. [2] I shall be sanctified amidst
Bnei Yisrael. I am Hashem Who sanctifies you." (Vayikra 22:32) The first
is the *mitzvah lo t'aseh* of *chillul Hashem*, which by itself, according to the
Gemara (Yoma 86a), has no *kaparah* absent death, being the most serious
of crimes. Yet Rabbeinu Bachaiya states that there is a *kaparah* available
based on the proximity of the *mitzvah aseh* that immediately follows in
the same *pasuk*: *Kiddush Hashem*! By speaking words of *Torah* in public
we make a *Kiddush Hashem*, which brings atonement for a *chillul Hashem*
(G-d forbid), without the necessity of dying.

5771

Dubner Maggid – The *pasuk* states "וַיֹּאמֶר ה' אֶל מֹשֶׁה אֱמֹר אֶל הַכֹּהֲנִים בְּנֵי אַהֲרֹן
וְאָמַרְתָּ אֲלֵהֶם לְנֶפֶשׁ לֹא יִטַּמָּא בְּעַמָּיו," "And Hashem said to Moshe: 'Speak to
the Kohanim, the sons of Aharon, and say to them: "Let none [of you]
defile himself for a dead person among his people."'" (Vayikra 21:1) The
double imperative of "say" is discussed in the Midrash Rabbah (26:5) as
an indication that, unlike in the case of angels, who need be commanded
but once, man often needs repetition of a command to overcome his

yetzer hara. Moreover, there is a distinction between the context of the first and second "say." Human nature being what it is, people need to hear an exhortation, in this case the negative commandment of not becoming impure, <u>once before</u> ignoring the admonition and <u>once after</u> suffering the resulting consequences. With the benefit of experience, one is then more apt to listen and internalize the directive.

5772

Rabbi Edward Davis – Why do we particularly celebrate *Rabbi Shimon bar Yochai* on *Lag B'Omer*? Are there not other great *Tannaim* worthy of having a special day of being remembered? Rav Moshe Feinstein quotes the *Gemara* (Shabbat 33b) as the basis for this *zechut* for *Rashbi*. *Rabbi Shimon* and his son were criticized by *Hashem*, after they emerged from thirteen years in a secluded cave, for being intolerant of the degree to which Jews were lax in *Torah* study. Yet they were successful in changing their perspective of an imperfect world when they saw an elderly Jew rushing *Erev Shabbat* with two *hadassim* in hand. When they asked the man what he intended to do with the myrtle, he replied "l'kavod Shabbat," "they are for the honor of Shabbat." When they inquired as to why he had <u>two</u> bundles, he replied that one was for "zachor" *Shabbat*, "remembering the Shabbat," and one was for "shamor" *Shabbat*," "guarding the Shabbat," to which *Rabbi Shimon* said to his son, *Rabbi Elazar*, "See how beloved are the mitzvot to the Jews!" With this *Rashbi* became worthy of a holiday in his honor, through coming to terms with the goodness in an imperfect world.

5773

Rabbi Avi Weiss – On the phrase "ayin tachat ayin," "an eye <u>instead of</u> an eye," (Vaykira 24:20) the *Talmud*, in many places, explains this is a reference to money equal to the value of an eye, rather than the actual removal of the eye. One proof from the *Gemara* (Bava Kama 83b), brings the pasuk from Parashat Masei which states "וְלֹא תִקְחוּ כֹפֶר לְנֶפֶשׁ רֹצֵחַ אֲשֶׁר הוּא רָשָׁע לָמוּת כִּי מוֹת יוּמָת," "You <u>shall not accept</u> ransom for the life of a murderer, who is guilty of death, for he shall be put to death." (Bamidbar 35:31) This implies that for the loss of something less than life, for example limbs that do not regenerate (i.e. an eye), one <u>shall accept</u> ransom.

BEHAR

5757
There is a *mitzvah* in Parashat Behar to prevent the decline of another Jew into poverty. (Vayikra 25:35) Rashi tells us that this is analogous to an overburdened donkey. While it is on its feet, an off-center load can be redistributed by a single person, but if left unfixed, the donkey will collapse and it will take many people to once again place it on its feet.

5759
The *Yovel* year, which takes place every fifty years, represents a relinquishment of physicality and a move towards spirituality, which reinforces *bitachon* in *Hashem* amongst the Jews.

5760
Rabbi Yissocher Frand – The laws of *ona'ah*, cheating in business (Vayikra 25:14) and verbal communication (Vayikra 25:17) appear near the laws of *Shemittah* to underscore that real faith and reliance on *Hashem* would make cheating an absurd behavior. If we understand that the physical assets and societal position we obtain come from *Hashem* and not from our own efforts, we must make our *hishtadlut* and then accept the results. Verbal "cheating" in the form of snide and cutting remarks are signs of one's belief that his own place is improper and that he deserves a more elevated existence, with more *kavod*. Acceptance of our social allotment is similar to our *parnassah*, and in the same way that cheating to get additional money or possessions will result in losing, snide remarks will not further elevate a person over his friend, but rather come back to harm him.

5762

Rabbi Yochanan Zweig – In regards to *Shemittah*, Rashi points out that because of the transgression of the laws of *Shemittah* the Jewish people were exiled. Specifically, he states that the seventy years of the Babylonian Exile corresponded to the seventy *Shemittah* years that the Jews failed to observe after coming into *Eretz Yisrael*. (Vaykira 25:18) This cannot mean that the Jews worked the Land in those years, for it clearly states in the *Torah* "וְצִוִּיתִי אֶת בִּרְכָתִי לָכֶם בַּשָּׁנָה הַשִּׁשִׁית וְעָשָׂת אֶת הַתְּבוּאָה לִשְׁלֹשׁ הַשָּׁנִים," "I will ordain My blessing for you in the sixth year and it will yield a crop sufficient for the three-year period." (Vaykira 25:21). With triple crops, there would be no reason to work the Land. Rather, the problem was that while, during that time, the Jews recognized the need to give *tzedakah*, they did not allow poor people onto their Land to remove the *hefker* fruit. Part of what brings *achdut* to the Jews is allowing each other into our "*dalet amot*" to feel and empathize together, and to the extent the Jews did not strive for *achdut* during that period they brought about the penalty of *galut*.

5763

Rabbi Mordechai Kamenetsky – Concerning the *Yovel* year, the verse says: "Proclaim liberty throughout the land and to all its inhabitants thereof." (Vaykira 25:10) Presumably, because the law of the *Yovel* year states that only slaves are set free, only they are impacted. Why then does the Torah direct us to proclaim liberty to <u>all</u> the inhabitants? In fact, employers are impacted as well. Since employers have a myriad responsibilities to their employees, they too are "unburdened" at the *Yovel*.

5765

Rabbi Avram Skurowitz – The miracle of *Shemittah* is not necessarily the three-year bounty in year six, which lasts until the next harvest (Vaykira 25:21) but, as explained by Rashi, the annual harvest in years one through six. (Rashi on Vaykira 25:19) Agricultural norms of that time dictated that one leave the land fallow on either the second or third year to ensure the best crops over time. Yet in *Eretz Yisrael*, the Jews are assured by *Hashem* that their Land will yield produce every year for six years without rest. This underscores the fact that observance of the *Shemittah* is not about allowing the Land its natural rest to maximize productivity, just as *Shabbat* is not about giving people a day off to maximize performance. The Land could, based on G-d's miracle, go on indefinitely producing bumper crops, yet *Hashem* ordered the Jews to stop every seventh year to ensure that we would not lose sight of the Source of this amazing *berachah*.

5768

Reb Ephraim Sobol – The number six represents "nature" (e.g. the six directions of space: up, down and four directions) and seven reveals "true essence." Once something is done seven times it becomes ingrained. *Shemittah* year ensures that, at most, *Bnei Yisrael* will focus on the physicality of farming only for six years, and will "unplug" thereafter to reconnect to the spirituality that is our essence. *Shabbat* is the same on a weekly basis. Once a week we need to get back to the freedom of serving *Hashem* rather than the race for acquisition. The *Torah* likewise commands the *eved Ivri* to serve a man (for stealing) only six years but not more, lest it become his essence. If he tells his master that he wants to remain a slave, married to a *goyah*, it has become his essence and he missed the Jewish message of *Har Sinai*. As a result, as Rashi famously points out in the beginning of Parashat Mishpatim, a hole is bored through his ear. (Shemot 21:6)

5771

Rabbi Yechezkel Shraga Halberstam – The *pasuk* says "וְקִדַּשְׁתֶּם אֵת שְׁנַת הַחֲמִשִּׁים שָׁנָה וּקְרָאתֶם דְּרוֹר בָּאָרֶץ לְכָל יֹשְׁבֶיהָ יוֹבֵל הִוא תִּהְיֶה לָכֶם וְשַׁבְתֶּם אִישׁ אֶל אֲחֻזָּתוֹ וְאִישׁ אֶל מִשְׁפַּחְתּוֹ תָּשֻׁבוּ," "And you shall sanctify <u>the year of the fiftieth year</u> and proclaim liberty in the Land for all its inhabitants; it shall be a Jubilee Year for you, you shall return each man to his ancestral heritage and you shall return each man to his family." (Vayikra 25:10) Why is the *Yovel* referred to as the "year of the fiftieth year?" *Yovel* can be compared to *Shavuot*. During *Sefirat HaOmer* we are supposed to advance in steps of Holiness towards a proper receiving of the *Torah*, yet if one fails to prepare he can actually make up for the entire *Omer* period on the fiftieth day (i.e. *Shavuot*). Similarly, the repetition of the word "year" in the *pasuk* indicates that in one year a person can attain everything he should have learned in the preceding forty-nine years (and seven *Shemittah* years). The Rambam (Hilchot Teshuvah 2:1) actually says that *teshuvah* at the end of one's life is accepted. But, one may ask, does that opportunity exist for all of *Bnei Yisrael*? The remainder of the *pasuk* provides the answer: it is an ancestral heritage for all Jews.

5772

Rabbi Ben Tzion Shafier – Why on *Yom Kippur*, at the start of the *Yovel*, is the *Shofar* sounded? Sefer HaChinuch states that it is to strengthen the slave owner who has grown dependent on the slave that he must now set free. It is a *nechamah* to such an owner that all slave owners are simultaneously experiencing the same challenge, and the reminder of this is the *Shofar* blast. The lesson is that *Hashem*, as our Creator, keenly understands the social psyche of the people He created, and provides us with exactly what we need to communally face our challenges through the ways of the *Torah*.

5773

Rabbi Edward Davis – The *Talmud* (Yevamot 46b) tells us that the conversion process can only be done before a tribunal of three Jewish adults. The *Torah* normally requires two witnesses for valid testimony in a Jewish court, so why are three needed to determine if the *geir* is well-intentioned or not? Beyond testing the sincerity of the potential convert, the conversion process is also designed to provide the convert with lessons that are central to Judaism. Among these is the importance of being a part of the *Kahal*, and in becoming a new person through the conversion process, the *geir* is immediately attaching to the *achdut* of a group (more than two) of observant Jews.

BECHUKOTAI

5759

Ibn Ezra – Parashat Bechukotai contains ten verses of blessing resulting from *Torah* study and observance, yet has thirty verses pertaining to curses. If it is true, as the *Gemara* (Sanhedrin 100b) says, that *Hashem* rewards in greater measure than he punishes, how can we understand this imbalance? The blessings are written generally and are meant to encompass many blessings that will come to *Bnei Yisrael*. Conversely, the curses are very limited and specific, and are meant to engender fear. (Ibn Ezra Vayikra 26:13)

5760

The *tochachah* of Parashat Bechukotai includes reference to the idol-worship of *Bnei Yisrael*, which begs the question: why would the Jews engage in idolatry? The answer is that while the Jews did not believe in idols per se, they wanted to engage in public immorality. Why specifically public immorality? Because to engage in private immorality would indicate that it is improper, thereby engendering guilt. However public immorality creates societal "buy-in" by creating a culture and philosophy of immorality that immunizes against guilt. This has been evident in the push to recognize "gay marriage" as a strategy of the so-called homosexual lobby in America.

Shelah HaKadosh – The *pasuk* states "וְזָכַרְתִּי אֶת בְּרִיתִי יַעֲקוֹב וְאַף אֶת בְּרִיתִי יִצְחָק וְאַף אֶת בְּרִיתִי אַבְרָהָם אֶזְכֹּר וְהָאָרֶץ אֶזְכֹּר," "And I will remember My covenant with Yaacov, and also my covenant with Yitzchak, and also My covenant with Avraham will I remember, and I will remember the Land." (Vayikra 26:42) This *pasuk* is inserted in a frightening list of curses that will befall the Jewish People if they abandon the *Torah*. Injecting *Hashem's* remembrance of our Ancestors there is an apparent interruption of the theme. This remembrance is actually also a condemnation. In passing sentence upon a criminal, a human judge will examine the wrongdoer's pedigree for facts that could mitigate his wrongdoing and his liability. If the criminal's evil can be traced to his evil ancestors, the judge may certainly take that into account. In the case of *Bnei Yisrael*, however, *Hashem* traces our lineage and declares to us "Look from whom you came from! Your abandonment of *Torah* is even more outrageous, and you therefore [G-d forbid] deserve an even harsher punishment!"

Rabbi Yosef Kalatsky – The *tochachah* of Parashat Bechukotai sets forth horrible punishments that will be inflicted upon *Bnei Yisrael* should we fail to follow *Hashem's* directives. When *David HaMelech* counted the Members of *Bnei Yisrael*, he was afflicted with a terrible plague, since *Hashem* had specifically instructed him not to count them. (II Shmuel, chapter 24) *Hashem* had previously told *Avraham Avinu* that He would make his offspring uncountable. (Rashi on Bereshit 13:16) *David* successfully counted them, seemingly disproving *Hashem's* promise. Of course, the ability of the Jew to transcend the physical universe makes an individual's worth and potential incalculable for, as the *Talmud* (Sanhedrin 37a) tells us, anyone that saves a Jewish life saves a universe. *David* sought to diminish the spiritual, undefinable essence of each Jew by counting them physically – in essence grounding *Bnei Yisrael* in a physical, not spiritual, reality. Accordingly, *Hashem* created a physical reaction in this world, in the form of a plague and resulting deaths, as punishment for not allowing *Bnei Yisrael* to fulfill its destiny as an "otherworldly" People. The *parashah* states (Vayikra 26:8) that five Jews will beat 100 enemies, and 100 Jews will overcome 10,000, clearly demonstrating that physical laws do not apply and should not be applied to the Jews.

5761

MRF Note – In this year's season finale to the popular television drama The West Wing, the fictitious President curses G-d. After instructing his Secret Service detail to seal the National Cathedral for his private session with his Creator, President Bartlett launches into an emotional, multi-lingual attack, purposefully blaming G-d for, among other things, the death of his longtime and beloved secretary in a car accident. At the core of his argument the President links his recent political and personal misfortunes to his having lied to the American public concerning his major, undisclosed illness. He objects not to the justice in his suffering, but to the suffering of innocent others like his secretary. In the end the President, like a teenager who is told he is grounded, succumbs to G-d's Will only after defiantly putting out a lit cigarette on his "Father's" living room carpet (the church floor). Far from offending the *Torah* mind, such an admission during prime time concerning the supremacy of G-d and his daily involvement in the affairs of men (even important men like the President) is as refreshing as it is unexpected. Such an understanding is at the core of traditional Jewish thought. The first of the Ten Commandments is most often misquoted. It reads in full: "I am Hashem, your G-d, Who delivered you from the land of Egypt, from the house of slavery." (Shemot 20:2) The ancient *Torah* Sages asked why G-d, in making this initial declaration, should, so to speak, mention His Greatness only in regard to the Exodus. Why not begin with mightier credentials; say, for instance, "I am *Hashem*, your G-d, who created the Universe." The answer is as instructive as it is provocative. G-d is reminding us that He is orchestrating every moment of history. Certainly He created the world, but He did not, as Aristotle would argue, wind it up and set it off running. He recreates it daily, making countless calculations and decisions concerning all its affairs. As President Bartlett appeared to understand, G-d is pulling the strings. But just when you may have thought that Hollywood, at least for one evening, had taken a break from its long-held philosophy of casting G-d, if at all, in a vague, undefined and uninterested television role, here comes the ghost of the President's deceased secretary to boldly go beyond even this dubious standard. In the show's climactic final scene, when the President, this time alone in the Oval Office, is preparing to announce to the nation his decision not to run for reelection (in essence conceding to himself and the public that G-d has won, that there was a cost for his lying, and that accountability to G-d dictates that he must endure an amount of personal suffering for atonement) he has an epiphany. As she did throughout his career, Mrs. Langingham explains to the President that far from being the result of G-d's judgment of his actions, the President's recent string of bad luck is, well, just that, some bad luck. "G-d doesn't cause car accidents," she sagely informs the President, as she reminds him of all the important societal programs he has yet to implement during his first term. Her message is clear: "You are G-d, Mr. President! By blaming G-d you are tilting at windmills. Instead, control your own destiny and take on the world!" (notwithstanding that you lied to the world for the last four years). In Parashat Bechukotai, read this week in synagogues worldwide, G-d informs the Jewish people of the blessings that will be granted them and the curses that will befall them in proportion to their communal adherence to His Will as expressed in the *Torah*. The straightforward disclosure makes the rules of the game painfully clear: "I am watching, I am involved, and if you contradict My Will, there will be penalties." This is a message most of the world, and especially Hollywood, will not, indeed <u>cannot</u>, hear. Such a structure is inconsistent with permissiveness and liberalism. It demands introspection and adoption of a G-d-given moral code, not a feel-good pop spiritualism that allows one to in one breath claim to believe in G-d and in the next minute, for instance, curse his neighbor. Instead, the world demands the Novocain. The world requires books like "When Bad Things Happen to Good People," (written, ironically, by a non-traditional Jewish author) which, at its core, decides that there are forces in the world that even G-d can't, or won't, overcome. If there is no answer then there need be no questions. That allows us to push on, and to do so with impunity. Last year, a very big to-do was made when a respected rabbi in Israel opined that the Jewish people, as a people, were in some respect responsible for the Holocaust. It's an idea that is contained in this week's *Torah* reading. It's an idea that President Bartlett was able to intuit and accept, if merely for a fleeting moment, until Hollywood set him straight.

5762

The *Mishnah* in Pirkei Avot states "al tifrosh min haTzibbur" "don't separate yourself from the Community." (Avot 2:5) Here, in Parashat Bechukotai, the *pasuk* indicates "v'radfu miken chamisha meiah u'meiah miken r'vava yirdofu ...." "Five of you will pursue a hundred and a hundred of you will pursue ten thousand ...." (Vayikra 26:8). We therefore see that the value of each Jew to the Community is greater than a single person, but rather represents exponential power that is essential to the well-being and safety of the Community.

5764

Rabbi Yaacov Menken – The *pasuk* says "וְזָכַרְתִּי לָהֶם בְּרִית רִאשֹׁנִים אֲשֶׁר הוֹצֵאתִי אֹתָם מֵאֶרֶץ מִצְרַיִם לְעֵינֵי הַגּוֹיִם לִהְיוֹת לָהֶם לֵאלֹקִים אֲנִי ה'," "And I will remember for them the covenant of the Early Ones, those whom I took out of the land of Mitzrayim before the eyes of the nations, to be a G-d unto them, I am Hashem." (Vayikra 26:45) The Kedushas Levi questions why here the *Torah* must again reference our predecessors (which it did at Vayikra 26:42). The reference to the Jews in *Mitzrayim* is here an allusion to our lowly state. In essence, we are reminded by *Hashem* that He "knew us when," at our beginning when we were an unreliable, problematic partner, so now it would not be proper to severely, unceasingly punish us in light of our background.

5765

Rabbi Yossi Jankovits – The *pasuk* contained in the *berachot* of *Bnei Yisrael* reads: "v'hishbati chaya ra'ah mi haaretz," "I will cause evil beasts to withdraw from the land." (Vayikra 26:6) We see in Parashat Vayeishev, when *Yosef's* brothers try to manufacture evidence of *Yosef's* death by natural means, they take his multi-colored tunic and dunk it in the blood of a slaughtered goat. (Bereshit 37:31) Upon their presentation of the bloody tunic to their father *Yaacov*, we see the use of significant language. "Kitonet b'ni chaya ra'ah achalatnu ..." "The tunic of my son! An evil beast has eaten him," exclaimed *Yaacov*. (Bereshit 37:33) On that verse, Rashi comments that *Yaacov*, through *Ruach HaKodesh*, is referring to the wife of *Potiphar*. *Potiphar* was *Yosef's* Egyptian master, whose wife unsuccessfully attempted to seduce *Yosef* to engage in illicit relations. (Bereshit 39:7-18) Therefore, we see that the reference in the *berachot* may be in regards to harlotry and the desire for illicit relations. The ultimate blessing would be that *Hashem* would eliminate such temptations from the Jewish Homeland. MRF Note – A cute vignette frames this point. Once a youngster in the local Jewish day school was preparing to travel to Israel with his family on vacation. His teacher conceived of a constructive way of letting the entire class partake in the exciting trip. Each student was asked to write a petition to Hashem on a *klaf* which their classmate would insert in the *Kotel* upon his arrival in Israel. The teacher reviewed the notes before passing them to the family. One student expressed a desire that *Hashem* end all warfare against the Jews living in Israel by writing as follows: "I hope there are no more <u>whores</u> in Israel." Amen v'amen! Incidentally, this interpretation of "chaya ra'ah" is bolstered by recalling the promise made by *Hashem* that he would never again visit the same *makot* of Egypt upon the Jewish People (Shemot 15:26). We know that the *maka* of *arov* was clearly one of the *makot* that decimated Egypt so here, wild beasts must have an entirely different meaning.

5768

Rabbi Yossi Jankovits – There is a *Gemara* (Berachot 20b) that indicates that *Hashem* favors *Bnei Yisrael* because they eat a *kazayit* of bread and *bentch*, despite the fact that having eaten only a small amount of bread they are not satiated (for the *pasuk* states (Devarim 8:10) that you will eat, and <u>be satisfied</u> and you will bless, thereby requiring the blessing by *Torah* law only when one is satisfied). Yet, in Parashat Bechukotai, *Hashem* indicates that if we go in His Statutes "v'ahaltem lachmichem lasaiva," "you will eat your bread in satiety." (Vayikra 26:5). On this *pasuk*, Rashi comments that the blessing indicates that one will eat but a little and it will bless his innards (i.e. a small amount will be unnaturally satisfying). If true, how can it be a *zechut* that *Bnei Yisrael* eats little and *bentches*, since eating a little creates satiety that requires *bentching*?! The answer lies in the opening *pasuk* of the *parashah*, which states "im bechukotai tailaichu," "if you go in My statutes," (Vayikra 26:3) then certain rewards will be granted, among them, a reality where a small amount of bread creates satiation. The *Gemara*, therefore, is not praising *Bnei Yisrael* for *bentching* when they are not satisfied, but rather for "going in" *Hashem's* statutes to the extent that a small amount of bread is, in fact, satisfying to them.

5769

Rabbi Yitzchak Salid – The admonitions of the *Torah* appear in Parashat Bechukotai and Parashat Ki Tavo, in each case preceding by two weeks (rather than one week) *Shavuot* and *Rosh Hashanah*, respectively. In both cases the warnings are required to properly prepare us for the essential aspects of these days, but we are not able to hear about the horrors of noncompliance with Hashem's Will on the *Shabbat* immediately preceding these *Yom Tovim*. One important message is that *Shavuot* has the awesome nature of *Rosh Hashanah* and should not be treated lightly.

5770

Rabbi Yosef Weinstock – In Parashat Bechukotai, the curses include a *pasuk* that reads "וְתַם לָרִיק כֹּחֲכֶם וְלֹא תִתֵּן אַרְצְכֶם אֶת יְבוּלָהּ וְעֵץ הָאָרֶץ לֹא יִתֵּן פִּרְיוֹ" "Your strength will be spent in vain; your land will not give its produce and the tree of the land will not give its fruit." (Vayikra 26:20) Rashi points out that physical efforts spent in vain are a greater curse psychologically than natural disaster, for when one works hard and sees no result, he is more frustrated than if he had no result from no toil. Yet this is a curse only with respect to non-spiritual striving, for the opening *pasuk* of the *parashah* adjures the Jew to "go in [Hashem's] decrees," (Vayikra 26:3) which Rashi interprets as the toil of *Torah* study. Our Rabbis tell us that there is tremendous merit and satisfaction in the toil of *Torah*, regardless of what results one is ultimately able to achieve, and that is a tremendous blessing to our People.

5771

Rabbi Eliezer Zusia Portugal – The first *pasukim* of the Parashat Bechukotai state "If you toil in My statutes [i.e. study *Torah*], observe My commandments and perform them [i.e. put *Torah* into action], then the Land will give produce, the tree will give fruit." (Vayikra 26:3, 4) *Hashem* is telling us that we need to be like the farmer who plants (i.e. studies the *Torah*) and harvests (i.e. performs the *Torah*), and that both aspects of service to *Hashem* are required.

SEFER BAMIDBAR
BAMIDBAR

5758

Rabbi Yissocher Frand – Parashat Bamidbar means "in the desert" or "wilderness." *Hashem* gave the *Torah* in the desert to People who had nothing, but only after he had offered it to the other nations of the world. The other nations had fixed ways and existing "baggage," and did not want to upset the routine of their lives. This can be compared to a king who wanted to build a palace and went to existing cities and was rejected in each case. Ultimately, he built the palace in a ghost town, for a small number of subjects who had nothing to lose. The message for us is that we must each make ourselves like a desert to properly receive the Torah. There is even a *Gemara* (Eruvin 54a) that indicates "a person should make himself into a desert." MRF Note – When one is in a city and he looks up, he can hardly see the stars of the heavens, but by going out into the "desert," without the "glare" of the big city lights, one can properly appreciate the number and brightness of the stars.

5759

Baal HaTurim – On his deathbed, four tribes are addressed by *Yaacov Avinu* in the first person (you): *Reuven, Yehudah, Dan* and *Yosef*. (Bereshit 49:1-27) All became flag-bearing tribes in the *midbar*. (Bamidbar 2:2)

5760

In Pirkei Avot (2:21), the Mishnah states: "Lo alecha hamelacha ligmor v'lo attah ben chorin l'hibatail mimenoh," "It is not for you to complete the work, but neither are you free to desist from it." The Chofetz Chaim says "It is not for you to achieve, but to act. Achievement is the province of the Al-mighty."

5761

Rabbi Yossi Jankovits – *Yaacov*, before dying, told the brothers that the tribe of *Gad* would ultimately be "upgraded" when traveling in the desert, and that they would become part of the legions with *Shimon* under the flag of *Reuven*. That *mesorah* was passed down and understood by the *Shevatim*. Therefore, when the time came to assemble for travel in the the *midbar* there was no *machloket*, much like with the modern understanding that the Kohanim and Leviim receive the first *aliyot* to the *Torah*.

5762

Rabbi Edward Davis – The Chida gives *mussar* from the *Gemara* (Yoma 21a), which states that in the *Beit HaMikdash*, when everyone stood in the *Haichal*, there was no room between them, but when they prostrated themselves there was plenty of room to do so. The lesson is that humbling ourselves for others allows for honor and space for all. This miracle took place in *Yerushalayim*, which itself is the ultimate manifestation of Jewish community. This year, *Yom Yerushalayim* was the day before Parashat Bamidbar was read.

5763

The Lubavitcher Rebbe – Rashi points out that the census of *Bnei Yisrael* at the beginning of Parashat Bamidbar is the fourth in the *Chumash*. (Rashi on Bamidbar 1:1) *Hashem* previously counted *Bnei Yisrael* when they left *Mitzrayim* (Shemot 12:37), when they sinned at the *cheit haeigel*

(Shemot 32:35), and in the aftermath of that episode (Shemot 38:26). Why are the Jews counted again at the beginning of Bamidbar? The answer is based on the *halachic* concept of "davar she b'minyan," "something that can be counted" never becomes nullified. For example, one drop of milk in sixty or more parts chicken soup is nullified and of no consequence, but one egg that is not kosher which is mixed in a basket of 60 kosher eggs makes all eggs in the basket *treif*, because the non-kosher egg is "davar she b'minyan." By counting each Jew, *Hashem* shows us a Jew can never be nullified or assimilated. Furthermore, Bamidbar is read before *Shavuot* in order to indicate that the *Torah* is the way to remain a "devar she b'minyan." This idea is also brought out by the Chidushei HaRim.

5764

Rabbi Berel Wein – The *Torah* goes to great lengths to specify the leaders of each tribe (Bamidbar 1:5-15), although they are not mentioned again and actually die in the desert. The lesson is one of personal accountability in Jewish leadership. These names are eternally recited as those who could not save the generation from the harsh decree. It underscores the Jewish concept of personal responsibility.

5765

Dr. David Epstein – The Book of "Numbers" (in Hebrew, Bamidbar) is unique among the *Chamishah Chumshay Torah* insofar as the English translation of the Greek/Latin name of this Book is used by the English-speaking world, rather than, as with the other four Books, the Greek/Latin name itself (e.g. Genesis, Exodus, Leviticus and Deuteronomous). It is also noteworthy that the "Book of Numbers" is the only one of the Five Books whose name translates accurately from the traditional Jewish name of the same Book, which was called Sefer HaPekudim – Book of the Counting/Numbers. Actually, only two of the Five Books even had a tradition of a discrete historical name. The *Talmud* names the fourth Book "Sefer HaPekudim" (Yoma 7:1) and the fifth Book (what today we refer to as Devarim– Deuteronomy) was called "Mishneh Torah," meaning "Repetition of the Torah." (Chullin 63b) Apparently, the first three Books had no vernacular name in early Jewish history, for it was not until the Middle Ages that they began to be referred to in Jewish rabbinical literature as Bereshit, Shemot, Vayikra, Bamidbar and Devarim. Dr. Epstein's theory is that the emergence of a distinct, modern, Jewish name for each of the *Chamishah Chumshay Torah* was a response to the appropriation by the gentile world of the central concepts of the Five Books in the names they used (i.e. "Creation of the World" (Genesis), "Leaving Egypt" (Exodus), "the Priestly Class" (Leviticus), "Counting the Jews" (Numbers), and "the Recap/Summary" (Deuteronomy)). He suggests that perhaps the Jews decided they would choose a different appellation for each book by taking a word from the first *pasukim* of the first *parashah* for each Book that hints to a major theme of the Book, but stands in contrast to the word chosen (or perhaps stolen) by the non-Jewish world. Hence "Beginning" (Bereshit), "Names" (Shemot), "Calling Out," (Vayikra), "In the Desert" (Bamidbar) and "Sayings" (Devarim).

5768

Rabbi Yossi Jankovits – The idea, set forth in the *Gemara* (Pesachim 6b), that at least a portion of the *Torah* is out of chronological order, which is the subject of a debate between Rashi and Ramban, is undeniable in *Sefer Bamidbar*, since two *parshiot* after Parashat Bamidbar an explicit reference is made to a prior date. Specifically, Bamidbar begins "on the first day of the <u>second month</u> in the second year," as it continues to provide the census of *Bnei Yisrael*. (Bamidbar 1:1) Yet in Parashat Behaalotecha, the *Torah* states "Hashem spoke to Moshe ... in the second year, in the <u>first month</u>," and then goes on to provide the mitzvah of bringing the *Korban Pesach* in the desert. (Bamidbar 9:1-3) This is regarded as something of an embarrassment to *Bnei Yisrael*, since they originally received the same *mitzvah* (in Parashat Bo) in connection with entering the Land. Having endured the sin of the *meraglim* (Bamidbar 14:20-23) they were prohibited from entering the Land and needed a separate mitzvah to do *Pesach* in the *midbar*. (Rashi on Bamidbar 9:1) However, why not make Parashat Nasso (which follows Bamidbar) begin the Sefer of Bamidbar? The seminal event in Nasso is the dedication of the *Mishkan*, which occurred *Rosh Chodesh Nissan* (the first day of the first month) of the second year, which, like Behaalotecha, occurred before the census described in Bamidbar. The answer may be that the *Torah* does not want to draw attention to the building of the *Mishkan* as a great event since, as Rashi holds, the *Mishkan* was a *tikkun* for the *cheit haegel*. (Rashi on 31:18) Had *Bnei Yisrael* not sinned, a *Mishkan* would not have been needed to bring *Hashem's* Presence. Therefore Nasso, like Behaalotecha, must defer to the more "pareve" *sedra* of Bamidbar to "lead" the fourth *Sefer* of the *Chumash*.

5769

The verses we say when wrapping our *Tefillin Shel Yad* around our fingers appear in the *Haftarah* for Parashat Bamidbar. "וְאֵרַשְׂתִּיךְ לִי לְעוֹלָם וְאֵרַשְׂתִּיךְ לִי בְּצֶדֶק וּבְמִשְׁפָּט וּבְחֶסֶד וּבְרַחֲמִים וְאֵרַשְׂתִּיךְ לִי בֶּאֱמוּנָה וְיָדַעַתְּ אֶת ה'," "And I will betroth you to Me forever, and I will betroth you to Me with righteousness and with justice and with loving-kindness and with mercy. And I will betroth you to Me with faith, and you shall know Hashem." (Hoshea 2:21, 22)

Rabbi Yitzchok Isaac Sher – Why were the Sons of *Levy* counted from age one month and older (Bamidbar 3:15), while the other *Shevatim* were counted from the age of twenty and older? (Bamidbar 1:3) The *Kohanim* risked their lives in performing their *avodah*, for a mental lapse would result in death. In doing so, they demonstrated extreme self-sacrifice, a trait that needed to be stressed and inculcated into every member of *Shevet Levy* from the earliest age.

5770

Rabbi Yosef Chaim Sonnenfeld – The *pasuk* says "behold, I have taken the Leviim from the midst of Bnei Yisrael ... ," (Bamidbar 3:12) meaning that, while they were counted separately, the *Leviim* were also an integral part of the Jewish People. In fact, if one takes the word "ישראל," "Yisrael," and takes the middle letter of the "spelled out" name of each letter (e.g. for the first letter "yud," which is spelled "yud, vav, dalet," the middle letter is "vav"), the resulting letters spell "Leviim," a word that is quite literally taken from the "midst" of "Yisrael!"

5771

Rabbi Shimon Schwab – The *pasuk* says that the *Leviim* males were counted and reported by the Torah from one month of age and older. (Bamidbar 3:15) What was unique about the Tribe of Levy that they should be thus counted? Rashi indicates that once a child lives for thirty days (and is presumed to be viable) he is counted as "one who safeguards the charge of that which is Holy." (Rashi on Bamidbar 3:15) But, again, why are they considered to be faithful to safeguarding Hashem's charge? The *pasukim* in Parashat Vzot HaBerachah (Devarim 33:8, 9) state "of Levy … the one who said of his father and mother, 'I have not favored him'; his brothers he did not give recognition and his children he did not know; …" Because from an early age (i.e. one month) the Tribe of *Levy* told their children "I love you more than everything else in the world except *Hashem*," their children could be counted upon to stay faithful always to the *Torah*, and this, says Rav Schwab, is the secret to proper Jewish parenting throughout the ages.

5773

Rabbi Yossi Jankovits – The *pasukim* say "וְאֵלֶּה תּוֹלְדֹת אַהֲרֹן וּמשֶׁה בְּיוֹם דִּבֶּר ה' אֶת משֶׁה בְּהַר סִינָי וְאֵלֶּה שְׁמוֹת בְּנֵי אַהֲרֹן הַבְּכֹר | נָדָב וַאֲבִיהוּא אֶלְעָזָר וְאִיתָמָר," "And these are the offspring [toldot] of Aharon and Moshe on the day that Hashem spoke with Moshe at Mount Sinai. These are the names of the sons of Aharon, the firstborn was Nadav, and Avihu, Elazar and Itamar." (Bamidbar 3:1-2) The obvious questions are: why are the sons of *Aharon* also called the sons of *Moshe*, and what does the day of revelation at *Har Sinai* have to do with that issue? Rashi states that they are called his sons because he taught them *Torah* (Rashi on Bamidbar 3:1), and clearly he taught them the *Torah* he had learned at *Har Sinai* from *Hashem*. In Parashat Shemot, we learn that *Moshe*, while grazing the sheep of *Yitro*, came "el Har HaElokim Choreiva," "to the Mountain of G-d, Choreiv." (Shemot 3:1) We know from Parashat Mishpatim (Shemot 24:13), that this mountain was *Har Sinai* (for there the *Torah* records the mountain where *Moshe* is to receive the *Luchot* as "Har HaElokim"). *Hashem* engages *Moshe* and charges him with his mission to redeem the Jews. When *Moshe* persistently attempts to forego the job, the *pasuk* says "vayichar af Hashem b'Moshe vayomar halo Aharon achicha Halevy ...." "The wrath of Hashem burned against Moshe and He said 'Is there not Aharon your brother the Levy?'" (Shemot 4:14) There, commenting on *Hashem's* anger, Rashi, loosely citing the *Gemara* (Zevachim 102a), posits that *Hashem* mentions *Aharon* to indicate that, based on *Moshe's* recalcitrance, he shall not receive the *Kehunah*, but rather it would pass to *Aharon* and his sons. Going back to the *pasuk* in Parashat Bamidbar, the word "toldot" can be read not only as "offspring," but also as "outcome" or "consequences," meaning as a result of that original day that *Hashem* spoke (in anger) to *Moshe* at *Har Sinai* / *Choreiv* (when *Moshe* refused his mission), the sons of *Aharon* are to be the *Kohanim*.

Rabbi Ben Tzion Shafier – The Sforno points out that *Hashem* counts the Jews by name less than one year after receiving the *Torah*, whereas thirty-eight years later, as the Jews were poised to enter *Eretz Yisrael*, they were counted not by name but number. This, says the Sforno, is a credit to those of the Exodus generation, who were greater. This can be compared to children of *baalei teshuva*, who achieve great things in *Torah* and *Yiddishkeit*, well beyond what was achieved by their parents, yet are lesser than their parents, who took the fateful and uncomfortable step of leaving their world and embracing *Torah*.

NASSO

5758
Parashat Nasso is the longest *parashah* in the *Torah*. There are many connections between Nasso and *Shavuot*, the holiday on which we celebrate the giving of the Torah and which is observed around the same time Parashat Nasso is read every year.

- The *Torah* has three parts: *Torah*, *Naviim* (Prophets) and the *Ketuvim* (Writings)
- There are three parts to the Jewish Nation: *Kohain*, *Levy* and *Yisrael*
- The *Torah* was given in the third month, counting from *Nissan* (i.e. *Sivan*)
- The *Torah* was given by the third child of the family (*Moshe*, who was the younger brother of *Miriam* and *Aharon*)
- In Nasso, the *Kohanim* are commanded to give the "Three-Fold Blessing," "*Birkat Kohanim*" (Bamidbar 6:22-27), which itself is given in the merit of the Three Patriarchs (we learn this from the fact that the fifteen words of the blessing allude to the fifteen years that *Avraham, Yitzchak* and *Yaacov* were all contemporaneously alive).

5759
Rabbi Yissocher Frand – The portion of *sotah*, the suspected adultress, begins as follows: "Ish, Ish ..." "Any man," or, more literally, "a man, a man." (Bamidbar 5:12) Rabbi Moshe Chafetz explains that sometimes a situation involving marital infidelity results from the husband being too much of an "ish," a "man." He asserts himself too much and is less concerned with the "isha," the "wife." Furthermore, the portion of *sotah* follows the portion of one who doesn't provide proper gifts to the *Kohanim*, to explain that being stingy and selfish in relation to the priests is similar to being selfish in our marriages.

In the inauguration of the *Mishkan* each *nasi* brought a bull, a ram and a sheep. (Bamidbar 7:12-83) Rashi says these offerings represent the Patriarchs as follows: the bull: *Avraham*, the pillar of *chesed*, ran to get a bull for his guests (Bereshit 18:7); the ram: *Yitzchak*, the pillar of spiritual strength, was replaced with a ram at *Akeidat Yitzchak* (Bereshit 22:13); the sheep: *Yaacov*, the pillar of *emet*, separated his sheep from his wicked father-in-law *Lavan* to be honest to a level above reproach. (Bereshit 30:33)

5760

Rabbi Pinchas Winston – We learn from the *parashah* of *sotah* the *halachah* of a married woman being required to cover her hair. The verse says the *Kohain* shall uncover her head (Bamidbar 5:18), which implies that it would normally be covered. One might argue that perhaps <u>all</u> women, not only those who were married, covered their hair at the time, and since current *halachah* holds that unmarried women do not cover their hair, that *halachah* (of unmarried women covering their hair) was changed with time. However, since *halachah* and *minhagim* rarely survive over time as adulterated pieces of prior practice, it is unlikely that unmarried women covered their hair in the times of the *Mishkan* and *Beit HaMikdash*, but currently do not. The *sotah* is followed by the portion on the *nazir*, who "shall grow his hair wild [פרע]." (Bamidbar 6:5) This word can be compared to the verse from the *sotah*, which reads that "the Kohain shall have the woman stand before Hashem and uncover [ופרע] the head of the woman ...." (Bamidbar 5:18) This connects *sotah* and *nazir*, as does the *Gemara* (Sotah 7a) that states that wine leads to the *sotah's* infidelity and, for that reason, one who observes the *sotah* in her disgrace should become a *nazir* and abstain from drinking wine. (Berachot 63a)

Rabbi Yossi Jankovits – Why does one reply to a greeting of "Shalom Aleichem" with the reverse: "Aleichem Shalom?" An answer is that one is prohibited from speaking *Hashem's* name (of which *Shalom* is one) in a situation where he may be unable to finish the sentence. Such a statement would be uttering *Hashem's* name in vain, as the *Talmud* (Nedarim 10b) says, one should not say "to *Hashem*, an offering," because he may die before he can complete the statement and would be uttering *Hashem's* name in vain. Rather he should say "an offering, to *Hashem*." The *Talmud*

guarantees a long life for one who greets a friend first. Therefore, we
are not concerned that the person initiating the greeting will die before
completing the statement. Since he is promised the blessing of a long life,
he can say "Shalom" and afterwards, "Aleichem," but no such protection
is made for the recipient of the greeting. Should the recipient die before
completing the returned greeting (i.e. having only said "Shalom") he
would be *chayav* and he therefore uses *Shalom* only at the end of his reply.
Another answer is that any interaction between Jews should begin and
end with *Hashem's* name.

5761

Rabbi Tzadok HaKohen of Lublin – Water has enormous power. It can
wash away anything that stands in its path and is always on the move,
resembling life. But if water becomes too cold, it freezes and goes nowhere.
The mission of *kiruv* is not merely to ignite a "pilot light" to unaffiliated
Jews, but to thaw the frozen *Torah* of Jews born into an observant environment whose observance has cooled.

Rabbi Yaacov Menken – When *Shevet Yehudah* had given its *korbanot* to
dedication of the *Mishkan* (Bamidbar 7:12-17), *Shevet Yissachar* purposefully
gave the identical gifts (Bamidbar 7:18-23) to avoid creating an environment
of jealousy and "one-upmanship." Every subsequent tribe did likewise.
This is a strong lesson in how all Jews should all act concerning material
wealth. *Hashem* rewarded this restraint with a verbatim recounting in the
Torah of each offering, although they were identical.

Rabbi Yissocher Frand – The Shemen HaTov writes in the name of the
Sefas Emes, that by accepting *nazeirut*, the *nazir* becomes elevated above
the regular *Kohain*, which is demonstrated by the fact that the *nazir* cannot
defile himself through contact with even one of the special seven close
family relatives who have died (Bamidbar 6:7), yet the regular Kohain may
do so. (Vayikra 21:1, 2) This shows that the *Kedushah* that one attains on
his own accord is greater than that gifted to him by his family.

5762

Kli Yakar – There is a relationship between the portion of *sotah* in Parashat Nasso and the incident of the golden calf in Parashat Ki Tisa. In applying the principle that the first five of the *Aseret HaDibrot* are related and matched, in order, to the second five commandments, we see that "לֹא יִהְיֶה לְךָ אֱלֹקִים אֲחֵרִים עַל פָּנָי," "You shall have no other gods before Me," the restriction on idol worship (Shemot 20:3), corresponds to the seventh *mitzvah* that one should not commit adultery. (Shemot 20:13) The reason is that idol worship amounts to being unfaithful to *Hashem*, so to speak. Therefore, those who fashioned the *eigel hazahav*, like the *sotah*, were forced by *Moshe* to drink dust (of the pulverized idol). (Shemot 32:20) If they were guilty, they died, just as the *sotah* did. (Rashi on Shemot 32:20)

Rabbi Yochanan Zweig – *Dan l'kaf z'chut*, giving the benefit of the doubt, requires one to make himself into a disinterested judge. Interested judges are automatically disqualified and we are commanded to judge, so we cannot be recused. Once we are of the proper mindset, we must apply the merit to the person we are judging, as if we had no personal stake. The *mitzvah* therefore does not mean to avoid judging, but to actively judge on the favorable, but not personal, side.

5763

Rabbi Yochanan Zweig – The *mitzvah* of *vidui* is found in Parashat Nasso (Bamidbar 5:7). The word used there for confess, "v'hitvadu," has the same root as "todah," "to thank." This is the essence of confession. The resolution not to sin again must be grounded in a context of gratitude for all that *Hashem* has done for us. In that context, sin is a treacherous betrayal. The same idea is central to marriage counseling, where a promise to work on one's anger is often an empty one. It takes years of concentrated effort to make a difference in one's approach to anger, yet by appreciating what one's spouse has done for him and focusing on those things at the time anger is rising, one can, through context, overlook what is admittedly a minor slight. This is the power of gratitude.

Rabbi Yossi Jankovits – The Chasam Sofer states that the connection between *Shavuot* and the *Haftarah* of Nasso is that *Galiyat*, the enemy of *David*, is the product of *Orpah* (*Rut's* sister/sister in law, who is mentioned in *Megillat Rut*, which is read on *Shavuot*) and *Shimshon*, whose birth is mentioned in the *Haftarah* for Nasso.

Rabbi Yossi Jankovits – Evidence of the fact that *Shevet Yissachar*, following *Shevet Yehudah*, affirmatively decided to match (but not transcend) the offering of Yehudah to the *Mishkan's* inauguration is found in the inclusion of the word "hikriv" (Bamidbar 7:19), which is not repeated as to the offerings of any of the other *nasiim*. Also, it is interesting to note that *Hashem's* name ("Keil") is contained in the name of the *nasi* for the second, fifth, eighth and eleventh Shevatim. The names are Nataneil, from Yissachar (Bamidbar 7:18), Shlumieil, from Shimon (Bamidbar 7:36), Gamlieil, from Menashe (Bamidbar 7:54), and Pagieil, from Asher (Bamidbar 7:72). Since *Bnei Yisrael* traveled in a square formation in the *midbar* with three tribes on each side, the middle tribe for each side of the square had a prince whose name included the *Sheim Hashem* protecting that side. This is illustrated as follows:

	Yehudah	*Yissachar*	Zevulun	
Naftali				Reuven
Asher				*Shimon*
Dan				Gad
	Binyamin	*Menashe*	Ephraim	

5765

Rabbi Michael Jablinowitz – The *Birkat Kohanim* described in Nasso (Bamidbar 6:22-27) is the subject of an interesting *Midrash*, which states that the *Kohanim* are commanded to bless *Bnei Yisrael* with feeling, since they are not mere conduits of *Hashem's* blessing, but rather are empowered to determine the time and place of giving the blessing. The Midrash Tanchuma (Bereshit 12:2) informs us that the power of the Priestly Blessing was inherited from *Avraham Avinu*, and was provided to the genetic descendants of *Aharon HaKohain* by *Hashem*. This inheritance might lead the *Kohanim* to assume a "pass-through posture," based on their perception that they really had not done anything to merit the right to bless the People of Israel. The Sefas Emes points out that the Midrash explains to the *Kohanim* that, like *Avraham* and *Aharon*, who were innovators in their own right (*Avraham* converted masses of people to monotheism (Rashi on Bereshit 12:5), and *Aharon* pursued peace among the People (Avot 1:12)), the *Kohanim* are partners in *Hashem's* desire to bless his Holy Nation.

5766

Rabbi Michael Jablinowitz – Parashat Nasso describes the three concentric camps of *Bnei Yisrael* in the *midbar*. (Rashi on Bamidbar 5:2) "Machaneh Yisrael," the outermost camp, was the Nation's camp at large, "Machaneh Leviim" was the encampment of those who worked daily in service to *Hashem*, and "Machaneh Shechinah" was the centralized dwelling place of the Divine Presence. Rav Tzadok HaKohen of Lublin compares these three camps to those who participate in the three required meals on *Shabbat*. The Friday night meal represents all of *Klal Yisrael*, as even not fully observant Jews will often partake in this "family time" event. *Shabbat* lunch represents a higher level of Jews who make the effort to observe the entire *Shabbat*. Those who eat *Seudah Shlishit* are a small minority who do so not necessarily because they are hungry but in order to fulfill the commandments of *Hashem*. This is a moment when such individuals are closely connected to the *Shechinah*.

5767

Rabbi Edward Davis – There is a *chassidishe vort* connecting three main items from Parashat Nasso: *nazir* (Bamidbar 6:1-21), *Birkat Kohanim* (Bamidbar 6:22-27) and the gifts of the *nasiim* (Bamidbar 7:12-83). The *nazir* wholly rejects physicality in an effort to *miKadaish* himself. For example, he will not eat grapes or drink wine. (Bamidbar 6:3) The *Kohanim* bless the Jews with physicality, for "yivarechecha" is a call for

Hashem to bless the Jews with wealth. (Rashi on Bamidbar 6:24) The gifts of the princes demonstrate the synthesis of these two attitudes, where material wealth is itself transformed into Holiness through incorporation into the *Mishkan*.

5769

Rabbi Yosef Weinstock – There is a *machloket* as to whether the *nazir* has done something laudable or disfavored. The Ramban (and the Ibn Ezra) feel he did something good, and that the *chatat* he brings at the end of his *nazirut* is only to indicate he is descending from a lofty plane. The Rambam, supported by Rashi, sees his actions as wrong, for prohibiting upon himself what the *Torah* allows, resulting in a sin offering. The ambiguity of the Sages in assessing the *nazir* reflects the alternative approach to combatting the modern assaults on spirituality, where we can separate from physicality or embrace it while remaining true to *Torah*. Both sides seem to have adherents based on the alternative approaches to the *nazir*.

5771

Rabbi Shlomo Katz – There is a *Midrash* that states that in *Birkat Kohanim* (Bamidbar 6:24), "yevarechecha Hashem," "May Hashem bless you," refers to "zachor et haShabbat" (Shemot 20:8), remembering the Shabbat and its positive commands (e.g. making *Kiddush*), while "vayishmerecha," "May [Hashem] guard you," refers to "shamor et yom haShabbat" (Devarim 5:12), safeguarding the Shabbat and its negative commands (e.g. not kindling a fire). Two types of people serve *Hashem*: those with a positive commands focus (who are outgoing influencers), and those with a negative commands focus (who are less outgoing, more reticent, and consistent followers). In fact, the Rashba says that "levarech" does not translate precisely to "bless," but rather to "spread" *Hashem's* goodness amongst all Jews, something a positive-minded person does. Accordingly, the *Kohanim* bless both types of Jews according to their personal orientations.

5772

Rabbi Eli Mansour – The Kli Yakar states that, despite the fact that *Gershon* was the oldest of the three sons of *Levy*, his brother *Kehat* is mentioned before him (Bamidbar 4:18) at the end of Parashat Bamidbar (Gershon is mentioned [Bamidbar 4:22] in Parashat Nasso). The distinction is given to *Kehat* because that family (so to speak) carried the *Aron* containing the *Luchot* and symbolizing the *Torah*, while *Gershon* bore the other *kaylim* of the *Mishkan*. This honor was given to *Kehat* only so as to emphasize that *Torah* precedes everything, including seniority, with respect to *kavod*. This is a lesson acutely necessary in our generation, where honor is often given to those of wealth and social status. Our rabbis – our *Torah* scholars – are deserving of our highest respect and honor.

5773

Rabbi Shlomo Wolbe – Rashi famously points out that the placement of the discussion of *nazir* (Bamidbar 6:1-21) adjacent to that of the *sotah* (Bamidbar 5:11-29) is teaching that one who sees a *sotah* in her disgrace should defer from drinking wine, which leads to immoral behavior. (Rashi on Bamidbar 6:2) This teaches a broader and more profound lesson: if *Hashem* orchestrated that a man be in the *Beit HaMikdash* at precisely the time of a *sotah* ceremony, it was to specifically teach him the lesson through another's difficulty. We should apply this to any situation we experience where a Jew acts immorally, and take precautions to avoid the same pitfall.

BEHAALOTECHA

5758

Parashat Behaalotecha begins with the *mitzvah* to light the *Menorah*. The language in the verse commands *Moshe* to tell *Aharon* "b'haalotecha et haneirot ... ," which literally translates as "raise up the candles ...." (Bamidbar 8:2) Rashi comments here that this amounts to lighting a candle so that the wick itself ignites and "raises up" into a flame.

The *Erev Rav* were a mixed multitude of non-Jews that went out of *Mitzrayim* with *Bnei Yisrael* and who instigated the complaints about the *Mon* provided by *Hashem*. (Rashi on Bamidbar 11:4)

Because *Miriam* told her brother *Aharon* that *Moshe* was like the other prophets she was stricken with *tzaraat*. (Bamidbar 12:1-10) *Moshe* prayed for *Miriam* and she was immediately cured. (Rashi on Bamidbar 12:13) Two simple points emerge from this episode: *Moshe* was, in fact, a superior prophet, and prayer actually works.

Chasam Sofer – In regards to the command of lighting the *Menorah*, the *pasuk* states "va'yaas kain Aharon," "and Aharon did so." (Bamidbar 8:3) *Aharon* did not delegate the *mitzvah* but did it himself. *Aharon* did exactly what *Hashem* commanded him to do. He did not try to imbue the *mitzvah* with his own imprimatur in order to leave a legacy. The lesson here is that we should question our motives when, as a result of our feelings of transience in this world, we strive to leave monuments and buildings bearing testimony to our having been here. Such actions may evince a lack of faith in *Olam HaBa* and, ultimately, in *Hashem*, since the implied message is that this is "all there is." For those who expect a reward and existence beyond this world, simply following *Hashem's* commandments is the most sensible approach.

5759

The *Talmud* (Shabbat 116a) states that there are actually <u>seven</u> Books of the *Torah* and that *Sefer Bamidbar* really contains three separate Books! One entire Book is contained in two *pasukim*: "וַיְהִי בִּנְסֹעַ הָאָרֹן וַיֹּאמֶר מֹשֶׁה קוּמָה | ה' וְיָפֻצוּ אֹיְבֶיךָ וְיָנֻסוּ מְשַׂנְאֶיךָ מִפָּנֶיךָ" and "וּבְנֻחֹה יֹאמַר שׁוּבָה ה' רִבְבוֹת אַלְפֵי יִשְׂרָאֵל," "When it was that the Ark would journey, Moshe would say 'Arise, Hashem, and let Your enemies be scattered'", "And when it rested he would say 'Return, Hashem, the myriad thousands of Israel.'" (Bamidbar 10:35, 36) The first *pasuk* represents the era of *galut*, and the need for *Hashem's* protection of the Jews. The second *pasuk* refers perhaps to the era of *Medinat Yisrael*, and the need to keep Jews Jewish and return all Jews to *Hashem*.

Parashat Behaalotecha includes the prophecies of *Eldad* and *Meidad* (Bamidbar 11:26), who the *Gemara* (Sanhedrin 17a) tells us were part of the original *Sanhedrin*. They prophesized *Yehoshua's* ascendancy to *Moshe's* role as leader of *Bnei Yisrael*. The commentators explain that this episode was an ecstasy experience of closeness to *Hashem*.

Sforno – Despite the urging of his son-in-law *Moshe* (Bamidbar 10:31, 32), *Yitro*, who had converted to Judaism, returned to his homeland of *Midian*. The reason, according to Rashi, was that as a *geir*, *Yitro* would not have a legal claim to a portion of land in *Eretz Yisrael*. But the convert, like the *Kohain* and the *Levy*, was not given a portion of the Land in order to demonstrate the intimacy between the *geir* and *Hashem*. "G-d is his portion." According to the Ramban (Bamidbar 10:29), *Yitro* remained with *Bnei Yisrael*.

5760

Parashat Behaalotecha contains the famous episode involving *lashon hara*, when *Miriam* is stricken with *tzaraat* for speaking against *Moshe*. (Bamidbar 12:1-15) This is followed by the slander of the *meraglim* against *Eretz Yisrael* as described in Parashat Shelach. (Bamidbar 13:1-33) The spies were severely faulted for not having learned from *Miriam's* very public example. (Rashi on Bamidbar 13:2) *Miriam* found out that *Moshe* had separated from his wife *Tzipporah* in order to be ready for *nevuah* at any time. She learned this fact from having been with *Tzipporah* at the time of the public prophesy of *Eldad* and *Meidad*. According to Rashi, at that time, *Tzipporah* commented to *Miriam* "Woe unto the wives of these men." (Rashi on Bamidbar 12:1) While *Miriam's* comment to her brother *Aharon* concerning *Moshe's* decision to separate from *Tzipporah* was for the sake of *shalom bayit*, it was still punishable as negative and potentially harmful information about another Jew. Rashi comments that *lashon hara* specifically intended to harm someone through shame is even more egregious. (Rashi on Bamidbar 13:1)

5761

There are two examples of complaining in Parashat Behaalotecha, each aimed at accomplishing a different goal. *Bnei Yisrael* first complain about their food because they want meat for themselves. (Bamidbar 11:1) They also complain about the inability of some of them to bring a *Korban Pesach* to fulfill *Hashem*'s Will concerning the sacrifice. (Bamidbar 9:6, 7) In the case of the complaints about the *Mon*, they were given quail in an episode that ultimately led to the death of many Jews. (Bamidbar 11:31-34) Alternatively, in the case of complaints of being disenfranchised from the opportunity to do the *mitzvot* of *Pesach*, they were give the holiday of *Pesach Sheini*. (Bamidbar 9:9-14) This demonstrates the difference in both motivation and result for complaints made only to satisfy a *taivah* and those made *l'Sheim Shamayim*.

The *pasuk* states: "וַיַּעַשׂ כֵּן אַהֲרֹן אֶל מוּל פְּנֵי הַמְּנוֹרָה הֶעֱלָה נֵרֹתֶיהָ כַּאֲשֶׁר צִוָּה ה' אֶת מֹשֶׁה," "Aharon did so; he lit the lamps toward the face of the Menorah, as Hashem had commanded Moshe." (Bamidbar 8:3) Rashi on this *pasuk* comments that the *Torah* is commending *Aharon* for not deviating from the *mitzvah*. There is a *mashal* that demonstrates the merit of *Aharon* in doing exactly what was commanded to him in lighting the *Menorah*. There once was a king who appointed one of his trusted noblemen to the position of ambassador to a foreign nation. Before sending his envoy to the foreign land, the king admonished him not to remove his shirt in public for any reason whatsoever. The ambassador agreed to the king's obscure directive and assumed his post in the faraway land. One day, the king of the foreign nation approached the ambassador with a wager. "I'll bet you $1,000 that you have a distinctive birthmark on your back," was his proposition. The ambassador knew full well he had no such mark on his back and reasoned that to prove this point, by removing his shirt, would have to be acceptable to his king back home, since it would mean $1,000 for the king's treasury.

Based on his analysis, the ambassador removed his shirt and proved the point to the foreign king, who paid him the $1,000 willingly. When the ambassador returned to his country he proudly presented the winnings to his king. "But how did you win this money," queried the king? When the ambassador explained that it was as simple as removing his shirt, the king flew into a rage. "Fool!" he shouted. "I bet the foreign king $10,000 that, as my trusted servant, you would never ignore my order not to remove your shirt! You have cost me $9,000!" The lesson for us is to perform the *mitzvot* as directed and leave the accounting to Hashem.

5762

Certain members of *Bnei Yisrael* who were *tamei* at *Pesach* and were therefore excluded from the privilege of bringing the *Korban Pesach* approached *Moshe* presenting their petition for a *Pesach Sheini* in order to bring the required offering. (Bamidbar 9:6,7) Even with all his *Torah* knowledge, *Moshe* readily admitted he did not know the answer and told the petitioners that fact from the outset. (Bamidbar 9:8) There is a strong lesson in this story for the practicing professional and anyone called up to solve the problems of others. One must be willing to admit what one does not know.

Rabbi Yossi Jankovits – The verse states that *Aharon* lit the *Menorah* "el mool pinay haMenorah," literally, "to the <u>face</u> of the Menorah." (Bamidbar 8:2) The *Menorah*, like one's face, has seven openings (two ears, two eyes, two nostrils, and one mouth). The mouth is at the center and all other openings are "towards" the mouth. The position of the mouth underscores its importance as the source of speech, which itself contains the incredible power described in the episodes of *Miriam* (Parashat Behaalotecha) and the spies (Parashat Shelach).

Rabbi Yossi Jankovits – In the *shishi aliyah* of Parashat Behaalotecha there are two *pesukim* set apart by two inverted letter ב ,"nuns." (Bamidbar 10:35, 36) This is an allusion to the original declaration of "naaseh v'nishma," "we will first do, then we will learn," which was the collective response by *Bnei Yisrael* at *Har Sinai* upon the giving of the *Torah*. (Shemot 24:7) However, the fact that the "nuns" are inverted demonstrates that "naaseh v'nishma" was, at this point in the *Torah*, forgotten by the People, such that their lack of faith began to create serious problems for the Nation. We read this *parashah* during the summer months, which is the time of year when we too begin to lapse. With its proximity to *Shavuot*, which itself commemorates the giving of the *Torah*, Parasha Behaalotecha comes to remind us what is essential and worthy of our attention. It calls upon us to rededicate ourselves to *Torah* and *mitzvot* precisely when it is hardest for us to do so.

5763

Rabbi Yochanan Zweig – Parashat Behaalotecha begins with a discussion of the *Menorah*, the third time in the *Torah* that the Menorah is mentioned. (Bamidbar 8:2) Rashi connects this mention to the end of Parashat Nasso and the gifts presented by the princes of the Jewish Nation, commenting that *Aharon* was upset that neither he nor the Tribe of *Levy* were allowed to give gifts for the dedication of the *Mishkan*. (Rashi on Bamidbar 8:2) This seems odd since *Aharon* was never jealous of *Moshe* despite, as the older of the two, having an arguable right to the mantle of Jewish Leadership. In reality, his concern was not for his own standing but in his desire to attach to the Community and to ensure that the Tribe of *Levy* would not become an exalted and distinct class of Jews, but rather that, through the *Menorah*, *Aharon* and, by extension, the *Kohanim*, would have a role in a central communal element of Judaism. As *Kohain Gadol*, Aharon was the CEO of the *Mishkan*, which was essentially service to G-d. The *Menorah* was not designed for giving off light (note, as proof, that the wicks pointed in towards the middle, not outward), but rather it was to bring the *Shechinah* into the camp of the People, which is essentially a communal activity. This desire to connect to the *Tzibbur* is a required attribute of the convert, as we see in *Rut's* declaration to *Naomi* of her intention to "go where you shall go," and that "your people shall be my people," (Rut 1:16) statements that clearly demonstrate the ideal of cleaving to the Community. Rabbi Zweig goes even so far as to say that this philosophy is the foundation of his belief that all Jews should give some kind of donation to their local Jewish Federation.

5764

Rabbi Yossi Jankovits – The *parashah* includes the exhortation by *Moshe* for *Yitro* to remain a part of *Am Yisrael* (Bamidbar 10:29-32), after which comes the "*sefer*" between the inverted "nuns." One of the *pasukim* there reads "וּבְנֻחֹה יֹאמַר שׁוּבָה ה' רִבְבוֹת אַלְפֵי יִשְׂרָאֵל," "and when it rested he would say 'Reside tranquilly, O Hashem, among the myriad thousands of Israel.'" (Bamidbar 10:36) There is a thought among the Rabbis that a certain number of Jews brings a deeper connection of the *Shechinah* to this world. Achieving that number can occur through the addition of a righteous convert. *Moshe* was citing *Yitro's* inclusion into *Am Yisrael* as a contributing factor to the *Shechinah* resting among them. A Tosafot in *Gemara* Kiddushin (70b, 71a) cites the opinion that *geirim* are like a "sepachat" (which is a *nega* or white skin blemish) on the Jews. Because *geirim* are often so careful with observation of the *mitzvot*, they have the potential of making the born Jews look lax by comparison. In the later part of the *parashah*, *Miriam* invokes this same argument in criticizing *Moshe*. The *pasuk* says "וַתְּדַבֵּר מִרְיָם וְאַהֲרֹן בְּמֹשֶׁה עַל אֹדוֹת הָאִשָּׁה הַכֻּשִׁית אֲשֶׁר לָקָח כִּי אִשָּׁה כֻשִׁית לָקָח," "Miriam and Aharon spoke against Moshe regarding the <u>Cushite woman</u> he had married, for he had married a <u>Cushite woman</u>." (Bamidbar 12:1) The dual language about the stranger's status (which, according to Rashi, indicates that she was beautiful in form and, significantly, deeds) demonstrates *Miriam's* concern that *Tzipporah* and *Yitro* would hurt the Jews by forcing a comparison of their righteous actions and the questionable actions of the Jewish People. *Hashem* responds that He told *Moshe* face to face and that *Moshe* is right and then, amazingly, Miriam is struck *middah keneged middah* with *tzaraat*.

5765

In many synagogues, there is a Hebrew phrase set forth above the *Aron Kodesh* that reads "da lifnei Mi ata omed," "know before Whom you stand," which obviously suggests that in praying, one is before the Al-mighty and therefore one should conduct himself accordingly. Yet in Pirkei Avot (2:19) it states "Rabbi Elazar omer ... da lifnei Mi atah amail," "Rabbi Elazar says ... know before Whom you toil." This would seem to be more appropriate in both the *shul* and in daily life. Participation in *davening* should not be a static or passive undertaking. Prayer is referred to as the "avodah she balev," "the service of the heart." Service suggests effort, indeed toil. If our efforts to know *Hashem* include struggling to understand and communicate with Him, we will no doubt achieve greater success in *devekut*.

5768

Rabbi Yossi Jankovits – The two *pasukim* that are embedded between inverted "nuns" in Sefer Bamidbar (Bamidbar 10:35, 36) contain a total of eighty five letters, which is the numerical value of "פה," or "mouth." It is notable that this place in the *Torah* marks the beginning of the descent by *Bnei Yisrael* through a series of incidents involving the misuse of the "mouth": for example *Miriam's lashon hara* against *Moshe*; the *meraglim*; *Korach's* rebellion; and the "curse" of *Bilaam*. It is also significant to note that these two *pasukim* contain the word "omer," "say," which is the use of the mouth.

5769

Rabbi Eliyahu Schlesinger – Parashat Behaalotecha references two Silver Trumpets used to summon the Assembly. (Bamidbar 10:1-10) The *Gemara* (Menachot 28b) teaches that all the *kaylim* that *Moshe* made were eligible for use by subsequent generations except these two Silver Trumpets. Perhaps the lesson is that the way a leader of one generation communicates with his congregants and students will not necessarily work in subsequent generations.

5770

Rabbi Aharon Kotler – At *Hashem's* Command, to form the *Sanhedrin*, *Moshe* gathered seventy men from the Elders of Israel, "whom you know to be Elders of the People and its Officers." (Bamidbar 11:16) Rashi on this *pasuk* indicates that the "Officers" referred to here are the Jews who were in charge of the Jewish workers in *Mitzrayim*. These men refused to follow the instructions of the Egyptians to beat their fellow Jews and were consequently beaten themselves. (Shemot 5:14) Why was this background a required *middah* for serving on the *Sanhedrin*? These men were meritorious only because of their relationship to the Jewish People. In order to be effective, a leader must be connected to the travails of the people he purports to represent. This is reflected in the Midrash Rabbah (Shemot 1:27) that tells us that *Moshe* himself, although exempted based on his royal station, engaged in the hard work in *Mitzrayim*.

5771

Rabbi Avram Skurowitz – Professor Nechama Leibowitz asks why, at the end of Parashat Behaalotecha, does Rashi indicate, with respect to the episode of *Miriam's lashon hara*, that when the *Torah* states "ki isha Cushit lakach," literally "he <u>took</u> a <u>Cushite</u> woman," (Bamidbar 12:1), Rashi goes out on the proverbial limb and states (a) "Cushit" means "beautiful in both physicality and actions," and (b) "lakach" means that *Moshe* "separated from," rather than married, *Tzipporah*. Earlier in the *parashah*, in reporting the episode of *Eldad* and *Meidad* to *Moshe*, the *Torah* tells us "vayaratz hanaar," "the youth ran." (Bamidbar 11:27) Rashi there comments that there are those who say this was *Gershom*, son of *Moshe*. In *Chumash*, the term "naar" is used to indicate a certain age, which here has to mean that, based on Gershom's birth (Shemot 2:22) and *brit milah* (Shemot 4:25) mentioned in *Sefer Shemot*, that this episode could not have occurred at the beginning of the forty year desert experience. Furthermore, the *Eldad* and *Meidad* episode is directly linked by Rashi to *Miriam's lashon hara*. He tells us that *Tzipporah* was standing beside *Miriam* when *Eldad* and *Meidad* were prophesizing, and lamented "woe to the wives of these men ... ," which was a catalyst for *Miriam's* complaint about *Moshe* to *Aharon*. (Rashi on Bamidbar 12:1) Since we know that both the episode of *Eldad* and *Meidad* and the episode of *Miriam's lashon hara* took place towards the end of the desert journey, we can now understand why Rashi expands the meaning of the *pasuk*. Since *Moshe* had been married to *Tzipporah* for many years, "lakach" must mean something other than "take." Similarly, *Tzipporah's* national origin (she was from *Midian*, not *Cush* – modern day Ethiopia) was well known to all. It would not make sense for *Miriam* to mention it after so many years, so "Cushit" must also hold other meaning.

5773

Rabbi Moshe Weinberger – In no less than thirty six places the *Torah* admonishes "v'ahavtem et hageir," "love the convert." Why should the *Torah*, in which every letter is carefully calibrated and nothing is superfluous, need to remind *Bnei Yisrael* repeatedly? Rabbi Joseph B. Soloveitchik indicated that this is because the *geir* has a history of not "belonging" to the Jews, which makes them less likely to love him. MRF Note – This is connected to Moshe's statement to *Yitro* in Parashat Behaalotecha: "v'hayita lanu l'ainayim," "you have been [will be] as eyes for us." (Bamidbar 10:31) *Moshe* understood that *Yitro's* non-Jewish background and adoption of Torah later in life would allow him the unique ability to scrutinize the conduct of the Jews against the *Torah* ideal to which the Nation was now bound. While *Yitro* may have declined to take on that role (Rabbi Weinberger stresses that he retained his love for his homeland despite his conversion), it is true that many *geirim* do play that role to some extent, whether in their families or more broadly. Reminding anyone, especially Jews, how they might improve is not always viewed as an act of love, to which one would respond with love. The *Torah* therefore needs to repeatedly reinforce the need to love those who are one's "eyes."

SHELACH

5757

The *pasuk* in Parashat Shelach states "... do not turn after your heart and after your eyes, after which you stray." (Bamidbar 15:39) The order of here seems reversed, for normally one would see with his eyes and then turn his heart to the matter. In actuality, the *Torah* is addressing two people in a single *pasuk*. The first has a yearning in his heart that he follows. His negative actions are thereafter observed by the eyes of a fellow Jew who emulates them. Both have gone astray. An obvious example is immodest dress, which breaks down an important Jewish tradition. The first individual dresses immodestly based on a heartfelt need (e.g. a desire for acceptance; insecurity and a wish to draw attention). The second individual notices the breach and adopts the same behavior.

5758

The *Gemara* (Pesachim 8a) tells us that "shluchei mitzvah aynan nizokin," "agents for a mitzvah will not come to any harm." If this is so, why did disaster ensue for the *meraglim* sent by *Moshe* to spy the Land? The spies did not act as true messengers, but rather injected their own will and perspective into their mission. As such, they were not protected like those who faithfully complete a mission, and they, and all of *Bnei Yisrael*, were punished as a result.

Rabbi Yissocher Frand – The *pasuk* states "אֵלֶּה שְׁמוֹת הָאֲנָשִׁים אֲשֶׁר שָׁלַח מֹשֶׁה לָתוּר אֶת הָאָרֶץ וַיִּקְרָא מֹשֶׁה לְהוֹשֵׁעַ בִּן נוּן יְהוֹשֻׁעַ," "These are the names of the men Moshe sent to scout the Land, and Moshe called Hoshea the son of Nun, Yehoshua." (Bamidbar 13:16) *Moshe* added a letter "yud" to *Hoshea's* name. The Daas Zakainim tells us that the "yud" had originally been appended to *Sarai's* name (before *Hashem* renamed her *Sarah*). Menachem Tzion draws the connection between *Sarai* and *Hoshea*. *Moshe* feared that *Hoshea* would not have the spiritual strength to lead and overcome the nefarious plans of the other spies. In providing him with "*Sarai's* yud," he was drawing on the demonstrated strength of *Sarai* in sending *Yishmael* out, away from *Yitzchak*, to maintain the spiritual integrity of her home. (Bereshit 21:9-14)

5759

Rabbi Chaim Leib Shmuelevitz – The *Torah* tells us that the *meraglim* were "anashim," "great men." (Bamidbar 13:3) If they were great, why did they slander the Land? They feared losing their status in the *midbar* as leaders of *Bnei Yisrael*, and therefore tried to dissuade the People from ascending to the Land. Their desire for honor was their undoing. Rabbi Yisroel Ciner asks why, after all, did *Hashem* imbue man with such a strong desire for honor? He answers that the pleasure we experience from honor inspires us to want to provide honor to others.

MRF Note – In the *Haftarah* for Parashat Shelach, *Yehoshua* sends *Caleiv* and *Pinchas* (Midrash Rabbah 16:1) into *Yericho* to spy the Land. (Yehoshua 2:1-24) There they encounter *Rachav HaZonah*, who was, according to Siduro Shel Shabbat (chelek 2, drosh 2, perek 1), an innkeeper or, according to other *mefarshim*, a harlot. After *Rachav* agrees to assist the spies, perhaps significantly, the *pasuk* states "וַתּוֹרִדֵם בַּחֶבֶל בְּעַד הַחַלּוֹן כִּי בֵיתָהּ בְּקִיר הַחוֹמָה וּבַחוֹמָה הִיא יוֹשָׁבֶת," "And she let them down by a rope through the window, for her house was in the town wall <u>and she dwelt in the wall</u>." (Yehoshua 2:15) The fact that *Rachav* could have been professionally engaged in either positive or negative conduct, combined with her living position "in the wall," could mean that she was "on the fence" theologically, and could have "gone either way," with respect to choosing righteousness. To her eternal credit, she choose wisely and, the *Gemara* (Megillat 14b) tells us, ultimately merited to join the Jewish People as the wife of *Yehoshua*.

The spies brought back grapes, pomegranates and figs (Bamidbar 13:23), then defamed the Land. As an atonement, at the time when the *Beit HaMikdash* is standing, we bring *Bikkurim*, While the *halachah*, as from the *Mishnah*, requires that we bring *Bikkurim* from the *Sheva Minim* (Bikkurim 1:3) about which *Eretz Yisrael* is praised, significantly, another

Mishnah (Bikkurim 3:1) mentions as examples only grapes, pomegranates and figs being brought!

Baal HaTurim – There is a correlation between the *meraglim* (Bamidbar 13:4-15) of Parashat Shelach and the Brothers who stood before *Yosef,* 210 years before. (Bereshit 42:3-6) In each case there were ten "accused" spies, since *Yosef* and *Binyamin* were excluded in *Mitzrayim* and *Yehoshua* and *Caleiv* were excluded in the *midbar.* Furthermore, the *pasuk* tells us that "וַיַּכֵּר יוֹסֵף אֶת אֶחָיו וְהֵם לֹא הִכִּרֻהוּ," "Now Yosef recognized his brothers, but they did not recognize him," (Bereshit 42:8) simply because the Brothers could not "see" the potential in *Yosef* to become viceroy of Egypt. So too, the *meraglim* could not see *Eretz Yisrael* for what it truly was. Once revealed, the true character of both *Yosef* and the Land became obvious.

5760

Rabbi Yosef Kalatsky – *Caleiv* is heroic in ways not seen in *Yehoshua.* *Caleiv* exposed himself to the evil counsel of the spies to "work from the inside" to change their feelings about *Eretz Yisrael.* While *Yehoshua* separated himself from the group, *Caleiv* made them think he was "one of them," which is how he was able to quiet the People and make a case for entering the Land. (Rashi on Bamidbar 13:30) *Caleiv* subordinated his will (to be apart from this evil group) to perform *Hashem's* Will (that all of *Bnei Yisrael* should enter the Land as One). And for his efforts, no matter that they were ultimately unsuccessful, *Caleiv* merited to be called "וְעַבְדִּי כָלֵב," "My servant Caleiv" by *Hashem* Himself. (Bamidbar 14:24) The lesson is that when we extend ourselves by engaging in *kiruv* with a sincere desire to effectuate G-d's Will, He rewards us at a very high level.

5761

Steipler Gaon – There is a less than obvious connection between Parashat Shelach and its *Haftarah.* The twelve spies in the *parashah* are rightfully condemned for going to great lengths to conclude that the Land swallowed its inhabitants rather than seeing the more obvious miracle that *Hashem* was creating deaths and resulting funerals throughout the Land in order to allow them to move about freely and undetected. (Rashi on Bamidbar 13:32) The proof of this open miracle is contained in the *Haftarah*, when a mere two spies (i.e. *Caleiv* and *Pinchas*) in the Land were pursued throughout the entirety of their mission. (Yehoshua 2:1-24)

Dr. David Epstein – The *pasuk* in the *Haftarah* for Parashat Shelach tells us "וַתִּקַּח הָאִשָּׁה אֶת שְׁנֵי הָאֲנָשִׁים וַתִּצְפְּנוֹ וַתֹּאמֶר כֵּן בָּאוּ אֵלַי הָאֲנָשִׁים וְלֹא יָדַעְתִּי מֵאַיִן הֵמָּה," "And the woman had taken the two men, and had hidden <u>him</u>, and she said, 'Indeed the men came to me, but I did not know from where they were.'" (Yehoshua 2:4) We know that the two men mentioned in the *pasuk* are *Caleiv* and *Pinchas* (Midrash Rabbah 16:1), and that *Pinchas* is also *Eliyahu HaNavi* (Pirkei d'Rabbi Eliezer 46). We also know that *Eliyahu* ascended to Heaven without dying (Derech Eretz Zuta; see Melachim II 2:11), and therefore possessed angelic powers. This explains why the *pasuk* in the *Haftorah* states that *Rachav* hid only "him," meaning one of the two spies. While she had to hide *Caleiv*, *Pinchas* was able to simple make himself invisible.

5762

Moshe charges the spies with determining whether the people of *Canaan* are strong or weak. (Bamidbar 13:18) Rashi states that he gave the spies a simple, if somewhat counterintuitive, equation: if the inhabitants dwell in fortified cities they are weak, for a strong people need not create walls to detach from their enemies. This formula can be applied to the separation barrier advocated by some in *Eretz Yisrael* as part of a strategy of detachment. As Rashi tells us, fortification of the Land is a sign of weakness.

Rabbi Yosef Kalatsky – The *Haftarah* for Parashat Shelach tells us *Yehoshua* told *Caleiv* and *Pinchas* to announce to those they met on their spy mission that they were "kedorim," "peddlers of earthenware." (Rashi on Yehoshua 2:1) The Sefas Emes says this term describes not their feigned profession but their true character. Each was like a vessel of clay. Unlike a vessel made from another material (e.g. metal), which has independent, intrinsic value and which, if broken, can be salvaged, an earthenware vessel has value only with respect to its function; what fills it defines it. *Caleiv* and *Pinchas* made themselves pure vessels for *Hashem's* Will and were thus able to prevail in their mission. Reb Ephraim Sobol adds that this idea is bolstered by the fact that neither *Caleiv* nor *Pinchas* is mentioned by name in the *Haftarah*.

5764

Rabbi Yossi Jankovits – *Caleiv ben Yefuneh* was the husband of *Miriam*, and the father of *Chur*. (Rashi on Shemot 24:14). *Chur* stood up to *Bnei Yisrael* at the *cheit haeigel* and was killed. (Rashi on Shemot 32:5) Learning from *Chur's* unfortunate lesson, *Caleiv* pretended to go along with the evil plot of the *meraglim* and "work from the inside." (Rashi on Bamidbar 13:30)

5765

Rabbi Michael Jablinowitz – In Parashat Shelach, the portion of taking the *challah* (Bamidbar 15:17-21) follows the episode of the *meraglim* for the purpose of providing a *nechamah* to *Bnei Yisrael*. The Sefas Emes states that the *meraglim* did not want to leave life in the *midbar* where *Hashem* provided all sustenance "min haShamayim" "from Heaven," in trade for a place where sustenance for the Jews would come "min haAretz," "from the Earth," meaning through physical toil. It was for this reason that they slandered the Land and gave a false report. Through the *mitzvah* of *challah*, *Hashem* was providing the Jews with a mechanism to remember that all bounty comes from Him, thus allowing *Bnei Yisrael* to continue the close relationship with *Hashem* that began in the desert.

5768

MRF Note – The evil report of the spies contained a large measure of truth. The "spin" of that truth is what resulted in the report being evil. One such item might be the assertion that *Eretz Yisrael* was "Eretz ochelet yoshveha," "a Land that eats its inhabitants." (Bamidbar 13:32) Rav Avraham Yitzchak Kook might actually agree with this assertion: that the ultimate *aliyah* is to become "one with the Land," and that being "eaten" by the Land could have a positive implication. Certainly the opposite is true, for the *Torah* warns us "וְלֹא תָקִיא הָאָרֶץ אֶתְכֶם בְּטַמַּאֲכֶם אֹתָהּ כַּאֲשֶׁר קָאָה אֶת הַגּוֹי אֲשֶׁר לִפְנֵיכֶם", "And let the Land not <u>vomit you out</u> for having defiled it, as it vomited out the nation that preceded you." (Vayikra 18:28) Vomiting is a physical rejection when something "eaten" is found to be toxic to the "eater," which is comparable to *Bnei Yisrael* settling the Land but failing to observe the *Torah*. We also find that when the *Torah* describes being consumed by the earth in a negative way, for example in the episode of *Korach*, it uses the word "tivla," "to swallow," rather than "ochel," "to eat." (Bamidbar 16:32; see also the episode of *Kayin* and *Hevel* – Bereshit 4:11) Rav Moshe Feinstein was once approached by a potential *baal teshuvah* who was willing to take on one, but only one, *mitzvah* as a first step towards a more observant life. Rav Feinstein instructed him to take on *kashrut*, because, he explained, "you are what you eat," and if one eats pure kosher food he will purify himself and ultimately take on more *mitzvot*. The message is that food becomes part of the corpus. As such, if the Jews are "eaten" by *Eretz Yisrael* they become wholly integrated and as one with the Land, which is *Hashem's* anticipated ideal state for His People.

5769

Rabbi Yosef Weinstock – What is the connection between the sin of the *meraglim* (Bamidbar 13:31-33) and the incident of *Korach's* rebellion? (Bamidbar 16:1-3) *Korach*, through the *nevuah* of *Eldad* and *Meidad*, knew that *Moshe* would not enter the Land as the leader of *Bnei Yisrael*, but rather would die before the National *aliyah*. (Rashi on Bamidbar 11:28) While *Korach* originally contemplated making his "power grab" for leadership at the moment of *Moshe's* death and the entry into the Land, when the sin of the spies caused that entry to be delayed forty years, *Korach* was forced to make his move while *Moshe* was still alive.

5770

Reb Ari Lieberman – While we all know of the opening story of Parashat Shelach as the "sin of the meraglim," the *Torah* does not refer to them as such. Rather, they are called "anashim," which Rashi indicates means "men of importance," pointing out that at the time they were sent by *Moshe* to spy the Land they were honorable. (Rashi on Bamidbar 13:3) The *pasuk* tells us "וַיַּעֲלוּ וַיָּתֻרוּ אֶת הָאָרֶץ מִמִּדְבַּר צִן עַד רְחֹב לְבֹא חֲמָת," "So they went up and spied the Land, from the desert of Zin until Rechov, at the entrance to Chamat." (Bamidbar 13:21) The *Torah* uses the word "tooroo," for "spying," a rather innocuous term. "Meraglim," as the spies are commonly known, connotes something much more clandestine and potentially negative, even sinister, and this is what Rashi himself calls them in his first comment on the *parashah*. (Rashi on Bamidbar 13:2) Putting the two Rashi comments together, it becomes clear that despite the acknowledgement of the *Torah* of the greatness of these men, due to the evil nature of their ultimate report, they are forever branded as the "meraglim." There is a parallel of sorts in the same *parashah*, by the *mitzvah* of *challah*. The *Torah* instructs us to set aside a portion of our bread dough as "challah" to be given to the *Kohain* (Bamidbar 15:17-21), yet in today's common vernacular we refer to the bread of our table as "challah," not the portion that we remove and burn (there being no *Kohain* to give it to) to satisfy the *mitzvah*. In this case, the *mitzvah* became the identity of the object, thereby elevating it. Conversely, in the case of the *meraglim*, their *aveirah* came to define them for eternity. MRF Note – It says in Pirkei Avot (2:5) "v'al taamin b'atzmicha ad yom motecha," "Don't trust yourself until the day of your death;" this is the *meraglim*. It also says in the *Gemara* (Avodah Zarah 17a) that one can acquire the World to Come in a single moment of *teshuvah* after a life of lowliness; this is the *challah*.

5771

Reb Moshe Stauber – Following the incident of the spies, *Hashem's* declaration that the Jews were barred from *Eretz Yisrael* (Bamidbar 14:23) was not, effectively, "You <u>may not</u> enter," but rather, "you <u>cannot</u> enter," meaning "you have created your own reality. I Commanded you to enter; you manufactured reasons not to go. You chose the reality with which you must now live. You said 'we can't,' and therefore you can't." As the well-known expression goes, "If you say you can or you say you can't; either way, you're right!"

5772

Reb Aaron Moses – Rabbi Shlomo Wolbe teaches that, following *Hashem's* decree that the Jews would not go into *Eretz Yisrael* (Bamidbar 14:23), the *mapilim* were unwilling to accept a fate of life outside of the Land. They defiantly ("vayapilu") tried to ascend to the Land and were decimated. (Bamidbar 14:40-46) Although misguided, the *mapilim* were compelled to act based on internal stirrings of "azut," "boldness," which Rashi connects to the word "vayapilu." (Rashi on Bamidbar 14:44) There is a positive side to *azut*, provided it is invoked to carry out the Will of *Hashem*. In the case of the *mapilim*, the *Torah* tells us "וַיֹּאמֶר מֹשֶׁה לָמָּה זֶּה אַתֶּם עֹבְרִים אֶת פִּי ה' וְהִוא לֹא תִצְלָח," "Moshe said, 'Why do you transgress the Word of Hashem? It will not succeed,'" (Bamidbar 14:41) clearly indicating that *Hashem* did not approve. Yet there are cases where one invokes *azut d'Kedushah* to go against the majority who desire to "eat, drink and be merry." Such a person seeks to attain Holiness despite the pressures of a world that rejects it. If this contrarian position is, in fact, in concert with *Hashem's Torah*, as expressed in his *mitzvot* and the guidelines of our Rabbis, it is a noble and praiseworthy approach.

5773

Rabbi Eliezer Ashkenazi – In cannot be that *Hoshea* was renamed *Yehoshua* at the event of the *meraglim* (Bamidbar 13:16), for he is referred to as *Yehoshua* throughout *Sefer Shemot* which preceded *Sefer Bamidbar*. Rather, he was known *Yehoshua*, but he was referred to as *Hoshea* in Parashat Shelach to draw attention to his "upgrade" from a "lad," to a "man among men," which was necessary for him to overcome the evil intent of the *meraglim.* (Rashi on Bamidbar 13:16) This is similar to the reference in Parashat Lech Lecha, when the *Torah* tells us "וַיֹּאמֶר אלקים אֶל אַבְרָהָם שָׂרַי אִשְׁתְּךָ לֹא תִקְרָא אֶת שְׁמָה שָׂרָי כִּי שָׂרָה שְׁמָהּ," "And Elokim said to Avraham, 'Your wife Sarai-you shall not call her name Sarai, for Sarah is her name,'" (Bereshit 17:15) implying that her true name was always *Sarah* but that she had been referred to as *Sarai*. Similar to *Yehoshua*, in order for *Sarah* to bear children, it was necessary to "raise her profile," and refer to her by her proper, destiny connected name.

KORACH

5757

The *Haftarah* for Parashat Korach is from *Shmuel HaNavi* (I Shmuel 11:14-12:22). The connection is that *Korach* was a progenitor of *Shmuel*. Through *Ruach HaKodesh, Korach* knew this fact, and therefore pressed on with his rebellion, thinking this would save him. (Rashi on Bamidbar 16:7)

The *pasuk* states "Vayikach Korach ben Yitzhar ben Kehat ben Levy ... ," "And Korach, son of Yitzhar, son of Kehat, son of Levy, took ...." (Bamidbar 16:1) Notably, the chain of *Korach's* ancestors does not mention *Yaacov Avinu*, who was the father of *Levy*. In Parashat Vayechi, on his deathbed, *Yaacov*, in addressing *Levy*, declares "Into their design, may my soul not enter," which Rashi indicates is a reference to the rebellious assembly of *Korach*. (Bereshit 49:6)

5758

The beginning of Parashat Korach makes mention of *Ohn ben Pelet*, who, along with the more notorious *Datan* and *Aviram*, was a part of *Korach's* group that rebelled against *Moshe Rabbeinu*. (Bamidbar 16:1) Strangely, unlike with his coconspirators, *Ohn ben Pelet* is never mentioned again in the text. The *Talmud* (Sanhedrin 109b) informs us that *Ohn's* wife saved him from the death that befell his comrades. She explained to him that the *machloket* was a sure-fire loser for him in any case, since regardless of whether *Moshe* or *Korach* won, he would not be the leader of *Bnei Yisrael*. She gave him wine and put him to bed, then sat with her hair uncovered and viewable from the door of their tent. Ironically, the rebels, who were willing to challenge *Moshe's* leadership, were not willing to violate the *Oral Law* he had provided them: namely that the hair of a married woman is *ervah*, and may not be seen by other men.

5759

The *pasuk* tells us that, in the face of *Korach's* rebellion, *Moshe* declared "וְאִם בְּרִיאָה יִבְרָא ה' וּפָצְתָה הָאֲדָמָה אֶת פִּיהָ וּבָלְעָה אֹתָם וְאֶת כָּל אֲשֶׁר לָהֶם וְיָרְדוּ חַיִּים שְׁאֹלָה וִידַעְתֶּם כִּי נִאֲצוּ הָאֲנָשִׁים הָאֵלֶּה אֶת ה'," "But if Hashem creates <u>a new creation</u>, and the earth opens its mouth and swallows them and all that is theirs, and they descend alive into the pit, you will know that these men have provoked Hashem." (Bamidbar 16:30) But is the "mouth of the earth" something new? The *Mishnah* in Pirkei Avot (5:8) describes the ten things that were created on *Erev Shabbat*, at twilight, and the first listed is "pee haaretz," "the mouth of the earth," which *Chazal* tell us is the very hole that swallowed *Korach*. Perhaps the answer is that the "mouth of the earth," was not a new thing to Creation but to *Korach*! The idea came to *Moshe* from the episode of *Kayin* and *Hevel*. In Parashat Bereshit, *Hashem* declared to *Kayin* "וְעַתָּה אָרוּר אָתָּה מִן הָאֲדָמָה אֲשֶׁר פָּצְתָה אֶת פִּיהָ לָקַחַת אֶת דְּמֵי אָחִיךָ מִיָּדֶךָ," "Therefore, you are cursed even more than the ground, which <u>opened its mouth</u> to take your brother's [Hevel's] blood from your hand." (Bereshit 4:11) The Arizal (Sefer HaGilgulim: ote kuf) tells us that *Korach* was the reincarnation of *Kayin*, and the Rema MiPano teaches that *Moshe* was the reincarnation of *Hevel*, demonstrating that Hashem punishes *middah keneged middah*.

5760

Rabbi Yissocher Frand – The *Mishnah* in Pirkei Avot (5:20) tells us that a *machloket l'Sheim Shamayim* will bear positive results, pointing to the disputes of *Hillel* and *Shammai* as proof. As an example of a *machloket* that is not *l'Sheim Shamayim*, and which therefore will yield negative results, the *Mishnah* points to "*Korach* and his community." Rabbi Shimon Schwab asks why mention "*Korach* and his community," rather than "*Korach* and *Moshe*," since *Moshe*, after all, was his adversary in their dispute. He answers that in an argument for the Sake of Heaven, each side recognizes there is another side to the dispute. Yet *Korach* and his followers were unwilling to even concede this point.

Rabbi Yaacov Menken – *Korach*, in challenging *Moshe's* leadership, declares "The entire Congregation, all of them, they are Holy ...." (Bamidbar 16:3) Earlier, in the incident of *Eldad* and *Meidad*, *Moshe* had wistfully touched on the same subject, stating "... would that the entire People of Hashem could be prophets, ..." (Bamidbar 11:29) *Korach* lost his ability to see that not all people are purely Holy, and hence, he lost focus as to the extraordinary Holiness of *Aharon* and *Moshe*. This is a problem with which we all struggle. It has been said that "American Jews know how to make *Kiddush*, but they do not know how to make *Havdalah*," meaning they view all things as "Holy" and acceptable, and cannot distinguish those things that are less Holy, or even unholy. This is the mindset of *Korach*.

5761

Rabbi Yossi Jankovits – Following the dramatic destruction of those involved with *Korach's* rebellion, *Moshe* directs *Aharon* to use *Ketoret* in order to stem the plague that resulted from the continuing complaints of *Bnei Yisrael*. (Bamidbar 17:11-15) Man was created through *Hashem's* "Breathing" into his nostrils, (Bereshit 2:7) and, according to Bnei Yissaschar (Adar), the sense of smell was the only one of the five senses that *Chavah* did not corrupt when sinning with the serpent (she saw, touched and ate the fruit, and she heard Hashem in the Garden and hid). (Bereshit 3:1-8) In the same way that we employ the sense of smell during "besamim," the *Havdalah* spices, to connect this remaining, unadulterated sense of the Holiness of *Shabbat*, so too did *Moshe* direct *Aharon* to use the sweet-smelling *Ketoret* to "appease" *Hashem* and restore Holiness to *Bnei Yisrael*.

5762

Rabbi Yosef Kalatsky – The *pasuk* says "Vayikach Korach … ," "And Korach took …." (Bamidbar 16:1) On this *pasuk*, Rashi tells us that when the *Torah* tells us that *Korach* "took" it means that *Korach* separated himself from the rest of the Community. The only way that *Korach* could challenge *Moshe's* leadership was to first remove himself from the Community that knew *Moshe* to be their true prophet. Perhaps it is in recognition of the dangers associated with such separation that, in two places in Pirkei Avot, *Hillel* (2:5) and *Rabbi Tzadok* (4:7) warn us "do not separate yourself from the community," for doing so is a precondition to rebellion against Jewish leadership and *Hashem* Himself.

Rabbi Yochanan Zweig – According to the *Gemara* (Sanhedrin 109b), both *Korach* and his co-conspirator *Ohn ben Pelet* were influenced by their wives. *Korach* was pressured to rebel; *Ohn* to abstain from rebellion. The underlying driver in each case is what each's wife wanted and was willing to accept. *Korach's* wife wanted to be married to the leader of *Bnei Yisrael* and pressured *Korach* into being someone that he was not. *Ohn's* wife wanted her husband as he was, and connived to extract him from the rebellion to preserve him as he was. A good wife is an anchor. Man is to blaze new trails and his wife is meant to preserve stability in his life and provide support. A wife who imposes a role on her husband that he is unwilling or incapable of fulfilling sets him up for a lifetime of misery. A woman can and should inspire a man to "be all <u>he</u> can be," not what <u>she</u> wants him to be.

5763

Rabbi Yosef Kalatsky – The *Midrash* Yalkut Shimoni (remez 752) tells us that, prior to their "final showdown," *Moshe* went to *Korach's* tent to try to work things out. The sons of *Korach* "covered their faces with the ground," when *Moshe* entered their home, which indicates that they were embarrassed to face him. They were in a quandary because *halachah* dictated that they should rise in respect for their *Rebbe*, but they knew he was their father's rival. This predicament embarrassed them yet they ultimately stood up. In doing so, they had the stirrings of *teshuvah*, which they eventually embraced, saving them from the death that their father suffered. This aspect of shame/conscience is a prerequisite to *teshuvah* and for being a Jew generally. The *Sanhedrin*, although comprised of *talmidei chachamim* of the highest order, had to sit adjacent to the Temple Mount (Rashi on Shemot 21:1), to remain humble and, therefore, effective. Without shame, even brilliance can lead to disaster.

5764

Rabbi Yosef Kalatsky – In Parashat Korach, after the rebellious group led by *Korach* had been swallowed up by the earth, the *Torah* tells us "וַיִּלֹּנוּ כָּל עֲדַת בְּנֵי יִשְׂרָאֵל מִמָּחֳרָת עַל מֹשֶׁה וְעַל אַהֲרֹן לֵאמֹר אַתֶּם הֲמִתֶּם אֶת עַם ה'," "The following day, the entire congregation of Bnei Yisrael complained against Moshe and Aharon saying, 'You have killed the Nation of Hashem.'" (Bamidbar 17:6) *Moshe* instructs *Aharon* to get up and offer a pan of *Ketoret* in order that *Hashem* not destroy the Jews, after which the *Torah* relates that "Vayikach Aharon kaasher deebair Moshe, vayaratz el toch hakahal ... ," "And Aharon did as Moshe spoke, and he ran into the midst of the Congregation ...." (Bamidbar 17:12) Why would the *Torah* need to tell us that *Aharon* ran? Is it not obvious that *Aharon*, who loved the People so deeply, would move with alacrity to save them and would stop at nothing to do so? Here the *Torah* is explaining that despite what happened to his sons, *Nadav* and *Avihu*, who died when bringing a strange fire and *Ketoret* into the *Mishkan* (Vayikra 10:1, 2), *Aharon* did not hesitate for even a moment about bringing the *Ketoret* offering to *Hashem*. Any normal human being with concern for himself would at least tread softly based on the family history. Yet *Aharon* was so connected to fulfilling the Will of *Hashem* that the "baggage" of the past never entered his mind.

5765

Rabbi Yossi Jankovits – Following the episode of the ground swallowing up those in *Korach's* rebellion, followed by the Divine Fire that annihilated the 250 remaining rebels (Bamidbar 16:31-35), *Moshe* devised a final test to demonstrate that the *Kehunah* would belong to *Aharon* and his family alone and forever. The leaders of the Twelve Tribes carved their names on staffs and placed them overnight in the *Ohel Moed*. In the morning, only *Aharon's* staff had blossomed, indicating that he was picked to be *Kohain*. (Bamidbar 17:21-23) The very next *pasuk* reads "וַיֹּצֵא מֹשֶׁה אֶת כָּל הַמַּטֹּת מִלִּפְנֵי ה' אֶל כָּל בְּנֵי יִשְׂרָאֵל וַיִּרְאוּ וַיִּקְחוּ אִישׁ מַטֵּהוּ," "Moshe took out all the staffs from before Hashem, to Bnei Yisrael; they saw and they took, each man his staff." (Bamidbar 17:24) Why would each Tribe retrieve and keep the staff that did not blossom? This is the equivalent of saving a losing lottery ticket. What is the point? These staffs became family heirlooms, demonstrating that each *Shevet* had at least desired and fought for the *Kehunah*, even if it was not granted to them. The point is strengthened by the fact that following this episode, the *Torah* describes the gifts that all of *Bnei Yisrael* were required to give to the *Kohanim* (Bamidbar 18:8-19), indicating that prior to the episode of the staffs, it was unclear as to how the *Kohanim* would support themselves. Nonetheless, the Tribes that participated in the test of the staffs were eager and willing to win the *Kehunah*, simply in order to grow closer in service to *Hashem*. This was a lesson worth remembering and passing down to the ensuing generations and that is why the *Shevatim* retrieved and kept their staffs.

5769

Rabbi Yitzchak Salid – The Midrash Rabbah (18:3) tells us that *Korach* used two questions to diminish *Moshe's* standing as a leader: he asked *Moshe* whether a *beged* made totally of *Techeilet* colored wool requires *Tzitzit*, and whether a house full of *sefarim* requires a *Mezuzah*. To both questions *Moshe* answered "yes," and *Korach* mocked him. Each of these *mitzvot* deals with remembering *Hashem* through the detail of the commandment, and *Korach* tried to argue that such minute details are unnecessary for serving G-d through Judaism. The result was that the offspring of his rebellious group were lost to the Jewish People, "swallowed up" by physicality. So it is with our *Avodat Hashem*. The Chofetz Chaim once said that if one does not *daven minchah* with a *minyan*, his children will not *daven minchah* at all! Like with *Korach's* assembly, those who spurn the small details of religious observance could, G-d forbid, lose their children to assimilation.

5770

Rabbi Yossi Jankovits – What is the connection between the end of Parashat Shelach and the beginning of Parashat Korach? Shelach ends with the mitzvah of *Tzitzit*, which we shall see and we "shall remember all the commandments of Hashem ...." (Bamidbar 15:39) On this *pasuk*, Rashi points out that the *gematria* of "ציצית" is 600, and when added to the eight strings and five <u>knots</u> of the <u>Tzitzit</u>, comes to a total of 613, which, of course, is the number of *mitzvot* in the *Torah*. This is certainly a non-standard *gematria*. Why focus on the strings and knots, rather than the letters of the words? There is a *Gemara* (Shabbat 31a) about a potential convert that approached *Shammai* and *Hillel* requesting that each teach him *Torah* "al regel achat," which translates as "on one foot," and is commonly understood to mean "in its essential form." "Regel," however, can also mean "moment," as with the dialogue between *Bilaam HaRasha* and his she-donkey. (Bamidbar 22:28) Thus translated, the potential convert's question was: "How can one keep the entire 613 mitzvot of the Torah simultaneously, in a single moment, or as a single person?" This question presents a real conundrum, since no one person can perform all the *mitzvot* (for example, *Kohanim* generally cannot bury the dead; non-*Kohain* Jews cannot do the *advodah* of the *Beit HaMikdash*, etc.). *Shammai* chased the questioner away, but *Hillel* replied "That which is disdainful to you, do not do to your fellow: This is the entire Torah, the rest is the explanation, go now and learn it," or, as stated in the positive, "v'ahavta l'rayacha komocha," "love your neighbor as yourself." (Vayikra 19:18) *Hillel* was conceding that it is, in fact, impossible for any individual to satisfy the entire *Torah* unless he is connected ("knotted") to all Jews, in love, in which case the *mitzvot* done by others are considered to be his, and vice versa. *Korach*, however, in his quest to be *Kohain Gadol* (and thereby fulfill the most prestigious *mitzvot* himself), challenged *Moshe* by clothing 250 men in cloaks made of *Techeilet* but lacking *Tzitzit*! (Rashi on Bamidbar 16:1) *Moshe* replied that despite the fact that the cloaks had *Techeilet*, they were nonetheless obligated to have *Tzitzit*, as they contain the knots that are the connection to all Jews and all *mitzvot*. *Korach* rejected the figurative *kesher* of *Tzitzit* and therefore the inherent *kesher* of all Jews. MRF Note – Perhaps this is evidenced by the first *pasuk* of Parashat Korach, which calls him "Korach ben Yitzhar ben Kehat ben Levy," but does not connect his ancestry to *Yaacov Avinu*, for to do so would be to connect *Korach* to the *Shevatim* and, through them, all of *Bnei Yisrael*.

5771

Rabbi Yosef Weinstock – *Korach* exhibited jealousy to the extreme. The Chofetz Chaim identifies two types of jealousy, one more pernicious than the other. These two jealousies can be reduced to two questions: "Why him?" and "Why not me?" The latter is essentially a positive statement, reflecting that one believes he is deserving. It is not an admirable trait but it is far superior than the former question. "Why him?" is an essentially negative outlook, reflecting that one believes that another person is not deserving of a *berachah*. MRF Note – "Why him?" is also an unanswerable question as one has no personal knowledge of the actual merits and *aveirot* of another that would justify (or not) his good fortune from *Hashem*.

5772

Rabbi Yosef Weinstock – The two questions used by *Korach* in an attempt undermine *Moshe* were whether a *beged* made of *Techeilet* needs *Tzitzit* and whether a room of *Sifrei Kodesh* requires a *Mezuzah*. *Moshe's* response to *Korach's* challenge was instructive. *Moshe* answered that, yes, such a *beged* needs *Tzitzit* and such a room requires a *Mezuzah*, because in each case the Jew is required to take an action to fulfill the commandment. This illustrates that ours is a religion of <u>deed</u>, not <u>creed</u>. MRF Note – Similarly, *Korach* wanted the *Kehunah* based on who he was, not based on what he did to deserve it.

5773

In Melachim א, in describing the "Pool of Solomon" where the *Kohanim* washed, the *pasuk* says "סָבִיב | וַיַּעַשׂ אֶת הַיָּם מוּצָק עֶשֶׂר בָּאַמָּה מִשְׂפָתוֹ עַד שְׂפָתוֹ עָגֹל", "וְחָמֵשׁ בָּאַמָּה קוֹמָתוֹ וְקָו (כתיב וְקָוה) שְׁלֹשִׁים בָּאַמָּה יָסֹב אֹתוֹ סָבִיב," "And he made [the pool], ten cubits from brim to brim; it [was] round all about, and the height thereof [was] five cubits; and a line of thirty cubits did compass it round about." (I Melachim 7:23) But a circumference of thirty and a diameter of ten results in a 3:1 ratio, or 3.0, which is <u>not</u> the measure of pi (which is 3.14159 ...). How can it be that *Shlomo HaMelech*, the "wisest of all men," could err on the measure of pi? The answer lies in the pasuk itself, where the word "וקוה," "v'kavah," "and a perimeter," is, based on our tradition, pronounced when the *Torah* is read as "וקו," "v'kav." The Vilna Gaon points out that the *gematria* of "kavah" is 111, and the *gematria* of "kav" is 106 (since it is missing the "ה"). If one divides 111 by 106 he arrives at 1.04717. Applying this value to the three *amot* of Shlomo's formula that seemed to "come up short," we arrive at 3.14151, which is accurate to the true value of pi far in excess of Archimedes, who came up with 3.14185, 600 years <u>after</u> Shlomo HaMelech figured it out!

CHUKAT

5757

Parashat Chukat sets forth the *mitzvah* of *Parah Adumah*. (Bamidbar 19:1-22) Rambam states that from the time of *Moshe Rabbeinu* until the destruction of the Second Temple, only nine such animals were slaughtered according to the *Torah's* edict. He further cites (Hilchot Parah Adumah

1:1) that the tenth and final *Parah Adumah*, which must be three years old, will be slaughtered in the times of *Moshiach*. This raises the question as to whether, upon the birth of a qualified *Parah Adumah*, the world will have to wait three years for *Moshiach's* arrival? Rav Moshe Feinstein is said to have stated that when Moshiach comes we will then find a three year old *Parah Adumah* with which to fulfill the *Torah's* directive.

5758

The times are violent, amoral, very depressing and even painful. Yet the coming of *Moshiach* is like childbirth. An uninformed person watching the process would think the woman's pain was leading her to death, and would be surprised at the joy and celebration that ultimately replaces the fear and concern experienced during the labor period. So too will it be with imminent coming of *Moshiach*, and our job is to have *emunah* that we are watching a similar process unfold.

The incident of *Moshe* striking the rock in anger to bring forth water, rather than speaking to it, as *Hashem* had commanded him (Bamidbar 20:9-11), is cited by some as the reason *Moshe* was not allowed to enter *Eretz Yisrael*. The argument for this result is that there was no reason for *Moshe* to become angry and that, when he did, he taught *Bnei Yisrael* that anger for no reason is permissible. This should give us pause to consider what messages we send to our children about the acceptability of anger in our lives.

The "rock-striking" incident in Parashat Chukat is referred to by the *Torah* as "mei merivah," "the waters of strife." (Bamidbar 20:13) The *Gemara* (Sanhedrin 101b) tells us that *Paroh's* astrologers in *Mitzrayim* foresaw that water would be the downfall of the savior of the Jewish People, which gave rise to the decree to throw all male Jewish babies into the water of the Nile. (Shemot 1:22) Ironically, *Moshe* survived the harsh decree in Egypt only to be undone by the miraculous water that flowed from the rock in the desert.

5759

At the unfortunate incident of the rock (Bamidbar 20:9-13), the damage was the loss of a lesson that could have positively impacted countless future generations of Jews. *Hashem* was telling *Moshe* that a hard stone could be made to change its nature through talking to it, not by striking it. The lesson is even more impactful when applied to the "softness" of the human heart. (Rashi on Bamidbar 20:12)

5760

Rabbi Yossi Jankovits – The Chanukas HaTorah points out that *Avraham's* gifts provided to his "visitors" correspond to the gifts that *Hashem* provided to *Bnei Yisrael* in the *midbar*, and the <u>way</u> *Avraham* came by each of his gifts (i.e. directly or indirectly) dictated whether they would be provided by *Hashem* Himself or a *shliach*. For bread, *Avraham* said "v'ekchah pat lechem," "and I will bring bread [direct]." (Bereshit 18:5) For water, *Avraham* said "יֻקַּח נָא מְעַט מַיִם וְרַחֲצוּ רַגְלֵיכֶם וְהִשָּׁעֲנוּ תַּחַת הָעֵץ," "Let some water be brought [indirect], and wash your feet, and recline beneath the tree." (Bereshit 18:4) Similarly, the *Mon*, representing bread, came directly from *Hashem* (Shemot 16:1-36), but the *mayim*, both before and after the death of *Miriam*, came through *Moshe* as *Hashem's shliach*. (Shemot 17:5-7 and Bamidbar 20:9-11) *Moshe* was made "hard of speech" by *Hashem* so that *Bnei Yisrael* would know that when *Moshe* was acting as a *shliach* for *Hashem*, his speech would improve. (see Ibn Ezra) *Chazal* tell us that "Shechinah Medaberet mitoch grono shel Moshe," "The Divine Presence Speaks from the throat of Moshe [Rabbeinu]," therefore, in the episode recorded in Parashat Beshalach (Shemot 17:6), had Moshe spoken to the rock, rather than hitting it, it would have been tantamount to Hashem Himself speaking to the rock directly, without a *shliach*. At the second incident in Parashat Chukat, *Moshe's* anger with *Bnei Yisrael* caused his *nevuah* (i.e. the *Shechinah*) to depart. Moshe therefore could have spoken to the rock as Hashem's *shliach*, but by hitting it, Moshe essentially made his staff an additional *shliach* for carrying out *Hashem's* Will. While the water was destined since *Avraham's* time to be delivered through a *shliach*, it was not meant to be delivered through two *shlichim*, and for this *Moshe* was punished by *Hashem*.

5761

Rabbi Yissocher Frand – In Parashat Beshalach, *Bnei Yisrael* sings to *Hashem*, with the *Torah* relating the following introductory words: "Az yashir Moshe u'Venei Yisrael et hashira hazot l'Hashem ... ," "Then Moshe and Bnei Yisrael chose to sing this song to Hashem ...." (Shemot 15:1) Later, in Parashat Chukat, there is also a *shir* that begins "Az yashir Yisrael et hashirah hazot ...." (Bamidbar 21:17) The Shemen HaTov cites the absence of *Moshe's name* in the subsequent *shir* as a credit, rather than a blemish, to *Moshe* and his leadership. At *Yam Suf, Moshe* was challenged with educating a newly freed Nation on how to praise *Hashem*, and he therefore sang along to instruct them. Thirty-nine years later, *Bnei Yisrael* was poised to enter the Land, and, upon experiencing the miracle of the water, they were able to praise *Hashem* without assistance from *Moshe*. This is comparable to the most successful parents whose missions are fulfilled when their children know how and when to "sing" alone. This is the only meaningful human relationship; where people who love each other strive for each other's independence.

5762

Rabbi Yossi Jankovits – The *pasuk* says "וְכֹל כְּלִי פָתוּחַ אֲשֶׁר אֵין צָמִיד פָּתִיל עָלָיו טָמֵא הוּא," "Any open vessel that has no seal fastened around it becomes unclean." (Bamidbar 19:15) This can be read as a warning toward the mouth that speaks *lashon hara*.

Rabbi Yochanan Zweig – Towards the end of Parashat Chukat, *Hashem* tells *Moshe* not to fear *Og, Melech HaBashan*. (Bamidbar 21:34) Rashi there tells us that *Og* had a merit from many years before, when he had reported to *Avraham* the capture of his nephew *Lot*. (Bereshit 14:13) What is startling is that, in commenting on *Og's* motivation during that incident, Rashi tells us "וּמִתְכַוֵּין שֶׁיֵּהָרֵג אַבְרָם וְיִשָּׂא אֶת שָׂרָה," "He intended that Avram would be killed and he would marry Sarah." (Rashi on Bereshit 14:13) The fact that *Og* intended that harm would come to *Avraham* (as he went off to save *Lot*) did not diminish the debt *Avraham* owed him, for the information *Og* provided was valuable. This is because the measure of a debt owed is what the favor is worth to the recipient, not the inconvenience or motive of the giver. This was something *Moshe* understood, which caused him to fear the merit *Og* had acquired. It is human nature to want to minimize the debts we owe, especially to *Hashem*, because in doing so we reduce the feeling of a need to repay, or to change our life, as an accommodation to the giver. For example, it is common expression among teenagers to declare "Hey! I didn't ask to be born," but the fact that the gift of life was made obligates one to *Hashem*.

5763

Rabbi Yochanan Zweig – In Parashat Chukat, *Miriam* dies and the well that, in her merit, provided *Bnei Yisrael* with water in the desert stopped flowing. (Bamidbar 20:1, 2) The second revolt among the People regarding water then ensued (the first being described in Parashat Beshalach (Shemot 17:1-3)). Our Sages tell us that *Bnei Yisrael* were never challenged in the same manner twice in the *midbar*, so the crisis described in Chukat must have been different than that described in Beshalach. Another distinction between the two episodes is that in the latter case, *Moshe* became overwhelmed, falling on his face (Bamidbar 20:6), which was not so in the first story. A hint is provided based on the complaint of the People in Chukat, who inquire of *Moshe* "וְלָמָה הֲבֵאתֶם אֶת קְהַל ה' אֶל הַמִּדְבָּר הַזֶּה לָמוּת שָׁם אֲנַחְנוּ וּבְעִירֵנוּ," "Why have you brought the Congregation of Hashem to this desert so that <u>we and our animals</u> should die here?" (Bamidbar 20:4) The mention of livestock causes Rashi to comment enigmatically that *Hashem* has pity on even the money of *Bnei Yisrael*, rather than the animals of *Bnei Yisrael*. (Rashi on Bamidbar 20:8) It is important to understand that the rock that provided the Jews with water in the desert gushed continually to the point where there were canals through the encampment. Therefore, at the time of *Miriam's* death, while the water ceased gushing from the rock, there was nonetheless plenty of water accessible to the People, which was not the case in the first story when there was no water at all. In Parashat Chukat, the People were not thirsty, but rather they were concerned over a problem they would have to manage tomorrow; but not today. Tomorrow's concern thereby became today's need, and despair set in because they were unable to fix today what they feared would affect them tomorrow. Problems have solutions, but a need is difficult to manage. The *Gemara* (Tamid 32a) tells us that a wise man is one who sees the future. This is not one who lives in the future, but rather who plans for it while in the present. In this case, *Bnei Yisrael* had made themselves thirsty, while the animals, with access to the residual water of the canals, were not. This is why Rashi does not mention that *Hashem* has pity on the animals, because the animals were not suffering from thirst at this time, but rather on the property of *Bnei Yisrael*. This is the equivalent of worrying about water for a car wash. The car is not worried, but the owner is. The only proper reaction for *Bnei Yisrael* in this situation was to trust that the world would ultimately respond to their needs. This is why *Hashem* told *Moshe* to merely speak to the rock, and it would provide. When *Moshe* hit the rock he missed the point. *Hashem* was telling the Jews "Don't worry, the Land of Israel is going to give you all you could want, merely through requesting it!" The support for this appears later in Parashat Chukat, when Rashi waxes poetically in commenting on how the mountains killed the *Amori*. (Rashi on Bamidbar 21:15) His anthropomorphic language underscores that nature is acting as servant, running to do the will of and protecting *Bnei Yisrael*. The Land is special; there is no need to be insecure. The Land wants to take care of us.

5764

Reb Shmuel Grundwerg – Rabbi Eliyahu Schlesinger once commented that *Bnei Yisrael* is to *goyim* as fire is to water. With a division they interact for good, as a fire boils the water. Yet absent a proper separation, the water extinguishes the fire.

5765

Rabbi Mendel Bluming – The incident of Moshe's hitting the rock (Bamidbar 20:11), and the resulting punishment of forfeiture of entry into the Land, are hard to understand. In fact, forty years prior, *Hashem* had told *Moshe* to bring forth water from a rock by hitting it (Shemot 17:6). The *Midrash* Yalkut Shimoni explains the problem with *Moshe's* action in Parashat Chukat with a reference to teachers. There are times when younger students may be subject to corporal punishment for teaching purposes, but such actions are forbidden for older students. The generation standing before *Moshe* after forty years was not the generation that left *Mitzrayim*. The prior generation required a tough style of leadership, and responded to the notion of hitting a rock to produce water. Yet the generation that stood poised to pass over the *Yarden* and inhabit *Eretz Yisrael* required a different teaching device. *Moshe* indicated through his actions that, while he was undisputedly the greatest rabbi the Jews had ever had, he was perhaps less equipped to lead the new generation into the Land, and for that he was excluded from entry. The message for parents and teachers is that there is no one proper approach for children and students, but each approach requires a separate calculation to determine the ideal way to effectively teach and impact the students.

5768

Parashat Chukat contains the *chok* of the *Parah Adumah*, whereby the *Kohain* who performs the purification process to a *tamei* person becomes *tamei* himself and is excluded from the Community. (Bamidbar 19:1-22) Also prominent in the *parashah* is the episode of "Mei Merivah," "the Waters of Strife," where *Moshe* famously hit the rock and, as a result, *Hashem* declared that he would not enter *Eretz Yisrael* with his Nation. (Bamidbar

20:9-13) Like the rationale for the *Parah Adumah*, the ultimate reason for the exclusion of *Moshe* from the Land is elusive. The lesson of leadership is that one may be doing exactly what is expected of him as a leader and yet will become reduced or be penalized in the process. However, like the *Kohain* who rejoins *Bnei Yisrael* the day after he is excluded, *Moshe Rabbeinu* will one day enter the Land and rejoin *Am Yisrael* in the coming days of *Moshiach*.

5769

Rabbi Yosef Weinstock – Rabbi Samson Raphael Hirsch challenges the popular understanding of the incident in Parashat Chukat when, after complaining about the *Mon, Bnei Yisrael* are attacked by snakes in the *midbar*. (Bamidbar 21:5-9) *Hashem* did not make a miracle in producing deadly snakes to attack, but rather He removed His Divine Protection that was keeping the already existing snakes at bay. The obvious lesson is that one must be grateful to *Hashem* for all the troubles He deflects and which one avoids based on His Protection. Rabbi Tzvi Nightingale mentions this idea in regard to an otherwise enigmatic line in *Hallel* that reads "הַלְלוּ אֶת ה' כָּל גּוֹיִם שַׁבְּחוּהוּ כָּל הָאֻמִּים כִּי גָבַר עָלֵינוּ | חַסְדּוֹ וֶאֱמֶת ה' לְעוֹלָם הַלְלוּיָהּ," "Praise Hashem all nations. Praise Him all states! For his kindness has overwhelmed us and the truth of Hashem is eternal, Hallelukah!" (Tehillim 117) Why would the non-Jewish nations praise *Hashem* for all the kindness He has done for the Jews? Perhaps because they, more than we, know the extent to which *Hashem* regularly intervenes on our behalf to frustrate their plans to harm us, G-d forbid. He is constantly holding back "the snakes," and really, only "the snakes" are fully aware. Reb Shmuel Grundwerg comments that perhaps this is also why the *Torah* relates the story of *Balak* and *Bilaam* (Bamidbar 22:2-24:25), despite the fact that it is not a part of the linear narrative that focuses on the *Avot* and the Jews. *Hashem* is giving us but one example where, based on His Divine Involvement, the curse was turned into a blessing.

5770

Biala Rebbe – The Kli Yakar states that the fact that the miraculous well that gave water in the merit of *Miriam* stopped providing water was a direct consequence of both *Miriam* dying (Bamidbar 20:1) and the failure of *Bnei Yisrael* to mourn her as they had mourned *Aharon*. (Bamidbar 20:29) From this we learn that a gift we receive in the merit of a third person obligates us to thank both the giver and the meritorious third person. This is always true with regard to blessings that come to us in the merit of our Holy wives, whom we should thank on a regular basis.

5771

Rabbi Edward Davis – Rashi makes clear at the beginning of Parashat Chukat that the incident of *Moshe's* "hitting the rock" took place in the fortieth year in the *midbar*. (Rashi on Bamidbar 20:1) Essentially, the *Torah* skips thirty eight years in recording what happened to the Jews in the desert! It is reasonable to conclude that, unlike the other recorded incidents in years 1, 2 and 40, for those intervening years, the Nation functioned in an ideal way, learning *Torah* and keeping *Hashem's mitzvot*. This is an extraordinary and uplifting understanding, which contains a lesson as powerful as those learned from the well-documented failings of *Bnei Yisrael*.

5772

Rabbi Edward Davis – A little known *pasuk* towards the end of Parashat Chukat reads "אֶת (כתיב ויירש) וַיִּשְׁלַח מֹשֶׁה לְרַגֵּל אֶת יַעְזֵר וַיִּלְכְּדוּ בְּנֹתֶיהָ וַיּוֹרֶשׁ הָאֱמֹרִי אֲשֶׁר שָׁם," "Moshe sent [spies] to spy out Yazeir and they captured its villages, driving out the Amori who lived there." (Bamidbar 21:32) *Moshe* sent these spies without the fanfare that accompanied the *meraglim*, and they successfully captured a city in *Eretz Canaan*. This could be viewed as something of a *tikkun*, as Rashi tells us that these spies specifically declared their intention not to act as the *meraglim* had, but rather to trust in *Hashem* and His servant *Moshe*. (Rashi on Bamidbar 21:32).

5773

Rabbi Avi Billet – Since there are at least ten answers as to what *Moshe* did wrong at the "rock" in Parashat Chukat, it is safe to say that we don't know exactly what sin he committed, at his elevated level. We might say, however, that *Moshe's* response to the People's complaints for water was a very human one. *Miriam*, of course, was responsible for the availability of water in the *midbar*, as the *Gemara* (Taanit 9a) tells us, in her merit the water flowed. Upon her death, *Moshe*, whose life was (at least) twice saved by *Miriam*, was in mourning. And yet, there is no indication in the *Torah* that *Bnei Yisrael* came to comfort him. Rather, they complained bitterly about the loss of water, not making the obvious connection of gratitude to *Miriam*, since now it would have been patently obvious to all what merit she possessed and what a loss her death was. Perhaps *Moshe* was overcome by the chutzpah and lack of *kavod* to his sister's memory. It is interesting to note that *Moshe* calls the People "הַמֹּרִים," which translates as "rebels," but is not the expected word "המורדים." (Bamidbar 20:10) "Hamorim" is a contraction of "Ha-Miriam," perhaps a veiled rebuke to their perceived callousness.

BALAK

5758

The evil prophet *Bilaam* was one of *Lavan's* sons, meaning he was *Yaacov's* brother-in-law. In fact, the *Gemara* (Sotah 11a) tells us that he actually advised *Paroh* concerning how to treat *Bnei Yisrael*, and he lived more than 300 years. *Hashem* gave him *nevuah* on par with *Moshe Rabbeinu's* so that the other nations of the world could not claim that if they had been granted a prophet as great as *Moshe* they would have accepted and followed the *Torah*. (Rashi on Bamidbar 22:5)

5759

Rabbi Bernard Weinberger – For three consecutive *parshiot* there is a "ק" "koof" in the *parashah's* name: "קרח" Korach (koof is the first letter); "חקת"

Chukat (koof is the middle letter); and "בלק" Balak (koof is the last letter). The letter koof represents *Kedushah*, and each *parashah* has an element of *Kedushah* contained within it. *Korach* was a *Levy*, the Holiest of the *Shevatim*; *Chukat* describes the *Parah Adumah*, which restored Holiness to the *tamei* Jew. And *Balak* was the progenitor of *Rut*, who contained and passed down the Holiness of the Messianic Davidic line. The Holiness is intrinsic and advances within the *parshiot*, even if it is not readily apparent.

5760

Rabbi Pinchas Winston – Parashat Balak opens "וַיַּרְא בָּלָק בֶּן צִפּוֹר אֵת כָּל אֲשֶׁר עָשָׂה יִשְׂרָאֵל לָאֱמֹרִי וַיָּגָר מוֹאָב מִפְּנֵי הָעָם מְאֹד כִּי רַב הוּא וַיָּקָץ מוֹאָב מִפְּנֵי בְּנֵי יִשְׂרָאֵל", "And Balak son of Tzippor saw all that Yisrael had done to the Amori. Moav was very frightened of the nation, because it was formidable; and Moav was disgusted in the face of Bnei Yisrael." (Bamidbar 22:2-3) The word "ha'am," literally, "the nation," usually refers to the *Erev Rav*, the mixed multitude of people that left *Mitzrayim* with *Bnei Yisrael* during the Exodus. The *Torah* would therefore be telling us that the Nation of *Moav* was frightened of the *Erev Rav* and disgusted/angered by *Bnei Yisrael*. This reflects the historical reality of the Jew-haters, for in their attempts to destroy the Jews they first seek to neutralize the potential allies for fear they will join the Jews in resistance.

5761

Rabbi Tzvi Nightingale – If *Bilaam* had such clarity as to the truth and righteousness of the Jewish People, why did he not convert? Rav Noach Weinberg answers based on a fundamental precept of human nature. When one is exposed to *emet* he cannot reject it outright without first undertaking to undermine it. Because he knows what he feels compelled to reject is right and true, an irreconcilable conflict arises within him. His only options are either to embrace the truth, however painful, or to actively attempt to change the essence of the true thing to make it untrue. *Bilaam* knew the Jewish People were chosen, but refused to accept the duties and discomfort that comes with "chosenness." He therefore had to try to undermine *Bnei Yisrael* so that their chosenness should be damaged. Only then could he live with his decision not to join the Chosen Nation. In fact, the name *Bilaam* is based on the language "bli am," "without a nation."

5762

Rabbi Edward Davis – The *Torah* devotes many verses to describe the dialogue between *Bilaam* and *Balak* during which no Jewish "voice" is included. Perhaps this is to underscore the degree to which the *goyim* will plot and focus on the Jewish People and, more importantly, the way in which all that plotting is for naught because of *Hashem's* protection of His People. MRF Note – There is a timeless lesson here for the current leaders of Israel, who should stop listening to today's "Bilaam" (Kofi Annan) and "Balak" (Colin Powell).

5763

The entire *Bilaam-Balak* story is a marked departure from the Jewish "narrative" of the *Torah*. We learn from this that *Hashem* is Omniscient, looking out for *Bnei Yisrael* even in the disconnected story of the plotting of the *goyim* against the Jews.

5764

Rabbi Eli Mansour – The *pasuk* says "וַיָּקׇם בִּלְעָם בַּבֹּקֶר וַיַּחֲבֹשׁ אֶת אֲתֹנוֹ וַיֵּלֶךְ עִם שָׂרֵי מוֹאָב," "And Bilaam arose early in the morning and saddled his she-donkey and went with the officers of Moav." (Bamidbar 22:21) The *Gemara* (Sanhedrin 105b) tells us it was beneath the dignity and station of *Bilaam* to saddle his own donkey, yet *Bilaam* did so nonetheless once *Hashem* commanded him to go. (Bamidbar 22:20). *Bilaam* meant to demonstrate his enthusiasm to follow *Hashem's* Will, and thereby to indict *Bnei Yisrael*, whom he wished to suggest were lax in their observance to *Hashem*. Rashi, on that *pasuk*, tells us that *Hashem* pointed out to *Bilaam* that *Avraham*, the father of the Jewish People, arose early to saddle his own donkey for the *Akeidah* (see Bereshit 23:3), thereby neutralizing *Bilaam's* claim.

5765

Rabbi Yossi Jankovits – It was the wicked *Bilaam* who uttered the famous verse "מַה טבו אֹהָלֶיךְ יַעֲקֹב מִשְׁכְּנֹתֶיךְ יִשְׂרָאֵל," "How goodly are your tents Yaacov, your meeting places Yisrael." (Bamidbar 24:5) These are the words that one recites when entering a synagogue. Why do we recite the words of the *rasha Bilaam* every day upon entering a *shul*? We are taught that on every occasion that *Bilaam* sought to curse *Bnei Yisrael*, *Hashem* converted his curse to a *berachah*. The *Talmud* (Sanhedrin 105b) indicates that of these many blessings that *Bilaam* recited in favor of *Bnei Yisrael*, only *Mah Tovu* remained a blessing forever. Other blessings ultimately had the effect of a curse. This is because none of these blessings were recited with the *kavanah* that they required. As such, they had no lasting power in a spiritual sense. Yet because Jews around the world recite *Mah Tovu* as they enter a *shul* to pray, despite *Bilaam's* lack of sincerity and *kavanah*, the *berachah* remains. Therefore *Mah Tovu* serves as a powerful reminder of the importance of *davening* to *Hashem* with *kavanah* in an effort to make our prayers and blessings everlasting.

5767

Rabbi Yossi Jankovits – Parashat Balak opens with a reference to all that "Yisrael," not, significantly, *Bnei Yisrael*, had done to the *Emori*, which frightened the people of *Moav*. (Bamidbar 22:2, 3) In Parashat Vayechi, *Yisrael* (i.e. *Yaacov*) says to his son *Yosef* on his deathbed "וַאֲנִי נָתַתִּי לְךָ שְׁכֶם אַחַד עַל אַחֶיךָ אֲשֶׁר לָקַחְתִּי מִיַּד הָאֱמֹרִי בְּחַרְבִּי וּבְקַשְׁתִּי," "And I have given you one portion over your brothers, which I took from the hand of the Emori <u>with my sword</u> and <u>with my bow</u>." (Bereshit 48:22) Rashi on this *pasuk* says that these are figurative names for spiritual weapons: a sword representing sharp wisdom and a bow representing prayer. *Balak* was fearful not of the physical strength of the Jews but of their spiritual strength passed down from *Yaacov Avinu*. Here we see the *goyim* recognizing the power of *yichus*.

5768

Rabbi Zalman Sorotzkin – At the end of Parashat Balak, the *pasuk* reads "vayachel ha'am liznot el bnot moav," "and the People <u>began</u> to commit harlotry with the daughters of Moav." (Bamidbar 25:1) It seems shocking that the same People who merited *Ma Tovu* would descend so rapidly. The *Gemara* (Sanhedrin 106a) explains the evil plan of *Bilaam* and *Balak*. The daughters of *Moav* would entice the Jewish men by having old women offer precious clothing for sale. Once interested, young, attractive women in the rear of the trading booths who were prepared for an immoral encounter would call to the Jewish men. Thus, the descent was gradual, with a seemingly innocuous "beginning." An interest in glamorous clothing brought about a cataclysmic sin. In this narrative is a warning to us to be vigilant in identifying and avoiding spiritual pitfalls.

5770

Rabbi Abraham J. Twerski – The *pasuk* says "וַיַּרְא בָּלָק בֶּן צִפּוֹר אֵת כָּל אֲשֶׁר עָשָׂה יִשְׂרָאֵל לָאֱמֹרִי," "Balak, the son of Tzippor, saw all that Yisrael had done to the Emori." (Bamidbar 22:2) What exactly had *Yisrael* done? *Moshe* sent messages to *Sichon*, king of the *Emori*, asking for passage though his land and provisions for which they would pay. (Bamidbar 21:21, 22) In response, *Sichon* attacked the Jews without provocation and was defeated. *Balak*, the classic Jew-hater, "heard" only that the Jews had destroyed the *Emori*, not the full background story of their prior attempts at peace, which is unfortunately still the case with modern-day Israel.

Rabbi Avram Skurowitz – The Kli Yakar teaches that there are four references to the Jews in the opening of Parashat Balak: (1) "Yisrael" (Bamidbar 22:2); (2) "haAm" (Bamidbar 22:3); (3) "Bnei Yisrael" (Bamidbar 22:3); and (4) "haKahal," in the pasuk "vayomer moav el ziknei midyan, atah y'lachachu haKahal et kol s'vivotainu kilchoch hashor eit yerek hasadeh," "Moav said to the elders of Midyan 'Now <u>the Congregation</u> will chew up our entire surroundings as <u>an ox</u> chews up the greenery of the field.'" (Bamidbar 22:4) The first three references appear straightforward, but the last one begs for interpretation. The first reference of *Yisrael* is to *Yaacov Avinu*, who had, in fact, conquered the *Emori* previously. (see Rashi on Bereshit 48:22). The second reference of "ha'am" is a reference to the *Erev Rav* who Moav feared would fight on the side of *Bnei Yisrael*. The third reference of *Bnei Yisrael* is to the Jews themselves. The fourth reference is to the descendants of *Yosef*, whom the *Midyanim* had sold into slavery so many years prior (Bereshit 37:28), which, incidentally, the "ziknei Midyan," the "elders of Midyan," would remember. *Yosef*, of course, is compared to an ox. (Devarim 33:17)

5771

Rabbi Eli Mansour – The *Gemara* (Sanhedrin 105b) tells us that nearly all the "blessings" that *Bilaam* recited about *Bnei Yisrael* were ultimately turned to a curse, save one: "מַה טֹּבוּ אֹהָלֶיךָ יַעֲקֹב מִשְׁכְּנֹתֶיךָ יִשְׂרָאֵל," "How goodly are your tents Yaacov, your meeting places Yisrael." (Bamidbar 24:5) The Ketav Sofer states that *Mah Tovu* was never converted to a curse because there is actually a curse already embedded in the blessing. This *pasuk* is essentially a recognition of the fragmentation amongst the Jews with respect to the places in which we learn and *daven*. The fact that Jews must have more than one tent or meeting place is testament to either our unwillingness or inability to come together as one.

5772

Rabbi Yosef Weinstock – Of all of the calamities the *Gemara* (Taanit 26a) says befell *Bnei Yisrael* on *Sheva Asar b'Tammuz* (e.g. the breaking of the *Luchot*, breaching of the walls of *Yerushalayim*, the burning of a *Sefer Torah*), perhaps the most tragic was the cessation of the *Korban Tamid*. Judaism (*l'havdil*), perhaps more than any other religion, appreciates consistency over extraordinary events. The *Korban Tamid* defined the day to day connection between the People and their G-d, and when it was discontinued, that consistency was lost. We try in our lives to build consistent service to *Hashem* and avoid ostentatious displays of single-feat religiosity.

5773

Rabbi Alexander Aryeh Mandelbaum – In an enigmatic *pasuk* towards the end of Parashat Balak, *Bilaam* declares "וַיִּשָּׂא מְשָׁלוֹ וַיֹּאמַר אוֹי מִי יִחְיֶה מִשֻּׂמוֹ קָאֵל," "he decimated his parable and said 'Woe, who will survive when He [G-d] imposes Keil?!'" (Bamidbar 24:23) The *Midrash* Pirkei d'Rabbi Eliezer (chapter 29), with respect to this *pasuk*, comments chillingly that *Bilaam* was stating that Hashem created seventy nations but only attached His Name "Keil" to two: "ישראל," "Yisrael," and "ישמעאל," "Yishmael," so who can survive in the days of *Yishmael*? The children of *Yishmael*, manifested in today's Arab and Muslim people, have the power to oppress the Jewish People because *Hashem's* name "Keil" is upon them. They are willing to kill and to be killed because of what they regard as G-d's Will.

PINCHAS

5758

Pinchas was *Aharon's* grandson who witnessed the sinfulness of *Zimri ben Salu*, a Jewish prince from the tribe of *Shimon*, who cohabitated with *Kozbi bat Tzur*, a Midianite woman. (Bamidbar 25:14, 15) *Pinchas* at the time had the *halachic* status of a zealot, who is allowed to kill such a man in an indignant rage. Yet had *Pinchas* gone to the *Beit Din* for permission to kill *Zimri*, they would have refused him (his inquiry being evidence that he was not truly a zealot at that moment). Based on *halachah*, if *Zimri* had stopped sinning prior to *Pinchas's* action, *Pinchas* would have had the status of a murderer. Moreover, the *Gemara* tells us (Sanhedrin 82a) that had *Zimri* killed *Pinchas* before *Pinchas* killed him, he would not have been found guilty of murder, because despite being a zealot, *Pinchas* would also have the halachic status of a *rodeiph*.

5759

Parashat Pinchas is one of five *parshiot* in *Chamishah Chumshay Torah* named for a person: Noach, Yitro, Korach, Balak and Pinchas. Chayei Sarah sometimes also makes the list.

Pinchas was not in line for the *Kehunah*, as he was alive at the time *Elazar*, his father, became a *Kohain*, and the original *Kehunah* was granted to *Aharon*, his sons and their future offspring only, not his then-living grandchildren. (Rashi on Bamidbar 25:13) The *Kehunah* transmits only to those sons born to a *Kohain*, which was not the case with *Pinchas*. Yet because of his meritorious action, *Pinchas* was rewarded with the *Kehunah*. (Bamidbar 25:13)

5760

Sforno – "Briti Shalom," "My Covenant of Peace," that *Hashem* gave to *Pinchas* (Bamidbar 25:12) was peace from death itself: immunity from the *malach hamavet*. This is supported by the opinion of Targum Yonatan ben Uziel that *Pinchas* was actually *Eliyahu HaNavi*, who ascended to *Shamayim* in a chariot of fire and never died.

5761

Rabbi Eli Mansour – Following the incident of immorality with the *Midyani* women, Hashem commands Moshe to "צָרוֹר אֶת הַמִּדְיָנִים וְהִכִּיתֶם אוֹתָם," "Harass the Midianites and kill them." (Bamidbar 25:17) *Moshe* ultimately appoints *Pinchas* to take vengeance in accordance with Hashem's directive. (Bamidbar 31:6) Although commanded by *Hashem* to do it, *Moshe* had gratitude for the refuge *Midyan* had provided him (when he fled from Egypt) and intuited that *Hashem* must have meant that *Moshe* should appoint another for the mission. *Hakarat hatov* resides among the highest of Jewish virtues. Gratitude is the basis for the custom of the *baal tefillah* repeating all of the *Shemoneh Esrei* on behalf of the *kehillah* except *modim* (the prayer of thanks). Given the importance of gratitude, we must all express thanks individually and personally, and not through a messenger.

5762

Rabbi Yochanan Zweig – Parashat Pinchas begins with Hashem describing the righteous actions of "Pinchas ben Elazar ben Aharon haKohain." (Bamidbar 25:11) Rashi states that *Hashem* noted *Pinchas's* pedigree in connection with his grandfather *Aharon* because his other grandfather was *Yitro*, a convert and former idolater. *Bnei Yisrael* had a valid complaint against *Pinchas*. Perhaps he had overreacted to the idolatry of *Zimri* based on *Pinchas's* idolatrous "spiritual genes," inherited from *Yitro*. Moreover, perhaps *Pinchas* acted zealously as overcompensation for this known issue in his background. *Hashem*, in mentioning *Pinchas's* connection with *Aharon*, was dispensing with the "ex-smoker syndrome" argument (ex-smokers are often the most virulent anti-smokers), confirming that *Pinchas* acted only *l'Sheim Shamayim* and not because of his fear of his own proclivities towards idolatry. (Rashi on Bamidbar 25:11)

Lubavitcher Rebbe – It was "unnatural" for a person to be "made" a *Kohain* if not born a *Kohain*. (Rashi on Bamidbar 25:13) But because *Pinchas*, in rising to kill *Zimri* and *Cozbi*, exhibited unnatural self-sacrifice in the face of possible physical and spiritual death, he transcended nature and was rewarded accordingly.

Rabbi Yossi Jankovits – The daughters of *Tzalaphchad* begin their plea for a portion of the Land of Israel by pointing out to *Moshe* that their father was not a part of *Korach* and his rebellious company. (Bamidbar 27:3) The *Torah* tells us "וַיַּקְרֵב מֹשֶׁה אֶת מִשְׁפָּטָן לִפְנֵי ה'," "and *Moshe* brought their petition before *Hashem*." (Bamidbar 27:5) The Chasam Sofer indicates that *Moshe* recognized the inherent conflict of interest, since the women were essentially intimating that their father sided with *Moshe* during the rebellion. Although *Moshe* knew the *halachah* with respect to their entitlement to their father's property, to avoid any hint of impropriety, he recused himself from the case.

5763

Dr. Mark Jaffee – The daughters of *Tzalaphchad* state "לָמָּה יִגָּרַע שֵׁם אָבִינוּ מִתּוֹךְ מִשְׁפַּחְתּוֹ כִּי אֵין לוֹ בֵּן תְּנָה לָּנוּ אֲחֻזָּה בְּתוֹךְ אֲחֵי אָבִינוּ," "Why should the name of our father be omitted [yigara] from among his family because he had no son? Give us a portion along with our father's brothers." (Bamidbar 27:4) The word "yigara" appears only one other place in *Chumash*, in connection with those who petitioned *Moshe Rabbeinu* for a *Pesach Sheni*, when those Jews who were ritually impure at the time *Bnei Yisrael* brought the *Korban Pesach* asked Moshe to allow them to do so thirty days later. (Bamidbar 9:7) As with these Holy Jews, the daughters of *Tzalaphchad* were clearly eager to attach themselves to the *mitzvot* and to connect in the greatest way to the Community and the Land.

5764

Rabbi Yossi Jankovits – Based on one opinion, *Rabbi Akiva* is the *gilgul* and *tikkun* of *Zimri ben Salu*. The *pasuk* states that when *Zimri* brought *Kozbi* for immoral purposes, *Bnei Yisrael* sat at the entrance of the *Ohel Moed* and cried (Bamidbar 25:6), and Targum Yonatan ben Uziel indicates that Bnei Yisrael were reciting *Shema* at that time. We also know that 24,000 Jews died in the plague brought about by the sinning with the *Midyani* women. (Bamidbar 25:9) Furthermore, the *Gemara* (Sanhedrin 82a) tell us that *Zimri* dragged *Kozbi* by her hair and had forced relations with her before *Moshe Rabbeinu*. In comparison, the *Gemara* (Berachot 61b) tells us that Rabbi Akiva famously recited the Shema just prior to his death *al Kiddush Hashem*. Moreover, the *Talmud* (Yevamot 62b) also indicates 24,000 students of *Rabbi Akiva* died during his lifetime. Furthermore, his tortuous death involved having his skin raked with metal combs (Berachot 61b), normally associated with hair. Perhaps most interesting, the *Gemara* (Nedarim 50b) tells us that the beautiful wife of Roman governor Turnus Rufus thought to defeat *Rabbi Akiva* (her husband's intellectual superior) by enticing him into impermissible relations. When she approached *Rabbi Akiva* he spat, wept and then laughed. Alarmed by his strange behavior she asked him to explain. He told her that while she was unquestionably beautiful, she, like everyone came from a putrid, spittle-like drop. Yet the fact that her beautiful form would eventually be worm-food in the grave warranted tears. The purpose of the laugh, he told her, was a secret. The woman was so taken with *Rabbi Akiva* that she divorced Turnus Rufus, married him, and thereafter had permitted relations with him. *Sefer* Emunat Itecha states that this woman was the *gilgul* of *Kozbi* and that *Rabbi Akiva* was the *gilgul* of *Zimri*. Rabbi *Akiva* knew this, and that is why he laughed.

5765

Rabbi Moshe Tzvi Neriah – Despite the trials and difficult stories in the string of *parshiot* beginning from the *pasuk* of the "inverted nuns" in *Behaalotecha* (Bamidbar 10:35, 36), and the slide downwards over five *parshiot* in *Sefer Bamidbar* for *Bnei Yisrael* (e.g. the matters of the *Mon* (Bamidbar 11:4-6), Miriam's *lashon harah* (Bamidbar 12:2), the *meraglim* (Bamidbar 13:27-29), *Korach* (Bamidbar 16:3), and *Baal Peor* (Bamidbar 25:3)) some of the happenings in Parashat Pinchas give cause for hope. There appears to be something of a youth-movement at work, where *Pinchas*, through an act of zealotry, is granted the Covenant of Peace and the *Kehunah* (Bamidbar 25:12, 13), the daughters of *Tzalaphchad* demonstrate strident love for *Eretz Yisrael* in demanding their father's inheritance (Bamidbar 27:1-11), and *Yehoshua* is named as the successor to *Moshe* (Bamidbar 27:18-23). Such activities surely must have inspired the youth of the generation that was anticipating entering the next phase of Nationhood through the annexation of the Land, and should equally inspire the Jews of today as we prepare for the difficult introspection and memories of the *Three Weeks*.

5767

Rabbi Yossi Jankovits – The pasuk states "וַתִּקְרַבְנָה בְּנוֹת צְלָפְחָד בֶּן חֵפֶר בֶּן גִּלְעָד בֶּן מָכִיר בֶּן מְנַשֶּׁה לְמִשְׁפְּחֹת מְנַשֶּׁה בֶן יוֹסֵף וְאֵלֶּה שְׁמוֹת בְּנֹתָיו מַחְלָה נֹעָה וְחָגְלָה וּמִלְכָּה וְתִרְצָה," "The daughters of Tzalaphchad, the son of Cheipher, the son of Gilad, the son of Machir, the son of Menashe, of the families of Menashe, the son of Yosef, came forward, and his daughters' names were Machlah, Noah, Chaglah, Milcah and Tirzah." (Bamidbar 27:1) Rashi states that the lineage of the daughters of *Tzalaphchad* is traced to *Yosef* because, like *Yosef*, they loved the Land. From where do we see love of the Land in their request? By all interpretations their father died in the first or second year of the *midbar* experience, yet their petition to inherit him came in the final, fortieth year. Rebbetzin Yocheved Rivka Kaminer states that this indicates that they were not interested in his movable wealth, which was available in the desert upon his death, but only his portion in the Land, which was only at issue as the *midbar* experience was ending.

5768

Rabbi Yossi Jankovits – As set forth in the *siddur*, the opening lines of Parashat Pinchas are recited at the commencement of a *brit milah* ceremony. *Pinchas* acted zealously to stop the illicit relations between *Zimri ben Salu* and *Kozbi bat Tzur*, as this was an adulteration of the covenant of *Avraham Avinu*. In the same way that when *Avraham* was commanded in circumcision, the *Torah* tells us he became "perfect" (Bereshit 17:1), *Pinchas* became "shaleim," "complete," through his deed. This is reflected in the *pasuk* "לָכֵן אֱמֹר הִנְנִי נֹתֵן לוֹ אֶת בְּרִיתִי שָׁלוֹם," "Therefore, say, 'I [Hashem] hereby give him My covenant of [shalom].'" (Bamidbar 25:12) In an actual Torah scroll, there is a "vav ketiyah," a "severed vav," in the word "שלום," "shalom," making it (absent the "vav") read as "שלם," "shaleim." Interestingly, the word "romach," "spear," used by *Pinchas* in his act of zealotry, is spelled in the *Torah* narrative without a "vav"

(רמח) (Bamidbar 25:7), and has a *gematria* of 248. The word "Avraham" also has a *gematria* of 248, for *Avraham's* act of *brit milah* sanctified all 248 of his limbs for the sake of *Hashem*. Since *Chazal* tell us that *Pinchas* is *Eliyahu HaNavi* (Targum Yonatan ben Uziel), and *Eliyahu* attends every *brit milah*, we begin the ceremony by remembering *Pinchas* and his noble deed.

5769

Rabbi Yitzchak Salid – What was the "Briti shalom," "[Hashem's] Covenant of peace" that *Pinchas* received (Bamidbar 25:12), and why did he get it? The Sforno says it was the freedom from stress, which he defines as the internal conflict one experiences in considering a decision. We worry before and after we decide something, and that worry results in mental and physical exhaustion and aging. Because *Pinchas* acted firmly and without reservation in the incident of *Zimri*, he was granted total serenity in future decisions, which may be why *Pinchas*, who is *Eliyahu HaNavi*, never died. This is a *berachah* for which we all should *daven*. In fact, in both *Mussaf Rosh Chodesh* and in *Birkat Hamazon* we pray for "yeshua v'nechama," "salvation and serenity." This petition raises a question. Would one not expect that serenity would be a natural, unavoidable product of utopian salvation? If so, we must say we are praying for serenity absent salvation, should *yeshuah* continue to be delayed. Essentially, either way we want what *Pinchas* received: serenity that will come from the coming of *Moshiach* (which *Pinchas*, as *Eliyahu*, will herald) or serenity that comes from *Hashem's* blessing of "Briti shalom," as we continue our long wait for our Messiah.

5770

Maharam Schick – The *Gemara* (Kiddushin 70b) states "if you see a Kohain who is arrogant you are assured his lineage is genuine." In Hoshea (4:4) it states "Your Nation is argumentative like a Kohain." By virtue of his act of *kanaut*, zealousness, *Pinchas* demonstrated the qualities of a true *Kohain*, and therefore the *Torah* reinforces his lineage back to his grandfather *Aharon HaKohain*. (Bamidbar 25:11)

5771

Rabbi Neal Turk – Rav Soloveitchik held that the *Three Weeks* period was an inverse of the progression of *aveilut* upon the death of a loved one (G-d forbid). The *Three Weeks* of national mourning correspond to the twelve months of personal mourning, the *Nine Days* correspond to the thirty day *shaloshim* period, and *Tisha B'Av* corresponds to the intensive seven day *shivah* period. Based on this understanding, the *dinim* of each stage may be reexamined. Because one is permitted to shave during the year of mourning (following the *shaloshim*), students of the Rav shave during the *Three Weeks*. Yet because a party of any kind is prohibited for the year of *aveilut*, these students would not have a party, even without music, during the same *Three Weeks* period. The points are (1) one needs to be consistent in following a particular *halachic* model and, more importantly, (2) during this time of year we need to internalize the concept that we are involved in a communal, yet very real, *aveilut*, based on having lost our Holy Temples.

5773

Rabbi Michael Jablinowitz – In Parashat Pinchas we read of the counting of *Bnei Yisrael* for the second time (Bamidbar 26:1-51), the first being in Parashat Bamidbar (Bamidbar 1:1-46). The Sefas Emes indicates that the first counting was related to receiving the *Torah* and the second to entering *Eretz Yisrael*. Both were significant events for *Bnei Yisrael*, and in each case every Jew received a portion, along with personal and national accountability.

MATOT

5757

The Lubavitcher Rebbe – The word "matot" means "tribes" or "staffs." A staff symbolizes strength and permanence. "Masei" means "journeys."

Parashat Matot and Parashat Masei are often read together as a "double" *parashah*, to indicate to us that even when we <u>journey</u> (especially in the summer months for vacation at the time when these *parshiot* are read), we must exhibit <u>strength</u> to be vigilant and steadfast in not changing the level of religious observance that we practice in our home life.

5758

After the war with *Midyan*, *Elazar* commanded Bnei Yisrael to immerse their vessels that had been contaminated by the *Midyanim*. (Bamidbar 31:21-24) The *Gemara* (Avodah Zarah 75b) states that from this command we learn the *halachot* of the *mitzvah* of *tevillat kaylim*.

5759

When the Tribes of *Reuven*, *Gad* and half of *Menashe* asked *Moshe Rabbeinu* to give them land on the east side of the *Yarden*, *Moshe* balked until they promised to go fight in *Eretz Yisrael* for *Bnei Yisrael*. (Bamidbar 32:21-24) When they did promise, "וַיִּגְּשׁוּ אֵלָיו וַיֹּאמְרוּ גִּדְרֹת צֹאן נִבְנֶה לְמִקְנֵנוּ פֹּה וְעָרִים לְטַפֵּנוּ, לֹא נָשׁוּב אֶל בָּתֵּינוּ עַד הִתְנַחֵל בְּנֵי יִשְׂרָאֵל אִישׁ נַחֲלָתוֹ..." "They approached him and said 'enclosures for our sheep we shall build here for our livestock and cities for our children. ... We shall not return to our homes until the Children of Israel will have inherited every man his inheritance.'" (Bamidbar 32: 16, 18) In responding to their request and pronouncement, *Moshe* taught *Bnei Yisrael* an important lesson. He declared "Binu lachem arim l'tapichem u'gidairot l'tzonachem," "Build for yourselves cities for your children and enclosures for your flocks" (Bamidbar 32:24), thus reversing the order of tasks. *Moshe's* point was that one must first care for his children, making them his first priority over his business. (Rashi on Bamidbar 32:15) Even if the Tribes meant to say that they would take care of their business for the sake of their children, *Moshe* rejected that message. He advocated that a Jew must work on making his children into *mentschen*, and the *parnassah* part will fall into place.

The Tribe of *Levy* was allowed to participate in the war against *Midyan* (Rashi on Bamidbar 31:4), but not against the inhabitants of *Eretz Yisrael* at the time of conquering the Land. Why? *Levy* was set aside to worship and serve *Hashem*. The war against *Midyan* was about sanctifying G-d's name and taking retribution for *Midyan's* spiritual attack on *Bnei Yisrael*. *Midyan* had caused the Jews to sin in immorality and *avodah zareh*, resulting in a deadly plague. (Bamidbar 25:1-9) Because the *Midyanim* were successful in damaging the spiritual essence of *Bnei Yisrael*, their spiritual representatives (i.e. the Tribe of *Levy*) were right to join the fight. The other wars, however, were struggles over money and the Land and, being rooted in physicality, *Levy* was excluded.

The *Midrash* Zohar (Balak) states that when, in Parashat Matot, the Tribes of *Reuven*, *Gad* and part of *Menashe* asked to remain on the east side of the *Yarden*, it was the beginning of the Babylonian Exile. It is interesting to note that the combination of the names *Balak* (בלק) and *Bilaam* (בלעם) yields two words associated with *galut*: Amalek (עמלק) and Bavel (בבל).

When *Reuven* and *Gad* asked *Moshe* to remain east of the *Yarden*, Moshe became very angry and rebuked them harshly and at length, assuming they were unwilling to assist their brethren in the conquest of the Land. (Bamidbar 32: 6-15) Notably, the Tribes did not interrupt *Moshe's* monologue and interject to clarify their intention to fight in the forefront of the battle. *Shlomo HaMelech* wrote "he who hates rebuke is a fool." (Mishlei 12:1) Criticism, even if off the mark to some extent, is valuable in our efforts towards self-perfection.

5761

In Parashat Matot, *Moshe* becomes angry with the officers of *Bnei Yisrael* who, in waging their war with the *Midyanim*, spared their women, who had been at the forefront of *Midyan's* spiritual attack. (Bamidbar 31:14) A few *pasukim* later, *Elazar* commands the Nation in the laws of *tevillat kaylim*, even while *Moshe* is yet present. (Bamidbar 31:21) Rashi there points out that *Moshe's* anger caused him to forget his learning in this area.

5762

Nachalat Tzvi – *Yaacov Avinu* thought that he was with *Rachel* when *Reuven*, his first born, was conceived, but, in reality, *Leah* bore *Reuven*. (Bereshit 29:23) Based on his misperception, *Yaacov* was unable to draw down the loftiest *neshamah* for *Reuven*. Similarly, when *Gad* was conceived, Yaacov assumed he was with *Leah*, but in reality it was *Zilpah* (for unlike *Rachel* who, when giving her maidservant to *Yaacov*, expressly told him so, *Leah* hid *Zilpah's* identity from *Yaacov*). The result was that *Reuven* and *Gad* became very successful with respect to physicality, but are somewhat impaired spiritually and thus, do not ultimately settle in *Eretz Yisrael*.

5764

Rabbi Yossi Jankovits – When *Moshe* concedes to the request of *Bnei Reuven* and *Bnei Gad* to settle east of the *Yarden* only after they help their brethren conquer and divide *Eretz Yisrael*, he says "then you shall be vindicated from Hashem and from Yisrael." (Bamidbar 32:22) This *pasuk* is the basis for the *inyan* of *maarit ayin*, which the *Talmud* (Pesachim 13a) tells us mandates that one's actions pass the scrutiny not only of *Hashem* but of the Jewish Community as well.

5765

Rabbi Michael Jablinowitz – The Sefas Emes teaches that the portion on *nedarim* contained in Parashat Matot (Bamidbar 30:2-17) follows the portion related to the *korbanot* brought on the *Yom Tovim* contained in *Parashat Pinchas*. (Bamidbar 29:1-39) It is a well know principle from the *Gemara* (Berachot 26b), that since the destruction of the *Beit HaMikdash*, our *tefillah* substitutes in a mystical way for the *korbanot* we would otherwise bring in service to *Hashem*. Furthermore, Parashat Matot falls out during the *Three Weeks*, a time of national mourning for, in part, the loss of the Second *Beit HaMikdash*, which the *Gemara* (Gittin 56a) tells us was destroyed based on *lashon hara* by the otherwise observant Jews living at that time. The clear message is that Jews must take stock of the way in which they use the power of speech, especially during this time in the Jewish calendar.

5767

Rabbi Eli Mansour – Every line of the *Torah* has meaning. The *pasukim* at the end of Parashat Matot read "וְיָאִיר בֶּן מְנַשֶּׁה הָלַךְ וַיִּלְכֹּד אֶת חַוֹּתֵיהֶם וַיִּקְרָא", "אֶתְהֶן חַוֹּת יָאִיר וְנֹבַח הָלַךְ וַיִּלְכֹּד אֶת קְנָת וְאֶת בְּנֹתֶיהָ וַיִּקְרָא לָה נֹבַח בִּשְׁמוֹ," "Yair, son of Menashe, went and captured their villages and called them 'the Villages of Yair.' And Novach went and captured Kinat and her suburbs and called it 'Novach,' after his name." (Bamidbar 32:41-42) Both men memorialized their names through naming these cities, but Rashi makes note that the word "לָה," in the phrase "v'yikra la Novach," is missing a "dagesh," or "dot" in the "heh," which he indicates can render the reading as "לֹא," meaning "no," in Aramaic. Thus translated, the phase can be translated as "and it is not called Novach," meaning the memory of *Novach's* name with respect to these cities did not endure. (Rashi on Bamidbar 32:42) Why would the property of *Yair* be sustained but the property of *Novach* not endure? There is a significant difference between the naming convention used by *Yair*, who called his villages "the Villages of Yair," and that used by *Novach*," who called his villages simply "Novach." Because *Novach* made no distinction between his possessions and himself, he nullified entirely his spiritual essence, which is the <u>enduring</u> component of a man. As a result, and contrary to his intention, his name was forgotten with respect to these places. MRF Note – This subtle lesson contained at the end of the Parashat Matot supports the earlier lesson taught by *Moshe* to the Tribes of *Reuven* and *Gad*, who initially prioritized their possessions over their children. (Rashi on Bamidbar 32:16)

5768

MRF Note – Although they did not ask to settle across the *Yarden*, half of the Tribe of *Menashe* was appointed by *Moshe* to remain there with the Tribes of *Reuven* and *Gad*. (Bamidbar 32:33) Perhaps this was due to their tribal heritage and skill in communicating and interpreting, as *Menashe ben Yosef* had originally done for his father in *Mitzrayim.* (Rashi on Bereshit 42:23) In the case of *Reuven* and *Gad*, the message of their willingness to fight alongside their brothers in the conquest of the Land and remain a part of *Am Yisrael* despite settling on the east side of the river seemed to get lost in their original request to *Moshe.* (Rashi on Bamidbar 32:7) Even when their intention was finally understood and their request was granted, it seemed likely that in the future there would be additional communication challenges. Accordingly, the Tribe most skilled in communications was appointed by *Moshe* to ensure the enterprise would succeed to everyone's benefit.

5769

Rabbi Yosef Weinstock – In Parashat Matot, *Hashem* commands *Moshe* "nikom nikmat Bnei Yisrael mayait haMidyanim … ," "take the vengeance of Bnei Yisrael on the Midyanim," (Bamidbar 31:2), in response to the earlier spiritual attack through prohibited relations. *Hashem* frames the vengeance as that of *Bnei Yisrael*, yet the next pasuk states "וַיְדַבֵּר מֹשֶׁה אֶל הָעָם לֵאמֹר הֵחָלְצוּ מֵאִתְּכֶם אֲנָשִׁים לַצָּבָא וְיִהְיוּ עַל מִדְיָן לָתֵת נִקְמַת ה' בְּמִדְיָן" "And Moshe spoke to the Nation, saying, 'Arm from among you men for the army, that they can be against Midyan, and carry out the vengeance of Hashem against Midian.'" (Bamidbar 31:3) One potential reason for the disparate phrasing lies in the mutual affection between *Hashem* and *Bnei Yisrael*. The Kedushas Levi teaches that *Hashem* refers to the holiday of *Pesach* as "Chag HaMatzot," and the Jews refer to the same holiday as "Chag HaPesach," with each "side" lauding the virtues of the other. But perhaps in this case the opposite is at play. *Hashem* tells *Moshe* that because the Jews succumbed to illicit relations with the *Midyani* women, they must fix the problem of their own making by attacking the *Midyani* nation. In reply, *Moshe* seems to indicate that the vengeance must be for *Hashem*, for in reality, He had created the problem! For had He not designated *Bnei Yisrael* as His Chosen Nation, *Midyan* (and most other enemies) would not have bothered to devise techniques to derail the Jews from their lofty mission. Since *Hashem* was the "project manager," it was His revenge that *Moshe* was commanded to actualize. This philosophy has provocative implications when considering the roots of persistent anti-Semitism. *Moshe* well-understood that being chosen is a magnet for hatred of the Jews.

5770

Rabbi Yosef Weinstock – In Parashat Balak, the *Torah* tells us that the Children of Israel began to act promiscuously with the daughters of *Moav*. (Bamidbar 25:1) While Rashi tells us this occurred at the advice of *Bilaam* to *Midyan*, the *Torah* does not. Yet in Parashat Matot, when *Hashem* commands the Jews to take vengeance on *Midyan*, *Moshe* rebukes *Bnei Yisrael* for having let the *Midyani* females live. (Bamidbar 31:15) There, he states about the *Midyanim* "hain hayna hayu l'Vnei Yisrael bidvar Bilaam limsar maal baHashem ... ," "see now, they were the ones who caused Bnei Yisrael, by the word of Bilaam, to commit a trespass against Hashem ...." (Bamidbar 31:16) The *Torah* is not a historical narrative but a book of life lessons. In not attaching responsibility to *Bilaam* at the time of the event, the *Torah* is teaching the Jews that they are ultimately responsible for their sins, despite the fact that an outsider was an instigator. Certainly *Bilaam* was liable and, in fact, he was later killed for his part in the sordid affair, but there was personal accountability for the Jews, which may be why the *Torah* waits for two *parshiot* to place any blame on *Bilaam*.

5771

Rabbi Eli Mansour – Rashi makes clear that *Elazar HaKohein* commanded *Bnei Yisrael* in regard to the laws of *kashering kaylim* because *Moshe* made a mistake. He became angry at the Jews based on their failure to kill the *Midyani* women who were the catalyst for the sin of *Baal Peor* and his anger led him to forget these laws. (Rashi on Bamidbar 31:21) The fact that anger led to *Moshe* being deprived of the merit of commanding *Bnei Yisrael* on these laws should not be viewed as a punishment per se, but a natural consequence of getting angry; simple cause and effect. This principle is set forth clearly in the *Mishnah* and attributed to *Hillel*: "v'lo hakapidan m'lameid," "an angry person cannot teach." (Avot 2:6) This is simply because one who is in anger cannot recall his learning due to that anger.

5773

Rabbi Avraham Yitzchak Kook – There is a marked difference between *Moshe's* reactions in Parashat Chukat and Parashat Matot. In Chukat, where the Jews were complaining about water, *Moshe* became angry and declared them rebels (Bamidbar 20:10), but in Matot, when *Reuven* and *Gad* asked to settle on the east side of the *Yarden*, *Moshe* became significantly more angry and animated, comparing them in detail to the *meraglim* that preceded them. (Bamidbar 32:6-15) From here we learn that when it comes to impediments to entering and settling *Eretz Yisrael* there is no room for polite talk, but rather forceful and passionate communication is the only way to respond.

MASAI

5759

Parashat Masai, the final *parashah* of *Sefer Bamidbar*, recounts the desert journeys of *Bnei Yisrael*. Rashi states that they made forty-two journeys in total, and fourteen of them happened in the first year. Moreover, eight journeys occurred after the death of *Aharon* in the final year in the *midbar*. Accordingly, for thirty-eight years, *Bnei Yisrael* made only twenty journeys, an average of one approximately every two years. This demonstrates *Hashem's* love for *Bnei Yisrael*, as He mitigated the harsh decree by not inconveniencing the Jews more than was required. (Rashi on Bamidbar 33:1)

5760

Rabbi Mordechai Kamenetsky – We learn a valuable lesson from the *Mitzrim* as described in Moshe's writings in Parashat Masai. In describing the departure of *Bnei Yisrael* from Egypt with "an upraised hand," the *pasuk* states "וּמִצְרַיִם מְקַבְּרִים אֵת אֲשֶׁר הִכָּה ה׳ בָּהֶם כָּל בְּכוֹר וּבֵאלֹהֵיהֶם עָשָׂה ה׳ שְׁפָטִים," "And the Mitzrim were busy burying because Hashem had struck down their firstborn and on their gods Hashem imposed judgments." (Bamidbar 33:4) Despite their moral depravity, the *Torah* uses the actions of the Egyptians to teach the world the importance of the essential ethical imperative of burying the dead.

5763

Rabbi Moshe Weinberger – In Parashat Masai, the death of *Aharon HaKohain*, which is originally described in Parashat Chukat, is again mentioned. (Bamidbar 33:38-39) Why is the repetition necessary and why in this *parashah*? Also mentioned in Masai are the *arei miklat*, the six cities of refuge for the unintentional murderer. (Bamidbar 35:9-28) The *Torah* informs us that the perpetrator remains in the city until the death of the *Kohain Gadol* (Bamidbar 35:25), the first of which was *Aharon HaKohain*. The *Torah* connects the two ideas as a *nechamah* for all Jews of all times. Mentioning the death of the first *Kohain Gadol* demonstrates that the event inevitably takes place, thus providing hope and encouragement to the exiled Jew. In the same way, we should be confident that our current *galut* will end with the coming of the Holy *Moshiach*, may it be soon and speedily, in our days.

The *parashah* references the death of *Aharon*, which the *Torah* tells us specifically was on *Rosh Chodesh* for the fifth month (what we know as *Av*). (Bamidbar 33:38) This is the only *yahrzeit* date that the *Torah* (rather than *mesorah*) states explicitly.

Rabbi Aviezer Heller – Contrary to normative *halachah*, one could marshal an argument for allowing learning on *Tisha B'Av*. The *Gemara* (Taanit 30a) tells us that children would be off from school on *Tisha B'Av* (implying they were otherwise in school year round), which could be viewed as a pleasurable thing, as Ramban (in the name of Tosafot on Shabbat 116a) tells us that *Bnei Yisrael* parted *Har Sinai* as would children leaving school (i.e. eager and with delight). We might think that so too an adult would receive no pleasure from studying a difficult *sugya*, and therefore it would be *mutar* on *Tisha B'Av* to learn in such a way. To the contrary, the Aruch HaShulchan explains that the soul of a Jew connects to *Torah* at all times and receives *hanaah*, even when his mind may be put off from the subject or difficulty. It is that soulful pleasure that is prohibited to us on *Tisha B'Av*.

5764

Rabbi Yossi Jankovits – In Parashat Masai, *Hashem* sets forth the boundaries of *Eretz Yisrael*. (Bamidbar 34:1-13) Like any land survey, it begins with a "point of beginning," where it also ends. Here, the "POB" is "Yam HaMelach," the "Salt Sea," what we know as the Dead Sea. One could question why something as exalted as *Eretz Yisrael* should be surveyed with such a prominent dismal primary reference. For the Dead Sea recalls the cities of *Sodom* and *Amorah*, and the incident of *Lot* and his daughters. There is a well-known idea that *Hashem* continually remakes the world to bring *geulah* and unlimited *Kedushah* to *Bnei Yisrael*. He also created the *Satan* to be vigilant in looking for means to reduce *Bnei Yisrael* and deprive us of opportunities to elevate ourselves and achieve our noble destiny. Therefore, *Hashem* orchestrates good for the Jewish People through unsuspected, unlikely, and even immoral channels. For example, the *Satan* seeks to foil *Moshiach's* emergence, so *Hashem* brings the seeds of redemption through *Tamar* and *Yehudah* and *David* and *Batsheva*. In fact, there is a *mesorah* recorded in the *Talmud* Yerushalmi (Berachot 2:4) that *Moshiach Tzidkenu* will be born on *Tisha B'Av*, thereby bringing us towards the final redemption through a sad, and therefore unexpected, origin. Similarly, the *Torah* hides the settling of *Eretz Yisrael*, a glorifying precondition for the ultimate redemption, in the unseemly reference to the Dead Sea, and connects the Land to *Lot*, who gave rise to *Moav*, from whom *Rut* came, who is the progenitor of *David HaMelech*, from whom our Redeemer will ultimately emerge.

5765

Rabbi Yossi Jankovits – One *pasuk* from Parashat Masai stands out as eerily prophetic. As *Moshe* admonishes *Bnei Yisrael* concerning *Hashem's* very explicit command to conquer the Land and drive out its inhabitants, he states the following: "וְאִם לֹא תוֹרִישׁוּ אֶת יֹשְׁבֵי הָאָרֶץ מִפְּנֵיכֶם וְהָיָה אֲשֶׁר תּוֹתִירוּ מֵהֶם לְשִׂכִּים בְּעֵינֵיכֶם וְלִצְנִינִם בְּצִדֵּיכֶם וְצָרְרוּ אֶתְכֶם עַל הָאָרֶץ אֲשֶׁר אַתֶּם יֹשְׁבִים בָּהּ," "But if you do not drive out the inhabitants of the Land before you, those of them whom you leave shall be "sichim" [nails] in your eyes and "tzininim" [a surrounding barrier of thorns] in your sides, and they will harass you upon the Land in which you dwell." (Bamidbar 33:55) Reb Ephraim Sobol points out that references to nails (soaked with rat poison, the terror weapon of choice of the Arabs) and surrounding barrier (Ariel Sharon's brainchild for separating Arab and Jewish communities) are, in our time, too explicit to ignore. Moreover, the Ohr HaChaim speaks on this issue, also in prophetic terms, stating that not only will they want our Land but they will fight us for it. Finally, it should be noted that this modern understanding of this *pasuk* is not to attribute "original inhabitant" status to the so-called "Palestinian" people (something they claim), but rather to describe the historical reality that would meet the Jews in every era where they attempt to exercise sovereignty over the Land.

5771

Rabbi Eli Mansour – In describing the travels of *Bnei Yisrael* in the desert, the *Torah* mentions "Marah" (Bamidbar 33:8), which is where, after traveling three days without anything to drink, the Jews discovered water. There, the *Torah* states "but they could not drink water from [the waters of Marah] because they were bitter." (Shemot 15:23) The Baal Shem Tov writes that it was the Jews, not the waters, that were "marah," bitter, and that their attitude actually impacted the taste they experienced. This is a profound lesson concerning the importance of maintaining a positive attitude to bring about a positive result. Further, the episode provides an express antidote to affliction of negativity. *Moshe* tosses a piece of "wood" into the water to sweeten it, and the *Torah* is compared to wood, as we saying in davening "Eitz Chayim hee ... ," "it [the Torah] is a Tree of Life ... ," (Mishlei 3:18) We must acknowledge that learning *Torah* will remove from us all bitter attitudes and improve a bitter environment.

5772

Rabbi Josef B. Soloveitchik – *Halachah* makes accommodations for the "istanis," a sensitive person. For example, as stated in the *Gemara* (Berachot 16b), during the *Nine Days*, bathing in warm water for pleasure is prohibited, yet bathing in warm water due to personal pain and discomfort is allowed. So too in the case of eating in the *Sukkah*, *halachah* states an individual decides for himself whether or not he is comfortable, and if he is not, then he is *patur*. In order to avail oneself of this regime, he must be willing to apply the same principle to others, meaning we must defer to the sensitivities of others and not offend them, even if by an objective standard what upsets them is not considered upsetting. An individual gets to decide what makes him uncomfortable, whether with relation to *mitzvot* or relations with other people. This goes well beyond *Hillel's* well-know maxim, set forth in the *Talmud* (Shabbat 31a), of "that which is offensive to you do not do to others."

SEFER DEVARIM
DEVARIM

5758

Rabbi Chaim Shmuelevitz – In rebuking *Bnei Yisrael, Moshe* lists all the places that they sinned, but only alludes to their actual sins. (Rashi on Devarim 1:1) This approach contains a *mussar* lesson that is a central principle of interpersonal communications. We should rebuke only as necessary and never derive enjoyment from it. This is an important lesson in the days preceding *Tisha B'Av* when the Second Temple was destroyed because of baseless hatred amongst Jews.

5759

The *Three Weeks* of mourning between *Shiva Asur b'Tammuz* and *Tisha B'Av* correspond to the three hours that *Adam HaRishon* did not wait before partaking of the Tree of Knowledge of Good and Evil. Had he waited, it would have been *Shabbat* and he would have had permission to eat it.

Sefer Devarim is also known as "Mishneh Torah." The root of the word "mishneh" is "sheni," "second," meaning "repeated," for much of the *mitzvot* of the *Torah* are repeated in *Sefer Devarim*. But *Sefer Devarim* also contains *mitzvot* introduced for the first time and related to the Land, which were ripe for imparting during that last year in the desert for *Bnei Yisrael*.

Tisha B'Av is closely tied to the story in the *Gemara* (Gittin 56a) about "Kamtza and Bar Kamtza." *Chazal* tell us that because of the incident of *Kamtza* and *Bar Kamtza* the Temple was destroyed. A party invite intended for *Kamtza* was inadvertently received by *Bar Kamtza*, who came nonetheless, was thrown out of the party by the host, and then set about to destroy the host and the attending rabbis who did nothing to protest his expulsion. We can understand why *Bar Kamtza* is blamed; after all he was involved in the *machloket* that spiraled out of control. But why would *Kamtza* be blamed? He never received the original party invitation! The problem with *Kamtza* is that he was socially connected to people like the party's host that were capable of excluding and publicly embarrassing other Jews. Such social associations helped fertilize the soil in which *sinat chinam* could grow, thereby making *Kamtza* guilty through that association.

5760

Rabbi Yosef Kalatsky – The destructions of the Temples represent the destruction of the relationship between *Hashem* and *Bnei Yisrael*. *Hashem* created a system of *avodah* that involve *mitzvot* that ask us to emulate our Creator (for example, to bury the dead, to visit the sick, etc.). This system is very effective in achieving commonality, to the extent possible, between G-d and the Jews. When *Bnei Yisrael* committed the three cardinal sins during the time of the First Temple and engaged in *sinat chinam* at the time of the Second Temple, we acted inconsistently with respect to what G-d expected of us and what G-d is, in His Essence. Under such conditions *Hashem* withdraws His Presence. He has nothing in common with us, as it were, and, like a spouse who is in a dead end marriage, He departs.

5761

The *Torah* prohibits marriage to a convert to Judaism from either *Moav* or *Amon* (Devarim 23:4), but allows a born Jew to marry a member of the nation of *Amalek* who converts. This is based on the sin of *Moav* and *Amon* of not showing *Bnei Yisrael* hospitality in the desert despite the fact that the progenitor of the Jews, *Avraham Avinu*, saved the progenitor of *Moav* and *Amon*, *Lot*, Avraham's nephew. (Devarim 23:5) Yet while this is bad, *Amalek* attacked and killed Jews (Shemot 17:8), which is seemingly much worse. The problem is that *Avraham* risked his life to save *Lot*, and *Lot's* descendants should have felt indebted to the Jews. The failure of *Moav* and *Amon* to acknowledge this debt is a genetic flaw that the *Torah* informs us cannot be overcome.

5762

Rabbi Yossi Jankovits – *Hashem* exhibited tremendous *chesed* by not letting *Moshe Rabbeinu* into *Eretz Yisrael*, for if he went in he would have established a *Beit HaMikdash* that would never have been destroyed. In such a case, says the Ohr HaChaim (Devarim 1:37), rather than applying His Wrath upon the Holy Temples, *Hashem* would have imposed His Wrath upon the Jewish People, G-d forbid, thereby destroying them. *Sarah Imeinu* foresaw this problem and therefore sent *Hagar* and *Yishmael* into the desert without water. When *Hagar* implored G-d for water for *Yishmael*, she was answered. (Bereshit 21:19) This amounted to a *kal v'chomer* that *Moshe* should have known. In essence *Sarah* "set him up," so that by striking the rock to obtain desert water, rather than merely speaking (Bamidbar 20:11), as *Hagar* and *Yishmael* had, *Moshe* committed a sin that would keep him out of *Eretz Yisrael* and save the Jewish People from destruction.

Rabbi Yosef Y. Jacobson – The *Midrash* (Eichah 1:1) states that there were three prophets who used the word "eichah": *Moshe, Yishaiyahu* and *Yirmiyahu*. *Moshe* wrote in Parashat Devarim "אֵיכָה אֶשָּׂא לְבַדִּי טָרְחֲכֶם וּמַשַּׂאֲכֶם וְרִיבְכֶם", "Alas, how can I alone carry your contentiousness, your burdens and your quarrels?" (Devarim 1:12) No alternative leader wanted to step forward to assume the challenge of properly shepherding the Jewish People. This progressed to *Yishaiyahu's* lament about moral depravity (Yishaiyahu 1:21) and led ultimately to *Yirmiyahu's Megillat Eichah*, describing the destruction of *Yerushalayim*. This negative progression is being played out in the so-called "Oslo Peace Process," when, as in *Moshe's* time, no one will step forward to avoid the negative consequences that are sure to ensue. Another modern example is American cultural assimilation amongst its Jews. Now more than ever *Am Yisrael* needs effective leadership to avoid tragedy.

5763

Abravanel – The *pasuk* states "Gam bi hitanaf Hashem b'glalchem," "With me [Moshe] as well Hashem became angry because of you [plural]." (Devarim 1:37) This declaration comes as *Moshe* is recounting the sin of the spies, which was a lapse on *Moshe's* part for letting *Bnei Yisrael* even contemplate sending a scouting party in apparent defiance of *Hashem's* directive to enter the Land. *Moshe* specifically asked about the Canaanites and their cities, and gave an opening for the ultimate negative report of the spies. (Bamidbar 13:18) While this was in fact a sin, because of his positive intention, *Hashem* did not punish *Moshe* until this sin was combined with that of striking (rather than talking to) the rock. (Bamidbar 20:11)

5764

The *Haftarah* for Parashat Devarim contains the famous words "לָמָּה לִּי רֹב "זִבְחֵיכֶם יֹאמַר ה' שָׂבַעְתִּי עֹלוֹת אֵילִים וְחֵלֶב מְרִיאִים וְדַם פָּרִים וּכְבָשִׂים וְעַתּוּדִים לֹא חָפָצְתִּי," "'Why do I need your numerous sacrifices?' Says Hashem – 'I am satiated with elevation offerings of rams and the choicest of fattened animals, and the blood of bulls and sheep and he-goats I do not desire.'" (Yishaiyahu 1:11) This is not, G-d forbid, a declaration of abrogation of the Temple *Avodah*. Rather, it is an indictment of Service devoid of love and pure intent. Further, the prophet tells us "לְמְדוּ הֵיטֵב דִּרְשׁוּ מִשְׁפָּט אַשְּׁרוּ חָמוֹץ שִׁפְטוּ "יָתוֹם רִיבוּ אַלְמָנָה," "Learn to do good, seek justice, strengthen the victim, perform justice for the orphan, do justice for the widow." (Yishaiyahu 1:17) These words are a present day indictment and a painful reminder of what we need to do to restore *Hashem's* Presence in the world. The formula in the *Haftarah* is clear: do *chesed* with love.

5765

Rabbi Edward Davis – Parashat Devarim is always read on "Shabbat Chazon," the Shabbat that falls during the *Nine Days* and which imme-diately precedes *Tisha B'Av*. The *Midrash* (Eichah:intro) tells us that, following the decree that all males from ages twenty to sixty would die in the desert (and thus never enter the Promised Land), a macabre annual event took place every *Tisha B'Av*. All men subject to the decree would dig a grave and lay down within it overnight on *Tisha B'Av*. In the morning, those who were destined to die that day would be buried, and those who woke up would return to their homes. Significantly, the tribe of *Levy*, which was not subject to the decree (not having participated in the sin of the *meraglim*), nonetheless undertook the same ritual annu-ally. Why would the men of *Levy* go through the trouble of digging a grave and lying within if they were not slated to die on that day? The answer is that *Levy* wanted to materially empathize with their distressed brothers. By participating in the annual event, they demonstrated the importance of *achdut* among the Jewish People. Regardless as to how one feels about the Disengagement/Expulsion of Jews from *Gush Katif,* it is necessary for every Jew to empathize in their plight and to say *kinot* on their behalf.

5769

In retelling the incident of the spies in Parashat Devarim, the *Torah* provides additional detail beyond what is mentioned in Parashat Shelach. Here, *Moshe* declares "the matter was good in my eyes ...." (Devarim 1:23) Rashi questions why, if it was good in *Moshe's* eyes, the event is listed as part of the admonitions here at the beginning of Parashat Devarim. Rashi goes to great lengths to describe how *Moshe* actually attempted to employ "reverse psychology" with *Bnei Yisrael.* He uses the example of a donkey seller who eagerly and willingly accepts his prospective buyer's request to try out the animal on every kind of terrain. The buyer will ultimately waive the right to test drive based on the seller's reaction to his request. (Rashi on Devarim 1:23) *Moshe* here is faulting himself for assuming his eager embrace of the doomed spy mission would cause *Bnei Yisrael* to abandon the plan and accept *Hashem's* exhortation to enter the Land. Essentially, *Moshe* is admitting that they "called his bluff" and the disastrous consequences are his to bear.

5770

Rabbi Avram Skurowitz – The Chanukas HaTorah states that, in outlining the places of their journeys where *Bnei Yisrael* sinned, *Moshe* mentions "Chatzeirot," followed by "Di Zahav." (Devarim 1:1) Rashi points out that "Chatzeirot" is a reference to the incident of *Korach,* while "Di Zahav" is a reference to the sin of the golden calf. One may question *Moshe's* order of presentation, since the golden calf preceded the story of *Korach.* In actuality, this reversal is itself a rebuke of *Bnei Yisrael.* In Parashat Yitro, in the first of the *Aseret HaDibrot,* Hashem says "Anochi Hashem Elokecha ... ," "I Am Hashem your [second person singular!]

G-d, ..." (Shemot 20:2) Hashem's use of the singular form of "your" is jarring, since this Statement was made at the Revelation at Sinai. Rashi on that *pasuk* tells us that *Hashem* was providing a future opening for *Moshe* to offer a defense of *Bnei Yisrael* following their sin of the golden calf: to wit, that *Hashem* commanded only *Moshe* <u>alone</u> regarding the prohibition of having other gods, thereby exonerating the Jews. This defense, however, was undermined thereafter by the words of *Korach*, when, in challenging *Moshe's* leadership, he declared "ki chol ha'eidah kulam kedoshim," "for the entire Assembly – all of them – are Holy, ..." (Bamidbar 16:3) Rashi expressly indicates on that *pasuk* that *Korach* was declaring that all of *Bnei Yisrael* heard the words at *Har Sinai* from *Hashem*, thereby making them all eligible to lead the Nation. *Bnei Yisrael* did not immediately refute *Korach's* statement, another error that retroactively undermined *Moshe's* defense from the first incident, a fact that *Moshe* notes in the beginning of his admonitions by reversing the order of the incident locations.

5771

Rabbi Shaanan Gelman – The three consecutive *Haftarot* of the *Three Weeks* begin, respectively, with the words "Divrei Yirmiyahu," "the <u>words</u> of Yirmiyahu" (Yirmiyahu 1:1); "Shimu D'var Hashem," "<u>Hear</u> the Word of Hashem" (Yirmiyahu 2:4); and "Chazon Yishaiahu," "the <u>vision</u> of Yishaiyahu." (Yishaiyahu 1:1) These three admonitions, says the Bnei Yissaschar, each contains a word representing an area that we must work to improve during this time of National introspection and *teshuvah:* what we <u>say</u>, what we <u>hear</u> and what we <u>see</u>.

5772

Rabbi Eli Mansour – The Kli Yakar writes that in Parashat Devarim, when *Moshe Rabbeinu* tells *Bnei Yisrael* that they took eleven days to journey from "Chorev" to "Kadesh Barnea" (Devarim 1:2), he is mystically alluding to *Asara b'Tevet*, *Shiva Asar b'Tammuz*, plus the first nine days of the month of *Av* – a total of eleven days. Here, "Chorev" is an allusion to the *churban* of the First and Second Holy Temples. The *Gemara* (Eruvin 18b) says that since the *churban*, the world is run by *Hashem* represented in an incomplete way by two letters: "י" "yud" and "ה" "heh." The two missing letters are "ו" "vav" and another "ה" "heh," which *gematria* totals eleven! We observe eleven days of mourning for the *Beit HaMikdash* in an attempt to restore *Hashem's* Name to the world.

5773

Rabbi Avraham Yitzchak Kook – We see that prior to entering *Eretz Yisrael*, *Bnei Yisrael* had to defeat *Sichon*, who was the king of the *Emori*, who lived in "Cheshbon." (Devarim 1:4) Rashi, in fact, comments on that verse that both *Sichon*, the king and *Cheshbon*, the city, were formidable. In response to our natural inclinations to make formidable "*cheshbonot*," as to why it will not be economically advantageous to make *aliyah* to *Eretz Yisrael*, Rav Kook says that, like those who preceded us, we must destroy the "*cheshbon*" and simply enter the Land.

VAETCHANAN

5757

The prohibition against *lashon hara* includes "avak lashon hara," literally, the "dust of evil talk." The *Gemara* (Bava Batra 164b) defines this as speech which, while itself not derogatory or harmful, promotes such talk. A Jew must resist speaking *lashon hara*, even at the risk of great financial loss, as it says in the *Shema*, as set forth in Parashat Vaetchanan, "וְאָהַבְתָּ אֵת ה' אלקיך בְּכָל לְבָבְךָ וּבְכָל נַפְשְׁךָ וּבְכָל מְאֹדֶךָ," "You shall love Hashem your G-d with all your heart, and all your soul and all your strength" (Devarim 6:5), which the *Talmud* (Berachot 54a) explains refers to all your possessions.

5758

The *Shabbat* on which Parashat Vaetchanan is read is referred to as *Shabbat Nachamu*, "the *Shabbat* of Comfort," which follows *Shabbat Chazon*, "the *Shabbat* of the Vision," on which Parashat Devarim is read, and which precedes *Tisha B'Av*.

5759

Rabbi Pinchas Winston – The *Shema* requires a Jew to love *Hashem* (1) with all his heart, (2) with all his soul (life), and (3) with all his possessions. (Devarim 6:4, 5) Under the common understanding, to demonstrate an ascending order of importance, the list should be as follows: (1) all your possessions, (2) all your heart, and (3) your life. Yet the *Torah's* order may reference three individual 2,000-year historical periods of the 6,000-year projected history of the world. These periods are (1) spiritual desolation, (2) Torah dissemination, and (3) the pain in advance of the *Moshiach's* arrival. (see Sanhedrin 97a) From year 0 to 2,000: Loving *Hashem* with your HEART – Man's test for the first 2,000 years of history was remaining loyal to *Hashem* (which is an issue of the <u>heart</u>). Note that the *Torah* wasn't given until 2,448. From 2000 to 4000: Giving your Life/SOUL for *Hashem* – In this period Israel as a nation was born and there was a "*mitzvah* period" lasting until 4,000 (239 BCE) with the death of the Ten Martyrs. During this time many Jews paid for their faith with their lives. From 4000 to 6000 (we are now in the year 5759): Giving Your POSSESSIONS to *Hashem* – The current issue of sacrifice in our era of comfort is whether or not the Jew is prepared to part with his possessions to acquire *Torah* and *mitzvot*.

5760

Rabbi Mordechai Kamenetsky – The *pasukim* say "כִּי שְׁאַל נָא לְיָמִים רִאשֹׁנִים אֲשֶׁר הָיוּ לְפָנֶיךָ לְמִן הַיּוֹם אֲשֶׁר בָּרָא אֱלֹקִים | אָדָם עַל הָאָרֶץ וּלְמִקְצֵה הַשָּׁמַיִם וְעַד קְצֵה הַשָּׁמָיִם הֲנִהְיָה כַּדָּבָר הַגָּדוֹל הַזֶּה אוֹ הֲנִשְׁמַע כָּמֹהוּ הֲשָׁמַע עָם קוֹל אֱלֹקִים מְדַבֵּר מִתּוֹךְ הָאֵשׁ כַּאֲשֶׁר שָׁמַעְתָּ אַתָּה וַיֶּחִי," "For inquire now regarding the early days that preceded you, from the day when Hashem created man on the earth, and from one end of the Heavens to the other end of the Heavens: Has there ever been anything like this great thing or has anything like it been heard? Has a people ever heard the voice of G-d speaking from the midst of fire, as you have heard, and survived?" (Devarim 4:32, 33) This refers to the unbroken chain from *Har Sinai* until the present. The "survival" that the *Torah* refers to is the survival of the Divine Message. This is in strong distinction to other religions (*l'havdil*) that claim a miraculous event to which there were no witnesses and therefore no reliable tradition of revelation upon which to rely.

Rabbi Edward Davis – The first sin of the *Torah* might be the violation by *Adam* and *Chavah* of the prohibition of "lo toseefu," the negative *mitzvah* regarding adding to the Commandments of *Hashem*, which appears in Parashat Vaetchanan. (Devarim 4:2) In Parashat Bereshit it says "וַיְצַו ה' אלקים עַל הָאָדָם לֵאמֹר מִכֹּל עֵץ הַגָּן אָכֹל תֹּאכֵל," "And Hashem commanded the man saying 'of every tree of the Garden you are free to eat, but as for the Tree of Knowledge of Good and Evil <u>you must not eat of it</u>, for as soon as you eat of it, you shall die.'" (Bereshit 2:16) When the serpent tempted *Chavah*, the *Torah* states "וַתֹּאמֶר הָאִשָּׁה אֶל הַנָּחָשׁ מִפְּרִי עֵץ הַגָּן נֹאכֵל וּמִפְּרִי הָעֵץ אֲשֶׁר בְּתוֹךְ הַגָּן אָמַר אלקים לֹא תֹאכְלוּ מִמֶּנּוּ וְלֹא תִגְּעוּ בּוֹ פֶּן תְּמֻתוּן," "and the woman said to the serpent 'we may eat of the fruit of the trees of the Garden; it is only from the fruit of the tree in the middle of the Garden that G-d said "you shall not eat of it <u>or touch it</u>, lest you die."'" (Bereshit 3:2, 3) When *Chavah* touched the fruit and didn't die, she figured the threat was hollow. By adding the additional prohibition, the Will of *Hashem* was violated through a sin that preceded the sin of eating the fruit. Rabbi Yossi Jankovits states that with regard to this concept the *Gemara* (Sanhedrin 29a) asserts the dictum "kol hamosif gorea," "anyone who adds [to Hashem's Word], [in fact] subtracts [from it]."

5761

Rabbi Yisroel Ciner – *Shabbat Nachamu* is about consolation. The *geulah* and arrival of *Moshiach* are approaching, but certainly it is easy to become depressed concerning his delayed arrival. This can be compared to a package containing valued merchandise that was supposed to arrive on a certain day. When the package fails to arrive on time, each successive day that passes thereafter brings reduced hope of ever getting the merchandise. But this is a false *mashal*. Rather, imagine that one had an extensive coin collection of 900,000 rare coins, all mixed together in a giant jar. You heard that another coin collector was willing to pay an enormous sum for a particular coin that you knew with certainty you possessed in your collection. You would grow happier, not sadder, with each coin you pulled from the jar that was not the coin for which you were looking, because for each wrong coin you pulled you would be one coin closer to the coin you were seeking. You would know you would eventually find the valuable coin and your mind would be completely at ease during the process. So too should it be with our wait for *Moshiach*. Since we are sure that he will come, every day that he doesn't brings us a day closer to his inevitable arrival.

5762

Meshech Chochmah – The Ten Commandments set forth in Parashat Yitro direct *Bnei Yisrael* to "zachor," "remember," the *Shabbat*. (Shemot 20:8) This makes sense, for in the *midbar* there was no toil, and the focus was recalling *Hashem's* command to keep the *mitzvot aseh* of *Shabbat* (e.g. *Kiddush*). Here, in Parashat Vaetchanan, when the Nation was poised to enter the Land, the second version of the Ten Commandments direct *Bnei Yisrael* to "shamor," "guard," the Shabbat. (Devarim 5:12) This also makes sense, for in the Land the Jews would be preoccupied with earning a livelihood, and therefore had to be warned concerning the *mitzvot lo'taseh* of *Shabbat* (e.g. the prohibition of harvesting).

5763

Rabbi Yossi Jankovits – In the first *aliyah* of Parashat Vaetchanan, we are told of *Hashem's* response to *Moshe's* plea to let him into *Eretz Yisrael*. "Rav lach," *Hashem* declares, "it is too much for you!" (Devarim 3:26) The *Gemara* (Sotah 13b) makes a startling connection between *Hashem's* response to *Moshe* and *Moshe's* response to *Korach's* rebellion (Bamidbar 16:7) The origins of this issue arose much earlier in the *Torah*. In Parashat Shemot, at the Burning Bush, *Moshe* expressed reluctance to accept the role of liberator of *Bnei Yisrael*. Rashi, quoting the *Gemara* (Zevachim 102a), comments there that, as a result of not wanting to be the leader of the Nation, *Moshe* was punished with the loss of the *Kehunah*, the ultimate leadership position. (Rashi on Shemot 4:14) Later, in Parashat Korach, *Moshe* declares to *Korach* and his band of rebels (many of whom were from the Tribe of Levi but wanted to be Kohanim), "rav lachem," "it is too much for you!" (Bamidbar 16:7) *Chazal*, including the Ibn Ezra, say that in the case of *Korach*, the "it" was the *Kehunah*. *Moshe* was, in essence, stating "Look, being a Levi is great. It's enough and you don't need the Kehunah. It's not such a big deal." At that moment *Moshe* was, in some respect, "slighting" the *Kehunah*. It was as a result of this statement that *Hashem* determined that, retroactively, *Moshe* had not been adequately punished for his sin at the Burning Bush, for his loss of the *Kehunah* seemed minor in his eyes. Therefore, here in Parashat Vaetchanan, Hashem tells *Moshe*, using the identical language of "rav lach," that he will need to be punished for his recalcitrance at the Burning Bush by being barred from entering the Land at the end of his life.

5764

Dr. Neal Weinreb – Parashat Vaetchanan is read on *Shabbat Nachamu*. In the *Bentching* it says "May the Merciful G-d send us *Eliyahu HaNavi* [in the times of *Moshiach*] ... to bring us good news, salvation and comfort." Why would "yeshuot," "salvation," precede "nechamot," "comfort?" Comfort is a state granted during times of distress, accompanied by a prospective outlook and longing for better times in the future. Once there is *yeshuah*, is there a need for *nechamah*? Perhaps there are two *nechamot*, as is evidenced by, G-d forbid, *shivah* situations. We can provide *nechamah* to someone who lost a loved one in a ripe old age, but it's much more elusive when they, for example, lose a young child to a tragedy (G-d forbid). There we cannot fathom *Hashem's* reasons. In such a case, the ultimate explanation, and the ultimate comfort, will be provided at the End of Days, after the Holy *Moshiach* has been revealed. Perhaps the *Haftarah* of Parashat Vaetchanan (Yishaiyahu 40:1-26) contains the double language of "Nachamu Nachamu" as an allusion to this idea. We may have received partial *nechamah* for the tragedies that have befallen us individually and as a Nation, but the true and complete *nechamah* for all our ills will be experienced after the *yeshuah*, may it be soon, speedily, in our days.

5765

Reb Ephraim Sobol – In describing the prospective conquest by *Bnei Yisrael* of the Land they are about to enter, *Moshe* states as follows: " וְהָיָה כִּי יְבִיאֲךָ | ה' אלקיך אֶל הָאָרֶץ אֲשֶׁר נִשְׁבַּע לַאֲבֹתֶיךָ לְאַבְרָהָם לְיִצְחָק וּלְיַעֲקֹב לָתֶת לָךְ עָרִים גְּדֹלֹת וְטֹבֹת אֲשֶׁר לֹא בָנִיתָ וּבָתִּים מְלֵאִים כָּל טוּב אֲשֶׁר לֹא מִלֵּאתָ וּבֹרֹת חֲצוּבִים אֲשֶׁר לֹא חָצַבְתָּ כְּרָמִים וְזֵיתִים אֲשֶׁר לֹא נָטָעְתָּ וְאָכַלְתָּ וְשָׂבָעְתָּ," "It shall be that when Hashem, your G-d, brings you to the Land that Hashem swore to your forefathers, to Avraham, to Yitzchak and to Yaacov, <u>to give you – great and good cities that you did not build, houses filled with every good thing that you did not fill, chiseled cisterns that you did not chisel, orchards and olive trees that you did not plant</u> – and you shall eat and be satisfied." (Devarim 6:10, 11) Clearly the reward for proper conquest is a veritable set table for *Bnei Yisrael* at the expense of the *goyim* that were there. But what would be the result of an incomplete or imperfect conquest? The answer is perhaps presented in Parshat Masai, where the following is set forth: "וְאִם לֹא תוֹרִישׁוּ אֶת יֹשְׁבֵי הָאָרֶץ מִפְּנֵיכֶם וְהָיָה אֲשֶׁר תּוֹתִירוּ מֵהֶם לְשִׂכִּים בְּעֵינֵיכֶם וְלִצְנִינִם בְּצִדֵּיכֶם וְצָרְרוּ אֶתְכֶם עַל הָאָרֶץ אֲשֶׁר אַתֶּם יֹשְׁבִים בָּהּ וְהָיָה כַּאֲשֶׁר דִּמִּיתִי לַעֲשׂוֹת לָהֶם אֶעֱשֶׂה לָכֶם," "But if you do not drive out the inhabitants of the Land before you, those of them whom you leave shall be pins in your eyes and a surrounding barrier in your sides, and they will harass you upon the Land which you dwell. And it shall be that what I meant to do to them, I shall do to you." (Bamidbar 33:55, 56) The final *pasuk* is chilling in light of the Gaza Deportation taking place currently, where Jewish families are being forcibly removed from their houses, farms and greenhouses leaving them intact to the Arabs to enjoy despite not having built or paid for them.

5766

Rabbi Yosef Y. Jacobson – *Moshe's* plea to be allowed to enter *Eretz Yisrael*, and *Hashem's* steadfast refusal, are rooted in the story of *Yosef HaTzaddik*. *Moshe* carried *Yosef's* coffin for the forty years in the desert in response to *Yosef's* expressed desire to be buried in *Eretz Yisrael*. (Bereshit 50:25) *Moshe*, understanding that *Yosef's* bones were now, at the end of the wandering, to be brought into and buried in the Promised Land, made a seemingly reasonable request. According to the *Midrash*, Moshe thought that he, like *Yosef*, at the very least, should be buried in *Eretz Yisrael*. Surprising, *Hashem* refused to allow *Moshe* to be buried there, indicating that, in distinction to *Yosef*, because *Moshe* did not remember the Land, he would not go into the Land, even for burial. This begs the question: how did *Yosef* remember the Land where *Moshe* did not? In two incidents *Yosef* demonstrated his affinity towards the Land. When the wife of *Potiphar* tried to seduce *Yosef*, the *Torah* tells us "וַתִּקְרָא לְאַנְשֵׁי בֵיתָהּ וַתֹּאמֶר לָהֶם לֵאמֹר רְאוּ הֵבִיא לָנוּ אִישׁ עִבְרִי לְצַחֶק בָּנוּ בָּא אֵלַי לִשְׁכַּב עִמִּי וָאֶקְרָא בְּקוֹל גָּדוֹל," "and she called to the people of her house, and she spoke to them, saying, 'Look! [My husband] brought us a <u>Hebrew man</u> to mock us. He came to me to lie with me, but I called loudly!'" (Bereshit 39:14) *Yosef* is falsely imprisoned as a result, and he tells the *Sar Hamashkim* "כִּי גֻנֹּב גֻּנַּבְתִּי מֵאֶרֶץ הָעִבְרִים וְגַם פֹּה לֹא עָשִׂיתִי מְאוּמָה כִּי שָׂמוּ אֹתִי בַּבּוֹר," "For indeed I was stolen from the <u>Land of the Hebrews</u>, and even here, I have done nothing, for which they have put me into the dungeon." (Bereshit 40:15) At the time, many tribes lived in *Eretz Canaan*. Moreover, *Yosef* could have decided to separate himself from his Jewish destiny and steep himself in Egyptian high society. Yet his connection and love for the Land and belief that it was Divinely granted to the Jews never wavered, and he was comfortable being referred to as a Hebrew, a designation understood to be connected to the Land. *Moshe* also greatly valued the Land and yearned to go into it. Yet after he met the daughters

of *Yitro* at the well in *Midyan*, the *Torah* relates "וַתֹּאמַרְןָ אִישׁ מִצְרִי הִצִּילָנוּ
מִיַּד הָרֹעִים וְגַם דָּלֹה דָלָה לָנוּ וַיַּשְׁקְ אֶת הַצֹּאן," "They said, 'A <u>Mitzri</u> man rescued
us from the hands of the shepherds, and he also drew [water] for us and
watered the flocks.'" (Shemot 2:19) Apparently, *Moshe* presented himself
more as a fugitive from Egypt than as one connected to the Land of the
destiny of the Jewish People. As such, he did not merit to be buried in
that Land.

5769

Rabbi Eli Mansour – What is the significance of the juxtaposition of the
admonition about adding or subtracting from the *Torah* (Devarim 4:2),
and the reference to the incident of *Baal Peor* which left 24,000 Jews dead?
(Devarim 4:3) Our Rabbis teach that the sin of *Baal Peor* began when the
Jews visited the markets of the *Moavim*, where they became ensnared in
immorality. The initial social interactions were not forbidden by the *Torah*
but small, incremental violations ultimately led to a National tragedy for
Bnei Yisrael. Stopping in the Moabite shops for innocent purposes, the
Jewish men were lured to a secluded place where a temptress was waiting.
Seemingly small deviations (here subtractions) from the *halachah* are
antithetical to *Torah* and lead to enormous problems for the Jewish People.

5770

Ramban – The *Torah* directs us as follows: "v'asita hayashar v'hatov
b'Ayney Hashem … ," "and you shall do what is fair and good in the Eyes
of Hashem." (Devarim 6:18) Rashi explains that this means a Jew is to go
"lifnim mishurat hadin," "beyond the letter of the law." Ramban indicates
that where not specifically commanded by the *Torah* we should nonetheless
apply the principles of the *mitzvot* to bring about a Holy result. The *Torah*
cannot legislate for every conceivable contingency, but it gives us the tools
to conduct ourselves in accordance with *Torah*, and do what is fair and
good in all situations. Rabbi Moshe Rosenstein says that this is an insight

into the high level of esteem that *Hashem* places on the human intellect, which he has empowered to undertake this critical analysis.

5771

Rabbi Eli Mansour – The *Gemara* (Eruvin 54a) states the importance of learning *Torah* out loud rather than merely reading it. The Baal HaTanya stated that one who learns silently has not fulfilled the *mitzvah* of *Torah* learning, since the *pasuk* from Parashat Vaetchanan requires "v'dibarta bam," "speak of them [the words of Torah]." (Devarim 6:7)

Rabbi Eli Mansour – Prayer is highlighted and contrasted in Parashat Vaetchanan. The *pasuk* states "כִּי מִי גוֹי גָּדוֹל אֲשֶׁר לוֹ אלקים קְרֹבִים אֵלָיו כהי אלקינו בְּכָל קָרְאֵנוּ אֵלָיו," "For which is a great nation that has a G-d Who is close to it, as is Hashem, our G-d, whenever we call to Him." (Devarim 4:7) This clearly indicates that *Hashem* is always available to be petitioned. Yet we see that the results of our prayers are not always predictable, as indicated by *Moshe's* declaration (at the beginning of the *parashah*) that he implored *Hashem* and that while he was heard, his request to enter the Land was not granted. (Devarim 3:23-26) Nonetheless all prayers make their mark in Heaven.

5772

Rabbi Avi Weiss – The reference in Parashat Vaetchanan to "shamor," "guard," with respect to the *Shabbat* (Devarim 5:12), is distinguished from the "zachor," "remember," reference in Parashat Yitro. (Shemot 20:8) Aside from the *halachic* impact of the two references, these two ideas represent our dual approaches to *Hashem*. "Zachor," relating to the *mitzvot asei*, connects to *ahavat Hashem*, whereas "shamor," relating to the *mitzvot lo t'asei*, evokes feelings of *yirat Hashem*. Because we love *Hashem*, we imitate him (e.g. making *Kiddush*) and focus on commonality (so to speak) with *Hashem*, yet based on the unlimited distinction between us and Him, we are in awe and don't do certain things on that day (e.g. kindle a fire). Rabbi Yosef Weinstock points out this same distinction with respect to interaction amongst Jews. The students of *Rabbi Akiva* who perished in a plague were, perhaps, capable of "v'ahavta l'reiacha komocha," "loving their friends like themselves," (after all this was the core belief of *Rabbi Akiva* – Rashi on Vayikra 19:18), but, perhaps, were not capable of honoring the distinctions between each other, leading to their demise.

5773

The Slonimer Rebbe – We can ask a strong question with respect to the destruction of *Bayit Sheni*. The *Gemara* (Yoma 9b) tells us that the cause of the destruction was *sinat chinam*, yet nowhere in the *Torah* is "baseless hatred" described as a sin worthy of such a severe punishment. How can it be that *Hashem* destroyed the Holy Temple and exiled *Am Yisrael* on this basis? The answer lies in the fact that the *churban* is not a punishment for *sinat chinam*, but a consequence of it! The supernatural structure of the Holy Temple requires *achdut* among the Jews as a foundational prerequisite. Struggles between Jews break the connection between Heaven and earth, without which those stones cannot remain standing. On the heels of *Tisha B'Av*, this provides an insight into how we must proceed if we genuinely wish to rebuild the Temple.

EIKEV

5758

The *pasuk* in Parashat Eikev, relating to *Tefillin*, reads "v'samtem et Divarai Aileh al l'vavchem … ," "And you should place these Words of Mine upon your heart," (Devarim 11:18) The *Gemara* (Kiddushin 30b) says the word "samtem," "you should place," can be read as "sam tam," "perfect medicine." The *Torah*, and more precisely the *Tefillin*, are the salve for the *yetzer hara*.

Rabbi Manis Friedman – The "chosenness" of the Jews is explained with a *mashal*. Imagine an adult came into a third grade class, sat on the floor with the children, and asked out loud "what are we learning today?", purporting to be just another student. The adult would arouse suspicion and distain among the kids, who know that the role of the adult is to teach, not to be "one of the gang." The adult might say "I'm just like you," but the kids will remind him "No! You are not!"

5759

Vedibarta Bam – The *pasuk* reads "v'atah Yisrael mah Hashem Elokecha shoail mayimach … ," "And now, Yisrael, <u>what</u> does Hashem your G-d ask of you … ?" (Devarim 10:12) The word "מה,""mah," meaning "what?" seems superfluous. The verse could simply have read "And now, Yisrael, Hashem your G-d expects the following of you: …." The word "mah" is included to showcase the letters "מ," and "ה," which are the two Hebrew letters that have an intrinsic and extrinsic similarity. The way to spell the letter "mem" is "מם," and the way to spell the letter "hey," is "הה." The "inside" of these letters is identical to the "outside" of these letters. The notion is that the Holiness that a Jew projects on the "outside" should be "identical" to how he is on the "inside," and this is the only necessary character trait that *Hashem* expects of us according to the *Torah*.

The *pasuk* states "וַאֲהֵבְךָ וּבֵרַכְךָ וְהִרְבֶּךָ וּבֵרַךְ פְּרִי בִטְנְךָ וּפְרִי אַדְמָתֶךָ דְּגָנְךָ וְתִירֹשְׁךָ וְיִצְהָרֶךָ שְׁגַר אֲלָפֶיךָ וְעַשְׁתְּרֹת צֹאנֶךָ עַל הָאֲדָמָה אֲשֶׁר נִשְׁבַּע לַאֲבֹתֶיךָ לָתֶת לָךְ," "And He will love you and bless you and multiply you; He will bless the fruit of <u>your womb</u> and the fruit of your soil, your grain, your wine, and your oil, the offspring of your cattle and the choice of your flocks, in the Land which He swore to your forefathers to give you." (Devarim 7:13) It is notable that the verse references "your womb" in the masculine form, where we would expect, based on biology, a feminine reference. The *Gemara* (Berachot 51b) relates that the *Torah* uses this language to indicate that the blessings a wife merits with respect to having children originate from her husband

5760

Torah Temimah – The language "u'vairach pri vitnicha … ," "and He will bless the fruit of your [second person; masculine] womb … ," (Devarim

7:13) indicates that a child receives his life – in the form of *middot* – from his father.

"Eikev" literally translates as "because," and the first *pasuk* of the *parashah* therefore reads "<u>Because</u> you harken to the mishpatim [statutes]", such and such will happen. (Devarim 7:12) Rashi states that "eikev" has the same letters (עקב) as the Hebrew word for "heel," as mentioned in regard to the birth of *Eisav* and *Yaacov*, when *Yaacov* emerged "v'yado ochezet ba'akeiv Eisav … ," "with his hand grasping the heel of Eisav." (Bereshit 25:26) This alludes to the *mitzvot* that one treats lightly (i.e. treads upon with his heel).

Rabbi Yossi Jankovits – In recounting their tribulations in the *midbar*, *Moshe* reminds the People "וָאֶתְפֹּשׂ בִּשְׁנֵי הַלֻּחֹת וָאַשְׁלִכֵם מֵעַל שְׁתֵּי יָדָי וָאֲשַׁבְּרֵם לְעֵינֵיכֶם," "I grasped the two Tablets and threw them down from my two hands, and I smashed them before your eyes." (Devarim 9:17) In doing so, he reminds them of his having sided with them for the purpose of creating unity. It is said that *Moshe* broke the *Luchot* out of anger, which is compared by the *Gemara* (Shabbat 105b) to *avodah zareh*. Upon seeing the sin of the golden calf, *Moshe* anticipated *Hashem's* proposal to destroy *Bnei Yisrael* and to begin anew with *Moshe* as progenitor of the Chosen Nation. *Moshe* wanted to foreclose this option, forcing *Hashem* (as it were) to deal with everyone together. This is said to be a reason why *Aharon* too participated in the sin.

Rabbi Eliyahu KiTov – Many good things happened for the Jews on *Tu B'Av*. One, as related in the *Talmud* (Taanit 31a), was that permission was granted by the Roman Emperor to bury the dead massacred at *Beitar*. *Hadrian's* massacre (which was carried out on *Tisha B'Av*) was matched in extreme cruelty by his order to take the thousands of slain Jews to his large vineyard and place them one atop another around its perimeter. A later emperor granted permission for a proper burial, after which the Sages enacted the fourth *berachah* of *Birkat HaMazon* (entitled "HaTov, v'HaMeitiv"), based on the *pasuk* says "Hu Haitiv, Hu Maitiv," "[Hashem] is Good and He does Good." The Rabbis recognized that *Hashem* <u>is</u> Good, for He miraculously preserved the bodies from decaying prior to their burial, and He <u>does</u> Good, in allowing for their eventual burial. The blessing we recite on a "better" bottle of wine brought to the table recalls the pain, and the miracle, in *Hadrian's* vineyard.

Rashi, quoting the *Gemara* (Berachot 33b), provides a profound insight in Parashat Eikev as to what one can control in his life, and what is outside of his control. On the *pasuk* "וְעַתָּה יִשְׂרָאֵל מָה ה׳ אלקיך שֹׁאֵל מֵעִמָּךְ כִּי אִם לְיִרְאָה אֶת ה׳ אלקיך לָלֶכֶת בְּכָל דְּרָכָיו וּלְאַהֲבָה אֹתוֹ וְלַעֲבֹד אֶת ה׳ אלקיך בְּכָל לְבָבְךָ וּבְכָל נַפְשֶׁךָ", "And now, Yisrael, what does Hashem, your G-d, ask of you? Only to fear Hashem, your G-d, to walk in all His Ways and to love Him, and to worship Hashem, your G-d, with all your heart and with all your soul," (Devarim 10:12), Rashi states "הכל בידי שמים חוץ מיראת שמים," "everything is in the control of Heaven except one's fear of Heaven."

Rabbi Pinchas Winston – Perhaps there is a parallel between the identified phenomenon of an elderly person, as they begin to realign priorities later in life, to start increasing religious observance, and the modern *baal teshuvah* movement. Because the Jewish People are collectively sensing that "time is limited" before our imminent National Redemption, many are turning to *Torah* as a system for conducting their lives.

5761

The *Gemara* (Berachot 41a) tells us that the priority order of *berachot* is set forth in the *pasuk* of Parashat Eikev describing *Eretz Yisrael* as "אֶרֶץ חִטָּה וּשְׂעֹרָה וְגֶפֶן וּתְאֵנָה וְרִמּוֹן אֶרֶץ זֵית שֶׁמֶן וּדְבָשׁ," "a Land of wheat and barley, vines and figs and pomegranates, a Land of oil producing olives and [date] honey." (Devarim 8:8) This pecking order is what necessitates covering the *challah* when making *Kiddush* on *Shabbat*, since wheat precedes grapes [wine], yet we are commanded to make *Kiddush* before *hamotzi*.

5762

Rabbi Shlomo Riskin – Why does bread require four *berachot achronot* (i.e. *Birkat HaMazon*) but grapes, figs and the like only one? The same could be asked about the *Kedushah* of *Har Moriah* relative to *Har Sinai*. In the latter case, we received the *Torah*, our reason for being, from *Har Sinai*, yet we don't even know where it is (and we probably gave it back to Egypt in the early 1980s). One answer is that there is more *Kedushah* in both bread and *Har Moriah*. How so? According to Rav Joseph B. Soloveitchik, *Kedushah* comes through a combination of human effort and G-d's grace. *Avraham* undertook a super-human effort to do the *Akeidah* at *Har Moriah*, yet the Jews were simply presented the *Torah* at *Sinai*. Similarly, a fruit that is picked from a tree cannot be compared to the labor-intensive production that brings bread.

Rabbi Aviezer Heller – The *pasuk* states "ki lo al halechem l'vado yichye haadam ki al kol mota Pi Hashem yichye hadam," "for not by bread alone does man live, rather by everything that emanates from the Mouth of Hashem does man live." (Devarim 8:3) The point that the *Torah* is making is that even if one has bread presently he cannot survive in the future without a replenished supply. Knowing that it is the recurring gift of bread (like the *Mon* in the *midbar*) that comes from *Hashem* gives man an insight into the wonderful *Chesed* of the Creator.

Rabbi Yitzchak Assouli – "Eikev" means "heel" (Rashi on Devarim 7:12), which is a reference to humility in the context of *mitzvah* performance, for the heel is content to be "in the back" of the foot, but the toes are compelled to "be out in front," and, accordingly, are most often injured as a result.

5763

Rabbi Aviezer Heller – The period on the Jewish calendar between *Shavuot* and *Yom Kippur* is approximately 120 days, which can be divided into three forty days periods: (1) *Shavuot* until *Shiva Asar b'Tammuz*, when *Moshe* received the first *Luchot*; (2) *Shiva Asar b'Tammuz* until *Rosh Chodesh Elul*; and (3) *Rosh Chodesh Elul* until *Yom Kippur*, when *Moshe* received the second *Luchot*. These three periods represent the time following the intense experience of *Matan Torah*: (1) separation in anticipation of marriage, which was before the *cheit haeigel*; (2) betrayal and abandonment, resulting in the loss of the Temple and forced *galut*; and (3) reconciliation and marriage, when *Hashem* took us back as His People. *Elul* is known as the *rashei teivot* of the first four words of the *pasuk* "אֲנִי לְדוֹדִי וְדוֹדִי לִי הָרוֹעֶה בַּשׁוֹשַׁנִּים," "I am my beloved's, and my beloved is mine, who grazes among the roses." (Shir HaShirim 6:3) The last letter of each of these same words is "yud," which has a *gematria* value of ten, adding up to forty – the days of each described period. The Vilna Gaon connects the primary *avodah* of *Elul*, which is *teshuvah*, to Parashat Eikev through the verse "וּמַלְתֶּם אֵת עָרְלַת לְבַבְכֶם וְעָרְפְּכֶם לֹא תַקְשׁוּ עוֹד," "You shall circumcise the barrier of your heart, therefore, and be no more stiffnecked." (Devarim 10:16)

5764

Rabbi Yosef Y. Jacobson – In Parashat Eikev we learn the Biblical command "וְאָכַלְתָּ וְשָׂבָעְתָּ וּבֵרַכְתָּ אֶת ה' אלקיך עַל הָאָרֶץ הַטֹּבָה אֲשֶׁר נָתַן לָךְ," "And you will eat and be satisfied, and you shall bless Hashem, your G-d, for the good Land He has given you." (Devarim 8:10) This is the *mitzvah* of *Birkat HaMazon*, or *Bentching*. In the blessing for the Land, the second in *Birchat HaMazon*, there is also reference to *brit milah* and to the *Torah*. The *Talmud* (Berachot 49a) states that whoever said the *berachah* for the Land without mentioning *brit milah* and *Torah* must repeat the *Birkat HaMazon*. Why should this be the rule? Perhaps because if "Zionism" is not based on the 3,700 year old covenant with *Avraham Avinu* and the 3,300 year old covenant from *Har Sinai*, then we have no real, authentic claim to the Land. This is reflected in the *Gemara* (Bava Batra 75a) which reads "The face of Moshe was like the sun; the face of Yehoshua was like the moon." *Moshe* gave us *Torah*, *Yehoshua* gave us the Land. Just as the moon has no independent significance beyond its reflection of the sun, so too the Land has no independent significance beyond its manifestation of the *Torah*. Both the moon and, *l'havdil*, the Land are pretty, to be sure, but neither is significant without its source of illumination.

5765

Rabbi Yosef Kalatsky – Wherever the *Torah* mentions both "chukim" (statutes for which there is no ready rational explanation) and "mishpatim" (judgments which are seemingly understandable and reasonable to the human mind), it mentions *chukim* first, to underscore that, ultimately, we do not know the reasons for the *mitzvot* and we do them simply because our Creator has thus commanded us. In the opening *pasuk* of the Parashat Eikev, it states "v'haya eikev tishmeun ait hamishpatim ... ," "this shall be the reward when you harken to these judgments ...." (Devarim 7:12) Obviously missing from the verse is any mention of *chukim*. Furthermore, Rashi famously comments here that the *Torah* uses the word "eikev," which also means "heel," to allude to those *mitzvot* that are often regarded as minor and, therefore, left under the heel of the average Jew. In mentioning only *mishpatim*, the *Torah* is warning the Jew that it is, in fact, those *mitzvot* for which we think we have a sensible explanation that we are most likely to fail to properly observe. An approach to *mitzvot* based on evaluation and measurement of the meaning and relative worth of any *mitzvah* is a very dangerous and self-destructive undertaking. If we instead treat all *mitzvot* as *chukim* for the purpose of observance, we will merit the reward that comes with keeping *Hashem's* Holy *Torah*.

5767

The *Talmud* (Berachot 34b; Sanhedrin 99a) indicates that in the place a *baal teshuvah* stands a total *tzaddik* cannot. Perhaps there is an analogy to be drawn with the struggle for weight loss. A person who has been greatly overweight feels exhilaration in losing a few pounds through dieting or exercise. Although he may yet be overweight, he celebrates his accomplishments and is inspired to continue improvement. The lifelong fitness adherent, however, would be aghast to be at even the reduced weight of the dieter, since he has never been more than a pound or two over his ideal weight. So it is also with the *tzaddik*, who never fell to a level of spiritual debasement, where the incremental journey back is a series of exhilarating victories.

5769

Rabbi Yaakov Moshe Charlap – The *pasuk* says "uvo tidbak … ," "and to [Hashem] you shall cleave." (Devarim 10:20) The *Gemara* (Ketubot 111b) reports that the Sages debated just how one could "cleave" to *Hashem*, Who is, after all, compared to fire. *Rabbi Elazar* taught that through clinging to *Torah* scholars, one clings to *Hashem*. This is an obvious but overlooked precept of Judaism. We must cling to the teachings of our Rabbis. When the Jews loosened their connection to *Moshe Rabbeinu*, their *Torah* authority, thinking he was not returning to them (see Rashi on Shemot 32:1), the result was the sin of the golden calf.

5770

Rabbi Moshe Gruenwald – The *Torah* tells us "עַל כֵּן לֹא הָיָה לְלֵוִי חֵלֶק וְנַחֲלָה עִם אֶחָיו ה' הוּא נַחֲלָתוֹ כַּאֲשֶׁר דִּבֶּר ה' אלקיך לוֹ," "Therefore, Levy has no portion or inheritance [in the Land] with his brothers; Hashem is his Inheritance, as Hashem, your G-d spoke to him." (Devarim 10:9) This *pasuk* is followed immediately by "וְאָנֹכִי עָמַדְתִּי בָהָר כַּיָּמִים הָרִאשֹׁנִים אַרְבָּעִים יוֹם וְאַרְבָּעִים לַיְלָה וַיִּשְׁמַע ה' אֵלַי גַּם בַּפַּעַם הַהִוא לֹא אָבָה ה' הַשְׁחִיתֶךְ," "And I remained on the mountain like the first days forty days and forty nights, and Hashem hearkened to me also at that time; and Hashem did not wish to destroy you." (Devarim 10:10) The juxtaposition of the two *pasukim* indicates a connection between *Levy's* lack of a portion in *Eretz Yisrael* and *Moshe's* return to *Har Sinai* after the *cheit haeigel*. The *Leviim* were teachers of *Torah* to *Bnei Yisrael*. As such, they could not be distracted with "working the Land." Yet had *Bnei Yisrael* not sinned at the *cheit haeigel*, *Moshe* would never had smashed the first *Luchot* and, as a result, the *Torah* would never have been forgotten (Eruvin 54a), which would have made the teachings of the *Leviim* unnecessary. Therefore, the sin brought about two results: *Moshe's* ascension for the second set of *Luchot* and the *Leviim* taking on the role of *Torah* teachers and, hence, losing their share of the Land.

5771

Rabbi Eli Mansour – While we cannot fathom why, G-d forbid, *Hashem* brings suffering upon us as individuals or even as a Nation, there is consolation in Parashat Eikev, as *Moshe* declares "וְיָדַעְתָּ עִם לְבָבֶךָ כִּי כַּאֲשֶׁר יְיַסֵּר אִישׁ אֶת בְּנוֹ ה׳ אלקיך מְיַסְּרֶךָ," "Know in your heart, that just as a father chastises his son, so does Hashem, your G-d, chastise you." (Devarim 8:5) Knowing the loving Source of our *yesurim* makes them bearable.

5772

Rabbi Yitzchak Salid – Occasionally (although not often), Parashat Eikev (rather than Parashat Re'eh) is read on *Shabbat Mevorchim* for *Elul*. There are no *Yom Tovim* (or fast days) in *Cheshvan* because they are not needed, since we are still very close to *Hashem* based on the activities of *Tishrei*. There is also no *Yom Tov* in *Elul*, but we blow *shofar* every day (except *Shabbat*) because we are farthest away from *Tishrei* based on the calendar progression. Reb Steven Jacoby points out that maybe "women are from *Cheshvan*" and "men are from *Elul*," in keeping with the idea that women are naturally closer to spirituality and, hence, do not require 613 *mitzvot* to achieve that connection.

5773

Me'am Loez – The *pasuk* states "בָּרוּךְ תִּהְיֶה מִכָּל הָעַמִּים לֹא יִהְיֶה בְךָ עָקָר וַעֲקָרָה וּבִבְהֶמְתֶּךָ," "You will be blessed from all the nations; there will not be a barren male or barren female among you or among your livestock." (Devarim 7:14) What does the guarantee of fertility have to do with being blessed by all the nations of the world? The blessing of *goyim* can have the effect of delaying the contemplated benefit. We see this in the blessing of fruitfulness imparted by *Lavan* to *Rivkah*, his sister. "לָהּ אֲחֹתֵנוּ אַתְּ הֲיִי לְאַלְפֵי רְבָבָה וְיִירַשׁ זַרְעֵךְ אֵת שַׁעַר שֹׂנְאָיו," "Our sister, may you become thousands of myriads, and may your seed inherit the cities of their enemies." (Bereshit 24:60) The Ohr HaChaim (Bereshit 25:20) states that because *Hashem* did not want *Rivkah's* blessing of children to be attributed to the wicked *Lavan*, He delayed her ability to have children. In the case of the *pasuk* from Parashat Eikev, *Hashem* is promising that despite the fact that the *goyim* will bless *Am Yisrael*, *Hashem* will not delay the manifestation of their blessings. MRF Note: It is interesting that we have still incorporated *Lavan's* blessing into the *bedekken* ceremony. Perhaps this is because when we, the Jews, articulate the *berachah*, it becomes an unqualified blessing.

RE'EH

5758
Rabbi Tzvi Hirsch miVilna – The *pasuk* states "... v'natatah et haberachah al har girizim v'et hak'lalah al har aival," "... then you shall place the blessing on Har Gerizim and the curse on Har Eival." (Devarim 11:29) Why should the blessings be given on one mountain and the curses on another? The distinction is made to show that blessings and curses have distinct sources. One cannot get a blessing by exposing oneself to evil; curses, not blessings, originate from a place of evil. This is demonstrated by the *Midrash* that says that the *Yam Suf* split in *Yosef's* merit, for *Bnei Yisrael* was transporting his coffin and bones for burial in *Eretz Yisrael*. *Moshe* commanded the sea to run away in honor of the one who ran away from *Potiphar's* wife. (Bereshit 39:12) *Yosef* knew that to stand and fight his *yetzer hara* would jeopardize his spirituality. He needed to completely separate himself from the curse and run to a place of blessing.

Rashi points out that there is a reference to the Oral Law in the Written Law here in Parashat Re'eh. The *pasuk* states "you may slaughter from your cattle and your flock that Hashem has given you as I [Moshe] have commanded you ...." (Devarim 12:21) Nowhere in the Written Torah is *shechitah* instructed. It must be that *Hashem* told *Moshe* how to slaughter animals in a kosher fashion and intended that *Moshe* orally pass that information on to *Bnei Yisrael*.

5759

Rabbi Samson Raphael Hirsch – The holidays of *Pesach*, *Shavuot* and *Sukkot* are described in Parashat Re'eh, but *Rosh Hashanah* and *Yom Kippur* are not. (Devarim 16:1-17) This may be because, unlike the *Shalosh Regalim*, there was no change in the observation of *Rosh Hashanah* and *Yom Kippur* when *Bnei Yisrael* transitioned from the *midbar* to living in *Eretz Yisrael*.

The *Talmud* (Menachot 43b) records the command of *Chazal* to recite 100 *berachot* a day, which breaks down as follows: 16 morning blessings; 3 (19 total) blessings on learning the *Torah*; 3 (21 total) blessings on *Tzitzit* and *Tefillin*; 2 (23 total) for *Baruch She'amar* and *Yishtabach*; 4 (27 total) blessings for *Shema* twice daily; 57 blessings (84 total) for three *Amidot* (19 x 3) daily; 16 blessings (100 total) for two daily meals (washing, *hamotzi*, *Bentching* (4) and *berachot* on wine (2)). On *Shabbat* we lack 13 *berachot* in our *Amidot* and therefore on *Shabbat* we should eat candy to make additional *berachot* and answer amen (without "Baruch Hu u'Varuch Shemo," "Blessed is He and blessed is His Name") for the blessings of the *Torah* and *Haftarah*.

Ibn Ezra – The first word of Parashat Re'eh is "re'eh," which means "behold," written in the singular form. (Devarim 11:26) The directive to observe the *mitzvot* is focused on the individual even as it impacts the *Kahal*. An individual's observance can result in a *berachah* for the Nation.

"Re'eh" means "behold," or "see." The *Torah* requires us to see value when it is not apparent to the naked eye. This trait can be explained in a *mashal* about a lottery winner. He is joyous on the day he learns that he bought the winning ticket, even though he has not yet seen a penny of his winnings and is only relying on the promise of payment. We too should "see" *Hashem's* promises as certain to come true and rejoice <u>now</u> in what will be in the future for *Bnei Yisrael*.

5760

Rabbi Yossi Jankovits – In warning *Bnei Yisrael* about false prophets, the *Torah* mentions "ki yisit'cha achicha ben imecha ... ," "if your brother, the son of your <u>mother</u>, entices you ...." to serve a foreign god. (Devarim 13:7) Notably absent is the enticement by a "brother, son of your <u>father</u>." The *Torah*, in its infinite wisdom, is alluding to future introduction of Christianity, which claims a fatherless ("immaculate") conception.

Rabbi Yossi Jankovits – The *Torah* provides the signs of a kosher animal as "mafris parsah," "split hooves," and "ma'aleh hageirah," "chews its cud." (Devarim 14:6) Alternatively, "mafris parsah" can be translated as "breaks off a slice of bread." A "geirah," is also a unit of money equal to 1/20 of a *shekel* (Shemot 30:13), so, accordingly, "ma'aleh hageirah," can be read "one who brings forth money." The proximity in the *parashah* of the rules of *kashrut* (Devarim 14:3-21) and the laws of giving *tzedakah* (Devarim 14: 22-29) teach that, as with animals, there is such a thing as a kosher *Yid*, and that is one who gives money and bread to the poor and needy.

Rabbi Zvi Miller – The foundation of "being" is "eirech atzmo," "self-worth": appreciating you were created "b'Tzelem Elokim," "in the Image of *Hashem*." This charges us to emulate His aspects in order to show the world His Holiness through our actions. This is analogous to the moon reflecting the light of the sun to those positioned on Earth. In our *tefillot* we beseech *Hashem* for insight into the aspects of His Essence so as to incorporate them and demonstrate them to the world. This is essentially what *Avraham Avinu* did while being visited by *Hashem*. (Bereshit 18:1, 2) He ran to do *chesed* (*hachnasat orchim*) for the "travelers," having had this revelation from *Hashem's* actions (*chesed* in the form of *bikur cholim*).

The *pasuk* implores *Bnei Yisrael* not to eat anything that died on its own, "ki Am Kadosh attah laShem," "for you [singular] are a Holy Nation to

Hashem." (Devarim 14:21) Rashi, quoting Sifrei, explains the subtle but important behavioral lesson the *Torah* is trying to convey. *Bnei Yisrael* is being instructed to make themselves Holy with that which is *mutar* to them; meaning to enjoy those things that the *Torah* allows. However, we are also admonished to be careful around those who are *nohaig* to treat such things as *assur* (who are attempting to obtain a higher sanctification). In such a situation, we are commanded to also treat such things as *assur* based on the higher standard of others.

5761

The *Mishnah* (Berachot 5:2) states that the addition to the *Shemoneh Esrei* concerning *Havdalah* is made in the blessing entitled "chonain hada'at," "You favor man with knowledge." The *Talmud* Yerushalmi (Berachot 39b) accepts the view that wisdom is a prerequisite to making distinctions, such as between the Holy and the secular, which is the essence of *Havdalah*. The point relies on the notion that there are definable extremes – Holy and profane – but that understanding the distinctions and into which category a particular action, thought or philosophy may fall requires wisdom. Wisdom, we know, requires work, time and desire to acquire. Often, the unwillingness on the part of an individual to undertake the required effort leads to a lazy (and unwise) determination of what is Holy and what is not.

5762

The second *pasuk* of Parashat Re'eh urges the Jews to observe the "Commandments of Hashem, your G-d, that I command you today." (Devarim 11:27) Yet we know that Parashat Re'eh takes place during the last year in the desert, which means the giving of the *Torah* at Mount Sinai took place thirty-nine years before! The mention of "today" is a reference to the importance of making the *Torah* fresh and new each day of one's life, as if one was commanded on this very day. Every day is a moment of truth for the Jew, and true *Torah* growth comes "one day at a time." One should resolve "<u>today</u> I will learn *Torah*;" "<u>today</u> I will not eat *treif*."

5763

Rabbi Edward Davis – Rav Joseph B. Soloveitchik spoke about our need to be sensitive to "Biblical jargon" in order to best understand otherwise seemingly repetitive portions of the *Torah*. An example is where the *Torah* in two places warns against eating the camel. (Vayikra 11:4 and Devarim 14:7) Chazal state that the second reference, found in Parashat Re'eh, pertains to the prohibition of the milk of a camel. Another example in Parashat Re'eh is the Torah's declaration "ki fatoach tiftach et yad'cha," translated as "for open, you shall open your hand." (Devarim 15:8) This means that one must be proactive in providing for the poor, rather than reactive when asked to do so. An example occurred in the Hollywood, Florida community, when a local widow announced her daughter's engagement. Rabbi Davis received unsolicited phone calls from congregants who desired to contribute to defray the costs of the wedding, even without having been asked to do so. This is an example of *Torah* in action.

5764

Reb Yossi Hahn – With respect to eating kosher animals, the *pasuk* states "רַק הַדָּם לֹא תֹאכֵלוּ עַל הָאָרֶץ תִּשְׁפְּכֶנּוּ כַּמָּיִם," "But you shall not eat the blood; you shall pour it onto the earth like water." (Devarim 12:16) It was customary at the time of the giving of the *Torah* that a conqueror of men or a hunter of animals would eat the heart and/or drink the blood of the vanquished, as it was widely believed that that heart and blood contained the life source, and therefore power, of all living creatures. Here, the *Torah* is bucking conventional wisdom in telling the Jews that true strength lies not in drinking blood but in *mitzvah* observance.

5765

Rabbi Michael Jablinowitz – There is a hint in Parashat Re'eh as to the essence of the Jew. The *Torah* provides us with a clear choice: blessings or curses, which flow respectively from doing good or, G-d forbid, doing evil. Yet the language used to describe each is inconsistent. Regarding "*berachah*," "blessing" the *Torah* states "asher tishm'u el mitzvot," "that you shall listen to the mitzvot," (Devarim 11:27) and as for "*klallah*," "curse," the *Torah* states "lo tishm'u el mitzvot," "if you don't listen to the mitzvot." (Devarim 11:28) One might expect that the key to blessing is doing *mitzvot* and the key to curses is doing sins. Yet both blessing and curse are referenced to *mitzvot*, which would suggest that a Jew's natural inclination is to harken and attach himself to the *mitzvot*.

5768

Rabbi Chaim Tuvi – The well-known double *lashon* in Parashat Re'eh reads "aseir, t'aseir," (Devarim 14:22) which is commonly interpreted as a command to "surely tithe," but the Vilna Gaon says that this language is meant to be taken literally, meaning one should take "עשׂר," (one tenth) of the word "תעשׂר." Ten percent of "tav" (400) is 40, or "mem"; ten percent of "ayin" (70) is 7, or "zayin"; ten percent of "sin" (300) is 30, or "lamed"; and ten percent of "reish" (200) is 20, or "chaf." Mem, Zayin, Lamed, Chaf (sofit) spells "מזלך," "your mazel," which is a reference to the secret of charitable giving; namely that one's *mazel* with regards to money is dependent upon the *tzedakah* that he gives.

5769

Rabbi Eli Mansour – Why does the *pasuk* charge *Bnei Yisrael* to "rak chazak l'vilti achol hadam," "only be strong, do not drink the blood" (Devarim 12:23) of the animals you slaughter? Blood is naturally repulsive. One would not think that extra strength is needed to avoid drinking it. Actually, even after leaving *Mitzrayim*, the Jews had an affinity for blood developed by the desensitizing experiences over hundreds of years of slavery in Egypt. The modern American analogs are today's "alternate lifestyles" and immodest attire, which we see all around us. The American Jew needs to be particularly strong in rejecting these trends which are anathema to *Torah*, so as not to grow accustomed and accepting of them.

5770
Rabbi Yosef Kalatsky – The prohibition in Parashat Re'eh of cutting oneself in grieving for a dead person, usually a relative (Devarim 14:1; see also Vayikra 19:28) is preceded by the language "Banim atem l'Hashem Elokaichem," "you are children of Hashem your G-d." We must realize that despite the loss of a loved one, our closest and most loving "Relative" is *Hashem*, Who perpetually remains in our lives. We are quite literally His Children, and we are comforted in knowing He will never abandon us.

5771
Rabbi Michael Jablinowitz – The *parashah* begins with the word "re'eh," "see" (Devarim 11:26) and ends with the same word employed in the directive that *Bnei Yisrael* shall be "yaira'eh," "seen" in *Yerushalayim* for the *Shalosh Regalim*. (Devarim 16:16) There, appearing in *Yerushalayim* is linked to obtaining *simchah*: "v'hayita ach sameach," "and you shall be completely happy!" (Devarim 16:15) The Sfas Emes states that *Eretz Yisrael* is a place of *simchah* that leads us to "*yirah*," fear of Hashem, whereas *chutz l'Aretz* is a place of *yirah* which can lead us to *simchah*. MRF Note – This provides all the more reason to celebrate *Z'man Simchateinu* in *Eretz Yisrael*!

5772
Rabbi Ephraim Wachsman – There are two *Rosh Hashanah* holidays that Jews observe: the first of *Tishrei* and the first of *Nissan*. When counting from the first day of *Nissan*, there are six full months representing the six days that precede the *Shabbat*: *Nissan, Iyar, Sivan, Tammuz, Av* and *Elul*.

Tishrei, then, is the seventh month, equivalent to *Shabbat*, and therefore *Elul* is the equivalent of *Erev Shabbat*. One's "Shabbat" (i.e. Tishrei, with all its holidays) will only be a successful as his "*Erev Shabbat*" in *Elul*. Proper preparation makes for a meaningful holiday season.

5773

Rabbi Eli Mansour – The *Torah*, in describing *Maaser Sheini*, famously states "aseir t'aseir," literally "tithe, you shall tithe." (Devarim 14:22) While this directive is commonly tied to *maaser kesafim*, the *pasuk* is written with direct reference to *Maaser Sheini*, which the *Torah* expressly indicates is "l'maan tilmad l'yira et Hashem Elokecha kol hayamim," "so that you will learn to fear Hashem your G-d all the days." (Devarim 14:23) The Chinuch indicates that one learns fear and awe of *Hashem* by going to *Yerushalayim* and eating one's produce (or spending the monetary proceeds). During that time one witnesses the *Beit HaMikdash* and the *Kohanim* in action, and in such an elevated spiritual setting, one cannot help but develop a strong sense of fear of G-d. In that sense, returning to the *pasuk*, we give our tithe to gain the wealth contained in *Yirat Shamayim*, through the atmosphere of *Kedushah* contained in the *Maaser Sheini* experience. In our times, the lesson is to put ourselves in such environments in order to enjoy the "wealth" that is gained in fearing *Hashem*.

SHOFTIM

5757

There are a number of potential reasons that a "black hat" is associated with Orthodox Judaism. 1. On a *Kabbalistic* level, there are five elements to the soul. Two of them ("chaya" and "yechidah") transcend the intellect. Wearing a hat and a *kippah* over the head represents these two elements. 2. Black is formal. 3. A hat demonstrates respect for *Hashem* during *davening*.

5758

Many lessons are contained in the handling of the *korbanot*. Part of the *korban* was given to the *Kohanim*, which is a reminder to think of others. Part was burnt for *Hashem*, which reminds us to think of Him, and the remainder was eaten by the individual, which transforms the physical slaughter into a Holy thing. Rambam (Moreh Nevuchim) explains that animals that were worshipped by pagans were specifically used for *korbanot* in a ritual where the animal died in place of the offerer.

5759

Rabbi Simcha Bunim Bonhart – Parashat Shoftim opens with the *pasuk* "Judges and police you shall appoint for <u>yourself</u> in your cities ...." (Devarim 16:18) This is a directive to judge yourself before judging others and to police yourself before policing others.

MRF Note – Parashat Shoftim is read in the month of *Elul*, as we prepare for the Days of Awe, *Rosh Hashanah* and *Yom Kippur*. Growing up in New Hampshire, I recall that there was a law that everyone inspect and fix his car every year in order to pass a state-mandated inspection. Problems that were left unaddressed during the year needed to be addressed in the pre-inspection period to ensure another year of operations. The same is true during *Elul*, the pre-inspection period of the soul.

5760

The *pasuk* states "Shoftim v'shotrim titen l'cha b'chol sh'arecha asher Hashem Elokecha notain l'cha ... ," "Judges and officers shall you appoint <u>for you</u> in all your gates which Hashem your G-d gives you ...." (Devarim 16:18) "For you" can be understood to mean "for your soul," the true essence of any person, and "your gates" can be understood as the "gates" or "windows" to your soul, namely one's mouth, ears and eyes. The message is that one must carefully judge what goes in and, in the case of the mouth, also what comes out in the form of words. One must make himself a judge and an officer in this regard, applying the *Torah's* laws to what is allowed through each "gate." To accomplish this, we are told in Pirkei Avot (1:6) "aseh l'cha rav," which enjoins a Jew to "establish <u>for himself</u> a teacher" to provide the relevant laws and strategies for effective self-improvement.

5761

Rabbi Yissocher Frand – In the exemptions from military service set forth in Parashat Shoftim is an exemption for a man who has built a house in which he has yet to take residence. Of him the *Torah* states "[l]et him go and return to his house, lest he die in the war and another man will inaugurate it." (Devarim 20:5) On this point, Rashi states that this would be a matter of great aggravation for the soldier. The *Torah* here is speaking to man as he is, which at times means as a jealous creature. When the thought of another man living in one's house outweighs his other concerns, even that he could die in war, his presence in an army could hurt morale and he therefore must leave. Ideally, one should think that should he die, at least his house will be put to good use by someone else, but the *Torah* understands that humans simply do not think in those terms.

5762

Rabbi Yosef Kalatsky – The *Torah* specifically warns that a king may not have too many horses so that he will not return to Egypt and should not have too many wives so that his heart will not go astray. (Devarim 17:16, 17) For most *Torah* prohibitions, the *Torah* does not provide an explicit reason. Here, where a reason is given, a danger emerges. *Shlomo HaMelech*, the wisest of all men, thought the reasons for these prohibitions would not apply to him based on his superior intellect and character, and stumbled in these areas. People usually fail in areas in which they believe they understand the basis for the *mitzvah* which they rationalize to be inapplicable to them. *Shlomo HaMelech* ended up sinning because he believed he knew himself better than *Hashem* knew him.

5763

Rabbi Yossi Jankovits – A question arises concerning the "eidim zomemin," the "conspiring witnesses." The *Torah* says if two witnesses come to give false testimony in a capital case and are exposed as fraudulent prior to the execution of the accused, "וַעֲשִׂיתֶם לוֹ כַּאֲשֶׁר זָמַם לַעֲשׂוֹת לְאָחִיו וּבִעַרְתָּ הָרָע מִקִּרְבֶּךָ," "You shall do to him as he conspired to do to his fellow, and you shall destroy the evil from your midst." (Devarim 19:19) This means that in such a case, the conspiring witnesses are put to death. Yet *halachah* states that if they are not exposed until after the execution of the accused, nothing is done to them! The *Gemara* (Makot 5b) explains that this law was a major grievance of the *Tzidukim* who drew a *kal v'chomer* in holding that where the accused is put to death, of course the false witnesses are also put to death. There are a number of reasons given for why we don't do anything to the false witnesses in such a case. One possible answer comes from the often misunderstood *pasuk* which follows the portion on the conspiring witnesses: "וְלֹא תָחוֹס עֵינֶךָ נֶפֶשׁ בְּנֶפֶשׁ עַיִן בְּעַיִן שֵׁן בְּשֵׁן יָד בְּיָד רֶגֶל בְּרָגֶל," "Your eye shall not pity; life for life, eye for eye, tooth for tooth, hand for hand, foot for foot." (Devarim 19:21) This we know must refer to monetary value, for there is no way to calculate the value of one man's eye relative to that of another. The classic case is where a two-eyed man knocks out the only eye of a one-eyed man. To remove one eye from the two-eyed man would not render him equivalent to his victim, who is now blind. Applying this logic we may not execute the false witnesses whose false testimony resulted in the death of an innocent man, because their situation is different from his. The wrongly executed died with knowledge of the falsity of his accusers' testimony, and without knowledge as to why he is being killed. The false witnesses, however, would know very well why they are dying and the justification for their execution, which would mean their deaths would not be an exact settlement for the erroneous death. The Gerrer Rebbe claims that another reason that we do not execute the false witnesses is that death brings *kaparah*, something that is denied to them.

Rabbi Yosef Kalatsky – The *Torah* requires a Jewish king to carry a *Sefer Torah*, to "read" it, and to fear *Hashem*. (Devarim 17:19) The Sforno notes that "read" means in-depth study. He states that a true study of the wisdom of the *Torah* will lead the king to see the unimaginable power and wisdom of *Hashem*, causing this mere worldly king to fear Him. Such a fear is a requirement for a man of flesh and blood with power over the life and death of other Jews.

5764

Rabbi Yossi Jankovits – The *pasuk* declares "Tzedek, tzedek tirdof ... ," "Righteousness, righteousness you shall pursue ... ," (Devarim 16:20), meaning that one should be a *tzaddik* in stages, not all at once. This is the message of *Elul*: that all meaningful change is lasting only if undertaken incrementally. The *Shofar*, the representative symbol of *Elul*, is blown from the small end with sound emerging from the wider end. To blow it the opposite way is *assur* according to *halachah*. (Rosh Hashanah 27b) The lesson is that little changes bring big results. We see this philosophy in *Yaacov Avinu*, when he rejects his brother *Eisav's* offer to "travel together." *Yaacov* tells *Eisav* "v'ani etnahalah l'iti l'regel ... ," "I will make my way at a slow pace ...." (Bereshit 33:14). The *rashei teivot* of his words are "vav," "aleph," "lamed," and "lamed." Unscrambled, that spells "אלול," "Elul!"

5765

Rabbi Yissocher Frand – One of the conditions that makes a Jew *patur* from participating in a war is where he has built, but not dedicated, a new home. (Devarim 20:5) There is a *machloket* amongst the commentators as to whether there is a *mitzvah* of *chanukat habayit* and, correspondingly, whether such a *mitzvah* applies only within *Eretz Yisrael* or worldwide. One opinion holds that there is a positive *mitzvah* to dedicate a new house which applies only in Israel. The basis of this opinion is the fact that there is a requirement upon all Jews of *yishuv Eretz Yisrael*. The Ramban counts this as one of the 613 commandments, while the Rambam declares it to be a *chovah*, but not among the 613. In any event, by purchasing or building a home in *Eretz Yisrael*, a Jew fulfils an important obligation and therefore is obligated to have a ceremony and, accordingly, a *seudat mitzvah* upon completing the construction or purchase.

5766

Rabbi Yosef Weinstock – The *Torah* commands that that king of Israel is compelled by the *Torah* to write and possess two *Sifrei Torah*. (Devarim 17:18, 19) The *Gemara* (Sanhedrin 21b) tells us that one he brings with him in his daily travels, from which he learns. The other remains pristine, locked away unused in his royal treasury. One possible lesson, appropriate for *Elul*, is that the king's daily *Torah* will be subject to the harsh elements of governing on a day to day basis, as the king hopefully strives to fulfil the *Torah's* commandments. Yet he must remember that there is an ideal to which he aspires, as represented in the second, pristine *sefer*. At this time of year, we too try to improve ourselves in an effort to match more closely to the ideal Jewish character model to which we aspire.

5767

Rabbi Ephraim Wachsman – The *arei miklat* contained people whose only hope for release was the death of the *Kohain Gadol*. (Bamidbar 35:25) The *Talmud* (Makot 11a) relates that the mother of the *Kohain Gadol* feared the people of the *ir miklat* would *daven* for the death of her son, and to counter that possibility she would deliver food to the inmates. She recognized the power of sincere *tefillah* of people desperate and "out of options" could result in the death of her Holy son who *davened* on behalf of all of *Klal Yisrael*. We should be inspired in *Elul* to unleash the same power in our prayers to *Hashem*, from Whom all blessings flow.

5768

Rabbi Yitzchak Salid – The common element of many of the *mitzvot* of Parashat Shoftim is the recognition of authority: the authority of a Jewish court (Devarim 16:18), authority of the Jewish king (Devarim 17:15), the authority of the *Kohanim* (Devarim 20:2) and authority of the rabbis (Devarim 21:2). It is important to recognize that freedom as the *Torah* ideal is not based on rejecting authority or eliminating authority, but rather to accede to *Hashem's* Divinely granted authority.

5769

Rabbi Eli Mansour – Parashat Shoftim describes the prohibition of a judge taking a bribe. (Devarim 16:19) The *Talmud* (Ketubot 105b) contains many examples where small, seemingly insignificant acts done on behalf of a rabbinical judge caused him to recuse himself from hearing a case. Examples include relatively minor assistance provided by a litigant to a judge, including extending a hand to help him across a bridge, brushing a feather off his clothing or covering spittle in the street where he was walking. These illustrations could lead one to conclude that the rabbis were hypersensitive to the issue of bribes, perhaps legalistic to an unhealthy degree. However the true nature of these great men is inspiring. They were so in tune with the concept of gratitude that, to them, minor favors were regarded as major gifts. Rather than "standing on ceremony" and allowing de minimis gifts and favors to disqualify them, they genuinely perceived these favors as large gifts, clearly arising to the status of bribes. This mindset should inspire us to seek out and identify the amazing things others do for us and to be eager to recognize and thank others for the good they bestow on us.

5770

Rabbi Mordechai Shifman – As described in Parashat Shoftim, the portion of *Eglah Arufah* requires a declaration by the *zakainim* concerning the discovered corpse. "וְעָנוּ וְאָמְרוּ יָדֵינוּ לֹא שָׁפְכוּ (כתיב שפכה) אֶת הַדָּם הַזֶּה וְעֵינֵינוּ לֹא רָאוּ," "They shall speak up and say 'our hands have not spilled this blood, and our eyes did not see.'" (Devarim 21:7) Rashi asks rhetorically whether it would occur to anyone that the Elders would murder someone. Rather, he brings the *Gemara* (Sotah 45b) that explains that they are stating that they did not see the man and send him off without food nor "u'valo lavayah," "without escort." Why is escorting a guest of such importance that failing to do so is equated to murder? The final impression one imparts upon his guest actually has an effect on his guest's wellbeing once he leaves. Police experts report that there is something called a "mugger's mark," where a person, unsure of himself and his surroundings, is targeted by criminals who detect a vulnerability. By giving one's guest directions and, perhaps more importantly, a sense of self-confidence that he is a person worthy of a meaningful escort, one makes him less vulnerable to attack and, G-d forbid, death.

5771

Rabbi Ben Tzion Shafier – The *Torah* warns us of the three dangers to a Jewish King: too many horses, too many wives and too much gold and silver. (Devarim 17:16, 17) The Daat Zakainim states that the prohibition of too much money centers around the concern that the king will become arrogant. This seems strange, for the Rambam informs us that it is required to show a king tremendous *kavod*, and outlines the many *halachot* dealing with the death penalty if one fails to do so. Insofar as the Jews are commanded to greatly honor their king, how can money itself be a catalyst for arrogance? Power and *kavod* are dependent on others, for a king cannot enjoy honor if his subjects do not provide it to him. A king realizes this and therefore can remain humble with the knowledge that he needs others to reign. But wealth by definition brings independence, which is very dangerous. The perception that one does not need others is the root of arrogance and, if activated by wealth, can lead to a king's downfall.

5772

Rabbi Chaim Yaacov Goldvicht – Parashat Shoftim begins with reference to judges. (Devarim 16:18) The Midrash Rabbah (Devarim: parashah 5, siman 5) quotes as follows: "Rabbi Eliezer says 'where there is judgment, there is no judgment. Where there is no judgment, there is judgment.'" How so? "Rabbi Eliezer says 'if judgment is performed below, it will not have to be performed Above. If judgment is not performed below, it will have to be performed Above.'" This can be understood on a societal level <u>and</u> on an individual level. *Hashem* need not judge and punish us if we, on our own, identify our errors and work to correct them, a powerful thought leading into *Rosh Hashanah*.

5773

Reb Steven Jacoby – The *pasuk* states "כִּי יִפָּלֵא מִמְּךָ דָבָר לַמִּשְׁפָּט בֵּין דָּם | לְדָם בֵּין דִּין לְדִין וּבֵין נֶגַע לָנֶגַע דִּבְרֵי רִיבֹת בִּשְׁעָרֶיךָ וְקַמְתָּ וְעָלִיתָ אֶל הַמָּקוֹם אֲשֶׁר יִבְחַר ה' אלקיך בּוֹ" "If a matter of judgment is hidden from you, between blood and blood, between verdict and verdict, between plague and plague, <u>matters of dispute within your gates</u>, you shall rise up and ascend to the place that Hashem, your G-d, shall choose." (Devarim 17:8) The Arizal points out that Jews over many centuries have been bloodied, subject to harsh verdicts and endured afflictions, and here the *Torah* tells us why: because of matters of dispute within our cities, between Jews! To the extent we can live in internal harmony, negative external forces will be diminished.

KI TEITZEI

5758

The verse in the Parashat Ki Teitzei reads "... a perfect and honest measure you shall have so that your days may be prolonged on the Land that Hashem your G-d gives you." (Devarim 25:15). While the *Torah* calls for a "perfect measure," the *Talmud* (Bava Batra 88b) describes the duty of a seller to add a little bit in favor of the buyer. The Olat Chodesh asks why the equation of a "perfect measure" results in long days, and answers that every person has a known measure of days in the world. Because of the concept of *middah keneged middah*, if one deceives his fellow man by using a defective measurement, thereby giving less than promised, *Hashem* will accordingly give the deceiver less days in his life than were originally promised. This is an important idea for the month of *Elul* as we prepare for *Rosh Hashanah* and our petitions for long life.

The *mitzvah* of maintaining honesty in our weights and measures (Devarim 25:13-16) immediately precedes the requirement to remember and eradicate *Amalek* (Devarim 25:17-19). This may be due to the fact that the Nation of *Amalek* represents lack of belief in G-d, because of which they attacked the Jews. There is another reference to *Amalek* in Parashat Beshalach, which is immediately preceded by *Bnei Yisrael* questioning "Is there Hashem in our midst or not?" (Shemot 17:7) Cheating with weights is not a matter of dishonesty, rather it is a declaration regarding a lack of faith in *Hashem's* ability to provide us with a *parnassah*. Cheating in business indicates that we do not accept or believe the *Gemara* (Beitzah 16a) which teaches that the amount we make in any given year is determined by *Hashem* on *Rosh Hashanah* and is fixed regardless of how much or how little we do thereafter. This rejection of G-d's centrality in our lives is a key feature of the mind of Amalek.

5759
Rabbeinu Bachaiya – In Parashat Mishpatim we are instructed to return the wandering ox of "your enemy" to him (Shemot 23:4), and in Parashat Ki Teitzei we have the same *mitzvah* regarding the ox, sheep and goat of "your brother." (Devarim 22:1) This is the same *mitzvah*, but presented in this order to demonstrate the primary objective (or rather an objective) of bringing about an interpersonal change in the Jew. The goal is to make he who was once your enemy into your brother by opening your heart to the concept of *Ahavat Yisrael*.

Rabbi Mordechai Kamenetsky – The verse states "כִּי תִבְנֶה בַּיִת חָדָשׁ וְעָשִׂיתָ מַעֲקֶה לְגַגֶּךָ וְלֹא תָשִׂים דָּמִים בְּבֵיתֶךָ כִּי יִפֹּל הַנֹּפֵל מִמֶּנּוּ," "When you build a new house you shall make a fence around your roofs that you shall not place blood in your house when <u>a fallen one falls</u>." (Devarim 22:8) Here the *Torah* is explicitly identifying Divine Providence as being the cause of the man's fall from the roof (hence, the reference to the "fallen one," even though he has not yet physically fallen), but leaves open the free will of the homeowner as to whether he should be the tool of *Hashem's* plan. The *Torah* warns us not to be an accomplice to such "blood" but only to be a conduit for "good" and "life."

5760

Chofetz Chaim- Man is essentially lazy concerning his limbs, as is demonstrated from the effort required to exercise and toil. Yet the opposite is true regarding man's tongue, as man would rather talk than refrain. *Chazal* say that the *pasuk* in *Iyov* (5:7) which states "Man was born to toil," refers to the lifelong struggle to curb one's inclination to gossip; to not speak when he is otherwise inclined to do so.

MRF Note – When Vice-Presidential candidate Al Gore passionately kissed his wife at the 2000 Democratic National Convention, he publicly, yet mistakenly, was asserting that fidelity absent modesty is acceptable public conduct. The public disenchantment with Clinton involves his utter lack of both of these virtues; virtues so critical in the preservation of the Jewish people over the millennia (adapted from a *shiur* by Rabbi Gedalya Glatt).

Rabbi Yossi Jankovits – Parashat Ki Teitzei provides the *Torah* basis for divorce. The *pasuk* states "כִּי יִקַּח אִישׁ אִשָּׁה וּבְעָלָהּ וְהָיָה אִם לֹא תִמְצָא חֵן בְּעֵינָיו כִּי מָצָא בָהּ עֶרְוַת דָּבָר וְכָתַב לָהּ סֵפֶר כְּרִיתֻת וְנָתַן בְּיָדָהּ וְשִׁלְּחָהּ מִבֵּיתוֹ," "If a man takes a wife and possesses her. She fails to please him because he finds immorality about her and he writes her a bill of divorce and presented into her hand, and sent her from his house" (Devarim 24:1) The *Talmud* (Gittin 90a) states that *Beit Shammai* claimed that divorce was proper only in cases of immoral activity by the wife. *Beit Hillel* said if a wife burned her husband's meal it is grounds for divorce, and *Rabbi Akiva* goes even further, saying that a man who finds a more attractive woman may divorce his current wife. The *Gemara* is startling, since we generally associate *Beit Hillel* with the more lenient and forgiving view in Jewish law, and *Rabbi Akiva* with his well-known dictum "v'ahavta l'raiacha komocha," "and you shall love your neighbor like yourself." (Vayikra 19:18) Where is the famous compassion of *Hillel* and *Rabbi Akiva* for the wife in this case? If suspected immorality was the only possible ground for divorce, any divorced woman would be "damaged goods," ineligible for remarriage. In fact, by dictating that a man may divorce his wife over petty things, *Hillel* and *Rabbi Akiva* increase the chances that she will remarry with a man who will not think the worst about her prior marriage.

5761

Parashat Ki Teitzei spells out the specific steps that a soldier in a voluntary war must undertake to take and live with a captive woman. (Devarim 21:10-14) Rashi makes clear that the *Torah* is recognizing that the *yetzer hara* may overcome the soldier on the battlefield. It may, in fact, be unconquerable in this regard. What is implied by the *Torah* is that in most other areas, where there is no special accommodation for the *yetzer hara*, we have the power to overcome it. The *Torah* does not ask a Jew to do anything he is incapable of, and in those few cases where a Jew cannot handle it, the *Torah* makes an accommodation for him.

5762

Rabbi Yissocher Frand – The Daat Zakainim teaches that the prohibition of plowing with an ox and a donkey together (Devarim 22:10) concerns the effect on the donkey. Because the ox chews its cud, the donkey may get the mistaken impression that the ox was recently fed while the donkey was not. This would cause jealousy and some level of pain in the donkey due to the misinformation received. The lesson is clear. If we need be concerned with the feelings of animals in this regard, how much more so should we seek to spare humans from such pain.

There is a connection between the *mitzvah* in Parashat Ki Teitzei of *shiluach hakein* (Devarim 22:6, 7) and the mitzvah of *kibbud av v'eim* (Devarim 5:16), aside from the obvious fact that in each case the *Torah* promises long life for observance of the *mitzvah*. In both cases the self-sacrifice of the parent(s) is recognized and forms the basis for the *mitzvah*. In the case of *shiluach hakain*, the mother bird endangers herself by remaining with her eggs, requiring one to send her away. We may therefore not benefit from the instinctive self-sacrifice of the mother bird without first recognizing it.

Rabbi Mordechai Kamenetsky – The *Torah* prohibits the nations of *Amon* and *Moav* from marrying into *Bnei Yisrael*. (Devarim 23:4-7) Why, in doing so, does the *Torah* inject a mention of *Hashem's* love for the Jews in prohibiting *Bilaam's* curse against His Nation? (Devarim 23:6) Perhaps this illustrated the same philosophy that causes a Jew to say "kain ayin hara," "there should be no 'evil eye'," or "chas v'shalom," "G-d forbid," when describing something. These phrases are themselves constant recognitions of *Hashem's* wonderful involvement in our lives. The *Torah* here sets the foundation for the way Jews will communicate with one another for millennia to come.

5763

Rabbi Yosef Kalatsky – Like *Avraham* who fetched provisions for the *malachim* who did not need them (Bereshit 18:2-8), the essence of the *mitzvah* of *chesed* is not dependent upon the need of the supposed recipient. Based on that reality, the nations of *Amon* and *Moav* can be faulted for failing to provide bread and water for the Jews during their sojourn in the desert. (Devarim 23:5) Although *Bnei Yisrael* had the Clouds of Glory (which provided shelter), the Well of *Miriam* (which provided water in abundance) and the *Mon* (which provided nourishment), the requirements of *chesed* would dictate that *Moav* and *Ammon* at least offer. Because they did not, they can never truly be Jews, since the essence of the Jew is *chesed*.

5764

Rabbi Yosef Kalatsky – The pasuk states "וְכִי יִהְיֶה בְאִישׁ חֵטְא מִשְׁפַּט מָוֶת וְהוּמָת וְתָלִיתָ אֹתוֹ עַל עֵץ," "If a man commits a sin for which he is sentenced to death, and he is put to death, you shall hang him <u>on a tree</u>." (Devarim 21:22) The Ohr HaChaim HaKadosh states here that the *Torah* is not merely referring to "gallows," but "eitz" refers to the *Torah* sage of that generation, meaning that such a sage (who is compared to a mighty tree) must bear some of the blame for the sin of the killer. However, the *Gemara* (Berachot 19a) connects the *mitzvah* that immediately follows, to bury the *meit* on that very day (Devarim 21:23), alludes to the requirement of assuming that the *Torah* sage has done *teshuvah* by the next day. The credibility of the sage must be maintained for the benefit of the community at large.

5765

Rabbi Yosef Weinstock – The *Torah* indicates that the reward for one who honors his father and mother is long life. (Devarim 5:16) The same reward is cited in Parashat Ki Teitzei for the *mitzvah* of *shiluach hakain*. (Devarim 22:7) The former of these *mitzvot* appears to be grounded in *chesed*, the latter in cruelty, for the *mitzvah* of *shiluah hakain* is a positive commandment that must be done even if one does not want the chicks or eggs. Perhaps the lesson is that kindness and cruelty are inadequate human interpretations of *mitzvot* that are above such labels. Our mission is to perform the *mitzvot* in faithfulness, not applying our limited viewpoint and judgments to the essence of the *mitzvot*. MRF Note – The failure to keep this lesson in mind was demonstrated in a "d'var Torah" published in an Israeli newspaper this week. The author argued that the *mitzvah* to eradicate *Amalek* (Devarim 25:17-19) must "undergo a dramatic change and renewal, drastic enough as to render it unrecognizable to the traditional understanding." This so-called "call to genocide" was described by the author as backward and cruel, and therefore inapplicable and unnecessary for the modern Jew who seeks to remove cruelty from the culture of its enemies. Such twisted thinking denies *Hashem's* dominion over the world and the immutable and perfect nature of His Holy *Torah*.

5768

Rabbi Yitzchak Salid – Parashat Ki Teitzei begins with the *inyan* of "ashet yifat toar," "a woman of beautiful form." The *pasuk* begins "v'raitah," "and you will see." (Devarim 21:11) This seems significant in light of Rashi's mention on this *pasuk* that the *Torah* accommodates (to some extent) the *yetzer hara* in man. It would be expected that Rashi would draw an explicit connection with the *inyan* of orlah (Vayikra 19:25), where he quotes Rabbi Akiva's mention that the *Torah* is accommodating the *yetzer hara* of man (by promising increased crop production for those who observe orlah). The fact that Rashi does not provide that cross reference may be demonstrating that a different lesson is at work in the case of the captive woman. For here, the *pasuk* mentions "seeing," that for which the heart is already searching. Because the *yetzer hara* caused the Jew in this case to seek out and "see" the captive woman, the *Torah* must therefore prescribe an antidote. The clear lesson here is that the eyes will very often see that for which the soul is searching. By controlling our desires we can avoid seeing the pitfalls in life. Reb Ephraim Sobol draws the connection told by the Kotzker Rebbe who was walking on a narrow street with a group of *talmidim*. As an immodestly dressed woman approached, one of his students turned aside to face the wall as she passed. The Kotzker whispered into his ear "I'd rather that you looked at her and thought about the wall!"

5769

Rabbi Michael Jablinowitz – Rabbi Gedalyahu Schorr, in his sefer Ohr Gedalyahu, teaches that Parashat Ki Teitzei is thematically devoted to elevating otherwise mundane life activities to imbue them with a measure of Holiness. For example, one who builds a house makes a *ma'akeh* (Devarim 22:8); one who wears clothing may not wear *shaatnez* (Vayikra 19:9). Perhaps primary among these *mitzvot* is "motza sifatecha tishmor v'asita," "what comes out of your mouth you shall keep and do." (Devarim 23:24) Something so mundane and natural as speaking must be carefully monitored to ensure proper intention and result.

5770

Rabbi Yossi Jankovits – There is "double *lashon*" in Parashat Ki Teitzei with regard to the *mitzvah* of *shiluach hakain*. The *pasuk* states "shalach t'shalach," which translates as "you shall surely send away," (Devarim 22:7) which suggests an active approach to finding and fulfilling this *mitzvah*. Yet the previous *pasuk* begins "ki yakray kan tzibur," "if you <u>happen upon</u> a bird's nest ... ," (Devarim 22:6) which is read by the *Gemara* (Chullin 138b) to instruct us <u>not</u> to actively seek out this *mitzvah*, but rather to perform it with alacrity when it presents itself. This is unique to this *mitzvah*, as is the fact that *shiluach hakain* is equated by *Chazal* with the coming of *Moshiach*. In two places in *Tanach* there is a reference to "sending" with regards to the *Moshiach* (e.g. Hashem's sending of *Eliyahu HaNavi* [Malachi 3:23]), using the same language as applies to the sending of the mother bird. Based on this connection between the two *inyanim*, the Rabbis apply the practicalities of *shiluach hakain* to our attitude towards the coming of *Moshiach*, meaning they learn that we do not engage in *cheshbonot* to determine when he will come, yet we apply alacrity to our yearning for him and our desire that he come speedily, in our days.

5771

Rabbi Mordechai Becher – When reciting the *Shema*, we do not recite aloud "baruch Shem Kavod Malchuto l'olam va'ed," "Blessed is the Name of His Honored Kingship forever," except on *Yom Kippur*, when we are compared to angels. But why do we say it out loud for *Maariv* after *Kol Nidre* rather than at *maariv* after *Neilah*? Are we not closer in emulating the attributes of *malachim* after a day of prayer and fasting, rather than merely one hour after eating? The proof is brought from the episode of *Yaacov* and his ladder, where the angels are famously moving up and down, rather than down (from Heaven) and then up. (Bereshit 28:12) *Chazal* famously indicate there that the angels dedicated to accompany *Yaacov* outside of *Eretz Yisrael* were descending for that purpose (apparently the angels escorting him within Israel could not leave the Land for that purpose). But commentators note that this took place on *Har Moriah*, where *Yaacov* was still separated by both time and geography from physically departing from the Land. (Rashi on Bereshit 28:11) The differentiator was direction or "vector." *Yaacov* was headed *chutz l'Aretz*, even while he was in the *Aretz*, and for that reason he needed exile angels to escort him even while he was still in the Land. The same applies to our approach to *Yom Kippur*. After *Kol Nidre* we are directed towards Holiness; afterwards, despite having been cleansed in the process, we are on a vector towards physicality. It's not necessarily where one is, but rather where one is going. MRF Note – The same can be used to distinguish the fate of *Yishmael* in the *midbar* from the fate of the *ben sorer u'moreh* (Devarim 21:21) in Parashat Ki Teitzei. As Rabbi Eli Mansour teaches, *Hashem* spared *Yishmael* (Bereshit 21:17) because he was engaged in *teshuvah* at the time of his judgment, while the rebellious son, despite having not yet sinned enough to warrant death, was clearly on a negative trajectory and therefore was killed.

5772

Maharam Schick – The *pasuk* states "שַׁלֵּחַ תְּשַׁלַּח אֶת הָאֵם וְאֶת הַבָּנִים תִּקַּח לָךְ לְמַעַן יִיטַב לָךְ וְהַאֲרַכְתָּ יָמִים," "You shall surely send away the mother, and take the children for yourself, so that it will be good for you and you will prolong your days." (Devarim 22:7) The reference to "children" is notable, since the previous *pasuk* mentions "efrochim," "young birds." The

Rambam stated to his son "fortunate is the one who completes his days quickly" (i.e. completes his life's mission quickly). This would suggest that the reward of long life for certain *mitzvot* (like *shiluach hakain*) would be undesirable, which cannot be the case. The Chasam Sofer understands a verse in Parashat Ki Tavo to answer this difficulty. "V'hotirecha Hashem l'tova bifri vitnecha … ," "Hashem shall give you bountiful goodness in the fruit of your womb …." (Devarim 28:11) This, he says, means that, despite having completed your mission in life, *Hashem* will retain you to teach your children (and your students, who are considered as children). By doing *shiluach hakain*, says Maharam Schick, the *Torah* tells us that we will merit to "take the <u>children</u> for ourselves," and it will be good and *Hashem* shall prolong our days to teach them *Torah*.

5773

Rabbi Avraham Shaag – The *pasukim* state "lo tirah et shor achicha … v'hitalamta …. lo tochal l'hitaleim." "You shall not see the ox of your brother … and <u>hide</u> …. you are not able to <u>hide</u> yourself." (Devarim 22:1, 3) Why the double *lashon* and why the mention of ability to hide? The intervening language also contains double *lashon*, stating "hashaiv t'shiveim," "and <u>return</u>, you shall <u>return</u> them," (Devarim 22:1) indicating one must go against his nature up to 100 times to return the lost ox. When combined, these *pasukim* teach that if one strives repeatedly to do a difficult thing, it will become second nature and one will be unable to avoid the responsibility of doing that thing in the future. People can, in fact, change their nature, and *Elul* is the time to strive to do so.

KI TAVO

5757

Throughout Parashat Ki Tavo, *Moshe* makes reference to "hayom hazeh," "*this* day," and specifically refers to *Bnei Yisrael* becoming greater, developing a heart and eyes, "as of *this* day." (Devarim 29:3) Rashi comments that on that particular day *Moshe* gave a *Sefer Torah* to the *Leviim*, his Tribe. While that may have been an important event, how can this be understood as a more seminal day in the history of the Jewish People than, for example, *Yam Suf* or *Matan Torah*? Rashi continues that on that very same day the other *Shevatim* protested that by giving the Torah Scroll only to *Levy*, *Moshe* was creating the possibility that at some time in the future *Levy* would claim that their Tribe alone received the *Torah*. (Rashi on Devarim 29:3) Admittedly this would need to be very far in the future, as the *Kahal* had recently stood at *Sinai* together, and were therefore very clear that *Matan Torah* applied to all Jews. Nevertheless, they protested, and *Moshe* correctly reasoned that *Bnei Yisrael* were standing up for the *Torah* of generations far removed from themselves, an accomplishment that may have transcended the awesome previous experiences of the Nation. Such devotion to the *Torah* was the highest level achieved to that date. *Bnei Yisrael* wanted *Torah* for their grandchildren's grandchildren. This is the best argument for combatting intermarriage. Raising dubiously Jewish children makes a mockery of the legacy put forth in Parashat Ki Tavo. Furthermore, by not preserving *Torah* for later generations, we are hardening the (one) heart and blinding our eyes as a Nation.

5758

The *Mishnah* (Bikkurim 1:4) indicates that the convert to Judaism brings *Bikkurim* but does not recite *Mikra Bikkurim* because of the language in Parashat Ki Tavo referencing the Land that *Hashem* swore "l'Avotainu," "to our Forefathers." (Devarim 26:15) The *geir* is excluded based on genealogy (his forefathers were not the Jewish forefathers), even though he may own land in *Eretz Yisrael* and be required, therefore, to bring *Bikkurim*. The *Mishnah* goes on to indicate that when *davening* publicly the *geir* alters his *tefillah* to say "Avoteichem," "your Fathers," and privately he recites "Avot Yisrael," "the Fathers of Israel," rather than "Avoteinu," "our Fathers." A *Baraita* in *Talmud* Yerushalmi (perek 1, halachah 4) quotes *Rabbi Yehudah's* challenge to this *Mishnah* and declares that the convert recites and brings *Bikkurim* in the normal fashion, as *Hashem* made *Avraham*, one of the Forefathers, the Father of the multitude of nations. There, *Rabbi Yehoshua ben Levy* indicates that the *halachah* follows *Rabbi Yehudah*. The Rambam rules as such in his Mishneh Torah, as *Avraham Avinu*, Father to all, was the first to inherit the promise of the Land. In regards to *Vidui Maasrot*, however, the *halachah* is clear that the *geir* is not included as, it is argued, this relates to the *Shevatim* at the time of *Yehoshua*, to which a *geir* cannot claim a connection.

5759

Rabbi Yitzchak Etshalom – There is a fundamental difference in the approach to Judaism for converts and born Jews, which is reflected in how they are addressed. Converts are referred to as "Bnei Avraham," "Sons of Avraham" and born Jews are referred to as "Bnei Yaacov," "Sons of Yaacov." *Avraham* left everything he knew and made himself uncomfortable in order to follow the *emet*. *Yaacov* was fortunate enough to have been born into a tradition of his father and his grandfather and had to continue, rather than begin, that *mesorah*.

5760

Rabbi Yossi Jankovits – The *pasuk* says "Yitzav Hashem itecha et haberachah ba'asamecha," "Hashem will command the blessing to you in your silos (storehouses)." (Devarim 28:8) This is an indication of two ideas. Firstly, in a silo the exact amount of the supply is unknown. *Hashem* seeks to bless us but desires to do so in a way that will not be contrary to the natural order of things. Hence, as with a silo, one should not keep strict accounting of his holdings, as *Hashem* will miraculously increase them in a seemingly natural, unnoticeable way. Secondly, one is obligated to be modest concerning his wealth, in order that it should endure. As stated in the *Gemara* (Taanit 8b), similar to a silo, one should keep wealth out of the public eye so that he should not cause others the pain of jealousy and create an *ayin hara*, G-d forbid.

5761

Rabbi Yissocher Frand – There are two occurrences of *tochachah* in the *Torah*, one is *Sefer Vayikra* (26:14-43) in Parashat Bechukotai and the one in *Sefer Devarim* (28:15-68) in Parashat Ki Tavo. The admonition in Bechukotai ends with words of comfort, but not so for Ki Tavo, where the comfort must wait until Parashat Nitzavim, fifty *pasukim* later! Rabbi Joseph B. Soloveitchik quotes the Rambam that each *tochachah* is representative of one of the two destructions of the *Batei Mikdash*. The first came with a predetermined restoration after seventy years, but not so with the second, which to this day has yet to be rebuilt. The Rambam says that repentance will eventually come, as it does fifty *pasukim* later, and restoration will follow. Presently, we are now in the "pause" between Ki Tavo and Nitzavim, eagerly awaiting salvation.

The Chofetz Chaim discussed the case of a person who, unbeknownst to himself, has inadvertently overpaid (but not excessively) in a one-time transaction, and who asks his friend for his opinion of the deal. It is, according to the *Gemara* (Ketubot 17a), a *mitzvah* for the friend to praise the transaction and avoid telling him the truth. But would this not be a violation of the *Torah* directive to separate oneself from falsehood? (Shemot 23:7) The Chofetz Chaim says "no," because pursuing peace is the highest form of *emet*. The bottom line is that in helping to ensure that the buyer does not engage in *machloket* with the seller, the friend is facilitating truth in the form of peace, which is the best deal for everyone.

5762

Rabbi Yissocher Frand – In Parashat Ki Tavo *Moshe* tells *Bnei Yisrael* that curses will come upon them "תַּחַת אֲשֶׁר לֹא עָבַדְתָּ אֶת ה' אלקיך בְּשִׂמְחָה וּבְטוּב לֵבָב מֵרֹב כֹּל," "because you did not serve Hashem your G-d amid gladness

and goodness of heart, when everything was abundant." (Devarim 28:47)
This must mean that *simchah* is a central *mitzvah* of the *Torah*, but Rabbi
Yochanan Zweig questions where in the *Torah* it can be found. He answers
that people who are always angry and upset are so because they are not
receiving what they believe the world owes them. In contrast, happy
people generally view everything they receive as a gift. The one who is
perpetually upset truly believes that he, rather than *Hashem*, is the center
of the universe. This is akin to *avodah zareh*, which perhaps would justify
the resulting curses.

5763

The Lubavitcher Rebbe – In the *Bikkurim* process, the *ani's* simple fruit
basket is kept by the *Kohain*, while the gold or silver basket of the rich
man is returned to him. The *Gemara* (Bava Kama 92a) cites this as an
example of where "the rich get richer." The Rebbe indicates that the
Bikkurim offering is comprised of two components: *ruchniut* (the fruits)
and *gashmiut* (the basket). The *ani's* basket, coming from an impoverished,
brokenhearted donor, is considered a valuable spiritual offering to *Hashem*
and He rewards the *ani* for it. He'll take the fruits of the rich man, but
<u>not</u> his unsanctified material possessions.

5764

Rabbi Eli Mansour – There is much commentary about the famous *pasuk*
that appears in the middle of the *tochachah*, which blames the curses
"תַּחַת אֲשֶׁר לֹא עָבַדְתָּ אֶת ה' אלקיך בְּשִׂמְחָה וּבְטוּב לֵבָב מֵרֹב כֹּל," "because you did
not serve *Hashem* your G-d amid gladness and goodness of heart, when
everything was abundant." (Devarim 28:47) The Kotzker Rebbi reads
the *pasuk* as follows: "because you <u>happily avoided</u> serving Hashem your
G-d ... ," meaning that apart from not serving Him, you delighted in the
fact that you were failing to do so. The *Torah* recognizes man's fallibility
and allows for a *teshuvah* process, but it should at least bother us when

we fall short of *Hashem's* directives. To relish our failure to properly serve our Maker is deserving of curses, G-d forbid.

5765

Ms. Nechama Schachter – The *mitzvah* of *Bikkurim* was not in effect until the conquest of *Eretz Yisrael* was completed, which took fourteen years. The Lubavitcher Rebbe states that this means those *Shevatim* who were settled in the first years did not bring *Bikkurim* for many years, until their brethren were also settled, so that all could bring *Bikkurim* together. While the essence of *Bikkurim* is gratitude to *Hashem* for the bounty of the Land, a greater and more precious principle to *Hashem* is the *achdut* of the Jewish People.

5768

Rabbi Edward Davis – There was a *mitzvah* for *Bnei Yisrael* to erect large stones once inside *Eretz Yisrael*, and to write the *Torah* upon them in the seventy languages of the world. (Rashi on Devarim 27:8) We know the rule that it is *assur* to teach *Torah* to the *goyim*, so it seems clear this exercise was to benefit *Bnei Yisrael*. Yet we also know that the Jews spoke *Lashon HaKodesh* in the *midbar*, which raises the issue of why they used the seventy languages to record the *Torah*. It seems clear that this was done not for the generation of the *midbar*, but for Jews of the future. It might be that the first mass *aliyah* set the groundwork for all *aliyah* movements of the future. *Hashem* was aware that we would ultimately sin and be dispersed amongst the seventy nations, and wanted to make clear that adopting the language (or other trappings) of these foreign cultures would not disqualify Jews from reclaiming our heritage of practicing the *Torah* upon our return to our Land.

Rabbi Yitzchak Salid – The *mitzvah* of *Bikkurim* is essentially about *hakarat hatov*, something with which men have more trouble than women. The proof is contained in the treatment of *Hallel*. *Hallel* is essentially acknowledging

Hashem's Chesed in connection with a particular event, and while men are *chayav* to recite *Hallel*, women are not. Women are obligated to light *Chanukah neirot*, since they were also saved in the miracle of *Chanukah*, but they are not required to say *Hallel*. A famous question is why we do not say *Hallel* on *Purim*. One opinion from the *Gemara* (Megillah 14a) is that the reading of *Megillat Esther* is itself *Hallel*. Yet how can women be exempted from reading *Hallel* when they are obligated in *Megillah*? Rabbi Salid answers that perhaps women are *chayav* not to read the *Megillah* but to hear the *Megillah*.

5769

Reb Zacharia Schwartz – Man needs *simchah* in his life just as he needs sleep, air and food. *Simchah* is a fundamental necessity that one pursues all his life (as memorialized in the Declaration of Independence). Knowing this, we can appreciate that the failure to serve *Hashem* with *simchah* results in the horrible curses set forth in Parashat Ki Tavo, G-d forbid. (Devarim 28:47) This is simply due to the fact that failing to find *simchah* in serving *Hashem* necessarily means that one sought and found *simchah* in other, more destructive, contexts. Those sources of *simchah* are also sources of *aveirot* and distance from *Hashem*, necessitating punishment to encourage course correction.

Reb Eitan Katz – In weekday *shacharit* we say "Mizmor l'Todah," "a Song of Thanksgiving," which includes the verse "d'oo ki Hashem, Hu Elokim, Hu Asanu, v'Lo anachnu ... ," "I know that Hashem is G-d, He Made us and His, we are ...." (Tehillim 100:3) The word "v'lo" is written "ולו," meaning "and His," but the Sages tell us the word could also be spelled as "ולא," meaning "and not!" Read this way, the *pasuk* is translated as "I know that Hashem is G-d, He Made us and we didn't [make us] ...." Both these readings capture the approaches to the *Yamei Noraim*. We can look at *Hashem* as "Malkeinu," the Sole Sovereign, Creator of everything including us; and we can also view him as "Avinu," our Father with Whom we seek intimacy. Interestingly, these two spellings of "lo": "לא," and "לו," when combined and reordered, spell "אלול," "*Elul*," the month preceding the High Holidays when we try so hard to establish these dual understandings.

5770

Rabbi Yaacov Galinsky – There are two sets of curses in the *Torah*, one in Parashat Ki Tavo (Devarim 28:15-68) and one in Parashat Bechukotai (Vayikra 26:14-43). Ki Tavo has almost twice as many curses and no words of consolation following them. The curses of Bechukotai are based on the following rationale: "וְאִם תֵּלְכוּ עִמִּי קֶרִי וְלֹא תֹאבוּ לִשְׁמֹעַ לִי וְיָסַפְתִּי עֲלֵיכֶם מַכָּה שֶׁבַע כְּחַטֹּאתֵיכֶם," "And if you treat Me casually, and you do not wish to listen to Me, I will add seven punishments corresponding to your sins." (Vayikra 26:21) The warning, repeated throughout Chapter 26 of *Sefer Vayikra*, is that if the Jews believe that mere coincidence – and not *Hashem* – is the cause of their misfortune, *Hashem* will be forced to correct their understanding through punishment, G-d forbid. For such a situation, where *Hashem* is not mentioned or recognized, *nechamah* is thereafter required to avoid despair, which is why there are words of *nechamah* in Parashat Bechukotai (Vayikra 26:44, 45) In comparison, Ki Tavo's curses, while more numerous and severe, make repeated references to *Hashem* as the Cause of the curses. In recognizing that *Hashem* is the Source of the suffering, the Jews do not require consolation.

5772

Rabbi Aharon Ziegler – The "curses" of Parashat Ki Tavo include the following *pasuk*: "אָרוּר מַשְׁגֶּה עִוֵּר בַּדָּרֶךְ וְאָמַר כָּל הָעָם אָמֵן," "Cursed is one who misguides a blind person on the path. And all the People shall say, 'Amen!'" (Devarim 27:18) Rashi comments that the "blind person" in the *pasuk* is one who is uninformed regarding a particular matter, the one who "misguides" him gives him bad advice, and the "path" has a figurative, not literal, meaning. Rashi states the same idea on the *pasuk* in Parashat Kedoshim that reads "... v'lifnei eevair lo titain michshol," "and before a blind person do not place an obstacle." (Vayikra 19:14) Rav Joseph B.

Soloveitchik asks why do we not accept a simple understanding of these *pasukim*; namely the physical prohibition against tripping a blind person. He answers that the *Torah* does not prohibit what is not worthy of mention. The *Torah* was given to a People who would never even consider such a cruel act as tripping or physically misguiding a blind man. One who could do such a thing would be rightfully investigated as <u>not</u> being Jewish. This prohibition is so obviously not applicable to Jews that *Chazal* ignore the literal case and discuss the figurative one only.

NITZAVIM

5757

This week in this year is the tenth completion of the *Daf Yomi* review of the *Shas*. The *Torah* does not tell us the final resting place of *Moshe*, and some have suggested that it is in the heart of every Jew in the form of the *Torah*, both Written and Oral (i.e. the *Talmud*), that he gave to the Jewish People.

5759

The *selichot* that we recite before the *Yamei Noraim* always start on a Saturday night/Sunday morning to benefit from the holiness of the *Shabbat* just passed. According to the Ateret Zekenim (siman 581), *selichot* must be said for a minimum of four days, which imitates the four day preparation process for blemish checking for *korbanot*.

Elul is the month of *teshuvah*. One component of *teshuvah* is sincere regret. There are two components to regret: regret due to fear of punishment and regret based on love of *Hashem*. Both components are required to fully wipe away an *aveirah*.

Winston Churchill once said that people occasionally stumble over the truth but most dust themselves off and hurry off as if nothing had happened. In line with this idea, the Ramchal, in his book Mesilat Yesharim, cites the *Gemara* (Kiddushin 30b) which states that the only antidote for the *yetzer hara* is *Torah*. By straying away from the *Torah*, he writes, "the darkness of earthliness advances by degree ... until one is so far sunk in evil it does not even occur to him to seek the truth."

5760

A gentile once challenged the great Maharal, a *Gadol* of *Am Yisrael* concerning the apparent lack of unity among G-d's supposed "Chosen People." The Maharal pointed out that, indeed, the worldwide dispersion of Jews both geographically and ideologically is a cause <u>and</u> effect of the lack of love between them. *Hashem* has separated the Jewish People one from another because they had already done that to themselves. *Sinat chinam* was the cause of the destruction of the *Beit HaMikdash* and the elimination of *sinat chinam* will bring about the *geulah*. Basically stated, Jews need to get together on every level. The newest Jewish singles fad of "speed-dating" is in line with this philosophy and is designed to make that happen. The first step of *achdut* is communication. By speaking to at least seven precious Jewish souls in a matter of one hour, one's *neshamah* is connecting to its People; in reality moving towards fulfilling its essential mission. While speed-dating is also about screening prospective mates for marriage (which itself is the ultimate expression of unity between Jews), what is going on is much simpler and yet more profound than that. It's about Jews relating to Jews, a process that, when totally manifested, will bring about the perfection of the world.

5761

This was the week of the World Trade Center/Pentagon Terror Attacks, which occurred on the twenty-third of *Elul*. On that day President George W. Bush quoted from the twenty-third *Tehillim*: "Though I walk in the valley of the shadow of death ...." *Pasuk* <u>twenty-three</u> of chapter twenty-nine of *Sefer Devarim* (appearing in this week's Parashat Nitzavim) is chilling: "וְאָמְרוּ כָּל הַגּוֹיִם עַל מֶה עָשָׂה ה' כָּכָה לָאָרֶץ הַזֹּאת מֶה חֳרִי הָאַף הַגָּדוֹל הַזֶּה," "even all the nations shall say, 'for what has Hashem done thusly to this land, what is the meaning of the heat of this great anger?'" (Devarim 29:23)

5762

Rabbi Yossi Jankovits – The *pasuk* states that "You will return to Hashem your G-d ... ," "Return" is "shavta," spelled "שבת," which is identical to "Shabbat." The authentic *Shabbat* experience has the power to prompt the "return" of the *baal teshuvah*.

Dr. David Epstein – The *pasuk* says "וַיִּתְּשֵׁם ה' מֵעַל אַדְמָתָם בְּאַף וּבְחֵמָה וּבְקֶצֶף גָּדוֹל וַיַּשְׁלִכֵם אֶל אֶרֶץ אַחֶרֶת כַּיּוֹם הַזֶּה," "And Hashem removed them from upon their Soil, with anger, with wrath, and with very great fury, and he cast them to another land as this very day!" (Devarim 29:27) "And he cast them," "vai yashlochaim" is spelled "וישלכם," in the *Torah* the "lamed" is enlarged. "Lamed" is similar to "limud," the Hebrew word for "teach." This may be an instruction that while in the Diaspora (or, perhaps more directly, because of our dispersion) Jews must teach the non-Jewish world about *Torah* values and assume the role of being a proverbial "Light unto the nations."

5763

Rabbi Yisroel Ciner – The *pasuk* states "Atem nitzavim hayom kulchem ...." "You are standing today all of you" before *Hashem*. (Devarim 29:9) *Chazal* state that this was the "Brit of Arvut" – the Covenant of Guaranteeing Responsibility for Other Jews. The Zohar says that "standing today," refers to *Rosh Hashanah*, and Parashat Nitzavim is always read the *Shabbat* before *Rosh Hashanah*. The Nesivos Sholom explains that by standing together on *Rosh Hashanah* and taking responsibility on for another, the Jewish People have the collective merit for a good judgment.

5764

Rabbi Yissocher Frand – The Chofetz Chaim points out that while *Hashem* no longer speaks to mankind through *Naviim* or a *Bat Kol*, he does send messages through natural phenomena such as hurricanes (which the Chofetz Chaim specifically mentioned in his writings). We must recognize the destructive power of wind as a metaphor for the destructive power of *lashon hara*, and all of *Klal Yisrael* must learn this lesson from recent Hurricanes Charlie, Frances and Ivan.

5765

Rabbi Ephraim Shapiro – In describing the reprehensible idolatry that *Bnei Yisrael* encountered among the nations of the world after leaving *Mitzrayim*, the *Torah* states "וַתִּרְאוּ אֶת שִׁקּוּצֵיהֶם וְאֵת גִּלֻּלֵיהֶם עֵץ וָאֶבֶן כֶּסֶף וְזָהָב אֲשֶׁר עִמָּהֶם," "And you saw their abominations and their detestable idols, of wood and stone, of silver and gold that were with them." (Devarim 29:16) The Brisker Rav questions the seeming progression of the characterization of idols: from wood to stone, then silver and finally gold. He concludes that the way of exile for *Bnei Yisrael* is that the worshiping of idols is first assessed to be of no value, but the more time that a Jew spends in the *tumah* of *galut*, the more appealing the worship of things other than *Hashem* can become. He gives proof from the story of *Avram* and *Sarai* in Parashat Lech Lecha and their descent into Egypt during the famine. The *pasuk* states "וַיְהִי כַּאֲשֶׁר הִקְרִיב לָבוֹא מִצְרָיְמָה וַיֹּאמֶר אֶל שָׂרַי אִשְׁתּוֹ הִנֵּה נָא יָדַעְתִּי כִּי אִשָּׁה יְפַת מַרְאֶה אָתְּ," "And it occurred as he was about to enter Mitzrayim, he said to his wife Sarai 'see <u>now</u> I know you are a beautiful woman.'" (Bereshit 12:11) Clearly *Sarai* had always been beautiful, yet it was only as *Avram* approached a society of *tumah* that the *gashmiut* of his wife was manifested to him. The obvious lesson is that a Jew is best suited for a life of *Kedushah* in *Eretz Yisrael*, in a society that is devoted to service to *Hashem*. To the extent that he wanders in the *galut* toward the societies of the *goyim*, he faces a constant and ever increasing danger, not merely by being exposed to acute impurity that will impair him in his mission to cleave to *Hashem*, but by becoming accustomed and attracted to such impurity over time.

Rabbi Yossi Jankovits – Parashat Nitzavim begins "Atem Nitzavim hayom kolchem lifnei Hashem Elokeichem, ... maichoteiv eitzecha ad shoeiv maimecha" "You are standing here today, all of you, before Hashem your G-d, ... from the hewer of wood until the drawer of water." (Devarim 29: 9, 10) Here Rashi comments that the reference to wood choppers and water carriers is to the quasi-converts from the Canaanite nations that were living among *Bnei Yisrael*. The Divrei Yoel, however, says that there may be a hidden message of *teshuvah* in the references to wood cutting and water drawing. The *Gemara* (Taanit 31a) states that annually, beginning on *Tu B'Av*, there was no longer wood chopping for use in the fires of the *Beit HaMikdash* (because the wood was so dry that no insect would eat it, therefore it need not be chopped). The Fifteenth of *Av* falls <u>forty</u> days before the twenty-fifth of *Elul*, which is the date of *Hashem's* Creation of the World (note that 1 *Tishrei*, or *Rosh Hashanah*, is the date on which *Adam*, not the World, was created). The number forty represents inception, gestation and manifestation (e.g. the forty weeks of pregnancy). *Tu B'Av* would therefore be a propitious time for initiating focus on *teshuvah* in preparation for the *Yamei Noraim*. Similarly, the Water Libations Service that was done in the Temple during *Sukkot* concluded on *Hoshana Rabbah* (Sukkot 42b), and required extensive carrying of water to complete the service. *Hoshana Rabbah*, coincidentally, is the day on which the Judgment rendered on *Rosh Hashanah* is finally sealed, thus ending the *teshuvah* period. (Zohar: Tzav 31b) We can now understand the deeper message of *Moshe's* speech in the beginning of the *parashah*. "Atem nitzavim hayom," "you are all standing here this day," which Targum (Iyov 2:1) indicates is *Rosh Hashanah*, the Day of Judgment, engaged in a critical *teshuvah* process "maichoteiv eitzecha ad shoeiv maimecha," "commencing on *Tu B'Av* and terminating on *Hoshana Rabbah*."

5768

Rabbi Avi Billet – The pasuk states "הַעִדֹתִי בָכֶם הַיּוֹם אֶת הַשָּׁמַיִם וְאֶת הָאָרֶץ הַחַיִּים וְהַמָּוֶת נָתַתִּי לְפָנֶיךָ הַבְּרָכָה וְהַקְּלָלָה וּבָחַרְתָּ בַּחַיִּים לְמַעַן תִּחְיֶה אַתָּה וְזַרְעֶךָ," "Today, I call upon the Heaven and the Earth to bear witnesses to you: I have set before you life and death, the blessing and the curse. You shall choose life, so that you and your offspring will live." (Devarim 30:19) It seems odd that the *Torah* directs us to "choose life" when presented with a choice of life and death. After all, human beings have a survival instinct that makes choosing life an involuntary reflex. The Ibn Ezra states simply: choose life for your body (present) and your memory (future). The latter is an obvious reference to children. We are commanded to choose to live eternally by raising Jewish children tied to our *mesorah*, who will survive us in death.

5770

Meshech Chochmah – The *pasuk* says "וְשָׁב ה' אלקיך אֶת שְׁבוּתְךָ וְרִחֲמֶךָ וְשָׁב וְקִבֶּצְךָ מִכָּל הָעַמִּים אֲשֶׁר הֱפִיצְךָ ה' אלקיך שָׁמָּה," "Then Hashem, your G-d, will <u>return</u> you from captivity and have mercy on you and <u>return</u> you for gathering." (Devarim 30:3) The double language of "return" alludes to the *geulah* that will occur in two stages. First will be all Jews who have always yearned for the Redemption and a return to *Eretz Yisrael*, for those Jews view their *galut* as "captivity." Only after these first Jews are redeemed will the second "return" commence for those who were not anxious to return.

5771

Rabbi Yosef Weinstock – Parashat Nitzavim begins with the *pasuk* "אַתֶּם נִצָּבִים הַיּוֹם כֻּלְּכֶם לִפְנֵי ה' אלקיכֶם רָאשֵׁיכֶם שִׁבְטֵיכֶם זִקְנֵיכֶם וְשֹׁטְרֵיכֶם כֹּל אִישׁ יִשְׂרָאֵל," "You are all <u>standing</u> today before Hashem, your G-d the leaders of your Tribes, your elders and your officers, every man of Yisrael." (Devarim 29:9) The *Torah* may have chosen the word "nitzavim" over "amudim" in order to denote "standing with resilience." The word comes from the same *shoresh* as "matzeivah," a "monument." The choice of this word was in reply to the concern of *Bnei Yisrael* that they would not be able to withstand the punishments that were destined to befall them as outlined previously in Parashat Ki Tavo. *Moshe* wanted to strengthen their resolve with assurances that they would, in fact, preserve and flourish in the future. (Rashi on Devarim 29:9)

5772

Reb Shmuel Sackett – Parashat Nitzavim makes conspicuous mention of *geulah*. We know that the ingathering of the exiles from lands in which we have grown fat and lazy is no simple feat. This is evidenced in the language of the tenth *berachah* in the *Shemoneh Esrei*, in which we *daven* for the Ultimate Redemption. The language reads "תְּקַע בְּשׁוֹפָר גָּדוֹל לְחֵרוּתֵנוּ. וְשָׂא נֵס לְקַבֵּץ גָּלֻיּוֹתֵינוּ. וְקַבְּצֵנוּ יַחַד מֵאַרְבַּע כַּנְפוֹת הָאָרֶץ," "Sound the great shofar for our freedom, raise the <u>banner</u> to gather our exiles and gather us together from the four corners of the earth." The word "nais," can mean "banner" or, more appropriately here, "miracle," the only place in the list of petitions in the *Shemoneh Esrei* that uses that word! Simply stated, it will take a miracle to get all Jews to come to Israel, but it will happen.

VAYAILECH

5758

Parashat Vayailech describes the *mitzvah* of *Hakhel* (Devarim 31:10-13), which occurs once every seven years. All of *Bnei Yisrael* gather to hear their king read the *Torah*, including "hataf," the small children. Rashi says that the *Torah* requires bringing them, regardless of their level of understanding and even if they will be disruptive, in order to reward their parents for bringing them. (Rashi on Devarim 31:12)

5759

The 613th and final *mitzvah* of the *Torah* (according to the Chinuch) is that every Jewish man must write a *Sefer Torah*. (Devarim 31:19) *Halachah* dictates that every letter of the *Torah* be "freestanding" (not touching another letter) and surrounded by parchment, while also ensuring that the letters comprising a word be close enough to be read together. The *mussar* lesson is that every Jew must independently embrace the *Torah* but also that *areivut* for one another applies.

5760

Rabbi Yosef Kalatsky – There is a thought in *Chazal* (see Iturei Torah quoting HaGra) that all elements of Creation are manifested in the composition of man. An example is that the salt water of the ocean corresponds to the salty tears of man. This means that every human being has the strength and ferociousness of a lion within him from which to draw strength for the study of *Torah*.

5761

Rabbi Kalman Packouz – Parashat Vayailech begins "וַיֵּלֶךְ מֹשֶׁה וַיְדַבֵּר אֶת הַדְּבָרִים הָאֵלֶּה אֶל כָּל יִשְׂרָאֵל," "and Moshe <u>went</u> and spoke these words to all of Yisrael." (Devarim 31:1) Why does it say "and Moshe went?" This seems unnecessary. The Ibn Ezra states that before he died *Moshe* went to each tribe to notify them of his impending death and to encourage them not to fear, for *Yehoshua* would be an adequate replacement. We learn from this that when we become aware of the fears of a loved one, we are obligated "to go" to alleviate those fears. This is a pertinent lesson in light of the recent terror attacks of September 11, 2001.

5764

Rabbi Eli Mansour – In the first *berachah* of the *Shemoneh Esrei*, *Hashem* is referred to as "Melech, Ozer u'Moshiah u'Magen," "King, Helper, and

Savior and Shield." This is a reference to the progression of the *Yom Tov* Season: "Melech" refers to *Rosh Hashanah* when *Hashem* is crowned King of the World; "Ozer" refers to *Hashem* as our Help in repenting during the *Aseret Yemei Teshuvah*; "Moshiah" refers to *Hashem* saving us from sin (and therefore death) on *Yom Kippur*; and "Magen" refers to the protection of the *sukkah* on *Sukkot*.

5766

Rabbi David Hollander – Parashat Vayailech begins "וַיֵּלֶךְ מֹשֶׁה וַיְדַבֵּר אֶת הַדְּבָרִים הָאֵלֶּה אֶל כָּל יִשְׂרָאֵל," "and Moshe went and spoke these words to all of Yisrael." (Devarim 31:1) *Chazal* question why the *Torah* must comment that *Moshe* <u>went</u> and then spoke. Would it not have been sufficient to indicate that he spoke? Perhaps the way in which he "went" in his life spoke more than the words he said. In essence, our actions speak louder than our words.

5769

Rabbi Yitzchak Salid – The Jewish People generally (and each Jew individually) can rise above the natural consequences of life by acting in a transcendent/supernatural way. This is accomplished by making decisions that are in line with the Will of *Hashem* as expressed in His Holy *Torah*, rather than by following our own selfish interests. MRF Note – There is a well-known dictum of *Rabbi Shimon bar Yochai* "הלכה היא בידוע שעשו שונא ליעקב," "it is an immutable truth that Eisav hates Yaacov." (Rashi on Bereshit 33:4). Perhaps this is true only when the Jews are acting like "Yaacov," but not when they act as "Yisrael," the more elevated and exalted spiritual status of the Chosen People. So too, perhaps the phrase in the *Gemara* (Nedarim 32a) that "ein mazal l'Yisrael," "there is no astrological influences on Yisrael," is meant to imply that the Jews acting as "Yaacov," would be subject to the slings and arrows of nature (even the stars), but that Jews acting as the more exalted "Yisrael" would be immune to such forces.

HAAZINU

5759

Ran – For the songs of *Az Yashir* and *Haazinu*, the *Torah* departs from the standard columned text format and presents its verses in a patterned fashion. The *Gemara* (Megillah 16b) explains that in a *Torah* scroll, *Haazinu* is written to resemble two stacks of bricks, while *Az Yashir* is presented as a single wall of interlocking bricks. *Haazinu* discusses *Hashem's* anger, the downfall of evil and the demise of the enemies of *Bnei Yisrael*. (Devarim 32:1-43) Like stacks of bricks, these things will not stand for long, and will eventually topple. Conversely, *Az Yashir* is a song about *Hashem's* kindness to the Jews (Shemot 15:1-19), which, like a solid brick wall with interlocking bricks, will stand forever.

5760

Towards the end of the first *aliyah* of Parashat Haazinu, there is a letter ה "hey" written larger than the others. If one takes the first letter of every word in the *parashah* from the beginning of the *parashah* until the enlarged "hey," and then adds their respective numerical values, the total is 345, which is the *gematria* of "Moshe." It is as if he signed the poem of Haazinu.

The *pasuk* states "וַיָּבֹא מֹשֶׁה וַיְדַבֵּר אֶת כָּל דִּבְרֵי הַשִּׁירָה הַזֹּאת בְּאָזְנֵי הָעָם הוּא וְהוֹשֵׁעַ בִּן נוּן," "And Moshe came and spoke all the words of this song in the ears of the People; he and Hoshea bin Nun." (Devarim 32:44) Rashi tells us that here the *Torah* reverts to *Yehoshua's* original name of *Hoshea* to indicate that he did not become haughty despite the honor afforded him by *Moshe* in making him his primary student.

5761

Rabbi Yissocher Frand – Parashat Haazinu contains the song that is referenced in Parashat Vayailech by *Hashem* when commanding *Bnei Yisrael* in the *mitzvah* of writing a *Sefer Torah*. The *pasuk* says "וְעַתָּה כִּתְבוּ

לָכֶם אֶת הַשִּׁירָה הַזֹּאת וְלַמְּדָהּ אֶת בְּנֵי יִשְׂרָאֵל שִׂימָהּ בְּפִיהֶם לְמַעַן תִּהְיֶה לִּי הַשִּׁירָה הַזֹּאת לְעֵד בִּבְנֵי יִשְׂרָאֵל," "And now, write for yourselves this song, and teach it to Bnei Yisrael. Place it into their mouths, in order that this song will be for Me as a witness for Bnei Yisrael." (Devarim 31:19) Rav Yitzchak HaLevi Herzog notes that the *Torah* is referred to as "a song." Unlike many areas of life such as the sciences and other technical disciplines, people enjoy music at all levels. Regardless of one's background or education, one can appreciate the beauty of a song. So too with the *Torah*, for both the *talmud chacham* and the *baal teshuvah* are each able to love and cherish the *Torah*, each on his own level.

Rabbi Yossi Jankovits – The *Haftarah* for *Shabbat Shuvah* is from *Hoshea* (14:2-10), who tradition tells us was a descendant of *Reuven*. The Midrash Rabbah (84:19) says that *Reuven* merited that his offspring would be a *navi* to guide *Bnei Yisrael* in the ways of *teshuvah* because *Reuven* was the first person in history to do *teshuvah*. What was Reuven's sin? In Parashat Vayishlach, following the death of *Rachel*, *Yaacov* moved his bed into *Bilhah's* tent, to the frustration of *Reuven*. *Reuven* proceeded to move the bed into the tent of *Leah*, his mother, thus impermissibly interfering with the personal marital arrangements of his father. (Rashi on Bereshit 35:22) The text tells us "vayishma Yisrael," "and Yisrael heard," (Bereshit 35:22) yet, significantly, the *Torah* does not indicate any rebuke or punishment for *Reuven*. Then, in Parashat Vayeishev which follows, *Reuven* convinces the Brothers not to kill *Yosef*, but instead to throw him into a pit. (Bereshit 37:22) The narrative tells us "וַיָּשָׁב רְאוּבֵן אֶל הַבּוֹר וְהִנֵּה אֵין יוֹסֵף בַּבּוֹר וַיִּקְרַע אֶת בְּגָדָיו," "and *Reuven* returned to the pit and, behold, *Yosef* was not in the pit! And he tore his clothing." (Bereshit 37:29) Rashi there tells us that in the time between putting *Yosef* in the pit and returning to find it empty, *Reuven* had engaged in *teshuvah* for his sin with respect to *Yaacov's* bed. Why would this be considered significant and the first instance of *teshuvah* in history? Why, for example, would not *Kayin* (Bereshit 4:13) or *Yishmael* (Rashi on Bereshit 25:9), each of whom predated *Reuven*, be deemed the first to do *teshuvah*? *Sefer* Zichron Menachem states that since *Reuven* came

392 — אַתָּה וְהַלֵּוִי וְהַגֵּר Attah, v'HaLevy, v'HaGeir

to the realization that he had to repent absent any prodding or punishment from either his father or *Hashem*, his was a higher level of repentance. Reb Ari Kirschenbaum points out that the big *chiddush* here is that one can be involved in a sin (the sale of *Yosef*) and still do *teshuvah* with respect to other sins (moving the bed), and that *Hashem* values and accepts that *teshuvah*. The *yetzer hara* will tell you that unless you are a *tzaddik* in <u>all</u> areas you are a hypocrite to do *teshuvah* in any <u>one</u> area. *Reuven's* story teaches us that this is not so.

5762

Rabbi Edward Davis – Parashat Haazinu begins with two references comparing *Torah* to water. The *pasuk* says "Yaarof kamatar likchi tizal katal imrati ... ," "May my teaching drip like <u>rain</u>, may my speech flow like <u>dew</u> ...." (Devarim 32:2) Homiletically, this could be applied in the *baal teshuvah* world, where one individual acquires a rushing, torrential connection to *Torah*, similar to a downpour of rain, and another develops a subtle, incremental internalization of *Torah*, akin to dew. Each is a valid approach, but a problem arises when spouses are separated into these two camps.

5763

There is a reference in Parashat Haazinu to *Techiyat HaMaytim*. The *pasuk* states "Ani amit v'achayeh ... ," "I [Hashem] bring forth death and I give life ...." (Devarim 32:39) Based on <u>natural</u> chronology, life should precede death, so the *pasuk* must therefore be referring to something <u>supernatural</u> – the Resurrection of the Dead.

5765

Rabbi Chaim Tzvi Teitelbaum – The *Haftarah* for *Shabbat Shuvah* begins with the following *pasuk*: "שׁוּבָה יִשְׂרָאֵל עַד ה׳ אלקיך כִּי כָשַׁלְתָּ בַּעֲוֹנֶךָ," "Return, Yisrael, until Hashem, your G-d, for you have <u>stumbled</u> in your <u>iniquity</u>."

(Hoshea 14:2) The choice of wording seems strange, for "stumbled" suggests accidental misstep, while "iniquity" connotes intentional sinning. One answer may be drawn from the reference in Pirkei Avot (3:1) to the fact that everyone will one day give "din v'cheshbon," "a judgment and an accounting" before *Hashem*. On this *Mishnah*, the Vilna Gaon indicates that "din" refers to man being called to answer for every sin he did, while "cheshbon" refers to answering for squandering time while sinning. Two repentances are therefore required. This is what is meant by the *pasuk* above. You lost precious time through <u>negligence</u> as a result of <u>intentionally</u> choosing to sin. The *Gemara* (Yoma 86b) tells us that "teshuvah may yirah," "repentance out of fear," converts one's intentional sins into the more favorable classification of unintended, but "teshuvah may ahava," "repentance out of love," results in intentional sins becoming *mitzvot*! When one regrets that, through his intentional sins, he has unintentionally squandered the opportunity for *deveikut* with *Hashem*, and he resolves to do better, since he is motivated by love, his *teshuvah* is in furtherance of the goal of Creation (i.e. closeness to *Hashem*), and therefore all of his failings are credited as merits.

5770

The *pasuk* states "וַיְדַבֵּר ה' אֶל מֹשֶׁה בְּעֶצֶם הַיּוֹם הַזֶּה לֵאמֹר," "And Hashem spoke to Moshe on that very day, saying ...." (Devarim 32:48) Rashi tells us that the language "b'etzem hayom hazeh" indicates the time at which *Hashem* imposes His Will, which is high noon, in order to publicly demonstrate that despite man's attempt to circumvent it, *Hashem's* Will must be done. Rashi mentions the three places in the *Chumash* where these words appear and which illustrate the point: (1) *Noach's* contemporaries attempted to keep him from entering the Ark (Bereshit 7:13); (2) the *Mitzrim* attempted to keep the Jews from leaving *Mitzrayim* (Shemot 12:51); and (3) here in Parashat Haazinu, the Jews were distraught at the notion of *Moshe's* impending death and tried to keep him from ascending *Har Nevo*. In each case *Hashem* took public action to bring about His intended result.

5771

Divrei Shaul – The Vilna Gaon, in Aderet Eliyahu, notes that there are 613 words in Parashat Haazinu, corresponding to the 613 *mitzvot* of the *Torah*. This reinforces the Ramban's teaching that all of the past, present and future of all worlds are contained within the *Torah*.

5772

Rabbi Abraham Stone – The *pasuk* says "הַאֲזִינוּ הַשָּׁמַיִם וַאֲדַבֵּרָה וְתִשְׁמַע הָאָרֶץ אִמְרֵי פִי," "Give ear, O Heavens, and I will speak; and may the earth hear the words of my mouth." (Devarim 32:1) The Daat Zakainim notes that for the Heavens, *Moshe* uses the word "Haazinu," indicating close proximity, and for the earth, "tishma," indicating, perhaps, greater distance, something that seems to be reversed based on *Moshe's* physical location. Daat Zakainim learns from this that *Moshe* was "closer" to the Heavens than the earth. The same language is presented in reverse in the *pasuk* in *Navi*: "Shimu Shamayim, v'haazini eretz ... ," "Hear O Heavens, and give ear to me O earth ...." (Yishaiyah 1:2), and Daat Zakainim comments that *Moshe* was closer to Heaven and *Yishaiyah* was closer to earth. This presents a problem, for if an exalted prophet was "bound to earth" in distinction to *Moshe*, what should the average Jew feel about his spiritual level and potential? After all, *Haazinu* is meant to be a message for every Jew, yet perhaps it only can apply to *Moshe* himself! The Shelah answers by noting the time of year that each of these *pasukim* are read. The prophesy of *Yishaiyah* is read on *Tisha B'Av*, when we are farthest from *Hashem*. *Haazinu*, which read during *Aseret Yemei Teshuvah*, informs us that at that time of year *Hashem* is nearest to us, all of us, not merely *Moshe Rabbeinu*, which is *chizuk* to redouble our efforts in *teshuvah* and *tzedakah*.

5773

Rabbi Eliyahu Ha'Itamari – The *pasuk* that ends the song of *Haazinu* reads "v'cheepair admato amo," "and He will appease His Land and

His People." (Devarim 32:43) Right after, *Moshe* admonishes *Bnei Yisrael*: "וַיֹּאמֶר אֲלֵהֶם שִׂימוּ לְבַבְכֶם לְכָל הַדְּבָרִים אֲשֶׁר אָנֹכִי מֵעִיד בָּכֶם הַיּוֹם אֲשֶׁר תְּצַוֻּם אֶת בְּנֵיכֶם לִשְׁמֹר לַעֲשׂוֹת אֶת כָּל דִּבְרֵי הַתּוֹרָה הַזֹּאת," "And he said to them, 'Apply your hearts to all of the words which I bear witness for you this day, so that you may command your children to observe to do all the words of this Torah.'" (Devarim 32:46) What is the connection between these successive *pasukim*? The word "אַדְמָתוֹ," "His Land," has the same letters as "ד אמות," "four amot," a measurement indicating one's immediate domain. The *Gemara* (Ketubot 111a) indicates that one who walks four *amot* in *Eretz Yisrael* is guaranteed a portion in the World to Come, and that whoever dwells in the Land lives without sin. One might think that merely living in *Eretz Yisrael* will suffice to ensure that the Jews will remain there forever. Not so, says *Moshe*, clarifying the next *pasuk*. Observe and perform all the words of the Torah, "כִּי לֹא דָבָר רֵק הוּא מִכֶּם כִּי הוּא חַיֵּיכֶם וּבַדָּבָר הַזֶּה תַּאֲרִיכוּ יָמִים עַל הָאֲדָמָה אֲשֶׁר אַתֶּם עֹבְרִים אֶת הַיַּרְדֵּן שָׁמָּה לְרִשְׁתָּהּ," "for it is not an empty thing for you, for it is your life, and through the matter <u>shall you prolong your days on the Land</u>." (Devarim 32:47) The message is that *Hashem* <u>will</u> appease His Land and His People, but the People must perform the *Torah* to remain in the Land.

VEZOT HABERACHAH

5760

Parashat VeZot HaBerachah is the only *parashah* not specifically read on any *Shabbat*.

The *Torah* indicates that *Moshe* died, but that "v'lo yada eesh et k'vurato ad hayom hazeh," "no one knows his burial place until this day." (Devarim 34:6) This can be taken to mean that *Moshe Rabbeinu* is not "buried," insofar as his teachings are still being absorbed even to this very day. No one knows his burial place because "he" has never been buried.

5761

Moshe was born and died on the seventh day of Adar. The proof is provided in the *Gemara* (Kiddushin 38a). *Bnei Yisrael* cried for *Moshe* on the Plains of *Moav* for thirty days following his death (Devarim 34:8), after which *Hashem* instructed *Yehoshua* "in another three days you will be crossing this *Yarden*." (Yehoshua 1:11) Rashi calculates that this is a total of thirty-three days preceding the crossing, which we know was on 10 *Nissan*. (Yehoshua 4:19) Thirty-three days preceding 10 *Nissan* is 7 *Adar* (10 days of *Nissan* and 23 days of *Adar*), the date of *Moshe's* death. It is clear that *Moshe* was also born on 7 *Adar* because on the day of his death he states in Parashat Vayailech "ben meiah v'esrim shana anochee hayom ... ," "I am 120 years old today," (Devarim 31:2), and Rashi confirms that this was his birthday, quoting the *Gemara* (Sotah 13b) which tells us that the *Torah* uses the word "today" to demonstrate that *Hashem* fills the days of years of the righteous to ensure they die on the very day of their birth.

5762

Rabbi Meyer Katznelson – We must each strive to do what we can in service to *Hashem*, and even if it is a small contribution, we should make the most of that contribution. This is reflected by the fact that a Jew who could not bring an animal *korban* to the *Beit HaMikdash* would bring a bird at the very least, and the *Torah* commanded the *Kohain* to retain the bird's feathers in the sacrifice process. (Vayikra 1:17) Rashi comments that one might think that the burning feathers would be repulsive, but the Torah mandates that the feather be included based on *Hashem's* appreciation of the sacrifice of one who has limited resources.

5764

Rabbi Yochanan Zweig – In describing the death of *Moshe*, the *Torah* states that *Bnei Yisrael* wept for thirty days. (Devarim 34:8) This can be contrasted with the death of his brother *Aharon*, where the *Torah* tells us that *Beit Yisrael* wept for thirty days. (Bamidbar 20:29) Rashi comments, with respect to *Moshe's* death, that the language indicates that only the males cried for him, whereas with *Aharon* both the men and women cried over his death. Rashi further explains that it was *Aharon's* reputation as a pursuer of peace between husband and wife that was valued and therefore missed by all Jews. *Chazal* tell us that it was in *Moshe's* merit that the *Mon* fell daily for *Bnei Yisrael*. The *Mon* represented *parnassah*, which the men especially appreciated, because providing a livelihood for one's family is the exclusive duty of a man. A husband should not burden his wife with the problems he encounters in securing a livelihood for himself and his family.

5765

Rabbi Yossi Jankovits – The *Torah* ends with the *pasuk* mentioning what *Moshe* performed "l'aynay kol Yisrael," "before the eyes of all Israel." (Devarim 34:12) Rashi says the *Torah* is referring to smashing the *Luchot*, which *Hashem* considered *Moshe's* greatest achievement. The *Gemara* (Eruvin 54a) states that *Moshe's* act of smashing the *Luchot* brought forgetfulness to the world, which requires *Bnei Yisrael* to begin again and learn the *Torah* anew from its beginning, immediately after we conclude reading it.

5770

Vilna Gaon – There is a debate in the *Gemara* (Gittin 60a) as to whether, if *Hashem* revealed the entire *Torah* to *Moshe* at *Har Sinai*, *Moshe* wrote the narrative of his own death, as recorded at the end of Parashat VeZot HaBerachah. (Devarim 34:5-12) The Vilna Goan indicates that the *Torah* was, indeed, given to *Moshe*, but as one long "run-on sentence" that was "decoded" over time. In this way, *Moshe* would not have known of his death until the end of the forty year period. Read in this manner, the fact that it was, as *Rabbi Shimon* states in the *Gemara* (Bava Batra 15a), written by *Moshe* "b'demah," "with a tear [of sadness] in his eye," could be read not as "with a tear," but rather "mixed-up," meaning unclear, until the very end.

5771

The Brisker Rav – The *Gemara* (Menachot 30a) tells us the manner by which *Hashem* conveyed the last eight verses of the *Torah* differed from the way he generally conveyed the text. The normal process was *Hashem* spoke the words to *Moshe* and he would repeat them, then later write them into a *Torah* scroll. But with the verses about his own death, *Moshe* wordlessly recorded *Hashem's* dictation. This is similar to the distinction between the writing of the *Naviim*, which *Hashem* commanded each respective *navi* to write, and the *Ketuvim*, which *Hashem* told the *navi* to record so that another could read it at a later date. Here, *Moshe* could record the verses describing his death, although they had not happened, and could then present a complete *sefer* to *Yehoshua*.

5772

Rabbi Avigdor Miller – The *pasuk* states "אֵין כָּאֵל יְשֻׁרוּן רֹכֵב שָׁמַיִם בְּעֶזְרֶךָ וּבְגַאֲוָתוֹ שְׁחָקִים," "There is none like G-d, O Yeshurun, a rider of the Heavens at your assistance, and in His Majesty, the skies." (Devarim 33:26) This *pasuk* is informing the Jews that all of *Hashem's* greatness and power is exercised on behalf of *Yeshurun* (i.e. *Bnei Yisrael*), and that this happens "in the skies," above and away from our awareness. *Hashem* gave us the seemingly obscure incident of *Balak* and *Bilaam* (Bamidbar 22:2-41) to illustrate this point, where, if the *Torah* had not told us, we would not be aware of the plotting of the *goyim* against us. We are mostly oblivious to these salvations, for, as Rabbi Miller indicates, they are provided on our behalf "in the skies."

5773

Rabbi Moshe Weinberger – The greatness of *Moshe* is difficult to fathom. The *pasuk* in Parashat Behaalotecha states "וְהָאִישׁ מֹשֶׁה עָנָיו (כתיב ענו) מְאֹד מִכֹּל הָאָדָם אֲשֶׁר עַל פְּנֵי הָאֲדָמָה," "Now the man Moshe was exceedingly humble, more than any person on the face of the earth." (Bamidbar 12:3) This is consistent with *Moshe's* hesitant response to *Hashem's* directive to approach

Paroh and liberate the Jews from *Mitzrayim*. (Shemot 3:11) Why then did he not object to the task of receiving the *Torah*, an event seemingly more momentous in world history than even the Exodus? Perhaps *Moshe* was more accepting of his *Torah* mission because he identified with the choice of *Har Sinai* as the venue, which we know was not the grandest of mountains. While he may have felt qualified to ascend a lowly mountain to accept the *Torah*, going head to head with the most exalted leader of his time would have been anathema to *Moshe's nature*, for it required positioning himself as an exalted counterbalance to *Paroh*, a status that gave him great discomfort.

CALENDAR CONVERTER

Hebrew Year	Fall to Summer of
5757	1996-1997
5758	1997-1998
5759	1998-1999
5760	1999-2000
5761	2000-2001
5762	2001-2002
5763	2002-2003
5764	2003-2004
5765	2004-2005
5766	2005-2006
5767	2006-2007
5768	2007-2008
5769	2008-2009
5770	2009-2010
5771	2010-2011
5772	2011-2012
5773	2012-2013

GLOSSARY OF TERMS, PLACES AND PERSONS

Achashveirosh (King): King in the *Purim* story, as mentioned in *Megillat Esther*

achdut: unity

Adam (HaRishon): man (the first)

Adar: twelfth (sixth) month in Hebrew calendar, during which *Purim* is celebrated

Aggadah / Aggadita: non-legal texts or stories set forth within the *Oral Law*

agunah: a woman who cannot remarry because she is unable to get a divorce either because her husband is unwilling or has disappeared

Aharon (HaKohain): Aaron, brother of *Moshe*; first *Kohain Gadol*

ahavah / ahavat: love (of)

Ahavat Yisrael: love for one's fellow Jews

aishet yefat toar: a beautiful foreign woman encountered on the battlefield by a Jewish soldier

Akeidah (Akeidat Yitzchak): the Binding (of *Yitzchak*); *Hashem* tells *Avraham* to offer his son as a sacrifice

aleph-beit: Hebrew alphabet

aliyah / aliyot: "going up"; refers both to going up to read from the *Torah* and emigration to Israel

aliyah l'regel: ascending to *Yerushalayim* for the holidays *Pesach, Shavuot, and Sukkot*

al Kiddush Hashem: sanctification of the Divine Name; martyrdom

amah / amot: cubit(s); measurement

Amalek: a nation that descended from Amalek, son of *Eisav;* attacked *Bnei Yisrael* in the desert and we are commanded to destroy them and their memory

am haaretz: "people of the land"; an uneducated person

Amidah / Amidot: the main section of daily prayer also known as *Shemoneh Esrei*

Am Kadosh: "Holy Nation"; the Jews

Amon: a nation that battled against *Bnei Yisrael* in the desert; descended from *Lot*

Amos: prophet; (786–746 BCE)

Amram: husband of *Yocheved;* father of *Moshe, Aharon* and *Miriam*

Am Segulah: "Treasured Nation"; the Jews

Am Yisrael: the Nation of Israel

Anaini HaKavod : Clouds of Glory; protected Jews in the desert

ani / aniyim: poor person(s)

Aram (Naharaim): birthplace of *Avraham*

Arba'ah Minim: "Four Species"; taken as a *mitzvah* on *Sukkot: lulav,* etrog, *hadassim* and aravot

Arba Leshonot Geulah: four expressions of redemption in the *Torah*

arbeh: locusts; eighth Egyptian plague

areivut: responsibility that every Jew has, one to another

Aretz: *Eretz,* Land of Israel

Aron (Kodesh): (Holy) Ark, in the *Beit HaMikdash* and also located in the *shul,* which houses the *Sifrei Torah*

arov: wild animals; fourth Egyptian plague

Asara b'Tevet: Tenth of *Tevet,* fast day commemorating siege of *Yerushalayim*

Aseret HaDibrot: Ten Commandments

Aseret Yemei Teshuvah: "Ten Days of Repentance"; ten days between *Rosh Hashanah and Yom Kippur*

Asher: son of *Yaacov* and *Zilpah*; one of the *Twelve Tribes*

Ashkenaz (nusach): (customs and prayers) pertaining to the Jews of middle and eastern Europe

Ashrei: Psalm 145, recited three times daily in prayer service

Asnat: *Osnat*, wife of *Yosef*, mother of *Menashe* and *Ephraim*

assur: forbidden

Av: fifth (eleventh) month of the Hebrew calendar, during which *Tisha B'Av* occurs; or father

aveilut: period of a year of mourning after the death of one's parent

aveirah / aveirot: transgression(s) of a *Torah* law

Avihu: son of *Aharon*; brother of *Nadav*

Avimelech: King of *Plishtim*

Aviram: with *Datan*, led the *Korach* rebellion in the *midbar*

avnei shoham: stones of onyx worn on the breastplate of the *Kohain Gadol*

avodah: service

avodah zareh: idol worship

Avodat Hashem : worship and service of *Hashem*

Avot: "Patriarchs"; *Avraham, Yitzchak* and *Yaacov*

Avraham (Avinu): Abraham (Our Father); husband of *Sarah*; father of *Yitzchak* and *Yishmael*

Avram: original name of *Avraham*

ayil: ram

ayin hara: evil eye

ayin ra'ah: "bad eye"; greedy

Ayin Tova: "good eye"; humble

Aza: Gaza

Azaryah: with *Chananya* and *Misha'el*, defied *Nevuchadnezair*

Az Yashir: prayer/song daily said during *Shacharit*, also known as *Shirat Hayam;* sung by *Bnei Yisrael* after *Yetziat Mitzrayim*

azut: boldness

azut d'Kedushah: boldness for Holiness

baal: master

baal chesed: one involved in acts of kindness

Baal Peor: idol worshipped by *Moav*

Balak: King of *Moav*, sent *Bilaam* to curse *Bnei Yisrael*

Bamidbar (Sefer Bamidbar): "in the desert / wilderness"; Book of Numbers, the fourth Book of *Chamishah Chumshay Torah*

Baraita: "outside"; body of teachings of the *Oral Law* not incorporated into the *Mishnah*

Barak: together with *Devorah,* led battle against Canaanites

Bar Kamtza: character from the *Gemara* story of the cause of the destruction of *Bayit Sheni*

Bar Mitzvah: "Son of the Commandment"; a male who has attained the age of thirteen and is therefore *chayav* in the *mitzvot*

Baruch Hashem: "Blessed be Hashem"; an exclamation of thanks and praise

Baruch She'amar: first blessing of *Pesukei d'Zimrah* in *Shacharit*

bashert: "meant to be"; one's soulmate

Basmat (bat Yishmael) : Basmat (daughter of Yishmael)

Bat Kol: Divine Voice

Batsheva: wife of *David HaMelech,* mother of *Shlomo HaMelech*

Batyah (bat Paroh): daughter of *Paroh,* found *Moshe* in the river and adopted him

Bavel: Babylon

bayit: house; home

Bayit Rishon: "first House"; the first *Beit HaMikdash*

Bayit Sheni: "second House"; the second *Beit HaMikdash*

Bayit Shlishi: "third House"; the third *Beit HaMikdash,* in the times of *Moshiach*

bechirah: choice; free will

bechor/ bochorot /bechorah: firstborn(s); the right of the firstborn son

bedekken: wedding ceremony where the *chatan* lowers the veil over the *kallah's* face

Be'er Miriam: The Well of *Miriam*, which miraculously provided water in the *midbar*

Be'er Sheva: "well of seven / oaths"; city in the south of *Eretz Yisrael*

beged: garment

Beitar: city southwest of *Yerushalayim*; last stronghold of Bar Kochba revolt; scene of massacre

Beit Din: "House of Law"; rabbinic court made up of at least three rabbis

Beit HaMikdash / Batei Mikdash: the First or Second Temple(s)

Beit Hillel: "house of Hillel"; a school of thought contrasted with *Beit Shammai* in the *Talmud*

beit midrash: "house of study"; room dedicated to the learning of *Torah*

Beit Shammai: "house of Shammai"; a school of thought contrasted with *Beit Hillel* in the *Talmud*

ben / bnei: son(s)

Ben Azai: Shimon ben Azzai, *Tanna* in second century

ben sorer u'moreh: rebellious son

Bentch / Bentching / Bentcher: "bless"; refers to *Birchat HaMazon;* the book used for *Bentching*

berachah / berachot: blessing(s)

berachah achronah / berachot achronot: blessing(s) said after consuming a snack

berachah l'vatalah: *berachah* said in vain

Bereshit (Sefer Bereshit): "in the beginning"; Book of Genesis; the first Book (and first *parashah*) of *Chamishah Chumshay Torah*

Betuel: father of *Lavan* and *Rivkah*

Betzalel: constructed the *Mishkan*

b'Ezrat Hashem: "with the help of *Hashem*"; G-d willing

Bigdei Kehunah: the clothing worn by the *Kohain* in his *avodah*

Bikkurim: first fruits, brought to the *Kohain* as a *korban*

bikur cholim: visiting the sick

Bilaam (HaRasha): Balaam (the Wicked One); sent by *Balak, King of Moav*, to curse *Bnei Yisrael* in the desert

Bilhah: wife of *Yaacov*; maidservant of *Rachel*, mother of *Dan and Naftali*

Binyamin: Benjamin; youngest son of *Yaacov* and *Rachel*; one of the Twelve Tribes

Birkat HaMazon: "Blessing of Food"; grace after meals

Birkat Kohanim: Three-Fold Blessing that the descendants of *Aharon* are commanded to impart to *Bnei Yisrael*

bitachon: trust (in *Hashem*)

Bnei Brak: city in both ancient and modern *Eretz Yisrael*

Bnei Cheit: "sons of Cheit"; Avraham bought the *Maarat HaMachpeilah* from them

Bnei Yisrael: Children of Israel

Boaz: married *Rut*

bris: *brit milah*

Brit Bein Habetarim: "Covenant Between the Parts"; when *Hashem* told *Avraham* that his descendants will inherit *Eretz Yisrael*

brit milah: "covenant of circumcision"; ritual circumcision on the eighth day of life; also known as a *bris*

brit: covenant

Caleiv (ben Yefuneh): Caleb (son of Yefuneh); one of the twelve spies sent to *Eretz Yisrael* from the desert; husband of *Miriam*

Canaan (Eretz Canaan): name in the *Torah* for *Eretz Yisrael* before it was settled by *Bnei Yisrael*; Canaanites were the foremost of the seven nations that occupied the land before *Bnei Yisrael*

Chabad: Lubavitch orthodox *chassidic* movement

Chachamim: Sages

Chag / Chagim: festival(s)

challah: braided bread loaf in honor of *Shabbat* or *Yom Tov*

Cham: son of *Noach*

chametz: products made from five grains that are prohibited on *Pesach*

Chamishah Chumshay Torah: "Five- Five Sections of the Torah"; the Pentateuch; five books of the *Torah* organized in order of weekly *Parshiot*

Chananya: with *Azaryah* and *Misha'el,* defied *Nevuchadnezair*

Chanukah: eight day holiday celebrating the rededication of the *Bayit Sheni*; Festival of Lights

chanukat habayit: "dedication of the house"

Charan: father of *Lot;* also city where *Avraham* settled before going to *Eretz Canaan*

chassid / chassidut / chassidishe / chassidic: "pious one"; hassidic; movement founded in eighteenth century Eastern Europe by the Baal Shem Tov

chatan: groom

chatat: a sacrifice used to atone for unintentional sins

Chavah: first woman; married *Adam*

chayav: guilty of transgressing; obligated

Chazal: acronym of "Chachameinu Zichronam Levrachah," "Our Sages of blessed memory"

cheit: sin

cheit haeigel (hazahav): sin of the (golden) calf

chesed: loving kindness towards others

Cheshbon: City of *Sichon*

cheshbon /cheshbonot: reckoning(s); accounting(s)

Cheshvan: eighth (second) month of the Hebrew calendar

Chevra Kadisha: "the Holy Society"; tends to the preparation and burial of the dead

Chevron: Hebron; city in *Eretz Yisrael* where *Maarat HaMachpeilah* is found

chiddush / chiddushim: novel *Torah* insight(s)

chillul Hashem: "profaning the Name"; an act that brings disrespect to the *Torah* or to *Hashem*

chinuch: training or education in the ways of *Torah*

chizuk: encouragement

chodesh: month

chok / chukat / chukim: *Torah* law(s) or *mitzvah (mitzvot)* for which no explanation is provided

Chol HaMoed: intermediate days of *Pesach* and *Sukkot* where some work is permissible

Choreiv: *Har Sinai*

Choshen: Breastplate worn the by *Kohain Gadol*

chovah: obligation

Chumash / Chumashim: "Five"; the Pentateuch; *Chamishah Chumshay Torah*

chumrah: strict interpretation of the law; also a prohibition that exceeds the *halachic* requirement, one can impose this upon himself or be universally accepted

chuppah: marriage canopy

Chur: Hur; son of *Miriam* and *Caleiv*

churban: "destruction"; the destruction of the *Beit HaMikdash*

Chushim (ben Dan): deaf son of *Dan*

chutz l'Aretz: "outside the Land"; outside of *Eretz Yisrael*

Cush: territory on coast of the *Yam Suf*

Daf Yomi: "page of the day"; refers to the practice of studying one page of *Gemara* a day, and finishing the entire *Talmud* in a seven and a half year cycle

dalet amot: "four square cubits"; vernacular for a person's private space

dam: blood; first Egyptian plague

Dan: son of *Yaacov* and *Bilhah*; one of the *Twelve Tribes*

Daniel: *sefer* in *Tanach*; or the person who prophesied in *Bavel*

dan l'kaf zechut: "judge on the side of merit"; giving the benefit of the doubt

Datan: with *Aviram*, led the *Korach* rebellion in the *midbar*

davash: honey

daven (davening): to pray (praying); *tefillah*

David (HaMelech): "King David"; second king of Israel, credited with writing most of *Sefer Tehillim*

derech eretz: proper ethical behavior

Devarim (Sefer Devarim): "word;" Book of Deuteronomy; the fifth Book of *Chamishah Chumshay Torah*

deveikut: "clinging"; spiritual attachment

Devorah: only female judge in *Sefer* Shoftim

din (dinim): law(s); judgment(s)

Dinah: daughter of *Yaacov* and *Leah*

Dor HaMabul: generation destroyed in the Flood

d'var Torah / divrei Torah: "word(s) of Torah"; thought-provoking *Torah* idea; *vort*

Edom: nation which descended from *Eisav*

Efrat: city in Judea, Israel

Eglah Arufah: "calf whose neck is broken"; ritual where a calf is killed as penitence for an unsolved murder

Eichah (Megillat): (Book of) Lamentations, read on *Tisha B'av*, part of *Tanach*

eidot: *Torah* laws of commemoration

eidut: testimony

eigel hazahav: "the golden calf"

Eisav: Esau, twin brother of *Yaacov*; son of *Yitzchak*

Eitz HaDa'at: "Tree of Knowledge"; produced fruit consumed by *Adam* and *Chavah*

Eiver: Ever; with *Shem* opened first yeshivah in history

Elazar: son of *Aharon HaKohain*; father of *Pinchas*; succeeded *Aharon* as *Kohain Gadol*

Eldad: with *Meidad* prophets in the *midbar*

Eliezer: servant to *Avraham;* or second son of *Moshe*

Eliphaz (ben Eisav): oldest son of *Eisav*

Eliyahu HaNavi: Elijah the Prophet

Elul: sixth (twelfth) month of the Hebrew calendar

emet: true

Emori: Amorites; ancient nomadic people; one of original nations of *Eretz Canaan*

emunah: faith; belief

Ephod: garment worn by the *Kohain Gadol*

Ephraim: son of *Yosef*; became like one of the *Twelve Tribes*

Ephron (haChiti): sold the *Maarat HaMachpeilah* to *Avraham*

Eretz Yisrael: Land of Israel

erev: "evening of"; the day proceeding *Shabbat or chag*

Erev Rav: non-Jews who accompanied the Jews out of *Mitzrayim*

Erev Shabbat: "eve of *Shabbat*"; Friday before sundown

eruv: "mixing, or merging"; a ritual enclosure constructed to integrate private and public properties into one private domain thereby permitting carrying of objects on *Shabbat*

ervah: nakedness

Esther: heroine of *Megillat Esther* and the *Purim* story

etzba: primary pointing finger

eved: servant

eved Ivri: "Hebrew servant"; bound because of debt or theft

frum: devout; fully observant of *halachah*

frumkeit: the state and lifestyle of being *frum*

gabbai /gabbaim: person responsible in *Shul* for organizing the services and calling people to read the *Torah*

Gad: son of *Yaacov* and *Zilpah*; one of the *Twelve Tribes*

Galiyat: Goliath; killed by *David*

galut: exile, the Diaspora

Gan Ayden: Garden of Eden

gashmiut: "materiality"; in contrast to spirituality

Gavriel: Gabriel; a *malach*

Gemara: "completion"; *Talmud Bavli*

geir / geirim: convert(s)

geir tzedek: "righteous convert"; someone who becomes fully Jewish according to *halachah*

gematria: tradition of interpreting meanings and significance by totaling the numerical equivalents of Hebrew letters

Gershom: son of *Moshe*

Gershon: son of *Levy*

geulah: redemption or deliverance

gevurah: strength

gezeirah: "decree"; a rabbinic law instituted to protect against violating a law of the *Torah*

gilgul: "cycle"; reincarnation

Goshen: place in *Mitzrayim* where *Bnei Yisrael* lived

goy / goyah / goyim: gentile(s); female gentile; non-Jew(s)

guf: body

Gush Katif: Israeli settlement in Aza, destroyed in August 2005 with displacement of 8,600 Jewish residents

Haazinu: *parashah* in *Devarim*; song of *Moshe* on his last day of life

hachnasat orchim: welcoming guests to one's home

hadassim : myrtle; one of the *Arba'ah Minim* used on *Sukkot*

Hadrian: Roman Emperor during Temple Period; renamed *Eretz Yisrael* "Palestine" is response to Jewish revolt

ha'eitz: "the tree"; blessing over fruit of trees

Haftarah / Haftarot: selected section from *Neviim*, recited following the weekly *Torah* reading on *Shabbat* and *Yom Tov*

ha'gafen: "the vine"; blessing over fruits of vine: wine and grape juice

Hagar: maidservant of *Sarah*; when *Sarah* could not conceive she gave *Hagar* to *Avraham*; mother of *Yishmael*

Hagbah: "lifting"; the act of lifting up the *Torah* before the congregation after it is read

Haggadah: "narration"; the book used to conduct the *Pesach Seder*

Haichal: inner room of the *Beit HaMikdash*

hakarat hatov: "recognizing goodness"; gratitude

Hakhel: *mitzvah* for all men, women, and children to hear the *Torah* read by the king once every seven years

halachah / halachot / halachic: (pertaining to) *Torah* Law

Halachah l'Moshe m'Sinai: "Law from Moshe at Sinai"; law whose source is not written but was transmitted orally from *Hashem* to *Moshe*

Hallel: "praise"; *tefillot* recited on *Rosh Chodesh* and *Chagim*

Haman: the villain of *Megillat Esther* and the *Purim* story

hamotzi: blessing on bread or *challah*

hanaah: pleasure

Har Eival: Mount Ebal; mountain that *Bnei Yisrael* encountered when first entering *Eretz Yisrael*; mountain of the curses

Har Gerizim: Mount Gerizim; mountain that *Bnei Yisrael* encountered when first entering *Eretz Yisrael*; mountain of the blessings

Har HaBayit: "Mountain of the House"; the Temple Mount

Har Moriah: site of *Akeidat Yitzchak*

Har Nevo: Mount Nebo; where *Moshe* was granted a view of *Eretz Yisrael*

Har Sinai: "Mount Sinai"; where the *Torah* was given

Hashem: "the Name"; G-d

hashgachah: "supervision"; most often used for *kashrut*

Hashgachah Pratit: concept that every event is determined by Divine Will

hashkafah: "outlook"; a worldview regarding philosophy and *halachah*

Havdalah: prayer to mark the conclusion of *Shabbat*

hefker: undisciplined; ownerless

Hevel: son of *Adam* and *Chavah*, killed by brother *Kayin*

Hillel: Sage of the *Talmud*

hishtadlut: required effort; working as diligently as possible, necessary to merit *Hashem's* assistance

Hoshana Rabbah: seventh day of *Sukkot*

Hoshea: *Navi*

Hoshea: original name of *Yehoshua*

inyan / inyanim: topic(s), center(s) of interest

ir miklat /arei miklat : city (cities) of refuge for an inadvertent killer

issur: prohibition

Ivrit: Hebrew language

Iyar: second (eighth) month of Hebrew calendar

Iyov: Job; Book of Job, part of *Tanach*

Kabbalah / Kabbalistic: (pertaining to) Jewish mysticism

Kabbalat Shabbat: Friday night service welcoming *Shabbat*

Kaddish: prayer recited by a mourner

Kadosh: Holy

Kahal: Congregation

kallah: bride

kal v'chomer: "light and heavy"; "all the more so," principle where a conclusion is drawn from a more lenient premise to a major one

Kamtza: character from the *Gemara* story of the cause of the destruction of *Bayit Sheni*

kanaut: zealousness

kaparah: atonement

kasher / kashering: kosher; to make kosher

kashrut: state of being kosher; *halachot* of kosher

kavanah: concentration; intention

kavod: honor; glory

Kayin: son of *Adam and Chava*, killed brother *Hevel*

kazayit: "like an olive"; a *halachic* food measurement

Kedushah: Holiness

Kehat: son of *Levy*

kehillah: community; the sense of community

Kehunah: Priesthood of *Kohanim*

keli / kaylim: utensil(s)

Keruvim: winged angelic figures made of gold on the *Aron*

kesher: knot; connection

Ketoret: incense offering

ketubah: marriage contract

Ketuvim: "writings"; the third division of the *Tanach*

kever / kevarot: grave(s)

kibbud av v'eim: honoring one's father and mother

Kiddush: prayer recited at the beginning of a festive meal on *Shabbat* and *Chag*

Kiddush Hashem: sanctification of the name of *Hashem*; martyrdom

kikar: unit of weight, approximately sixty five pounds

kinim: lice; third Egyptian plague

kinot: "lamentations"; read on *Tisha B'av*

kinyan: an act that formalizes a legal transaction

kippah: yarmulke

kiruv: "bringing closer"; the outreach movement to non-orthodox Jews to enhance their belief and practice

Kiryat Arba: "Town of Four"; location of *Maarat HaMachpeilah, Chevron,* Israel

Kislev: ninth (third) month of Hebrew calendar

kivshon haaish: fiery furnace

Kiyor: wash basin in the *Mishkan* and *Beit HaMikdash*

klaf: small piece of paper or parchment

klal : general principle

klallah: curse

Klal Yisrael: the Jewish community as a whole

Kodesh: Holy

Kodesh HaKadoshim: "Holy of Holies"; inner sanctuary of the *Mishkan* and *Beit HaMikdash*

Kohain / Kohanim: Priest(s); descendants of *Aharon*

Kohain Gadol: High Priest

Kohelet: Book of Ecclesiastes, part of *Tanach*

kollel: "gathering"; an institute for full-time advanced *Torah* study

Kol Nidre: "all the vows"; opening prayer for *Yom Kippur*

Korach: cousin of *Moshe* and *Aharon* who led a revolt against them

korban / korbanot: sacrifice(s) offered in the *Mishkan* and *Beit HaMikdash*

Korban Pesach: Passover sacrifice

Korban Tamid: daily sacrifice

Korban Todah: Thanksgiving sacrifice

Kotel: Western Wall

Kozbi (bat Tzur): *Midyani* princess killed with *Zimri ben Salu* by *Pinchas*

Kriyat Yam Suf: Splitting of the Sea of Reeds

Lag B'Omer: thirty-third day of the *Omer*; festive day

lashon: tongue; language

Lashon HaKodesh: "Holy tongue"; Hebrew

lashon hara: word (or non-verbal communication) that is either derogatory or potentially harmful to another

Lavan: brother of *Rivkah*; father of *Rachel* and *Leah*

Leah: daughter of *Lavan*; sister of *Rachel*; wife of *Yaacov*; mother of *Reuven, Shimon, Levy, Yehudah, Yissachar, Zevulun* and daughter *Dinah*

Levy: son of *Yaacov* and *Leah*; one of the *Twelve Tribes*

Levy / Leviim: descendant(s) of *Levy*, tasked with assisting the *Kohanim*

l'havdil: "to make distinction"

Lot: nephew of *Avraham*

l'Sheim Shamayim: "for the Name of Heaven"; done with no ulterior motive by to serve *Hashem*

Luchot: Tablets; the Stones upon which were transcribed the Ten Commandments

lulav: palm branch; one of the *Arba'ah Minim* used on *Sukkot*

ma'akeh: a fence around a roof; required as a *mitzvah*

Maarat HaMachpeilah: "Cave of Patriarchs"; burial site of *Avraham, Sarah, Yitzchak, Rivkah, Yaacov* and *Leah* in *Chevron*

maarit ayin: "appearance of the eye"; refraining from a permissible action because it may appear to be improper to others

Maariv: evening prayer service

maaser: "tenth"; tithe given to *Leviim*

maaser kesafim: "tenth of money"; obligation to give ten percent of one's income to *tzedakah*

Maaser Sheini: "second tenth"; tithe of first, second, fourth, and fifth years of seven year agricultural cycle; produce (or cash equivalent) is brought to be eaten in *Yerushalayim*

maasim tovim: good deeds

Mabul: the Flood

Machlat (bat Yishmael): *Eisav's* third wife

machloket: disagreement, debate

machzit hashekel: "half of a shekel"; given on *Purim*

madraygah: spiritual level

Maftir: "he who concludes"; the last *aliyah* of the *Shabbat* or *Yom Tov* *Torah* reading

Mah Tovu: "how good it is"; first prayer said when entering a *shul*

makah / makot: plague(s)

Makat Arbeh: eighth Egyptian plague of locusts

Makat Bechorot: tenth Egyptian plague of the death of the firstborn sons

Makat Kinim: third Egyptian plague of lice or gnats

malach / malachim: angel(s), messenger(s)

malach hamavet: "angel of death"

Malkitzedek (Melech Shaleim): King of Salem; *Shem*

mapilim: those of *Bnei Yisrael* who unsuccessfully tried to enter *Eretz Yisrael* after the sin of the *meraglim*

Mara Datra: "master of the house"; local authority on *halachah*

Marah: "bitter"; location of misfortune for the Jews in the *midbar*

Masah u'Merivah: desert location where *Bnei Yisrael* complained about lack of water

mashal: example, allegory

mashgiach: supervisor of *kashrut* for a kosher establishment

Matan Torah: "the Giving of the *Torah*" at *Har Sinai*; celebrated on *Shavuot*

matzah: unleavened bread eaten on *Pesach*

mayim: water

mayim achronim: "after-waters"; used to wash hand in preparation of *Birchat HaMazon*

mechillah: forgiveness

Medinat Yisrael: the modern State of Israel

mefaraish / mefarshim: commentary; commentaries

megadef: blasphemer

megillah: scroll

Megillat Esther: "Scroll of Esther"; read on *Purim*

Meidad: with *Eldad*, prophets in the *midbar*

meirkavah: chariot

meit: "dead"; a dead body

melachah / melachot: "labor(s)"; action(s) within thirty nine categories of labor forbidden on *Shabbat* and, with some exceptions, *Yom Tov*

Melachim: Book of Kings, part of *Tanach*

melech: king

Menashe: son of *Yosef*; brother of *Ephraim*; became like one of the *Twelve Tribes*

Men of the Great Assembly: a panel of 120 Sages that constituted the religious authority at the onset of *Beit Sheini*

Menorah: Candelabra used in the *Mishkan* and *Beit HaMikdash*

mentsch / mentschen: "person(s)"; person(s) of integrity

meraglim: spies

mesorah: tradition

metzora: one afflicted with *tzaraat*

Mezuzah: "doorpost"; the parchment affixed to the doorpost containing portions of *Shema*

midbar: desert

middah / middot: attribute(s) of character

middah keneged middah: "measure for measure"; the principle of "what goes around comes around," as directed by *Hashem*

Midrash (Peliah): non-legal commentary and interpretative teachings (especially wondrous or perplexing)

Midyan / Midyanim / Midyani: Midian; Midianites; Midianite

Migdal Bavel: Tower of Babel

miKadaish: to make Holy

mikareiv: to bring close (to *Torah)*

mikoshaysh: gatherer of wood who desecrated *Shabbat*

Mikra Bikkurim: "declaration of first fruits"; the prayer that accompanies bringing of *Bikkurim*

mikvah: ritual bath

milah: *brit milah*

Minchah: afternoon prayer service; or flour offering

minhag : binding custom, as opposed to *halachah*

minyan: quorum of ten men required for a prayer service or *Torah* reading

Miriam: sister of *Aharon and Moshe;* wife of *Caleiv;* mother of *Chur*

Misha'el: with *Azaryah* and *Chananya,* defied *Nevuchadnezair*

Mishlei: Book of Proverbs, part of *Tanach*

Mishkan: Tabernacle; portable sanctuary used in the *midbar;* replaced by the *Beit HaMikdash*

Mishloach Manot: "sending of portions"; gifts of food sent on *Purim*

Mishnah: first written compilation of *Oral Law*, divided into six *sedarim*

mishpat/ mishpatim: rational *Torah* law(s)

Mitzrayim / Mitzri /Mitzrim: Egypt; Egyptian(s)

mitzvah / mitzvot: commandment(s) of the *Torah*

mitzvah (mitzvot) aseh: positive commandment(s) of the *Torah;* "thou shall . . ."

mitzvah (mitzvot) bein adam l'atzmo: commandments of the *Torah* between a human being and himself

mitzvah (mitzvot) bein adam l'chaveiro: commandments of the *Torah* involving interpersonal relations

mitzvah (mitzvot) bein adam l'Makom: commandments of the *Torah* between man and God

mitzvah (mitzvot) lo t'aseh: negative commandment(s) of the *Torah;* "thou shall not . . ."

Mizbeach: Altar in the *Mishkan* or *Beit HaMikdash*

Moav / Movaim: Moab; (land of) nation descended from *Lot*; Moabites

modim: "we thankfully acknowledge"; a blessing in the *Shemoneh Esrei*

Mon : Manna

Moshe (Rabbeinu): Moses (our Teacher)

Moshiach (Tzidkenu): "Messiah (the Righteous One)"; bringer the ultimate redemption

Motzei Shabbat: evening following *Shabbat* day

motzei shem ra: "putting out a bad name"; slander

m'samaiach chattan v'kallah: bringing joy to the bride and groom

Mussaf: additional prayer service recited on *Shabbat, Yom Tov, Chol HaMoed*, and *Rosh Chodesh*

mussar: morality, ethics, methods for personal improvement in character

mutar: permissible

Naaman: an Aramite general

naaseh v'nishmah: "we will do and we will hear"; declaration of *Bnei Yisrael* at *Matan Sinai*

nachas / nachat: pride, pleasure

Nadav: eldest son of *Aharon*; brother of *Avihu*

Naftali: son of *Yaacov* and *Bilhah*; one of the *Twelve Tribes*

Naomi: mother in law of *Rut*

nasi / nasiim: leader(s); prince(s)

Navi / Naviim: Prophet(s); second division of the *Tanach*

nazir / nazirut: "consecrated"; one who sets himself apart for Divine service by undertaking certain ascetic restrictions

nechamah: comfort

nevuah: prophecy

Nevuchadnezair: Babylonian king, destroyed the first *Beit HaMikdash* and exiled the Jews

neder / nedarim: vow(s)

nega: skin mark, plague

Neilah: "closing"; the closing service of *Yom Kippur*

ner / neirot: candle(s)

neshamah / neshamot: soul(s)

neshamah yetairah: additional soul received on *Shabbat*

netilat yadayim: ritual handwashing

niddah: "separated"; in the context of Jewish marital Laws, when a woman is prohibited to her husband based on her menstrual state

Nimrod: King of Shinar; great grandson of *Noach*

Nine Days: first nine days of the month of *Av,* during which there is a period of mourning

Nissan: first (ninth) month of the Hebrew calendar

Noach: built the Ark and survived the Flood; father of *Shem,* Yafet and *Cham*

nohaig: accustomed to

Novach: conqueror of Kenat; forgotten to history

Og (Melech HaBashan): Og the King of Bashan

Ohel Moed: "Tent of Meeting"; *Mishkan*

Ohn ben Pelet: initial follower of *Korach*

olah: whole burnt offering

Olam HaBa: "the World to Come"

Olam HaZeh: this world

oleh: immigrant to Israel

Omer: formal counting of forty-nine days between *Pesach* and *Shavuot,* named for the grain offering

ona'ah: "overreaching"; the act of selling an item for more than its worth

oneg: delight, spiritual pleasure

onen: state of a mourner from the time one hears of the death until burial

Oral Law: laws, statutes and legal interpretations that were not recorded in *Chamishah Chumshay Torah* but given to *Moshe* at *Har Sinai;* includes *Talmud, Mishnah* and *Gemara*

orlah: fruit of a tree prohibited for the first three years after planting

Orpah: sister and sister-in-law of *Rut*

Ovadiah: prophet who converted from *Edom*; part of *Tanach*

Parah Adumah : "Red Heifer"

parashah/

parashat / parshiot: *Torah* portion(s)

parashat hashavua: weekly *Torah* portion

pareve: for food, containing neither dairy nor meat products; neutral

parnassah: livelihood

Parochet: Curtain concealing the *Kodesh HaKadoshim* in the *Mishkan* and *Beit HaMikdash*

Paroh: "Pharaoh"; Egyptian king

pasuk / pasukim: verse(s)

patur: exempt

Pesach: Passover, festival commemorating Exodus from Egypt

Pesach Sheini: "second Passover"; opportunity for those unable to offer the *Korban Pesach* to do so a month later

Pesukei d'Zimrah: "Verses of Song"; *Tehillim* recited daily in *Shacharit* service

Pidyon HaBen: rite of redeeming first born male child from *Kohain*, thirty days after birth

Pinchas: son of *Elazar HaKohain*; grandson of *Aharon*; known for his zeal

Pirkei Avot: "Ethics of Our Fathers"; tractate in *Mishnah*

Plishtim: enemy nation of *Bnei Yisrael*

Potiphar / Potiphera: one of *Paroh*'s officials who acquired *Yosef*

Puah: *Miriam*; one of the midwives in *Mitzrayim* who helped save male Jewish babies, with *Shifrah*

Purim: "lots"; holiday celebrating the victory over *Haman*

Rabbi Akiva: *Akiva Ben Yosef*, *Tanna* in latter part of first century

Rabbi Chananya: a sage of the *Mishnah*

Rabbi Elazar ben Azaryah: *Tanna* in first century

Rabbi Elazar ben Shimon: son of *Rabbi Shimon bar Yochai*

Rabbi Meir: *Tanna*, student of *Rabbi Akiva*

Rabbi Shimon bar Yochai: Rashbi; second century *Tanna*

Rabbi Shimon ben Pazi: Rabbi of second half of third century

Rabbi Tzadok: second generation *Tanna*

Rabbi Yehoshua ben Levy: third century *Talmudic* Scholar

Rabbi Yehudah: Yehuda bar Ilai, second century *Tanna*

Rabbi Yishmael: Yishmael ben Elisha; *Tanna* of the first and second centuries

Rabbi Yochanan: second century *Tanna*, contributor to the *Mishnah*

Rabbi Yose bar Yehudah: second century *Tanna*

rachamim: compassion

Rachav (HaZonah): a woman who lived in *Yericho*; either an innkeeper or harlot

Rachel: daughter of *Lavan*; sister of *Leah*; wife of *Yaacov*; mother of *Yosef* and *Binyamin*

Ramses: Egyptian *paroh*

rasha: wicked person

rashei teivot: Hebrew abbreviation based on first letter of each word of a phrase

Rav: scholar, teacher

Rebbe: *Torah* teacher; head of *chassidut* movement

rebbetzin: wife of a rabbi

rechilut: *lashon hara* that causes ill will between people

re'eim: legendary enormous creature

Refidim: place visited by the Jews in the *midbar*

refuah: healing

Reish Lakish: Shimon ben Lakish, third century, known for his great strength

reshut: optional or voluntary action

Reuven: son of *Yaacov* and *Leah*; one of the *Twelve Tribes*

Rivkah: daughter of *Betuel*; sister of *Lavan*; wife of *Yitzchak;* mother of *Yaacov* and *Eisav*

rodeiph: homicidal pursuer, worthy of death

Rosh Chodesh: "head of the month"; one or two semi-festive days when new moon appears marking the beginning of each month

Rosh Hashanah: "head of the Year"; Jewish New Year

ruach: spirit

Ruach HaKodesh: "Divine Spirit"; prophecy

ruach ra'ah: evil spirit

ruchniut: spirituality

Rut: Ruth, *Moavi* princess who converted to Judaism; married *Boaz*; *Megillat Rut* is part of *Tanach*

Sanhedrin: "sitting together"; religious court assembly

Sarah (Imeinu): Sarah (Our Mother); wife of *Avraham*; mother of *Yitzchak*

Sarai: original name of *Sarah*

Sar Hamashkim: *Paroh*'s wine bearer, butler

Sar Haofim: *Paroh*'s baker

satan: accuser, Heavenly prosecutor

Schem: Hivvite prince who abducted *Dinah*; name of city where *Dinah* was held

S'dom (and Amorah): Biblical cities Sodom (and Gomorrah)

Seder: "order"; the festive meal on *Pesach*

sedra: "order"; *parashah*

sefer / sifrei / sefarim: book(s)

Sefer Torah: *Torah* Scroll

Sefirah (Sefirat HaOmer): "counting"; counting of *Omer* for forty-nine days between *Pesach* and *Shavuot*

selichot: "forgiveness"; penitential prayers said in the week before *Rosh Hashanah*

Semicha: Rabbinic ordination

seudat hoda'ah: meal of thanksgiving

seudat mitzvah: "commanded meal"; festive meal following fulfillment of a *mitzvah*

Seudah Shlishit: "the third meal"; the third required meal for *Shabbat* eaten before sunset

shaatnez: prohibited mixture of wool and linen in a garment

Shabbat / Shabbatot: Sabbath(s); Day(s) of Rest

Shabbat Chazon: "Sabbath of the Vision"; *Shabbat* immediately preceding *Tisha B'Av*

Shabbat HaChodesh: "Sabbath of the Month"; *Shabbat* preceding month of *Nissan*

Shabbat HaGadol: "Great Sabbath"; *Shabbat* preceding *Pesach*

Shabbat Mevorchim: "Sabbath of Blessing"; *Shabbat* preceding *Rosh Chodesh*

Shabbat Nachamu: "Sabbath of Comfort"; *Shabbat* following *Tisha B'Av* and the *Three Weeks*

Shabbat Parah: "Sabbath of the [Red] Heifer"; *Shabbat* before *Shabbat HaChodesh*, *Torah* portion describing *Parah Adumah* is read

Shabbat Shekalim: "Sabbath of Shekel"; *Shabbat* before month of *Adar*

Shabbat Shuvah: "Sabbath of Return"; *Shabbat* between *Rosh Hashanah* and *Yom Kippur*

Shabbat Zachor: "Sabbath of Remembrance"; *Shabbat* preceding *Purim*

Shabbos: Sabbath; *Shabbat*

Shacharit: morning prayer service

shalom: peace; hello; or goodbye

Shalom Aleichem: "Peace be Upon You"; greeting

shalom bayit: "peace in the home"; domestic tranquility

Shalom Zachor: "welcoming the male"; a festive gathering on first Friday night after a baby boy is born

shaloshim: thirty day mourning period following burial

Shalosh Regalim: three annual pilgrimage festivals: *Pesach, Shavuot* and *Succot*

shalshelet: "chain"; accent symbol for *Torah* reading

Shamayim: Heaven

Shammai: first century Sage of *Mishnah*

Shas: "six orders"; *Talmud*

shavua / shavuot: week(s)

Shavuot: "Feast of Weeks"; the holiday commemorating the giving of the *Torah*

Shechinah: Divine Presence

shechitah / shecht / shechted: ritual animal slaughter

shehakol: blessing for certain foods

Sheim Hashem: "the Name of *Hashem*"; for the Sake of *Hashem*

Sheish Zichronot: "Six Remembrances"; verses recited daily at the end of *Shacharit*

shekel: coin in the Temple era; Israeli coin

sheker: falsehood

Shelomit bat Divri: Shelomit, the daughter of Divri; mother of *megadef*

Shel Rosh: "of the head"; *Tefillin* worn on the head

Shel Yad: "of the arm;" *Tefillin* worn on the arm

Shem: son of *Noach*; established *Yeshivat Shem v'Eiver*; *Malkitzedek*

Shema (Yisrael): "Hear (Israel)"; daily prayer declaration of faith recited at *Shacharit* and *Maariv*

Shemini Atzeret: "Eighth Day of Assembly"; holiday immediately following *Sukkot*

Shemittah: "sabbatical year"; seventh year of agricultural cycle when the land lies fallow

Shemoneh Esrei: "Eighteen" benedictions; also known as *Amidah,* main section of daily prayer service

Shemot (Sefer Shemot): "names"; Book of Exodus; the second Book of *Chamishah Chumshay Torah*

Sheva Berachot: "Seven Blessings"; recited during Jewish wedding; the week of festivities following wedding

Sheva Minim: "Seven Species"; special agricultural species of *Eretz Yisrael*: wheat, barley, grape, fig, pomegranate, olive, and date

Sheva Mitzvot Bnei Noach: "Seven Laws of the Children of Noah"; universal obligations binding all people including non-Jews

Shevet / Shevatim: Tribe(s) descended from the twelve son(s) of *Yaacov*

shibud: enslavement

shidduch: match or arranged marriage

Shifrah: *Yocheved*; one of the midwives in *Mitzrayim* who helped save male Jewish babies, with *Puah*

shiluach hakein: *mitzvah* of sending away a mother bird before taking her eggs or chicks

Shimon: son of *Yaacov* and *Leah*; one of the *Twelve Tribes*

Shimshon: Samson; one of the Judges

shir / shirah: song

Shir HaShirim: "Song of Songs"; part of *Tanach*

Shir Shel Yom: "Song of the Day"; *Tehillah* sung at end of every *Shacharit* particular to that day

shishi: sixth

shiur: *Torah* class; or a defined measure

Shiva Asar b'Tammuz: seventeenth day of the month of *Tammuz*, a fast day; beginning of the *Three Weeks*

shivah: week-long mourning period for first-degree relatives: father, mother, son, daughter, brother, sister, and spouse

Shivil HaZahav: "Golden Mean"

shliach / shlichim: messenger(s)

Shlomo (HaMelech): (King) Solomon

Shmuel HaNavi: Samuel the Prophet; the last of the Judges

shochet: ritual slaughterer

Shofar: ram's horn blown of *Rosh Hashanah* and *Yom Kippur*

shoresh: root, origin

shtetl: small village

shul: synagogue

Shulchan: ceremonial Table in the *Mishkan* and *Beit HaMikdash*

Sichon: *Emori* king

siddur: Jewish prayer book

simchah: joyous occasion; or happiness

Simchat Torah: "Rejoicing with the *Torah*"; holiday that immediately follows *Sukkot*

Sinai: mountain in the desert where the *Torah* was given

sinat chinam: baseless hatred

Sisra: commander of the Canaanite army

Sivan: third (ninth) month of the Hebrew calendar; month of *Shavuot*

sofer / soferim: scribe(s)

sotah: woman suspected of infidelity

sugya: unit of organization of the *Gemara*

sukkah/ sukkot: temporary structure(s) for dwelling in the *midbar* and during *Sukkot*

Sukkot: "Feast of Tabernacles"; holiday in month of *Tishrei* celebrated with *sukkot* and *Arb'ah Minim*

tachanun: "supplication"; part of weekday *Shacharit* and *Mincha* services

Taharat HaMishpachah: laws of family purity

tahor: pure

taivah: physical desire

talmid / talmidim: student(s)

Talmud (Bavli): most widely used repository of *Oral Law*, composed in Babylonia; *Gemara*

talmud chacham / talmidei chachamim: *Torah* scholar(s)

Tamar: daughter-in-law of *Yehudah*

tamei: ritually impure

Tammuz: fourth (tenth) month in Hebrew calendar

Tanach: *rashei teivot* of *Torah, Naviim* [and] *Ketuvim*; the three parts of the *Torah*

Tanna / Tannaim: scholar(s) from the *Mishnah* period

Techeilet: turquoise or blue dye used for *Tzitzit*

Techiyat HaMaytim: resurrection of the dead

tefach (tefachim): unit of measurement corresponding to the length of a fist

tefillah / tefillot: prayer(s); see also *davening*

Tefillin: "phylacteries"; ritual object worn on the forehead and arm by men during *Shacharit*

Tefillin Shel Rosh: "Tefillin of the Head"; worn on the head

Tefillin Shel Yad: "Tefillin of the Arm"; worn on the arm

Tehillah / Tehillim: Psalm(s); part of *Tanach*

Teivah: The Ark (of *Noach*)

teivah: small ark that hid *Moshe* as a baby

teraphim: idols

terumah: gift, offering; given to *Mishkan* or *Kohanim* in *Beit HaMikdash*

teshuvah: repentance

tevillat kaylim: immersion of certain culinary utensils in a *mikvah*

Three Weeks: twenty-one day National mourning period between the fast days of *17 Tammuz* and *Tisha B'av*

tikkun: improvement, correction

Tisha B'Av: "Ninth of Av"; fast day commemorating the destruction of the first and second *Batei Mikdash*

Tishrei: first (seventh) month of the Hebrew calendar

tochachah: rebuke

todah: thanksgiving offering

Torah: "teaching"; broadly refers to the written and oral history and laws given at *Sinai* and thereafter, including *Tanach*; narrowly, *Chamishah Chumshay Torah*

Torah Shebaal Peh: "The *Oral Law*"; also given to *Moshe* at *Har Sinai* with *Chamishah Chumshay Torah*

Torah Shebichtav: "The *Written Law*"; *Chamishah Chumshay Torah*

treif / treifa: "torn"; colloquialism meaning non-kosher

Tu B'Av: fifteenth of the month of Av

tumah: impurity

Twelve Tribes: *Shevatim*

tzaddik / tzaddikim: righteous one(s)

tzaraat: a leprous, disfigurative condition of the skin reflecting a spiritual failing

Tzalaphchad: father of five daughters; died in the *midbar* with no male heir

tzedakah: charity

tzfardaya : frog(s); second Egyptian plague

Tzibbur: community, congregation

Tzidukim: Sadducees; break away sect from Judaism that rejected the *Torah she b'al Peh*

Tzipporah: wife of *Moshe*; daughter of *Yitro*

Tzitzit: *mitzvah* ritual fringes

tzniut: concept and laws of modesty and privacy in attire and behavior

tzohar: window; or luminous stone

Urim v'Tumim: "lights and perfections"; the stones on the *Choshen* of the *Kohain Gadol*

Ur Kasdim: birthplace of *Avraham*

Ushpizin: "guests"; seven patriarchal figures welcomed into the *sukkah*

Vayikra (Sefer Vayikra): "and he called"; Book of Leviticus; the third Book of *Chamishah Chumshay Torah*

vidui: confession of sins

Vidui Maasrot: "confession of a tithing"; recited every three years on the last day of *Pesach*

vort: "word"; thought-provoking *Torah* idea

Written Law: *Torah* laws set forth in *Chamishah Chumshay Torah*

Yaacov (Avinu): Jacob (our Father); son of *Yitzchak*; husband of *Leah* and *Rachel*; father of the *Shevatim* and daughter *Dinah*

Yael: woman who killed *Sisra*

yahrzeit: anniversary of a death

Yair: son of *Menashe*

Yamim Noraim: "Days of Awe"; High Holy Days of *Rosh Hashanah* and *Yom Kippur*

Yam Suf: "sea of reeds"

Yarden: Jordan (River)

Yechezkel: Ezekiel; fifth century *Navi* in *Bavel*, part of *Tanach*

Yefet: son of *Noach*

Yehoshua: Joshua, *Moshe's* successor; or Book of Joshua, part of *Tanach*,

Yehudah: Judah; son of *Yaacov* and *Leah*; one of the *Twelve Tribes*

Yekkish: German-Jewish, exhibiting high attention to detail and punctuality

yemach shemo / yemach shemam: may his (their) name be obliterated

Yericho: Jericho; first city in *Eretz Yisrael* conquered by *Yehoshua*

yerida: "going down"; emigration from Israel

yerushah: inheritance

Yerushalayim: Jerusalem, Israel!

Yerushalmi (Talmud): the version of *Talmud* compiled in *Eretz Yisrael* in the fourth century

yeshivah: Torah academy

Yeshivat Shem v'Eiver: *Yeshivah* of Shem and Eiver; first *yeshivah* in history

yeshuah: salvation

Yeshurun: elevated name of *Bnei Yisrael*

yesurim: suffering

yetzer hara: evil inclination

yichus: family status or pedigree

Yid: Jew

Yiddishkeit: Jewishness; Judaism

yirah / yirat: fear (of)

Yirat Shamayim: fear of Heaven; piety

Yirmiyahu (HaNavi): Jeremiah the *Navi*; part of *Tanach*

Yishaiyah (Yishaiyahu): Isaiah the *Navi*; part of *Tanach*

Yishmael: Ishmael; son of *Avraham* and *Hagar*; brother of *Yitzchak*

Yishtabach: prayer of praise in *Shacharit* service concluding *Pesukei d'Zimrah*

yishuv: settlement

Yisrael: *Yaacov Avinu*; also sometimes referring to *Bnei Yisrael*

Yissachar: Issacher; son of *Yaacov* and *Leah*; one of *Twelve Tribes*

Yitro: father in law of *Moshe*; father of *Tzipporah*

Yitzchak: Isaac; son of *Avraham*; husband of *Rivkah*; father of *Yaacov* and *Eisav*

Yitziat

Mitzrayim: "the going out of Egypt"; the Exodus

Yocheved: wife of *Amram*; mother of *Moshe*

Yom HaAtzmaut: Israeli Independence Day

Yom HaDin: "Day of Judgment"; final judgment after death

Yom HaShoah: Holocaust Remembrance Day

Yom Kippur: "Day of Atonement"; fast day on tenth of *Tishrei*

Yom Tov / Yom Tovim: "Good Day(s)"; Jewish holiday(s)

Yosef (HaTzaddik): Joseph (the Righteous); son of *Yaacov* and *Rachel*; father of *Ephraim* and *Menashe*; one of the *Twelve Tribes*

Yovel: Jubilee year; fiftieth year after seven *Shemittah* cycles

zakain / zakainim: elder(s)

zechut: merit

zemer / zemeriot: *Shabbat* song(s)

Zevulun: Zebulun; son of *Yaacov* and *Leah*; one of *Twelve Tribes*

Zilpah: maidservant of *Leah*; mother of *Gad* and *Asher*

Zimri (ben Salu): leader of *Shevet Shimon*, killed by *Pinchas*

z'man: time specific to *halachah*

Z'man Simchateinu: "the Time of our Happiness"; *Sukkot* and *Shemini Atzeret/Simchat Torah*

ZT'L: *rashei teivot* for "zekher tzadik l'vrachah"; "may his memory be a blessing"

SOURCES AND INFLUENCES

Abramsky	Rabbi Yechezkel	(1886-1976); Belarus; *Chazon Yechezkel*
Abravanel	Rabbi Don Isaac	(1437–1508); Portugal
Alpert	Rabbi Nisson	(1927–1986); Poland; New York
Alshich	Rabbi Moshe	(1508–1593); Safed, Israel
Alter of Kelm		Rabbi Simcha Zissel Ziv Broida; (1824–1898); Lithuania; mussar movement.
Alter of Slabodka		Rabbi Nosson Tzvi Finkel; (1849–1927); Lithuania
Anidjar	Reb Shalom	Hollywood, Florida
Arizal		Ari; Rabbi Yitzchak ben Shlomo Luria Ashkenazi; (1534–1572); Yerushalayim, Tzfat, Israel; *Sefer HaGilgulim*
Aruch HaShulchan		Rabbi Yechiel Michel Epstein; (1829–1908); Lithuania
Ashkenazi	Rabbi Eliezer	(1512–1585); Egypt; Prague; Poland
Assouli	Rabbi Yitzchak	Yerushalayim, Israel
Ateret Zekenim		Rabbi Menachem Mendel Auerbach; (1620–1689); Austria
Auman	Rabbi Kenneth	Young Israel of Flatbush; Brooklyn

Baal HaTanya		Rabbi Shneur Zalman of Liadi; (1745–1812); Belarus; first Rebbe of Chabad
Baal HaTurim		Rabbi Jacob Ben Asher; (1269–1340); Germany; *Arba'ah Turim*
Baal Shem Tov		Rabbi Yisroel ben Eliezer; (1698–1760); Ukraine; founder of Chassidut
Barr	Reb Louis	Baltimore
Be'er Yosef		Rabbi Yosef Tzvi Salant; (1885–1981); Yerushalayim, Israel
Becher	Rabbi Mordechai	Gateways; Yeshiva University; Australia; New Jersey
Beis HaLevi		Rabbi Yosef Dov Soloveitchik; (1820–1892); Belarus
Ben Ish Chai		Rabbi Yosef Chaim; (1835–1909); Baghdad
Berditchever Rebbe		Rabbi Levi Yitzchak of Berditchev; (1740–1809); Ukraine; *Kedushas Levi*
Bergman	Rabbi Meir Tzvi	Bnei Brak, Israel; Rosh Yeshivah of Rashbi Yeshivah
Biala Rebbe		Rabbi Ben Zion Rabinowitz; Switzerland
Billet	Rabbi Avi	Anshei Chesed Congregation; Boynton Beach, Florida
Bixon	Rabbi Donald	Beth Israel Congregation; Miami Beach
Bluming	Rabbi Mendel	Chabad of Potomac, Maryland
Bnei Yissaschar		Rabbi Tzvi Elimelech Spira; (1783–1841); Munkatch, Galicia
Bogomilsky	Rabbi Moshe	see *Vedibarta Bam*
Bonhart	Rabbi Simcha Bunim	of Peshischa; (1767–1827); Poland
Brander	Rabbi Asher	Kehillah of Westwood; Los Angeles
Breslov	Rabbi Nachman of	(1772–1810); Uman, Ukraine; *Likutei Moharan*

Breuer	Rabbi Shlomo Zalman	(1850–1926); Hungary; Frankfurt am Main, Germany
Brisker Rav		see Rabbi Yitzchak Zev Halevy Soloveitchik
Bunim	Reb Irving	(1901–1980); Lithuania; United States; Founder of Young Israel movement
Chafetz	Rabbi Moshe	Rabbi Moshe ben Gershom; (1663–1711); Italy
Chanukas HaTorah		Rabbi Avraham Yehoshua Heschel; (1595–1663); Krakow, Poland
Charlap	Rabbi Yaakov Moshe	(1882–1951); Rosh Yeshivah of Yeshivat Mercaz Harav; Yerushalayim, Israel
Chasam Sofer		Rabbi Moshe Schreiber; (1762–1839); Germany; Austria
Chaver	Rabbi Yitzchak Isaac	(1789–1852); Lithuania; second generation student of the Vilna Gaon
Chernobyl Rebbe		Rabbi Menachem Nachum of Chernobyl; (1730–1797); Ukraine; student of the Baal Shem Tov and the Maggid of Mezritch
Chida		Rabbi Chaim Yosef David Azulai; (1724–1806); Israel; Italy
Chidushei HaRim		Rabbi Yitzchak Meir Rotenberg–Alter; (1799–1866); Poland; first Rebbe of Gerrer Chasidim
Chinuch		*Sefer HaChinuch*; published anonymously in 13th century Spain
Chizkuni		Rabbi Chizkiyahu ben Manoach; mid–13th century; France
Chofetz Chaim		Rabbi Yisrael Meir Kagan; (1839–1933); Russian Empire; Radin, Poland; *Mishnah Berurah*
Choueka	Rabbi Shmuel	Congregation Ohel Simha; Long Branch, New Jersey

Ciner	Rabbi Yisroel	Beth Jacob Congregation; Irvine, California
Cohen	Rabbi J. Simcha	(1936–2014); Rabbi of Congregation Aitz Chaim; West Palm Beach, Florida;
Cohn	Reb Levy	Coral Springs, Florida
Daat Zakainim		Collection of Torah commentary by various Baalei HaTosafot, disciples of Rashi; 13th Century
Damesek Eliezer		Rabbi Eliezer Hager; (1890–1945); Vizhnitz, Ukraine
Dancyger	Rabbi Yechiel	(1828–1894); Poland; first rebbe of the Aleksander dynasty
Davis	Rabbi Edward	Mara Datra, Young Israel of Hollywood–Fort Lauderdale; Florida
Derech Eretz Zuta		Supplement to the Talmud Bavli
Dessler	Eliyahu Eliezer	(1892–1953); Gateshead, England; Bnei Brak, Israel
Divrei Shaul		Rabbi Yosef Shaul (ben Aryeh Leibush) HaLevi Nathanson; (1810–1875); Galicia
Divrei Yoel		Rabbi Yoel Teitelbaum; (1887–1979); Satmar Rebbe; Hungary; New York
Dubner Maggid		Rabbi Jacob ben Wolf Kranz of Dubno; (c. 1740–1804); Lithuania
Eidut B'Yosef		see Divrei Shaul
Eiger	Rabbi Akiva	(1761–1837); Hungary; Poland
Ein Yaakov		compilation of all the Aggadic material in the Talmud
Elefant	Dr. Ronen	Hollywood, Florida; West Hartford, Connecticut
Emes L'Yaakov		Rabbi Yaakov ben Yaakov Moshe Lorberbaum; (1760–1832); Poland
Emunat Itecha		Rabbi Moshe Wolfson; Brooklyn

Epstein	Dr. David	Hollywood, Florida
Etshalom	Rabbi Yitzchak	Los Angeles
Ezer MiYehudah		Rabbi Azriel Yehuda Lebowitz; (1910–1992); Hungary
Feiglin	Reb Moshe	Israeli politician; Yerushalayim, Israel
Feinstein	Rabbi Dovid	Rosh Yeshivah of Mesivta Tifereth Jerusalem; New York
Feinstein	Rabbi Moshe	(1895–1986); Belarus; New York; *Igros Moshe*
Feivel	Rabbi Uri	Rabbi Aaron Hart; (1670–1756); Holy Roman Empire; United Kingdom
Flamm	Rabbi Avraham Dov Berish	(1804–1873); Poland; Lithuania
Flom	Rabbi Chaim	(d. 2008); Yeshivat Ohr David; Jerusalem, Israel
Frand	Rabbi Yissocher	Yeshivas Ner Yisroel; Baltimore
Frank	Mrs. Jamie	Eishet Chayil; Hollywood, Florida
Freedman	Rabbi Binny	Rosh Yeshivah of Orayta; Yerushalayim, Efrat, Israel
Friedman	Rabbi Manis	Founder of Bais Chana Institute of Jewish Studies; Saint Paul, Minnesota
Frier	Reb Avi	Hollywood, Florida
Galinsky	Rabbi Yaacov	(1920–2014); Bialistock; Bnei Brak, Israel
Gelman	Rabbi Shaanan	Kehillat Chovevei Tzion; Skokie, Illinois
Gerrer Rebbe		See Chidushei HaRim
Gifter	Rabbi Mordechai	(1915–2001); Rosh Yeshivah of Telshe Yeshivah–Cleveland; Baltimore; Lithuania; Cleveland; Yerushalayim, Israel
Ginsberg	Rabbi Dr. Paul	Hollywood, Florida
Ginsparg	Rabbi Mordechai	Fasman Yeshivah High School; Chicago

Glatt	Rabbi Gedalya	Director of Jewish Legacy; Bais Yaakov of Miami High School; North Miami Beach
Goldvicht	Rabbi Chaim Yaakov	(1924–1995); Founding Rosh Yeshiva at Yeshivat Kerem B'Yavneh; Israel
Greenberg	Reb Ben	Hollywood, Florida
Greenblatt	Rabbi Ephraim	(1932–2014); Memphis; *Rivevos Ephraim*
Greenwald	Reb Michael	Hollywood, Florida; Ramat Beit Shemesh, Israel
Groundland	Rabbi Ephraim	(1932–2009); Scotland; Israel
Gruenwald	Rabbi Moshe	Rabbi Moshe Greenwald; (1853–1911); Hungary; Ukraine
Grumet	Rabbi Zvi	Yerushalayim, Israel
Grundwerg	Reb Shmuel	Sammy; Efrat, Israel
Hahn	Reb Yossi	Hollywood, Florida
Ha'Itamari	Rabbi Eliyahu	(c. 1650–1729); Turkey; *Shevet Mussar*
HaK'tav v'HaKabbalah		Rabbi Jacob Zvi Mecklenburg; (1785–1865); Germany; Prussia
Halberstam	Rabbi Yechezkel Shraga	Stropkover Rav; (1811–1899); Poland
Halberstam	Rabbi Yekutiel Yehuda	(1905–1994); Poland; Israel; founding rebbe of the Sanz–Klausenburg Chasidim
Heller	Rabbi Aviezer	Manhattan
Herzog	Rabbi Yitzhak HaLevi	(1888–1959); first Chief Rabbi of Ireland; Ashkenazi Chief Rabbi of the British Mandate of Palestine and Israel
Hirsch	Rabbi Samson Raphael	(1808–1888); Hamburg, Germany
Hirschhorn	Reb Tevi	Chicago
Hizkiya	Reb Arie	Weinbaum Yeshivah High School; Boca Raton, Florida

Hollander	Rabbi David	(1913–2009); Hungary; New York
Ibn Ezra		Rabbi Abraham Ben Meir Ibn Ezra; (1089–1167); Spain
Imrei Emes		Rabbi Avraham Mordechai Alter; (1866–1948); Poland; Israel; third Rebbe of Gerrer Chasidim
Imrei Yosef		Rabbi Joseph Meir Weiss; (1838–1909); Hungary; first Spinka rebbe
Iturei Torah		Reb Aharon Yaacov Greenberg; (1900–1963); Israel
Jablinowitz	Rabbi Michael	Yeshivat Ateret Yerushalayim; Israel
Jacobson	Rabbi Yosef Y.	Chovevei Torah Seminary and Congregation Beis Shmuel; editor of *Algemeiner* journal; Brooklyn
Jacoby	Reb Steven	Hollywood, Florida
Jaffee	Dr. Mark	Hollywood, Florida
Jaffee	Ms. Yael	daughter of Dr. Mark Jaffee; Hollywood, Florida
Jankovits	Rabbi Yossi	GIL Torah Outreach; Hollywood, Florida
Jungreis	Rebbetzin Esther	Hineni Movement; Hungary; New York
Kalatsky	Rabbi Yosef	Yad Avraham Institute; New York
Kalter	Rabbi Naftali	Boca Raton, Florida
Kamenetsky	Rabbi Binyomin	son of Rabbi Yaakov Kamenetsky; founder of Yeshivah of South Shore; Long Island, New York
Kamenetsky	Rabbi Mordechai	son of Rabbi Binyomin Kamenetsky; Dean of Yeshivah of South Shore; Long Island, New York
Kamenetsky	Rabbi Yaakov	(1891–1986); Lithuania; Slobodka; Lakewood, New Jersey; Brooklyn
Kaminer	Rebbetzin Yocheved Rivka	(1846–1900); mother of Imrei Emes; Poland

Katz	Reb Eitan	Singer; Israel; California; New York
Katz	Rabbi Shlomo	Project Genesis; Baltimore
Katz	Rebbetzin Toby	North Miami Beach
Katznelson	Rabbi Meyer	(1908–2002); Maryland; Hollywood, Florida
Kedushas Levi		see Berditchever Rebbe
Ketav Sofer		Rabbi Avraham Shmuel Binyamin Sofer;(1815–1871); Hungary
Kirschenbaum	Reb Ari	North Miami Beach
KiTov	Rabbi Eliyahu	(1912–1976); Poland; Yerushalayim, Israel
Kli Yakar		Rabbi Shlomo Ephraim ben Aaron Luntschitz; (1550–1619); Prague
Kook	Rabbi Avraham Yitzchak	(1865–1935); Russian Empire, Palestine; First Ashkenazi Chief Rabbi of Palestine and founder of Yeshivat Merkaz HaRav
Kotler	Rabbi Aharon	(1891–1962); founder of Beth Medrash Govoha; Lakewood, New Jersey
Kotzker Rebbe		Rabbi Menachem Mendel Morgensztern; (1787–1859); Poland
Krasner	Rabbi Shimon	Ner Israel Rabbinical College; Baltimore
Krohn	Rabbi Paysach	Mohel and lecturer; New York
Kunstler	Rabbi Daniel	Ahavas Chaim Yeshivah; Yerushalayim, Israel
Lebowitz	Rabbi Ezriel Yehuda	Hudhazer Rov; (1910–1992); Hungary; New York; Congregation Kehal Yeraiem Vein
Leff	Rabbi Baruch	Torah Institute; Baltimore
Leibowitz	Prof. Nechama	(1905–1997); Latvia; Germany; Israel
Lieberman	Reb Ari	Stamford, Connecticut
Levovitz	Rabbi Yerucham	(1873–1936); Mashgiach at Mir Yeshivah; Poland

Lewis	Rabbi Yehuda Leib	Amsterdam
Librati	Reb Eli	Hollywood, Florida
Likutei Kerem Shlomo		Rabbi Shlomo Halberstam; (1907–2000); New York; third Bobover Rebbe
Lopian	Rabbi Elya	(1876–1970); Poland; England; Israel; mussar movement
Lubavitcher Rebbe		Rabbi Menachem Mendel Schneerson; (1902–1994); Ukraine; New York
Ma'ayanah shel Torah		Rabbi Alexander Zusia Friedman; (1897–1943); Poland
Maggid of Mezritch		Rabbi Dov Ber ben Avraham of Mezeritch; Maggid of Mezritch; (d. 1772); disciple of Baal Shem Tov
Maharal		Rabbi Judah Loew ben Bezalel; (1520–1609); Prague
Maharam Schick		Rabbi Moshe Schick; (1807–1879); Hungary
Maharil Diskin		Rabbi Yehoshua Yehuda Leib Diskin; (1818–1898); Poland; Belarus; Israel
Maharsha		Rabbi Shmuel Eidels; (1555–1631); Poland
Malbim		Rabbi Meir Leibush ben Yechiel Michel Wisser; (1809–1879); Russian Empire
Mandelbaum	Rabbi Alexander Aryeh	Yerushalayim, Israel
Mansour	Rabbi Eli	Congregation Beit Yaakob; Brooklyn
Me'Am Loez		commentary on Tanach written in Ladino; initiated by Rabbi Yaakov Culi; (d. 1732); Turkey
Mechilta		Halachic Midrash on Sefer Shemot
Menachem Tzion		Rabbi Menachem Mendel of Rimanov; (1745–1815); Poland

Menashe ben Yisrael	Rabbi	Rabbi Manoel Dias Soeir; Menasseh Ben Israel; (1604–1657); Portugal; Netherlands
Menken	Rabbi Yaacov	Project Genesis; Baltimore
Meshech Chochmah		Rabbi Meir Simcha of Dvinsk; (1843–1926); Lithuania; Poland
Mesilat Yesharim		see Ramchal
Midrash Rabbah		collection of aggadic midrashim on the books of the Tanach
Midrash Tanchuma		Three different collections of aggadic midrashim on the five books of the Torah, consisting partly of Midrashim originating with Rebbe Tanchuma
Mikdash Mordechai		Rabbi Mordechai Ilan; (1917–1981); Tel Aviv, Israel
Miller	Rabbi Avigdor	(1908–2001); Lithuania; Maryland; New York
Miller	Rabbi Zvi	Salant Foundation; Yerushalayim, Israel
Minchat Chinuch		Rabbi Yosef ben Moshe Babad; (1800–1874); Ukraine; Galicia
Minchat Yehudah		Rabbi Yehudah Petaya; (1859–1942); Iraq; Israel
Moses	Reb Aaron	Hollywood, Florida
Nachalat Tzvi		Reb Meshulam Feivish Tzvi Gross; (1863–1947); Hungary; New York
Nayman	Rabbi Yaakov	(1909–2009); Belarus; Lithuania; Chicago
Neriah	Rabbi Moshe Tzvi	(1913–1995); Israeli politician; Russian Empire; Israel
Nesivos Sholom		Rabbi Sholom Noach Berezovsky; Slonimer Rebbe; (1911–2000); Belarus; Yerushalayim, Israel

Netziv		Rabbi Naftali Zvi Yehuda Berlin; (1816–1893); Russia; Poland
Neuwirth	Rebbetzin Dr. Pnina	Ra'nanah, Israel
Nightingale	Rabbi Tzvi	Aish HaTorah South Florida; Hollywood, Florida
Noam Elimelech		Rabbi Elimelech Weisblum of Lizhensk; (1717–1787); Galicia
Noda B'Yehudah		Rabbi Yechezkel ben Yehuda Landau; (1713–1793); Poland; Prague
Ohr HaChaim (HaKaddosh)		Chaim ben Moshe ibn Attar; (1696–1743); Morocco; Israel
Olat Chodesh		Rabbi Eleazar ben David Fleckeles; (1754–1826); Prague
Oznayim L'Torah		Rabbi Zalman Sorotzkin; Lutzker Rav; (1881–1966); Lithuania; Belarus; Israel
Packouz	Rabbi Kalman	Aish HaTorah Shabbat Shalom Internet Weekly; Oregon; Miami Beach
Pam	Rabbi Avraham	(1913–2001); Rosh Yeshivah of Torah V'Daas; Brooklyn
Panim Yafos		Rabbi Pinchas HaLevi Horowitz (1731–1805); Ukraine; Germany
Pardes Yosef		Rabbi Yosef Patzanovski; (1875–1942); Poland
Perlman	Rabbi Mordechai	Yerushalayim, Israel
Pesikta Zutra		Midrash on Chumash
Pirkei d'Rabbi Eliezer		aggadic/midrashic work on the Torah composed by Rabbi Eliezer ben Hyrcanus; (80–118 C.E.)
Portugal	Rabbi Eliezer Zusia	(1898–1982); Russia; Romania; Israel; United States; first Skulener Rebbe
Premishlan	Rabbi Meir of	(1703–1773); Ukraine; disciple of the Baal Shem Tov

Rabbeinu Bachaiya		Rabbi Bachaiya ben Asher ibn Halawa; (1255–1340); Spain
Ralbag		Gersonides; Rabbi Levi ben Gershon; (1288–1344); France
Rambam		Rabbi Moshe ben Maimon; Maimonides; (1135–1204); Cordoba, Spain; *Mishneh Torah, Moreh Nevuchim*
Ramban		Rabbi Moshe ben Nachman; Nachmanides; (1194–1270); Spain
Ramchal		Rabbi Moshe Chaim Luzzatto; (1707–1746); Italy; Netherlands; Israel; *Mesilat Yesharim*
Ran		Rabbeinu Nissim; Rabbi Nissim ben Reuven Gerondi; (1310–1375); Spain
Rashba		Rabbi Shlomo ben Aderet; (1235–1310); Spain
Rashbam		Rabbi Samuel ben Meir; (c. 1085–c. 1158); Troyes, France
Rashi		Rabbi Shlomo Yitzchaki; (1040–1105); France
Reiss	Dr. Larry	Hollywood, Florida
Rema MiPano		Rabbi Menachem Azariah da Fano; (1548–1620); Italy; *Gilgulei Neshamot*
Riskin	Rabbi Shlomo	Chief Rabbi of Efrat; Founder of Ohr Torah Stone; New York; Israel
Rogow	Rabbi Mordechai	(1900–1967); Lithuania; Illinois; Rosh Yeshivah of Hebrew Theological College in Skokie, *Ateres Mordechai*
Rosenstein	Rabbi Moshe	(1880–1941); Lithuania
Rosh		Rabbi Asher ben Yechiel; Rabbeinu Asher; (1250–1327); Germany;, Spain
Rovner	Rabbi Aron	Yad Avraham Institute; Manhattan
Sackett	Reb Shmuel	Manhigut Yehudit; Karnei Shomron, Israel

Salid	Rabbi Yitzchak	Project for the Advancement of Torah in Hollywood (PATH); Israel; Hollywood, Florida
Schachter	Ms. Nechama	Hollywood, Florida
Schepansky	Rabbi Israel	(d. 1998); New York; *Or HaMizrach*
Schlesinger	Rabbi Eliyahu	Jerusalem Religious Council; Gilo, Israel
Schorr	Rabbi Gedalyahu	(1910–1979); Poland; New York; Rosh Yeshivah of Torah V'Daas; *Ohr Gedalyahu*
Schroeder	Dr. Gerald Lawrence	Aish HaTorah; Yerushalayim, Israel
Schwab	Rabbi Shimon	(1908–1995); Germany; New York
Schwartz	Rabbi Elias	Yeshivah Toras Emes–Kaminetz; Brooklyn, New York
Schwartz	Reb Zacharia	Hollywood, Florida; New York
Seder Hadorot		Rabbi Yechiel Heilprin; (1660–1746); Lithuania
Sefas Emes		Rabbi Yehuda Aryeh Leib Alter; (1847–1905); Poland; second Rebbe of Gerrer Chasidim
Sefer Yetzirah		Kabbalah work attributed to Avraham Avinu
Senter	Rabbi Chaim Zvi	Aderes HaTorah; Yerushalayim, Israel
Sforno		Rabbi Ovadia Ben Jacob Sforno; (1475–1550); Italy
Shaag	Rabbi Avraham	(1801–1876); Hungary; Israel
Shafier	Rabbi Ben Tzion	Director at Tifereth Bnei Torah and TheShmuz.com; New York
Shapiro	Rabbi Ephraim	Congregation Shaarei Tefillah; North Miami Beach
Shelah (HaKadosh)		Rabbi Yeshaya Halevi Horowitz;(c. 1565–1630); *Shnei Luchot HaBrit*

Shemen HaTov		Rabbi Shmuel Shmelka ben Tzvi Hirsch Horowitz; (1726–1778); Czech Republic
Shem MiShmuel		Rabbi Shmuel Bornsztain; (1855–1926); Poland ; second Sochatchover Rebbe
Sher	Rabbi Yitzchok Isaac	(1875–1952); founder of Slabodka yeshivah, branch of Hebron Yeshivah; Bnei Brak, Israel
Shifman	Rabbi Mordechai	RASG Hebrew Academy; Miami Beach
Shmuelevitz	Rabbi Chaim Leib	(1902–1979); Poland; China; Israel; *Sichos Mussar*
Shocher Tov		Midrash on Tehillim
Siduro Shel Shabbat		Rabbi Hayyim ben Solomon; (ca. 1760–1816); Ukraine
Sifrei		Midrash on Bamidbar and Devarim
Sipper	Rabbi Yaacov	senior lecturer, Beis Chaya Rochel Seminary; Gateshead, England
Skurowitz	Rabbi Avram	Hollywood, Florida
Slonimer Rebbe		See Nesivos Shalom
Sobol	Reb Ephraim	Hollywood, Florida
Soloveitchik	Rabbi Ahron	(1917–2001); Russia; Poland; New York; Illinois
Soloveitchik	Rabbi Joseph B.	The Rav; (1903–1993); Belarus; Boston; New York; *Lonely Man of Faith*
Soloveitchik	Rabbi Moshe	(1879–1941); Lithuania; Russia; Poland; New York
Soloveitchik	Rabbi Yitzchak Zev Halevi	the Brisker Rav; the Gryz; (1886–1959); Belarus; Israel
Sonnenfeld	Rabbi Yosef Chaim	(1848 –1932); co–founder Eidah HaChareidis; Hungary; Yerushalayim, Israel
Sorotzkin	Rabbi Zalman	See Oznayim L'Torah

Spiro	Rabbi Mark	Executive Director of LivingJudaism. com; Managing Director of Hebrew High; Seattle
Stauber	Reb Moshe	Hollywood, Florida
Steif	Rabbi Yonasan	Viener Rov; (1877–1958); Hungary; New York
Steipler Gaon		Rabbi Yaakov Yisrael Kanievsky; (1899–1985); Ukraine; Poland; Bnei Brak, Israel
Sternbuch	Rabbi Moishe	GR"A Shul of Har Nof; England; South Africa; Yerushalayim, Israel
Stone	Rabbi Abraham	Congregation Adath Yeshurun; Brooklyn
Tanna D'vei Eliyahu		Midrash; end of 10th century
Targum Yonatan (ben Uziel)		Targum to the Nevi'im written in Aramaic by Rabbi Yonatan ben Uziel
Tatz	Rabbi Dr. Akiva	Jerusalem Medical Ethics Forum; South Africa; England
Teitelbaum	Rabbi Chaim Tzvi	(1879–1926); Hungary; Sigheter Rebbe
Tiferet Yonatan		Rabbi Yonatan Eybeschutz; (1690–1764); Poland; Germany
Torah Temimah		Rabbi Baruch Epstein; (1860–1941); Belarus
Tosafot		medieval commentaries on the Talmud; France
Tuvi	Rabbi Chaim	Yismach Moshe Charity; Yerushalayim, Israel
Twersky	Rabbi Dr. Abraham J.	founder of Gateway Rehabilitation Center in Pittsburgh, associate professor of psychiatry at University of Pittsburgh's School of Medicine, founder of the Shaar Hatikvah rehabilitation center for prisoners in Israel; Wisconsin; Pennsylvania; New Jersey

Turetsky	Reb Ricky	Miami Beach
Turk	Rabbi Neal	Director of Professional Rabbinics at Rabbi Isaac Elchanan Theological Seminary (RIETS); New York
Tzadok HaKohen of Lublin	Rav	Rabbi Tzadok haKohen Rabinowitz of Lublin; (1823–1913); Poland
Tzedah Laderech		Rabbi Menachem ben Aharon ibn Zerach; (d. 1385); Spain
Tzror Hamor		Rabbi Abraham Saba; (1440–1508); Iberian Peninsula; Portugal; Morocco
Tzvi Hirsch miVilna	Rabbi	Rabbi Tzvi Hirsch ben Azriel of Vilna;(d. 1733); *Beit Lechem Yehudah*
Vayikra Rabbah		homiletic Midrash to the Book of Vayikra
Vedibarta Bam		Rabbi Moshe Bogomilsky; Khal Beis Rivkah; Brooklyn, New York
Viener Rav		Rabbi Yonasan Steif; (1877–1958); Hungary, New York
Vilna Gaon		Rabbi Eliyahu ben Shlomo Zalman Kremer; GR"A; (1720–1797); Lithuania; *Aderet Eliyahu*
Vital	Rabbi Chaim	(1542–1620); Tzfat, Israel; Scribe and editor of the Arizal's teachings
Volozhin	Rabbi Chaim	Rabbi Chaim Ickovitz; Rabbi Chaim ben Yitzchak; (1749–1821); Lithuania; *Nefesh HaChaim*
Wachsman	Rabbi Ephraim	Rosh Yeshiva of Yeshivah Meor Yitzchak; Monsey, New York
Wasserstrom	Rabbi Keith	Hollywood, Florida
Wein	Rabbi Berel	Beit Knesset HaNasi; Yeshivah Ohr Sameach; Israel
Weinberg	Rabbi Noach	(1930–2009); founder of Aish HaTorah; New York, Israel

Weinberger	Rabbi Bernard	Young Israel of Brooklyn
Weinberger	Rabbi Moshe	Congregation Aish Kodesh; Woodmere, New York
Weinreb	Dr. Neal	Hollywood; Boca Raton, Florida
Weinstock	Rabbi Yosef	Young Israel of Hollywood–Fort Lauderdale; Florida
Weiss	Rabbi Avi	Hebrew Institute of Riverdale; Bronx
Weiss	Rabbi Moshe Meir	Agudas Yisroel of Staten Island; New York
Winston	Rabbi Pinchas	Canada; Israel
Winter	Rabbi Kalman	(1945–2012); Silver Spring, Maryland
Wolbe	Rabbi Shlomo	(1914–2005); Berlin; Yerushalayim, Israel
Yalkut Shimoni		early 13th century compilation of Aggadot Midrashim on the Tanach
Yerushalmi		Talmud Yerushalmi; collection of Rabbinic notes on the Mishnah
Yonah	Rabbeinu	Rabbi Yonah ben Avraham Gerondi; (d. 1263); Spain; France; *Shaarei Teshuvah*
Yudelevitch	Rabbi Avraham Aharon	(1850–1930); Russia; England; Boston; New York
Zichron Menachem		Rabbi Menachem Mendel Levkovitch; Poland
Ziegler	Rabbi Aharon	Yerushalayim, Israel
Zohar		Kabbalistic commentary on the Torah and mysticism, thought to be written by Rabbi Moshe Shem Tov de Leon; (1250–1305); Spain; based on the writings of Rabbi Shimon Bar Yochai
Zweig	Rabbi Yochanan	Yeshivah V'Kollel Beis Moshe Chaim; Miami Beach

A collection of *divrei Torah* about the *Yom Tovim*
is available in a second book, compiled by Menashe R. Frank,
entitled *Ach Sameach*.

www.ingramcontent.com/pod-product-compliance
Lightning Source LLC
Chambersburg PA
CBHW051848090426

42811CB00034B/2256/J